Date: 2/18/20

**004.16 MCD
McDonald, Rick,
CompTIA A+ Core 1 (220-
1001) and Core 2 (2...**

CompTIA® A+
Core 1 (220-1001)
and Core 2 (220-1002)
Cert Guide

Fifth Edition

Rick McDonald

Pearson

CompTIA® A+ Core 1 (220-1001) and Core 2 (220-1002) Cert Guide

Fifth Edition

Rick McDonald

Copyright © 2020 Pearson Education, Inc.

Published by:
Pearson Education
221 River Street
Hoboken, NJ 07030

ISBN-13: 978-0-7897-6051-7

ISBN-10: 0-7897-6051-7

Library of Congress Control Number: 2019908201

1 2019

Warning and Disclaimer

This book is designed to provide information about the CompTIA Core 1 (220-1001) and Core 2 (220-1002) A+ exams. Every effort has been made to make this book as complete and accurate as possible, but no warranty or fitness is implied. The information provided is on an "as is" basis. The author and the publisher shall have neither liability nor responsibility to any person or entity with respect to any loss or damages arising from the information contained in this book or from the use of the supplemental online content or programs accompanying it.

Microsoft and/or its respective suppliers make no representations about the suitability of the information contained in the documents and related graphics published as part of the services for any purpose all such documents and related graphics are provided "as is" without warranty of any kind. Microsoft and/or its respective suppliers hereby disclaim all warranties and conditions with regard to this information, including all warranties and conditions of merchantability, whether express, implied or statutory, fitness for a particular purpose, title and non-infringement. In no event shall Microsoft and/or its respective suppliers be liable for any special, indirect or consequential damages or any damages whatsoever resulting from loss of use, data or profits, whether in an action of contract, negligence or other tortious action, arising out of or in connection with the use or performance of information available from the services.

The documents and related graphics contained herein could include technical inaccuracies or typographical errors. Changes are periodically added to the information herein. Microsoft and/or its respective suppliers may make improvements and/or changes in the product(s) and/or the program(s) described herein at any time. Partial screen shots may be viewed in full within the software version specified.

Microsoft® Windows®, and Microsoft Office® are registered trademarks of the Microsoft Corporation in the U.S.A. and other countries. This book is not sponsored or endorsed by or affiliated with the Microsoft Corporation.

Special Sales

For information about buying this title in bulk quantities, or for special sales opportunities (which may include electronic versions; custom cover designs; and content particular to your business, training goals, marketing focus, or branding interests), please contact our corporate sales department at corpsales@pearsoned.com or (800) 382-3419.

For government sales inquiries, please contact governmentsales@pearsoned.com.

For questions about sales outside the U.S., please contact intlcs@pearson.com.

Trademark Acknowledgments

All terms mentioned in this book that are known to be trademarks or service marks have been appropriately capitalized. Pearson IT Certification cannot attest to the accuracy of this information. Use of a term in this book should not be regarded as affecting the validity of any trademark or service mark.

Editor-in-Chief
Mark Taub

Product Line Manager
Brett Bartow

Acquisitions Editor
Paul Carlstroem

Managing Editor
Sandra Schroeder

Development Editor
Christopher Cleveland

Project Editor
Mandie Frank

Copy Editor
Kitty Wilson

Technical Editors
Chris Crayton

Editorial Assistant
Cindy Teeters

Designer
Chuti Prasertsith

Composition
codeMantra

Indexer
Ken Johnson

Proofreader
Abigail Manheim

Credits

Figure Number	Attribution/Credit Line
Chapter Opener Images	Charlie Edwards/Getty Images
Figure 1-1	Rick McDonald
Figure 1-2	Rick McDonald
Figure 1-3	Rick McDonald
Figure 1-4	Rick McDonald
Figure 1-5	Rick McDonald
Figure 1-6	Rick McDonald
Figure 1-7a	Rick McDonald
Figure 1-7b	Scanrail/123RF
Figure 1-8	Rick McDonald
Figure 1-9	Rick McDonald
Figure 1-10	Rick McDonald
Figure 1-11a	Rick McDonald
Figure 1-11b	Rick McDonald
Figure 1-12	Rick McDonald
Figure 1-13	Rick McDonald
Figure 1-14	Rick McDonald
Figure 1-15	Rick McDonald
Figure 1-16	Rick McDonald
Figure 1-17	Rick McDonald
Figure 1-18	Rick McDonald
Figure 1-19	Rick McDonald
Figure 1-20	Rick McDonald
Figure 1-21	Rick McDonald
Figure 1-22	Rick McDonald
Figure 1-23	Rick McDonald
Figure 1-24	Rick McDonald
Figure 1-25	Rick McDonald
Figure 1-26	Rick McDonald
Figure 1-27	Rick McDonald
Figure 1-28a	Rick McDonald
Figure 1-28b	Rick McDonald
Figure 1-29	Rick McDonald
Figure 2-1	Rick McDonald
Figure 2-2	Rick McDonald
Figure 2-3a	Rick McDonald
Figure 2-3b	Rick McDonald
Figure 2-4	Rick McDonald
Figure 2-5	Screenshot of Microsoft Windows © Microsoft 2019
Figure 2-6	Courtesy of Cisco Systems, Inc.
Figure 2-7	Courtesy of Cisco Systems, Inc.
Figure 2-8	Screenshot of Microsoft Windows © Microsoft 2019
Figure 2-9	Es sarawuth/Shutterstock
Figure 2-13	Screenshot reprinted with permission from Apple Inc.
Figure 2-14	Screenshot of Linux © Linux Kernel Organization, Inc.

Contents at a Glance

Table of Contents

About the Author

Rick McDonald is a professor in the IT Specialist program at the University of Alaska in Fairbanks, Alaska. He holds degrees and certificates from Gonzaga University in Spokane, Washington, and University of Illinois Springfield. After several years in the airline industry, he returned to full-time teaching in North Carolina and then in Ketchikan, Alaska. Previous publication projects include CCNA Companion Guides and technical editing of various certification textbooks. He is currently teaching A+, CCNA, and AWS certification classes in Fairbanks and across Alaska via the Web.

About the Technical Reviewer

Chris Crayton (MCSE) is an author, technical consultant, and trainer. He has worked as a computer technology and networking instructor, information security director, network administrator, network engineer, and PC specialist. Chris has authored several print and online books on PC repair, CompTIA A+, CompTIA Security+, and Microsoft Windows. He has also served as technical editor and content contributor on numerous technical titles for several of the leading publishing companies. He holds numerous industry certifications, has been recognized with many professional teaching awards, and has served as a state-level SkillsUSA competition judge.

Dedication

I would like to dedicate this book to my wife, Becky, whose unending patience allowed deadlines be met. And to my mother, Frances McDonald, who taught me that learning is a life-long adventure.

I also dedicate this book to my two young grandsons, Hank and Walt. Considering the changes in the past 10 years in IT, it is fun to wonder what this book will hold when you are ready for your own copy.

Acknowledgments

This book is a result of concerted efforts of many dedicated people, without whom this book would not be a reality. I wish like to thank the technical reviewer, Chris Crayton, whose efforts and patience made this a better book for all to use, and to the development editor, Chris Cleveland, who helped me navigate the adjustments to a new CompTIA A+ version. Thanks also to Kitty Wilson, Copy Editor, whose thorough work makes this book much more approachable.

Thanks also to Paul Carlstroem, portfolio manager, for his help and continuous support during the development of this book. I wish to also express my appreciation to Mary Beth Ray, executive editor at Pearson/Cisco Press, for her confidence in me throughout years of working on book projects. Thank you and best to you in your new adventures.

I also wish to thank Professors Josh Peter and Mel Denning, and Ivan Gallagher, Ken Moneymaker, David Mattice, and Cheri Renson, my colleagues and friends at the Community and Technical College at the University of Alaska. Their patience and support as ideas and details were discussed and parsed are greatly appreciated. I learned much from their generous sharing of IT experiences.

It has been a huge undertaking to pull all the pieces of this project together. It is due to the dedication of those mentioned above that this book is not only large in scope but high in quality. It is my sincerest hope that our combined efforts will help you, the readers and users of this book, achieve your goals in an IT career.

Introduction

CompTIA A+ certification is widely recognized as the first certification you should receive in an information technology (IT) career. Whether you are planning to specialize in PC or mobile device hardware, operating systems management, security, or network management, the CompTIA A+ certification exams measure the baseline skills you need to master to begin your journey toward greater responsibilities and achievements in IT.

CompTIA A+ certification is based on a vendor-neutral exam that measures your knowledge of industry-standard technology.

Goals and Methods

The number-one goal of this book is a simple one: to help you pass the CompTIA A+ certification Core 1 (220-1001) and Core 2 (220-1002) exams.

Because CompTIA A+ certification exams now stress problem-solving abilities and reasoning more than memorization of terms and facts, our goal is to help you master and understand the required objectives for each exam.

To aid you in mastering and understanding the A+ certification objectives, this book uses the following methods:

- The beginning of each chapter defines the topics to be covered in the chapter; it also lists the corresponding CompTIA A+ objective numbers.

- The body of the chapter explains the topics from hands-on and theory-based standpoints. Each chapter includes in-depth descriptions, tables, and figures that are geared toward building your knowledge so that you can pass the exam. The chapters are broken down into several topics each.

- The key topics indicate important figures, tables, and lists of information that you should know for the exam. They are interspersed throughout the chapter and are listed in table format at the end of the chapter.

- You can find memory tables online in Appendix C, "Memory Tables," and Appendix D, "Answer Key to Memory Tables." Use them to help memorize important information.

- Key terms without definitions are listed at the end of each chapter. Write down the definition of each term and check your work against the key terms in the glossary.

How the Book Is Organized

Each chapter in this book maps one-to-one with the domains of the A+ Core 1 (220-1001) and Core 2 (220-1002) exam domains:

Chapter	Core 1 (220-1001) Domain Covered	Percentage of Exam
Chapter 1, Mobile Devices	1.0 Mobile Devices	14%
Chapter 2	2.0 Networking	20%
Chapter 3	3.0 Hardware	27%
Chapter 4	4.0 Virtualization and Cloud Computing	12%
Chapter 5	5.0 Hardware and Network Troubleshooting	27%
Chapter	**Core 2 (220-1002) Domain Covered**	
Chapter 6	1.0 Operating Systems	27%
Chapter 7	2.0 Security	24%
Chapter 8	3.0 Software Troubleshooting	26%
Chapter 9	4.0 Operational Procedures	23%

Chapter 10, "Final Preparation," lists the complete set of all objectives and subobjectives for both exams. Also, be sure to visit CompTIA's web page at https://certification.comptia.org to ensure that you have the latest information for the CompTIA A+ exams.

Book Features

To help you customize your study time using this book, the core chapters have several features that help you make the best use of your time:

- **Foundation Topics:** These are the core sections of each chapter. They explain the concepts for the topics in each chapter.

- **Exam Preparation Tasks:** After the "Foundation Topics" section of each chapter, the "Exam Preparation Tasks" section lists a series of study activities that you should do at the end of the chapter.

- **Review All Key Topics:** The Key Topic icon appears next to the most important items in the "Foundation Topics" section of the chapter. The Review All Key Topics activity lists the key topics from the chapter, along with their page numbers. Although the contents of the entire chapter could be on the exam, you should definitely know all the information highlighted with Key Topic icons, so you should review this activity.

- **Define Key Terms:** This section lists the most important terms from the chapter. To ensure that you know them, write a short definition of each and compare your answer to the glossary at the end of the book.

- **Review Questions:** Confirm that you understand the content that you just covered by answering these questions and reading the answer explanations.

- **Web-based practice exam:** The companion website includes the Pearson Cert Practice Test engine, which allows you to answer practice exam questions. Use it to prepare with a sample exam and to pinpoint areas where you need more study.

What's New?

You'll find plenty that's new and improved in this edition, including:

- Increased content concerning the troubleshooting of computer hardware and software

- Addition of Windows 10 content

- Addition of Chrome OS content

- A large increase in operational procedures content

- Addition of basic scripting

- Addition of remote access technologies

- Increased virtualization concepts

- Addition of cloud computing concepts

- Reorganized text to minimize duplication of coverage between objectives

- New coverage of Linux and OS X features and troubleshooting

- New coverage of MacBook features, such as Thunderbolt 2

- Updated processor coverage

- Updated BIOS dialogs, including more UEFI/BIOS examples

- USB 3.1 and USB-Type C

- mSATA and M.2 SSDs

- Improved photos and illustrations

- Enhanced laptop teardown and subassembly replacement procedures
- Updated memory coverage (DDR4 DIMMs and UniDIMMs)
- Updated coverage of mobile devices, including teardown tips
- Enhanced coverage of desktop and laptop upgrades, including Thunderbolt and the miniPCIe card
- Updated coverage of docking stations and video cable adapters
- Updated power supply and cooling system information
- Improved coverage of network hardware and cabling
- Enhanced coverage of device troubleshooting, teardown, and upgrades
- New coverage related to dealing with prohibited content/activity
- Enhanced coverage of Windows features
- Enhanced discussion of Windows upgrade paths and methods
- New Windows 8/8.1/10 features
- Enhanced coverage of ESD protection issues
- Enhanced coverage of Windows OS troubleshooting
- Enhanced Control Panel discussion
- Enhanced coverage of iOS and Android devices
- Enhanced coverage of security issues (physical, digital, wireless network, wired network, workgroup, and homegroup folders)
- New coverage of network and cloud computing concepts
- Enhanced coverage of security issues
- New coverage of Linux and OS X OS troubleshooting

For more information about how the A+ certification can help your career or to download the latest official objectives, access CompTIA's A+ web page at https://certification.comptia.org/certifications/a.

In this book, we cover the major objectives but combine some of them when necessary to make a topic easier to understand. To make sure you can relate the book's contents to the CompTIA A+ certification objectives, each chapter contains cross-references to the appropriate objectives, as needed, and we provide a master cross-reference list later in this introduction.

Who Should Read This Book?

The CompTIA A+ exams measure the necessary competencies for an entry-level IT professional with knowledge equivalent to what you would learn in 6 to 12 months of hands-on experience in a lab or in the field. This book is written for people who have that amount of experience working with desktop PCs, laptops, and mobile devices. Average readers will have attempted in the past to replace a hardware component within a PC or mobile device; they should also understand how to navigate through Windows, access the Internet, and have (or be willing to learn) a basic knowledge of OS X and Linux features.

Readers will range from people who are attempting to attain a position in the IT field to people who want to keep their skills sharp or perhaps retain their job due to a company policy that mandates that they take the new exams.

This book is also aimed at readers who want to acquire additional certifications beyond the A+ certification (Network+, Security+, and so on). The book is designed to provide an easy transition to future certification studies.

Strategies for Exam Preparation

Strategies for exam preparation vary depending on your existing skills and knowledge, as well as the equipment you have available. Of course, the ideal exam preparation would consist of building a PC from scratch and installing and configuring the operating systems covered.

Chapter 1 contains lists of the tools, software, and operating systems recommended by CompTIA for exam study and preparation and how to track down the best deals.

The next best step you can take is to read through the chapters in this book, jotting down notes about key concepts or configurations in a dedicated notepad. Each chapter contains a quiz that you can use to test your knowledge of the chapter's topics. It's located near the end of the chapter.

After you have read through the book, take a look at the current exam objectives for the CompTIA A+ certification exams listed at https://certification.comptia.org/certifications/a. If there are any areas shown in the certification exam outline that you would still like to study, find those sections in the book and review them.

When you feel confident in your skills, attempt the practice exams included on the companion website with this book. As you work through the practice exam, note the areas where you lack confidence and review those concepts or configurations in the book. After you have reviewed the areas, work through the practice exam a second time and rate your skills. Keep in mind that the more you work through the practice exam, the more familiar the questions will become.

After you have worked through the practice exam a second time and feel confident with your skills, schedule the real CompTIA A+ Core 1 (220-1001) and Core 2 (220-1002) exams through Pearson VUE (www.vue.com). To prevent the information from evaporating out of your mind, you should typically take the exam within a week of when you consider yourself ready to take the exam.

Companion Website

Register this book to get access to the Pearson IT Certification test engine and other study materials plus additional bonus content. Check this site regularly for new and updated postings written by the authors that provide further insight into the more troublesome topics on the exam. Be sure to check the box indicating that you would like to hear from us about updates and exclusive discounts on future editions of this product or related products.

To access this companion website, follow these steps:

Step 1. Go to www.pearsonitcertification.com/register and log in or create a new account.

Step 2. Enter the ISBN for this book: **9780789760517**.

Step 3. Answer the challenge question as proof of purchase.

Step 4. Click the **Access Bonus Content** link in the Registered Products section of your account page to be taken to the page where your downloadable content is available.

Please note that many of our companion content files are very large, especially image and video files.

If you are unable to locate the files for this title by following these steps, please visit www.pearsonITcertification.com/contact and select the **Site Problems/ Comments** option. Our customer service representatives will assist you.

Pearson Test Prep Practice Test Software

As noted previously, this book comes complete with the Pearson Test Prep practice test software, including two full exams. These practice tests are available to you either online or as an offline Windows application. To access the practice exams that were developed with this book, please see the instructions in the card inserted in the sleeve in the back of the book. This card includes a unique access code that enables you to activate your exams in the Pearson Test Prep software.

Accessing the Pearson Test Prep Software Online

The online version of this software can be used on any device with a browser and connectivity to the Internet, including desktop machines, tablets, and smartphones. To start using your practice exams online, simply follow these steps:

Step 1. Go to https://www.PearsonTestPrep.com.

Step 2. Select **Pearson IT Certification** as your product group.

Step 3. Enter your account email and password. If you don't have an account on PearsonITCertification.com or CiscoPress.com, you need to establish one by going to PearsonITCertification.com/join.

Step 4. In the **My Products** tab, click the **Activate New Product** button.

Step 5. Enter the access code printed on the insert card in the back of your book to activate your product. The product will now be listed in your My Products page.

Step 6. Click the **Exams** button to launch the exam settings screen and start your exam.

Accessing the Pearson Test Prep Software Offline

If you wish to study offline, you can download and install the Windows version of the Pearson Test Prep software. You can use the download link for this software on the book's companion website, or you can just enter this link in your browser:

http://www.pearsonitcertification.com/content/downloads/pcpt/engine.zip

To access the book's companion website and the software, simply follow these steps:

Step 1. Register your book by going to PearsonITCertification.com/register and entering the ISBN: **9780789760517**.

Step 2. Answer the challenge questions.

Step 3. Go to your account page and click the **Registered Products** tab.

Step 4. Click the **Access Bonus Content** link under the product listing.

Step 5. Click the **Install Pearson Test Prep Desktop Version** link under the Practice Exams section of the page to download the software.

Step 6. After the software finishes downloading, unzip all the files on your computer.

Step 7. Double-click the application file to start the installation and follow the onscreen instructions to complete the registration.

Step 8. After the installation is complete, launch the application and click the **Activate Exam** button on the My Products tab.

Step 9. Click the **Activate a Product** button in the Activate Product Wizard.

Step 10. Enter the unique access code found on the card in the sleeve in the back of your book and click the **Activate** button.

Step 11. Click **Next** and then click **Finish** to download the exam data to your application.

Step 12. Start using the practice exams by selecting the product and clicking the **Open Exam** button to open the exam settings screen.

Note that the offline and online versions will sync together, so saved exams and grade results recorded on one version will be available to you on the other as well.

Customizing Your Exams

Once you are in the exam settings screen, you can choose to take exams in one of three modes:

- **Study mode:** Allows you to fully customize your exams and review answers as you are taking the exam. This is typically the mode you would use first to assess your knowledge and identify information gaps.

- **Practice Exam mode:** Locks certain customization options, as it is presenting a realistic exam experience. Use this mode when you are preparing to test your exam readiness.

- **Flash Card mode:** Strips out the answers and presents you with only the question stem. This mode is great for late-stage preparation, when you really want to challenge yourself to provide answers without the benefit of seeing multiple-choice options. This mode does not provide the detailed score reports that the other two modes do, so you should not use it if you are trying to identify knowledge gaps.

In addition to choosing among these three modes, you will be able to select the source of your questions. You can choose to take exams that cover all of the chapters, or you can narrow your selection to just a single chapter or the chapters that make up specific parts in the book. All chapters are selected by default. If you want to narrow your focus to individual chapters, simply deselect all the chapters and then select only those on which you wish to focus in the Objectives area.

You can also select the exam banks on which to focus. Each exam bank comes complete with a full exam of questions that cover topics in every chapter. The two exams printed in the book are available to you as well, along with two additional exams of unique questions. You can have the test engine serve up exams from all four banks or just from one individual bank by selecting the desired banks in the exam bank area.

There are several other customizations you can make to your exam from the exam settings screen, such as the time of the exam, the number of questions served up, whether to randomize questions and answers, whether to show the number of correct answers for multiple-answer questions, and whether to serve up only specific types of questions. You can also create custom test banks by selecting only questions that you have marked or questions on which you have added notes.

Updating Your Exams

If you are using the online version of the Pearson Test Prep software, you should always have access to the latest version of the software as well as the exam data. If you are using the Windows desktop version, every time you launch the software while connected to the Internet, it checks to determine whether there are any updates to your exam data and automatically downloads any changes made since the last time you used the software.

Sometimes, for many reasons, the exam data may not fully download when you activate your exam. If you find that figures or exhibits are missing, you may need to manually update your exams. To update a particular exam you have already activated and downloaded, simply click the **Tools** tab and click the **Update Products** button. Again, this is only an issue with the desktop Windows application.

If you wish to check for updates to the Windows desktop version of the Pearson Test Prep exam engine software, simply click the **Tools** tab and click the **Update Application** button to ensure that you have the most up-to-date version of the software.

This chapter covers the seven A+ 220-1001 exam objectives related to knowledge of mobile devices. These objectives may comprise 14% of the exam questions:

- **Core 1 (220-1001): Objective 1.1:** Given a scenario, install and configure laptop hardware and components.

- **Core 1 (220-1001): Objective 1.2:** Given a scenario, install components within the display of a laptop.

- **Core 1 (220-1001): Objective 1.3:** Given a scenario, use appropriate laptop features.

- **Core 1 (220-1001): Objective 1.4:** Compare and contrast characteristics of various types of other mobile devices.

- **Core 1 (220-1001): Objective 1.5:** Given a scenario, connect and configure accessories and ports of other mobile devices.

- **Core 1 (220-1001): Objective 1.6:** Given a scenario, configure basic mobile device network connectivity and application support.

- **Core 1 (220-1001): Objective 1.7:** Given a scenario, use methods to perform mobile device synchronization.

Mobile Devices

The mobile device category includes laptops, tablets, and smartphones. Due to the variety of operating systems, form factors, port types, and capabilities, supporting these devices is a bigger challenge than ever before.

"Do I Know This Already?" Quiz

The "Do I Know This Already?" quiz allows you to assess whether you should read the entire chapter. Table 1-1 lists the major headings in this chapter and the "Do I Know This Already?" quiz questions covering the material in those headings so you can assess your knowledge of these specific areas. The answers to the "Do I Know This Already?" quiz appear in Appendix A, "Answers to the 'Do I Know This Already?' Quizzes and Review Question Sections."

Table 1-1 "Do I Know This Already?" Section-to-Question Mapping

Foundation Topics Section	Questions
Install and Configure Laptop Hardware and Components	1–2
Install Components Within the Display of a Laptop	3
Use Appropriate Laptop Features	4
Characteristics of Other Mobile Devices	5
Accessories and Ports Used by Other Mobile Devices	6–7
Basic Mobile Device Network Connectivity and Application Support	8–11
Methods to Perform Mobile Device Synchronization	12–14

CAUTION The goal of self-assessment is to gauge your mastery of the topics in this chapter. If you do not know the answer to a question or are only partially sure of the answer, you should mark that question as wrong for purposes of the self-assessment. Giving yourself credit for an answer you correctly guess skews your self-assessment results and might provide you with a false sense of security.

1. You are researching options for adding a hard drive to your laptop. You want speed, but price is a consideration. Which of these is the middle-of-the-road option for speed and price?

    a. HDD

    b. SSD

    c. SSHD

    d. OLED

2. Which of these are generally accessed through the bottom of a laptop? (Choose all that apply.)

    a. Battery

    b. Wireless adapter

    c. SODIMM RAM

    d. SSHD

3. Which screen type would you choose for maximum brightness and efficiency?

    a. LCD with IPS

    b. OLED

    c. LCD with TN

    d. LED with CCFL

4. Which of the following is not featured on a common docking station?

    a. SSD

    b. Power connection

    c. USB ports

    d. Display output port

5. A Fitbit is an example of which technology?

    a. VR/AR headset

    b. GPS

    c. Wearable technology

    d. E-reader

6. Which of the following is an Apple proprietary connector?

    a. USB-C

    b. USB-on-the-Go

    c. Lightning

    d. AppleUSB

7. Which term describes using a phone and USB cable to provide secure Internet access to a laptop in an airport lounge?

    a. Mobile-Web

    b. OGWiFi (On-the-Go WiFi)

    c. Tethering

    d. Hotspot

8. You are using your iPhone to pay for your groceries. Your receipt is sent to your email. Which technology is used in this payment transaction?

    a. IR

    b. HTTP

    c. NFC

    d. Hotspot

9. Which two transmissions are always disabled in Airplane mode? (Choose two.)

    a. Bluetooth

    b. GPS

    c. Cellular

    d. WiFi

10. What unique identifier does each phone have?

    a. IMSI

    b. IMEI

    c. SSO

    d. S/MIME

11. Which of the following mobile operating systems support VPN connections? (Choose all that apply.)

    a. Windows 7

    b. Android

    c. iOS

    d. Windows 10 Mobile

12. Which of the following are considered to be main methods of data synchronization?

    a. Synchronization to the automobile

    b. Synchronization to the desktop

    c. Synchronization to the cloud

    d. All of the above

13. What does SSO stand for to?

    a. Sudden Service Outage

    b. Source Signal Only

    c. Single Sign-On

    d. Subscriber Service Overage

14. Which two of the following are required for cloud-based synchronization on a mobile device? (Choose two.)

    a. Bluetooth 2.0

    b. App or Web service installed

    c. Web access

    d. USB 2.0 port

Foundation Topics

Install and Configure Laptop Hardware and Components

220-1001: Objective 1.1: Given a scenario, install and configure laptop hardware and components.

220-1001
Exam

Because the display, keyboard, and network hardware are integrated into a laptop, the laptop uses specialized or proprietary components for hard drive, optical drive, system board, memory, CPU, and other components. Replacing these devices involves much different procedures than on a desktop computer.

Some of the general differences include:

- **Component sources:** Replacement components such as display, keyboard, wireless network card, and system board are available only from the original equipment manufacturer (OEM). These are known as *OEM parts*. Other components, such as optical drives and hard drives, memory, and the CPU, can be purchased from third-party sources but differ greatly from their desktop counterparts.

- **Power sources:** A laptop is powered by an internal battery and an AC adapter that also charges the battery. As with other laptop components, the original vendor is the most typical source for replacements, although some third-party vendors may sell "universal" replacement AC adapters that work.

- **Components unique to laptops:** Laptops include several components typically not included on desktop computers, including an antenna in the display that is connected to a mini-PCIe card to provide wireless networking, a keyboard with an integrated touchpad or pointing stick, a touchscreen or non-touchscreen display, and integrated speakers.

These differences, along with the extensive use of plastics and the use of tiny screws, make servicing a laptop a major challenge, even for those who are experienced with servicing a desktop computer.

Laptop Access

Whether you need to disassemble a laptop to upgrade internal hardware or to replace a defective component, there are several best practices you should use to make the reassembly process as easy as possible:

- **Refer to manufacturer documentation:** Documentation helps you properly identify screw types, screw lengths, number of screws (some laptops have more than 100), cable and component locations, and other information needed. Most vendors offer this information online, but some manufacturers insist on doing the repairs themselves and do not provide documentation for access to these components.

- **Use appropriate hand tools for case disassembly and component removal:** Using recommended tool types and sizes helps prevent problems such as damaging screw heads by using a screwdriver that is too large. Repair documentation typically lists the recommended tools for each procedure. Proceed with caution! If you break a part of the laptop, you won't be able to buy it locally but will usually have to order a replacement.

- **Document and label cable and screw locations:** Laptops typically use a mixture of screw lengths and sometimes screw types. Mix them up, and you could damage components or end up being unable to secure them properly. Taking photos at different stages of disassembly may help in the reassembly process.

- **Organize parts:** Consider using a multiple-compartment parts tray with a lid (available at hardware stores) for parts sorting and storage. A magnetic dish also helps prevent loss of parts.

NOTE The Laptop Repair 101 website (www.laptoprepair101.com) provides many useful resources, including links to major vendors' laptop service manuals, illustrated step-by-step procedures for the removal of many components, and links to parts sources.

If you need to replace the battery, mass storage (hard disk, SSD, SSHD, or optical drive), SODIMM RAM, or wireless adapter on a typical laptop, you need to access these components from the bottom of the laptop. Figure 1-1 shows the underside of a typical laptop and its access panels. Figure 1-2 shows the same laptop after the access panels have been removed for component upgrades or replacements.

NOTE Some laptops use a single cover for all upgradable components rather than multiple covers. Some laptops require disassembly to access the hard disk drive or SSD mass storage. Check the system documentation for details.

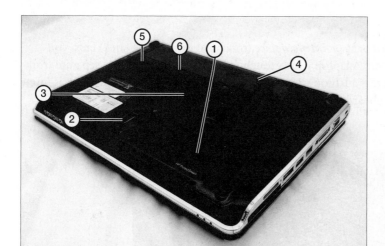

1. Access panel for hard disk or SSHD and wireless card
2. Optical drive ejector switch
3. Access panel for SODIMM RAM
4. Battery
5. Battery ejector switch
6. Access panel for CMOS battery

FIGURE 1-1   The Underside of a Typical Laptop, with Removable Panels

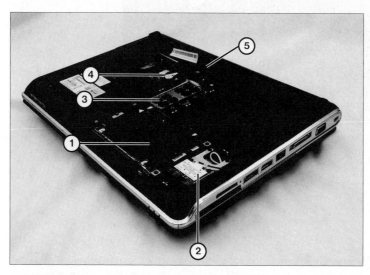

1. Hard disk
2. Wireless card
3. SODIMM RAM
4. CMOS battery
5. Main battery compartment after battery removal

FIGURE 1-2   The Same Laptop as in Figure 1-1 After Opening Access Panels to Permit
Component Replacements or Upgrades

Keyboard

If a laptop *keyboard* or its *pointing device* (touchpad or pointing stick) fails, you must replace the unit. A laptop with a touchpad has a keyboard that is separate from the touchpad, whereas a laptop with a pointing stick has a pointing stick that is integrated with the keyboard. Some laptops have both types of pointing devices (see Figure 1-3).

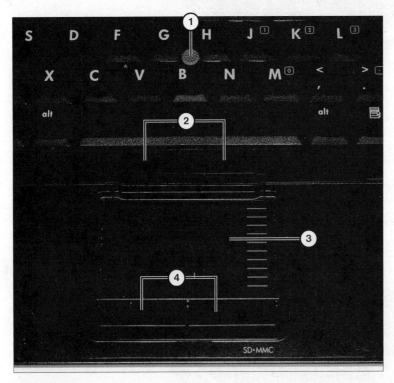

1. Pointing stick
2. Buttons for pointing stick
3. Touchpad
4. Buttons for touchpad

FIGURE 1-3   A Business-Class Laptop with a Pointing Stick and Touchpad

NOTE   Touchpads are generally located in the palm rest (which extends below the keyboard), while pointing sticks, such as the IBM/Lenovo TrackPoint and Toshiba AccuPoint, are located in the middle of the keyboard (with buttons located in the palm rest).

To replace a keyboard (with or without a pointing stick), follow this basic procedure:

Step 1. Disconnect the laptop from AC power and remove the battery.

Step 2. Remove the screws that hold the keyboard in place.

Step 3. Turn the laptop upright.

Step 4. Open the screen so that the keyboard is visible.

Step 5. If necessary, remove the bezel that holds the keyboard in place.

Step 6. Lift up the keyboard to expose the keyboard cable.

Step 7. Remove any hold-down devices used to hold the keyboard cable in place.

Step 8. Disconnect the keyboard cable from the system board (see Figure 1-4).

FIGURE 1-4   Removing the Keyboard Cable

Step 9. Remove the keyboard.

To install a replacement, reverse these steps.

NOTE   On some laptops, you must remove the display assembly first before you can remove the keyboard.

Hard Drive Storage (HDD)

Most laptop computers use one 2.5-in. storage drive that comes in one of three common choices: HDD, SSD, or SSHD. Each has strengths and weaknesses, and each could be the right choice, depending of the scenario presented:

- **Hard disk drive (HDD):** These magnetic disks have been a standard option for years and combine low cost with large capacity. However, they are slower than the other options. With magnetic disks and moving parts that can wear down, they are the least reliable of the three options.

- **Solid-state drive (SSD):** SSD is a flash memory drive with no moving parts. It is much faster than an HDD when booting and storing or retrieving data. Although SSDs currently cost more than HDDs, their prices are dropping, and their capacity is improving. Many newer laptops have M.2 expansion ports and can support an M.2 SSD card that is directly mounted to the circuit board for even faster reading.

- **Solid-state hybrid drive (SSHD):** An SSHD combines a solid-state cache with magnetic capacity. It uses a memory manager to choose the most common files for the fast cache.

Table 1-2 highlights the differences among these three hard drive options.

Table 1-2 Comparison of HDD, SSD, and SSHD

Type of Hard Drive	Cost	Capacity	Speed	Reliability
HDD	Least expensive and readily available	Highest capacity	Slowest due to moving parts and magnetic disks	Has moving parts that can wear over time
SSD	Most expensive but price is dropping	Lowest capacity but improving	Fastest	Has no moving parts
SSHD	Midrange cost	Blends high HDD capacity with fast solid-state cache for most used files	Blends fast solid-state cache with slower magnetic storage	Has moving parts that can wear out but spins less than HDD

NOTE   Some Ultrabooks use the 1.8-in. or 2.5-in. SSD form factor (hard disks or SSD). The larger 3.5-in. drive form factor is used in desktop drive enclosures or in desktop computers.

Although a few laptop computers require you to remove the keyboard to access the hard drive, most laptops feature storage devices that can be accessed from the bottom of the system. Follow this procedure to remove and replace a storage device (HDD, SSD, or SSHD) accessible from the bottom:

Step 1.   Disconnect the laptop from AC power and remove the battery.

Step 2.   Loosen or remove the screw or screws used to hold the drive cover in place.

Step 3.   Slide the cover away from the retaining lug or clips and remove it.

Step 4.   Remove the screws holding the drive to the chassis.

Step 5.   Slide the drive away from the retaining screw holes and lift it out of the chassis (see Figure 1-5).

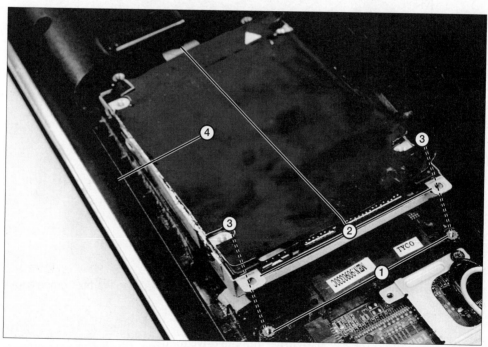

1. Retaining screw holes
2. Drive mounting frame tabs
3. Remove/attach bolts through tabs into screw holes
4. Protective cover over hard disk circuit board

FIGURE 1-5   Removing a Laptop Hard Disk After Removing the Retaining Screws

Step 6.   If the computer uses an interposer—that is, a proprietary connector linking the drive's SATA connector and the drive bay—remove it and save it for reuse.

Step 7.   Remove the screws fastening the drive to the drive frame.

Step 8.   Remove the drive from the drive frame (see Figure 1-6).

1. Mounting tabs
2. Mounting holes for drive
3. Matching screw holes in drive
4. SATA data and power connectors

FIGURE 1-6   A Laptop Hard Disk After Being Removed from Its Mounting Frame (Compare to Figure 1-5)

Step 9.   Insert the new hard drive into the drive frame.

Reverse these steps to install a new hard drive.

After the system is restarted, start the computer and enter the BIOS or UEFI setup program to verify that the new hard drive has been properly recognized by the system.

Memory

The variety of available computer memory can cause confusion. Table 1-3 provides a brief list of memory types, including memory specifically for laptops.

Table 1-3   RAM Review

Type of RAM	Description
RAM (random access memory)	Volatile memory not for storage
SDRAM (synchronous dynamic RAM)	Combines static RAM and dynamic RAM
SDR SDRAM (single data rate SDRAM)	Single data rate means internal clock rate and input/output are the same.
DDR SDRAM (double data rate SDRAM) DDR2, DDR3, DDR4	Xxx; DDR4 is the latest generation
DIMM (dual in-line memory module)	Form factor used in desktops
SODIMM (small outline DIMM)	Form factor used in laptops

You need to note the following before you can select the right memory upgrade for a laptop:

- **Form factor:** Most laptops in service use DDR2, DDR3, or DDR4 SODIMMs.

- **Memory speed:** If you plan to add a module, make sure it is the same speed as the existing module. If you plan to replace the modules, buy a matched set of modules in the fastest speed supported by the system.

- **Memory timing:** The most common way to refer to memory timing is by its column address strobe (CAS) value. If you install memory modules that use different CAS values, the laptop could become unstable and crash or lock up.

To determine the correct memory to use for a memory upgrade, use one of the following methods:

- **Use the interactive memory upgrade tools available from major third-party memory vendors' websites:** These tools list the memory modules suitable for particular laptops, and some use an ActiveX web control to detect the currently installed memory. Crucial System Scanner is a very useful tool for showing what's currently installed and what is compatible. For more information, visit https://www.crucial.com/usa/en/systemscanner.

■ **Check the vendor's memory specifications:** You can determine part numbers by using this method, but this method is best if memory must be purchased from the laptop vendor rather than from a memory vendor.

Generally, laptops have two connectors for memory, typically using small outline DIMMs (SODIMMs), which are reduced-size versions of DIMM modules. Figure 1-7 compares a typical DDR3 SODIMM with a DDR2 SODIMM, a DDR3 DIMM, and a DDR4 DIMM.

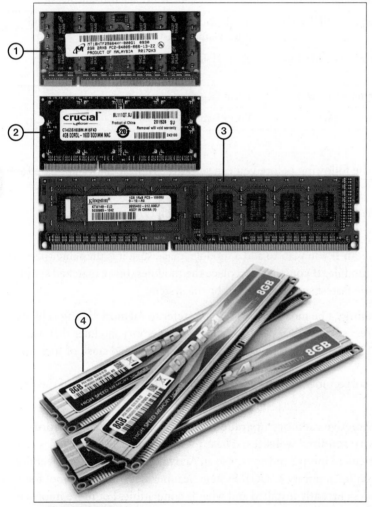

1. DDR2 SODIMM
2. DDR3L (low voltage) SODIMM
3. DDR3 DIMM
4. DDR4 DIMM

FIGURE 1-7   Comparison of SODIMMs and DIMMs (DDR4 Image © scanrail. 123rf.com)

Table 1-4 compares the major features of SODIMMs (also known as SO-DIMMs).

Table 1-4 SODIMM Features

Memory Type	Number of Pins	Notch Location	Notes
DDR	200	After pin 20	67.6mm long and 30mm high
			Notch closer to short end* than with DDR2
DDR2	200	After pin 20	Notch closer to long end* than with DDR
DDR3	204	After pin 36	Same dimensions as DDR, DDR2
DDR4	260	After pin 144	69.7mm long and 30mm high

* Short end = left side (20 pins); long end = right side (80 pins) front view

TIP The best memory upgrade for a portable system is to add the largest-capacity memory modules that can be installed in the system. Use matched sets on systems that support multichannel memory to improve performance.

Follow these steps to perform a typical memory upgrade:

Step 1. Disconnect the laptop from AC power and remove the battery.

Step 2. Remove any screws or hold-down devices.

Step 3. Remove the old memory module(s), if necessary. To remove a memory module, pull back the clips on both sides and swing the memory up and out.

Step 4. Insert the new memory upgrade, making sure the contacts on the edge of the module make a firm connection with the connector.

Step 5. Push the top of the module down until the latches lock into place (see Figure 1-8).

1. Push the SODIMM into the connector at the appropriate angle
2. Push the SODIMM down until the latches lock into place
3. The latches hold the SODIMM in place

Step 6.   If the memory socket requires screws to secure the memory in place, install them.

Step 7.   Close the cover and secure it to complete the upgrade.

Step 8.   Test the upgrade by starting the system and running a memory diagnostic tool. (Windows includes memory testing software, and you can also download a memory testing program.)

Smart Card Reader

A *smart card reader* is typically used on corporate laptops for access control (do not confuse it with a flash memory card reader). Smart cards are usually plastic with an embedded chip to authenticate a user for access. They are not a common option for home use.

To remove a smart card reader (see Figure 1-9):

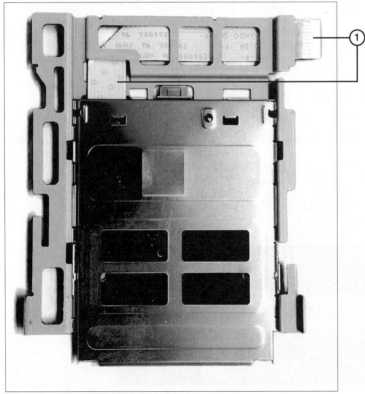

1. Ribbon cable connector to motherboard

FIGURE 1-9   A Typical Smart Card Reader from a Dell Laptop

Step 1.   Disconnect the laptop from AC power and remove the battery.

Step 2.   Remove the bottom cover.

Step 3.   Locate the ribbon cable connecting the reader to the motherboard.

Step 4.   Disconnect the ribbon cable.

Step 5.   Remove the screws holding the reader in place.

Step 6.   Remove the reader from the system.

To replace the smart card reader, reverse these steps.

Optical Drives

Although built-in optical drives are moving toward legacy status, some laptops feature modular USB optical drives designed for being swapped. However, for an optical drive that is not designed for being swapped, follow this procedure to remove it:

Step 1.   Disconnect the laptop from AC power and remove the battery.

Step 2.   Locate the latch that holds the drive in place or locate the mounting screw that holds the drive in place. It might be located inside the access panel for another component. Slide open the latch or remove the mounting screw.

Step 3.   Slide the drive out of the system. See Figure 1-10 for a typical example.

To reinstall the drive, reverse these steps. If a range of drives are available for a laptop, you can use this method to upgrade to a better drive.

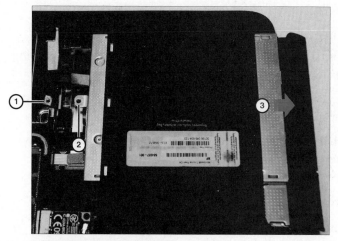

1. Screw hole for mounting bolt
2. Retaining lug on optical drive
3. Pull drive from drive bay

Mini PCIe

A Peripheral Component Interconnect (**PCI**) slot in a computer is a slot for plugging in add-on peripherals. This slot provides access to the motherboard for a device such as a WiFi modem, a video graphics processing unit (GPU), or added storage with an M.2 card. miniPCI Express (**mPCIe**) cards perform functions similar to those of the PCIe card, but they are designed for the compact space of a laptop. The mPCIe slots in a laptop are used for plugging in wireless cards and also for M.2 memory modules. Other examples of modules that can plug into mPCIe slots are GPS units, cellular cards, and analog-to-digital converter (ADC) cards.

Wireless Card

A laptop with WiFi or Bluetooth support typically uses either an mPCIe expansion card or an M.2 card to provide wireless network support. The M.2 card form factor (also called NGFF, for next-generation form factor) is also used for SSD and other I/O devices. Note that an M.2 card slot made for SSD cannot be used for WiFi or Bluetooth cards.

Regardless of which *wireless card* a laptop uses, there are two antennas that lead from the WiFi antennas built into the display panel that need to be connected to the card.

To remove a wireless card, follow this basic procedure:

Step 1. Verify the location of the card. Some laptops have the card under the keyboard, whereas others have the card under a removable cover on the bottom of the computer.

Step 2. Disconnect the laptop from AC power and remove the battery.

    a. If the card is located under the keyboard, remove the keyboard.

    b. If the card is located under an access panel, remove the screws holding the access panel in place.

Step 4. Disconnect any wires connected to the adapter. They might be screwed into place or snapped into place. Note their positions.

Step 5. Unscrew any bolts holding the card in place. A miniPCIe card (refer to Figure 1-11) uses two mounting bolts, while an M.2 card (refer to Figure 1-12) uses a single mounting bolt.

Step 6. Rotate the card upward at a slight angle and remove it from the slot.

Step 7. If the card is attached to a bracket, remove the card from the bracket.

To reinstall the card or replace it with a different card, reverse these steps.

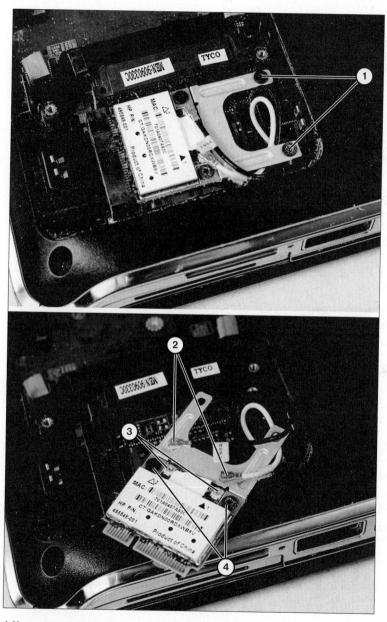

1. Unscrew mounting bolts
2. Antenna wires
3. Antenna wire attachment points
4. Unscrew mounting bolts to remove card from bracket

FIGURE 1-11   Removing a miniPCIe Wireless Card

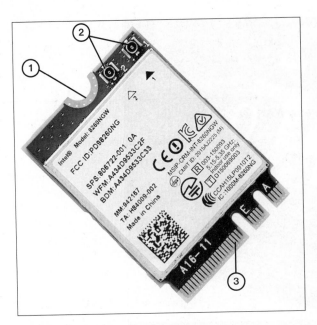

1. Mounting screw fits here
2. Antenna connectors
3. M.2 connector

FIGURE 1-12   A Typical M.2 Wireless Adapter

Cellular Card

Some laptop users require connectivity no matter where they are in the field. Because cellular access is sometimes needed because WiFi is not available, some business-class laptops come with slots for cellular LTE wireless connectivity. Cell providers offer data-only services for data access, but these plans are not set up for calling or messaging. Cell providers also offer service plans for external USB LTE modems.

To enable cellular on a laptop, it is best to start by consulting the manufacturer's documentation for the location of the slot for the SIM card. Then follow these steps:

Step 1.   Activate the SIM card.

Step 2.   Insert the SIM card into the laptop, making sure the gold contacts connect.

Step 3.   If the SIM card does not auto-configure, access the settings by selecting the **Cellular** option from the Network Connections area in the system tray (Windows 10).

Step 4.   Select the **Cellular** tab and choose **Add an APN (access point name)**.

Step 5.   Enable a PIN if you want to specify what users have access to the cellular connection.

USB Travel Routers and Wireless WAN Cards

Another option for traveling users is a mobile hotspot. Each cell provider has its own version of a hotspot and can add a hotspot with a data plan to the user's cell account.

Video Card

As mentioned earlier, the mPCIe slot in a laptop may be used for a video graphics processing unit (GPU). Gaming users often enhance the GPUs on their gaming machines. To install a GPU, follow these steps:

Step 1.   Disconnect cables and remove the old graphics card. Remove the card drivers, if necessary.

Step 2.   Align the new GPU to the slots in the PCIe card and insert carefully.

Step 3.   Connect cables and place them away from the fan.

Step 4.   R-connect any other cables and close the case.

Step 5.   Boot the computer. When online, check for driver updates and install them.

Laptop Screens

A computer display screen typically consists of a liquid crystal display (LCD) or an organic light-emitting diode (OLED) display, and any communication peripherals are added separately. Laptop screens are specially designed to accommodate a web-cam, microphone, WiFi antennas, and often touchscreen digitizers and inverters.

An LCD screen uses a backlight to illuminate light-modulating liquid crystals. When an electric current passes through the crystals, they arrange into patterns that become the image on the screen. LCD screens are customized to different device types, and some have WiFi antennas attached.

OLED screens are in many ways advanced compared to LED screens. They are brighter and use less energy (saving on battery use) and are flexible and foldable. But the screens themselves are much thinner and more subject to cracking or breaking when dropped or mishandled.

Screens are covered in more detail later in this chapter.

DC Jack

The *DC* jack (also referred to as the *power adapter port*) receives DC power from the AC/DC power adapter and passes it to the battery. If the DC jack fails, the laptop's battery cannot be charged, and the laptop cannot run on external power either. To replace the DC jack on a typical laptop:

Step 1.   Remove power from the laptop and then remove any components that block access to the DC jack and cable. These might include mass storage, WLAN card, service cover, optical drive, keyboard, palm rest, memory modules, display assembly, other ports, and bottom cover (see Figure 1-13).

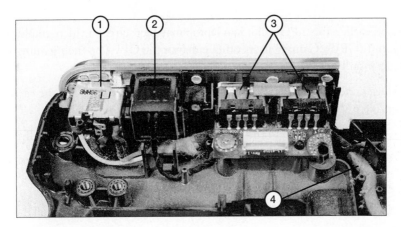

1. DC jack
2. RJ-11 modem port
3. USB 2.0 ports
4. DC jack power cable

FIGURE 1-13   Access to the DC Jack May Be Blocked by Other Ports That Must Be Removed First

Step 2.   Unplug the DC jack power cord from the system board.

Step 3.   Remove the DC jack power cord from the guides holding it in place on the system board.

Step 4.   Remove the screw or clip that holds the DC jack in place.

Step 5.   Lift out the DC jack (see Figure 1-14).

To replace the DC jack, reverse these steps.

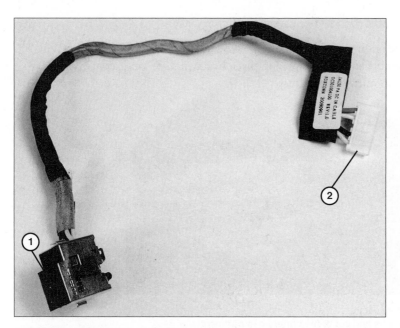

1. DC jack connection to power adapter
2. Motherboard power connector

FIGURE 1-14   A DC Jack Successfully Removed from a Laptop

Battery

A failing laptop battery can be a source of all kinds of problems for the user. Most manufacturers have diagnostic software that reports on the health of the battery and estimates how many cycles are left. It is best to be proactive in battery replacement. If you need to purchase a replacement battery for a laptop, you may consider a larger-capacity battery, if one is available for the model being repaired.

Before performing any replacement of internal components, the system must be removed from all power sources. Follow this procedure:

Step 1.   Turn off the computer.

Step 2.   Disconnect the AC adapter from the computer.

Step 3.   Open the battery compartment in the unit; it might be secured by a sliding lock or by screws.

Step 4.   If the battery is under a removable cover, remove the battery compartment cover.

Step 5. Open the lock that holds the battery in place.

Step 6. Slide out or lift out the battery (see Figure 1-15). If the battery is a flat assembly, it might be held in place by a clip; if so, push the clip to one side to release the battery.

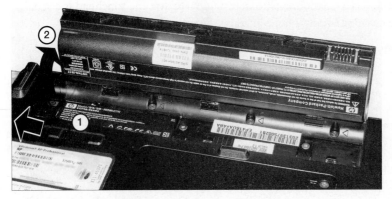

1. Releasing the battery catch
2. Rotating the battery up and out of the battery compartment

FIGURE 1-15   Removing a Battery from a Typical Laptop Computer

Step 7. Examine the battery contacts inside the computer for dirt or corrosion and clean dirty contacts with a soft cloth.

To replace the battery, follow these steps:

Step 1. Line up the replacement battery with the contacts inside the battery compartment. Make sure you insert the battery so that the positive and negative terminals are in the right directions.

Step 2. Slide in or clip the battery into place.

Step 3. Replace any cover over the battery compartment.

Step 4. If the battery must be charged before use, plug in the AC adapter to both the computer and wall outlet. Check the computer's manual for the proper charge time for a new battery.

CAUTION   Take precautions against ESD when you change the battery. Discharge any static electricity in your body by touching a metal object before you open the battery compartment and don't touch the contacts on the battery or the contacts in the battery compartment with your hands.

Touchpad

If you need to replace the touchpad, you must partially disassemble the portable computer. Details vary from unit to unit (check with your vendor for details), but the basic procedure is described here. To remove the touchpad, follow these steps:

Step 1. Check service documents to determine whether the touchpad is a separate component or is built into the top cover.

Step 2. Remove all power from the laptop.

Step 3. If the touchpad is built into the top cover, remove the top cover. If the touchpad is a separate component, remove components that block access to the screws that hold the touchpad in place. These might include the storage devices, wireless adapter, optical drive, keyboard, keyboard cover, display assembly, and top cover.

Step 4. Place the system so it is bottom side up.

Step 5. Disconnect the cable from the pointing devices to the motherboard.

Step 6. Remove the clips or screws holding the touchpad in (see Figure 1-16).

Step 7. Remove the touchpad assembly.

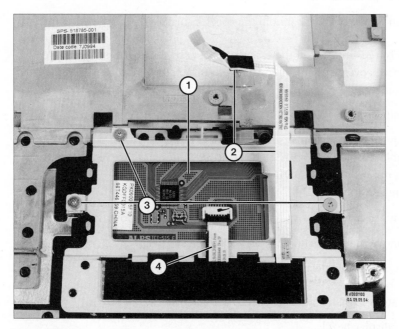

1. Touchpad
2. Ribbon cable to motherboard
3. Mounting screws to remove
4. Ribbon cable for touchpad buttons

To replace the touchpad, reverse these steps.

Plastics/Frames

Most laptops use plastic bezels, case covers, and frames (sometimes referred to collectively as *plastics/frames*). These can be cracked during normal use or during replacement or upgrades to internal components.

To replace a service cover on the bottom of a laptop, such as the access cover to storage, RAM, or the wireless adapter:

Step 1. Loosen the screws that hold the cover in place or use the unlocking latch (varies by system).

Step 2. Lift the cover by the edge(s) recommended in the service manual. It might need to be unsnapped from the base enclosure through careful use of a straight-blade screwdriver or pry tool. YouTube can be a big help at this point.

Step 3. When the cover comes off, set it aside.

Step 4. Place the new service cover in place of the old one. Snap it down or swing it into position.

Step 5. Tighten the screws that hold the cover in place.

The base enclosure is the part of the case that covers the entire bottom of the computer. The service covers either snap or screw into the base enclosure. To remove the base enclosure:

Step 1. Remove the service cover.

Step 2. Remove any components that cover up screws that must be removed to enable the base enclosure to be removed. These might include mass storage, optical drives, SODIMMs, or WiFi adapters. See the laptop's service manual for details.

Step 3. Remove the rubber feet if they are used to conceal mounting screws.

Step 4. Remove the screws holding the base enclosure in position.

Step 5. Lift the base enclosure from the computer frame.

Reverse these steps to install a replacement base enclosure.

To remove the display bezel:

Step 1. Remove the display assembly from the computer.

Step 2. The display bezel might be held in place by screws or might be snapped into place. If the bezel uses screws, remove any screw covers and remove the screws. If the bezel snaps into place, pry up the display bezel from the inner edges.

Step 3. Lift the display bezel away from the display assembly.

Reverse these steps to install a replacement display bezel.

NOTE Remember that access to the inside of a laptop is not the same for all manufacturers. Check the documentation for instructions or special tool requirements.

Speaker

If you have failed speakers, you can check for several possible problems before resorting to replacing them. Things you should check before replacing speakers include the obvious, such as volume settings and audio output settings, and the not-so-obvious, such as audio cable connections, audio driver updates, and secure the seating on the sound card. If speakers are broken or worn out and need to be replaced, follow these steps to remove a laptop speaker or speakers:

Step 1. Disconnect power to the laptop and remove any components that block access to the speakers. These might include the hard drive, WLAN cover, optical drive, keyboard, keyboard cover, display assembly, and top cover.

Step 2. If necessary, turn the laptop so it's bottom side up.

Step 3. Disconnect cables, as indicated in the manufacturer's directions.

Step 4. Remove the screws holding the speakers in place.

Step 5. Lift out the speakers.

To replace the speakers, reverse these steps.

System Board

To remove a typical system board (motherboard), follow these basic instructions:

Step 1. Remove all mass storage devices (hard disk, SSD, SSHD, optical drive).

Step 2. Remove the base enclosure. Disconnect the fan from the motherboard if it is part of the base assembly.

Step 3.   Remove the display assembly.

Step 4.   Disconnect all cables from the system board. (A photo of the assembly before unplugging cables may be of great use in the reassembly process.) These might include a fingerprint reader cable, power connector, display panel cable, webcam and microphone cables, wireless antenna cables, connector board cables, speaker cables, touchpad and keyboard cables, fan connector, and power button board cable. Some of these are round cables, and others are flat ribbon cables.

Step 5.   Remove all screws holding the top cover in place. Remove the top cover and turn it upside down so the motherboard is visible.

Step 6.   Remove any additional screws holding the motherboard to the top cover (see Figure 1-17).

Step 7.   Remove the system board from the bottom plate. This might require lifting one end of the board at an angle and sliding it out.

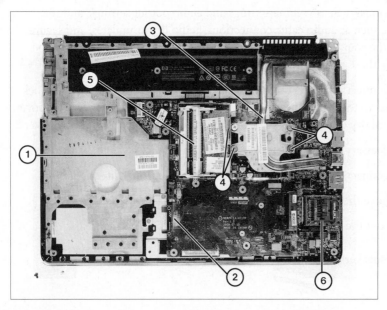

1. Top cover
2. Motherboard
3. Heat sink assembly
4. Mounting screws for heat sink
5. SODIMM memory sockets
6. Flash memory card reader (built into motherboard)

FIGURE 1-17   Preparing to Remove the Motherboard After Removing All Mounting Screws

Figure 1-18 illustrates a typical motherboard after being removed from a laptop.

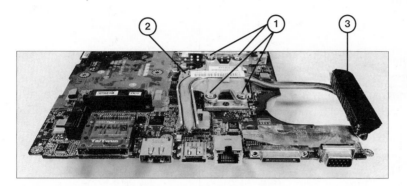

1. Mounting screws for heat sink
2. Retaining assembly for heat sink pipe
3. Fan exhaust/heat exchanger for heat sink

FIGURE 1-18   A Typical Laptop Motherboard After Removal

After removing the system board, remove any components you plan to use on the new system board, such as the heat sink, CPU, and memory.

After attaching the heat sink and CPU to the new system board and installing the memory, reverse the preceding steps to replace the system board.

CPU

Before replacing the CPU in a laptop, you must determine which models are supported by the installed motherboard. Laptop motherboards are customized for a narrow range of CPUs. A UEFI/BIOS update might enable additional CPUs to be used successfully. Install any required UEFI/BIOS update before disassembling the laptop.

You cannot replace the CPU without removing the heat sink module. Laptop heat sinks are typically one-piece or two-piece units that pull heat away from the chipset and the processor. Some units incorporate the fan. To remove the heat sink (see Figures 1-19 and 1-20), follow these steps:

Step 1.   Remove the screws holding the heat sink in place.

Step 2.   If the heat sink incorporates a fan, disconnect the fan power lead from the motherboard.

Step 3.   Lift up on the heat sink to remove it. (Move it from side to side if necessary to loosen the thermal material.) Set aside the heat sink.

Figure 1-19 shows what a typical heat sink looks like after being removed from a working system.

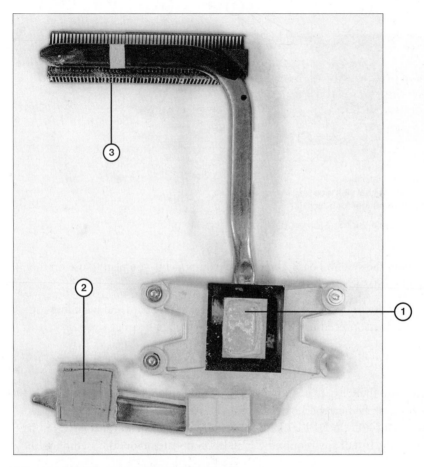

1. Remove thermal compound from CPU heat sink
2. Phase-change thermal material on chipset heat sink can be reused
3. Use compressed air to clean fan exhaust/heat exchanger before reusing heat sink

FIGURE 1-19   A Heat Sink After Removal

To remove the CPU, follow these steps:

Step 1.   Loosen the processor locking screw. Note the markings on the CPU and the socket. The CPU must be aligned in the same position when installed.

Step 2.   Remove the CPU from the socket (see Figure 1-20). Retain it for possible reuse.

If you are using a factory CPU assembly, use the new CPU and heat sink in the reassembly process. Before doing so, be sure to remove the old thermal material from the fan and other motherboard components that use the heat sink. The new heat sink includes thermal material (thermal pads and/or paste). Use 70% or higher isopropyl alcohol for cleaning these components.

NOTE   Laptop processors use different sockets than desktop processors. Laptop and desktop sockets are not interchangeable.

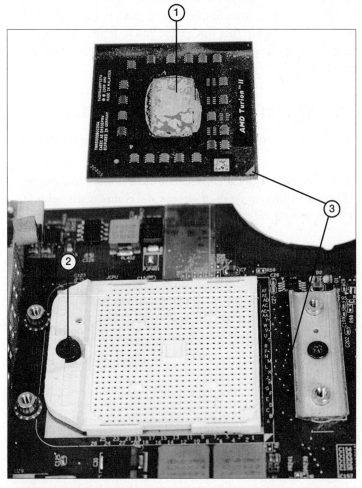

1. Thermal material residue on CPU must be removed before reuse
2. Clamping mechanism for CPU socket
3. Pin 1 markings for correct orientation of processor in socket

FIGURE 1-20   A Typical Laptop Processor and Its Socket

If you are reinstalling the same processor and heat sink, or if you are using a heat sink and processor from a vendor other than your laptop vendor, you typically need to supply your own thermal material. Be sure to clean old thermal material from the fan, processor, heat sink, and other motherboard components before applying new material.

Install the processor first, followed by the heat sink, the fan (if it is not built in to the heat sink), and the remainder of the components you removed.

Cooling Fan

The cooling fan in a laptop might be part of the heat sink or might be attached to the laptop's enclosure. If you plan to reuse a fan, be sure to clean it. However, if you are performing a disassembly of a laptop that will enable you to replace the fan, we recommend replacing it. If the cooling fan in a laptop fails, many components may be damaged or destroyed.

Install Components Within the Display of a Laptop

220-1001: Objective 1.2: Given a scenario, install components within the display of a laptop.

We refer to the display of a laptop simply as a *screen*, but there is more to a display than meets the eyes. There are different types of screens and components behind the glass that make it work, and the following sections cover the essentials of screen technology.

Screens

Replacing screens can be a difficult task, and it involves expensive and delicate parts. Some vendors provide online documentation that guides you through the entire process of reducing an intact portable into a pile of parts and rebuilding it. However, this information is primarily intended for professional computer service staff.

LCD

A liquid crystal display (**LCD**) is made with either a passive or active-matrix display grid. Active matrix is considered the better technology, and it is the type used in the vast majority of current laptops. An active-matrix screen uses a transistor for every dot onscreen; for example, a 1,600×900 active-matrix LCD screen has 1,440,000 transistors. Each pixel intersection in an active-matrix screen has a transistor, and a small current is sent across the screen grid. The transistors can manage the current on the screen very quickly, giving the user an experience of smoothly flowing motion.

LCD screen replacement on laptops can be complex, especially if you need to replace the display panel or the backlight, or if the screen assembly includes the WiFi antenna, as is the case with most recent models. LCD display panels built into portable computers are customized for each model of portable computer. You need to disassemble a computer in order to remove and replace an LCD screen. You can get replacements from either the vendor or an authorized repair parts depot. Many vendors require that only authorized technicians remove or replace display panels in portable computers. However, the process of replacing the entire LCD display assembly is simpler and might be possible for you to perform in the field. This section focuses on LCD display replacement.

LCD Screen Replacement

The details of the process for removing an LCD display assembly from a portable computer vary by model, but they involve these basic steps:

Step 1. After removing power from the system, if the system has an integrated wireless card, disconnect the antenna leads attached to the adapter.

Step 2. Remove the keyboard frame and keyboard.

Step 3. Disconnect the display cable from the system board; this cable transmits power and data to the display assembly. On touchscreen-equipped models, this cable also carries touchscreen data.

Step 4. If the system has integrated wireless, remove the antenna leads from the clips in the top cover.

Step 5. Rotate the display assembly to a 90-degree angle to the base unit.

Step 6. Remove the screws that secure the display assembly.

Step 7. Pull the display assembly free from the base unit. Figure 1-21 illustrates a typical 15.6-in. display assembly after removal.

Step 8. Be sure to save all screws, ground springs, and other hardware that you removed during the disassembly process.

NOTE If you need to replace the inverter, the backlight, or the webcam, further disassembly is necessary.

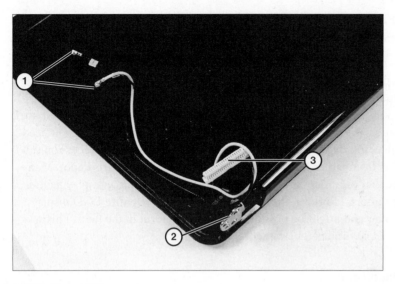

1. WiFi antenna wires
2. Display hinge mount
3. Display connector

FIGURE 1-21   Detail of a Typical Laptop LCD Panel After Removal

Many vendors offer replacement LCD display assemblies that can be installed by following the previous steps in reverse order. Although you can also purchase components of the assembly, such as the LCD display panel or backlight, this type of repair is difficult and time-consuming and should be performed at a repair depot. If you do repair on your own, it is a good idea to remove the old screen first to make sure you can do the job of replacement without special tools. You may have to search for specific brand coaching on YouTube or other sites to get the task completed safely. By observing others completing the task you can visually compare the connectors on your laptop to the ones on the replacement to assure compatibility.

OLED

An organic LED (*OLED*) display uses a layer of organic compounds between two electrodes to emit light. As a consequence, the brightness of each OLED pixel can be individually controlled. OLED displays have been developed in two forms: passive matrix (PMOLED) and active matrix (AMOLED). A defective OLED display should be swapped out.

Replacing OLED screens is more difficult than damage during the replacement process, and specialized tools are necessary for the more delicate steps. If the need to replace OLED screens is infrequent, it may be safer and more cost-effective to take cracked or broken screens to a professional who is equipped to replace them.

The advantages of OLED can be summarized as follows:

- **Brighter:** OLEDs can be larger than other types of screens and offer higher resolutions.

- **Thinner in size and lighter in weight:** OLEDs are a good choice for smartphones, tablets and convertible (two-in-one) units that switch between laptop and tablet modes.

- **Energy efficient:** Only the lit pixels draw power; with good application design, this can greatly extend battery life.

- **Faster refresh rates:** OLEDs can refresh quickly, which makes them a favorite of gamers who value quick response time.

WiFi Antenna Connector/Placement

Although the miniPCIe card that contains the WiFi radio is located in the base of a laptop, the WiFi antenna is usually part of the screen assembly (see Figure 1-22). If a laptop screen is damaged, the WiFi antennas might also be damaged. In an OLED display, the inverter is not present, but the rest of the components are in the same locations.

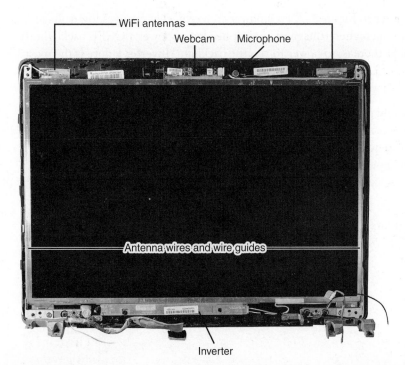

FIGURE 1-22   WiFi Antennas, Wires, CCFL Inverter, Webcam, and Microphone in a Typical LCD-CCFL Display

Webcam

Almost every laptop display assembly includes a webcam at the top-center edge of the display assembly (refer to Figure 1-22). If a webcam fails, you can replace it after performing a partial teardown of the laptop assembly. However, if you need a higher-resolution webcam, you can use an external webcam that plugs into a USB port.

Microphone

A microphone is also part of the display assembly. It is used by the webcam or for other recording purposes, as needed (refer to Figure 1-22). If a microphone fails, you can replace it after performing a partial teardown of the laptop assembly. However, if you need a higher-quality microphone, you can use a microphone as part of a headset that plugs into an audio port or a USB port.

Inverter

An LCD-CCFL laptop display is easy to read because of two components: the inverter and the backlight. If either fails, the laptop display becomes so dim that it is almost impossible to use.

The inverter (refer to Figure 1-22) is a power converter that changes low-voltage DC power into the higher-voltage AC power needed to power a CCFL backlight. If the inverter fails, there is no power to run the backlight. Inverter failure is the most common cause of LCD display failure. However, inverters are relatively inexpensive to replace, and they can be purchased for do-it-yourself (DIY) replacement.

A CCFL backlight failure is far less common than an inverter failure. If a CCFL backlight fails, a complete disassembly of the display, down to the individual component level, is required. If a CCFL backlight failure occurs, swapping the screen assembly for a known-working replacement often makes more sense than attempting a repair unless you are experienced with screen disassembly.

NOTE   Some vendors offer kits that can be used to convert laptop LCD or other types of CCFL displays to use LED backlights instead. To learn more, see www.lcdparts.net.

Digitizer/Touchscreen

A touchscreen display differs from a standard laptop display in that it has a digitizer layer on top of the display panel. The digitizer detects and transmits touches to the laptop processor. Digitizers are also used on touchscreen smartphones, tablets, fitness monitors, smart watches, phablets, e-readers, and smart cameras.

If the digitizer layer is damaged, but the display panel is intact, the digitizer layer can be replaced separately.

NOTE   For examples of pricing and availability of digitizers, see http://touchscreendigitizer.net.

Use Appropriate Laptop Features

220-1001: Objective 1.3: Given a scenario, use appropriate laptop features.

220-1001
Exam

Recent generations of laptops have become as powerful as and more versatile than desktops. Laptops have developed features common to those of larger computers, but they have had to overcome the issues that come with a smaller form factor. The following sections describe some of the ways to enable a laptop to perform functions of a larger computer.

Special Function Keys

Because laptop computers incorporate multimedia and networking components, they include special function (*Fn*) keys on the keyboard and special controls for displays, wireless functions, volume, screen brightness, Bluetooth networking, and (in some cases) keyboard backlighting. These keys provide all the functions of a desktop but in significantly less space.

Most laptop keyboards combine two functions on one key, and the user presses the Fn key on the keyboard to toggle between functions much as the Shift key is used with the numbers of a keyboard to use special characters. While the Fn key is held down, pressing any key with an additional Fn function performs the Fn function; when the Fn key is released, the key reverts to its normal operation. Fn functions are usually printed below or beside the normal key legend and sometimes in a contrasting color.

Newer MacBook Pro models come with a touch bar that replaces physical function keys with a touch strip. This strip is interactive and can change depending on user preference for each application. While the touch bar is currently beyond the scope of the A+ exam, this innovation may be an indicator of future evolution in laptop keyboards.

Laptops also have special provisions for expansion, such as docking stations, and physical security, through locking mechanisms. Learn more in the following sections.

NOTE   Be sure to make special note of features such as docking stations, physical laptop locks and cable locks, and rotating/removable screens for the 220-1001 exam.

NOTE   On some laptops, the special functions are the default. On such systems, to use the function keys for normal operating system functions (for example, refresh Windows Explorer/File Explorer view in Windows), hold down the Fn key and press the function key (for example, F5 to refresh).

Features available with typical Fn key or other special function keys include:

- Dual displays (secondary monitor or projector)
- Wireless (on/off)
- Cellular (on/off)
- Volume settings
- Screen brightness
- Bluetooth (on/off)
- Keyboard backlight (on/off)
- Touch pad (on/off)
- Screen orientation
- Media options (fast forward/rewind)
- GPS (on/off)
- Airplane mode (on/off)

In Figure 1-23, the top keyboard is on a MacBook Air—a model that does not have a touch bar. The lower keyboard is from a Samsung ATIV-500 convertible tablet.

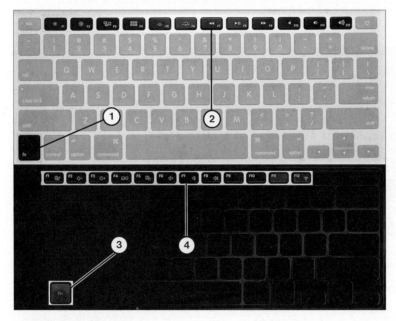

1. Fn key on MacBook Air
2. Special keys that work with Fn key
3. Fn key on Samsung ATIV-500 (Windows)
4. Special keys that work with Fn key

FIGURE 1-23 Examples of Fn Keys

To determine exactly which features are controlled through the Fn key, check the documentation for your mobile device.

Docking Station

A *docking station* expands the capability of a portable computer by adding features such as:

- One or more expansion slots
- Additional I/O ports, such as Ethernet, display output ports (for HDMI or DisplayPort), Thunderbolt ports, USB ports (USB 2.0, 3.0, USB 3.1 Type C), and others
- Power connection for the laptop
- Connectors for a standard keyboard and mouse

Most docking stations are produced by portable computer vendors, although some third-party products are also available. Business-class laptops that support docking stations might feature a proprietary expansion bus on the rear or bottom of the computer (see Figure 1-24).

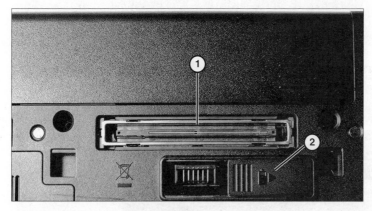

1. Laptop connection to docking station
2. Open door to permit battery charging by docking station

FIGURE 1-24   A Typical Proprietary Bus for a Docking Station on a Business-Class Laptop

However, docking stations made for tablets or thin and light laptops might connect via a high-speed bus such as Thunderbolt or USB 3.0/3.1 or via a proprietary charging/data cable (see Figure 1-25).

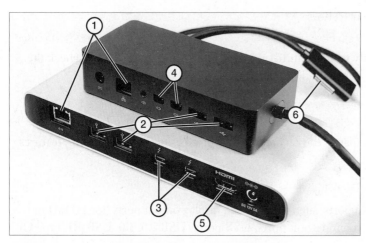

1. Ethernet   4. Mini DisplayPort
2. USB   5. HDMI
3. Thunderbolt   6. Proprietary charging/docking cable

FIGURE 1-25   Microsoft Dock for Surface Pro 3 and 4 (Top) and a Third-Party Dock for MacBook Air and Pro with Thunderbolt Ports (Bottom)

Wireless docking stations are now available for mobile systems running fifth-generation or newer Intel Core vPro (business-class) processors with the Intel Tri-Band Wireless-AC 17265 adapter. For an example, see https://www.dell.com/en-us/shop/accessories/apd/452-bbux?sku=452-BBUX.

Regardless of how a docking station connects to a portable computer, the user can leave desktop-type peripherals connected to the docking station and can access them quickly and easily by connecting the portable computer to the docking station.

NOTE   The term *mobile docking station* is often used to describe a device that is used to securely hold a laptop or tablet in place in a vehicles (police, insurance, EMS, and other industries). These devices are not used for additional ports. The term *vehicle mount* is more appropriate for such a device.

Port Replicator

A port replicator is a device that allows a laptop or notebook to expand the number of ports so additional devices can be attached. For example, a user can attach a port replicator to a USB port on a notebook and then attach other devices, such as printers, cameras, mice, speakers, and so on, to the port replicator. The replicator may have DVI and HDMI ports to host additional displays. As features are added, port replicators come to resemble non-proprietary docking stations.

Physical Laptop and Cable Locks

Most laptops as well as other mobile devices such as projectors and docking stations feature security slots. On a laptop, this slot is typically located near a rear corner (see Figure 1-26).

1. Security slot

FIGURE 1-26   A Security Slot on a Laptop

This slot is used with a laptop *cable lock* such as the one shown in Figure 1-27. A laptop lock may be a combination or keyed lock, but either way, it is designed to lock the laptop (or other secured device) to a fixed location such as a table.

FIGURE 1-27   A Combination Laptop Security Lock

To prevent data theft from occurring, you should also use the password-lock function in your operating system to require a password whenever the keyboard is locked. In Windows, press **Windows+L**. For maximum protection, use some type of full-disk encryption, such as Windows BitLocker, macOS FileVault, or a third-party solution such as PGP or Symantec Endpoint Encryption.

Rotating/Removable Screens

One of the fastest-growing categories of mobile devices is those with *rotating/ removable screens*. Bridging the gap between tablet and laptop, this category includes all performance levels from low-end 32-bit processors with 32GB storage and 2MB RAM to systems running high-performance multicore 64-bit processors.

Devices with removable keyboards (see Figure 1-28) typically feature screen sizes under 12 in. When used without the keyboard, such a device functions as a large tablet. Many models have additional ports built into the keyboard.

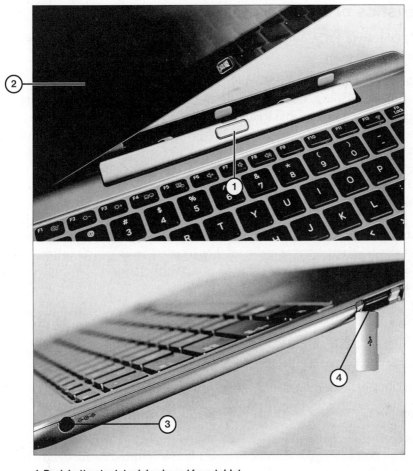

1. Push button to detach keyboard from tablet
2. Tablet
3. Keyboard includes charging jack
4. Keyboard includes two USB ports (only one visible here)

FIGURE 1-28   A Samsung ATIV-500 Windows Tablet with a Removable Keyboard

Devices with rotating screens feature larger displays and more ports, and they have more powerful processors. Although the display size and port availability of these devices rival those of conventional laptops, these devices are not intended to be easily upgradable. Memory, storage, and wireless upgrades typically require a major disassembly process.

Characteristics of Other Mobile Devices

220-1001: Objective 1.4: Compare and contrast characteristics of various types of other mobile devices.

Manufacturers are continuously developing new apps and mobile devices that further integrate technology into our daily lives. Users are more readily accepting smartphones, tablets, and wearable technology such as smart watches and fitness trackers as part of their routine daily life. With the vast range of available products you might need to use or support, it's important to have a working knowledge of their basic functions.

Tablets

Tablets, which use a touchscreen instead of a mouse or keyboard for user input, are available in a wide variety of types and sizes. The most common tablets currently in use are the iPad Pro, Samsung Galaxy Tab S4, and Microsoft Surface Pro. Tablets typically include the following features:

- Use of iOS, Android, Windows 10 Mobile, or Chrome OS operating systems

- Video camera enabled for video chat

- Stylus device for writing

- Keyboard and other devices attached using Bluetooth

- Limited or nonexistent port and storage expansion options

- Apps installed or updated through the operating system's app store (App Store or iTunes for Apple devices, Google Play for Android devices, and The Microsoft Store for Microsoft)

- The requirement for plenty of power (either by being plugged into AC power or having most of the battery life remaining) to update the operating system

NOTE   Windows tablets with screens larger than 8 in. typically run standard editions of Windows 8.1 or Windows 10. Smaller Windows tablets typically use Windows 10 Mobile.

Smartphones

No device has had a greater impact on human communication in recent history than the use of smartphones. Smartphones typically use either Android or iOS operating systems, although a few use Windows 10 Mobile.

With the exception of phone calls, most of the apps available in smartphones are available in tablets, too, including video chat and messaging. Some differences between tablets and smartphones include:

- Wireless carriers provide operating system updates for Android phones, but Apple provides operating system updates.

- Wireless carriers provide network-specific updates for iPhones (iOS), but Apple provides operating system updates.

- Phone carriers provide data-only services to tablets, and regular cellular voice calling is not available on all of them. Some tablet apps, however, provide real-time voice communication via the data connection.

You may come across the term "phablet" in discussions of smartphones. This term usually refers to phones with screen sizes of 5.5 in. or larger. Most feature Quad HD (QHD) (four times the pixels of HD) or HD resolution panels, and some include dedicated styluses. Although smaller smartphones typically don't include flash memory storage, some phablets do. As the phone market expands, encompassing an ever-increasing array of devices, the phablet distinction will likely become less important.

Wearable Technology Devices

Wearable technology devices such as the Fitbit (which is a fitness monitor) and the Apple Watch (which is a fitness monitor and smart watch) have expanded the reach of personal technology and computing. These devices connect to a smartphone via Bluetooth and can be charged in as little as 15 minutes.

When selecting wearable technology, it's important to verify compatibility with your device's operating system and features. If Bluetooth is not enabled in your smartphone, it must be turned on before a wearable technology device can connect with it.

VR/AR (virtual reality/augmented reality) headsets used with smartphones—such as the Oculus Rift and Gear VR—are a growing part of the gaming market. Virtual reality refers to computer simulations projected into a headset that covers the user's entire field of vision, creating a virtual world experience. With augmented reality apps on smartphones and tablets, generated images are layered on top of real-world images captured by the device's camera.

E-readers

E-readers such as the Amazon Kindle and Kobo Clara are optimized for text reading. Because these devices are similar in size to a paperback, they are widely used for recreational reading.

Low-end e-readers with monochrome screens do not display graphic designs well, which limits their suitability for reading graphic novels or technical documents. Some users have also complained of poor formatting and the lack of indexing with some e-reader books. Most e-readers, however, now have at least some kind of edge lighting for easier reading.

Because e-readers are designed for a single function, they can be very compact and efficient. For example, the Kindle Paperweight is 6.7×4.6×0.36 in. and weighs only 7 ounces, but it is WiFi enabled and has 8GB of RAM and a battery that can last several weeks.

E-readers that support ePub and PDF formats are more suitable for graphically rich books. E-readers from Kobo (kobobooks.com), Amazon, and others (as well as the Google Books app) support ePub.

GPS

Standalone Global Positioning System (**GPS**) devices such as TomTom GO and Garmin provide turn-by-turn navigation in vehicles. Although smartphone mapping apps such as Apple Maps and Google Maps also provide these features, standalone GPS units are still useful because they can feature larger screens and easier user interface (requiring less driver distraction).

One potential drawback to standalone GPS device usage is the need to keep maps updated. Many of these units do not include map updates in the purchase price, and these updates must be purchased separately. If you manage standalone GPS units, you should familiarize yourself with the devices' map update cycles and with subscription renewal information. Whether a user will use a standalone GPS or a smartphone as a GPS in a vehicle, a suitable mount and 12V power adapter should be made available.

GPS has spread into several non-mapping markets. Fitness trackers and sports apps use GPS for training, and GPS has applications in the medical mobile health care market and for tracking pets with GPS collars. Tracking personal property such as cars and drones is becoming more common as GPS technology becomes cheaper and integration into the Internet of Things (IoT) becomes commonplace.

Accessories and Ports Used by Other Mobile Devices

220-1001: Objective 1.5: Given a scenario, connect and configure accessories and ports of other mobile devices.

Many different types of connections, ports, and accessories are available for mobile devices. The following sections review the essential features of a number of them.

Connection Types: Wired

Wired connections have long been moving from proprietary design to universal standards such as USB 3. The following sections describe a few wired connection types that a technician will likely encounter while USB 3 proliferates in the market.

Micro-USB/Mini-USB for Android and Windows

For a brief period, the 5-pin *mini-USB* port was used for Android smartphones. Most recently, the USB-on-the-Go connector has become the de facto standard for both Android smartphones and tablets. However, some recent Android tablets use the reversible USB Type C connector.

Most Windows tablets and smartphones (depending on the model) use the USB-on-the-Go (micro-USB) connector or the USB Type C connector.

Figure 1-29 compares 30-pin, Lightning, 5-pin mini-USB, micro-USB, and USB Type C cables. All these cables have the standard USB Type A connector on the other end.

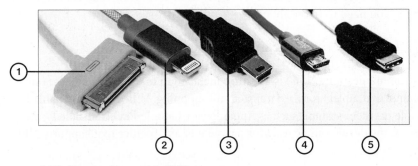

1. 30-pin power/sync cable (iOS)
2. Lightning power/sync cable (iOS)
3. 5-pin miniUSBpower/sync cable (Android)
4. microUSB (USB-on-the-Go) power/sync cable (Android smartphones and tablets, Windows tablets)
5. USB Type C power/sync cable (several smartphone brands and the iPad Pro)

FIGURE 1-29   The Most Common Mobile Power/Sync Cables

Lightning for Apple iOS

Older iOS devices (up through the iPhone 4 series and the third-generation iPad) used the 30-pin connector. However, starting in 2012, Apple standardized on the 8-pin reversible *Lightning* connector for iPhones, iPads, iPods, and other mobile devices. (The iPad Pro, however, uses USB Type C.)

Tethering

Most smartphones can share a cellular data connection by using tethering. Wired tethering involves attaching the phone to a laptop or tablet with a phone cable with a USB connection. When tethering is done wirelessly, the phone becomes a *hotspot*. For details, see Chapter 2, "Networking."

Proprietary Vendor-Specific Ports (Communication/Power)

Until recently, every smartphone and tablet used its own proprietary connection for charging and file synchronization. Older Android tablets and smartphones used various proprietary chargers. To support these, multiple-head AC or 12V DC chargers were sold, as were dedicated cables.

Connection Types: Wireless

While wired connections can offer high-speed data coupled with battery charging benefits, there are times when wires get in the way or simply are not a practical solution for device connection. There are a few types of wireless connections in common use today that you need to know about.

NFC

Near field communication (*NFC*) is a feature included in many mobile devices such as smartphones and tablets for data transfer and shopping. When NFC is enabled and a suitable payment system (such as Apple Pay or Google Pay) is installed on a mobile device, the device can be used for payment at any retailer that supports NFC payments.

NFC can also be used to automatically turn on Bluetooth and transfer files between devices (a feature sometimes referred to as "tap and go" or, on Android devices, Android Beam). It can be enabled separately from NFC for payments.

Apple does not currently permit its devices with NFC to work for file transfers except with iTunes purchasing and Apple Pay. Apple's AirDrop feature uses peer-to-peer WiFi for file sharing.

Bluetooth

Bluetooth began as a short-range, low-speed wireless network technology primarily designed to operate in peer-to-peer (or ad hoc) mode between PCs and other devices, such as printers, projectors, smartphones, mice, and keyboards. Before a

Bluetooth device can work with your computer or mobile device, it must be paired with the device.

By default, Bluetooth is usually disabled on Android devices but is enabled on iOS devices such as iPads or iPhones. To connect a Bluetooth device to a mobile device, Bluetooth first needs to be enabled; then the Bluetooth device needs to be synchronized to the mobile device. This is known as *pairing*, or *linking*. It sometimes requires a PIN code. Once synchronized, the device needs to be connected. For more information on Bluetooth, see Chapter 2.

IR

Some recent and current-model smartphones include built-in **IR** (infrared) capabilities. However, this feature is designed for use with TV and home theater remote control apps rather than for data transfer, as with older mobile devices. If your smartphone can be used to control your TV, it has an IR blaster onboard.

Hotspot

When a smartphone enables sharing of its Internet connection, it becomes a hotspot. Creating a hotspot enables wireless tethering, creating a small WiFi network. The phone generates a default password (which the phone user can change) that other WiFi devices can use to access the network and share the phone's access to the Web. Setting up a hotspot is covered later in this chapter.

Accessories

Mobile devices can be quite expensive, and users want to get the most use from a mobile device while protecting their investment. The accessories listed here are aftermarket add-ons that enhance the experience of using a mobile device and, in some cases, physically protecting it against damage.

Headsets

For music listening, mobile devices feature the same 3.5mm mini-jack that is available on computers for headsets or earbuds. However, for hands-free telephone use, you can pair a wireless headset with a smartphone via Bluetooth.

Speakers

Portable speakers use rechargeable batteries, and the USB cable on portable speakers is used only for recharging. Some low-cost speakers use a 3.5mm mini-jack speaker cable, but most use Bluetooth. By using Bluetooth, you can place the speaker in the midst of the action while keeping your smartphone or tablet out of harm's way.

Game Pads

Game pads are video game controllers with Bluetooth connections that can be used with smartphones or tablets for game play. They can contain joystick controls and thumb controls. Game pads are sometimes known as joy pads. Some iOS controllers connect via Lightning rather than with Bluetooth.

Extra Battery Packs/Battery Chargers

Although a few smartphones and tablets have user-replaceable batteries, a much more convenient solution is a portable battery charger, also known as a portable power bank. This type of device has a battery onboard and a USB connection, and it can be used to charge a smartphone or tablet via its USB charging cable.

These devices differ in terms of the following characteristics:

- **mAh (milliampere-hour) rating:** The higher the rating, the more charges the device can supply before it needs to be recharged.

- **Amperage output:** An output rating of 2.1A or higher is needed to charge an iPad or Android tablet.

- **Number of USB charging ports:** A portable battery charger may have one or more charging ports. Having two or more USB charging ports can be useful when you have multiple devices to charge.

Protective Covers/Waterproofing

Two ways to protect a smartphone or tablet from damage are to apply protective covers and waterproofing.

Without a protective cover, a smartphone or tablet is very vulnerable to impact damage. Broken screens are the most common problem, and a clear plastic screen protector is highly recommended as it absorbs the scratches of daily use and abuse for a fraction of the cost of screen replacement.

Damage to the case can cause failures to other systems. A rubberized protective cover with raised edges to protect the screen is a good investment for any tablet or smartphone. For better protection against dampness, look for a cover that has good weather sealing.

The IP (ingress protection) rating scale, developed to measure dust and dirt protection of an electronic enclosure, is a convenient way to rate the dust and water protection features of a smartphone. The maximum level of protection, IP68, has been achieved by a few smartphones. To learn more, see www.dsmt.com/resources/ip-rating-chart/.

Credit Card Readers

Credit card readers for smartphones and tablets enable credit card transactions almost anywhere. Readers plug into the 3.5mm headset jack and are available in versions for magnetic strip cards, chip cards, and NFC (contactless) payment devices. As we move toward a cashless economy, card chip and swipe readers are becoming very common. The Square reader is the most recognizable and popular mobile card reader.

Some systems are designed to work as commercial-grade point-of-sale (POS) systems, with support for cash drawers and receipt printer. Before selecting a system, make sure it is compatible with your operating system. Check for usage fees as well.

Memory/MicroSD

Although the amount of onboard storage in smartphones and tablets has increased in recent years, users who download a lot of media or take a lot of photos can always use more storage.

Some Android-based and Windows-based tablets and smartphones have microSD card slots, but iOS devices do not have upgradable storage. Depending on the operating system a device uses, it might be possible to store some apps on the memory card.

Basic Mobile Device Network Connectivity and Application Support

220-1001: Objective 1.6: Given a scenario, configure basic mobile device network connectivity and application support.

220-1001
Exam

When people are connected to mobile devices, they manage to keep moving while staying connected to their networks and Internet. Mobile phone users are handed off from cell tower to cell tower as they drive down a road, and office people move between access points and networks as they move through buildings with their tablets and mobile devices. But these systems are far from perfect, and there are times when user authentication causes a drop in service, or perhaps a user wanders away from WiFi and needs to access cellular data. This section covers the methods for getting connected when out and about using mobile connections.

Wireless/Cellular Data Network Connectivity for Mobile Devices

This chapter has already introduced the different kinds of device networks. The following sections show how to configure these settings.

Enabling/Disabling Hotspots

To use the mobile hotspot feature on an Android device, follow these steps (which are based on a Samsung phone running on Android):

Step 1.   Enable the mobile hotspot feature in the device's setup.

Step 2.   Select how you want to share the connection wirelessly. Provide the SSID and password listed to any devices that will share the connection.

Step 3.   If you decide to permit only allowed devices to connect, you must provide a name for each device and its MAC address. The MAC address is listed on a label attached to an external adapter. To find the MAC (physical) address for an internal network adapter, see the sidebar "Finding the Network Adapter's MAC (Physical) Address."

Step 4.   Open the Allowed Devices menu (see Figure 1-30), click **Add**, enter the device name and address, and click **OK**.

Finding the Network Adapter's MAC (Physical) Address

If you cannot view the label on an external device, or if your network adapter is internal, use one of these methods to display it. On a Windows device, open a command prompt window and use the command **ipconfig /all** to see the MAC (physical) address for the device. With macOS 10.4 (Tiger) and newer, the address is located under the Apple menu in the upper-left corner (select **WiFi** and **Advanced**. With most Linux distros, run the command **ifconfig -a**. MAC addresses can be listed in uppercase or lowercase. The MAC address for an iOS device is called its WiFi address. To see it, open **Settings > About**. The MAC address for an Android device is called its WiFi MAC address. To see it, open **Settings > About > Status**.

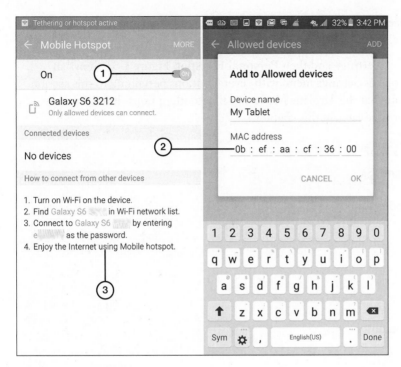

1. **Enabling mobile hotspot**
2. **Entering MAC address of device that will connect to mobile hotspot**
3. **Instructions for devices that will connect to mobile hotspot**

FIGURE 1-30   Entering the MAC Address of the Device Sharing the Hotspot's Internet Connection

Step 5.   Make the connection from your device just as you would with any other wireless Internet router or hotspot. Enter the password when prompted.

Step 6.   When your devices are finished using the Internet, disable the hotspot setting in your smartphone or tablet.

CAUTION   Some cellular providers charge an additional fee if you turn your cellular device into a hotspot or if you use tethering. Check with your mobile service provider for details. And keep in mind that the data usage of every device connected to a mobile hotspot is counted toward your total data allocation. If you're not careful, using a mobile hotspot could cost you extra money in overages.

The same process on an iPhone is similar. To use the mobile hotspot feature on an Android device, follow these steps:

Step 1.   Select **Settings** and then **Personal Hotspot**. Figure 1-31 shows an iPhone 6s Settings menu with several options pertaining to this section. (Note that the Airplane Mode and Bluetooth options shown here are addressed later in this chapter.)

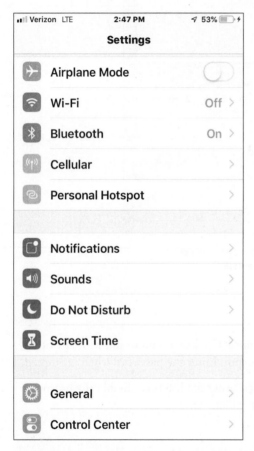

FIGURE 1-31   iPhone Settings Menu

Step 2.   Slide the **Personal Hotspot** toggle to turn it on. The menu now shows a WiFi password for the hotspot. The phone generates a password by default, or the user can configure one by selecting the password menu.

Step 3.   Choose the method of connection. Figure 1-32 shows the options for connecting. For the hotspot, select to use either WiFi or Bluetooth and follow the instructions for your selection. (There is also an option for USB, which is used for tethering, as described in the next section.)

FIGURE 1-32   iPhone Personal Hotspot Menu

Enabling/Disabling Tethering

To use USB *tethering*, follow these steps (which are based on a Samsung phone running Android 5.x):

Step 1.   Connect a USB cable from your computer to the data port on your device.

Step 2.   Select the USB tethering option on your device.

Step 3.   If you are connecting a Windows computer, select the network type (Home) on the computer when prompted.

Step 4.   Use your computer's web browser and other network features normally.

Step 5.   When you're finished, disable USB tethering.

> **NOTE**   In Windows Device Manager, the tethered USB connection is listed as Remote NDIS Based Internet Sharing Device in the Network Adapters category.

To tether using an iPhone, see the directions in the preceding section, "Enabling/Disabling Hotspots."

Enabling/Disabling Airplane Mode

A device cannot typically shut off the cellular antenna by itself. However, every device manufactured is required to have an *Airplane mode*, which, depending on the version, turns off any wireless antenna in the device, including cellular and GPS. Some airlines offer in-flight Web access, and to enable a device to use that access in flight, you may need to turn on Airplane mode and then activate WiFi. You might also need to activate Bluetooth for your headset.

On a typical Android device, you can enable Airplane mode by going to **Settings > Connections** and then enabling **Airplane Mode**, as shown in Figure 1-33. Note the airplane icon in the upper portion of the figure. On Android devices, you can also access Airplane mode by pressing and holding the power button.

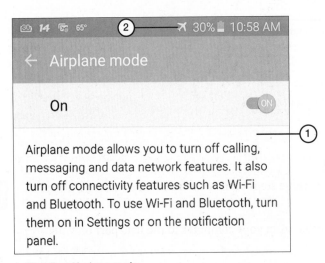

1. Enabling Airplane mode
2. When Airplane mode is enabled, the airplane icon is shown in place of WiFi or cellular connection signal strength

FIGURE 1-33   Enabling Airplane Mode on a Samsung Smartphone Using Android

To enable Airplane mode on an iOS tablet, go to **Settings > Airplane Mode**, as shown in Figure 1-34. Again, note the icon of an airplane at the top left of the figure. Another option is to swipe the screen up to access the control center and then tap the airplane icon to toggle Airplane mode on or off.

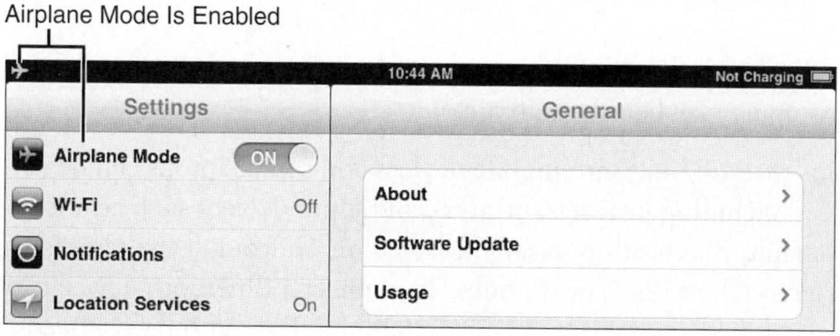

Airplane Mode Is Enabled

FIGURE 1-34   Airplane Mode on a Typical Apple Tablet

Some airlines don't consider Airplane mode to be sufficient, and they ask you to turn off your device, either for the duration of the flight or at least during takeoff and landing.

Bluetooth

As mentioned earlier in the chapter, Bluetooth is a short-range, low-speed wireless network technology primarily designed to operate in peer-to-peer (or ad hoc) mode between PCs and other devices. Bluetooth runs in virtually the same 2.4GHz frequency used by IEEE 802.11b, 802.11g, and 802.11n wireless networks but uses a spread-spectrum frequency-hopping signaling method to help minimize interference. Bluetooth devices connect to each other to form a personal area network (PAN).

Some systems and devices include integrated Bluetooth adapters, and others need a Bluetooth module connected to a USB port to enable Bluetooth networking.

Bluetooth 4.0, also known as Bluetooth Smart, is designed for use with very low-power applications such as sensors. Bluetooth 4.1, a software update to 4.0, enables Bluetooth to perform multiple roles at the same time and to work better with LTE cellular devices. Bluetooth 4.2 adds features to support the Internet of Things (IoT). Most Bluetooth mice, keyboards, and headsets on the market today support version 4.0. Bluetooth is covered more extensively in Chapter 2.

> **NOTE** The Internet of Things (IoT) refers to the network of physical objects (devices, buildings, vehicles, appliances, and so on) that are connected to each other through embedded electronics, sensors, software, and network connectivity for the collection and exchange of data. For more information, see the Chapter 2.

The most common Bluetooth devices have a range of 10m (for example, portable printers, headsets, computer keyboards, and mice).

The Bluetooth radios that are built into mobile devices and some laptops can be used for many devices, including headsets, printers, and input devices such as mice and keyboards. By default, Bluetooth is usually disabled on Android devices but is enabled on iOS devices such as iPads or iPhones. To connect a Bluetooth device to a mobile device, Bluetooth first needs to be enabled; then the Bluetooth device needs to be synchronized to the mobile device. This is known as *pairing*, or linking, and it sometimes requires a *PIN* code. Once synchronized, the device needs to be connected. Finally, the Bluetooth connection should be tested.

The following sections show the steps involved in connecting a Bluetooth headset to a typical Android-based device and to an iOS device. Before you begin, make sure the Bluetooth headset is charged.

Steps to Configure a Bluetooth Headset on an Android-Based Device

Following these steps to connect a Bluetooth headset to a typical Android-based device:

Step 1. Go to **Settings > Connections** and then enable **Bluetooth**.

Step 2. Tap **Bluetooth** to display the Bluetooth Settings screen.

Step 3. Prepare the headset. How you do this varies from headset to headset.

Step 4. If the Android device is not scanning automatically, tap **Scan**. Keep holding the button on the headset until the Android device finds it.

Step 5. On the Android device, tap the device to pair with. Most Android devices pair the Bluetooth headset to the mobile device and then complete the connection automatically, allowing full use of the device.

Step 6. Enter a PIN code, if prompted to do so. Many devices come with the default pin 0000.

When finished, the screen on the Android device looks similar to the screen shown in Figure 1-35. Note the Bluetooth icon at the top of the screen. This icon indicates whether Bluetooth is running on the device. It remains even if you disconnect the Bluetooth device. For this headset device, you would test it simply by making a phone call.

To disconnect the device but retain the pairing, turn off the device. To unpair the device, tap the settings (gearbox) icon on the screen and tap **Unpair**. To use it again, pair it again.

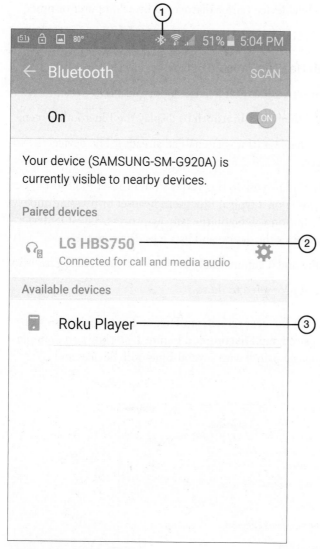

1. Bluetooth device connected
2. Newly connected device
3. Other nearby devices

FIGURE 1-35   Bluetooth Screen on an Android Smartphone Showing the LG HBS750 Headset Connected

Android devices can also connect to other Bluetooth-enabled devices (forming a PAN) or to a computer equipped with a Bluetooth dongle. To create such connections, you must set the mobile device to discoverable (which generally lasts only two minutes). In the same way that the headset is discovered by the mobile device in the previous procedure, a mobile device can be discovered by a computer or other mobile device.

Steps to Configure a Bluetooth Headset on an iOS Device

Following these steps to connect a Bluetooth headset to a typical iOS device:

Step 1.   Go to **Settings** and then tap **Bluetooth** to display the Bluetooth screen.

Step 2.   Tap **Bluetooth** to enable it (if it isn't enabled already). The device searches for devices.

Step 3.   Prepare the headset. How you do this varies from headset to headset. For example, switching on a typical Bluetooth headset or pressing and holding the power button will begin the pairing process. The iOS device automatically recognizes the device and lists it as discoverable.

Step 4.   Tap the device name, and it automatically connects, as shown in Figure 1-36.

Step 5.   Enter a PIN code, if prompted to do so.

To remove the device, tap it. On the next screen, tap **Forget This Device**. To stop using the device but keep it paired, tap **Disconnect**. Figure 1-36 shows an example of an iPhone 6 that has previously paired with several Bluetooth devices and is currently connected to one.

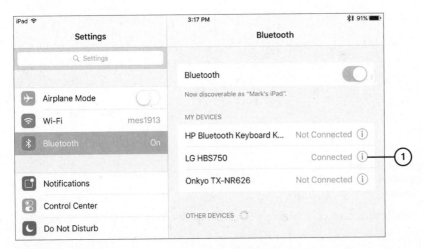

1. Connected device

FIGURE 1-36   A Connected Bluetooth Headset on an iOS Device

NOTE Most Bluetooth devices can be connected to only one mobile device at a time. If you need to switch a Bluetooth device from one mobile device to another, be sure to disconnect it or "forget" it from the current connection before making a new one.

NOTE To make driving and using a cell phone at the same time safer, take advantage of Bluetooth pairing with your car stereo system. It's the ultimate "hands-free" device.

Corporate and ISP Email Configuration

A key function of a smartphone is its ability to send and receive email while away from a desk. Sending and receiving email is also an important function of tablets. This section shows how to configure email on Android and iOS devices.

Corporations and ISPs use two different types of email services: *POP3* (Post Office Protocol 3) and *IMAP4* (Internet Message Access Protocol v4). Depending on how you receive email, you might need to configure your device to receive either or both types of email services.

To set up a POP3 email account, you must know the server that you want to connect to, the port you need to use, and whether security is being employed.

Use the following steps to connect a typical Android smartphone to a POP3 account:

Step 1.   Go to the Home screen and tap the **Menu** button. Then select **All Apps.**

Step 2.   Scroll down until you see the email app.

Step 3.   Select whether you want a POP3, IMAP, or Exchange account. (In this case, select **POP3.**) If the device already has email accounts set up on it, you might need to open **Settings** and then tap the **Add account** button.

Step 4.   Type the email address and the password of the account and then tap **Next**.

Step 5.   Configure the incoming settings, if prompted to do so. Change the username, if desired, to something different from the email address and then type the POP3 server name. This is typically the domain name portion of the email address. If security is being used, select SSL or TLS. Type the port number, which is **110** by default for POP3. Then tap **Next**. (If you need any of this information, ask the network administrator.)

Step 6.   Configure the outgoing settings. Type the SMTP server. Organizations often use the same server name as for the POP3 server. However, small office/home office (SOHO) users might have to use their ISP's SMTP server. If security is being used, select SSL or TLS. Type the port number, which is **25** for SMTP. Then tap **Next**.

Step 7.   Configure the account options, such as how often to check for mail and whether to notify you when it arrives. Tap **Next**. At this point, new email should start downloading.

Step 8.   Finally, you can give the account an easier-to-remember name and then tap **Done**.

Use the following steps to connect an iOS device to a POP3 account:

Step 1.   Go to the **Home** screen and tap the **Settings** button.

Step 2.   Tap **Mail, Contacts, Calendars.**

Step 3.   Tap **Add Account.**

Step 4.   Tap **Other** at the bottom of the list.

Step 5.   Tap **Add Mail Account.**

Step 6.   Type the name, email address, and password (and, if you like, an optional description) and tap **Next**.

Step 7.   Tap **POP**. Then, under Incoming Mail Server, type the POP3 server name and the username. Under Outgoing Mail Server, type the SMTP server. Then tap **Save**.

Step 8.   The system verifies the address and password. If successful, the process is finished. If not, check that everything was typed correctly and that the correct parameters, such as the type of server and security, have been configured.

Connecting to IMAP or Exchange Servers

To connect to an IMAP account, you must enter the IMAP server (for receiving mail), which uses port 143 by default, and the outgoing SMTP server (for sending mail). If you connect to a Microsoft Exchange mail server, that server name often takes care of both receiving and sending email. You might need to know the domain of which the Exchange server is a member. Secure email sessions require the use of SSL or TLS on port 443. Check with the network administrator to find out which protocol to use. POP3 also has a secure derivative known as APOP, a challenge/response protocol that uses a hashing function to prevent replay attacks during an email session. This protocol can be chosen from the Android platform and is also used by Mozilla Thunderbird and Apple Mail.

If you want your email to be encrypted for security and authentication, you can enable Secure/Multipurpose Internet Mail Extensions, better known as *S/MIME*. To enable encryption support for an email account, turn on the **Sign All Outgoing Emails** option and create public key encryption keys for your email accounts.

Integrated Commercial Provider Email Configuration

To set up web-based services such as Apple's iCloud, Google/Inbox (Gmail), Microsoft's Outlook or Exchange Online, and Yahoo! Mail, you can use or install the appropriate app from your device's app store.

For example, Android devices come with a Gmail application built in, so a user can access Gmail directly, without having to use the browser. Apple iOS devices allow connectivity to Gmail, Yahoo!, iCloud Mail, Exchange, Outlook, AOL, and a host of other email providers.

Connecting to these services is simple, and it works similarly to using a desktop or laptop computer. Choose the type of provider you use, enter a username (the email address) and password (and, on Apple devices, an Apple ID as well), and the user will have access to web-based email.

When troubleshooting issues with email, make sure that the username and password are typed correctly. Using onscreen keyboards often leads to mistyped passwords. Also make sure that the mobile device is currently connected to the Internet.

PRI Updates/PRL Updates/Baseband Updates

Updates to your smartphone's Preferred Roaming List (*PRL*) and *baseband* (the portion of the smartphone that makes connections to the cellular network for phone and data) are performed automatically by mobile providers.

When a smartphone or cellular-equipped tablet reports that a system update is available, PRL and baseband are two of the items that might be updated. Primary rate interface (PRI) updates (not to be confused with PRL updates) are used to control the speed at which data is sent from a mobile device to a cell tower. PRI updates are also sent automatically and help ensure that the cell tower receives data at an acceptable rate.

Resetting the PRL can help if you are experiencing issues connecting to the cell towers. To reset the connection, go to the phone's dialer (*not* the messaging app) and enter the appropriate code. For example, on an Android, type **##72786#**; on an iOS device, type **##873283#**. Different carriers may have different requirements for phones.

Radio Firmware

In mobile phones, whenever an operating system update is sent, the manufacturers update their firmware along with it. This firmware, which is separate from the operating system, updates the radio modem that manages connections for cellular, WiFi, GPS, Bluetooth, and NFC. These are usually small updates that improve reliability. If just the phone operating system were updated but not the radio firmware, the cellular modem would eventually go out of sync with the operating system, and performance would become unreliable.

IMEI vs. IMSI

Two international standards are used to identify cell phones and other devices with cellular service:

- **IMEI**: IMEI (International Mobile Equipment Identity) is a unique number given each cell phone and it is used to identify phones on the GSM, UMTS, LTE, and iDEN networks. The IMEI can be used to block access to a stolen phone. MEID numbers used by CDMA networks (Sprint, Verizon, and US Cellular) work in the same way as IMEI numbers. Some vendors refer to these numbers as IMEI/MEID numbers.

- **IMSI**: IMSI (International Mobile Subscriber Identity) is used to identify a subscriber using a cell network. It is usually stored in the phone or tablet's SIM card.

In the event that a cell phone is stolen, the owner can contact the cell phone provider and request that the phone be blocked from being used. The cell phone provider usually has a record of the IMEI number and can block the phone from being used even if the SIM card is changed. Support for cell phone blocking by IMEI number varies from provider to provider and from country to country.

If the owner of a stolen cell phone replaces the phone, the new SIM card can be provisioned with the same IMSI code because that code identifies the user of the phone rather than the phone itself.

TIP   To see the IMEI or MEID numbers for an Android phone, type *#06# as if you are dialing a phone number. The code is displayed immediately. On an iOS device, go to **Settings** > **About** and scroll to the number. You can copy it from this display if necessary.

VPN

A virtual private network (*VPN*) is a secure private network connection that is carried over a less secure network, such as the Internet. A VPN connection requires a VPN server at the remote site and a VPN client at the client site. VPN traffic between client and server is encrypted and encapsulated into packets suitable for transmission over the network. VPN connections aren't just for laptop and desktop computers. VPN connections are also supported by iOS, Android, and Windows 10 Mobile devices. VPNs are discussed further in Chapter 2.

VPN settings vary by the VPN type, so be sure to know the VPN type and settings needed for the VPN before you create a connection to a VPN from a mobile device:

- To create a connection to a VPN with an iOS device, open **Settings > General > VPN > Add VPN Configuration.**

- To create a connection to a VPN with an Android device, open **Settings > More connection settings > VPN** and then choose **Basic VPN or Advanced IPsec VPN.**

- To create a connection to a VPN with a Windows 10 Mobile device, open **Settings > Network & Internet > VPN > Add a VPN connection.**

Methods to Perform Mobile Device Synchronization

220-1001: Objective 1.7: Given a scenario, use methods to perform mobile device synchronization.

Data Synchronization

Keeping things in sync means having the same information on your different devices. We use synchronization to bring files in line with each other and to force devices to coordinate their data. For example, when a salesperson makes a change to a sales proposal document on a laptop, it is important that the other people involved in the transaction—such as sales managers, ordering specialists, and customers— have access to the updated information when they access the document on their devices. Synchronizing data to the cloud is how the salesperson updates the others. Synchronizing data from the cloud to the desktop (or another device) is how others gather the updated information.

Synchronizing to the Cloud and to the Desktop

Each cloud provider carefully designs a system for synchronizing users' data, and different kinds of data may require different levels of synchronization. Most cloud storage providers offer their customers choices related to how often data is synchronized. Sometimes transfers are scheduled by time, and sometimes they are triggered by events, such as a change to a document or a device coming online. Sometimes, as with Google Drive documents, it is possible for several users to simultaneously access documents for group editing.

A mobile device can synchronize by connecting to a PC via USB (or some other serial connection), or, commonly, using WiFi or Bluetooth.

Synchronizing to the Automobile

Documents are not the only data that requires synchronization. Automobiles have evolved into very complex machines that run many kinds of software internally as well as utilizing the driver's devices while in motion. The driver is not always aware that software updates to mechanical systems are improved by the manufacturers and pushed out to the cars they service. These updates sync data from the manufacturer to the auto and also may involve sending data gathered by the auto uploaded to the manufacturer for research or product improvement.

The more common scenario is when a driver gets into a car and wants to sync a phone or tablet to the car's display and sound system. The advantage of this is that the driver can have the benefit of technology—say a map program providing directions to a destination—along with improved safety by having hands-free access to the data. The auto can also access the device's music library and personal assistant for making calls and sending voice messages.

Types of Data to Synchronize

Synchronization is the matching up of files, email, and other types of data between one computer and another. The types of data we synchronize are too numerous to list in one chapter. This section lists data types that you should be aware of as data types that commonly need to be synchronized. Brief examples of use are provided, though more are possible.

The types of files that can be synchronized include:

- **Contacts:** From phones or email applications
- **Applications:** Including business and government documents
- **Email:** So that the same messages appear on all of a user's devices
- **Pictures:** Synced and sorted in Google or shared with people close by using AirDrop on Apple devices
- **Music:** To access user collections on multiple devices
- **Videos:** To access user collections on multiple devices

- **Calendar:** So that all meeting attendees know the right time and place

- **Bookmarks:** For common browsing between devices or among groups

- **Documents:** So that all revisions are shared

- **Location data:** So that you know where your shipped items are located and when they will arrive

- **Social media data:** For keeping up with family members and friends

- **e-books:** So you can finish the book you started somewhere else

- **Passwords:** So that only certain users can access applications or documents

NOTE   For the 220-1001 exam, you should know the preceding list along with:

- Synchronization methods, such as synchronizing to the cloud, synchronizing to the desktop, and synchronizing to the automobile

- Mutual authentication for multiple services (Single Sign-On, or SSO)

- Software requirements to install an application on a PC

- Connection types to enable synchronization

Synchronization Methods

Three main methods are used for synchronization, as briefly discussed in the preceding sections:

- Synchronization to the cloud

- Synchronization to the desktop

- Synchronization to the automobile

Cloud-Based Synchronization

With cloud-based synchronization, apps on a mobile device send data to the cloud, where it is downloaded by other mobile apps, by web browsers, or by programs running on Windows or macOS computers. Examples of providers that enable cloud-based synchronization include:

- Dropbox (www.dropbox.com)

- Samsung Smart Switch (www.samsung.com)

- Apple iCloud (www.apple.com/icloud)

- Microsoft OneDrive (https://onedrive.live.com)

- Google Drive (www.google.com)

Data that is synced via cloud-based synchronization is encrypted and secured by passwords and usernames. Mutual authentication is used by each side of the connection to verify its identity to the other side.

If synchronization to a cloud application is interrupted, the problem can usually be resolved by closing and re-launching the application.

Mutual Authentication for Multiple Services (SSO)

Apple, Microsoft, and Google allow mutual authentication for multiple services (also known as SSO, or Single Sign-On) to enable a single login to provide access to multiple services. For example, a single Microsoft account login provides access to Outlook email, the Microsoft Store, and OneDrive. A single Apple login provides access to iTunes, iCloud, and other services. A single Google login provides access to Gmail, Android services, and other services.

Desktop-Based Synchronization

With desktop-based synchronization, the user connects a mobile device via a USB cable. With Android-based devices connected to Windows, the mobile device is treated as a drive, and data can be dragged and dropped between devices. Third-party options such as Android File Transfer (www.android.com) enable macOS to have simple browse and copy file transfers, similar to Windows. Files can be transferred and viewed between Mac systems and Android devices. On an iOS device, iTunes is used for file transfer and synchronization for music and media files.

Automobile Synchronization

It is always a good idea—and usually the law—to have both hands on the steering wheel when driving. Having your device synced for hands-free use in most newer cars that are equipped with onboard Bluetooth is a fairly straightforward process:

Step 1.   Turn on the car stereo and your mobile phone.

Step 2.   Select the **Bluetooth** pairing button on the car stereo console so it will discover your phone.

Step 3.   Select **Bluetooth** from the settings menu on your phone and then select your car stereo from the list when it appears.

Step 4.   Enter the PIN displayed on the car stereo into your phone and select **OK**.

Email Synchronization

Email synchronization options depend on the email service in use. For example, Microsoft Exchange email uses Exchange ActiveSync. When an email account is configured on a mobile device, synchronization settings are configured as part of the process and can be adjusted, disabled, or reenabled as needed.

Software Requirements for Synchronization Software

Most desktop synchronization software for all current versions of Windows requires the PC to have 4GB of RAM or more, at least one USB 2.0 port., and 300MB of free space on the hard drive. Most desktop synchronization software for macOS requires macOS 10.5 or greater and an available USB port, although some, such as Dropbox, may require macOS 10.9 or newer versions.

Connection Types for Synchronization Software

USB and WiFi are the most common connection types for synchronizing software, especially on mobile devices.

For desktop-based synchronization, USB 2.0 ports are the minimum requirement, although some also support Bluetooth connections. For cloud-based synchronization, the appropriate app or web service must be loaded on the mobile device, and the computer used for file synchronization and Internet access must be available.

Exam Preparation Tasks

Review All the Key Topics

Review the most important topics in the chapter, noted with the key topics icon in the outer margin of the page. Table 1-5 lists these key topics and the page number on which each is found.

Table 1-5 Key Topics for Chapter 1

Key Topic Element	Description	Page Number
Figure 1-1	The Underside of a Typical Laptop, with Multiple Removable Panels for Access to Storage, RAM, and Other Components	9
Figure 1-2	The Same Laptop as in Figure 1-1 After Opening Access Panels to Permit Component Replacements or Upgrades	9
Steps	Replacing a laptop keyboard	11
Table 1-2	Comparison of HDD, SSD, and SSHD	12
Steps	Replacing a laptop storage device (HDD, SDD, SSHD)	13
List	Laptop memory upgrade considerations	15
Table 1-4	SODIMM Features	17
Steps	Performing a memory upgrade	17
Steps	Removing/replacing a smart card reader	18
Steps	Removing/replacing an optical drive	19
Steps	Removing/replacing a wireless card	20
Steps	Removing/replacing a DC jack on a laptop	24
Steps	Removing a system from all power sources before replacing internal components	25
Steps	Replacing a touchpad	27
Steps	Replacing a service cover on a laptop	28
Steps	Removing/replacing laptop speakers	29
Steps	Removing a laptop motherboard	29
Steps	Removing/replacing a heat sink/CPU	31
Steps	Removing/replacing an LCD display assembly	35
List	Special function keys	40
Section	Laptop/cable locks	43
Figure 1-28	A Samsung ATIV-500 Windows Tablet with a Removable Keyboard	45
List	Tablet features	46
List	Differences between tablets and smartphones	47
Section	Wired connection types	49

Key Topic Element	Description	Page Number
Section	Wireless connection types	50
Section	Enabling/disabling hotspots	54
Section	Enabling/disabling tethering	57
Section	Enabling/disabling airplane mode	58
Steps	Configuring Bluetooth on Android devices	60
Steps	Configuring Bluetooth on iOS devices	62
		63
List	Creating VPNs with mobile devices	67
List	Files that can be synchronized	68
List	Synchronization methods	69

Complete the Tables and Lists from Memory

Print a copy of Appendix C, "Memory Tables" (found online), or at least the section for this chapter, and complete the tables and lists from memory. Appendix D, "Answers to Memory Tables," also online, includes completed tables and lists to check your work.

Define Key Terms

Define the following key terms from this chapter, and check your answers in the glossary:

keyboard, pointing device, hard disk drive (HDD), solid-state drive (SSD), solid-state hybrid drive (SSHD), smart card reader, PCI, mPCIe, wireless card, DC, LCD, OLED, Fn, docking station, cable lock, rotating/removable screen, VR/AR (virtual reality/augmented reality), GPS, mini-USB, Lightning, hotspot, NFC, Bluetooth, IR, tethering, Airplane mode, pairing, PIN, POP3, IMAP4, SSL, S/MIME, PRL, baseband, IMEI, IMSI, VPN

Answer Review Questions

1. Which of the following is best for updating RAM in most laptops?

   a. DDRSD4

   b. DIMM

   c. SODIMM

   d. SDR SDRAM

2. Match each operating system with its application download site.

Operating System	Application Download Site
a. Android	
b. Apple iOS	
c. Windows 10 Mobile	

Answer Options:

1. Microsoft Store

2. Google Play

3. App Store

3. You have been asked to upgrade an aging laptop without replacing it. Which options can you add to provide the fastest possible update?

   a. DIMM

   b. HDD

   c. SSD

   d. SSHD

4. You have been called to check on a laptop that belongs to a user just returning from vacation. The laptop keeps crashing after a few minutes of use. The documentation for the laptop indicates that additional RAM was added during a system tune-up earlier in the week. What are two considerations worth revisiting when troubleshooting? (Choose two.)

   a. Memory speed

   b. iOS update history

   c. Voltage rating of the power cable

   d. Memory timing

5. Pokémon GO is a gaming app that creates game images on a smartphone or tablet as the player walks around a neighborhood. Which technology is used in this game?

   a. AR

   b. VR

   c. NFC

   d. IR

6. Which one of the following is not commonly done using a function key command?

   a. Screen orientation change

   b. Volume control

   c. Fast-forward

   d. Uber summons

7. Which of the following are methods of sharing a wireless connection? (Choose all that apply.)

   a. IMAP

   b. Hotspot

   c. Tethering

   d. SSL

8. Which statement best describes Airplane mode?

   a. Airplane mode allows mobile devices to communicate safely via Bluetooth and WiFi while in flight but turns off cellular transmission.

   b. Airplane mode is an FCC regulation controlling the use of mobile devices in airports.

   c. Airplane mode allows mobile devices to communicate only when they are attached to each other by cable.

   d. Airplane mode turns off all wireless antennas so that mobile devices cannot transmit or receive data while in flight.

9. Bluetooth uses which of the following networking standards?

   a. Tethering

   b. WEP

   c. Ethernet

   d. 802.11

10. Which of the following statements best describes Bluetooth? (Choose all that apply.)

    a. Bluetooth devices form short-range, low-speed wireless networks.

    b. Bluetooth devices connect to form a PAN.

    c. Bluetooth devices create peer-to-peer networks.

    d. Bluetooth devices allow dissimilar devices to communicate on the same network.

11. When setting up a POP3 email account, which types of security protocol might you select for incoming mail? (Choose two.)

   a. HTTP

   b. HTTPS

   c. TLS

   d. SSL

12. Which of these is an email extension that adds a level of encryption support?

   a. IMAP

   b. POP3

   c. S/MIME

   d. NFC

13. Which port is used for POP3?

   a. 25

   b. 53

   c. 80

   d. 110

14. If your phone is stolen, which of the following enables the phone to be blocked so that the thief cannot use it?

   a. NFC

   b. IMEI

   c. S/MIME

   d. IMSI

15. Which of these is not among the three basic methods of synchronization?

   a. Synchronization to the cloud

   b. Synchronization to the app

   c. Synchronization to the car

   d. Synchronization to the desktop

This chapter covers the eight A+ 220-1001 exam objectives related to knowledge of computer networks. These objectives may comprise 20% of the exam questions:

- **Core 1 (220-1001): Objective 2.1:** Compare and contrast TCP and UDP ports, protocols, and their purposes.

- **Core 1 (220-1001): Objective 2.2:** Compare and contrast common networking hardware devices.

- **Core 1 (220-1001): Objective 2.3:** Given a scenario, install and configure a basic wired/wireless SOHO network.

- **Core 1 (220-1001): Objective 2.4:** Compare and contrast wireless networking protocols.

- **Core 1 (220-1001): Objective 2.5:** Summarize the properties and purposes of services provided by networked hosts.

- **Core 1 (220-1001): Objective 2.6:** Explain common network configuration concepts.

- **Core 1 (220-1001): Objective 2.7:** Compare and contrast Internet connection types, network types, and their features.

- **Core 1 (220-1001): Objective 2.8:** Given a scenario, use appropriate networking tools.

## CHAPTER 2

Networking

Networking support requires a sound understanding of how different types of computer networking hardware and software work together to enable communication between computing devices. This chapter covers several networking devices and protocols, both wired and wireless, that you will need to master to be a successful network technician.

"Do I Know This Already?" Quiz

The "Do I Know This Already?" quiz allows you to assess whether you should read the entire chapter. Table 2-1 lists the major headings in this chapter and the "Do I Know This Already?" quiz questions covering the material in those headings so you can assess your knowledge of these specific areas. The answers to the "Do I Know This Already?" quiz appear in Appendix A, "Answers to the 'Do I Know This Already?' Quizzes and Review Question Sections."

Table 2-1 "Do I Know This Already?" Foundation Topics Section-to-Question Mapping

Foundation Topics Section	Questions
TCP and UDP Ports, Protocols, and Their Purposes	1–6
Networking Hardware Devices	7–9
Install and Configure a Basic Wired/Wireless SOHO Network	10
Compare and Contrast Wireless Networking Protocols	11–13
Summarize the Properties and Purposes of Services Provided by Networked Hosts	14–15
Network Configuration Concepts	16–17
Internet Connection Types, Network Types, and Their Features	18
Using Networking Tools	19

> **CAUTION** The goal of self-assessment is to gauge your mastery of the topics in this chapter. If you do not know the answer to a question or are only partially sure of the answer, you should mark that question as wrong for purposes of the self-assessment. Giving yourself credit for an answer you correctly guess skews your self-assessment results and might provide you with a false sense of security.

1. Which of the following application tasks would likely require TCP?

   a. A DHCP request on a network

   b. Sending an Excel spreadsheet to a coworker

   c. A web-based phone conversation

   d. Streaming a sports event on the Web

2. Which two statements about UDP are true? (Choose two.)

   a. UDP is User Data Profile, which is sent in a packet.

   b. UDP is connection oriented.

   c. UDP is connectionless.

   d. UDP is User Datagram Protocol.

3. Which protocol uses TCP but not UDP?

   a. IMAP

   b. HTTPS

   c. FTP

   d. DNS

4. Which protocol requires less processing by networking equipment: TCP or UDP?

   a. TCP because it is connectionless

   b. UDP because it is connectionless

   c. UDP because it requires reliability

   d. TCP because it is unreliable

5. Which port is used for FTP?

   a. 35

   b. 27

   c. 23

   d. 21

6. When a file is sent and part of the file is missing, which protocol is used to request that the sender re-send the missing parts?

   a. File Transfer Protocol

   b. Simple Network Transfer Protocol

   c. Transmission Control Protocol

   d. Server Message Block

7. Which three network devices connect users within a LAN? (Choose three.)

   a. Router

   b. Hub

   c. Switch

   d. DNS server

   e. Access point

8. Which two devices have functions combined into a standard SOHO router?

   a. Hub and switch

   b. Switch and router

   c. Router and hub

   d. Wireless bridge and hub

9. What is the chief difference between a wireless bridge and a WAP?

   a. A WAP connects wired devices, while a wireless bridge connects wireless devices.

   b. A WAP is for connecting wireless devices, and a bridge is for connecting LANs.

   c. A WAP uses Ethernet, and a bridge uses RIP.

   d. There is no difference; these are two names for the same device.

10. Which one of the following is a device that enables remote management of wireless LANs?

    a. Web hub

    b. SOHO router

    c. Cloud-based network controller

    d. WEB LAN manager

11. If you have been asked to place a switch in a ceiling area where there is no AC outlet, which technology would be part of a possible solution?

    a. STP

    b. TCP

    c. DNS

    d. PoE

12. Which is the correct pairing for wireless encryption standards and types?

    a. WEP: TKIP

    b. WPA: PSK

    c. WPA2: AES

    d. WPS: Common shared key

13. On a 2.4GHz network, which channel is the best choice for avoiding interference from other channels?

    a. 6

    b. 10

    c. 5

    d. 2

14. Which technology can assign an IP address to wireless devices in a local coffee shop?

    a. TCP

    b. Static IP

    c. DNS

    d. DHCP

15. Which acronym refers to a feature that makes streaming media and voice services a better experience?

    a. TCP

    b. QoS

    c. PnP

    d. DNS

16. Which is an example of a subnet mask?

    a. fe80::

    b. 10.20.10.1

    c. 255.255.0.0

    d. 192.168.1.0

17. Which is an example of a valid IPv6 address?

    a. FF02::2

    b. 2001:db8:aaaa:1::200

    c. fe80::c1c6:bd64:f9c7:2c9d

    d. All of the above

18. Which is a secure network connection that is carried on the Internet?

    a. NAT

    b. VLAN

    c. PNS

    d. VPN

19. You have just installed an Ethernet jack in an office and need to connect it to the patch panel in the wiring closet. When you get to the wiring closet, you see that there are several unused cables that are not identified by room number, and you can't tell which one to connect. Which tool in your networking toolkit will best help you solve this problem?

    a. Multimeter

    b. Tone generator

    c. Cable tester

    d. Ohmmeter

Foundation Topics

TCP and UDP Ports, Protocols, and Their Purposes

220-1001: Objective 2.1: Compare and contrast TCP and UDP ports, protocols, and their purposes.

When humans want to share ideas with each other, they agree to use common communication protocols, or rules, to make sure they are understood. *Protocols* help us know when to speak, when to listen, and how to start and finish conversations. We constantly use protocols but rarely think about them. When people have a communication failure, a protocol failure is likely involved.

Protocols serve the same purpose in computer network communication. Because the processes involved in computer communication can be very complex, ways of using protocols and ports have been developed to keep the processes of communication sorted out and flowing smoothly. This section describes some of the protocols and ports that are typically used in networks.

When an application needs to send or receive data, it must use a particular protocol designed for that application and open up a *port* on the network adapter to make a connection to another computer. Computers use port numbers to identify protocols and keep the different processes sorted out. For example, if you want to visit www.google.com, you open a browser and type http://www.google.com. The protocol being used is HTTP (short for Hypertext Transfer Protocol), and it makes the connection to the web server: google.com. HTTP selects an unused port on your computer (known as an *outbound port*) to send and receive data to and from google.com. On the other end, Google's web server has a specific port open at all times, ready to accept sessions. In most cases, the web server's port is 80, which corresponds to HTTP. This is known as an *inbound port*.

TCP

Transmission Control Protocol (TCP) sessions are known as *connection-oriented sessions*. This means that every packet that is sent is checked for delivery. If the receiving computer doesn't receive a packet, it cannot assemble the message and must ask the sending computer to transmit the missing packet again. No packet is left behind. For example, if a computer sends a picture of a cat but for some reason the packets containing part of the picture (say the nose) don't arrive, TCP allows the receiving computer to tell the sending computer that some expected packets went missing and to send them again. This way, the whole picture arrives for the user application at the receiving end and not some strange picture of a nose-less cat.

UDP

User Datagram Protocol (**UDP**) sessions are known as *connectionless sessions*. This means the messages are sent without an expectation of communication from the receiver. UDP does its best to send a message, but errors are not accounted for.

UDP is used in streaming media sessions, such as Voice over IP (VoIP) and gaming, and for protocols that use a simple query and response, such as DNS. If you were listening to some streaming music and you heard a break in the song or a blip of some kind, that would likely indicate some missing packets. TCP would try to replace the missing packets, but you wouldn't want them back because by the time they arrived, you would be listening to a totally different part of the music stream, and the updated information would not make any sense out of place.

The two examples of the cat picture and the music stream demonstrate that different situations call for different protocols. UDP is the better choice for time-sensitive information, even though it is less reliable than TCP. In other situations, where reliability is important, TCP is beneficial.

Both TCP and UDP utilize ports to make connections. Remember that it's the inbound ports that you are concerned with on a server. For example, an FTP server that stores files for customers must have inbound port 21 open by default because that is the common port for FTP. Table 2-2 displays some common protocols and their default corresponding inbound ports. Most common protocols use the same TCP and UDP port numbers, but Table 2-2 lists exceptions.

Table 2-2   Common Protocols and Their Ports

Port Number(s)	Protocol	Port Type
21	FTP	TCP, UDP
22	SSH	TCP, UDP
23	Telnet	TCP, UDP
25	SMTP	TCP, UDP
53	DNS	TCP, UDP
80	HTTP	TCP, UDP
110	POP3	TCP, UDP

Port Number(s)	Protocol	Port Type
143	IMAP	TCP
443	HTTPS	TCP, UDP
3389	RDP	TCP, UDP
137–139	NetBIOS/NetBT	TCP, UDP
445	SMB/CIFS	TCP
427*	SLP	TCP, UDP
548	AFP	TCP
67/68	DHCP	UDP
389	LDAP	TCP, UDP
161/162	SNMP	TCP, UDP

* Can also be used for AFP.

TIP   Know these protocols and their corresponding port numbers for the 220-1001 exam.

The following sections provide more details about these protocols.

FTP

File Transfer Protocol (*FTP*) is a protocol used by both web browsers and specialized FTP programs to access dedicated file transfer servers for file downloads and uploads. When you access an FTP site, the site uses the prefix ftp://.

Windows and Linux contain a command-line FTP program; type **ftp**, press **Enter**, and then type **help** at the FTP prompt to see the commands you can use. See http://linux.about.com/od/commands/l/blcmdl1_ftp.htm.

For macOS, see http://osxdaily.com/2011/02/07/ftp-from-mac/ or use **ftp** from the command line.

FTP sites with downloads available to any user support anonymous FTP. If any credentials are required for FTP, they are typically the username anonymous and the user's email address as a password. Some FTP sites require the user to log in with a specified username and password. FTP is not considered secure because FTP users can authenticate in clear-text sign-ins. For greater security, you can use FTP secured with SSL/TLS (FTPS) or Secure File Transfer Protocol (SFTP). FTP uses port 21.

TIP   Although you can use an operating system's built-in FTP client for file uploads and downloads with both secured and unsecured FTP sites, you should consider using third-party FTP products such as FileZilla (https://filezilla-project.org). Such programs enable you to create a customized setup for each FTP site you visit and store passwords, server types, and other necessary information. They also enable faster downloads than typical web browsers running in ftp:// mode.

SSH

Secure Shell (*SSH*) allows data to be exchanged between computers on a secured channel. This protocol is more secure than FTP and Telnet. The Secure Shell server housing the data you want to access would have port 22 open. (SSH uses port 22.) Several other protocols use SSH in order to make secure connections. One of these is Secure FTP (SFTP), as previously mentioned. Regular FTP can be insecure. SFTP combats this by providing file access over a reliable data stream, generated and protected by SSH.

Telnet

Telnet enables a user to make a text-based connection to a remote computer or networking device and use it as if he were a regular user sitting in front of it rather than simply downloading pages and files as he would with an http:// or ftp:// connection.

Windows and Linux contain a command-line Telnet program. To open a connection to a remote computer, open a command prompt (Windows) or Terminal session (Linux) and type **telnet** and press the **Enter** key. This command opens the Telnet command prompt. For help with commands, type **help** and press the **Enter** key.

macOS includes a menu-driven Telnet program available from Terminal. Due to the standard practice of using SSH, Telnet has been removed from later versions of macOS. But if Telnet is still needed, it is possible to install it. See http://osxdaily.com/2018/07/18/get-telnet-macos/.

NOTE   A remote computer must be configured to accept a Telnet login. Typically, TCP port 23 on the remote computer must be open before a login can take place.

SMTP

Simple Mail Transfer Protocol (*SMTP*) is used to send email from a client system to an email server, which also uses SMTP to relay the message to the receiving email server. SMTP uses port 25.

> **NOTE** When configuring email settings on a client, check with the ISP or organization that provides Internet access for the correct settings. You need to know the server type(s) used (SMTP, POP3, or IMAP), the ports used (default values may be changed by some ISPs), the username and password for the email service, and the security settings (for example, whether SSH is used).

DNS

Domain Name System (*DNS*) is the name for the network of servers on the Internet that translate *domain names*, such as www.informit.com or www.comptia.org, and individual hostnames into their corresponding IP addresses. When manually configuring an IP address, you typically provide the IP address of a DNS server (or the IP addresses of multiple DNS servers) as part of the configuration process. DNS uses port 53. Some technicians refer to DNS as Domain Name Service, which may not be technically correct, but it is understandably a common translation of DNS.

HTTP/HTTPS

Hypertext Transfer Protocol (*HTTP*) is the protocol used by web browsers, such as Internet Explorer, Microsoft Edge, Firefox, and Chrome, to access websites and content. Normal (unsecured) sites use the prefix http:// when accessed in a web browser. Sites that are secured with various encryption schemes such as HTTP Secure or HTTP over SSL (*HTTPS*) are identified with the prefix https://. HTTP uses port 80, and HTTPS uses port 443.

> **NOTE** Most browsers connecting with a secured site also display a closed padlock symbol onscreen.

POP3

Post Office Protocol version 3 (*POP3*) is one of two leading protocols for receiving email; IMAP is the other one. In an email system based on POP3, email is downloaded from the mail server to folders on a local system. POP3 is not a suitable email protocol for users who frequently switch between computers and mobile devices because email might be spread over multiple computers. POP3 is the current standard. Users who utilize POP3 servers to retrieve email typically use SMTP to send messages. POP3 uses port 110.

TIP For users who must use POP3-based email and who use multiple computers, a remote access solution, such as Windows Remote Desktop Connection or a service such as GoToMyPC, is recommended. A remote access solution enables a user to remotely access the system that connects to the POP3 mail server so she can download and read email messages no matter where she is working.

IMAP

Internet Message Access Protocol (*IMAP*) is an email protocol that enables messages to remain on the email server so they can be retrieved from any location. (Recall that POP3, the other leading protocol for receiving email, downloads messages to the mail client.) IMAP also supports folders, so users can organize their messages as desired. IMAP4 is the current version of IMAP.

To configure an IMAP-based email account, you must select IMAP as the email server type and specify the name of the server, your username and password, and whether the server uses SSL. IMAP uses port 143.

NetBIOS/NetBT

NetBIOS, also known as NetBT (RFC 1001), is a protocol that allows some legacy applications that were developed in the 1980s (before the TCP/IP environment became the standard) to work on larger networks and the Internet. Many of those early applications could not scale to the TCP environment, so the NetBIOS/NetBT protocol was designed in 1987 to provide the needed compatibility. NetBIOS/NetBT uses ports 137–139.

SMB/CIFS

Server Message Block (*SMB*) provides access to shared items such as files and printers. SMB uses packets that authenticate remote computers through what are known as *interprocess communication mechanisms*. SMB uses ports 137–139 for SMB traffic using NetBIOS over TCP (NetBT) and 445 for SMB hosted on TCP.

Port 445 is also used by the Common Internet File System (*CIFS*). CIFS was widely used after its introduction as a standard method for sharing files across corporate intranets and the Internet. CIFS is an enhanced version of Microsoft SMB, which is an open, cross-platform protocol. CIFS has now been widely replaced by updated versions of SMB (SMB 2.0 and 3.0).

NOTE   If traffic on ports 137–139 is blocked, you must use the device's IP address to access shared files or printers. When these ports are open, you can use the name of the device to access its shared files or printers.

SLP

Service Location Protocol (**SLP**) was designed to allow networked hosts to find services of other devices, such as printers on the local network. Prior to SLP, devices needed to have services specifically configured. With SLP, devices providing services can announce their presence to hosts and provide configuration information. SLP uses port 427.

AFP

Apple Filing Protocol (**AFP**), which uses port 548, was previously known as Apple-Talk Filing Protocol. AFP uses TCP/IP for transport. macOS 10.9 (Mavericks) and newer versions use AFP to connect to devices running older macOS versions and for Apple's Time Machine backup app.

Starting with macOS 10.9, macOS uses SMB2 to connect between macOS devices or with Linux devices or Windows devices. In newer versions of macOS (High Sierra, Mojave, and newer), AFP is used for backward compatibility, but it is no longer being supported or developed.

RDP

The Remote Desktop Protocol (**RDP**) port, 3389, is used by Remote Desktop Services (RDS), which is the Windows Server–based companion of Remote Desktop Connection. RDP is discussed in detail in Chapter 6, "Operating Systems."

DHCP

Dynamic Host Configuration Protocol (**DHCP**) is used to automatically assign IP addresses to hosts. These hosts could be computers, printers, servers, routers, and so on. In most SOHO networks, a router uses DHCP to assign IP addresses to the client computers. In addition, your ISP uses DHCP to assign an IP address to you, and usually your router gets this address. The DHCP service makes life easier for a network administrator by automatically assigning IP addresses, subnet masks, gateway addresses, DNS servers, and so on. If you get your address from a DHCP server, you are getting your address assigned dynamically, and it could change periodically. However, some computers and printers require a static address—that is, an address that is assigned by the network administrator manually. It is better in many situations for servers and printers to use static addresses that DHCP doesn't change. This way, access to printers and servers is more reliable over time. DHCP uses ports 67 and 68, where UDP port number 67 is the destination port of a server, and UDP port number 68 is used by the client.

SNMP

Simple Network Management Protocol (**SNMP**) is used as the standard for managing and monitoring devices on a network. It manages routers, switches, and computers and is often incorporated into software known as a *network management system* (*NMS*). The NMS is the main software that controls everything SNMP based; it is installed on a computer known as a *manager*. The devices to be monitored are known as *managed devices*. NMS installs a small piece of software known as an *agent* that allows the NMS to monitor those managed devices. SNMP uses ports 161 and 162.

LDAP

Lightweight Directory Access Protocol (**LDAP**) is used to access and maintain distributed directories of information such as the kind involved with Microsoft domains. Microsoft refers to this as *directory services*. LDAP uses port 389.

Networking Hardware Devices

220-1001: Objective 2.2: Compare and contrast common networking hardware devices.

Understanding how computers communicate on a network is essential for any IT professional. Network environments can range from simple home networks to very complex corporate designs, but there are essential elements and functions that apply to all networks. The following sections describe basic networking hardware devices used to build small networks and describes how they contribute to the communication process.

Router

A *router* connects one network to another. For example, a router connected to a cable modem or DSL modem enables multiple devices on a LAN to share a single broadband connection to the Web.

Most routers sold for SOHO configurations are WiFi (802.11 family) wireless routers with integrated Fast Ethernet or Gigabit Ethernet switches. Both wired and wireless devices can be on the same network and can share folders and printers as well as Internet access.

Figure 2-1 shows the rear of a typical 802.11ac router for cable Internet from ASUS.

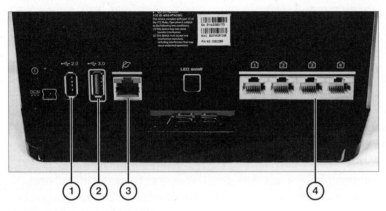

1. USB 2.0 port for external storage
2. USB 3.0 port for external storage
3. WAN (Internet) port to cable modem
4. Gigabit Ethernet switch for LAN

FIGURE 2-1   Many Wireless Routers Can Now Be Used as Hosts for USB Drives for Shared Network Storage

A router used for DSL is similar in appearance to a router used for cable Internet but features a DSL port. The switches built into routers are also stackable. If a router needs more ports, you can add a switch.

Routers are specialized computing devices that are controlled by *firmware*. When you log into a router to view or change its configuration, the options available are limited by the router's firmware. Buggy firmware can cause network problems and can make a network more vulnerable to attack.

Use a router's configuration program to determine the firmware date and version it uses. If the router is using an older version of firmware, check the vendor's website for an update. Before downloading the update, read the technical notes to see what issues the firmware affects and whether any other problems are caused by the update. Download the update and follow the vendor's instructions for installing the firmware.

If you want more features than the vendor-provided firmware includes, check for third-party firmware. DD-WRT is Linux-based alternative open source firmware suitable for a great variety of WLAN routers and embedded systems. DD-WRT is the most popular replacement firmware for routers, and some vendors now use it in their high-end routers.

Switch

A *switch* provides connectivity to devices in a local network. Each port on a switch works independently, allowing more than one concurrent session. A switch makes a direct connection between the sending and receiving devices by identifying the Media Access Control (MAC) address of each device. In today's networks, switches are very common in 100Mbps, 1000Mbps, and 10Gbps networks. Switches can be stacked to increase the number of connection ports in a network. Stacked switches are daisy-chained together, and in theory there is no limit to the number of switches possible in a network.

A switch resembles a hub but creates a dedicated full-speed connection between the two computers that are communicating with each other. A five-port 10/100/1000 switch, for example, provides the full 100Mbps bandwidth to each port connected to a Fast Ethernet or 10/100 card. If the network adapters are configured to run in full-duplex mode (that is, to send and receive data simultaneously), and the switch supports full-duplex mode (as most modern switches do), the bandwidth is doubled; for example, Fast Ethernet bandwidth (100Mbps) on the network would be doubled to 200Mbps, and Gigabit Ethernet (1000Mbps) bandwidth would be doubled to 2Gbps. Low-cost switches used in small office/home office (*SOHO*) networks (see Figure 2-2) cannot be configured to perform complex switching functions and are considered *unmanaged*. *Managed* switches, which are common in corporate and enterprise networks, also support SNMP for diagnostics and performance measurement, virtual LANs (VLANs) to enable multiple workgroups to use the same physical switch but keep their traffic separate, and redundancy.

1. 100Mbps connection
2. Unused RJ-45 port
3. Ethernet cable

FIGURE 2-2   An Unmanaged Fast Ethernet (10/100) Five-Port Switch

Wireless Access Point

Whereas hubs and switches deal with wired networks, a *wireless access point (WAP)* extends a wired network to wireless connections. It is also based on Ethernet, but it involves the IEEE 802.11 group of standards, which define wireless LANs (WLANs). A WAP acts as a central connecting point for computers equipped with wireless network adapters; like a switch, a WAP identifies each computer by its MAC address.

To turn a wireless router into a WAP (which would then need to connect to a separate router), check the configuration options available for the router.

Cloud-based Network Controller

Cloud-based networking has emerged in the past few years as the next generation of computer networks. Using a *cloud-based controller*, administrators can manage wireless LANs and branch offices that are located anywhere on the Internet from a central location. With wireless networking becoming more common than wire-based networks, cloud management solutions are expected to grow.

Firewall

A *firewall* is a hardware appliance or software application that protects a computer from unwanted intrusion. The networking world is especially concerned with hardware-based devices that protect an entire group of computers, such as a LAN. When it comes to small offices and home offices, firewall functionality is usually built into the router. In larger organizations, it is a separate device. A firewall stops unwanted connections from the outside and can block basic network attacks.

Network Interface Card

A network interface card (*NIC*) is the interface on a computer (or other device) that connects to the LAN. A NIC was traditionally a circuit board (card) that mounted to the motherboard, but now NICs are built-in interfaces. A NIC connects to a cable with an RJ-45 connecter. The NIC is designed to take communication off the physical cable (or wireless signal from the air) and present it to the computer for processing. A NIC has a unique physical address, known as a MAC address, that identifies the device to other hosts on the network. NICs have evolved to also provide wireless and virtual access to networks.

Repeater/Extender

Wireless network signals can be blocked by masonry, steel, or concrete walls and can weaken over distance. A signal repeater or extender can enable areas of weak or no signals to take advantage of a wireless network.

A wireless *repeater* (see Figure 2-3) resembles a wireless router and might include a switch, but instead of connecting to a cable or DSL modem, it connects wirelessly to a wireless router.

1. Front view
2. Gigabit Ethernet switch on rear of unit

FIGURE 2-3   A Wireless Repeater

Hub

A *hub* is the simplest device used on an Ethernet network for connecting devices to each other. As networks have become more complex, simple hubs have become rare in networks. A hub features multiple RJ-45 ports, a power supply, and signal lights to indicate network activity. Hubs were used to connect computers together and to boost the communication signal between computers.

Hubs have been almost completely replaced by switches because a hub splits the bandwidth of a connection among all the computers connected to it. For example, a five-port 10/100 Ethernet hub divides the 100Mbps speed of Fast Ethernet among the five ports, providing only 20Mbps of bandwidth to each port for Fast Ethernet and 10/100 adapters. A hub also broadcasts data to all computers connected to it.

NOTE   The sharing of all traffic in a LAN caused traffic jams for the computers involved. One solution that came along was the now-legacy Ethernet bridge, which divided a LAN into two parts. The Ethernet bridge was a precursor to the wireless bridge (discussed later in this chapter).

DSL Modems: Dial-up, Cable, and DSL

A modem connects a LAN to an Internet service provider (ISP). The term *modem* (short for *modulator/demodulator*) was originally used only for analog (dial-up) modems when most computer networks were connected by phone systems. A dial-up modem is a device that allows a computer (or, in rare cases, multiple computers) access to the Internet by changing the digital signals of the computer to analog signals used by a typical land-based phone line. Dial-up modems are slow devices and are usually used today only if no other Internet option is available. However, they might be used in server rooms as a point of remote administration as well.

Today, the term modem is typically applied to any device that connects to the Internet. *Cable modems* and *DSL modems*, the devices most commonly used to connect small networks to the Internet, are referred to as modems even though they work quite differently than dial-up modems. They are further discussed later in the chapter, in the section, "Internet Connection Types, Network Types, and Their Features."

Wireless Bridge

A *wireless bridge* is a device (or a setting on many access points) that is used to connect two wireless LANs together in order to expand a wireless network or to connect wireless clients to an Ethernet network.

Patch Panel

A *patch panel* is a box designed as a junction point for twisted pair (TP) cable and fiber cable used in networks. Patch panels are typically built into wiring closets or added to equipment racks in a 1U or taller form factor.

After removing any connector on the cable, each wire in the TP cable must be untwisted before being punched into the appropriate connection on the back of the panel. The twisted cables are color coded so they can be properly terminated at the other end. The most common standards for color-coding are known as T568A or T568B. Be sure to use the color coding that matches the rest of your network. T568A and T568B are covered in Chapter 3, "Hardware."

The front of the patch panel uses RJ-45 connectors for short standard network cables.

Ethernet over Powerlines

A powerline extender kit can be a practical solution when there is a need to extend a wired or wireless Internet connection. Powerline adapters are sold in pairs:

One unit plugs into an AC wall socket near the router and is connected to the router via a switch, and the other unit plugs into an AC wall socket in the room or area that needs network/Internet access. The AC wiring in the home or office (as long as it's on the same circuit) carries network signals between units. With a wired extender, you can plug a computer or switch into the Ethernet port. With a wireless extender, you need to log into the network via the wireless extender's SSID.

Figure 2-4 illustrates a typical wired powerline extender.

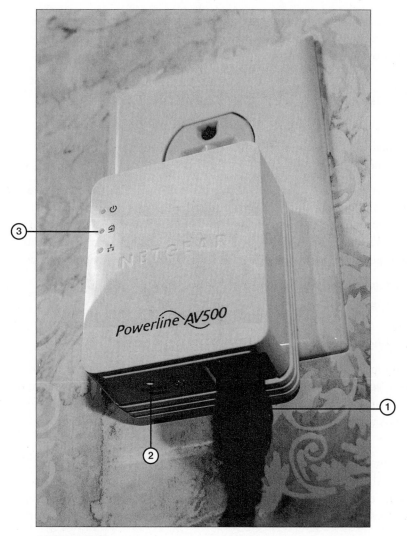

1. Ethernet cable
2. Reset button
3. Activity lights

FIGURE 2-4   A Powerline Extender

Power over Ethernet

A Power over Ethernet (*PoE*) switch is a switch with added capability (a built-in *endspan*) to send power out a port using CAT5 or better grades of twisted pair cable. The switch can send up to 25.5 watts of power on the unused twisted pairs (pins 4–5, 7–8) in 10BASE-T or 100BASE-T Ethernet (PoE Mode B) or by using all four wire pairs (PoE Mode A), enabling it to be used with Gigabit Ethernet. PoE enables wireless access points, IP security cameras, VoIP phones, routers, and other Ethernet devices to be installed in areas away from traditional power sources.

A *PoE switch endspan* is built into a switch. Another type of POE device, known as a *power over Ethernet injector*, is installed between a standard Ethernet switch and a PoE device to provide power only.

Install and Configure a Basic Wired/Wireless SOHO Network

220-1001: Objective 2.3: Given a scenario, install and configure a basic wired/ wireless SOHO network.

Wireless Ethernet, also known as IEEE 802.11, is the collective name for a group of wireless technologies compatible with wired Ethernet; these technologies are referred to as wireless LAN (WLAN) standards. Wireless Ethernet is also known as WiFi, after the Wireless Fidelity (Wi-Fi) Alliance (www.wi-fi.org), a trade group that promotes interoperability between different brands of wireless Ethernet hardware.

The following sections describe factors to consider when implementing these wireless technologies into a SOHO environment.

Access Point Settings

A small office/home office (SOHO) wired or wireless router can provide a secure way for users to access the Internet and local network resources; it can also become a magnet for attack. The difference is in how it is configured. In the following sections, we look at how to configure SOHO routers to meet typical network requirements.

To configure a router's settings, connect to the router with an Ethernet cable or wirelessly, using the manufacturer's instructions on the default IP address to use. (In the following examples, the router IP address is 192.168.1.1.) To connect, open a browser and enter the IP address of the router in the address bar and press **Enter**.

Channels

The wireless spectrum is divided into 11 *channels*, and part of installing a router on a 2.4GHz wireless network is selecting an appropriate channel for the signal. For best results, avoid overlapping channels. Only channels 1, 6, and 11 do not overlap with other channels, so it is best to use one of these three channels.

Some routers feature an Auto setting that enables the router to use the least-active channel, but if you prefer (or must) select a channel manually, use a WiFi diagnostic utility (discussed later in this chapter) to find the least-used channel. (More information on channels follows in the next section.)

To change the channel used by a wireless network:

Step 1.   Log into the router.

Step 2.   Navigate to the wireless configuration dialog.

Step 3.   Select a different channel (typically 1, 6, or 11 when using 2.4GHz networking because they have less interference than other channels).

Step 4.   Save your changes and exit the wireless configuration dialog.

Figure 2-5 shows a typical wireless channel configuration dialog on a dual-frequency (2.4GHz and 5.0GHz) Wireless-N router from Western Digital. Most SOHO routers have similar options.

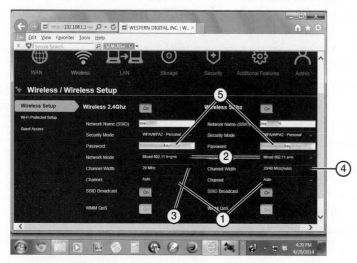

1. Auto channel selection lets router decide which channel works best
2. Mixed mode supports older network devices
3. Default channel width supported by all 2.4GHz devices
4. Auto channel width uses 40MHz channels with Wireless-N or AC clients and 20MHz channels with Wireless-A clients
5. Pre-shared key (blanked out for security)

FIGURE 2-5   Configuring Wireless Frequencies and Channels

NAT

Network address translation (*NAT*) is the process of modifying IP addresses as information crosses a router. Generally, this functionality is built into a router. It hides an entire IP address space (for example, 192.168.0.1 through 192.168.0.255) on the LAN. Whenever an IP address on the LAN wants to communicate with the Internet, the IP address is converted to the public IP address of the router (for example, 68.54.127.95). This way, it appears as if the router is the only device making the connection to remote computers on the Internet, which provides safety for the computers on the LAN. It also allows a single IP address to do the work for many other IP addresses in the LAN.

SOHO routers perform NAT automatically when connected to an IPv4 network. NAT is not necessary on an IPv6 network because IPv6 is much more secure and has no shortage of IP addresses.

Port Forwarding, Port Triggering, and DNAT

Port forwarding involves forwarding external visitors through a router to a specific computer. Instead of opening up the entire LAN, port forwarding directs particular traffic where you want it to go. Say that you set up an FTP server internally on your LAN. The FTP server might have the IP address 192.168.0.250 and have port 21 open and ready to accept file transactions (or you could use a different inbound port if you wanted). Clients on the Internet that want to connect to your FTP server would have to know the IP address of your router—so, for example, the clients would connect with an FTP client by using the IP address 68.54.127.95 and port 21. Once you create the appropriate port forwarding rule, the router sees these packets and forwards them to 192.168.0.250:21 (or whatever port you choose). Many ISPs block this type of activity, but port forwarding is a common and important method in larger networks.

Figure 2-6 illustrates port forwarding for an incoming VPN that uses PPTP. PPTP uses two non-contiguous ports and thus needs two rules—one for each port.

Port forwarding is also called destination network address translation (*DNAT*).

Port triggering, which is available on some routers, involves a particular service, such as Internet Relay Chat (IRC), opening an outgoing port or range of ports on demand. Port triggering can be used without being tied to a specific IP address.

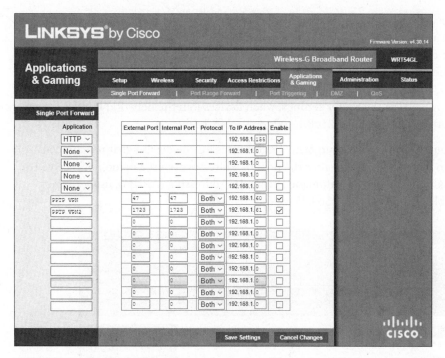

FIGURE 2-6 Configuring Port Forwarding to Permit Incoming VPN Connections

DMZ

A demilitarized zone (**DMZ**) allows outside traffic through to a particular IP address on a LAN. In a SOHO router, any device assigned to the DMZ receives traffic that is not specified for a particular device. Using a DMZ host makes sense for gaming and other types of traffic where you cannot specify in advance the ports needed. However, the DMZ host must have its own firewall because DMZ hosts are not protected by the router firewall.

> **TIP** Use static IP addresses for any devices that use port forwarding or the DMZ to ensure that the correct device is being specified. Dynamic IP (server-assigned DHCP) addresses can change according to the number of devices on the network and based on whether some devices leave the network and then return to it.

DHCP

By default, SOHO routers have the DHCP service turned on so they can provide IP addresses to any wired or wireless devices that connect. Most routers enable you to specify the range and number of IP addresses available via DHCP. Figure 2-7 illustrates a router with DHCP enabled and a range of IP addresses the DHCP server can assign. In this example, the default address of the router is 192.168.1.1, and the subnet mask is 255.255.255.0. This means the router has the first address on the 192.168.0 network, which is a private network that can't be used on the Internet. As shown in the router settings, when devices join the network, DHCP assigns addresses in the range 192.168.1.100 to 192.168.1.149.

If a router does not have sufficient IP addresses for the devices that need to connect to it, devices arriving after the pool of addresses are used up do not receive IP addresses but switch to Automatic Private IP Addressing (APIPA), using the nonroutable IP address range 169.254.x.x.

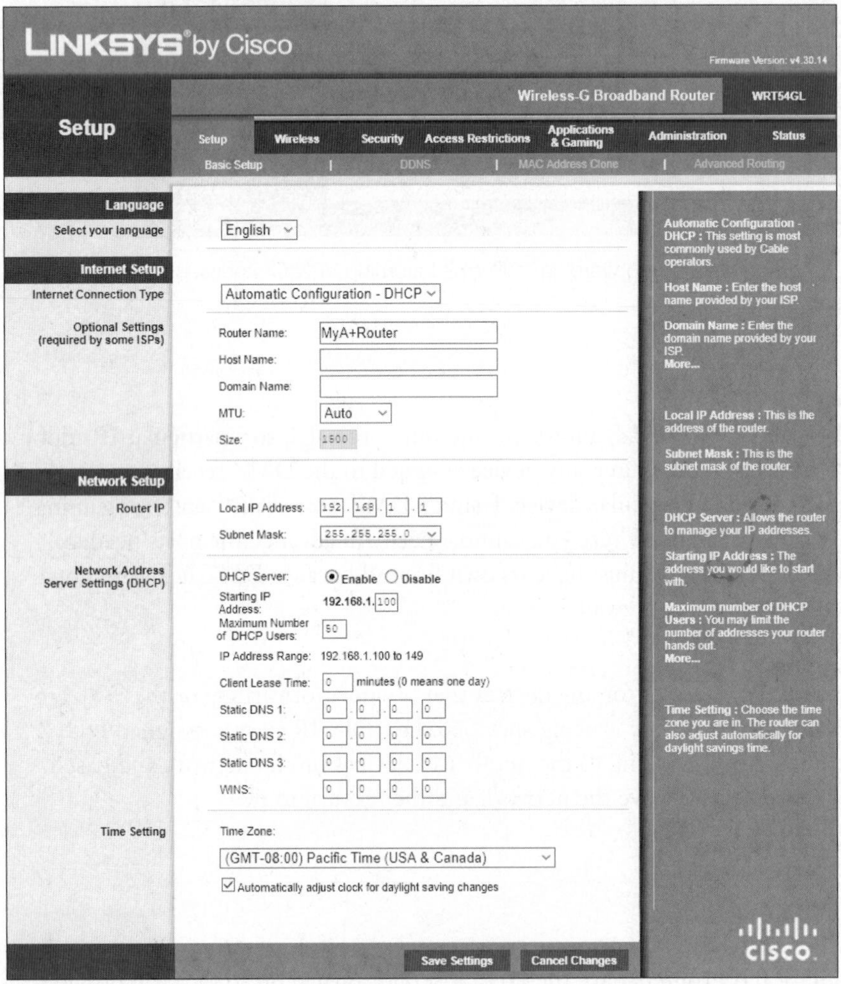

FIGURE 2-7   Configuring DHCP to Provide a Range of 50 IP Addresses

TIP   When you need to use static IP addresses on some devices, make sure to reserve some IP addresses and keep them out of the range of addresses assigned by the DHCP server. For example, in the network illustrated in Figure 2-7, IP addresses below 100 and above 149 in the 192.168.1.x network could be used for devices needing static IP addresses.

IP Addressing

A SOHO router comes with a default IP address. This IP address is a special type known as a *private address*.

NIC Configuration

A PC may have several different NICs to make it possible to connect to networks over the wire, via WiFi, or virtually. Once you select the NIC that matches the method of connecting, you can choose the protocol and configure network access. You do this configuration in one of the windows shown earlier in this chapter, in the section "DHCP."

NIC Configuration Steps

The following steps are shown in Figure 2-8, starting with the largest window and moving down:

Step 1.   Click the **Windows** icon and select the **Windows Settings** gear.

Step 2.   In the Windows Settings window select the **Network & Internet** link.

Step 3.   When you see the different connection options, select the one you want and click **Change adapter options** on the right side of the window.

Step 4.   Choose the adapter you want to configure (in this case, **Ethernet**) and click on the **Properties** button. A list of items available to the NIC are listed. Note that in the example, both IPv4 and IPv6 are checked, making them available to the NIC.

Step 5.   Double-click on **Internet Protocol Version 4 (TCP/IPv4)**. You now see the window where the IP address is configured dynamically or statically (refer to Figure 2-7).

Step 6.   Assign the address or leave the default DHCP options and click **OK** to accept any changes.

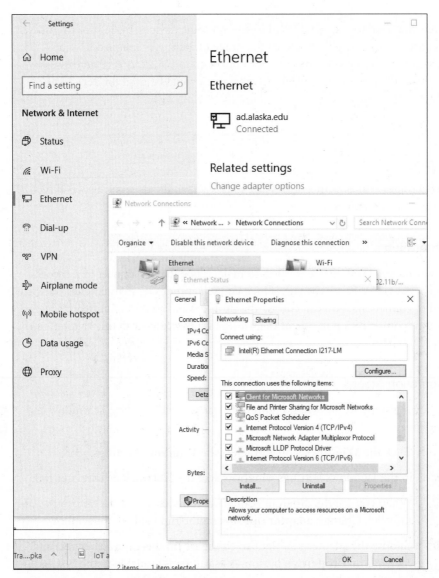

FIGURE 2-8   Descending from the Largest Window to the Smallest, the Steps in NIC Configuration

End-User Device Configuration

The steps to configure a NIC are essentially the same steps used for other end-user devices, such as printers and mobile phones. If the default on an end-user device is DHCP, the device is likely to auto-configure. If the device needs to be configured, the process is mostly the same as described for NICs. To access the configuration windows, you may need to visit the manufacturer's support site.

Internet of Things (IoT) Device Configuration

The Internet has long connected people together, but in recent years the explosive growth of the Web has involved connections between people and a number of things that people use. As communication protocols such as Bluetooth and Z-Wave have evolved, so have production techniques that have made it easier to embed communication capability into smaller and less expensive objects that have become common in people's everyday life. Markets for IoT devices are ever-expanding and include phones, cars, home appliances, door locks, wall outlets, lights, and video-enabled doorbells, among many other devices. Industrial uses are being developed as well, and there are now devices that measure soil moisture, noise, motion, air pressure, and water pressure. Many billions of things are now talking to each other and sharing data, and the number of such devices is expected to grow exponentially. Figure 2-9 depicts some of the many IoT functions you may already enjoy on your mobile device.

FIGURE 2-9   IoT Applications on a Mobile Device (Image ©Es sarawuth. Shutterstock)

The software to manage IoT devices can be installed on computers or mobile devices. Typically, a vendor of an IoT product develops a mobile app to monitor and manage the product. While some systems are complex, many are quite simple and easy to set up on a home network. The following are some of the items that can participate in the IoT that are noted in the A+ objectives:

- Thermostats
- Light switches
- Security cameras
- Door locks
- Voice-enabled smart speakers/digital assistants

Figure 2-10 shows the user interface for an IoT-enabled wall outlet adapter that is being used to monitor energy use for a refrigerator. Off/on and scheduling capability are built into the application, and the device can be managed from anywhere on the Web.

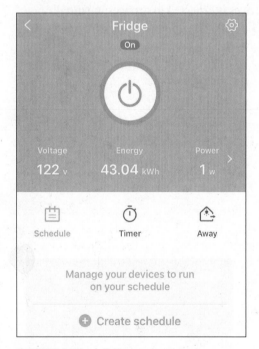

FIGURE 2-10   IoT Device App Interface

Cable/DSL Modem

Setting up a cable modem or DSL modem is a fairly simple task on the user's end. Most SOHO networks use a wireless router, and it must be connected to the modem. Simply plug one end of an Ethernet cable into the cable or DSL modem and plug the other end into the RJ-45 jack labeled "Internet." Attach the local devices to the wireless router with Ethernet cables in the remaining ports or via WiFi.

Basic QoS

Quality of service (*QoS*) is an important feature to enable on any network that provides streaming media, gaming, or VoIP services. QoS prioritizes real-time and streaming traffic. Depending on the router, QoS can simply be turned on and off (basic QoS), or it can be tweaked by specifying services to prioritize, whether to optimize for gaming, and uplink/downlink speeds to use.

QoS can be configured by an ISP or by a router. If your ISP is already performing QoS optimization, any changes you make on your router will not improve your traffic.

UPnP

Universal plug and play (*UPnP*) is a router feature that enables devices on a network to add themselves to a network without the need to reconfigure the router. UPnP is widely used for media streaming across a network.

UPnP can be vulnerable to attacks. If you don't use media streaming or other services that use UPnP, you can disable it.

WiFi Encryption Types

Although many public WiFi hotspots are not encrypted, encryption is a necessity for both SOHO wired or wireless routers and larger business wireless networks to preserve privacy and to prevent criminals from borrowing the network. Several types of encryption are available on most SOHO routers, and you need to select and enable the appropriate one.

WEP (Wired Equivalent Privacy)

WEP is the oldest and weakest WiFi encryption standard. If WEP is enabled, all network devices must use the same WEP key and encryption strength.

For the best security, use the highest setting supported by both WEP and adapters. Small-office or home-office hardware might use 64-bit encryption with a 40-bit key (10 hexadecimal characters or 5 ASCII characters); business-market hardware often uses 128-bit encryption with a 104-bit key (26 hexadecimal characters or 13 ASCII characters). WEP encryption keys cannot include punctuation marks.

WEP can be configured using a pre-shared key (PSK) or Open System Authentication (OSA). PSK is easier to break than OSA, but either form is easier to break than newer encryption methods and should not be used unless some network devices don't support WPA or WPA2 encryption. 802.11n and 802.11ac do not support WEP.

WPA (WiFi Protected Access)

WPA uses a variable-length encryption key (up to 63 ASCII characters, including punctuation marks) and Temporal Key Integrity Protocol (*TKIP*) 128-bit encryption, so it is much more secure than WEP.

WPA can use PSK or a RADIUS authentication server to generate unique keys (such as in enterprise and government WiFi networks).

WPA has been replaced by WPA2, but some routers can be configured to support both WPA and WPA2 clients on the same network.

WPA2 (WiFi Protected Access 2)

Unlike most sequels, WPA2 is a sequel that's better (in the sense of being more secure) than the original. *WPA2* replaces TKIP with Advanced Encryption Standard (*AES*), a 128- to 256-bit encryption protocol used in technologies such as hard drive encryption as well as networking. AES can be used exclusively or in conjunction with TKIP, which is the recommended option. Some router configurations use the term *WPA-AES* to refer to WPA2. If you use a mixture of WPA and WPA2 devices and can't update the firmware on the older devices to support AES, use the WPA's-TKIP-AES setting on your router. WPA2 certification is mandatory for all new devices that bear the WiFi trademark.

WPS (WiFi Protected Setup)

WPS provides an easier way to configure a wireless network than entering the router's IP address on each device connecting to it. Routers that support WPS typically have the default WPS key on the bottom of the device. To use WPS, use the setup software provided with the router on each computer and follow the directions on devices such as printers or multifunction devices. Note that WPS should be used only if all devices on a wireless network support it.

There are two ways to use WPS: the default PIN method, in which the PIN on the router is used to set up clients, and a pushbutton method, in which a physical or software button is pushed on the router and clients to set up the network. In December 2011, researchers announced that the PIN and the pre-shared key could be compromised by brute-force attacks. Since that time, users have been encouraged to use the pushbutton method or to forgo using WPS for configuration.

Table 2-3 compares WEP, WPA, and WPA2 to each other.

Table 2-3 Wireless Encryption Types

Setting	Encryption Type	Encryption Key Length	Encryption Key Rules	Strength
Open	None	N/A	N/A	None
Wired Equivalent Privacy (WEP)	RC4	10 hex/5 ASCII characters (64-bit) 26 hex/13 ASCII characters (128-bit)	ASCII: alphanumeric (no punctuation)	Very weak
WiFi Protected Access (WPA)	TKIP (128-bit)	Up to 63 ASCII characters	Punctuation is okay; some devices can't use a full-length encryption key	Strong
WiFi Protected Access 2 (WPA2)	AES (128-bit)	Up to 63 ASCII characters	Punctuation is okay; some devices can't use a full-length encryption key	Very strong

Compare and Contrast Wireless Networking Protocols

220-1001: Objective 2.4: Compare and contrast wireless networking protocols.

Computer networking protocols are generally accepted procedures and rules for communication between devices. There are different protocols for communication, security, data, and so on. When computers communicate on any network, they have to follow these very strict rules and conventions in order to minimize errors. Wireless network protocols are developed by the Institute of Electrical and Electronics Engineers (IEEE), and understanding them and how they have evolved will help you in servicing wireless networks.

WiFi Standards

There are five different WiFi standards:

- *802.11b* has a maximum speed of 11Mbps and can fall back to 5.5Mbps or slower if necessary. It uses the 2.4GHz frequency band with 20MHz-wide channels.

- **802.11a** has a maximum speed of 54Mbps and supports slower speeds from 6Mbps to 48Mbps, as needed, and uses the 5GHz frequency band.

- **802.11g** has a maximum speed of 54Mbps and supports slower speeds from 6Mbps to 48Mbps, as needed. Unlike 802.11a, 802.11g uses the 2.4GHz frequency band, so it is backward compatible with 802.11b.

- **802.11n** has a maximum speed of 150Mbps when using a single 20MHz channel, or it can run at up to 300Mbps with channel bonding (40MHz channel). All 802.11n devices use the 2.4GHz frequency by default, but 802.11n can optionally support 5GHz frequencies as well. 802.11n supports MIMO (multiple input multiple output) antennas to improve performance and range, although not all devices include multiple antennas.

- **802.11ac** uses only the 5GHz band and supports up to 80MHz-wide channels compared to 20MHz for 802.11b/g and 40MHz for 802.11n using channel bonding. It supports multiuser MIMO (MU-MIMO). The speed of 802.11ac is up to 433Mbps per stream when 80MHz-wide channels are used.

Table 2-4 compares the five wireless Ethernet standards to each other.

Table 2-4   Wireless Ethernet Standards

Wireless Ethernet Type	Frequency	Maximum Speed	MIMO Support	Estimated Range Indoors/ Outdoors	Channel Width/ Number of Channels	Interoperable With
802.11a	5GHz	54Mbps	No	35m/120m	20MHz/12*	Requires dual-mode (802.11a/b or 802.11a/g) hardware; 802.11n networks supporting 5GHz frequency
802.11b	2.4GHz	11Mbps	No	32m/140m	20MHz/3**	802.11g
802.11g	2.4GHz	54Mbps	No	32m/140m	20MHz/3**	802.11b, 802.11n

Wireless Ethernet Type	Frequency	Maximum Speed	MIMO Support	Estimated Range Indoors/ Outdoors	Channel Width/ Number of Channels	Interoperable With
802.11n	2.4GHz	72Mbps per stream (20MHz channel)	Yes***	70m/250m	20MHz/3**	802.11b, 802.11g (802.11a on networks also supporting 5GHz frequency)
802.11n (optional)	5GHz	150Mbps per stream (40MHz channel)	Yes***	70m/250m	20MHz or40MHz/12*	802.11a (20MHz-wide channels only)
802.11ac	5GHz	433Mbps per stream (80MHz channel)	Yes***	70m/250m	20MHz or 40MHz or 80MHz	802.11a, 802.11n (5GHz). 802.11ac routers also support previous standards.

* Non-overlapping channels; exact number varies by country.

** Non-overlapping channels.

*** Up to four streams supported. Most devices have up to three antennas but can receive/transmit only two streams at a time.

NOTE WiFi-certified hardware is 802.11-family wireless Ethernet hardware that has passed tests established by the Wi-Fi Alliance. Most, but not all, 802.11-family wireless Ethernet hardware is WiFi certified.

Frequencies

Wireless routers use either the 2.4GHz band or the 5GHz band. Each has advantages and disadvantages. The 2.4GHz band has a longer range but may perform at slower speeds. The 5GHz band may provide faster rates but has a shorter range. There are a couple reasons for the differences. One is that lower frequencies travel better through obstacles such as floors and walls. Another is that the 5GHz band is less used and has more channels than 2.4, and its channels do not overlap. This means 5GHz devices do not contend with other devices for bandwidth, as do devices in the more popular 2.4GHz range.

Many wireless routers offer both 2.4GHz and 5GHz, and each can be configured separately; some routers are capable of switching between the two frequencies if a signal becomes weak. Table 2-5 summarizes the two wireless bands.

Table 2-5   2.4GHz vs. 5GHz Wireless Bands

Frequency	Estimated Range	Channels	Advantages	Disadvantages
2.4GHz	50m (160 feet) indoors	11	Longer range	Slower performance, channels easily overlap
5GHz	15m (50 feet) indoors	23	Shorter range	Faster performance, channels do not overlap

Understanding MIMO

The number of antennas supported by the router and the adapters (either built-in or add-on devices) is one of the reasons for different performance levels in a given 802.11n or 802.11ac device. MIMO devices are available in the following configurations:

- **1x1:** One transmit, one receive antenna
- **2x2:** Two transmit, two receive antennas
- **2x3:** Two transmit, three receive antennas
- **3x2:** Three transmit, two receive antennas
- **3x3:** Three transmit, three receive antennas

The number of transmit antennas generally corresponds to the number of spatial streams (data streams) the device can support. In the case of a router that supports both 2.4GHz and 5GHz signals, the specifications include this information for each band.

NOTE   When a device has different numbers of receiving antennas and sending antennas, the device might be identified by the number of spatial (data) streams it can send and receive. For example, a device with a 2x3 antenna configuration can also be identified as having a 2x3:2 configuration (two send antennas, three receive antennas, and send/receive support for two spatial [data] streams). Some smartphones and tablets simply use the term MIMO (multiple input multiple output) if they support two or more 802.11n or 802.11ac streams.

Bluetooth

Bluetooth began as a short-range, low-speed wireless network technology primarily designed to operate in peer-to-peer (or ad hoc) mode between PCs and other devices, such as printers, projectors, smartphones, mice, and keyboards. Bluetooth runs in virtually the same 2.4GHz frequency used by IEEE 802.11b, 802.11g, and 802.11n wireless networks but uses a spread-spectrum frequency-hopping signaling method to help minimize interference. Bluetooth devices connect to each other to form a personal area network (PAN).

Some systems and devices include integrated Bluetooth adapters, and others need a Bluetooth module connected to a USB port to enable Bluetooth networking.

Bluetooth version 1.2 offers a data transfer rate of 1Mbps, and version 2 offers 3Mbps. Bluetooth version 3.0 + HS can reach speeds of up to 24Mbps because it uses Bluetooth only to establish the connection, and the actual data transfer happens over an 802.11 link. This feature is known as Alternative MAC/PHY (AMP). Bluetooth 4.0, also known as Bluetooth Smart, is designed for use with very low-power applications such as sensors. Bluetooth 4.1, a software update to 4.0, enables Bluetooth to perform multiple roles at the same time and to work better with LTE cellular devices.

Bluetooth 4.2 includes additional features to support the Internet of Things (IoT), and Bluetooth 5.0 was designed with the IoT in mind. IoT devices can be spread around a home, factory, or farm and can send a day's worth of stored data back to a network. Bluetooth 5 can provide up to twice the speed and up to four times the range of Bluetooth 4 while keeping power consumption low. As IoT growth continues at a rapid rate, Bluetooth 5 will be a common solution for IoT gateway devices.

Bluetooth is divided into classes, each of which has a different range. Table 2-6 shows these classes, their ranges, and the amount of power their corresponding antennae use to generate signal.

Table 2-6 Bluetooth Classes

Class	Power (mW)	Range
Class 1	100mW	100m (328 feet)
Class 2	2.5mW	10m (33 feet)
Class 3	1mW	1m (3 feet)

As you can see, Class 1 generates the most powerful signal, and as such has the largest range. The most common Bluetooth devices are Class 2 devices, with a range of 10m (for example, portable printers, headsets, computer dongles).

The Bluetooth radios that are built into mobile devices and some laptops can be used for many devices, including headsets, printers, and input devices such as mice and keyboards. By default, Bluetooth is usually disabled on Android devices but is enabled on iOS devices such as iPads or iPhones. To connect a Bluetooth device to a mobile device, Bluetooth first needs to be enabled; then the Bluetooth device needs to be synchronized to the mobile device. This is known as *pairing*, or linking, and it sometimes requires a PIN code. Once synchronized, the device needs to be connected. Finally, the Bluetooth connection should be tested.

The following sections show the steps involved in connecting a Bluetooth headset to typical Android-based and iOS devices. Before you begin, make sure the Bluetooth headset is charged.

Steps to Configure a Bluetooth Headset on an Android-Based Device

Following these steps to connect a Bluetooth headset to a typical Android-based device:

Step 1. Go to **Settings > Connections** and then enable **Bluetooth** if not already enabled.

Step 2. Tap **Bluetooth** to display the Bluetooth Settings screen.

Step 3. Prepare the headset. How you do this varies from headset to headset, but simply powering on a typical Bluetooth headset begins the pairing process.

Step 4. If the Android device is not scanning automatically, tap **Scan**. Keep holding the button on the headset until the Android device finds it.

Step 5. On the Android device, tap the device to pair with. Most Android devices pair the Bluetooth headset to the mobile device and then complete the connection automatically, allowing full use of the device.

Step 6. Enter a PIN code, if prompted to do so. Many devices come with the default pin 0000.

When finished, the screen on the Android device looks similar to the screen shown in Figure 2-11. Note the Bluetooth icon at the top of the screen. This icon indicates whether Bluetooth is running on the device. It remains even if you disconnect the Bluetooth device. For this headset device, you would test it simply by making a phone call.

To disconnect the device but retain the pairing, turn off the device. To unpair the device, tap the settings (gearbox) icon on the screen and tap **Unpair**. To use it again, pair it again.

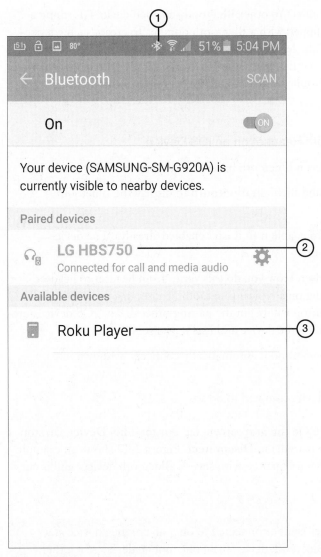

1. Bluetooth device connected
2. Newly connected device
3. Other nearby devices

FIGURE 2-11   Bluetooth Screen on an Android Smartphone Showing the LG HBS750 Headset Connected

Android devices can also connect to other Bluetooth-enabled devices (forming a PAN) or to a computer equipped with a Bluetooth dongle. To create such connections, you must set the mobile device to discoverable (which generally lasts only two minutes). In the same way that the headset is discovered by the mobile device in the previous procedure, a mobile device can be discovered by a computer or other mobile device.

Steps to Configure a Bluetooth Headset on an iOS Device

Follow these steps to connect a Bluetooth headset to a typical iOS device:

Step 1. Go to **Settings** and then tap **Bluetooth** to display the Bluetooth screen.

Step 2. Tap **Bluetooth** to enable it (if it isn't enabled already). The device searches for devices.

Step 3. Prepare the headset. How you do this varies from headset to headset. For example, switching on a typical Bluetooth headset or pressing and holding the power button will begin the pairing process. The iOS device automatically recognizes the device and lists it as discoverable.

Step 4. Tap the device name, and it automatically connects, as shown in Figure 2-12.

Step 5. Enter a PIN code, if prompted to do so.

To remove the device, tap it. On the next screen, tap **Forget This Device**. To stop using the device but keep it paired, tap **Disconnect**. Figure 2-12 shows an example of an iPhone 6 that has previously paired with several Bluetooth devices and is currently connected to one.

> **NOTE** Most Bluetooth devices can be connected to only one mobile device at a time. If you need to switch a Bluetooth device from one mobile device to another, be sure to disconnect it or "forget" it from the current connection before making a new one.

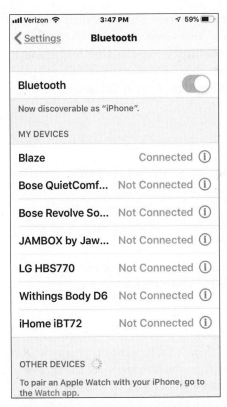

FIGURE 2-12   A Connected Bluetooth Headset on an iOS Device

NFC

Near field communication (***NFC***) is a feature included in many mobile devices such as tablets for data transfer and shopping. When NFC is enabled and a suitable payment system (such as Apple Pay or Android Pay) is installed on a mobile device, the device can be used for secure payments at any retailer that supports NFC payments.

NFC can also be used to automatically turn on Bluetooth and transfer files between devices (a feature sometimes referred to as "tap and go" or, on Android devices, Android Beam). It can be enabled separately from NFC for payments. Apple uses NFC for purchases and other limited functions requiring secure data. The technology is expected to grow.

RFID

Radio frequency identification (***RFID***) technology consists of an RFID tag that can broadcast information about an item, as well as an RFID reader to accept the broadcast information and deliver it to a computer system for use. An example would be RFID security badges that allow doors to be unlocked in a secure environment, giving access to some while denying use to others. In some retail environments, an item for sale has an RFID badge identifying the item name and price. The badges on the items in a shopping cart broadcast their information to a checkout reader, and customers can simply walk out the door, and the items are counted, priced, and paid for just by passing the reader. Passports and other identification documents may also have RFID information embedded in them.

Zigbee and Z-Wave

Zigbee is similar to Bluetooth in that it is a near-range wireless protocol designed to allow communication using low power. Zigbee is most commonly used to connect IoT data-sharing devices in a home, industry, or medical environment. A Zigbee device, such as a motion sensor or leak sensor, contains a Zigbee chip to send and receive data. Zigbee operates at the 2.4GHz frequency.

Z-Wave is a more recent version of Zigbee that uses less power and operates on the much lower 908.42MHz frequency. Zigbee and Z-Wave are not interoperable.

3G, 4G, 5G, and LTE

Any user of a mobile phone has used a 3G, 4G, 5G, or LTE network. This technology does not come from the phones but rather from the provider's cell tower. The G stands for "generation," and each new generation of network service provides advanced signaling and available services. Most cell phones in use now support 3G, 4G, and LTE. 5G, as of this writing, is still in development and testing and is not widely available. Table 2-7 lists the differences in these four generations.

Table 2-7   3G, 4G, 5G, and LTE Comparison

Generation	Year Released	New Features
3G	1998	Video calling
		High-speed Internet
		More data
4G	2008	Live streaming of HD TV
		Video conferencing
		100Mbps Internet speed while moving and 1Gbps when stationary
LTE (Long-Term Evolution)	2010	Improved coverage
		Faster speed
5G	In development	Much faster data
		Fewer delays

Summarize the Properties and Purposes of Services Provided by Networked Hosts

220-1001: Objective 2.5: Summarize the properties and purposes of services provided by networked hosts.

As computer networks have evolved over time, different technologies have emerged to perform specific tasks, or server roles, for the network. The following sections describe some of the common server roles that perform specialized tasks for the users on a network. A server might not necessarily be a computer. For example, routers often incorporate one or more of the server functions described in the following sections.

Web Server

Web servers are specialized computers that host websites and provide various types of content to clients via the Internet. A web server uses Hypertext Transfer Protocol (HTTP) to communicate with computers on other networks that are requesting information. Web hosting has become essential in business and education, and setting up a web server is a common task for an IT professional.

File Server

A *file server* is used to provide shared storage on a network. A file server is typically a computer with a single large drive or a RAID array for storage. Dedicated servers are used only for storage; a computer that shares storage and also performs standalone tasks (as in a Windows workgroup or HomeGroup) is known as a nondedicated server.

A network-attached storage (*NAS*) device is a special kind of file server designed to store large amounts of data in a central location for users on the network. A NAS is essentially one or more drives fitted with an Ethernet connection; it is assigned its own IP address.

Print Server

A *print server* manages the printing tasks for multiple users sharing one or more printers in an office. Printing a document in a large office was once a complicated task because printers were expensive, and access to them was limited. Eventually a designated computer and printer became hosts on an office network, and managing printing tasks for the whole office became more efficient. Because print jobs might be requested faster than a printer can deliver them, print servers queue print jobs and deliver them to appropriate printers when they are available. They can also track the usage of printers on the network. Print servers and printers can be either wired or wireless.

DHCP Server

A *DHCP server* supports Dynamic Host Configuration Protocol, the protocol that automatically assigns IP addresses to connected devices on a network. DHCP server functions are included in SOHO routers and are typical roles for domain controllers on small to medium business (SMB) networks. On larger networks, DHCP servers are often separate physical or virtualized servers.

DNS Server

A *Domain Name System (DNS)* server has a database containing public IP addresses and their associated domain names. The purpose of a DNS server is to translate domain names used in web page requests into IP addresses. DNS server functions are included in SOHO routers. For larger networks, a separate DNS server can be used. A DNS server communicates with other, larger DNS servers if the requested addresses are not in its database.

Proxy Server

A *proxy server* is an intermediary between a client and another network, such as the Internet. A proxy server stores web pages that have been requested, and if a client requests a web page, the proxy server checks its cache for the page. If the page exists and is up to date, the proxy server uses its cached copy to supply the client request. If the proxy server does not have the requested page, it downloads the page on behalf of the client, sends the page to the client, and retains a copy of the page in its cache.

A proxy server helps reduce traffic between a network and the Internet, and it can also be used to block requests for undesirable traffic. Proxy servers can also be used for anonymous surfing. See https://whatis.techtarget.com/definition/proxy-server for more information about how proxy servers are used.

Mail Server

A *mail server* sends or receives email on a network. An SMTP (Simple Mail Transfer Protocol) server is used to send outgoing email, and either a POP3 (Post Office Protocol version 3) or IMAP (Internet Message Access Protocol) server is used to receive mail. Mail server apps are available from many vendors.

Authentication Server

An *authentication server* is used to examine and verify or deny credentials to a user attempting to log into secured networks. Usernames and permissions are stored in this central server, which provides security certificates to users and records user logins to the network.

Syslog Server

Syslog servers track events that happen on devices on a network. Devices on a network usually have a way to track their system events, such as user logins and crashes, as well as other activities that the network administrator has determined to be important. The reports are sent to a central syslog server for network managers to analyze, as needed.

Internet Appliances

Internet appliances are single-purpose devices that are used to perform specific tasks on an IP network.

UTM

Unified threat management (*UTM*) devices provide firewall, remote access, virtual private network (VPN) support, web traffic filtering with anti-malware, and network intrusion prevention. UTM devices may be specialized boxes that are placed between the organization's network and the Internet, but they can also be virtual machines using cloud-based services. UTM devices unite the functions of several earlier devices and have largely replaced IDS and IPS devices (described next). Barracuda Networks, Check Point, Cisco, and other networking equipment manufacturers offer versions of UTM devices.

IDS

An intrusion detection system (*IDS*) device or program detects network intrusions that might not be detected by a firewall. Typical threats detected by an IDS include attacks against services, malware attacks, data-driven attacks, and host-based attacks. To detect these threats, a typical IDS uses signature-based detection, detection of unusual activities (anomalies), and stateful protocol analysis. An IDS device or program must be updated frequently with new signatures and rules to maintain protection.

A true IDS does not block attacks, but some products and services referred to as IDSs actually have characteristics of IPSs (intrusion prevention systems).

IPS

An intrusion prevention system (*IPS*) uses methods similar to those used by an IDS, but unlike an IDS, an IPS blocks attacks. Dedicated IDS and IPS devices are not widely used today, but their features are incorporated into UTM devices.

An IPS can also be implemented in software with a package such as the open source Snort (www.snort.org) for Windows and some Linux distributions.

End-point Management Server

An *end-point management server* keeps track of devices using the network and ensures that they comply with the security parameters of the entire network. End-points are the end users and devices that use a network. It is vital that those devices on the network all comply with security policies to keep the network secure. End-point servers can manage security policies for all the different devices and can consolidate the data into one dashboard for the network security administrator.

Legacy and Embedded Systems

The term *legacy* refers to things handed down from predecessors. *Legacy systems*, therefore, are systems that use outdated operating systems, programming languages, applications, or hardware. Maintaining legacy systems is often necessary when newer products are not compatible with legacy applications (for example, applications that can run only under MS-DOS or old versions of Windows).

If a legacy operating system and its applications can be run in a virtualized environment, the problems of maintaining old hardware are eliminated.

Embedded systems, which are dedicated computing devices used for specific tasks such as machine control, point-of-sale systems, or ATMs, are often also legacy systems. As long as they work, they are maintained. Embedded systems often use older operating systems; for example, experts estimated that 80% of worldwide ATMs were still using Windows XP at the time support for XP ended in April 2014.

Perhaps the biggest risk to both legacy and embedded systems is security. If a legacy system or an embedded system has network or Internet connectivity, it theoretically could be attacked or used as a bot to attack other systems. Although operating systems designed for embedded uses have more security than standard operating systems, the older the operating system, the greater the risks.

Because of the potential for security risks, some organizations have paid for extended security updates for otherwise-legacy systems such as Windows XP.

When considering whether and when to update legacy sy
systems, consider these issues:

- Will the existing data be usable with newer apps?
- Can the existing program run with current opera
- Will changes in network security, wireless, or In
  changeover to IPv6) cause problems with the application.
- Can a proprietary application be licensed to run in a virtual machine?
- Does existing hardware used in the embedded system work with the new
  operating system?
- Does the embedded application run on current embedded operating systems?
  If not, is an updated version available?

Evaluation, testing, troubleshooting, and running both systems in parallel are highly
advisable when updating legacy systems or embedded systems.

Network Configuration Concepts

220-1001: Objective 2.6: Explain common network configuration concepts.

220-1001
Exam

Computer network technologies evolve at a rapid pace, and keeping track of all the
different technologies and protocols can be daunting, but a fundamental understanding of the communication processes is essential for a computer technician.
This will become even more true as people increase the use of computers for communication and as the number of devices talking to each other grows exponentially.
The following sections cover some of the most commonly encountered networking
terms and technologies.

IP Addressing

The Internet protocol (IP) is the communication protocol that computers and
other devices use to communicate with computers outside of their local networks.
IPv4 and IPv6 are two current versions of IP addressing commonly in use today. All
devices that communicate on a local network have a physical address that is unique
and unchanging. IP addresses are changeable, logical addresses and are assigned to
devices for communicating outside their local networks.

ic vs. Static IP Addresses

The term *static* means *unchanging*, or *always the same*. *Dynamic* means *constantly changing*. We use these terms to describe the two most common ways to configure a computer's IP address settings:

- **Static IP address:** Assigned to a device by the administrator and not subject to change until reconfigured by the administrator. Note that there is more than just the IP address to configure. Other areas are the subnet mask, the default gateway, and DNS servers.

- **Dynamic (DHCP server-assigned) IP address:** Assigned by a DHCP server and will likely change each time a device leaves and then re-joins the network or when the address is used beyond its lease time and expires.

Table 2-8 describes the various settings related to static and dynamic addressing.

Table 2-8 Static vs. Dynamic IP Addressing

Setting	What It Does	Static IP Address	Dynamic IP Address
IP address	Identifies a computer on the network; unique value for each device	Entered manually on the device	Automatically assigned by the DHCP server
Subnet mask	Determines which bits in the IP address are the network portion and which are the host portion	Entered manually on the device, but a default subnet mask appears when the IP address is assigned	Automatically assigned by the DHCP server
DNS configuration	Identifies Domain Name System servers	IP addresses of one or more DNS servers, hostname, and domain name must be entered	Automatically assigned by the DHCP server
Gateway	Identifies IP address of device that connects the computer to the Internet or another network; same values for all devices on the network	IP address for the gateway must be entered	Automatically assigned by the DHCP server

Windows, macOS, and Linux default to using dynamic IP addresses. As Table 2-8 makes clear, this is the preferable method for configuring a TCP/IP network. Use a manually assigned IP address if a DHCP server (which provides IP addresses automatically) is not available on the network—or if you need to configure a firewall or router to provide different levels of access to some systems (in which case you must specify those systems' IP addresses).

It is possible to configure a DHCP reservation with a specific address from the DHCP pool of addresses. This is a permanent lease that is assigned to a DHCP client. It is similar to a static address in that it doesn't change, but it is configured into the DHCP server, and the address is from the range of addresses that DHCP gives out to clients.

NOTE   Routers, wireless gateways, and computers that host an Internet connection shared with Windows Internet Connection Sharing or a third-party sharing program all provide DHCP services to other computers on the network.

To configure an IP address in Windows, access the Internet Protocol Properties window. This window contains several dialogs used to make changes to an IP address. To open the General tab of the Internet Protocol Properties window, open Network Connections, right-click the network connection, select **Properties**, click **Internet Protocol v4 (TCP/IPv4)** or **TCP/IPv6** in the list of protocols and features, and click **Properties**.

IP configuration in Linux is performed by editing the /etc/network/interfaces file. If you use a GUI that features a Network configuration panel, you can use it to make changes for you.

To configure TCP/IP in macOS, go to System Preferences, open the Network panel, and select the appropriate tab.

APIPA IP Addresses/Link Local Addresses

Most IP networks use addresses provided automatically by Dynamic Host Configuration Protocol (DHCP). However, in the event that the DHCP server becomes unavailable and an alternate IP address has not been set up, devices on the network assign themselves APIPA/link local addresses. These addresses are in the IPv4 address range 169.254.0.1 to 169.254.255.254 (with the subnet mask 255.255.0.0); the IPv6 version is called a link local address and has the FE80::/64 prefix. A device with an APIPA address cannot connect to the Internet.

If a DHCP problem causes APIPA/link local addresses to be assigned, you can resolve the problem by checking the device's network connection and try using the **ipconfig/release** and **ipconfig/renew** commands at the command prompt. This causes the computer to obtain a new IP address from the DHCP server. If these actions don't solve the problem, the DHCP server (often located in the router on a SOHO network) should be checked and restarted, if necessary.

APIPA was originally developed by Microsoft, but it is now a standard (RFC 3927) that is also supported by macOS and Linux.

IPv4

An IP version 4 (IPv4) address consists of a group of four numbers that each range from 0 to 255 (for example, 192.168.5.1). An IP address is divided into two sections: the network portion, which is the number of the network the computer is on, and the host portion, which is the individual number of the computer. Using the IP address just mentioned as an example, the 192.168.5 portion would typically be the network number, and .1 would be the host number. A *subnet mask* is used to distinguish between the network portion of the IP address and the host portion. For example, a typical subnet mask for the IP address just used would be 255.255.255.0. The 255s correspond to the network portion of the IP address. The 0s correspond to the host portion, as shown in Table 2-9.

Table 2-9   An IPv4 Address and Corresponding Subnet Mask

IP Address/Subnet Mask	Network Portion	Host Portion
192.168.5.1	192.168.5	1
255.255.255.0	255.255.255	0

The subnet mask is also used to define subnetworks, if subnets are being implemented. (Subnetting is beyond the scope of the CompTIA A+ exam.)

Both computers and other networked devices, such as routers and network printers, can have IP addresses, and in some cases a device can have more than one IP address. For example, a router typically has two IP addresses: one to connect the router to a LAN and the other that connects it to the Internet, enabling it to route traffic from the LAN to the Internet and back.

Each number in an IP address is called an *octet*. An octet is an 8-bit byte. This means that in the binary numbering system, the number can range from 00000000 to 11111111. For example, 255 is actually 11111111 when converted to the binary numbering system. As another example, 192 decimal equals 11000000 binary. Because there are four octets in an IPv4 address, it is a 32-bit address. IPv4 supports up to 4.3 billion addresses (that is, $4.3×10^9$).

> **NOTE**   To convert numbers from decimal to binary and vice versa, use the Windows calculator. Press **Windows+R** to bring up the Run prompt and then type **calc** to open the Windows Calculator application. There are several types of calculators available from the Calculator menu in the upper left. Select the Programmer calculator. (7/8/8.1/10). Now you will see a list on the left that allows you to change between numbering systems. Simply type any number and then select the numbering system you want to convert it to.

IPv6

IP version 6 (IPv6) greatly increases the number of available IP addresses for computers, smartphones, and other mobile devices. IPv6 uses 128-bit source and destination IP addresses (compared to 32-bit for IPv4), theoretically enabling up to 340 undecillion addresses ($3.4×10^{38}$). (This number is largely unimaginable to humans; 340 undecillion is said to exceed the number of grains of sand on Earth.) IPv6 also features built-in security and provides better support for quality of service (QoS) routing, which is important to achieve high-quality streaming audio and video traffic. Windows, macOS, and Linux all support IPv6.

IPv6 Addressing

IPv6 addresses start out as 128-bit addresses that are each then divided into eight 16-bit blocks. The blocks are converted into hexadecimal, and each block is separated from the following block by a colon. Leading zeros are typically suppressed, but each block must contain at least one digit.

Here is a typical IPv6 address:

   21DA:D3:0:2F3B:2AA:FF:FE28:9C5A

A contiguous sequence of 16-bit blocks set to zero can be represented by :: (double colon). This technique is also known as *zero compression*. To determine the number of zero bits represented by the double colon, count the number of blocks in the compressed address, subtract the result from 8, and multiply the result by 16. An address can include only one zero-compressed block.

Here is an IPv6 address that uses the double colon:

FF02::2.

There are two blocks here: FF02 and 2. So, how many zero bits are represented by the double colon? Subtract 2 from 8 (8 – 2 = 6 and then multiply 6 by 16 (6 × 16 = 96). This address includes a block of 96 zero bits.

The loopback address on an IPv6 system is 0:0:0:0:0:0:0:1, which is abbreviated as ::1. Thus, if you want to test your network interface in Windows where IPv6 is enabled by default, you can type **ping ::1** at a command prompt.

IPv6 Address Types

IPv6 supports three types of addresses: unicast, multicast, and anycast. There are five types of unicast addresses:

- **Global unicast addresses:** Global unicast addresses are used in the same way as IPv4 public addresses. The first 3 bits are set to 001, and the following 45 bits are used for the global routing prefix; these 48 bits are collectively known as the public topology. The subnet ID uses the next 16 bits, and the interface ID uses the remaining 64 bits.

- **Link local addresses:** Link local addresses correspond to the Automatic Private IP Addressing (APIPA) address scheme used by IPv4 (addresses that start with 169.254). The first 10 bits are set to FE80 hex, followed by 54 zero bits, and 64 bits for the interface ID. Using zero compression, the prefix would thus be FE80::/64. As with APIPA, link local addresses are not forwarded beyond the link.

- **Site local addresses:** Site local addresses correspond to IPv4 private address spaces (10.0.0.0/8, 172.16.0.0/12, and 192.168.0.0/16).

- **Special addresses:** Special addresses include unspecified addresses (0:0:0:0:0:0:0:0 or ::), which are equivalent to IPv4's 0.0.0.0 and indicate the absence of an IP address; a loopback address (0:0:0:0:0:0:0:1 or ::1) is equivalent to the IPv4 loopback address 127.0.0.1.

- **Compatibility addresses:** Compatibility addresses are used in situations in which IPv4 and IPv6 are both in use. In the following examples, *w.x.y.z* are replaced by the actual IPv4 address. An IPv4-compatible address

(0:0:0:0:0:0:*w.x.y.z* or ::*w.x.y.z*) is used by nodes that support IPv4 and IPv6 communicating over IPv6. An IPv4-mapped address (0:0:0:0:0:FFFF:*w.x.y.z* or ::FFFF:*w.x.y.z*) represents an IPv4-only node to an IPv6 node. A 6to4 address is used when two nodes running both IPv4 and IPv6 connect over an IPv4 link. The address combines the prefix 2002::/16 with the IPv4 public address of the node. ISATAP can also be used for the connection; it uses the locally administered ID::0:5EFE:*w.x.y.z* (where *w.x.y.z* could be any unicast IPv4 address, either public or private); Teredo addresses are used for tunneling IPv6 over UDP through network address translation (NAT); they use the prefix 3FFE:831F::/32.

Both IPv4 and IPv6 support multicasting, which enables one-to-many distribution of content such as Internet TV or other types of streaming media. IPv6 multicast addresses begin with FF.

Anycast addressing sends information to a group of potential receivers that are identified by the same destination address. This is also known as *one-to-one-to-many association*. Anycast addressing can be used for distributed services, such as DNS or other situations in which automatic failover is desirable. IPv6 uses anycast addresses as destination addresses that are assigned only to routers. Anycast addresses are assigned from the unicast address space.

Viewing IP Address Information

To see the IPv4 and IPv6 addresses assigned to a Windows device using both IPv4 and IPv6, use the command-line **ipconfig** utility at the command prompt. Here's an example of the output from a system using a wireless Ethernet adapter:

```
Wireless LAN adapter Wireless Network Connection:
Connection-specific DNS Suffix . :
Link-local IPv6 Address . . . . . : fe80::5cf1:2f98:7351:b3a3%12
IPv4 Address. . . . . . . . . . . : 192.168.1.155
Subnet Mask . . . . . . . . . . . : 255.255.255.0
Default Gateway . . . . . . . . . : 192.168.1.1
```

For more information, see http://technet.microsoft.com/en-us/library/dd392266(WS.10).aspx.

macOS provides IPv4 and IPv6 address information through the TCP/IP tab of the Network utility (see Figure 2-13).

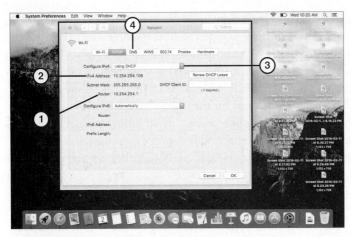

1. IPv4 address
2. Router (gateway) address
3. Open this menu to configure IP address manually
4. Click DNS tab to view or edit DNS addresses

FIGURE 2-13   macOS's TCP/IP Tab

Many Linux distros include a GUI-based network utility similar to the one used in macOS, but with any Linux distro (as well as with macOS), you can open Terminal and use the command **ifconfig -a** to view this information. Figure 2-14 shows a portion of the output for a wireless connection.

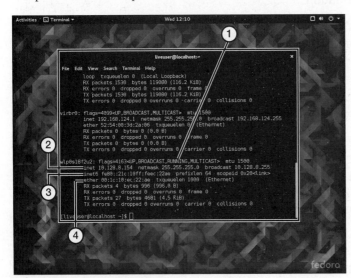

1. RUNNING = active connection
2. inet = IPv4 address information
3. inet6 = IPv6 address information
4. ether = MAC (physical) address

FIGURE 2-14   Linux **ifconfig** Output for a Wireless Connection

With macOS, use the TCP/IP tab (refer to Figure 2-13) to configure IPv4 or IPv6 address information. macOS uses the term *router* to refer to the default gateway. Use the DNS tab to configure DNS server information.

With Linux, you can use the network configuration tool provided in the GUI, or you can edit the network configuration scripts from Terminal, using the distro's text editor, if no GUI-based network configuration program is available. Two scripts need to be edited:

- **ifcfg-*connection name*** is used to identify IP addresses for IPv4 and IPv6 and the default gateway as well as other IP settings. It is located in the /etc/sysconfig/network-scripts/ folder. The loopback script is called **ifcfg-lo**. There is a separate **ifcfg** file for each connection (wired, wireless, and so on).

- The file resolv.conf is used to identify DNS servers. It is located in the /etc/ folder.

For syntax, see the documentation for the distribution in use.

TIP   For the 220-1001 exam, be sure you understand the difference between static and dynamic IP addressing and where to go within a given operating system to set or change client-side DHCP, DNS, subnet mask, and default gateway settings.

VPN

A virtual private network (*VPN*) is a private (secure) network connection that is carried by an insecure public network, such as the Internet. A VPN connection requires a VPN server at the remote site and a VPN client at the client site. VPN traffic between client and server is encrypted and encapsulated into packets suitable for transmission over the network. VPNs can be used in place of leased lines for connections between locations and for telecommuting workers.

The most common types of VPNs are PPTP and L2TP/IPsec VPNs. PPTP uses 128-bit encryption, while L2TP combined with IPsec (L2TP/IPsec) uses 256-bit encryption.

VLAN

A virtual local area network (*VLAN*) is a grouping of some computers on a local area network (LAN) that are configured to behave as if they have their own separate LAN. Usually LANs are separated by a router, but a switch may have the capability of grouping ports together to behave like a LAN inside the switch. Because the LAN exists in software configuration rather than in hardware, it is considered a VLAN. For example, if a LAN of 10 computers is divided evenly into VLAN 1 and VLAN 2, the computers in VLAN 2 will be able to communicate among themselves but not with any hosts on VLAN 1. The hosts in each VLAN will even have IP addresses on different networks, and communicating between VLANs will require the services of a router.

NAT

The details of network address translation (NAT) is covered earlier in this chapter under Access Point Settings.

Internet Connection Types, Network Types, and Their Features

220-1001: Objective 2.7: Compare and contrast Internet connection types, network types, and their features.

Different methods of accessing the Internet have come and gone over the decades since it was developed. This section describes the most common methods an A+ technician will likely encounter.

Internet Connection Types

One of the best reasons to create a network of any size is to provide access to the Internet. The many types of connectivity technologies that can be used for Internet access are discussed in the following sections.

> **NOTE**   As you review the following sections, try to determine which type of Internet connections you use at home and at the workplace. When you are shopping for Internet service, the BroadbandNow website (www.broadbandnow.com) is a useful source for finding the types of broadband Internet access available in a specified zip code.

For the 220-1001 exam, it is important to know the different network connection types and their speeds. Table 2-10 compares the network types from fastest to slowest.

Table 2-10 Comparison of Network Connection Speeds

Wired	Fiber	Cable	DSL	ISDN	Dial-up
← Fastest ----------------------------------- Slowest →					
Wireless	Cellular	Fixed line-of-sight			Satellite

Cable

Cable is broadband Internet service that is provided by a cable TV company. Broadband can deliver voice, data, and video at one time. Virtually all cable Internet service today is built on the fiber-optic and coaxial network used for digital cable and music services provided by most cable TV vendors. In most cases today, separate coaxial cables are used for TV and for Internet service into a home or an office. A cable modem is required in the home or office to receive the service.

Cable Internet can reach download speeds anywhere from 3Mbps up to 300Mbps or faster. Upload speeds are typically about 10%–20% of download speeds but vary by vendor. Speed can be impacted by longer distances between the modem and the provider's termination point in the neighborhood. Cable is faster and has more range than DSL.

> **NOTE** You can have cable Internet service without having cable TV.

Most cable modems connect to a computer or a router via an RJ-45 cable, but some use USB. When a cable provider also provides telephone service, a special modem is used that also includes a backup battery.

A cable Internet connection can be configured through the standard Network properties sheet in the operating system.

DSL

DSL (Digital Subscriber Line) was originally designed to work on the same telephone line used by a telephone and fax machine if the telephone line can carry a digital signal. For home use, DSL is designed strictly for Internet access. But for business use, DSL can be used for additional services and can be used in site-to-site scenarios between organizations.

While telephone line–based DSL is still available, it is much slower than cable Internet. Newer types of DSL use the same signaling methods but use fiber to provide speed comparable to that of high-performance cable.

Two major types of DSL use telephone lines: *ADSL* (Asynchronous DSL) and *SDSL* (Synchronous DSL). Two newer types of DSL—VDSL (Very High Bit-Rate Digital Subscriber Line) and VDSL2—use fiber for at least part of the signal path. These features are compared in Table 2-11.

Table 2-11   Common DSL Services Compared

Service Type	Line Type	User Installation Option	Typical Downstream Speeds	Typical Upstream Speeds	Supports HDTV Service
ADSL	Existing telephone line	Yes	384Kbps to 24Mbps	128Kbps to 3.3Mbps	No
SDSL	New telephone line	No	384Kbps to 2.0Mbps	384Kbps to 2.0Mbps	No
VDSL	Fiber + telephone line	No	Up to 55Mbps	15Mbps	Yes
VDLS2	Fiber + telephone line	No	Up to 200Mbps	Up to 100Mbps	Yes

NOTE   *Downstream* refers to download speed; *upstream* refers to upload speed. SDSL gets its name from providing the same speed in both directions; ADSL is always faster downstream than upstream.

Both VDSL and VDSL2 use fiber for most of the distance from the telephone company's central office (where all DSL services connect to the Internet).

A device known as a *DSL modem* is used to connect a computer to DSL service. A DSL modem connects to a PC through the RJ-45 (Ethernet) port or the USB port.

Many companies offering ADSL, VDSL, and VDSL2 services now provide a wireless router with DSL support and an integrated Gigabit Ethernet switch. Some of these devices also support HPNA, which was developed by the Home Phone Networking Alliance and uses coaxial wiring in the home as a network, or connections to a cable modem.

As Figure 2-15 indicates, DSL uses the same telephone lines as ordinary telephone equipment. However, a telephone on the same wire can interfere with the DSL connection. To prevent this, in some cases a separate DSL line is run from the outside service box to the computer with the DSL modem. However, if the DSL provider supports the self-installation option, small devices called *microfilters* are installed between telephones, answering machines, fax machines, and other devices on the same circuit with the DSL modem. Microfilters can be built into special wall plates but are more often external devices that plug into existing phone jacks, as shown in Figure 2-15.

A DSL connection may be configured as an always-on connection similar to a network connection to the Internet. However, many vendors now configure DSL connections as PPPoE (Point-to-Point Protocol over Ethernet) connections instead. A PPPoE connection requires the user to make a connection with a username and password. PPPoE connections are supported in Windows, macOS, and Linux.

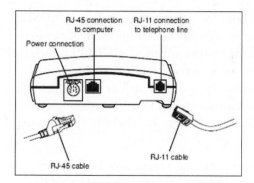

FIGURE 2-15 A Typical Self-Installed DSL Setup

Dial-up

Until the late 1990s, ***dial-up networking*** (DUN) was the most common way for home and small businesses to connect to the Internet. Today, dial-up connections are used when no other Internet connection is available. Dial-up connections are often referred to as *analog* connections because the device used to make the connection is an analog modem, which connects to the Internet through an ordinary telephone line. Dial-up is sometimes referred to as public switched telephone network (PSTN) or plain old telephone service (POTS).

Dial-up is relatively slow, with rates ranging from 28.8Kbps to 56Kbps, but it is available anyplace that has a landline telephone system. A modem is used to send data by modulating digital computer data into analog data suitable for transmission over telephone lines to a receiving modem, which demodulates the analog data back into computer form.

A disadvantage of telephone dial-up is that voice and data cannot share the wire simultaneously.

NOTE   Technically, the term *modem* (modulator/demodulator) refers only to a device that connects to the telephone line and performs digital-to-analog or analog-to-digital conversions. However, other types of Internet connections such as satellite, wireless, DSL, fiber, and cable Internet also use the term modem, even though they work with purely digital data. When used by itself in this book, however, *modem* refers only to dial-up (telephone) modems.

Fiber

Instead of using a copper connection to a home or business the way dial-up, ADSL/SDSL, or cable Internet do, many companies offer *fiber* (fiber-optic cable) connections to the home (FTTH, also known as fiber to the premises, or FTTP) at their highest service levels. Fiber network download speeds can reach up to 2Gbps, and some vendors provide the same upload speed. DSL vendors such as Verizon, AT&T, and CenturyLink offer fiber connections in some service areas, as does Google Fiber. Contact your ISP to determine if fiber connections are available in or coming to your area.

The conversion between the fiber connection entering a home and the Ethernet or coaxial WAN connection used to connect a router or gateway is performed by an optical network terminal (ONT), which is supplied by the fiber provider and installed in the home.

Fiber users rent the router or gateway, which resembles the router or gateway included with cable or DSL Internet service, from the fiber provider. The fiber router or gateway connects to the ONT. Some vendors offer a network box that incorporates a wireless router as an alternative to a separate ONT and router or gateway.

Fiber has the highest speeds and the longest distances of any network connection type. It is more expensive to install than other types of cable and wire, and it is more fragile as well. A key advantage of fiber is that because data is carried in light, it is not subject to data interruptions from electrical interference, as the other media can be. Fiber is discussed further in Chapter 3.

Satellite

Satellite Internet providers, such as HughesNet, StarBand, and WildBlue, use dish antennas similar to satellite TV antennas to receive and transmit signals between geosynchronous satellites and computers. Separate antennas are needed for satellite

Internet and TV services. Satellite is ideal for areas where cable infrastructure is unavailable and for ships at sea. Weather such as rain, snow, and fog can impact satellite speeds.

NOTE   Geosynchronous satellites orbit Earth's equator at a distance of more than 22,000 miles (approximately 35,000km). Because of their orbits and altitudes, they remain in the same location in the sky at all times. In the Northern Hemisphere, you need an unobstructed view of the southern sky to make a connection. In the Southern Hemisphere, you need an unobstructed view of the northern sky to make a connection.

Satellite Internet services use external devices often called *satellite modems* to connect computers to satellite dishes. A satellite modem connects to the USB or Ethernet (RJ-45) port in a fashion similar to that used by DSL or cable modems.

The FCC requires professional installation for satellite Internet service because an incorrectly aligned satellite dish with uplink capabilities could cause a service outage on the satellite it's aimed at. Setup software supplied by the satellite vendor is used to complete the process.

NOTE   Satellite connections can also be made between buildings to allow for high-speed exchange of data. In this scenario, a satellite dish would need to be installed on each building, and the dishes would need to be in direct line of sight of each other. Internet access can also be offered in this manner.

ISDN

ISDN (Integrated Services Digital Network) was originally developed to provide an all-digital method for connecting multiple telephone and telephony-type devices, such as fax machines, to a single telephone line and to provide a faster connection for teleconferencing for remote computer users. ISDN is used on PSTN lines with a terminal adapter (TA) on multiple channels of 64Kbps each.

NOTE   The telephone network was originally designed to support analog signaling only, which is why an analog (dial-up) modem that sends data to other computers converts digital signals to analog for transmission through the telephone network. The receiving analog modem converts analog data back to digital data.

To make an ISDN connection, a PC (and any other devices that share the ISDN connection) needs a device called an ISDN terminal adapter (TA). A TA resembles a conventional analog modem. Internal models plug into the same PCIe or PCI slot used by analog modems, and external models use USB or serial ports.

ISDN connections (where available) are provided through the local telephone company. There are two types of ISDN connections:

- **Primary Rate Interface (PRI):** A PRI connection provides 1.536Mbps of bandwidth, whereas a BRI interface provides 64Kbps (single-channel) or 128Kbps (dual-channel) of bandwidth. PRI is sold to large organizations.

- **Basic Rate Interface (BRI):** BRI was sold to small businesses and home offices before DSL and cable became widely available. BRI offers up to 128Kpbs of bandwidth.

Both types of connections enable you to use the Internet and talk or fax data through the phone line at the same time.

A direct individual ISDN connection is configured through the network features of the operating system with the same types of settings that are used for analog modem connections. You configure a network-based ISDN connection through the network adapter's TCP/IP properties window.

NOTE   Most telephone companies have largely phased out ISDN in favor of DSL, which is much faster and less expensive for Internet connections.

Cellular

Mobile devices offer many ways to connect to other devices, including sharing their WiFi or cellular connections with one or more computers. The following sections discuss these and other topics.

> **NOTE**   For the 220-1001 exam, you should know the following:
>
> - Wireless/cellular data network configuration, including enabling/disabling hotspot, tethering, and Airplane mode
> - Bluetooth configuration, including enabling Bluetooth, enabling pairing, finding a device for pairing, entering the appropriate PIN code, and testing connectivity
> - Corporate and ISP email configuration, including POP3, IMAP, port and SSL settings, Exchange, and S/MIME
> - Awareness of PRI updates, PRL updates, and baseband updates
> - Radio firmware settings
> - IMEI vs. IMSI definitions
> - VPN configuration

Wireless/Cellular Data Network

WiFi connectivity is enabled the same way on a smartphone or tablet as with laptops or other types of computers. In addition, smartphones or tablets with cellular radios can also be used to share their connections with others.

To enable mobile device use on airplanes, where electronic communications are usually not permitted, Airplane mode is used to turn off WiFi, cellular, and Bluetooth signals.

Learn more in the following sections.

Tethering

To use USB tethering, follow these steps (which are based on a Samsung phone running Android 5.x):

Step 1.   Connect a USB cable from your computer to the data port on your device.

Step 2.   Select the USB tethering option on your device.

Step 3.   If you are connecting a Windows computer, select the network type (Home) on the computer when prompted.

Step 4.   Use your computer's web browser and other network features as usual.

Step 5.   When you're finished, disable USB tethering.

NOTE   In Windows Device Manager, the tethered USB connection is listed as Remote NDIS-based Internet Sharing Device in the Network Adapters category.

Hotspots

To use the mobile hotspot feature, follow these steps (which are based on a Samsung phone running Android 5.x):

Step 1.   Enable the mobile hotspot feature in the device's setup.

Step 2.   Select how you want to share the connection wirelessly. Provide the SSID and password listed to any devices that will share the connection.

Step 3.   If you decide to permit only allowed devices to connect, you must provide a name for each device and its MAC address. The MAC address is listed on a label attached to an external adapter. To find the MAC (physical) address for an internal network adapter, see the sidebar "Finding the Network Adapter's MAC (Physical) Address" in Chapter 1, "Mobile Devices."

Step 4.   Open the Allowed Devices menu (see Figure 2-16), click **Add**, enter the device name and address, and click **OK**.

Step 5.   Make the connection from your device just as you would with any other wireless Internet router or hotspot. Enter the password when prompted.

Step 6.   When your devices are finished using the Internet, disable the hotspot setting in your smartphone or tablet.

CAUTION   Some cellular providers charge an additional fee if you turn your cellular device into a hotspot or if you use tethering. Check with your mobile service provider for details. And keep in mind that the data usage of every device connected to a mobile hotspot is counted toward your total data allocation. If you're not careful, using a mobile hotspot could cost you extra money in overages.

If you prefer to use a standalone mobile hotspot for your home, business, or vehicle, check with your wireless provider.

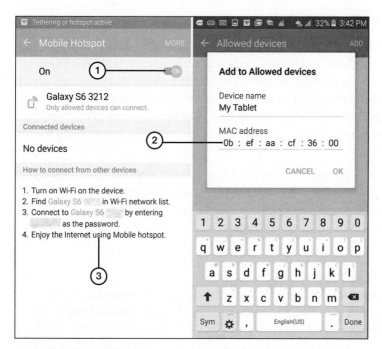

1. Enabling mobile hotspot
2. Entering MAC address of device that will connect to mobile hotspot
3. Instructions for devices that will connect to mobile hotspot

FIGURE 2-16   Entering the MAC Address of the Device Sharing a Hotspot's Internet Connection

Line-of-Sight Wireless

Line-of-sight wireless, sometimes referred to as *terrestrial wireless*, involves using small antennas to connect users to Internet service transmitted from microwave towers. As the name indicates, a clear line of sight must be available from the transmission tower to the customer site. In some cases, this means that the customer antenna must be placed on the roof or on its own stand, and trees may need to be trimmed to provide adequate signal quality.

To bring the network signal into the premises, coaxial cable connects from the antenna to a line-of-sight wireless modem, which is similar to a cable modem. Connect the modem to a router to provide Internet access to multiple devices. Typical download speeds range from 256Kbps up to 10Mbps.

Network Types

A *network* is a group of computers, peripherals, and software that are connected to each other and can be used together. Special software and hardware are required to make networks work.

LAN

A *LAN* (local area network) is a group of computers and other devices usually located in a small area, such as a house, a small office, or a single building. The computers all connect to one or more switches, and a router allows the computers access to the Internet. A LAN is defined as a group of connected computers under one administrative organization. LANs can contain a wide variety of connected devices, such as computers, servers, routers, switches, printers, intrusion detection appliances, and firewalls.

LANs can be wired or wireless LANS (WLANs). Wired LANs can have high-speed connections with Ethernet unshielded twisted pair cable (UTP), shielded twisted pair cable (STP), or fiber. Legacy LANs were often connected by coax cables. Cables are discussed in more detail in Chapter 3.

WAN

A *WAN* (wide area network) is a group of one or more LANs over a large geographic area. Let's say a company has two LANs, one in New York and one in Los Angeles. Connecting the two would result in a WAN. However, to do this would require the help of a telecommunications company. This company would create the high-speed connection required for the two LANs to communicate with each other quickly. Each LAN would require a router to connect to the other.

WANs are administered by several different Internet service providers (ISPs), and the links are usually slower than LAN connections.

PAN

A *PAN* (personal area network) is larger than a LAN and smaller than a WAN. This type of computer network is used for communication by smartphones, tablets, and other small personal computing devices, typically using Bluetooth, IrDA (an infrared technology), wireless USB, Zigbee, or Z-Wave protocols. A PAN can be wired or wireless. Additional examples of devices in a PAN are wireless headsets, keyboards, mice, printers, and bar code readers.

MAN

A smaller version of a WAN is known as a *MAN* (metropolitan area network). This type of network results when a company has two offices in the same city and makes a high-speed connection between them. A telecommunications company or ISP is needed for the high-speed links. MANs often consist of fiber networks around a city, and each one is administered by a single organization.

WMN

A wireless mesh network (*WMN*) is a communications network made up of a cloud of radio nodes organized in a mesh topology—that is, with many interconnections among devices or nodes. Wireless mesh networks often consist of mesh clients, mesh routers, and gateways. WMNs can range from very small home networks to large city-wide networks. Management of a WMN is decentralized. Without a central connection device, it can take time for all the wireless devices to find each other if they are moving around.

Using Networking Tools

220-1001: Objective 2.8: Given a scenario, use appropriate networking tools.

220-1001
Exam

If you plan on building a physical network, you need to stock up on some key networking tools that can help you in running, terminating, and testing cable. For this short section, imagine a scenario where you are the network installer and are required to install a wired network for 12 computers.

To start, you should check with your local municipality to see if any rules and regulations govern running networking cable. Some municipalities require a person to have an electrician's license to run networking cable, but most only require an exemption of some sort that anyone can apply for at the town or county seat. Due to the low-voltage nature of network wiring (for most applications), some municipalities have no rules regarding running it. But in urban areas, you need to apply for a permit and have at least one inspection done when you are finished with the installation.

Permits and regulations aside, let's say that in this scenario, you have been cleared to install 12 wired connections to computers (known as *drops*) and have diagrammed where the cables will be run and where they will terminate. All cables will come out of a wiring closet, where you will terminate them to a small patch panel. On the other end, they will terminate at in-wall RJ-45 jacks near each of the computers. Let's discuss each of the tools that you will use to complete this job.

NOTE When working with computers and computer network equipment, standard household tools are not adequate for the job. A specialized network technician's toolkit is necessary for quality work. A quick Internet search for "networking toolkit" will return a full range of options in many price ranges. Networking toolkits are also available from nearly every place that sells computers and accessories.

Cutting Tool

One tool you should have is a good, sharp cutting tool. You need to make a clean cut on the end of the network cable; scissors will not do. Either cut pliers or other cable cutting tools are necessary. Klein Tools (www.kleintools.com) is an excellent manufacturer of these types of tools.

Cable Stripper

A *cable stripper* is used to strip a portion of the plastic jacket off the cable to expose the individual wires. Once the wires are exposed, you can separate them and get ready to terminate them. Figure 2-17 illustrates a typical cable stripper.

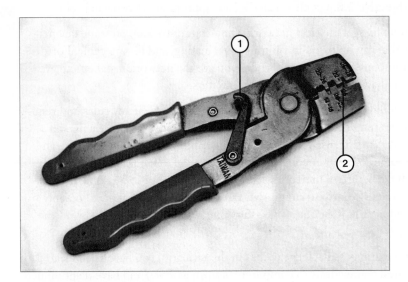

1. Release this clip to use the tool
2. Select the appropriate wire thickness based on the cable type

FIGURE 2-17   A Cable (Wire) Stripper

Crimper

A *crimper* attaches a connector to the end of raw twisted pair (TP) or coaxial cable. There are two types of crimpers you might need. If you are working with TP, you need an RJ-45 crimping tool (which often also work with RJ-11 telephone cable). After untwisting the wire pairs and aligning them according to the appropriate standard (typically T568B), insert them into an RJ-45 connector and push the cable and connector assembly into the crimper. Line up the crimper jaw with the recessed area of the connector and squeeze (see Figure 2-18).

If you are working with coaxial using F connectors, a compression-crimping tool is recommended. It produces a better, more water-resistant connection than a hex-type crimper. F connectors are discussed in Chapter 3.

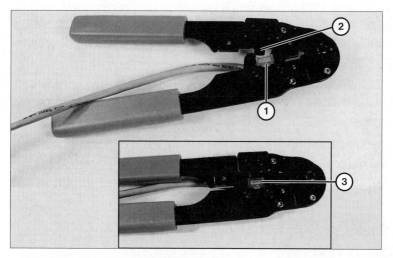

1. Connector and cable assembly inserted into crimper
2. Crimping jaw lined up and ready to crimp
3. Squeeze handles to complete crimp

FIGURE 2-18 Crimping an Ethernet Cable

Punchdown Tool

A *punchdown tool* (see Figure 2-19) punches the individual wires down into the 110 IDC clips of an RJ-45 jack and the patch panel. This "punching down" of the wires is the actual termination. The patch cables connect the various ports of the patch panel to a switch and the RJ-45 jacks to the computers.

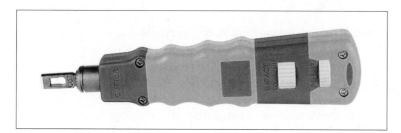

FIGURE 2-19 A Typical Punchdown Tool

Multimeter

A *multimeter* is a very flexible tool that can be used for testing both coaxial and TP cabling as well as AC and DC voltage. (However, it is easier to test cables with specially made cable testers.) When set for DC voltage, a multimeter can be used to test computer power supplies and AC adapters. When set for continuity (CONT), it can be used as a cable tester. It can also be used to test ohm (resistance) and ampere (amp, or current) levels.

All multimeters are equipped with red and black test leads. When used for voltage tests, the red lead is attached to the power source to be measured, and the black lead is attached to ground.

Multimeters use two different readout styles: digital and analog. Digital multimeters are more common today as their costs have dropped. Figure 2-20 shows a typical digital multimeter. For more on multimeters, see Chapter 3.

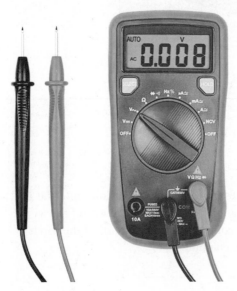

FIGURE 2-20   Typical Digital Multimeter (Image ©fotosv. Shutterstock)

Tone Generator and Probe

A *tone generator and probe* kit consists of two parts:

- **Tone device:** This device connects to one end of the network cable and, when turned on, sends a tone along the length of the cable.

- **Probing device:** This device, also known as an inductive amplifier, can pick up the tone anywhere along the cable length and at the termination point.

A tone generator and probe is not as handy as a proper network cable tester because it only tests one of the pairs of the wires. However, it is an excellent tool for finding individual phone lines and is commonly used for that.

Cable Tester

A necessary item for a PC technician's toolkit is a proper network *cable tester*. This device includes a LAN testing unit that you plug into a port on the patch panel and a terminator that you use to plug the other end of the cable into the corresponding RJ-45 jack. This tool tests each wire in the cable and makes sure everything is wired properly.

Some cable testers, such as the one shown in Figure 2-21, can also be used to test coaxial cable using F connectors, BNC connectors, or RCA connectors.

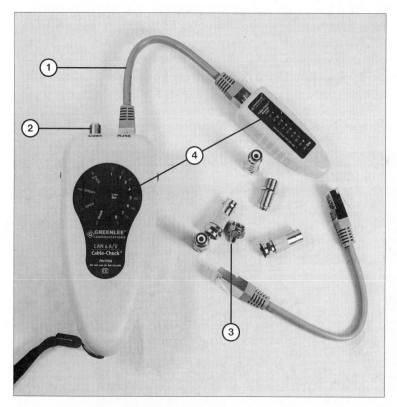

1. STP cable for testing patch panels
2. Threaded connector for testing coaxial cable
3. Adapters for various types of coaxial cable
4. Lights on remote and main unit light up as each line is tested

FIGURE 2-21   A Typical Cable Tester Equipped for Testing RJ-45 and Coaxial Cable

Loopback Plug

A *loopback plug* connects directly to the RJ-45 port of a PC's network adapter. When you use a loopback plug with a network diagnostic program, it simulates a network and tests whether the network adapter and TCP/IP are functioning properly.

WiFi Analyzer

A *WiFi analyzer* provides an easy-to-use view of both 2.4GHz and 5.0GHz wireless networks in the area. A WiFi analyzer can be a standalone device, a program for a desktop computer, or an app on a smartphone.

The InSSIDer WiFi analyzer program for Windows and Mac (www.metageek.com) is a commercial product as of version 4 ($19.95), but free downloads of the previous 3.x version are still available from some download sites, such as MajorGeeks (www.majorgeeks.com) and Softpedia (www.softpedia.com). Figure 2-22 shows InSSIDer v3 is displaying both 2.4GHz and 5GHz wireless networks in an office building. Most 2.4GHz networks in this example are using channels 1 or 11, making channel 6 (the only other non-overlapping channel) the best one to use for the selected network. InSSIDer also lists which networks are secure and the MAC address of each router.

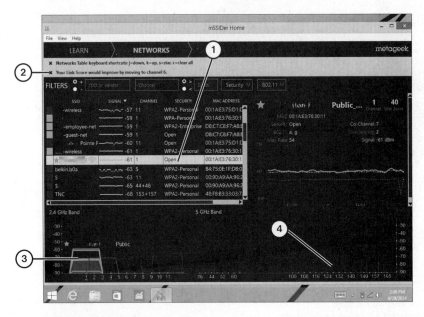

1. Selected network
2. Recommendation to use Channel 6
3. Lots of interference on Channel 1
4. Hardly any usage of 5GHz band with many more channels available

FIGURE 2-22   Using InSSIDer v3 to View Wireless Networks in an Office Building

You can also use smartphone apps such as WiFi Analyzer (from farproc, available on Google Play), the built-in Wireless Diagnostics feature in macOS, and the **iwlist** command in Linux to learn about the channels used by wireless networks in the vicinity.

Exam Preparation Tasks

Review All the Key Topics

Review the most important topics in the chapter, noted with the Key Topic icon in the outer margin of the page. Table 2-12 lists these key topics and the page number on which each is found.

Table 2-12   Key Topics for Chapter 2

Key Topic Element	Description	Page Number
Table 2-2	Common Protocols and Their Ports	85
Section	Channels	99
Steps	NIC configuration steps	103
Table 2-3	Wireless Encryption Types	109
Table 2-4	Wireless Ethernet Standards	110
Table 2-7	3G, 4G, 5G, and LTE Comparison	118
Table 2-8	Static vs. Dynamic IP Addressing	124
Table 2-9	An IPv4 Address and Corresponding Subnet Mask	126
Section	IPv6 Address Types	128
Table 2-10	Comparison of Network Connection Speeds	133
Table 2-11	Common DSL Services Compared	134
Steps	Steps to set up tethering	139
Steps	Steps to set up hotspots	140

Complete the Tables and Lists from Memory

Print a copy of Appendix C, "Memory Tables" (found online), or at least the section for this chapter, and complete the tables and lists from memory. Appendix D, "Answers to Memory Tables," also online, includes completed tables and lists to check your work.

Define Key Terms

Define the following key terms from this chapter, and check your answers in the glossary:

> protocol, port, Transmission Control Protocol (TCP), UDP, FTP, SSH, Telnet, SMTP, DNS, domain name, HTTP, HTTPS, POP3, IMAP, NetBIOS, SMB, CIFS, SLP, AFP, RDP, DHCP, SNMP, LDAP, router, firmware, switch, SOHO, wireless access point (WAP), cloud-based controller, firewall, NIC, repeater, hub, modem, cable modem, DSL modem, wireless bridge, patch panel, PoE, channel, NAT, port forwarding, port triggering, DNAT, DMZ, QoS, UPnP, WEP, WPA, TKIP, WPA2, AES, WPS, 802.11b, 802.11a, 802.11g, 802.11n, 802.11ac, Bluetooth, pairing, NFC, RFID, file server, NAS, print server, DHCP server, syslog server, UTM, IDS, IPS, end-point management server, legacy system, embedded system, subnet mask, VPN, VLAN, DSL, ADSL, SDSL, dial-up networking, fiber, satellite, ISDN, line-of-sight wireless, LAN, WAN, PAN, MAN, WMN, cable stripper, crimper, punchdown tool, multimeter, tone generator and probe, cable tester, loopback plug, WiFi analyzer

Answer Review Questions

1. Complete the following chart with the information provided below.

Wired					
← Fastest --------------------------------- Slowest →					
Wireless					

Answer options:

    a. ISDN

    b. Fixed line-of-sight

    c. Satellite

    d. Dial-up

    e. DSL

    f. Fiber

    g. Cable

    h. Cellular

2. Which of the following situations would require the use of UDP but not TCP? (Choose all that apply.)

  a. Video streaming

  b. Email

  c. Voice

  d. Online gaming

  e. SMS messaging

3. When you pay online through your browser for an item in a shopping cart, which port is your browser likely using to transport information?

  a. 68

  b. 80

  c. 443

  d. 53

4. Which device enables communication outside a LAN?

  a. Router

  b. Switch

  c. Wireless bridge

  d. Hub

5. You have been asked to create a VLAN inside the company LAN. Which device will you configure?

  a. A wireless bridge

  b. A managed switch

  c. The router sub-interface

  d. The central hub

6. Match the following devices with their definitions.

Device	Definition
Bridge	
Router	
Switch	
Modem	
Firewall	
Hub	
Patch panel	

   a. Converts digital signals to analog and analog signals to digital

   b. Uses a MAC address to direct data to a specific computer

   c. Acts as a junction point for network cabling

   d. Allows networks to communicate with each other

   e. Broadcasts data to all attached computers

   f. Extends wired LANs into wireless space

   g. Prevents unwanted intrusion from outside the network

7. Under what circumstances would you use a cloud-based network controller?

   a. To extend the LAN to work on adjacent wireless networks

   b. To improve Internet speeds to the LAN

   c. For remote management of wireless LANs

   d. To control costs of web connectivity at the network operations center

8. Which protocol that is used to access the Internet is used by all major operating systems, including Windows, macOS, Linux, Android, and iOS?

   a. APIPA

   b. DHCP

   c. Telnet

   d. TCP/IP

9. 192.168.28.10 is an example of which type of IP address?

   a. IPv6

   b. Link local

   c. IPv4

   d. APIPA

10. Given the IP address 192.168.28.10 and the subnet mask 255.255.0.0, which is the network portion of the address, and which is the host portion?

    a. 192. = host, 168.28.10 = network

    b. 192.168. = network, 28.10 = host

    c. 192.168.28. = network, 10 = host

    d. 192.168 = host, 28.10 = network

11. Which of the following is the subnet mask for a network with 255 hosts?

    a. 255.255.255.255

    b. 255.255.255.0

    c. 255.255.0.0

    d. 255.0.0.0

12. 127.0.0.1 and ::1 are both IP addresses. Which of the following statements are true? (Choose all that apply.)

    a. 127.0.0.1 is a useable address on a network.

    b. ::1 is an IPv6 address.

    c. 127.0.0.1 is an M.

    d. ::1 is a CIPS address.

    e. Both addresses are loopback addresses.

13. 10.0.0.1 is which type of IP address?

    a. Public

    b. Private

    c. APIPA

    d. Loopback

14. 169.254.0.1 is which type of IP address?

   a. Loopback

   b. Subnet mask

   c. DHCP

   d. APIPA

15. Which of the following statements best describes an advantage of IPv6 over IPv4?

   a. IPv6 is less complicated and easier to use.

   b. IPv6 automatically assigns IP addresses on a network.

   c. IPv6 translates domain names into IP addresses.

   d. IPv6 provides a dramatic increase in the number of available IP addresses.

16. Which of the following protocols is used to automatically assign IP addresses on a network?

   a. APIPA

   b. DHCP

   c. TCP/IP

   d. DNS

17. When you enter the Web address www.mycompany.com, the address is translated to a numeric IP address to establish a connection. Which of the following is the service that provides the translation?

   a. TCP

   b. UPnP

   c. DNS

   d. DHCP

18. As an IT technician, it is important for you to be familiar with the protocols and ports used by various applications to send and receive information across a network. Complete the following chart by adding the port numbers associated with each of the protocols listed.

   a. 443

   b. 80

   c. 22

    d. 21

    e. 110

    f. 143

    g. 53

    h. 25

Protocol	IMAP	FTP	HTTP	HTTPS	SMTP	DNS	SSH	POP3
Port								

19. Which of the following statements best describes SMTP?

    a. SMTP is a protocol for sending email from your computer to a server.

    b. SMTP is a naming system that links your computer's name with its IP address.

    c. SMTP is a method for automatically assigning IP addresses to computers on a network.

    d. SMTP is a protocol used to access the Internet.

20. Which of the following is the family of IEEE standards used by WiFi networks?

    a. 802.5

    b. 802.11

    c. 802.9

    d. 802.3

21. Which of the following WiFi encryption methods is the strongest?

    a. WPA

    b. WPA2

    c. WEP

    d. WAP3

22. Which of the following statements best describes the function of NAT?

   a. NAT changes a private IP address for use inside a LAN into a public IP address for use outside a LAN.

   b. NAT automatically assigns IP addresses to computers on a LAN.

   c. NAT automatically assigns a 169.254.x.x address to a computer on a LAN.

   d. NAT is a secure wireless encryption standard.

23. You have been asked to install a web-enabled soil monitor system for an agricultural company. What term is used to describe this kind of device?

   a. Remote sensing router

   b. Cloud-based network controller

   c. NAT device

   d. IoT device

24. Identify the tool in the following figure.

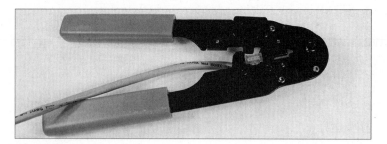

   a. Cable tester

   b. Crimper

   c. Punchdown tool

   d. Cable stripper

Understanding the physical aspects of computing is an essential requirement for a certified support technician. While most working technicians become specialized in a few areas of hardware support, it is important to demonstrate a broad knowledge of the different components of computing on the A+ exam. This chapter covers the 11 A+ 220-1001 exam objectives related to knowledge of hardware. These objectives may comprise 27% of the exam questions:

- **Core 1 (220-1001): Objective 3.1:** Explain basic cable types, features, and their purposes.

- **Core 1 (220-1001): Objective 3.2:** Identify common connector types.

- **Core 1 (220-1001): Objective 3.3:** Given a scenario, install RAM types.

- **Core 1 (220-1001): Objective 3.4:** Given a scenario, select, install, and configure storage devices.

- **Core 1 (220-1001): Objective 3.5:** Given a scenario, install and configure motherboards, CPUs, and add-on cards.

- **Core 1 (220-1001): Objective 3.6:** Explain the purpose and uses of various peripheral types.

- **Core 1 (220-1001): Objective 3.7:** Summarize power supply types and features.

- **Core 1 (220-1001): Objective 3.8:** Given a scenario, select and configure appropriate components for a custom PC configuration to meet customer specifications or needs.

- **Core 1 (220-1001): Objective 3.9:** Given a scenario, install and configure common devices.

- **Core 1 (220-1001): Objective 3.10:** Given a scenario, configure SOHO multifunction devices/printers and settings.

- **Core 1 (220-1001): Objective 3.11:** Given a scenario, install and maintain various print technologies.

## CHAPTER 3

Hardware

As a computer technician you will need knowledge of how the hardware components of a PC work together, and be able to make appropriate hardware choices that best suit client's needs. This chapter discusses fundamental hardware topics covered on the CompTIA A+ exam.

"Do I Know This Already?" Quiz

The "Do I Know This Already?" quiz allows you to assess whether you should read the entire chapter. Table 3-1 lists the major headings in this chapter and the "Do I Know This Already?" quiz questions covering the material in those headings so you can assess your knowledge of these specific areas. The answers to the "Do I Know This Already?" quiz appear in Appendix A, "Answers to the 'Do I Know This Already?' Quizzes and Review Question Sections."

Table 3-1 "Do I Know This Already?" Section-to-Question Mapping

Foundation Topics Section	Questions
Basic Cable Types	1–2
Common Connectors	3–4
Installing RAM Types	5–6
Installing Storage Devices	7–8
Installing Motherboards, CPUs, and Add-on Cards	9–10
Peripheral Types	11–12
Power Supplies	13–14
Custom Components	15–16
SOHO Multifunction Devices	17–18
Print Technologies	19–20

CAUTION The goal of self-assessment is to gauge your mastery of the topics in this chapter. If you do not know the answer to a question or are only partially sure of the answer, you should mark that question as wrong for purposes of the self-assessment. Giving yourself credit for an answer you correctly guess skews your self-assessment results and might provide you with a false sense of security.

1. What is the most commonly used cable in an Ethernet network?

    a. STP

    b. Coax

    c. UTP

    d. Plenum

2. What kind of cables are used in video cards for home theaters?

    a. DisplayPort

    b. HDMI

    c. Mini-USB3

    d. DVI

3. What is the latest version of USB?

    a. 3.1 Generation 2

    b. 3.2

    c. 3.0 Generation 3

    d. 3.5

4. Which of the following is not a video cable connector?

    a. S-Video

    b. VGA

    c. RJ-45

    d. HDMI

5. Which RAM type is a legacy type?

    a. SODIMM

    b. DDR2

    c. SDRAM

    d. DIMM

6. Which RAM type is designed for laptops?

   a. SODIMM

   b. DDR2

   c. SDRAM

   d. DIMM

7. Which one of the following is not used with an SSD?

   a. M.2

   b. PCIe

   c. mSATA

   d. HDD

8. What is the method for replicating a single drive from two or more physical drives?

   a. RAID

   b. Incremental backup

   c. Hot swappable

   d. Hard drive duplication (HDD)

9. You have been asked to overclock a gaming system. Which two places might you go to perform this task?

   a. System Settings

   b. BIOS

   c. Control Panel

   d. UEFI

10. While fixing a PC, you notice that its date and time are wrong. What are two possible problems you should check? (Choose two.)

    a. Date and Time settings

    b. System Updates log

    c. CMOS battery

    d. Internal power supply connection

11. Which of the following can be used to expand the number of PCI slots on a motherboard?

   a. Riser card

   b. Slot extension

   c. GPU controller

   d. Card extender

12. Which peripheral device uses NFC?

   a. Cameras

   b. Touchpads

   c. Tap/pay systems

   d. Wireless headsets with microphones

13. What function does a power supply perform?

   a. Reduces DC power to protect components

   b. Converts DC power to AC

   c. Converts AC power to DC

   d. Reduces AC power to safe levels for components

14. How are power supply capacities rated?

   a. Watts

   b. Amps

   c. Voltage

   d. Joules

15. Which of the following is most likely to host a RAID array?

   a. Thin client workstation

   b. NAS

   c. GPU controller

   d. Thick client desktop

16. Which type of PC configuration is likely to need high-end cooling systems due to overclocking?

    a. Thick client

    b. Audio/video workstation

    c. Network-attached storage

    d. Gaming PC

17. Which of the following is not a common print configuration option on a multifunction device?

    a. Orientation

    b. Collation

    c. Ink flow

    d. Duplex printing

18. Which Apple technology provides shared printing on both macOS and Windows 10 devices?

    a. LAN Printing

    b. AirPrint

    c. Cloud Print

    d. Apple Print

19. Which three of these are examples of virtual printing? (Choose three.)

    a. Print to 3D

    b. Print to PDF

    c. Print to file

    d. Print to XPS

20. Which of the following is not part of the laser imaging process?

    a. Exposing

    b. Developing

    c. Compacting

    d. Fusing

Foundation Topics

Basic Cable Types

220-1001: Objective 3.1: Explain basic cable types, features, and their purposes.

The array of cable types in computing can be overwhelming, especially since cable technology is in a constant state of evolution. You need to know not only the kinds of cable but also different versions of some types. This section organizes cables by their purpose, which should help you keep them straight. While some cables are uncommon and rarely encountered, you need to be familiar with all of the types in this section.

Network Cables

Networking cables covered here are different types of Ethernet cable. **Ethernet** is a term that is commonly used but not often completely understood. Briefly, Ethernet is a system of communication rules that allow computers to work together. Ethernet is considered a networking protocol (which is a bit different from an application protocol). It is concerned with physical cables and wireless standards as well as the computer's network interface card (NIC). Ethernet cables are designed to standards that allow the protocols to send and receive messages between devices. Ethernet is not the only communication protocol in use, but it is by far the most common.

Ethernet

Ethernet cable companies are always improving their product, and over time higher data speeds have been achieved through better engineering of both cables and interface cards. This has created a necessity for categories defining the equipment they can be used with. Between the categories are grades of enhancement that are noted with letters (for example, Category 5e, or CAT 5e).

Ethernet cables carry small voltage pulses (1 is voltage, 0 is no voltage) over a single frequency. This is known as *baseband transmission*. It is bidirectional, which means hosts can send and receive data on one cable. The various capabilities are indicated in cable categories. For example, 10BASE-T indicates the cable carries 10Mbps on a baseband signal over twisted pair (TP) cables. Cable categories and TP are explained below.

CAT5e, CAT6, and CAT6e

Category 5e (*CAT5e*), Category 6 (*CAT6*), and Category 6a (*CAT6a*) are the most common of the standard cabling grades. They are suitable for use with both standard 10BASE-T and Fast Ethernet networking and can also be used for Gigabit Ethernet networks if they pass compliance testing. CAT6, CAT6a, and Category 7 (*CAT7*) are capable of supporting 10GBASE-T (10GB) Ethernet networks. Table 3-2 provides the essential information about each of the TP cable types you need to know for the exam. Categories 5 through 6 are covered on the exam; Categories 3 through 7 are included in Table 3-2 to add perspective. You should know the table well and be able to identify the bandwidth of each category.

All of the copper Ethernet cable categories, no matter how fast, have a distance limitation of about 100m (about 300 ft.) before the data signal weakens and needs to be boosted by a switch, a hub, or a repeater.

Table 3-2   Categories and Uses for TP Cabling

Category	Network Type(s) Supported	Supported Speeds	Notes
CAT3	10BASE-T Ethernet	Up to 10Mbps	Legacy; also supported Token Ring networks at up to 16Mbps
CAT5	10BASE-T, 100BASE-T (Fast Ethernet)	Up to 100Mbps	Uses 24-gauge wires
CAT5e	10BASE-T, 100BASE-T, 1000BASE-T (Gigabit Ethernet)	Up to 1000Mbps	Enhanced version of CAT5
CAT6	10BASE-T, 100BASE-T, 1000BASE-T (Gigabit Ethernet)	Up to 1000Mbps (1Gbps)	Often uses 22-gauge or 20-gauge wire pairs (both of which are thicker than 24-gauge wire)
CAT6a*	10BASE-T, 100BASE-T, 1000BASE-T, 10GBASE-T (10Gbps Ethernet)	Up to 10Gbps	Enhanced version of CAT6
CAT7	10BASE-T, 100BASE-T, 1000BASE-T, 10GBASE-T (10Gbps Ethernet)	Up to 10Gbps	Uses 12-connector GG45 connector (backward compatible with RJ-45)

* Some vendors sold an enhanced version of CAT6 that they called CAT6e before the release of CAT6a. CAT6e is not an official standard.

Plenum and PVC

There are two categories of TP cable in terms of fire rating:

- **Standard:** Standard cable is suitable for patch cables between a NIC and a network jack or in a patch panel. This type of cable typically has a PVC jacket, which can create a lot of smoke when burned.

- **Plenum:** *Plenum* cable is designed for use in plenum space (that is, space used for HVAC air exchanges), such as ventilator shafts, under floors, or between suspended ceilings and the permanent ceiling. Plenum cable produces less smoke when burned, produces a lower level of toxic chemicals when burned, and is typically self-extinguishing. Plenum cable jackets might be made from Teflon or from a modified version of PVC that produces less smoke when burned than standard PVC.

Shielded Twisted-Pair (STP) vs. Unshielded Twisted-Pair (UTP)

Twisted-pair (TP) cabling is the most common of the major cabling types. The name refers to its physical construction: four twisted pairs of wire surrounded by a flexible jacket (unshielded TP, or *UTP*) or various types of metal foil or braid (shielded TP, or *STP*). STP uses the same RJ-45 connector as UTP but includes a metal shield for electrical insulation between the wire pairs and the outer jacket. It's stiffer and more durable but also more expensive and harder to loop through tight spaces than UTP. It is used where electromagnetic interference (EMI) prevents the use of UTP cable.

Figure 3-1 compares the construction of STP and UTP cables.

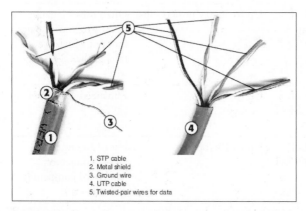

1. STP cable
2. Metal shield
3. Ground wire
4. UTP cable
5. Twisted-pair wires for data

FIGURE 3-1   An STP Cable (Left) Includes a Metal Shield and a Ground Wire for Protection Against Interference, While a UTP Cable (Right) Does Not

UTP and STP cable can be purchased in prebuilt assemblies or can be built using bulk cable and connectors.

T568B (EIA-568B) and T568A (EIA-568A) Standards

The de facto wire pair standard for all types of Ethernet UTP cables is known as *T568B*, or EIA-568B. The wire order, from left to right when looking at the top of the connector, is:

1. Pin 1—Orange/white stripe
2. Pin 2—Orange
3. Pin 3—Green/white stripe
4. Pin 4—Blue
5. Pin 5—Blue/white stripe
6. Pin 6—Green
7. Pin 7—Brown/white stripe
8. Pin 8—Brown

The *T568A* (EIA-568A) standard swaps the positions of the orange and green wires used in T568B. The wire order, from left to right when looking at the top of the connector, is:

1. Pin 1—Green/white stripe
2. Pin 2—Green
3. Pin 3—Orange/white stripe
4. Pin 4—Blue
5. Pin 5—Blue/white stripe
6. Pin 6—Orange
7. Pin 7—Brown/white stripe
8. Pin 8—Brown

Figure 3-2 illustrates cable pairings for a T568B cable, a T568B cable with connector, and the cable pairings for a T568A cable.

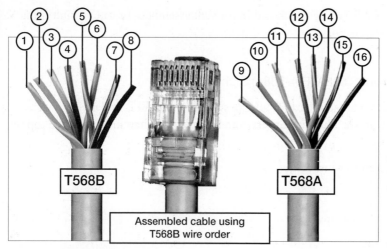

1. Pin 1 – Orange/white stripe
2. Pin 2 – Orange
3. Pin 3 – Green/white stripe
4. Pin 4 – Blue
5. Pin 5 – Blue/white stripe
6. Pin 6 – Green
7. Pin 7 – Brown/white stripe
8. Pin 8 – Brown
9. Pin 1 – Green/white stripe
10. Pin 2 – Green
11. Pin 3 – Orange/white stripe
12. Pin 4 – Blue
13. Pin 5 – Blue/white stripe
14. Pin 6 – Orange
15. Pin 7 – Brown/white stripe
16. Pin 8 – Brown

FIGURE 3-2   T568B (Left) and T568A (Right) Wire Pairs and an Assembled T568B Cable

NOTE   You can create a crossover cable by building one end to the T568B standard and the other end to the T568A standard.

Fiber

Fiber-optic cabling transmits signals with light rather than with electrical signals, which makes it immune to electrical interference. Fiber is more expensive than copper and requires more experience to install, but it offers the benefit of longer distances for large amounts of data and can be used in areas where electrical interference would make copper cable problematic. Because of the expense, fiber is used primarily as a backbone between networks.

Fiber-optic cable comes in two major types:

- **Single-mode fiber:** Has a thin core (between 8 and 10 microns) and is designed to carry a single light ray long distances (up to 60km or farther). Single-mode cable uses a laser diode as a light source. It is typically used by cable TV and telephone companies.

- **Multi-mode fiber:** Has a thicker core (62.5 microns) than single-mode and carries multiple light rays for short distances (up to 10km). Multi-mode cable uses an LED light source. It is typically used in local area networks (LANs) and metropolitan area networks (MANs).

An important thing to remember about the two fiber types is that single mode, with the smaller core, carries less data up to 60km (36 mi.) before the signal needs to be boosted. Multi-mode carries much more data but only for about 10km (6 mi.).

Fiber-optic cabling can be purchased prebuilt, but if you need a custom length, it should be built and installed by experienced cable installers because of the expense and risk of damage. Some network adapters built for servers are designed to use fiber-optic cable. Otherwise, media converters are used to interconnect fiber-optic to conventional cables on networks.

Fiber-optic devices and cables use one of several connector types. The most common include:

- **SC:** Uses square connectors

- **LC:** Uses square connectors

- **ST:** Uses round connectors

These connectors can be used singly or in pairs, depending upon the implementation. Figure 3-3 illustrates duplex (paired) SC, LC, and ST multi-mode cables.

NOTE   If you need to interconnect devices that use two different connector types, use adapter cables that are designed to match the connector types and other characteristics of the cable and device.

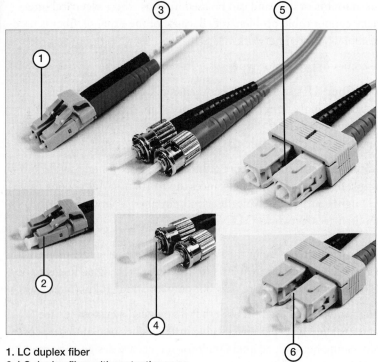

1. LC duplex fiber
2. LC duplex fiber with protective caps
3. ST duplex fiber
4. ST duplex fiber with protective caps
5. SC duplex fiber
6. SC duplex fiber with protective caps

FIGURE 3-3   SC, LC, and ST Fiber-Optic Cable Connectors Compared

Coaxial

Coaxial cabling is the oldest type of network cabling; its data wires are surrounded by a wire mesh for insulation. Coaxial cables, which resemble cable TV connections, are not popular for network use today because they must be run from one station directly to another rather than to or from a hub/switch. However, coaxial cabling is used for most cable TV, cable Internet, and satellite TV installations as well as CCTV cameras used for security.

Legacy 10Mbps Ethernet Coaxial Cable Standards

Coaxial cabling creates a bus topology. With an Ethernet bus topology, all network members are added to the same physical coaxial cable line to communicate with each other. Each end of the cable must be terminated so that signals are contained. A big disadvantage of the bus is that if any part of the bus fails, the entire network fails.

The oldest Ethernet standard, 10BASE5, uses a very thick coaxial cable (RG-8) attached to a NIC through an AUI transceiver that uses a "vampire tap" to connect the transceiver to the cable. This type of coaxial cable is also referred to as *Thick Ethernet*, or *Thicknet*.

Thin Ethernet, also referred to as *Thinnet*, *Cheapernet*, and *10BASE2 Ethernet*, was used for low-cost Ethernet networks before the advent of UTP cable. The coaxial cable used with 10BASE2 is referred to as RG-58. This type of coaxial cable connects to network cards through a T connector that bayonet-mounts to the rear of the network card using a BNC connector. The arms of the *T* are used to connect two cables, each running to another computer in the network.

If the workstation is at the end of a network, a terminating resistor is connected to one arm of the *T* to indicate the end of the network. If a resistor is removed, the network fails; if a station on the network fails, the network fails. Figure 3-4 shows both of these connection types. Note that some 10Mbps Ethernet cards are combo cards that might feature both legacy connector types as well as, on some models, an RJ-45 jack.

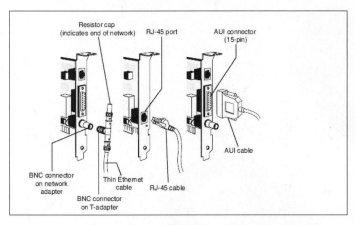

FIGURE 3-4 Combo UTP/BNC/AUI Ethernet Network Cards (Left and Right) Compared with a UTP/STP-Only Ethernet Card (Center) and Cables

RG-59 and RG-6 Coaxial Cable

Two other types of coaxial cable are common in cable Internet, satellite Internet, and fixed wireless Internet installations:

■ **RG-59:** Used in older cable TV or satellite TV installations as well as in CCTV security installations; 75-ohm resistance. RG-59 uses a 22-gauge (AWG) center conductor and a single outer shield. It is designed for signals up to 50MHz.

■ **RG-6:** Uses same connectors as RG-59 but has a larger diameter with dual shielding; used in cable TV/Internet, satellite TV/Internet, fixed wireless Internet/TV service, and closed-circuit (security) TV; 75-ohm resistance. RG-6 uses an 18-gauge (AWG) center conductor, which can carry a signal farther than RG-59. RG-6 is also available in quad-shielded versions. RG-6 can carry signals up to 1.5GHz, making it much better for HDTV signals.

BNC connectors are used for CCTV cameras and for some types of video projectors. BNC connectors are crimped to the coaxial cable and use a positive-locking bayonet mount.

F connectors are used for cable, satellite, and fixed wireless Internet and TV service. F connectors can be crimped or attached via compression to the coaxial cable. High-quality cables use a threaded connector. However, some F connector cables use a push-on connector, which is not as secure and can lead to a poor-quality connection. Figure 3-5 compares BNC and F connectors on an RG-6 coaxial cable.

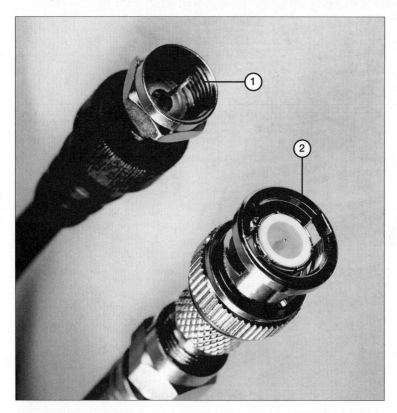

1. F-connector
2. BNC connector

FIGURE 3-5   F Connector and BNC Connector on RG-6 Cables

A two-way splitter such as the one shown in Figure 3-6 reduces signal strength by 50% (3.5dB) on each connection. Splitting the signal only once usually does not cause issues with your TV or Internet signal. However, if you need to split your signal, contact your TV or Internet provider for a splitter or ask what type of booster is recommended for your installation.

FIGURE 3-6   A Two-Way Coaxial Splitter

NOTE   Many antennas used for over-the-air digital TV now include a small inline booster that is powered by a 500mA USB connection or a small AC adapter. The booster helps improve range and bring in more stations.

Video Cables

When selecting a monitor or projector for use with a particular video card or integrated video port, it's helpful to understand the physical and feature differences between different video connector types, such as VGA, DVI, HDMI, DisplayPort component/RGB, BNC, S-video, and composite. Table 3-3 provides an overview of these connector types.

Table 3-3   Video Connector Types Overview

Connector	Signal Type	Base Resolution	Maximum Resolution (60Hz refresh rate)	HDCP Support	3D Support	Audio
VGA	Analog	640×480 graphics, 720×480 text	2048×1536*	No	No	No
HDMI	Digital, analog	VGA	1920×1200† 4K‡	Yes	Yes‡	Yes
DVI	Digital, analog§	VGA	1920×1200** 2560×1600††	Varies	No	No
DisplayPort	Digital, Analog	VGA	4K	Yes	Yes	Yes
BNC	Analog	VGA	1080p	No	No	No
Composite	Analog	480i	480i	No	No	No
S-Video‡‡	Analog	480i	480i	No	No	No
Component	Analog	720p	1080i	No	No	No

* Recommended resolutions are lower due to excessive interference

† HDMI 1.0 through 1.3c

‡ HDMI 1.4b or higher; also known as 4K resolution

§ DVI-D is digital only; DVI-I supports analog and digital signals; DVI-A is analog only

** Single-link

†† Dual-link

‡‡ S-video splits luma and chroma signals for a better picture than composite; composite combines these signals

VGA

Video Graphics Array, commonly known as *VGA*, is an analog display standard. It is largely a legacy technology, but you may still encounter it on older systems. By varying the levels of red, green, or blue per dot (pixel) onscreen, a VGA port and monitor can display an unlimited number of colors, but practical color limits are based on the video card's memory and the desired screen resolution.

The base resolution (horizontal×vertical dots) of VGA is 640×480. An enhanced version of VGA is Super VGA, or *SVGA*, which typically refers to 800×600 VGA resolution.

A VGA card made for use with a standard analog monitor uses a DB15F 15-pin female connector, which plugs into the DB15M male connector used by the VGA cable from the monitor. Figure 3-7 compares these connectors.

DB15M VGA cable   DB15F VGA port

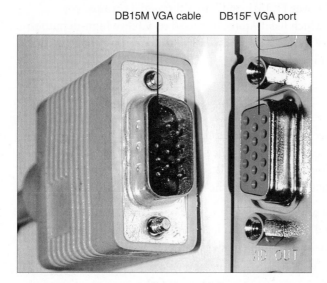

FIGURE 3-7   DB15M (Cable) and DB15F (Port) Connectors Used for VGA Video Signals

Most video cards with DVI ports use the DVI-I dual-link version, which provides both digital and analog output and supports the use of a VGA/DVI-I adapter for use with analog displays. (See Figure 3-23 in the "DVI-I to VGA" section, later in this chapter, to see some adapters and refer to Figure 3-11 in the "DVI" section, later in this chapter, to see a DVI-D cable and DVI-I port.)

The less-common DVI-A version supports analog signals only. The maximum length for DVI cables is 5m.

HDMI

Video cards and systems with integrated video that are designed for home theater use support a standard known as *High-Definition Multimedia Interface (HDMI)*.

HDMI has the capability to support digital audio as well as video through a single cable. HDMI ports are found on most late-model HDTVs as well as home theater hardware such as amplifiers and Blu-ray and DVD players, and many recent laptop and desktop PCs running Windows or Linux. All versions of HDMI support HDCP and digital rights management (DRM) for copyright protection.

The most recent HDMI standard, version 2.1, supports video resolutions and refresh rates including 8K60 and 4K120, as well as resolutions up to 10K. The earlier version, version 1.4b, supports 1080p HDTV and resolutions up to 4096×2160 (also known as 4K×2K), 48-bit color depths, various types of uncompressed and compressed digital audio, 3D over HDMI, and Fast Ethernet. The most common HDMI port is Type A, which has 19 pins. It is used to achieve high-definition resolutions such as 1920×1080 (known as 1080p or 1080i). For more about HDMI specifications, visit www.hdmi.org.

Mini-HDMI

The HDMI 1.3 and later specifications also define a ***mini-HDMI*** connector (Type C). It is smaller than the Type A plug but has the same 19-pin configuration. The HDMI 1.4 specification defines a micro-HDMI connector (Type D), which uses the same 19-pin configuration but in a connector the size of a micro-USB plug.

HDMI hardware, regardless of the version in use, uses connectors similar to the ones shown in Figure 3-8 and the ports shown in Figure 3-9. Typical cable lengths range up to 40 ft., but higher-quality copper cables can be longer.

1. DVI-I dual-link
2. DVI-D single-link
3. HDMI
4. Mini-HDMI
5. DisplayPort
6. Mini DisplayPort

FIGURE 3-8   HDMI Cable Connectors Compared to DVI and DisplayPort Cable Connectors

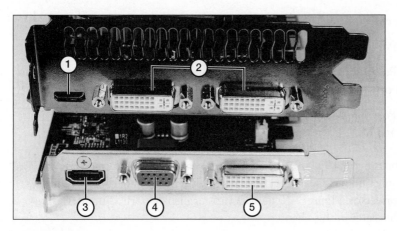

1. Mini HDMI
2. DVI-I Dual-link
3. HDMI
4. VGA
5. DVI-D Dual-link

FIGURE 3-9   HDMI, DVI, and VGA Ports on the Rear of Two Typical PCIe Video Cards

DisplayPort

DisplayPort was designed by the Video Electronics Standards Association (VESA) as a royalty-free digital interface to replace DVI and VGA. It offers similar performance to the HDMI standard.

Unlike HDMI or DVI, which can connect only one display per port, DisplayPort enables multiple displays to be connected via a single DisplayPort connector.

DisplayPort utilizes packet transmission similar to Ethernet and USB. Each packet transmitted has the clock embedded (whereas DVI and HDMI utilize a separate clocking signal).

DisplayPort connectors are not compatible with USB, DVI, or HDMI; however, devices that support dual-mode DisplayPort (DisplayPort++) technology are capable of sending HDMI or DVI signals with the use of the appropriate adapter. DisplayPort offers a maximum transmission distance of 3m over passive cable and in theory up to33m over active cable. There are 20 pins in a DisplayPort connector, with pins 19 and 20 being used for 3.3V, 500mA power on active cables. The mini-DisplayPort cable shown in Figure 3-8 also uses a 20-pin connector.

DisplayPort cables can be up to 15m long, but quality decreases with length.

Figure 3-10 shows a high-performance video card with a DisplayPort connector.

DisplayPort is currently available in three versions:

- **DisplayPort 1.1:** Maximum data transfer rate of 8.64Gbps

- **DisplayPort 1.2:** Maximum data transfer rate of 17.28Gbps; introduces mini-DisplayPort connector, and support for 3D

- **DisplayPort 1.3:** Maximum data transfer rate of 32.4Gbps with support for 4K, 5K, and 8K UHD displays

The Thunderbolt digital I/O interface is backward-compatible with mini-DisplayPort, so you can connect mini-DisplayPort displays to either a Thunderbolt or mini-DisplayPort connector. Figure 3-10 depicts various display ports. Thunderbolt is explained further later in this chapter.

1. DisplayPort
2. HDMI
3. DVI-I dual-link
4. DVI-D dual-link

FIGURE 3-10   DisplayPort, HDMI Port, and DVI Ports

DVI

The Digital Visual Interface port, or **DVI** port, is a digital video port that is used by many LED and LCD displays with a 25-in. or smaller diagonal measurement. The DVI-D supports only digital signals and is found on digital LCD displays. Most of these displays also support analog video signals through separate VGA ports. Figure 3-11 depicts DVI-I digital and DVI-D analog cable.

NOTE DVI single-link omits some of the connectors in the DVI interface, limiting the maximum resolution. DVI dual-link uses all of the connectors, enabling higher resolutions than are possible with DVI single-link.

DVI-D video cable supports digital signals only

DVI-I video port supports
analog and digital signals

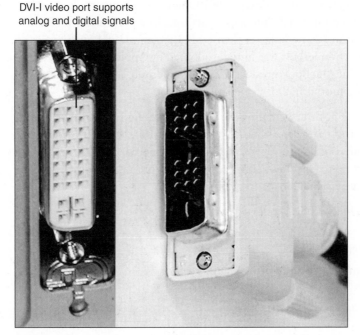

FIGURE 3-11 DVI-I Video Port and DVI-D Video Cable

Multipurpose Cables

Cables are highly engineered for the specific tasks they are intended to perform, but the growing number of cable types can become a burden. Designing cables that perform more than one function, such as combining the ability to charge batteries and transfer data, is an appreciated option by technology users.

Lightning

Older iOS devices (up through the iPhone 4 series and third-generation iPad) used the 30-pin connector. However, starting in 2012, Apple standardized on the 8-pin reversible *Lightning* connector for iPhones, iPads, iPods, and other mobile devices. The Lightning connector is used for both charging batteries and transferring data.

The data transfer rates are about the same as with the USB 2.0 standard. As of this writing, a replacement for Lightning has been patented by Apple but not applied to any products.

Thunderbolt

Thunderbolt is a high-speed interface capable of supporting hard disk drives, SSDs, HDTVs up to 4K resolution, and other types of I/O devices. Thunderbolt includes PCIe and DisplayPort digital signals into a compact interface that runs from 2x to 8x faster than USB 3.0, and 2x to 4x faster than USB 3.1 Gen 2. Intel introduced Thunderbolt in 2011. Thunderbolt was initially adopted by Apple, which uses it in the recent and current MacBook product lines. Thunderbolt is also available on some high-end desktop motherboards using Intel chipsets.

Thunderbolt is available in three versions that use two different port types: Thunderbolt 1 and Thunderbolt 2 use the same physical port as mini-DisplayPort. The newest version, Thunderbolt 3, uses the same physical connector as USB Type C. All three versions support up to six Thunderbolt devices per port and use daisy chaining to connect devices to each other.

Table 3-4 compares Thunderbolt versions to each other.

Table 3-4   Thunderbolt Interface Overview

Interface Version	Maximum Interface Speeds	Connection Type	Supported Protocols	Maximum Cable Length*
Thunderbolt 1	10Gbps	Thunderbolt 1*	Thunderbolt 1, DisplayPort	3m (9.8 ft.)
Thunderbolt 2	20Gbps	Thunderbolt 1*	Thunderbolt 1–2, DisplayPort 1.2	3m (9.8 ft.)
Thunderbolt 3	40Gbps	USB Type C	Thunderbolt 1–3, DisplayPort 1.2, PCIe 3, USB 3.0, USB Power Delivery	3m (9.8 ft.)

* Using copper cable. Some vendors are now shipping optical cable in lengths up to 30m.

Figure 3-12 compares a Thunderbolt 2 cable with a USB Type C cable (the cable used by Thunderbolt 3) and a mini-DisplayPort cable, which uses the same physical connector as a Thunderbolt cable. USB is explained in greater detail in the next section.

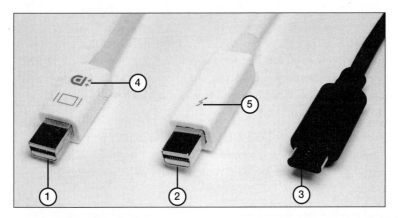

1. Mini-DisplayPort+ cable
2. Thunderbolt 1/Thunderbolt 2 cable
3. USB Type C – Thunderbolt 3 cable
4. DisplayPort++ icon
5. Thunderbolt icon

FIGURE 3-12   Mini-DisplayPort, Thunderbolt 1/Thunderbolt 2, and USB Type-C/Thunderbolt 3 Cables

Because of Thunderbolt's high bandwidth, it can be connected to docks that feature multiple port types. Figure 3-13 shows a typical Thunderbolt 2 dock that also provides USB 3.0 ports, an HDMI video port, a Gigabit Ethernet port, and audio headphone and microphone jacks.

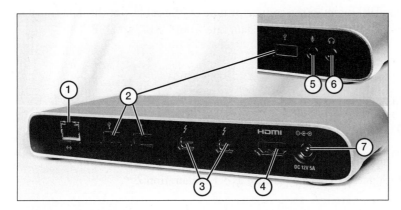

1. Gigabit Ethernet port
2. USB 3.0 ports
3. Thunderbolt 2 ports
4. HDMI port
5. Microphone port
6. Headset port
7. AC power jack

FIGURE 3-13   A Typical Thunderbolt 2 Dock

USB

Universal Serial Bus (*USB*) ports have replaced PS/2 (mini-DIN) mouse and keyboard ports on recent systems and can be used for printers, mass storage, and other external I/O devices. Some form of USB port is also used by most mobile devices, game consoles, many network devices, cars and trucks, smart TVs, and other electronics, making it truly "universal."

Most recent desktop systems have at least 8 USB ports, and many systems support as many as 10 or more front- and rear-mounted USB ports. Laptops typically have 3 or 4 USB ports, and Windows and Android typically have at least one USB or USB-On-the-Go port.

USB ports send and receive data digitally.

USB-C

The traditional USB Type A (USB-A) has been the standard USB connector for years, but USB Type C (USB-C) is now the industry standard for transmitting power and data. Hundreds of technology companies came together to develop the initial USB-A connector, and the same group has moved forward with *USB-C*, a connector that is easier to connect (reversible; no up or down side to the plug) and with the appropriate adapter allows backward compatibility to USB 2.0. (USB-C connectors are shown previously in Figures 3-12 and 3-13 and are shown again in Figures 3-16 and 3-17 in the sections that follow.)

The USB-C standard refers to the connector type on the cable, not the data transfer rate of the cable. USB-C can handle any data rate from USB-2 to USB-3.1.

USB 2.0, USB 3.0, and USB 3.1

Three standards for USB ports are included on the A+ certification exam:

- *USB 2.0* (Hi-Speed)
- *USB 3.0* (SuperSpeed); also known as USB 3.1 Generation 1
- *USB 3.1* (SuperSpeed+); also known as 3.1 Generation 2

USB packaging and device markings frequently use the official logos shown in Figure 3-14 to distinguish the four versions of USB in common use. The industry uses the term *Hi-Speed USB* for USB 2.0, *SuperSpeed USB* for USB 3.0, and *SuperSpeed+* USB for USB 3.1 Gen 2. USB 1.0 is largely legacy and not on the A+ exam.

FIGURE 3-14 The Evolution of USB from USB 1.1 (left) to USB 3.1 Gen 2–. (Images courtesy of USB-IF)

With any version of USB, a single USB port on an add-on card or motherboard is designed to handle up to 127 devices through the use of multiport hubs and daisy chaining hubs. USB devices are Plug and Play (PnP) devices that are hot swappable (which means they can be connected and disconnected without turning off the system).

Need more USB ports? You can add USB ports with any of the following methods:

- Motherboard connectors for USB header cables

- Hubs

- Add-on cards

Some motherboards have USB header cable connectors, which enable you to make additional USB ports available on the rear or front of the computer. Most recent cases also include front-mounted USB ports, which can also be connected to the motherboard. Because of vendor-specific differences in how motherboards implement header cables, the header cable might use separate connectors for each signal instead of the more common single connector for all signals.

USB generic hubs are used to connect multiple devices to the same USB port, distribute both USB signals and power via the USB hub to other devices, and increase the distance between the device and the USB port. There are two types of generic hubs:

- **Bus-powered:** Bus-powered hubs might be built into other devices, such as monitors and keyboards, or they can be standalone devices. Different USB devices use different amounts of power, and some devices require more power than others. A bus-powered hub provides no more than 100 milliamps (mA) of power to each device connected to it. Thus, some devices fail when connected to a bus-powered hub.

- **Self-powered:** A self-powered hub, on the other hand, has its own power source; it plugs in to an AC wall outlet. A self-powered hub designed for USB 1.1 or USB 2.0 devices provides up to 500mA of power to each device connected to it, whereas a self-powered hub designed for USB 3.0/3.1 devices provides up to 900mA of power to each device. Note that USB hubs are backward compatible with previous USB versions. A self-powered hub supports a wider range of USB devices than a bus-powered hub.

Add-on cards can be used to provide additional USB ports as an alternative to hubs. One advantage of an add-on card is its capability to provide support for more recent USB standards. For example, you can add a USB 3.0 card to a system that has only USB 1.1/2.0 ports to permit use of USB 3.0 hard drives at full performance. Add-on cards for USB 1.1 or USB 2.0 ports connect to PCI slots on desktop computers and CardBus or ExpressCard slots on laptop computers, whereas USB 3.0 cards connect to PCIe x1 or wider slots on desktop computers and ExpressCard slots on laptop computers.

Figure 3-15 illustrates a typical USB 3.0 card, a USB 2.0 self-powered hub, and a USB 2.0 port header cable.

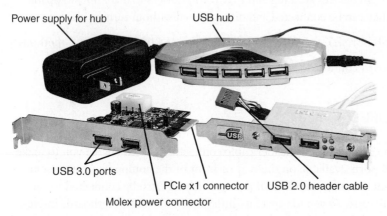

FIGURE 3-15   USB 2.0 and 3.0 Hardware

Table 3-5 provides an overview of USB standards.

Table 3-5   USB Standards Overview

Version	Marketing Name	Speeds Supported	Maximum Cable Length*	Notes
1.1 (legacy)	USB	12Mbps 1.5Mbps	3m	
2.0	Hi-Speed USB	480Mbps	5m	Also supports USB 1.1 devices and speeds
3.1 Gen 1 (also known as USB 3.0)	SuperSpeed USB	5Gbps	†	Also supports USB 1.1 and 2.0 devices and speeds
3.1 Gen 2	SuperSpeed+ USB	10Gbps	†	Also supports USB 1.1, 2.0, 3.0/3.1 Gen 1 devices and speeds

* To exceed recommended or maximum cable lengths, connect the cable to a USB hub or use an active USB extension cable.

† 3m is the recommended length, but no maximum cable length has been established for these versions of USB.

USB 3.0

USB 3.1 is actually two standards in one:

- **_USB 3.1 Gen 1_** is the new name for USB 3.0. Anytime you see a reference to USB 3.0, keep in mind that USB 3.1 Gen 1 is the same standard. Although USB 3.1 Gen 1 is the same standard as USB 3.0, vendors continue to use the original USB 3.0 name.

- **_USB 3.1 Gen 2_** has new USB 3.1 features. USB 3.1 Gen 2 (often referred to simply as USB 3.1) runs at speeds up to 10Gbps (2x the speed of USB 3.0/USB 3.1 Gen 1). It is backward compatible with USB 1.1, 2.0, and 3.0/3.1 Gen 1.

Both USB 3.1 Gen 1 and Gen 2 use the same cables and connectors as USB 3.0. However, some USB 3.1 Gen 2 ports support a new reversible connector, USB Type C, which can be used by both hubs and devices. Some systems, such as the second motherboard similar to the ones shown in Figure 3-16, include both a Type C USB 3.1 port and a standard Type A USB 3.1 Gen 2 port.

NOTE   Although USB Type-C connectors also support older USB standards, it is unlikely that vendors would use it for USB 3.0, USB 2.0, or USB 1.1 ports.

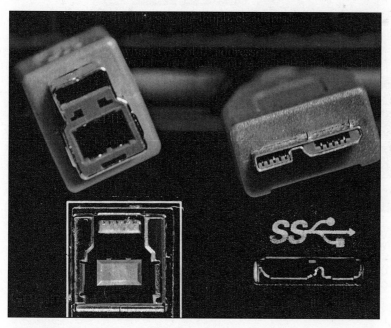

FIGURE 3-16   USB 3.0 Standard-B (Left) and Micro-B (Right) Cables and Receptacles

Other USB standards, such as USB Power Delivery and USB Battery Charging, take advantage of other features in the USB Type C port. For more information about USB 3.1, USB Type C, USB Power Delivery, or USB Battery Charging, see the official USB website, www.usb.org.

Figure 3-17 illustrates USB 3.0 Type A and Type C cable and USB 3.1 Gen 2 ports.

1. USB 3.0/3.1 Type A cable
2. USB 3.0/3.1 Type A port
3. USB 3.1 Type A port
4. USB 3.1 Type C port
5. USB 3.1 Type C cable

FIGURE 3-17   USB 3.0/3.1 Type A and Type C Ports and Cables

USB Adapters

USB cable adapter kits enable a single cable with replaceable tips to be used for the following tasks:

- Type A male to female to extend a short cable

- Type A female to Type B connectors to enable a single cable with multiple adapter tips to work with various types of peripherals (see Figure 3-18)

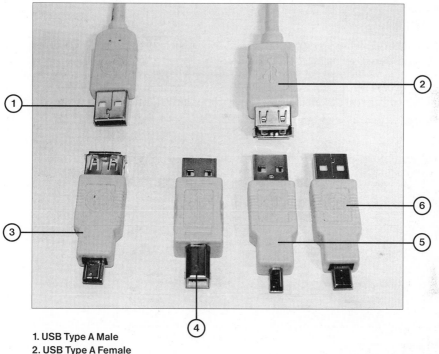

1. USB Type A Male
2. USB Type A Female
3. USB Mini-AB
4. USB Type B
5. USB Mini-B four pin
6. USB Mini-B five pin

FIGURE 3-18   USB 2.0 Cable Kit, Including a Type A Male/Female Cable and Several B-Type Connectors

- Type A female to USB-On-the-Go for use with tablets or smartphones (see Figure 3-19)

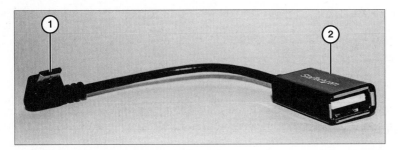

1. USB-on-the-Go
2. USB Type A Female

FIGURE 3-19   USB-on-the-Go to Type A Adapter, Which Enables a Standard USB Cable to Work with Devices That Use the Micro-A Connector

■ USB to Ethernet to enable a device without an Ethernet port to connect to a wired network (see Figure 3-20)

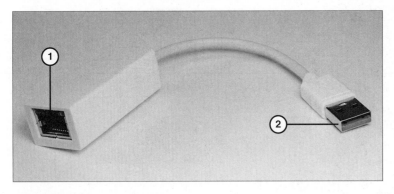

1. Gigabit Ethernet
2. USB 3.0 Type A

FIGURE 3-20   A Typical USB 3.0 to Gigabit Ethernet Adapter

Peripheral Cables: Serial

In years past, a device connected to a computer via a serial cable plugged into a serial port. *Serial* means that the data bits flow in a line, one after the other, over the cable. Serial connections were designed for the relatively low speed of telephone modem communication but were also used for other devices, such as keyboards, mice, and other peripheral devices.

Serial ports and cables were usually compared to parallel ports and cables, where multiple bits flow at once. Serial cables conformed to the RS-232 standard. Printers were the most common devices to be connected with parallel ports, but now most printers are connected with USB cables or via Ethernet cables on networks.

USB cables have replaced serial cables, but it is possible to use a USB to serial adapter to connect to an older machine, if necessary.

Hard Drive Cables

Hard drive cables are built to carry data to and from the motherboard. As data rates have increased, cable designs have changed to keep up with the data speeds. This section describes some of the hard drive cables encountered by technicians.

SATA Cables

At one time hard drives were connected to motherboards with Advanced Technology Attachment (ATA) cables. These cables had a ribbon-like appearance, with multiple wires carrying data between the bus and the hard drive.

Serial ATA (*SATA*) cables are next-generation serial cables that carry high-speed data. SATA cables are used inside computer cases and offer not only the advantage of high speed but the benefit of better airflow inside the box.

External SATA (eSATA) cables allow for external drives to be mounted at the same data rate. eSATA has better shielding to protect the cable and the data. To prevent the use of thinner SATA cables from being used outside the case, eSATA cables have a different connecter. Figure 3-21 depicts SATA and eSATA cables. (Note the thicker cable and different keying between cables 3 and 4).

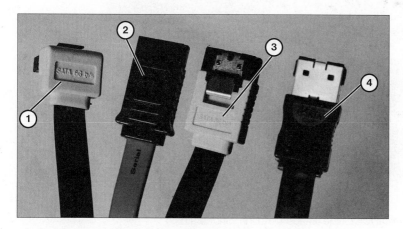

1. **Right-angle SATA 6Gbps cable end with locking clip**
2. **Standard SATA 1.5-3Gbps cable end**
3. **Straight SATA 6Gbps cable end with locking clip**
4. **eSATA cable end**

FIGURE 3-21 SATA and eSATA Cables Compared

IDE Cable

An Integrated Drive Electronics (***IDE***) cable is a standard cable type for connecting devices to a motherboard inside a computer case. Older hard drives have IDE connecters, and an IDE cable is one that accommodates them. SATA and SSD storage drives are more common, but you should be able to recognize an IDE hard drive and an IDE connector on a motherboard so you will know if you need an IDE cable to get them working.

An IDE cable typically has three: one for the motherboard that splits into two connectors. This way, you can attach two hard drives to a motherboard with only one cable.

If you need to service an older computer that has only IDE connectors but you have a SATA drive, you can solve the problem with a SATA to IDE adapter. Figure 3-22 depicts a typical IDE connector.

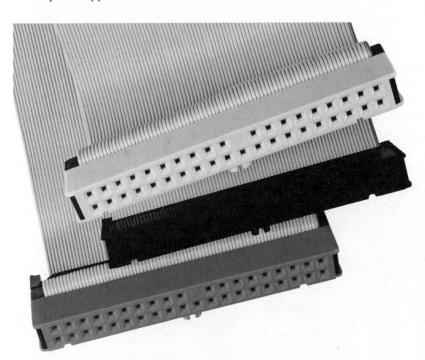

FIGURE 3-22   A Typical IDE Cable (Image © Kaspri, Shutterstock)

SCSI

Small Computer System Interface (***SCSI***) cables, like their IDE cable cousins, have been replaced by SATA cables inside computers. Most motherboards were designed for SATA and IDE connections, but SCSI, because it is less common, requires an expansion card to connect a hard drive.

The advantages of a SCSI drive system is that up to 7 (or sometimes 15) SCSI drives can be daisy chained together; for comparison, an IDE connector supports only 2 drives. At one time, SCSI drives were the fastest option, but that is no longer the case; SATA and SSD are faster. On the downside, SCSI was more expensive to purchase and more complicated to configure. The advantages and disadvantages have been rendered moot, however, by the newer technologies.

Adapters

With any advance in technology, there tends to be a period of time when the old overlaps with the new, or when competing technologies need to find a way to get along. Physical cable adapters are often the short-term (and economical) answer to technical compatibility problems during an upgrade cycle. This section briefly explains the three types of cable adapters listed in the A+ objectives.

DVI to HDMI

Because HDMI uses the same video signals as DVI, DVI to HDMI cables or adapters are widely available. Usually only the video transmits through these adapter cables, but some newer graphics cards allow for HDMI audio over DVI, which eliminates the need for a separate sound cable connection.

USB to Ethernet

USB to Ethernet adapters (refer to Figure 3-20) enable a device without an Ethernet port to connect to a wired network. These common connectors are available in a wide range of prices and qualities.

DVI-I to VGA

DVI-I includes both VGA-compatible analog video and DVI digital video. The DVI-I to VGA adapters shown in Figures 3-23 and 3-24 enable VGA displays to work with DVI-I ports on video cards.

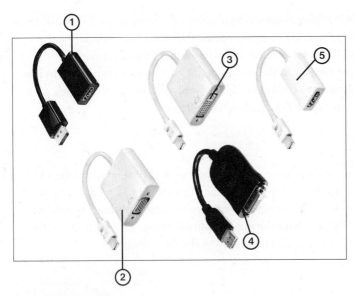

1. DisplayPort to HDMI
2. Mini-DisplayPort to VGA
3. Mini-DisplayPort to DVI-I
4. DisplayPort to DVI-D
5. Mini-DisplayPort to HDMI

FIGURE 3-23   Adapters for mini-DisplayPort and DisplayPort to Other Display Types

1. DVI-I dual-link
2. VGA (DB15)
3. DVI-I single-link

FIGURE 3-24   Single-Link and Dual-Link DVI-I to VGA Adapters

Common Connectors

220-1001: Objective 3.2: Identify common connector types.

As mentioned earlier, the array of cable types in computing can be daunting, but even more so can be the connector types, since many cables may use more than one connector type. To help keep them straight, this section reviews all of the networking connector types listed in the A+ objectives. Some of them are legacy types—and they are identified as such—but there is a lot of legacy equipment that you may encounter, and you should be familiar with all the types listed.

Table 3-6 briefly summarizes the connector types you should know. Most are discussed in this chapter. If a figure is available to show each connector, it is listed in the last column of the table.

Table 3-6   Network Connector Types

Type	Description	Status	Figure
RJ-11	Standard phone jack; smaller than RJ-45	Current	
RJ-45	Standard Ethernet cable connector	Current	Figures 3-2 and 3-4
RS-232	Most commonly found in DB9 or DB15 connections on PCs for printers, mice, and modems; mostly replaced by USB cables	In decline	
BNC	Bayonet Neill Connector; the male connector for 10BASE2 coax cables	Legacy	Figures 3-4 and 3-5
RG-59	Coax cable with 20AWG; common CCTV (non-broadcast)	Current	
RG-6	Coax with 18AWG; larger copper core than RG-59, so more signal and bandwidth; used for CATV (common cable TV)	Current	
USB	Universal Serial Bus; most common connector currently in use	Current	Figures 3-16 and 3-17
Micro-USB	Smallest of the USB connector types; the USB type for many non-Apple phones	Current/to be displaced by USB-C	
Mini-USB	About half the size of USB-A; common for external storage, cameras, and so on	Legacy but still in use	Figures 3-12 and 3-18
USB-C	Newest reversible USB connector; should replace other USB types	Current	Figure 3-12

Type	Description	Status	Figure
DB9	9-pin serial connector once common on PCs; once used for peripherals like mice and keyboards; can be used for serial communications to networking equipment; also used with a DB9 to USB adapter to PCs without DB9 ports	Legacy but still in specialized use	
Lightning	Apple mobile device connector used for data and power	Current	
SCSI	Used internally (hard drives) or externally (printers, storage, and so on)	Legacy	
eSATA	Used for connecting external storage; thicker than internal SATA cables	Current	Figure 3-21
Molex	Not a networking connector; delivers power from power supply to various drives and motherboard inside a PC	Legacy but still around; replaced by SATA	

Installing RAM Types

220-1001: Objective 3.3: Given a scenario, install RAM types.

RAM is like a work table in that it holds every project that the CPU is working on. The operating system, open applications, and all kinds of hidden processes use the RAM workspace when the device is running. If you get too many projects piled up onto a small work table, things get awkward and inefficient—and the work won't go as smoothly as it could with more workspace. For a computer, adding more RAM is like getting a bigger table so that things can be sorted and spread out for smoother working. Installing more RAM improves transfers between the CPU and both RAM and hard drives.

The contents of RAM are temporary; RAM is much faster than magnetic or SSD storage; RAM speed is measured in nanoseconds (billionths of a second), while magnetic and SSD storage is measured in milliseconds (thousandths of a second).

Ever-increasing amounts of RAM are needed as operating systems and applications get more powerful and add more features. Because RAM is one of the most popular upgrades to add to any laptop or desktop system during its lifespan, you need to understand how RAM works, which types of RAM exist, and how to add RAM to provide the biggest performance boost to the systems you maintain.

RAM is in a continual state of evolution, and it is no surprise that the list of RAM types has grown to be quite complicated—not just because there are so many developments but because RAM is so often described in acronyms that don't define the differences of the types. Table 3-7 provides a review of RAM development from Chapter 1, "Mobile Devices."

Table 3-7   RAM Review

Acronym	Meaning	Note:
RAM	Random access memory	Volatile memory not for storage
SDRAM	Synchronous dynamic RAM	Combines static RAM and dynamic RAM
SDR SDRAM	Single data rate SDRAM	Legacy
DDR SDRAM *DDR2*, *DDR3*, and *DDR4*	Double data rate SDRAM	DDR 2 through 4 are currently in use in most computers
DIMM	Dual inline memory module	Form factor used in desktops
SODIMM	Small outline DIMM	Form factor used in laptops

When you upgrade a computer, you need to know a few important details:

- **Form factor:** Most computers in service use DDR2, DDR3, or DDR4, and laptops use SODIMMs of each DDR type.

- **Memory speed:** If you plan to add a module, make sure it is the same speed as the existing module. If you plan to replace the modules, buy a matched set of modules in the fastest speed supported by the system.

- **Memory timing:** The most common way to refer to memory timing is by its column address strobe (CAS) value. It is usually marked on the label with a CL value. If you install memory modules that use different CAS values, the computer may become unstable and crash or lock up.

Memory modules of the same type with memory chips of the same speed can have different CAS latency (CL) values. CL refers to how quickly memory column addresses can be accessed. A lower CL value provides faster access than a higher CL value. CL values increase when comparing different types of memory.

Most, but not all, memory module labels indicate the CL value. For modules that aren't labeled, look up the part number for details.

To determine the correct memory to use for a memory upgrade, use one of the following methods:

- **Use the interactive memory upgrade tools available from major third-party memory vendors' websites:** These tools list the memory modules suitable for particular laptops, and some use an ActiveX web control to detect the currently installed memory. Crucial System Scanner is a very useful tool for showing what's currently installed and what is compatible. For more information, visit https://www.crucial.com/usa/en/systemscanner.

■ **Check the vendor's memory specifications:** You can determine part numbers by using this method, but this method is best if memory must be purchased from the laptop vendor rather than from a memory vendor.

Synchronous DRAM (SDRAM) and DDR (double data rate) SDRAM were the first two generations of RAM in sync with the processor bus (the connection between the processor, or CPU, and other components on the motherboard). They used 168-pin and 184-pin DIMMs to attach to the motherboard. These are legacy versions and are mentioned here for perspective on the evolution of RAM. The following types or RAM are part of the A+ objectives, and knowing your RAM is essential to being a good technician.

SODIMM Memory

As mentioned in Chapter 1, laptops have a more compressed form factor than desktops, and RAM for laptops therefore needs to be smaller to fit the form factor. Laptops use small outline DIMMs (SODIMMs), which are reduced-size versions of DIMM modules. Figure 3-25 compares a typical DDR3 SODIMM with a DDR2 SODIMM and a DDR3 DIMM.

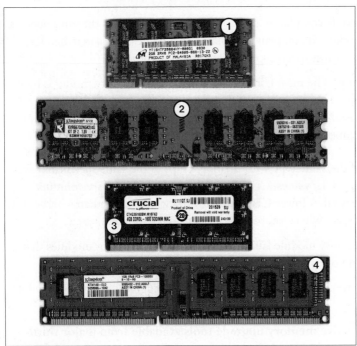

1. DDR2 SO-DIMM
2. DDR2 DIMM
3. DDR3 SO-DIMM
4. DDR3 DIMM

FIGURE 3-25   DDR2 SODIMM and DIMM Modules Compared to DDR3 SODIMM and DIMM Modules

Table 3-8 lists common DIMM and SODIMM form factors and their uses.

Table 3-8 RAM Comparison

RAM Type	Pins (DIMM)	Pins (SODIMM)	Common Type and Speed	Defining Characteristic
DDR SDRAM	184	200*	PC3200 = 400MHz/3200Mbps	Double the transfers per clock cycle compared to regular SDRAM.
DDR2 SDRAM	240^2	200*	DDR2-800 (PC2-6400) = 800MHz/6400Mbps	External data bus speed (I/O bus clock) is 2x faster than DDR SDRAM.
DDR3 SDRAM	$240^\dagger$	204	DDR3-1333 (PC3-10600) = 1333MHz/10,600Mbps	External data bus speed (I/O bus clock) is 2x faster than DDR2 SDRAM (4x faster than DDR SDRAM).
DDR4 SDRAM*	$288^\ddagger$	260	DDR4-2400 (PC4-19200) = 2400MHz/19200Mbps	External data bus speed (I/O bus clock) is 2x faster than DDR3 SDRAM (8x faster than DDR SDRAM).

*DDR SODIMM keying is closer to the middle of the motherboard than with SDRAM SODIMMs

†The keying on DDR3 is offset to one side compared to DDR2

‡The keying on DDR4 is different from the keying on DDR3, and they are not interchangeable

DDR2 SDRAM

Double data rate 2 SDRAM (DDR2 SDRAM) is the successor to DDR SDRAM. DDR2 SDRAM runs its external data bus at twice the speed of DDR SDRAM and features a 4-bit prefetch buffer, enabling faster performance.

DDR2 SDRAM memory might be referred to by the effective memory speed of the memory chips on the module (the memory clock speed x4 or the I/O bus clock speed x2)—for example, DDR2-533 (133MHz memory clock x4 or 266MHz I/O bus clock x2)=533MHz—or by module throughput (DDR2-533 is used in PC2-4200 modules, which have a throughput of more than 4200Mbps). *PC2* indicates that the module uses DDR2 memory; *PC* indicates that the module uses DDR memory.

Other common speeds for DDR2 SDRAM modules include PC2-3200 (DDR2-400; 3200Mbps throughput), PC2-5300 (DDR2-667), PC2-6400 (DDR2-800), and PC2-8500 (DDR2-1066).

DDR3 SDRAM

Compared to DDR2, double data rate 3 SDRAM (DDR3 SDRAM) runs at lower voltages, has twice the internal banks, and (with most versions) runs at faster speeds than DDR2. DDR3 also has an 8-bit prefetch bus. As with DDR2 vs. DDR, DDR3 has greater latency than DDR2. Typical latency values for mainstream DDR3 memory are CL7 or CL9, compared to CL5 or CL6 for DDR2. Although DDR3 modules also use 240 pins, their layout and keying are different from those of DDR2, and they cannot be interchanged.

DDR3 SDRAM memory might be referred to by the effective memory speed of the memory chips on the module (the memory clock speed x4 or the I/O bus clock speed x2); for example, DDR3-1333 (333MHz memory clock x4 or 666MHz I/O bus clock x2)=1333MHz) or by module throughput (DDR3-1333 is used in PC3-10600 modules, which have a throughput of more than 10,600MBps or 10.6GBps). *PC3* indicates that the module uses DDR3 memory.

Other common speeds for DDR3 SDRAM modules include PC3-8500 (DDR3-1066; 8500MBps throughput), PC3-12800 (DDR3-1600), and PC3-17000 (DDR3-2133).

Figure 3-26 compares DDR, DDR2, DDR3, and DD4 memory modules.

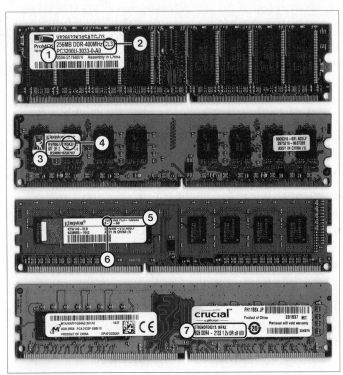

1. 256MB DDR module, PC3200 (DDR400)
2. CL3 latency
3. 2GB DDR2 module (from matched set), DDR2-667 (PC2-5300)
4. CL5 latency
5. 2GB DDR3 module, PC3-10600 (DDR3-1333)
6. CL9 latency
7. 8GB DDR4 module, DDR4-2133 (PC4-17000)

FIGURE 3-26   DDR, DDR2, DDR3, and DDR4 DIMM Desktop Memory Modules with Different Notch Locations

DDR4 SDRAM: The Current Standard

DDR4 SDRAM, introduced alongside Intel's X99 chipset for Haswell-E Core i-series processors in 2014, is the fourth generation of DDR memory. Compared to its predecessor, DDR3, DDR4 runs at lower voltage (1.2V) than either DDR3 or lower-voltage DDR3L. DDR4 supports densities up to 16GB per chip (twice the density of DDR3) and twice the memory banks, and it uses bank groups to speed up burst accesses to memory; however, it uses the same 8-bit prefetch as DDR3. Data rates range from 1600Mbps to 3200Mbps, compared to 800Mbps to 2133Mbps for DDR3. To improve memory reliability, DDR4 includes built-in support for CRC and parity error checking rather than requiring the memory controller to support error-checking (ECC) with parity memory, as in DDR3 and earlier designs.

Single Channel

Originally, all systems that used SDRAM were *single-channel* systems. Each 64-bit DIMM or SODIMM module was addressed individually.

Since RAM services the CPU, it would be best to have RAM with enough speed to match the processing the CPU performs. Dual-channel (and later triple-channel and quad-channel) RAM represent efforts to increase RAM speed for more efficient performance.

Dual Channel

Some systems using DDR and most systems using DDR2 or newer memory technologies support *dual-channel* operation. When two identical (same size, speed, and latency) modules are installed in the proper sockets, the memory controller accesses them in interleaved mode for faster access. This is why almost all RAM upgrades are done in pairs of chips.

Most systems with two pairs of sockets marked in contrasting colors implement dual-channel operation in this way: Install the matching modules in the same color sockets (see Figure 3-27). See the instructions for the system or motherboard for exceptions.

1. **Installed DIMM**
2. **Install identical module here for dual-channel operation**
3. **Use a matched pair (same speed and CL value as the first pair) in these sockets for best performance.**
This pair need not be the same size as the first pair.

FIGURE 3-27   Adding an Identical Module to the Light-Colored Memory Socket to Use Dual Channel Operation on a Motherboard

Triple Channel

Triple-channel RAM is designed to triple the speed of the RAM bandwidth. Some systems using Intel's LGA series chipsets support triple-channel addressing. Most of these systems use two sets of three sockets. Populate at least one set with three chips with identical memory. Some triple-channel motherboards use four sockets, but for best performance, the last socket should not be used on these systems.

Quad Channel

Some systems using Intel's LGA series chipset support quad-channel addressing. Most of these systems use two sets of four sockets. As in dual and triple channel, with quad channel you populate one or both sets with four chips of identical memory. Quad channel is mentioned here for comparison but is not on the A+ objectives.

NOTE   One thing to remember about dual, triple, and quad memory is that the chips are not different for each; the difference is in the way the motherboard accesses the chips. So it would be technically possible (although not technically resourceful) to use only two of the same RAM chips in a quad system.

Parity vs. Non-Parity

Two methods have been used to protect the reliability of memory:

- Parity checking

- ECC (error-correcting code or error-correction code)

Both methods depend upon the presence of an additional memory chip over the chips required for the data bus of the module. For example, a module that uses 8 chips for data would use a 9th chip to support parity or ECC. If the module uses 16 chips for data (two banks of 8 chips each), it would use the 17th and 18th chips for parity. *Parity checking*, which goes back to the original IBM PC, works like this: Whenever memory is accessed, each data bit has a value of 0 or 1. When these values are added to the value in the parity bit, the resulting checksum should be an odd number. This is called *odd parity*. A memory problem typically causes the data bit values plus the parity bit value to total to an even number. This triggers a parity error, and the system halts with a parity error message. Note that parity checking requires parity-enabled memory and support in the motherboard. On modules that support parity checking, there's a parity bit for each group of 8 bits.

The method used to fix this type of error varies depending on the system. On museum-piece systems that use individual memory chips, you must open the system, push all memory chips back into place, and test the memory thoroughly if you have no spares (using memory-testing software). Or you must replace the memory if you have spare memory chips. If the computer uses memory modules, replace one module at a time and test the memory (or at least run the computer for a while) to determine whether the problem has gone away. If the problem recurs, replace the original module, swap out the second module, and repeat.

TIP   Some system error messages tell you the logical location of the error so you can refer to the system documentation to determine which module or modules to replace.

NOTE   Parity checking has always been expensive because of the extra chips involved and the additional features required in the motherboard and chipset, and it fell out of fashion for PCs starting in the mid-1990s. Systems that lack parity checking freeze up when a memory problem occurs and do not display any message onscreen.

Because parity checking "protects" you from bad memory by shutting down the computer (which can cause you to lose data), vendors created a better way to use the parity bits to solve memory errors: using a method called ECC.

Error Correction: ECC vs. non-ECC Memory

For critical applications, network servers have long used a special type of memory called *error-correcting code (ECC)*. This memory enables the system to correct single-bit errors and notify you of larger errors.

Although most desktops do not support ECC, some workstations and most servers do offer ECC support. On systems that offer ECC support, ECC support might be enabled or disabled through the system BIOS, or it might be a standard feature. The parity bit in parity memory is used by the ECC feature to determine when the content of memory is corrupt and to fix single-bit errors. Unlike parity checking, which only warns you of memory errors, ECC memory actually corrects errors.

ECC is recommended for maximum data safety, although parity and ECC do provide a small slowdown in performance in return for the extra safety. ECC memory modules use the same types of memory chips used by standard modules, but they use more chips and might have a different internal design to allow ECC operation. ECC modules, like parity-checked modules, have an extra bit for each group of 8 data bits.

To determine whether a system supports parity-checked or ECC memory, check the system BIOS memory configuration (typically on the Advanced or Chipset screens). Systems that support parity or ECC memory can use non-parity-checked memory when parity checking and ECC are disabled. Another name for ECC is EDAC (error detection and correction).

Installing Memory

As mentioned earlier, upgrading RAM is one of the most (if not the most) common tasks a technician will perform to improve a computer's performance. This is an essential skill to learn and understand, so it is covered here. This section largely applies to both desktops and laptops.

> ### Installing Memory Safely
>
> When you install memory, be sure to follow the important safety procedures listed in Objective 4.4 of the 220-1002 Core 2 exam (see Chapter 9, "Operational Procedures").

Preparations for Installing DIMM Memory

Before working with any memory modules, turn off the computer and unplug it from the AC outlet. Be sure to employ electrostatic discharge (ESD) protection in the form of an ESD strap and ESD mat. Use an antistatic bag to hold the memory modules while you are not working with them. Before actually handling any components, touch an unpainted portion of the case chassis in a further effort to ground yourself. Try not to touch any of the chips, connectors, or circuitry of the memory module; hold them from the sides.

To install a DIMM module, follow these steps:

Step 1.   Line up the modules' connectors with the socket. DIMM modules have connections with different widths to prevent backward insertion of the module.

Step 2.   Verify that the locking tabs on the socket are swiveled to the outside (open) position. Some motherboards use a locking tab on only one side of the socket.

Step 3.   After verifying that the module is lined up correctly with the socket, push the module straight down into the socket until the swivel locks on each end of the socket snap into place at the top corners of the module (see Figure 3-28). A fair amount of force is required to engage the locks. Do not touch the metal-plated connectors on the bottom of the module as doing so can cause corrosion or ESD.

For clarity, the memory module installation pictured in Figure 3-28 was photographed with the motherboard out of the case. However, the tangle of cables and components around and over the DIMM sockets in Figure 3-29 provides a much more realistic view of the challenges you face when you install memory in a working system.

When you install memory on a motherboard inside a working system, use the following tips to help your upgrade go smoothly and the module to work properly:

- If the system is a tower system, consider placing the system on its side to make the upgrade easier. Doing this also helps prevent tipping the system over by accident when you push on the memory to lock it into the socket.

- Use a digital camera or smartphone set for close-up focusing so you can document the system's interior before you start the upgrade process.

- Move the locking tab on the DIMM sockets to the open position before you try to insert the module (refer to Figure 3-28). The memory module must be pressed firmly into place before the locking tab (left) will engage. The sockets shown in Figure 3-29 have closed tabs.

- If an aftermarket heat sink blocks access to memory sockets, try to remove its fan by unscrewing it from the radiator fin assembly. This is normally easier to do than removing the heat sink from the CPU.

■ Move power and drive cables away from the memory sockets so you can access the sockets. Disconnect cables if necessary.

■ Use a flashlight to shine light into the interior of the system so you can see the memory sockets and locking tabs clearly; this enables you to determine the proper orientation of the module and to make sure the sockets' locking mechanisms are open.

■ Use a flashlight to double-check your memory installation to make sure the module is completely inserted into the slot and locked into place.

■ Replace any cables you moved or disconnected during the process before you close the case and restart the system.

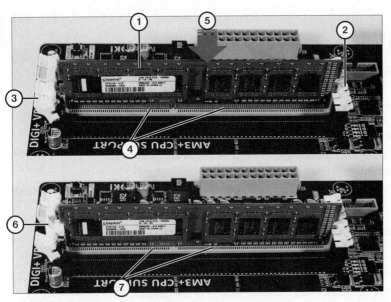

1. DDR3 module lined up for installation.
2. Many recent motherboards use fixed guides on one side.
3. Motherboards have at least one locking tab per module.
4. Connectors visible when module is not fully inserted.
5. Push module firmly into place.
6. Locking tab holds module in place when fully installed.
7. Connectors are no longer visible when module is fully inserted.

FIGURE 3-28   A DDR3 DIMM Partly Inserted (Top) and Fully Inserted (Bottom)

TIP   Note the positions of any cables before you remove them to perform an internal upgrade. You can use self-stick colored dots on a drive and its matching data and power cables. Marking masking tape with matching symbols works as well.

1. Memory sockets (some blocked by fan and heat sink)
2. Aftermarket fan and heat sink for CPU
3. Power and data cables

FIGURE 3-29   DIMM Sockets Surrounded and Covered Up by Power and Data Cables or Aftermarket CPU Fans and Heat Sinks, Making It Difficult to Properly Install Additional Memory

Installing Storage Devices

220-1001: Objective 3.4: Given a scenario, select, install, and configure storage devices.

Many ways to store computer data are discussed throughout this book. In this section the focus is on hardware storage attached to the computer—specifically optical storage, magnetic storage, and flash memory. Each type can be a viable solution for a storage problem, and you should be able to discuss the differences between them.

Optical Drives

Optical drives fall into three major categories:

- Those based on CD technology, including *CD-ROM*, CD-R (recordable CD), and *CD-RW* (rewritable CD)

- Those based on DVD technology, including *DVD-ROM*, DVD-ROM/ CD-RW combo, DVD-ROM/*DVD-RW/DVD-RW DL*, DVD-RAM, DVD-R/RW, DVD+R/RW, DVD±R/RW, and DVD±R/RW DL

- Those based on *Blu-ray* technology, including BD-ROM, Combo BD-ROM/ DVD Super Multi, *BD-R*, and *BD-RE*

All three types of drives store data in a continuous spiral of indentations called *pits* and *lands* that are burned into the non-label side of the disc from the middle outward to the edge. All these drives use a laser to read the data.

The difference between the storage capacities of Blu-ray, DVD, and CD is due to the differences in laser wavelengths. The shorter the wavelength, the smaller the pits and lands on the disc—and shorter wavelengths enable more data to be stored in the same space. Each type has a different capacity:

- Blu-ray, which has the highest capacity, uses a blue laser with a shorter wavelength than DVD or CD.

- DVD uses a red laser with a longer wavelength than Blu-ray but shorter than that of CD.

- CD, which has the lowest capacity, uses a near-infrared laser with the longest wavelength.

Most CD, DVD, and Blu-ray drives are tray-loading, but some use a slot-loading design (especially in home and automotive electronics products).

CD-ROM/CD-RW

CD-R and CD-RW drives use special media types and a more powerful laser than that used on CD-ROM drives to write data to the media. CD-R media is a "write-once" media; that is, the media can be written to during multiple sessions, but older data cannot be deleted. CD-RW media can be rewritten up to 1,000 times. 80-minute CD-R media has a capacity of 700MB, whereas the older 74-minute CD-R media has a capacity of 650MB. CD-RW media capacity is up to 700MB but is often less, depending on how the media is formatted. CD-RW media is available in four types:

- CD-RW 1x–4x

- High-speed CD-RW 4x–12x

- Ultra-speed CD-RW 12x–24x

- Ultra-speed+ CD-RW 32x

Drives compatible with faster media types can usually work with slower media types but not the other way around.

DVD Recordable and Rewritable Standards

DVD-R and DVD+R media is recordable but not erasable, whereas DVD-RW and DVD+RW media uses a phase-change medium similar to CD-RW and can be rewritten up to 1,000 times.

Here's more about the many members of the DVD family:

- **DVD-R:** A single-sided, single-layer, writable/nonerasable media similar to CD-R; capacity of 4.7GB. Some DVD-RAM and all DVD-RW drives can use DVD-R media.

- **DVD-R DL:** A single-side writable/nonerasable media similar to CD-R but with a second recording layer; capacity of 8.4GB.

- **DVD-RW:** A single-sided rewritable/erasable media similar to CD-RW; capacity of 4.7GB. DVD-RW drives can also write to DVD-R media.

- **DVD+RW:** A rewritable/erasable media. Also similar to CD-RW but not interchangeable with DVD-RW or DVD-RAM; capacity of 4.7GB.

- **DVD+R:** A single-side, single-layer writable/nonerasable media. Also similar to CD-R but not interchangeable with DVD-R; capacity of 4.7GB.

- **DVD+R DL:** A writable/nonerasable media with a second recording layer. Also similar to CD-R but not interchangeable with DVD-R DL; capacity of 8.4GB.

SuperMulti DVD drives can read and write all types of DVD media as well as CD media. Sometimes these drives are also referred to as DVD±R/RW. Some early DVD+R/RW and DVD-R/RW drives cannot write to DL media.

> **NOTE** The CompTIA A+ 220-1001 exam objectives erroneously refer to DVD-RW DL, which is a media type that does not exist. Only recordable DVD media is dual layer.

Blu-ray (BD)

Blu-ray disc (BD) technology is an enhancement of the DVD technology that offers greater storage capacity. It was developed by a consortium of electronics companies. BD drives are compatible with BD-ROM (read-only Blu-ray media), such as the media used for Blu-ray movies. To play back Blu-ray movies, you must have a compatible player app installed. Standard-capacity BD media types include:

- **BD-R:** Recordable, not erasable; similar to CD-R, DVD+R, DVD-R; 25GB capacity.

- **BD-R DL:** Dual-layer recordable media; similar to DVD+R DL, DVD-RW DL. 50GB capacity.

- **BD-RE:** Recordable and rewritable; similar to CD-RW, DVD-RW, DVD+RW. 25GB capacity.

- **BDXL:** BDXL drives and media represent a large jump in capacity over standard BD drives and media. The BDXL specification was released in April 2010. It supports multilayer 100GB and 128GB recordable media (BD-R 3.0) and multi-layer 100GB rewritable media (BD-RE Revision 4.0). Many, but not all, BD-RE compatible drives are compatible with BDXL standards. Check the drive's specifications to determine compatibility.

Drive Speed Ratings

Drive speeds are measured by an X-rating:

- **CD media:** 1X equals 150KBps, the data transfer rate used for reading music CDs. Multiply the X-rating by 150 to determine the drive's data rate for reading, writing, or rewriting CD media.

- **DVD media:** 1X equals 1.385MBps; this is the data transfer rate used for playing DVD-Video (DVD movies) content. Multiply the X-rating by 1.385 to determine the drive's data rate for reading, writing, or rewriting DVD media.

- **Blu-ray (BD) media:** 1X equals 4.5MBps; this is the data transfer rate for playing Blu-ray movies. Multiply the X-rating by 4.5 to determine the drive's data rate for reading, writing, or rewriting Blu-ray media.

Note that Blu-ray drives are also compatible with CD and DVD media. Check the specifications for a particular drive to determine the specific types of media it supports and the maximum read/write/rewrite speeds for each media type.

Recording Files to Optical Discs

You can use the following methods to record files onto optical discs:

- Built-in recording features in Windows or other operating systems
- Third-party disc mastering programs
- Third-party drag-and-drop programs

All optical media must be formatted, but depending on how you write to the media, the formatting process might be incorporated into the writing process or might require a separate step. Due to digital rights management, there are significant differences between Windows 8 and 10 when it comes to writing copyright-protected files. Third-party software, such as VLC, is commonly used to play and manage media.

Hard Drives

Hard drives are the most important storage devices used by personal computers. A hard drive stores the operating system (Windows, macOS, Linux, or others) and loads it into the computer's memory (RAM) at startup. Hard drives also store applications, system configuration files used by applications and the operating system, and data files created by the user.

Hard disk drives (HDDs) have traditionally been magnetic drives, but in recent years solid-state drives (SDDs) and hybrid magnetic/SSD (SSHDs) have become viable options for storage. These are discussed in the sections that follow.

Solid-State Drive (SSD)

An *SSD* is a flash memory drive with no moving parts. Because the drive does not spin to retrieve data, it is much faster than a magnetic hard drive for storing and retrieving data. SSD is currently more expensive with less capacity than HDD, but SSD capacity is improving, and costs are dropping.

A typical SSD (see Figure 3-30) has a 2.5-inch form factor, but an optional 2.5-inch to 3.5-inch adapter enables it to be installed in desktop computers that lack 2.5-inch drive bays. While SSDs placed in drive bays are faster, they still connect via the hard drive cables to connect to the motherboard.

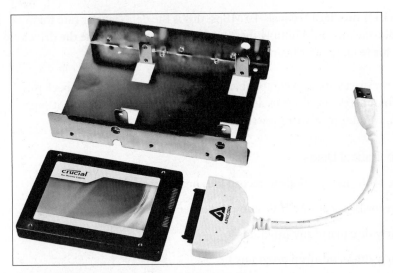

FIGURE 3-30   An SSD with Optional Data Transfer Cable and 2.5-inch to 3.5-inch Bay Adapter

A common upgrade to improve speed and capacity to a computer is to install an SSD to replace an older, slower, and smaller HDD. Since only newer motherboards and chipsets support M.2 drives, adapting an SSD into a desktop is a common solution. (A good time to do this is when upgrading to Windows 10, since loading the OS on the SSD makes the booting and updating processes much faster and avoids a cloning process to migrate the OS to the new drive.) Having the OS image copied to a USB flash drive makes installation easy.

While M.2 SSDs are currently more expensive, they have the potential to be both faster and lighter than standard SSDs. It is possible, depending on the motherboard and operating system, to upgrade to either an SSD or an M.2 SSD (pictured later in this section, in Figure 3-32). The M.2 SSD requires an available PCIe slot. If the motherboard does not have a PCIe slot, a PCIe adapter can be purchased to enable the drive. In BIOS, the M.2 drive can be enabled by locating the drive in the PCI drive settings.

The steps that follow describe how to install an SSD in a desktop with a new OS image:

Step 1.   Be sure the desktop has room for another drive, a bay to hold the drive and a SATA connection on the motherboard, and a Molex cable to power the SSD. If replacing the hard drive, back up files first. Follow the safety procedures outlined in Chapter 9.

Step 2.   Gather a new SSD, adapter bracket and, if necessary, SATA cable. The bracket screws are very small, so be sure to also have a quality small Phillips screwdriver. Follow the instructions to mount the SSD into the bracket.

Step 3.   Mount the bracket into the spare drive bay. Attach the SATA cable from the SSD to the motherboard. Attach the Molex power connector to power the drive. Tuck the cables away, close up the box, and reconnect the external power.

Step 4.   Boot the computer and enter the BIOS to set the boot drive to the USB flash with the new OS. If installing Windows 10, when you see the prompt for choosing which drive for the installation, choose the new SSD drive. Let the install run.

Step 5.   Upon reboot, enter the BIOS and set the boot order to boot from the new SSD with the OS.

To perform this process in a laptop, a visit to the manufacturer support page may be necessary to determine the best method to access the hard drive. The process is mostly the same but on a smaller scale. Laptops do not have room for additional drives, so backing up to an external drive will be necessary. Figure 3-31 depicts the tight workspace encountered when removing a hard drive from a laptop.

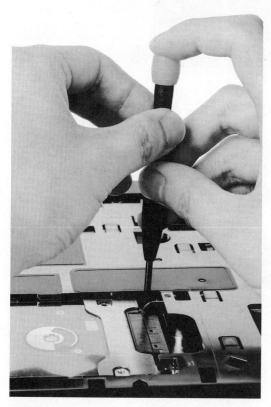

FIGURE 3-31   Laptop HD Removal (Image © JIPEN, Shutterstock)

SSDs are also available in these form factors:

- **mSATA (miniPCIe form factor):** Used by some high-performance laptops and desktops.

- **M.2 (smaller than miniPCIe; pronounced "M-dot-2"):** Faster than mSATA; used in some of the high-performance desktops and laptops but increasingly popular as prices drop. Needs a specific form factor as it attaches directly to the motherboard.

- **PCIe card:** For high-performance desktops. This is a way for SSDs to access the CPU by directly attaching to the motherboard and bypassing the traditional hard drive infrastructure.

Figure 3-32 depicts an M2 card, and Figure 3-33 illustrates an M.2 card installed in a high-performance desktop computer.

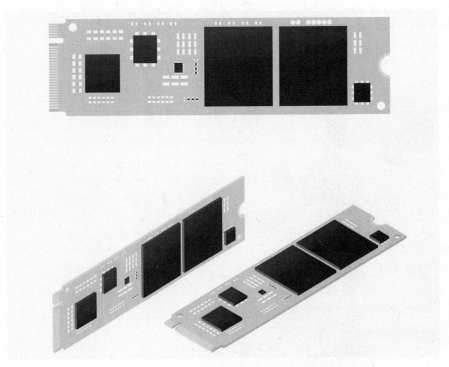

FIGURE 3-32   An M.2 SSD (Image © Andrush, Shutterstock)

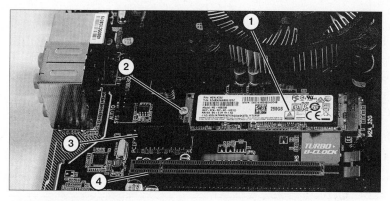

1. M.2 SSD installed in slot
2. Retaining screw for M.2 SSD
3. PCIe x1 slot (for comparison)
4. PCIe x16 slot (for comparison)

FIGURE 3-33   An M.2 SSD Installed in a High-Performance Desktop Computer

SSDs use one of two types of flash memory: multilevel cell (**MLC**) or single-level cell (**SLC**). MLC memory has lower performance than SLC and doesn't support as many write cycles, but it is much less expensive per gigabyte than SLC memory. Almost all SSDs sold in the consumer space use MLC flash memory. The differences in performance for similarly sized drives are based on the controller used, the firmware version in use, and whether the drive uses separate memory for caching or uses a portion of the SSD.

Although SSDs emulate hard disks, there are differences in their operation. Because unnecessary writing to flash memory causes premature failure, SSDs should not be defragmented, and newer SSDs use a feature known as TRIM to automatically deallocate space used by deleted files and make it available for reuse. TRIM is supported by Windows 8/8.1/10, but older SSDs require you to use vendor-supplied utilities to perform this task.

When Windows 8/8.1/10 detects an SSD, it enables TRIM (if the drive supports this command), disables defragment, and disables other utilities, such as SuperFetch and ReadyBoost, that are designed for use with traditional hard disks.

M.2 Drives

M.2 (pronounced "M-dot-2") is an SSD that can mount directly onto the motherboard or an expansion card, giving the drive more direct access to the CPU for much faster reading than is possible with an SSD. An M.2 has an appearance closer to that of a RAM chip than to that of a standard hard drive.

A motherboard must be specifically designed to accept an M.2 SSD, so M.2s are not a likely option for a legacy system.

SSHD

A solid-state hybrid drive (SSHD) combines a solid-state cache with magnetic capacity. It uses a memory manager to choose the most common files for the fast cache. An SSHD can be a good choice if improved performance and high capacity are desired but the cost of large SSDs is prohibitive, especially in laptops, which lack the capacity for multiple drives.

Table 3-9 highlights the differences among the three types of hard drives.

Table 3-9   Comparison of the Three Hard Drive Types

Type	Cost	Capacity	Speed	Reliability
HDD	Least expensive and readily available	Highest	Slowest due to moving parts and magnetic storage	Moving parts that can wear over time
SSD	Most expensive but price is dropping	Lowest but improving	Fastest	Solid state; no moving parts
SSHD	Midrange	Blends high HDD capacity with fast SSD cache for most used files	Blends fast solid-state cache with slower magnetic storage	Moving parts that can wear out but spins less than HDD

NVMe

One of the big reasons SSD is faster than HDD is the lack of moving parts. But this benefit created another problem: With all the available capacity to access data, the SSDs still had to funnel all the data through communication infrastructure designed for much slower HDDs. To solve this problem, a consortium of electronics companies put their resources together to develop *Non-Volatile Memory Express (NVMe)*. NVMe is a protocol designed to allow SSDs to transfer data between the motherboard and the SSD at staggeringly higher rates. It involved redesigning the command queueing method AHCI to create NVMe.

NVMe is not a physical form factor like M.2, nor is it an interface like PCIe; in fact, both of these can use NVMe. It is a protocol (or set of communication rules) that allows SSD data to bypass the bottleneck that happens with HDD infrastructure. The older protocol Advanced Host Controller Interface (AHCI) uses a process called *command queuing* to send requested data to the controller and motherboard. It is capable of handling one command queue with 32 commands at a time. NVMe, in contrast, can process more than 65,000 queues at one time, with each queue containing up to 65,000 commands. Needless to say, such data rates are having a huge impact on the kinds of applications being designed.

For NVMe to work, the computer's BIOS/UEFI and hardware needs to be designed for the high traffic, so only newer computers can physically support NVMe. On the software side, NVMe is supported by Windows, macOS, Linux, and Chrome.

SATA 2.5

SATA 2.5 refers to an HDD with 2.5-inch form factor. These are usually found in laptops, and larger 3.5-inch HDDs are found in desktops. The 2.5 inches refers to the size of the spinning platters inside the HDDs. They are connected to the motherboard with a SATA cable internally.

Magnetic Hard Disk Drives

Traditional hard disk drives use one or more double-sided platters formed from rigid materials such as aluminum or glass. These platters are coated with a durable magnetic surface divided into sectors. Each sector contains 512 bytes of storage, along with information about where the sector is located on the disk medium. Sectors are organized in concentric circles from the edge of the media inward toward the middle of the platter. These concentric circles are called *tracks*.

Hard disk drives are found in many desktop PCs, and many newer PC systems and most newer mobile computers typically use some form of SSD.

External drives typically include SATA hard disks with a bridge controller for use with USB 2.0 or USB 3.0 ports. Drives made for macOS include USB or Thunderbolt ports. Some external drives can also connect to eSATA ports. External drives that use 3.5-inch desktop hard disks require AC power, but most external drives that use 2.5-inch or smaller mobile hard disks can be bus powered, receiving power from the USB port on the host computer.

Spin Rate

The speed at which hard disk media turns, its ***spin rate***, is measured in revolutions per minute (rpm). Low-performance hard disks typically spin at 5400rpm. Mid-performance drives spin at 7200rpm. High-performance desktop drives spin at 10000rpm. Drives designed for use in enterprise computing, such as servers, spin at rates up to 15000rpm.

NOTE   It is generally felt that the 15000rpm drives are being built mostly for existing system replacements as their speed comes with higher power use. SSDs are leaping forward in speed and capacity with a fraction of the energy use of the 15000rpm drives.

Table 3-10 is a quick-reference table of hard disk spin rates with examples.

Table 3-10   Hard Disk Spin Rate Comparison

Spin Rate (RPM)	Typical Use	Desktop Drive Example	Laptop Drive Example
5400	"Green" power-saving drives	WD Blue Seagate 4TB Desktop HDD*	WD Blue Seagate Laptop HDD
7200	Midrange performance	WD Black Seagate Barracuda	WD Black Seagate Laptop Thin
10000	High performance	WD VelociRaptor	—
15000	Servers and enterprise	Servers	—

* Actual spindle speed 5900RPM

Form Factors

Internal hard disk drives for desktop computers use 3.5-inch form factors. Their capacities range up to 8TB, but most installed desktop drives in recent systems have capacities ranging from 500GB to 2TB.

Internal hard disk drives or SSDs for laptop computers use the SATA 2.5-inch form factors. Their capacity ranges up to 3TB, but most laptop drives in recent systems have capacities ranging from 500GB to 1TB.

Figure 3-34 compares front and rear views of a DVD drive, 3.5-inch desktop hard disk, SATA 2.5-inch laptop hard disk, and 2.5-inch laptop SSD.

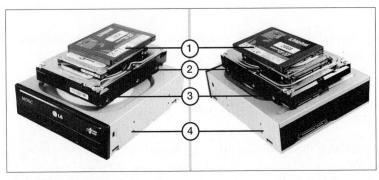

1. 2.5-inch laptop SSD
2. 2.5-inch laptop hard disk
3. 3.5-inch desktop hard disk
4. 5-25-inch DVD rewriteable drive

FIGURE 3-34   Front (Left) and Rear (Right) Internal Optical, Desktop and Mobile Internal Hard Disks, and Mobile Internal SSD Drives

Cache Sizes and Performance

Aside from interface type and spin rate, another influence on hard disk performance is the drive's cache size. In a hard disk, the cache is used to hold recently read information for reuse. Just as with processor cache memory, which often enables the CPU to read cache memory instead of slower main memory to reuse previously read information, hard disks with larger buffers can reread recently transferred information more quickly from cache than from the drive's magnetic storage.

In general, high-performance drives have larger caches than lower-performance drives. The larger-capacity drives in any given series typically have larger caches than the smallest-capacity drives in the same drive series.

Hybrid Drives

A *Hybrid drive* combines a standard SATA hard disk with up to 8GB of the same type of solid-state (SS) memory used in SSDs. The SATA hard disk is used for most of the storage, but the recent files are kept in the SS cache for fast access. Just as in SSD drives, the SS memory provides much faster data access than do purely mechanical hard disk drives. Consequently, when information needed by the CPU is available in the hybrid drive's flash memory, it is read from that memory, which boosts performance. Hybrid hard disk (also known as SSHD) drives are available in both 3.5-inch and 2.5-inch form factors. SSHDs are the middle ground in terms of cost and performance between HDDs and SSDs. Refer to Table 3-9 to review how SSHD compares to other drive types.

Flash Drives

Flash memory is a type of memory that can retain its contents without electricity. It has no moving parts, so it is very durable. Standard flash memory is used in digital media players, memory cards for cameras and digital media devices, digital camcorders, and USB thumb drives.

SSDs and flash drives are related, but they are not the same. SSD means *solid-state drive*, which defines the drive as having no moving parts. Flash is a type of memory that SSDs currently use. SSD flash also operates at a much higher level than the flash drives discussed here. (Refer to the earlier section "Solid-State Drive (SSD)" for information on SLC and MLC.)

Figure 3-35 illustrates the most common types of flash memory cards.

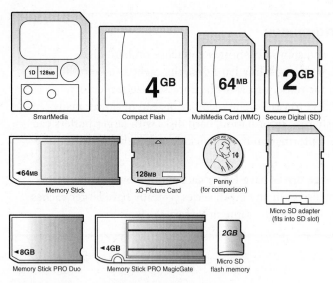

FIGURE 3-35   Common Flash Memory Card Types

Table 3-11 describes the most common types of flash memory.

Table 3-11   Flash Memory Card Capacities and Uses

Media Category	Common Capacity	Common Uses	Notes
SmartMedia (SM)	Up to 128MB	Digital cameras	Now obsolete. Replaced by xD-Picture Card.
CompactFlash (CF)*	Up to 512GB	Professional Digital SLR cameras	Check manufacturer's speed rating for best performance in burst mode.
MultiMedia Card (MMC)	Up to 4GB	Various devices	Obsolete. Replaced by SD, SDHC, and SDXC.
Memory Stick	Up to 128MB	Older Sony point-and-shoot digital cameras and digital media devices; also PlayStation 3 (PS3)	Obsolete. Replaced by SD, SDHC, and SDXC.
Memory Stick PRO MagicGate	Up to 4GB	Older Sony point-and-shoot digital cameras and digital media devices, including PlayStation Portable (PSP) and PS3	Obsolete. Replaced by SD, SDHC, and SDXC.
Memory Stick PRO Duo	Up to 32GB**	Older Sony point-and-shoot digital cameras and camcorders, and digital media devices, including PSP and PS3 (but not PS4)	Obsolete. Replaced by SD, SDHC, and SDXC.

Media Category	Common Capacity	Common Uses	Notes
Secure Digital (SD)*	Up to 2GB	Most models of point-and-shoot digital cameras; some digital SLR cameras; many flash memory–based media players	Has write-protect switch on left side of media. Can also be used in place of SDHC or SDXC memory.
Secure Digital High Capacity (SDHC)	4GB to 32GB	Many models of point-and-shoot digital cameras, digital SLR cameras, and flash memory–based media players	SDHC media has the same physical form factor as SD; however, only devices made for SDHC can use SDHC. These devices are also compatible with SD. Check with device vendor for details.
Secure Digital Extended Capacity (SDXC)	64GB to 512GB	Some high-performance digital SLR cameras	SDXC media has the same physical form factor as SD and SDHC; however, only devices made for SDXC media can use it.
miniSD*	2GB	Mobile phones and cameras	Obsolete. Replaced by microSD. Can be used in SD or SDHC slots with an optional adapter.
miniSDHC	32GB	Mobile phones and cameras	Obsolete. Replaced by microSDHC. Can be used in SDHC slots with an optional adapter.
microSD*	2GB	Various portable devices: smartphones, video games, and expandable USB flash memory drives	Can also be used in place of microSDHC; can be used in SD or SDHC slots with an optional adapter.
microSDHC	32GB	Various portable devices: smartphones, video games, and expandable USB flash memory drives	Device must support microSDHC; can be used in SDHC slots with an optional adapter.
xD-Picture Card*	Up to 512MB (standard) Up to 2GB (Type M, Type M+, Type H)	Older Fujifilm and Olympus digital point-and-shoot cameras	Obsolete. Replaced by SD Card. Some cameras also support SD Card.

* This type of memory is noted in the CompTIA A+ 220-1001 objectives.

** Original version up to 8GB; Mark 2 version up to 32GB.

Flash Card Reader

A card reader enables flash memory cards to be used with a computer. Figure 3-36 shows a typical external multi-slot card reader, and Figure 3-37 shows a typical internal multi-slot card reader. Most card readers assign a separate drive letter to each slot.

NOTE Do not confuse flash card readers with smart card readers. Smart card readers are used as part of a security system to read ID cards with embedded security.

1. SDHC card inserted into card reader

FIGURE 3-36 An External Multi-Slot Card Reader That Supports a Wide Variety of Flash Memory Cards and Connects to a USB 3.0 Port

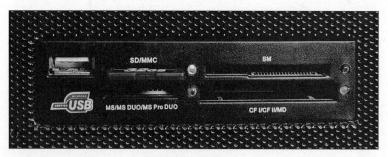

FIGURE 3-37 An Internal Card Reader That Connects to an Unused USB 2.0 Port Header on the Motherboard

NOTE   Some printers and multifunction devices also include card readers. Some card readers built into printers and multifunction devices are used only for printing, whereas others can be used to transfer files to and from the host computer.

When you insert a flash memory card containing files in Windows 10, Windows might display a simplified AutoPlay dialog (see Figure 3-38). If AutoPlay does not appear, open Computer, This PC, Windows Explorer, or File Explorer and navigate to the appropriate drive letter to use the files on the card.

FIGURE 3-38   A Typical AutoPlay Menu Displayed by Windows 10 When a Flash Memory Card Containing Files Is Inserted into a Card Reader

Storage Device Configurations

When adding or replacing a storage drive, it is necessary to optimize it for its intended purpose. A common reason for adding storage is to create a fault-tolerant set of drives that will protect data in case a drive fails. This section details the process of building data security into a system using RAID and hot-swappable drives.

RAID Types

Redundant array of independent (or inexpensive) disks (**RAID**) is a method for creating a faster or safer single logical hard disk drive from two or more physical drives. The most common RAID levels include:

- **RAID Level 0 (RAID 0):** Two drives are treated as a single drive, and both drives are used to simultaneously store different portions of the same file. This method of data storage is called **striping**. Striping boosts performance, but if either drive fails, all data is lost. Don't use striping for data drives.

- **RAID Level 1 (RAID 1):** Two drives are treated as mirrors of each other, and changes to the contents of one drive are immediately reflected on the other drive. This method of data storage is called *mirroring*. Mirroring provides a built-in backup method and provides faster read performance than a single drive. Suitable for use with program and data drives.

- **RAID Level 5 (RAID 5):** Three or more drives are treated as a logical array, and parity information (used to recover data in the event of a drive failure) is spread across all drives in the array. Suitable for use with program and data drives.

- **RAID Level 1+0 (RAID 10):** Four drives combine striping plus mirroring for extra speed plus better reliability. Suitable for use with program and data drives. RAID 10 is a striped set of mirrors.

Most PCs with RAID support include support for Levels 0, 1, and 10. Some high-performance desktop systems also support RAID 5. Systems that lack the desired level of RAID support can use a RAID add-on card. Table 3-12 provides a quick comparison of these types of RAID arrays.

Table 3-12   Comparisons of Common RAID Levels

RAID Level	Minimum Number of Drives Required	Data Protection Features	Total Capacity of Array	Major Benefit over Single Drive	Notes
0	2	None.	2 × capacity of either drive (if same size) OR 2 × capacity of smaller drive.	Improved read/write performance	Also called *striping*
1	2	Changes to contents of one drive immediately performed on other drive.	Capacity of one drive (if same size) OR capacity of smaller drive.	Automatic backup; faster read performance	Also called *mirroring*
5	3	Parity information is saved across all drives.	Capacity of smallest drive (where x equals the number of drives in the array).	Full data redundancy in all drives; hot swap of damaged drive supported in most implementations	
10	4	Changes on one two-drive array are immediately performed on the other two-drive array.	Capacity of smallest drive × number of drives / 2.	Improved read/write performance and automatic backup	Also called *striped and mirrored*

Creating a SATA RAID Array

The advent of SSDs has disrupted the normal acceptance of RAID as the most reliable backup method, but RAID is still in widespread use, and you should know about it. Many argue that because SSDs are several times more reliable than HDDs that the use of an SSD with an HDD backup may be the more reliable and cost-effective option. This thinking will likely change again as SSD prices continue to fall while capacity improves.

That said, here are the basics of setting up RAID on a PC.

Many recent desktop systems include SATA RAID host adapters on the motherboard. SATA RAID host adapter cards can also be retrofitted to systems lacking onboard RAID support. These types of RAID arrays are also referred to as *hardware RAID arrays*. RAID arrays can also be created through operating system settings and are sometimes called *software RAID arrays*. However, software RAID arrays are not as fast as hardware RAID arrays.

Motherboards that support only two drives in a RAID array support only RAID 0 and RAID 1. Motherboards that support more than two drives can also support RAID Level 1+0 (also known as RAID 10), and some support RAID 5 as well. RAID-enabled host adapters support varying levels of RAID.

NOTE   A nonstandard definition of "RAID 10" was created for the Linux MD driver; Linux "RAID 10" can be implemented with as few as two disks. Implementations supporting two disks, such as Linux RAID 10, offer a choice of layouts. Arrays of more than four disks are also possible.

A SATA RAID array requires:

- **Two or more drives:** It's best to use identical drives (same capacity, buffer size, and RPMs). However, you can mix and match drives. If some drives are larger than others, the additional capacity will be ignored. You can use standard hard disk drives, hybrid hard disks, or SSDs.

- **A RAID-compatible motherboard or add-on host adapter card:** Both feature firmware supporting RAID.

Because RAID arrays typically involve off-the-shelf drives, the only difference in the physical installation of drives in a RAID array is where they are connected. They must be connected to a motherboard or an add-on card that has RAID support.

NOTE   Sometimes RAID connectors are made from a different color of plastic than other drive connectors. However, the best way to determine whether a system or motherboard supports SATA RAID arrays is to read the manual for the system or motherboard.

After the drives used to create the array are connected to the RAID array's host adapter, restart the computer. If you are using the motherboard's RAID interface, start the system BIOS setup program and make sure the RAID function is enabled (see Figure 3-39). Save changes and exit the BIOS/UEFI setup program.

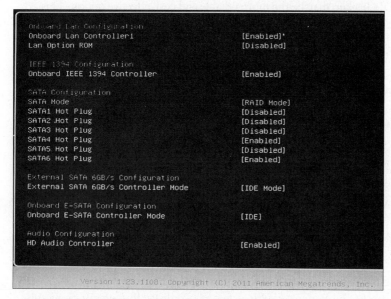

FIGURE 3-39   Enabling SATA RAID in a Typical System BIOS

When you restart the computer, watch for a prompt from the RAID BIOS to start the configuration process (see Figure 3-40).

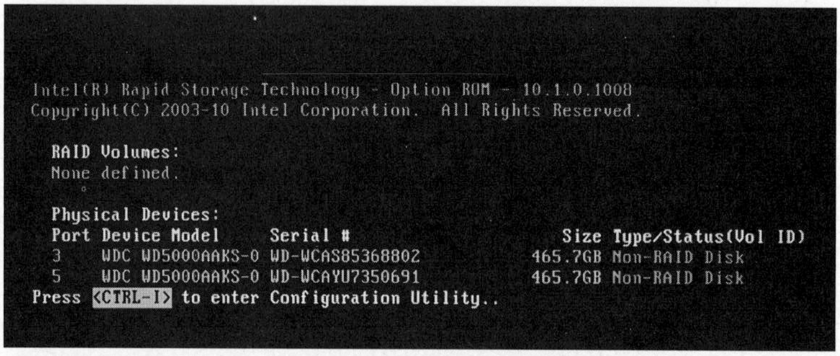

FIGURE 3-40   A Typical Prompt to Start RAID Array Setup

Specify the RAID setting wanted and any optional settings you want to use (see Figure 3-41). After the RAID array is configured, the system handles the drives as a single physical drive. If drivers for the array are not already installed, you need to install them when prompted by the computer. For Windows, you can provide driver files via USB or on optical discs, if necessary.

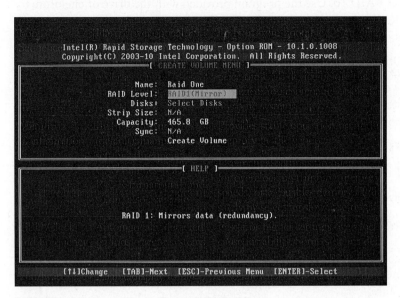

FIGURE 3-41   Preparing to Create a RAID 1 Array

CAUTION   If one or more of the drives to be used in the array already contains data, back up the drives before starting the configuration process! Most RAID array host adapters delete the data on all drives in the array when creating an array—sometimes with little warning.

If you do not have RAID adapters in a system, you can create a software RAID volume, also known as a *disk array*, by using Windows.

NOTE   Some hard disk drive vendors now produce drives especially made for SOHO RAID arrays of eight or fewer drives. Compared to normal SATA hard disk drives, RAID-optimized drives (also known as NAS drives) typically include features such as vibration reduction, optimization for streaming, disabled head parking, intelligent recovery from errors, and longer warranties.

To add a RAID array to a laptop, convertible (two-in-one), or all-in-one PC, use an external RAID drive or drive enclosure that connects to a USB 3.0 (or greater),

Thunderbolt, or eSATA port. An external RAID drive contains two hard disks that can be configured as RAID 0 or RAID 1. Enclosures with support for three or more drives can also be configured as RAID 5. Enclosures with support for four drives can be configured as RAID 10. Use the program provided with the drive or enclosure to configure the RAID array.

Hot-Swappable Drives

Hot-swappable drives are drives that can be safely removed from a system or connected to a system without shutting down the system. In Windows, the following drives can be hot swapped:

- USB drives
- eSATA drives
- SATA drives
- Flash memory drives

NOTE   eSATA and SATA drives must be configured as AHCI in the system BIOS/UEFI firmware.

In most enterprise systems, the RAID drives are hot swappable.

Safely Ejecting a Drive in Windows

To safely eject a hot-swappable drive from a Windows system, follow these steps (see Figure 3-42):

Step 1.   Open the Eject/Safely Remove Hardware and Eject Media icon in the notification area. If the icon is not visible, click the up arrow to display hidden icons.

Step 2.   Select the drive to eject from the menu.

Step 3.   When the Safe to Remove Hardware message appears, disconnect the drive.

Click or tap the up arrow to   Click or tap the drive to eject.   When this message appears, it is
display icons and then   safe to eject the drive
click or tap the Eject icon.

FIGURE 3-42   Safely Ejecting a Hot-Swappable Drive from a System Running Windows 10

If the drive is still in use, a Problem Ejecting *type* Storage Device dialog appears, informing you that the drive is in use. Click **OK**, make sure no apps or processes are using the drive, and then try the process again.

Safely Ejecting a USB Drive in macOS

To safely eject a USB drive in macOS, follow these steps:

Step 1.   Open Finder.

Step 2.   Click the up arrow next to the USB drive icon in the left pane.

Step 3.   When the drive icon is removed from the left pane of Finder, disconnect the drive (see Figure 3-43).

1. Click to open Finder
2. Click to eject USB drive

FIGURE 3-43   Safely Ejecting a Hot-Swappable Drive from a macOS System

Safely Ejecting a USB Drive in Linux

Some Linux distributions include support for safely ejecting a USB drive. However, the terminal commands **df** can be used to list mounted devices. If the USB drive is not listed as mounted, it can be removed immediately. If the USB drive is listed as mounted, you can use the following command:

sudo unmount /dev/*sdb1* (where *sbd1* is the mounted USB drive)

When the drive access light goes out, disconnect the drive.

Installing Motherboards, CPUs, and Add-on Cards

220-1001: Objective 3.5: Given a scenario, install and configure motherboards, CPUs, and add-on cards.

Everything on a computer connects to the motherboard, where the CPU—the brains of a computer—resides. With so many different uses of computers, it follows that there are many different designs for how parts and devices attach to the motherboard to access the CPU. The A+ objectives cover the form factors that you will most likely encounter at some point as a technician.

Motherboard Form Factor: ATX, ITX, and Smaller Sizes

Form factor refers to the size, shape, and other specifications of a motherboard. These other specifications can include the location of the mounting holes, type of power supply, external ports, and so on. Computer chassis are designed to accommodate specific form factors, and knowing these common standard form factors is essential for an A+ technician:

- ATX (Advanced Technology eXtended)
- mATX (microATX)
- ITX (Information Technology Extended)
- mITX (Mini-ITX)

ATX and mATX

The *ATX* family of motherboards has dominated desktop computer designs since the late 1990s. An ATX motherboard has the following characteristics:

- A rear port cluster for I/O ports

- Expansion slots that run parallel to the short side of the motherboard

- Left-side case opening (as viewed from the front of a tower PC)

There are three members of the ATX family, as listed in Table 3-13. In practice, though, the mITX design is not widely used.

Table 3-13 ATX Motherboard Family Comparison

Motherboard Type	Maximum Width	Maximum Depth	Maximum Number of Expansion Slots	Typical Uses
ATX	12 in. (30.5 cm)	9.6 in. (24.4 cm)	7	Full tower
mATX	9.6 in. (24.4 cm)	9.6 in. (24.4 cm)	4	Mini tower
mITX	6.7 in. (70 cm)	6.7 in. (70 cm)	1	Mini tower

Figure 3-44 illustrates the dimensions of ATX, mATX, and mITX motherboards.

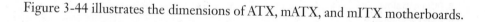

NOTE mATX and ATX have matching mounting holes, and an mATX can usually be placed in an ATX case. Similarly, mITX boards can usually mount in ATX cases.

NOTE ITX is a family of form factors including mITX and smaller versions used in tablets and mobile devices. mITX is the only ITX that is designed for a desktop.

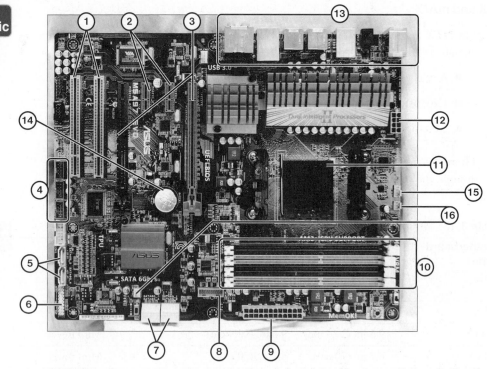

1. PCI slots
2. PCIe x1 slots
3. PCIe x16 slots
4. USB Port headers
5. SATA ports
6. Front-panel cable headers
7. Front-facing SATA ports
8. USB 3.0 header
9. ATX 24-pin power connector
10. DDR3 memory slots (dual-channel)
11. CPU socket
12. EPS12V power connector
13. Port cluster
14. CMOS battery (CR2032)
15. CPU fan header
16. Case fan header

FIGURE 3-44   A Typical Late-Model ATX Motherboard

Figure 3-45 illustrates a typical microATX (*mATX*) motherboard.

Key
Topic

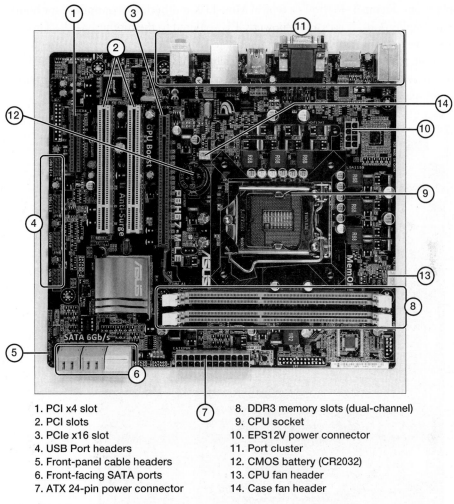

1. PCI x4 slot
2. PCI slots
3. PCIe x16 slot
4. USB Port headers
5. Front-panel cable headers
6. Front-facing SATA ports
7. ATX 24-pin power connector

8. DDR3 memory slots (dual-channel)
9. CPU socket
10. EPS12V power connector
11. Port cluster
12. CMOS battery (CR2032)
13. CPU fan header
14. Case fan header

FIGURE 3-45 A Typical Late-Model microATX (mATX) Motherboard

ITX Family

The ITX family of motherboards was originally developed by VIA Technologies in 2001 for use with its low-power x86 C3 processors. The original ITX motherboard form factor was quickly superseded by the smaller Mini-ITX form factor. Mini-ITX (*mITX*) measures 6.7×6.7 inches and has been adopted by many vendors for use with AMD and Intel processors. These processors may be socketed or soldered in place. Original designs featured a single PCI expansion slot, but most recent designs include a PCIe x1 or x16 expansion slot instead. A Mini-ITX motherboard can typically fit into a case made for ATX-family motherboards and uses a similar port cluster; however, Mini-ITX motherboards are used in small form factor PCs and in home theater applications. Figure 3-46 shows a typical Mini-ITX motherboard optimized for home theater applications. It uses a low-power CPU soldered to the motherboard, a fanless passive heatsink, and SODIMM memory to reduce heat and allow for very quiet operation. It includes a *miniPCIe* slot (normally found in laptops) for use with a WiFi card. Some Mini-ITX motherboards feature socketed processors and a PCIe x16 slot for high-performance 3D video, making them suitable for gaming.

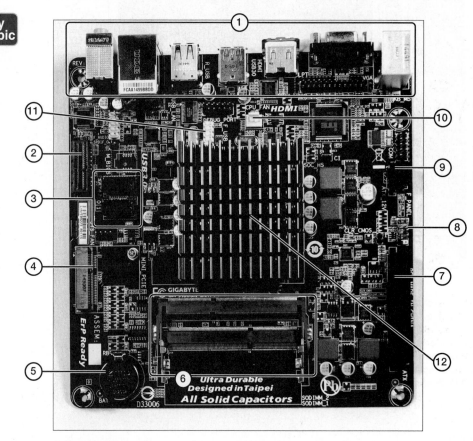

1. Port cluster
2. PCIe x1 slot
3. SATA ports
4. Mini-PCIe slot
5. CMOS battery (CR2032)
6. SO-DIMM DDR3 memory sockets
7. ATX 24-pin power connector
8. Front panel cable headers
9. ATX12V power connector
10. CPU fan header (not used with this processor)
11. USB header
12. Processor heat sink

FIGURE 3-46 A Typical Mini-ITX (mITX) Motherboard Optimized for Home Theater Applications

Comparing ATX, MicroATX, and Mini-ITX Motherboards

Figure 3-47 compares the general sizes and layouts of ATX, microATX (mATX) and Mini-ITX (mITX) motherboards.

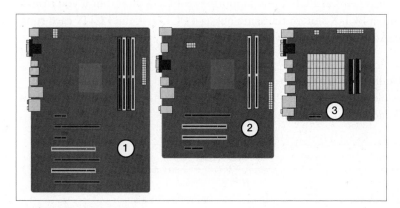

1. ATX motherboard
2. microATX motherboard
3. Mini-ITX motherboard

FIGURE 3-47   ATX, microATX, and Mini-ITX Motherboard Component Layouts Compared

Expansion Slot Types

Motherboards use *expansion slots* to provide support for additional input/output (I/O) devices and high-speed video/graphics cards. The most common expansion slots are PCI Express (also known as PCIe).

PCI Slots

A *PCI* slot (developed in 1992) mounts to the motherboard and is used for many types of add-on cards, including network, video, audio, I/O, and storage host adapters for SATA drives. There are several types of PCI slots, but the one found in desktop computers is the 32-bit slot running at 33MHz (see Figure 3-48 in the next section). PCI slots are also available in 66MHz versions and in 64-bit versions.

NOTE   Early PCI cards used 5V DC power, but virtually all 32-bit PCI cards in use for a number of years have used 3.3V DC power.

PCI-X Slots

PCI-X is a faster version of 64-bit PCI, running at speeds of 133MHz. PCI-X slots also support PCI cards. In fact, the PCI-X slot uses the same connectors as 64-bit PCI slot (see Figure 3-48). A PCI-X bus supports two PCI-X slots, but if you install a PCI-X card into a PCI-X slot on the same bus as a PCI card, the PCI-X card runs at the same speed as the PCI card. PCI-X slots are typically used in servers and workstations.

PCI-X 2.0 (introduced in 2008) also supports 266MHz and 533MHz speeds; however, both types of PCI-X have been replaced by PCIe. Figure 3-48 compares 32-bit and 64-bit PCI and PCI-X slots and card connectors.

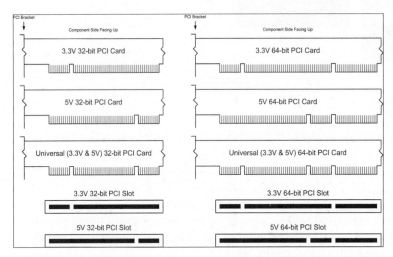

FIGURE 3-48   32-bit PCI Cards and Slots (Left) Compared to 64-bit PCI/PCI-X Cards and Slots (Right). (Image courtesy of Wikimedia Commons; see http://en.wikipedia.org/wiki/File:PCI_Keying.png for details)

PCIe (PCI Express) Slots

PCI Express (often abbreviated *PCIe* or PCIE) began to replace both PCI and Accelerated Graphics Port (AGP) slots in system designs starting in 2005. PCIe slots are available in four types:

- x1
- x4
- x8
- x16

Each x refers to an I/O lane. The most common versions include the x1, x4, and x16 designs, as shown in Figure 3-49.

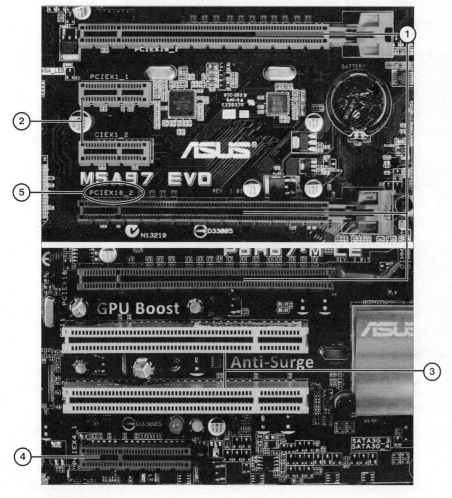

1. PCIe x16 slots
2. PCIe x1 slots
3. PCI slots
4. PCIe x4 slot
5. Slot identification

FIGURE 3-49 PCI Express Compared to PCI Slots

Some motherboards have two or more slots that use the x16 connector; however, the additional slots might actually support only x4 or x8 transfer rates (see Figure 3-50).

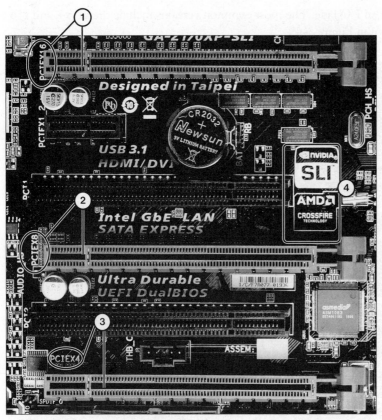

1. PCIe x16 slot
2. PCIe x16 connector, slot supports x8
3. PCIe x16 connector, slot supports x4
4. Multi-GPU (graphics processor) standards supported

FIGURE 3-50   A Motherboard Built for Multi-GPU Gaming That Has Three PCIe x16 Physical Connectors but Only One That Actually Provides x16 Speeds

PCI Express x1 and x4 slots were designed to replace the PCI slot, and x8 and x16 were designed to replace the AGP and PCI-X slots. Table 3-14 compares the performance of PCI, PCI-X, and PCIe.

Table 3-14   Technical Information About Expansion Slot Types

Slot Type	Performance	Suggested Uses
PCI 32-bit, 33MHz	133Mbps	Video, network, mass storage (SATA/RAID), sound card
PCI 32-bit, 66MHz	266Mbps	Network, mass storage (workstation and server)
PCI 64-bit, 33MHz	266Mbps	Network, mass storage (workstation and server)
PCI 64-bit, 66MHz	533Mbps	Network, mass storage (workstation and server)
PCI-X 66MHz	533Mbps	Network, mass storage (workstation and server)
PCI-X 133MHz	1.6Gbps	Network, mass storage (workstation and server)
PCI-X 2.0 266MHz	2Gbps	Network, mass storage (workstation and server)
PCI-X 2.0 533MHz	4.3Gbps	Network, mass storage (workstation and server)
PCIe x1 v1	500Mbps*	Network, I/O
PCIe x4 v1	2Gbps*	Network
PCIe x8 v1	4Gbps*	Multi-GPU (graphics processing unit) video secondary card
PCIe x16 v1	8Gbps*	Video primary and secondary cards
PCIe x1 v2	1Gbps*	Network, I/O
PCIe x4 v2	4Gbps*	Network
PCIe x8 v2	8Gbps*	Video secondary card
PCIe x16 v2	16Gbps*	Video primary and secondary cards
PCIe x1 v3	2Gbps*	Network, I/O
PCIe x4 v3	8Gbps*	Network
PCIe x8 v3	16Gbps*	Video secondary card
PCIe x16 v3	32Gbps*	Video primary and secondary cards
PCIe x32 v4	64Gbps*	Video primary and secondary cards
PCIe x	128Gbps*	Video primary and secondary cards

* Bidirectional data rates (full-duplex simultaneous send/receive); unidirectional data rates are one-half of values listed. All versions of PCIe use the same connectors.

NOTE   miniPCI and miniPCIe are reduced-size versions of the PCI and PCIe standards. They are used in laptop computers.

Riser Cards

Riser cards are used to work around limited space in some systems. Riser cards can make multiple ports available from a single slot bracket or slot, or they can enable full-size cards to be mounted horizontally in low-profile systems.

Figure 3-51 illustrates a two-slot (PCIe and PCI) riser card with cards attached.

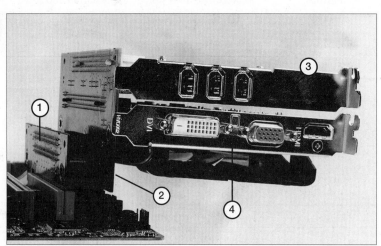

1. PCI portion of riser card
2. PCIe x16 portion of riser card
3. PCI card plugged into riser card
4. PCIe x16 plugged into riser card

FIGURE 3-51   An Example of How a Right-Angle Riser Card Enables Tall Cards to Fit in a Low-Profile Case (Such as a Small Form Factor or 1U/2U Rack-Mount Chassis)

Socket Types

Although Intel and AMD processors share two common architectures—x86 (used for 32-bit processors and for 64-bit processors running in 32-bit mode) and x64 (an extension of x86 that enables larger files, larger memory sizes, and more complex programs)—these processor families differ in many ways from each other, including:

- Different processor sockets
- Differences in multicore processor designs (Two or more processor cores help run multiple programs and programs with multiple execution threads more efficiently.)
- Cache sizes

Table 3-15 provides a quick reference to Intel and AMD sockets and processor family code names. The following sections provide additional detail.

Table 3-15 CPU Manufacturers, Sockets, and Code Names Quick Reference

CPU Manufacturer	Socket	Compatible Processor Code Name(s)
Intel	LGA 775	Prescott, Presler, Conroe, Wolfdale, Kentsfield, Yorkfield
Intel	LGA 1366	Bloomfield, Gulftown
Intel	LGA 1156	Clarkdale, Lynnfield
Intel	LGA 1155	Sandy Bridge, Ivy Bridge
Intel	LGA 1150	Haswell, Broadwell
Intel	LGA 2011	Sandy Bridge E, Ivy Bridge E
Intel	LGA 2011-v3	Haswell E
AMD	Socket AM3	Thuban, Zosma, Deneb, Propus, Heka, Rana, Callisto, Regor, Sargas
AMD	Socket AM3+	Vishera, Zembezi
AMD	Socket FM1	Llano
AMD	Socket FM2	Trinity, Richland
AMD	Socket FM2+	Kaveri
Intel	LGA 1151	Skylake, Kaby Lake, Coffee Lake
Intel	LGA 2066	Skylake-X, Kaby Lake-X
AMD	Socket AM4	Ryzen 7, 5, 3
AMD	Socket TR4	Ryzen Threadripper

Intel

Intel has used many processor sockets over the years, including the following:

- LGA 775
- LGA 1155
- LGA 1156
- LGA 1366
- LGA 1150
- LGA 2011

CAUTION   There are two versions of the LGA 2011 socket: the original LGA 2011 supports high-performance second-generation (Sandy Bridge E) and third-generation (Ivy Bridge E) Core i7 processors. LGA 2011-v3 uses the same physical layout but is compatible only with high-performance, fourth-generation Haswell E) processors. See the Intel ARK website (http://ark.intel.com) for details.

NOTE   The latest Intel desktop platform, Skylake, which uses LGA 1151, uses 100-series chipsets and supports both DDR3 and DD4 memory.

Land Grid Array Sockets

All of the Intel processor sockets listed in the previous sections use the ***Land Grid Array (LGA)*** design. The LGA design uses spring-loaded lands in the processor socket (see Figure 3-52) that connect to bumps on the backside of the processor (see Figure 3-53). The number of lands in the processor socket is used for the numeric part of the socket name. For example, LGA 775 has 775 lands in the processor socket.

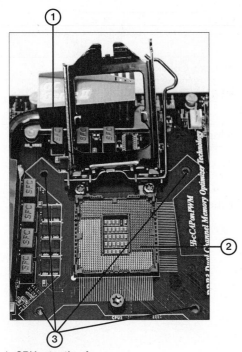

1. CPU retention frame
2. LGA1155 socket
3. Heat sink mounting holes

FIGURE 3-52   An LGA 1155 Socket Prepared for Processor Installation

1. Processor notch for assuring proper installation
2. Pin 1 triangle marking

FIGURE 3-53   The Front and Back Sides of an LGA Processor Before Installation

Processor Code Names

The code names referred to in the following sections refer to differences in the processor die design, such as the size of the processor, the location of cache memory, the type of integrated memory controller (when present), and so on. The same code name is used for a variety of processor models, which are distinguished from each other by clock speed, cache size, presence of integrated graphics, and features such as virtualization.

In Socket 775, the ranking is roughly in this order:

1. Celeron/Celeron D (slowest)
2. Pentium 4
3. Pentium D (two Pentium 4 CPUs in the same processor die)
4. Pentium 4 EE (Extreme Edition)
5. Pentium EE
6. Core 2 Duo
7. Core 2 Quad
8. Core 2 Extreme (fastest)
9. Starting with the Core i series and its offshoots, the ranking goes like this:

   1. Celeron (slowest)
   2. Pentium

3. Core i3

4. Core i5

5. Core i7 (fastest)

See the following sections for more information about multicore processors, cache sizes, and other technical differences.

NOTE   The processor information in the following tables is based on desktop processor series and is extremely simplified. Look up information for specific processor numbers and code names at the Intel ARK website (http://ark.intel.com). To learn how to decode processor model number series, see "About Intel Processor Numbers" at https://www.intel.com/content/www/us/en/processors/processor-numbers.html. Mobile processors with similar model numbers might vary in features.

LGA 775

LGA 775 replaced the older Socket 478 (though some Pentium 4 processor models were produced in versions for both sockets) and was the first Intel desktop processor socket to support 64-bit operations. Table 3-16 lists the processor code names and major features used by LGA 775 processors.

Table 3-16   LGA 775 Processor Technologies and Features

Code Name	Processor Family	Cores	Intel 64	L2 Cache	HT Tech	Intel VT-x	FSB Speed
Prescott	Pentium 4 EE	1	Yes	2MB	Yes	No	1066MHz
	Pentium 4	1	Varies	1MB–2MB	Varies	No	533MHz–800MHz
	Celeron D	1	Varies	256KB	No	No	533MHz
Presler	Pentium EE	2	Yes	4MB	Yes	No	1066MHz
	Pentium D	2	Yes	4MB	Varies	Varies	800MHz
Conroe	Core 2 Extreme	2	Yes	4MB	Yes	No	1066MHz
	Core 2 Duo	2	Yes	2MB, 4MB	Varies	Varies	800MHz–1066MHz
	Pentium	2	Yes	1MB	No	No	800MHz

Code Name	Processor Family	Cores	Intel 64	L2 Cache	HT Tech	Intel VT-x	FSB Speed
	Celeron	1, 2	Yes	512KB	No	No	533MHz–800MHz
Wolfdale	Core 2 Duo	2	Yes	3MB–6MB	No	Varies	1333MHz–1066MHz
	Pentium	2	Yes	2MB	No	Varies	800MHz
	Celeron	2	Yes	1MB	No	Yes	800MHz
Kentsfield	Core 2 Extreme	4	Yes	8MB	No	Yes	1066MHz–1333MHz
	Core 2 Quad	4	Yes	8MB	No	Yes	1066MHz
Yorkfield	Core 2 Extreme	4	Yes	12MB	No	Yes	1333MHz–1600MHz
	Core 2 Quad	4	Yes	4MB	No	Varies	1333MHz

Processors using LGA 775 range in clock speed from as low as 2.30GHz (Celeron Desktop) to as high as 3.73GHz (Pentium 4 EE, Pentium Desktop EE).

NOTE   Several chipsets have been used with LGA 775 processors; different chipsets support different processors. To determine a particular system compatibility with a particular processor, check the motherboard or system documentation.

LGA 1366

LGA 1366 was used by the Core i7 9xx series Extreme Edition CPUs for desktops and by Xeon processors used for workstations and servers. LGA 1366 uses a newer interconnect method called Quick Path Interconnect (QPI) to connect to the I/O controller hub (North Bridge/northbridge); the memory controller is built into the CPU and supports triple-channel DDR3 memory. Table 3-17 compares the technologies supported by the Core i7 and Extreme Edition CPUs for desktops. All LGA 1366 processors support Intel 64 (x64).

Table 3-17   LGA 1366 Desktop Processor Technologies and Features

Code Name	Processor Family	Cores	Turbo Boost Version	L2 Cache	HT Tech	Intel VT-x	Bus Speed
Blooomfield	Core i7 Extreme Edition	4	1.0	8MB	Yes	Yes	6.4GTps
	Core i7	4	1.0	8MB	Yes	Yes	6.4GTps
Gulftown	Core i7 Extreme Edition	6	1.0	12MB	Yes	Yes	6.4GTps
	Core i7	6	1.0	12MB	Yes	Yes	6.4GTps

NOTE   GT stands for Gigatransfers. In the tables throughout this section, GTps stands for Gigatransfers per second, which is different from Gbps. It has to do with clocking embedded into the data of PCIe traffic. Using GT clarifies that some of the data being counted is "overhead" data used to make the transfer reliable. The nature of GTs is beyond the scope of the A+ exam.

Processors using LGA 1366 range in clock speed from as low as 2.66GHz (Core i7-920) to as high as 3.46GHz (Core i7 Extreme-990X). Turbo Boost maximum Turbo frequency ranges from as low as 2.93GHz (920) to 3.73GHz (990X).

LGA 1156

LGA 1156 was used by the first-generation Core i3 and Core i5 processors and by Core i7 CPUs that did not use LGA 1366. (These processors are listed on the Intel ARK website as "previous-generation" Core i3, i5, and i7 processors.) LGA 1156, like LGA 1366, is designed to connect to a memory controller built into the CPU. LGA 1156-compatible CPUs support dual-channel DDR3 memory. Some processors that use LGA 1156 also include CPU-integrated video. All LGA 1156 processors support Intel 64 (x64).

Table 3-18 compares the technologies supported by these processors.

Table 3-18 LGA 1156 Processor Technologies and Features

Code Name	Processor Family	Cores	Smart Cache	Turbo Boost Version	HT Tech	Intel VT-x	Bus Speed
Gulftown	Core i7	6	12MB	1.0	Yes	Yes	2.5GTps
Lynnfield	Core i7	4	8MB	1.0	Yes	Yes	2.5GTps
	Core i5	4	8MB	1.0	Yes	Yes	2.5GTps
Clarkdale	Core i5	2	4MB	1.0	Yes	Yes	2.5GTps
	Core i3	2	4MB	No	Yes	Yes	2.5GTps
	Pentium	2	3MB	No	No	Yes	2.5GTps
	Celeron	2	2MB	No	No	No	2.5GTps

Processors using LGA 1156 range in clock speed from as low as 2.26GHz (Celeron G1101) to as high as 3.06GHz (Core i7-880). Turbo Boost maximum Turbo frequency ranges from 3.20GHz (Core i5-750) to 3.86GHz (Core i5-680).

LGA 1155

LGA 1155 is used by the second-generation (Sandy Bridge) and third-generation (Ivy Bridge) architecture Intel CPUs. Compared to the first-generation processors, these processors feature better L1 and L2 caches, CPU integrated video, two load and store operations per CPU cycle, and better performance for advanced mathematical operations. Both of these processor families use integrated memory controllers supporting DDR3.

Compared to Sandy Bridge, Ivy Bridge processors:

■ Use a smaller die size using a new 3D Tri-Gate transistor and supporting low-voltage DDR3 (DDR3L) memory to use less power

■ Support PCIe version 3.0

■ Feature faster 3D graphics

Most motherboards made for Sandy Bridge can support Ivy Bridge after a firmware update. Check with the motherboard or system manufacturer for details.

Table 3-19 compares the technologies used by these processors.

Table 3-19 LGA 1155 Processor Technologies and Features

Code Name	Processor Family	Cores	Smart Cache	Turbo Boost Version	HT Tech	Intel VT-x	Bus Speed
Sandy Bridge	Core i7	4	8MB	2.0	Yes	Yes	5GTps
	Core i5	2, 4	3MB–6MB	2.0	Yes	Yes	5GTps
	Core i3	2	3MB	No	Yes	Yes	5GTps
	Pentium	2	3MB	No	Varies	Yes	5GTps
	Celeron	1, 2	1MB, 1.5MB, or 2MB	No	Varies	Yes	5GTps
Ivy Bridge	Core i7	4	8MB	2.0	Yes	Yes	5GTps
	Core i5	4	6MB	2.0	Varies	Yes	5GTps
	Core i3	2	3MB	2.0	No	Yes	5GTps
	Pentium	2	3MB	2.0	No	Yes	5GTps
	Celeron	2	2MB	2.0	No	Yes	5GTps

Sandy Bridge processors using LGA 1155 range in clock speed from as low as 1.60GHz (Celeron G440) to as high as 3.40GHz (various Core i5 and i7 models). Turbo Boost 2.0 maximum Turbo frequency ranges from 3.10GHz (Core i5-2300) to 3.90GHz (Core i7-2700K). Sandy Bridge processors support PCIe version 2.0.

Ivy Bridge processors using LGA 1155 range in clock speed from as low as 2.30GHz (Celeron G1610T) to as high as 3.50GHz (Core i7-3770K). Turbo Boost 2.0 maximum Turbo frequency ranges from 3.30GHz (Core i5-33xx series) to 3.90GHz (Core i7-3770 series).

LGA 1150

LGA 1150 is used by fourth-generation (Haswell) and fifth-generation (Broadwell) Intel CPUs. The Haswell processor was the first processor to feature an integrated voltage regulator. Broadwell uses a smaller die size than Haswell for improved power efficiency and allows overclocking of the integrated GPU. All Haswell and Broadwell processors support PCIe version 3.0 along with standard and low-voltage DDR3. Motherboards built for Haswell need a BIOS/UEFI firmware update for Broadwell to ensure reliable operation. Table 3-20 compares the major features of processors using LGA 1150.

Table 3-20 LGA 1150 Processor Technologies and Features

Code Name	Processor Family	Cores	Smart Cache	Turbo Boost Version	HT Tech	Intel VT-x	Bus Speed
Haswell	Core i7	4	8MB	2.0	Yes	Yes	5GTps
	Core i5	4	4MB–6MB	2.0	No*	Yes	5GTps
	Core i3	2	3MB–4MB	No	Yes	Yes	5GTps
	Pentium	2	3MB	No	No	Yes	5GTps
	Celeron	2	2MB	No	No	Yes	5GTps
Broadwell	Core i7	4	6MB	2.0	Yes	Yes	5GTps
	Core i5	4	4MB	2.0	No	Yes	5GTps

* Core i5-4570T supports HT Tech

Haswell processors using LGA 1150 range in clock speeds from as low as 2.40GHz (Celeron G1820T) to as high as 3.50GHz (various Core i7 models). Turbo Boost 2.0 maximum Turbo frequency ranges from 3.10GHz (Core i5-2300) to 3.90GHz (Core i7-4770 series).

Broadwell processors using LGA 1150 range in clock speed from as low as 3.1GHz (Core i5-5675C) to as high as 3.30GHz (Core i7-5775C). Turbo Boost 2.0 maximum Turbo frequency ranges from 3.60GHz (Core i5-5675C) to 3.70GHz (Core i7-5775C).

LGA 2011

The LGA 2011 socket form factor is actually available in two versions. The original LGA 2011 supports high-performance Sandy Bridge E and Ivy Bridge E processors. LGA 2011-v3 supports high-performance Haswell E processors. These sockets and the processors designed for each are not interchangeable. None of these processors include onboard graphics. Table 3-21 lists processor technologies supported by LGA 2011. These processors support DDR3.

Table 3-21 LGA 2011 Processor Technologies and Features

Code Name	Processor Family	Cores	Smart Cache	Turbo Boost Version	HT Tech	Intel VT-x	Bus Speed
Sandy Bridge E	Core i7 Extreme Edition	6	15MB	2.0	Yes	Yes	5GTps
	Core i7	4	10MB–12MB	2.0	Yes	Yes	5GTps
Ivy Bridge E	Core i7 Extreme Edition	6	15MB	2.0	Yes	Yes	5GTps
	Core i7	4	10MB–12MB	2.0	Yes	Yes	5GTps

Table 3-22 lists processor technologies supported by LGA 2011-v3. These processors support DDR4.

Table 3-22   LGA 2011-v3 Processor Technologies and Features

Code Name	Processor Family	Cores	Smart Cache	Turbo Boost Version	HT Tech	Intel VT-x	Bus Speed
Haswell E	Core i7 Extreme Edition	8	20MB	2.0	Yes	Yes	5GTps
	Core i7	6	15MB	2.0	Yes	Yes	5GTps

> **NOTE**   Intel's latest socket for desktop processors, Socket 1151, supports Intel's Skylake processors. Skylake, the sixth generation of the Core I family, is supported by Intel's 150-series and 170-series chipsets and DDR4 memory. The fastest current Skylake desktop processor is the Core i7-6700K processor with a top speed of 4.2GHz, and the most powerful chipset is the Z170. To learn more about Skylake processors and matching chipsets, visit http://ark.intel.com and search for "Skylake."

AMD

AMD has used many processor sockets over the years, but the 220-1001 exam specifically cites the following recent and current socket designs:

- Socket AM3
- Socket AM3+
- Socket FM1
- Socket FM2
- Socket FM2+

All of these sockets use the micro Pin Grid Array (mPGA) design. All the AMD processors on the 220-1001 exam have integrated memory controllers.

> **NOTE**   In the following sections, only processors with thermal design power (TDP) over 25 watts are covered. Processors with 25 watts or less TDP are typically used in laptops or all-in-one units rather than typical desktops.

mPGA Sockets

The micro Pin Grid Array (mPGA) design uses pins on the back side of the CPU to connect to pins in the processor socket. To hold the CPU in place, a zero insertion force (ZIF) socket mechanism is used. Open the arm and insert the processor; then close the arm to clamp the CPU pins in place.

The heat sink clips to mounting lugs on two sides of the processor socket. All mPGA sockets listed at the beginning of this section work in the same way.

Socket FM2, which uses mPGA, is shown in Figure 3-54. The back side of a processor designed for Socket FM2 is shown in Figure 3-55.

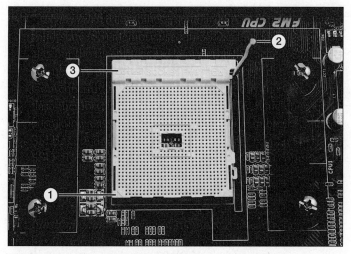

1. Triangle corresponds to pin 1 marking on processor
2. ZIF socket locking lever raised to unlock clamping mechanism
3. Processor socket name embossed here

FIGURE 3-54   Socket FM2 Before Processor Installation

1. Pin 1 triangle also visible on top side of processor

FIGURE 3-55   The Back Side of an AMD A10 5800K Processor Made for Socket FM2

Socket AM3

Socket AM3 supports processors with dual-channel DDR3 or DDR2 memory controllers onboard, including the Phenom II as well as lower-cost processors based on the Phenom II's architecture. See Table 3-23 for the technologies and features supported by AMD desktop processors using Socket AM3.

Table 3-23   Socket AM3 Desktop Processor Technologies and Features

Code Name	Processor Family	Cores	AMD 64 (x64)	L2 Cache Size	L3 Cache Size	RAM Type	Turbo CORE	AMD-V	Hyper Transport Speed
Thuban	Phenom II X6	6	Yes	3MB	6MB	DDR3	Yes	Yes	8GBps*
Zosma	Phenom II X4	4	Yes	2MB	6MB	DDR3	Yes	Yes	8GBps*
Deneb	Phenom II X4	4	Yes	1.5MB	4MB–6MB (most models)	DDR3	No	Yes	8GBps*
Propus	Athlon II X4	4	Yes	2MB	None	DDR2, No DDR3		Yes	8GBps*
Heka	Phenom II X3	3	Yes	1.5MB	6MB	DDR3	No	Yes	8GBps*
Rana	Athlon II X3	3	Yes	1.5MB	None	DDR2, No DDR3		Yes	8GBps*
Callisto	Phenom II X2	2	Yes	1MB	6MB	DDR3	No	Yes	8GBps*
Regor	Athlon II X2	2	Yes	1MB–2MB	None	DDR2, No DDR3		Yes	8GBps*
Sargas	Athlon II 1xxu	1	Yes	1MB	None	DDR2	No	Yes	8GBps*
Sargas	Sempron 1xx	1	Yes	1MB	None	DDR2	No	Yes	8GBps*

* 16GBps in HyperTransport 3.0 mode

NOTE   Processors built for Socket AM3 can also be used in Socket AM3+.

Desktop processors using Socket AM3 range in speed from as low as 1.8GHz (Athlon II 1xxu) to as high as 3.7GHz (Phenom II X4). Processors built for Socket AM3 can also be used in Socket AM3+.

SATA

The motherboard's Serial Advanced Technology Attachment (SATA) connectors are adjacent to the CPU. SATA connectors replaced IDE connectors, which were ribbon-like cables that were slower and more cumbersome and that needed to be assigned priority to hard drives.

The most important improvement was speed, with first-generation SATA cables transferring data up to 1.5Gbps. As SSDs came to market, SATA specifications improved to 3Gbps to match the faster data capabilities of the solid-state drives. The latest SATA version transfers data at 6Gbps.

Each generation of SATA cable had some differences in connectors, but the speed difference came from the controllers on the devices they connected to the motherboard and the ability of the motherboard controllers to handle the faster speeds.

IDE

An Integrated Drive Electronics (*IDE*) interface connects the motherboard to drives like CD-ROM/DVD or a hard drive. It uses a ribbon cable that connects two devices with one cable. IDE has largely been replaced by SATA connectors.

Front and Top Panel Connectors

Typical motherboards feature one or more audio connectors designed for different purposes:

- **Front/top-panel audio:** Microphone and headphones; found on almost all motherboards.

- **Music CD playback from optical drives:** This feature is rarely needed because Windows Media Player and other media player programs can play music through the SATA interface, and newer optical drives no longer include separate music CD playback connectors.

- **SPDIF header:** Designed to support an optional SPDIF bracket for digital audio playback; the bracket is provided by the motherboard vendor but is not always bundled with compatible motherboards.

Figure 3-56 illustrates these connectors on a typical motherboard.

Front-panel audio | Connects to SPDIF port

Connects to CD or DVD drive for audio playback

FIGURE 3-56 Front/Top-Panel Audio, Music CD, and SPDIF Bracket Headers on a Typical Motherboard

NOTE Front-panel audio cables often have two sets of connectors: one for HD audio and one for the older AC'97 audio standard. Use the connector that corresponds to the audio version supported by your motherboard.

ATX and ITX-family motherboards include several front/top-panel connectors for the power button, power light, drive activity lights, reset button, USB, and audio case speaker (if present). These connectors are grouped together on or near the front edge of the motherboard (see Figure 3-57).

Because front-panel leads are small and difficult to install, some motherboard vendors provide a quick-connect extender for easier installation: Connect the leads to the extender and then connect the extender to the front-panel headers. See Figure 3-58 for a typical example.

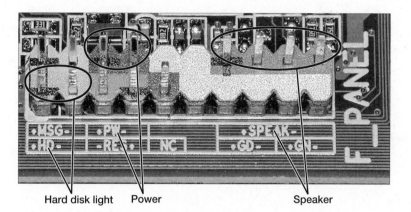

Hard disk light   Power   Speaker

FIGURE 3-57   A Typical Two-Row Front/Top-Panel Connector

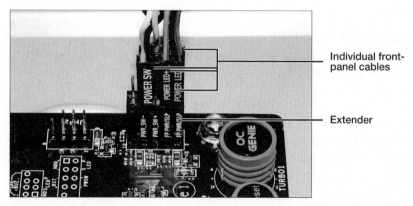

Individual front-panel cables

Extender

FIGURE 3-58   Individual Front-Panel Cables Connected via an Extender to a Motherboard

Internal USB Connector

The USB connectors on the outside of the case or laptop need to connect to the motherboard so that external devices can access the motherboard. On the inside of the case, the external USB connectors are attached to the USB header on the motherboard via cable. Figure 3-59 shows this type of connector.

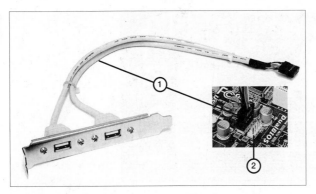

1. USB 2.0 header cable
2. USB 2.0 headers

FIGURE 3-59   External USB Connector and Attachment to Motherboard

BIOS/UEFI Settings

The *Basic Input/Output System (BIOS)* is an essential component of the mother-board. This boot firmware, also known as System BIOS or, on most recent systems, Unified Extensible Firmware Interface (UEFI), is the first code run by a computer when it is booted. It prepares the machine by testing it during bootup and paves the way for the operating system to start. It tests and initializes components such as the processor, RAM, video card, hard drives, optical drives, and USB drives. If any errors occur, the BIOS/UEFI reports them as part of the testing stage, known as the *power-on self-test (POST)*. The BIOS/UEFI resides on a ROM chip and stores a setup program that you can access when the computer first boots up. From this pro-gram, it is possible to change settings in the BIOS and upgrade the BIOS as well.

NOTE   From this point on in the chapter, the term *BIOS* refers to both traditional BIOS and UEFI firmware except when they differ in function.

BIOS/UEFI Configuration

The system BIOS has default settings provided by the system or motherboard maker, and these settings work fine for most people out of the box, but as a system is built up with storage devices, memory modules, adapter cards, and other components, it is sometimes necessary to alter the default settings to get the best use of the devices.

The changes to BIOS are made using the BIOS setup program and then saved to the CMOS (complementary metal-oxide semiconductor) chip on the motherboard.

NOTE   macOS provides operating system menus for making changes to system devices rather than permitting direct access to the BIOS.

Accessing the BIOS Setup Program

The BIOS configuration program is stored in the BIOS chip itself. Just press the key or key combination displayed onscreen (or described in the manual) when the system starts booting to access the BIOS program menu.

Although these keystrokes vary from system to system, the most popular keys on current systems include the Escape (Esc) key, the Delete (Del) key, the F1 key, the F2 key, and the F10 key.

Most recent systems display the key(s) necessary to start the BIOS setup program at startup, as shown in Figure 3-60. If you don't know which key to press to start your computer's BIOS setup program, however, check the system or motherboard manual for the correct key(s).

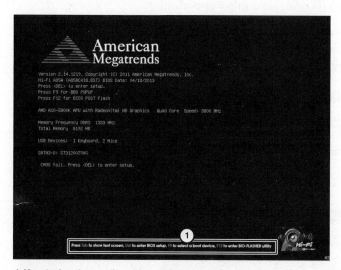

1. Keystrokes for configuration options at startup

FIGURE 3-60   A Typical Splash Screen That Displays the Keystrokes Needed to Start the BIOS Setup Program

NOTE   Because the settings you make in the BIOS setup program are stored in the nonvolatile CMOS, the settings are often called *CMOS settings* or *BIOS settings*. The contents of CMOS are maintained by a battery.

CAUTION   BIOS configuration programs vary widely, but the screens used in the following sections are representative of the options available on typical recent systems; your system might have similar options but place the settings on screens different from those shown here. Laptops, corporate desktops, and tablets generally offer fewer options than those shown here.

Be sure to consult the manual that came with your computer or motherboard before changing the settings you find here. Fiddling with the settings can improve performance, but it can also wreak havoc on an otherwise healthy device if settings are changed in error.

UEFI and Traditional BIOS

All desktop and laptop computers from 2014 on use a new type of firmware called the Unified Extensible Firmware Initiative (UEFI) to display a mouse-driven GUI or text-based menu for BIOS setup. macOS computers all use UEFI firmware. Compared to a traditional flash ROM BIOS, UEFI has the following advantages:

- Support for hard drives of 2.2TB and higher capacity. These drives require the use of the GUID Partition Table (GPT) to access full capacity.

- Faster system startup (booting) and other optimizations.

- Larger-size ROM chips used by UEFI make room for additional features, better diagnostics, the ability to open a shell environment for easy flash updates, and the ability to save multiple BIOS configurations for reuse.

UEFI firmware offers similar settings to those used by a traditional BIOS (see Figure 3-61) along with additional options (refer to Figures 3-62 and beyond). Most desktop systems with UEFI firmware use a mouse-driven graphical interface. However, many laptops with UEFI firmware use a text-based interface similar to BIOS.

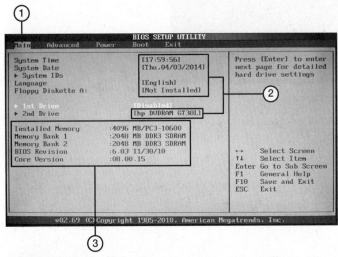

1. Selected menu
2. Editable items
3. Reported by system; not editable

FIGURE 3-61 A Computer That Uses a Traditional BIOS

To learn more about UEFI, visit http://www.uefi.org.

BIOS Settings Overview

The following sections review the typical setup process using various UEFI firmware versions on systems running Intel Core i3 3227U, Intel Core i5 i6600, AMD FX-8350, and AMD A10-5800K processors.

Table 3-24 provides detailed information about the most important CMOS/BIOS settings. Use this table as a quick reference to the settings you need to make or verify in any system. Examples of these and other settings are provided in the following sections.

Table 3-24 Major CMOS/BIOS/UEFI Settings

Option	Settings	Notes
Boot Sequence	Hard drive, optical (CD/DVD, Blu-ray), USB, network ROM; order as wanted	To boot from bootable OS or diagnostic CDs or DVDs, place the CD or DVD (optical) drive before the hard drive in the boot sequence. To boot from a bootable USB device, place the USB device before the hard drive in the boot sequence. You can enable or disable additional boot devices on some systems.
Memory Configuration	By SPD or Auto (default); manual settings (Frequency, CAS Latency [CL], Fast R-2-R turnaround, and so on) also available	Provides stable operation using the settings stored in memory by the vendor. Use manual settings (frequency, CAS latency, and so on) for overclocking (running memory at faster than normal speeds) or to enable memory of different speeds to be used safely by selecting slower settings.
CPU Clock and Frequency	Automatically detected on most recent systems	Faster or higher settings overclock the system but could cause instability. Some systems default to low values when the system doesn't start properly.
Hardware Monitor	Enable display for all fans plugged into the motherboard	Also known as PC Health on some systems; can be monitored from within the OS with vendor-supplied or third-party utilities.
Onboard Audio, Modem, or Network	Enable or disable	Enable when you don't use add-on cards for any of these functions; disable each setting before installing a replacement card. Some systems include two network adapters.
USB Legacy	Enable when USB keyboard is used	Enables USB keyboard to work outside the OS.
Serial Ports	Disable unused ports; use default settings for port you use	Also known as COM ports. Most systems no longer have serial ports.
Parallel Port	Disable unused port; use EPP/ECP mode with default IRQ/DMA when parallel port or device is connected	Compatible with almost any parallel printer or device; be sure to use an IEEE-1284-compatible printer cable. Most recent systems no longer include parallel (LPT) ports.

Option	Settings	Notes
USB Function	Enable	When motherboard supports USB 2.0 (Hi-Speed USB) ports, be sure to enable USB 2.0 function and load USB 2.0 drivers in the OS.
USB 3.0 Function	Enable	USB 3.0 ports also support USB 3.1, 2.0, and USB 1.1 devices. Disable when USB 3.0 drivers are not available for operating system.
Keyboard	NumLock, auto-repeat rate/delay	Leave at defaults (NumLock On) unless keyboard has problems.
Plug-and-Play OS	Enable for all except some Linux distributions	When enabled, Windows configures devices.
Primary VGA BIOS	Varies	Select the primary graphics card type (PCIe or onboard).
Shadowing	Varies	Enable shadowing for video BIOS; leave other shadowing disabled.
Quiet Boot	Varies	Disable to display system configuration information at startup.
Boot-Time Diagnostic Screen	Varies	Enable to display system configuration information at startup.
Virtualization	Varies	Enable to run hardware-based virtualization programs such as Hyper-V or Parallels so that you can run multiple operating systems, each in its own window.
Power Management (Menu)	Enable unless you have problems with devices	Enable CPU fan settings to receive warnings of CPU fan failure.
S1 or S3 standby	Enable S3	Use S1 (which saves minimal power) only when you use devices that do not properly wake up from S3 standby.
AC Pwr Loss Restart	Enable restart or full on	Prevents the system from staying down when a power failure takes place.
Wake on LAN (WOL)	Enable when you use WOL-compatible network card or modem	WOL-compatible cards use a small cable between the card and the motherboard. Some integrated network ports also support WOL.
User/ Power-On Password	Blocks system from starting when password is not known	Enable when physical security settings are needed but be sure to record the password in a secure place.
Setup Password	Blocks access to setup when password is not known	Both passwords can be cleared on both systems when CMOS RAM is cleared.
Write-Protect Boot Sector	Varies	Enable for normal use, but disable when installing drives or using a multiboot system. Helps prevent accidental formatting but might not stop third-party disk prep software from working.

Option	Settings	Notes
Boot Virus Detection (Antivirus Boot Sector)	Enable	Stops true infections but allows multiboot configuration.
SATA Drives	Varies	Auto-detects drive type and settings at startup time. Select CD/DVD for CD/DVD/Blu-ray drive; select None when drive is not present or to disable an installed drive.
SATA Drive Configuration	IDE, AHCI, RAID	IDE setting emulates now-obsolete PATA drives. To take advantage of hot swapping and native command queuing (NCQ) to improve performance, select AHCI. Use RAID when the drive will be used as part of a RAID array.

As you can see in Table 3-24, there are many options to select when configuring BIOS settings. Many BIOS firmware versions enable you to automatically configure your system with a choice of these options from the main menu:

- BIOS defaults (also referred to as Original/Fail-Safe on some systems)
- Setup defaults (also referred to as Optimal on some systems)

These options primarily deal with performance configuration settings in the BIOS firmware, such as memory timings, memory cache, and the like. The settings used by each BIOS setup option are customized by the motherboard or system manufacturer.

Use BIOS defaults to troubleshoot the system because these settings are conservative in memory timings and other options. Normally, the setup defaults provide better performance. As you view the setup screens in this chapter, you'll see that these options are listed.

CAUTION   If you use automatic setup after you make manual changes, all your manual changes will be overridden. Use the setup defaults and then make any other changes you want.

With many recent systems, you can select optimal or setup defaults, save your changes, and then exit; the system will then work acceptably. However, to configure drive settings, USB settings, or to enable or disable ports, you also need to work with individual BIOS settings, such as the ones shown in the following sections.

> **TIP** On typical systems, you set numerical settings, such as date and time, by scrolling through allowable values with keys such as + and – or page up/page down. However, to select settings with a limited range of options, such as enable/disable or choices from a menu, press Enter or the right-arrow key on the keyboard and then choose the option you want from the available choices.

Boot Options: Settings and Boot Sequence

Most computers include settings that control how the system boots and the sequence in which drives are checked for bootable operating system files. Depending on the system, these settings might be part of a larger menu, such as an Advanced Settings menu, a BIOS Features menu (see Figure 3-62), or a separate Boot menu (see Figure 3-63).

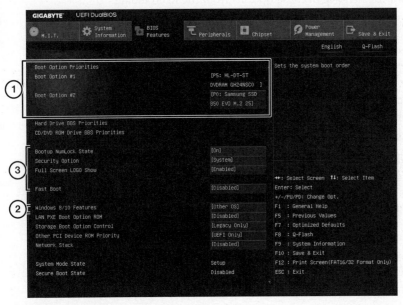

1. **Boot sequence**
2. **Other OS setting secure boot disabled**
3. **Other boot options**

FIGURE 3-62   Boot Sequence and Other Boot Settings in the UEFI/BIOS Features Menu

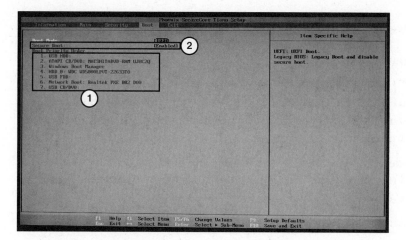

1. CD/DVD and USB flash boot before windows boot manager or hard disk drive
2. Secure boot enabled

FIGURE 3-63   A Typical Boot Menu Configured to Permit Booting from a CD/DVD or USB Flash Drive Before the Hard Drive

Enabling Fast Boot skips memory and drive tests to enable faster startup. Enabling Boot Up NumLock turns on the keyboard's NumLock option.

The menus shown in Figures 3-62 and 3-63 are used to adjust the order in which drives are checked for bootable media. For faster booting, set the hard drive with system files as the first boot device. However, when you want to have the option to boot from an optical (CD/DVD/Blu-ray) disc or from a USB flash or hard drive for diagnostics or operating system installations, put those drives before SATA hard drives in the boot order.

NOTE   Even when the first boot drive is set up as CD/DVD, some discs prompt the user to press a key to boot from the CD/DVD drive when a bootable disc is found. Otherwise, the system checks the next available device for boot files.

Firmware Updates

Interestingly, a flash BIOS update is not available from BIOS manufacturers (Phoenix, Insyde, AMI, and Award/Phoenix). They don't sell BIOS updates because their basic products are modified by motherboard and system vendors. Following are the general steps to locate a flash BIOS update and install it:

Step 1.   For major brands of computers, go to the vendor's website and look for "downloads" or "tech support" links. The BIOS updates are listed by system model and by version; avoid beta (prerelease) versions.

> **TIP** If your system is a generic system (that is, it came with a mainboard or mother-board manual and other component manuals rather than a full system manual), you need to contact the motherboard maker.

You can also buy a replacement flash BIOS file from www.eSupport.com if you cannot get an updated BIOS code from your system or mother-board vendor.

To determine the motherboard's make and model, you can download and run Belarc Advisor (free for personal use) from www.belarc.com/free_download.html.

See the following websites for additional help:

- Wims BIOS page (www.wimsbios.com)
- BIOSAgentPlus (www.biosagentplus.com)
- American Megatrends's BIOS/UEFI Firmware Support page (https://ami.com/en/support/bios-uefi-firmware-support/)

Step 2. Locate the correct BIOS update for your system or motherboard. For generic motherboards, the Wims BIOS page also has links to the mother-board vendors' websites.

Step 3. Determine the installation media needed to install the BIOS image. Many recent systems use a Windows-based installer, but some use a bootable CD or USB flash drive.

Step 4. Be sure to download all files needed to install the BIOS image. In most cases, a download contains the appropriate loader program and the BIOS image, but for some motherboards, you might also need to download a separate loader program. If the website has instructions posted, print or save them for reference.

Step 5. If you need to create bootable media, follow the vendor's instructions to create the media and place the loader and BIOS image files on the media.

Step 6. **Installation.** To install from Bootable media, follow Step 6a. To install from within Windows, follow Step 6b.

Step 6a. To install from bootable media, make sure the drive is the first item in the BIOS boot sequence. Insert or connect your media and restart the system. If prompted, press a key to start the upgrade process. Some upgrades run automatically, others require you to choose the image from a menu, and still others require the actual filename of the BIOS. The BIOS update might also prompt you to save your current BIOS image. Choose this option if possible so that you have a copy of your current BIOS in case there's a problem. After the process starts, it takes approximately three min-utes to rewrite the contents of the BIOS chip with the updated information.

Step 6b.   For installation from Windows, close all Windows programs before starting the update process. Navigate to the folder containing the BIOS update and double-click it to start the update process. Follow the prompts onscreen to complete the process. It takes approximately three minutes to rewrite the contents of the BIOS chip with the updated information.

CAUTION   While performing a flash upgrade, make sure you don't turn off the power to your PC and that you keep children or pets away from the computer to prevent accidental shutdown. Wait for a message indicating that the BIOS update has been completed before touching the computer. If the power goes out during the flash update, the BIOS chip could be rendered useless.

Step 7.   Remove the media and restart the system to use your new BIOS features. Reconfigure the BIOS settings if necessary.

Recovering from a Failed BIOS Update

If the primary system BIOS is damaged, keep in mind that some motherboard vendors offer dual BIOS chips on some products. The secondary BIOS performs the same functions as the primary BIOS so the system can continue to run.

If you use the wrong Flash BIOS file to update your BIOS, or if the update process doesn't finish, your system can't start. You might need to contact the system or motherboard maker for service or purchase a replacement BIOS chip.

In some cases, the BIOS contains a "mini-BIOS" that can be reinstalled from a reserved part of the chip. Systems with this feature have a jumper on the motherboard called the *flash recovery jumper*.

To use this feature, download the correct flash BIOS, make a bootable disc from it, and take it to the computer with the defective BIOS. Set the jumper to Recovery, insert the bootable media, and then rerun the setup process. Because the video won't work, you need to listen for beeps and watch for the drive light to run during this process. Turn off the computer, reset the jumper to Normal, and then restart the computer.

If the update can't be installed, your motherboard might have a jumper that write-protects the flash BIOS. Check the manual to see whether your system has this feature. To update a BIOS on a system with a write-protected jumper, you must follow these steps:

Step 1.   Disable the write protection.

Step 2.   Perform the update.

Step 3.   Reenable the write protection to keep unauthorized people from changing the BIOS.

Security Features

Security features of various types are scattered around the typical system BIOS/ UEFI dialogs. Features and their locations vary by system and might include:

- **BIOS password:** BIOS Settings Password or Security dialogs

- **Power-on password:** Configured through the Security dialog

- **Chassis intrusion**: Various locations

- **Boot sector protection:** Advanced BIOS Features dialog

These features support drive encryption:

- **TPM (trusted platform module):** Security dialog

- **LoJack for laptops:** An after-market product embedded in firmware or installed by the end user; not managed with BIOS dialogs

- **Secure Boot:** Boot or other dialogs

Enable the BIOS password feature to permit access to BIOS setup dialogs only for those with the password. The power-on password option prevents anyone without the password from starting the system. Note that these options can be defeated by opening the system and clearing the CMOS memory.

When *intrusion detection/notification*, also known as chassis intrusion, is enabled, the BIOS displays a warning on startup that the system has been opened.

Boot sector protection, found primarily on older systems, protects the default system drive's boot sector from being changed by viruses or other unwanted programs. Depending on the implementation, this option might need to be disabled before an operating system installation or upgrade.

Windows editions that support the BitLocker full-disk encryption feature use *TPM (Trusted Platform Module)* to protect the contents of any specified drive (Windows 7/8/8.1/10). Although many corporate laptops include a built-in TPM module, desktop computers and servers might include a connection for an optional TPM.

LoJack for laptops (and other mobile devices) is a popular security feature embedded in the laptop BIOS of a number of systems and can be added to other systems. It consists of two components: a BIOS-resident component and the Computrace Agent, which is activated by LoJack when a computer is reported as stolen. To learn more about LoJack for laptops, tablets, and smartphones see https://homeoffice. absolute.com.

Secure Boot (see the last line of Figure 3-62 and also see Figure 3-63)—blocks installation of other operating systems and also requires the user to access UEFI setup by restarting the computer in a special troubleshooting mode from within Windows 8 or later. Secure Boot is enabled by default on systems shipped with Windows 8, 8.1, or 10. Linux users or those who want more flexibility in accessing UEFI/BIOS (for example, technicians making changes in UEFI firmware) should disable Secure Boot.

Interface Configurations

Typical desktop systems are loaded with onboard ports and features, and the menus shown in Figures 3-64, 3-65, 3-66, and 3-67 are typical of the BIOS menus used to enable, disable, and configure storage, audio, network, and USB ports.

SATA Configuration

Use the SATA configuration options (such as those shown in Figure 3-64) to enable or disable SATA and eSATA ports and to configure SATA host adapters to run in compatible (emulating PATA), native (AHCI), or RAID modes. AHCI supports native command queuing (NCQ) for faster performance and permits hot swapping of eSATA drives.

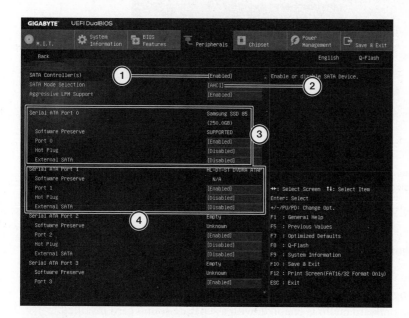

1. SATA ports enabled
2. SATA ports configured to run in AHCI mode
3. Port 0 is connected to a 250GB SSD
4. Port 1 is connected to a DVD optical drive

FIGURE 3-64 A UEFI Configuration Dialog for SATA Ports

USB Host Adapters and Charging Support

Most systems have separate settings for the USB (2.0) and USB 3.0 (a.k.a. SuperSpeed) controllers (on systems that have USB 3.0 ports). If you don't enable USB 2.0 or USB 3.0 in your system BIOS, all your system's USB ports will run at the next lower speed.

Some USB configuration utilities can also be used to enable a specified USB port to output at a higher amperage than normal to enable faster charging of smartphones. Figure 3-65 illustrates a system with USB 3.0 support enabled and battery charging support being enabled.

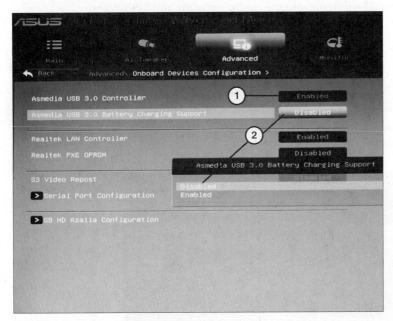

1. USB 3.0 host adapter enabled
2. Charging option being edited

FIGURE 3-65   Configuring a USB Host Adapter for Battery Charging

Audio and Ethernet Ports

Depending on the system, audio and Ethernet ports and other integrated ports might be configured using a common menu or on separate menus. In Figure 3-66, the HD Azalia onboard audio is enabled; with a separate sound card installed, onboard audio should be disabled. SPDIF audio can be directed through the SPDIF digital audio port (default) or the HDMI AV port (optional) using this menu.

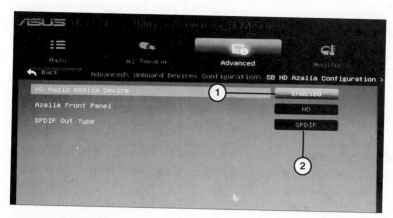

1. HD Audio enabled
2. Change to HDMI to permit HDMI cable to carry audio as well as video signals

FIGURE 3-66   Configuring Onboard HD Audio

In Figure 3-67, the option Onboard LAN Option ROM is disabled on this system. Enable it when you want to boot from an operating system that is stored on a network drive.

1. Ethernet network adapter enabled
2. LAN Option ROM (for booting from network) disabled

FIGURE 3-67   Configuring an Onboard Network Adapter

NOTE   Systems with support for legacy ports such as floppy, serial (COM), and parallel (LPT) ports use a separate BIOS settings menu for configuration. Do not enable these ports unless you use them.

CMOS Battery

The system BIOS is responsible for configuring the ports and features controlled by the chipset, and the CMOS chip on the motherboard stores the settings. The CMOS battery provides power to maintain the contents of the CMOS chip (see Figure 3-68). Battery life is several years, but a low CMOS battery can cause problems with drivers and sometimes booting. Since date and time settings are stored in CMOS, date and time errors can be a good indication that it is time to check or change the battery.

To clear CMOS on most systems, place a jumper block over two jumper pins.

1. CR2032 CMOS battery
2. Jumper block for clearing CMOS memory

FIGURE 3-68   A Typical CMOS Battery (CR2032)

NOTE   Some systems feature a port-cluster-mounted push button to clear the CMOS. If you need to clear the CMOS on a particular system, check the documentation for details.

CPU Cores: Single Core and Multicore

A processing core is the part of the CPU that gets instructions from software and performs the calculations for output. Early computers had *single-core processors* to do all the work. As demands on CPUs grew, single-core processors could not keep up.

Two or more physical processors in a system enable it to perform much faster when multitasking or running multithreaded applications. However, systems with multiple processors are expensive to produce. ***Multicore processors***, which combine two or more processor cores into a single physical processor, provide virtually all the benefits of multiple physical processors and are lower in cost and work with any operating system that supports traditional single-core processors.

Current gaming and desktop processors from Intel have 8 cores (i9), and AMD has one with up to 32 cores (Ryzen), but both companies are constantly updating their offerings with faster processors.

Virtualization

Creating and managing a virtual version of a computer (or any device) is a rapidly growing sector in computing. (See Chapter 4, "Virtualization and Cloud Computing," for further discussion of virtualization.) Most current AMD and Intel processors feature ***virtualization support***, also known as ***hardware-assisted virtualization***. Virtualization technology enables a host program (known as a hypervisor) or a host operating system to support one or more guest operating systems running at the same time in different windows on the host's desktop. Hardware-assisted virtualization enables virtualized operating systems and applications to run faster and use fewer system resources. The benefits are too many to discuss here, but think of it as getting two or more computers running in software but buying only one piece of hardware to run them.

Some of the best-known virtualization programs include Microsoft's Windows Virtual PC and Hyper-V Manager. Major third-party virtualization programs include VMware (www.vmware.com), Oracle VM VirtualBox (https://www.virtualbox.org/), and DOSBox (www.dosbox.com).

Hyperthreading

Hyperthreading technology was developed by Intel for processing two execution threads within a single processor core. Essentially, when hyperthreading is enabled in the system BIOS and the processor is running a multithreaded application, the processor is emulating two physical processors. The Pentium 4 was the first desktop processor to support hyperthreading, which Intel first developed for its Xeon workstation and server processor family. Hyperthreading is supported by Core i9. In mid-2019 Intel advised disabling hyperthreading in i7 and below due to security vulnerabilities.

CPU Speeds

Different components of the motherboard—such as the CPU, memory, chipset, expansion slots, storage interfaces, and I/O ports—connect with each other at different speeds. The term ***bus speeds*** refers to the speeds at which different buses in the motherboard connect to different components. On a motherboard, the bus is the path data takes between the internal components of the computer.

Some of these speeds, such as the speed of I/O ports and expansion slots (USB, Thunderbolt, and SATA ports; PCI and PCIe slots), are established by the design of the port or by the capabilities of the devices connected to them. However, depending on the motherboard, you might be able to fine-tune the bus speeds used by the processor, the chipset interconnect, and memory. These adjustments, where available, are typically performed through BIOS/UEFI firmware settings in menus such as Memory, Overclocking, and AI Tweaker.

Figure 3-69 shows the CPU (processor) overclocking UEFI firmware dialog from a system with an Intel i5 processor. The dialog indicates the current CPU and memory multipliers that can be adjusted.

Figure 3-70 illustrates the memory overclock adjustments dialog on the same system. To change CPU speed, memory timing, or other adjustments, change the Auto setting and enter the desired values. On this system and others, you can select a CPU overclocking value, and other settings are adjusted automatically as needed.

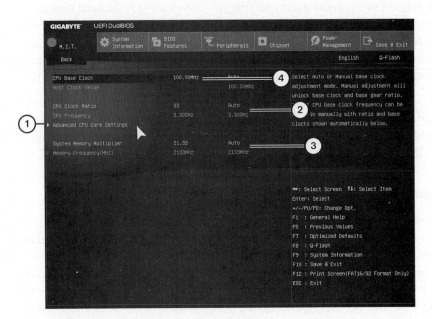

1. Enter this menu to overclock processor (CPU)
2. CPU clock speed based on current base clock speed and ratio
3. Memory speed based on current base clock speed and ratio
4. CPU base clock speed

FIGURE 3-69   CPU and Memory Speed Information on a System That Allows Speed Adjustment

1. Change from [Auto] to overclock memory

FIGURE 3-70 Preparing to Overclock Memory

Overclocking

Overclocking refers to the practice of running a processor or other components, such as memory or the video card's graphics processing unit (GPU), at speeds higher than normal. Overclocking methods used for processors include increasing the clock multiplier or running the front side bus (FSB) at speeds faster than normal. These changes are performed by altering the normal settings in the system BIOS setup for the processor's configuration.

Most processors feature locked clock multipliers. That is, the clock multiplier frequency cannot be changed. In such cases, the only way to overclock the processor is to increase the FSB speed, which is the speed at which the processor communicates with system memory. Increasing the FSB speed can lead to greater system instability than changing the clock multipliers.

Some processors from Intel and AMD feature unlocked clock multipliers so that the user can choose the best method for overclocking the system. Intel refers to these processors as Extreme Edition or Extreme Processor or uses the *K* suffix at the end of the model number; AMD uses the term *Black Edition* or uses the *K* suffix. Overclocked processors and other components run hotter than normal, and several techniques are often used to help maintain system stability at faster speeds, including using additional cooling fans, replacing standard active heat sinks with models that feature greater cooling, and adjusting processor voltages.

Intel's Core i9, i7, and i5 and AMD's Ryzen7 and Ryzen 5 processors support automatic overclocking according to processor load. Intel refers to this feature as *Turbo Boost*, whereas AMD's term is *Turbo CORE*.

Overclocking may provide the benefit of speed, but of course there is a cost. Excessive heat can cause problems with the CPU and shorten its life, so it is not a good idea for critical tasks. Manufacturers therefore don't recommend overclocking. However, many gaming-oriented systems have the heavy-duty cooling and extensive BIOS adjustments needed to make overclocking successful.

To monitor system clock and bus speed settings, check the processor and memory configuration dialog typically available on gaming-oriented systems or others designed for overclocking (see Figure 3-71). On these systems, you can disable the normal Auto settings and manually tweak speeds, voltages, and other timing settings.

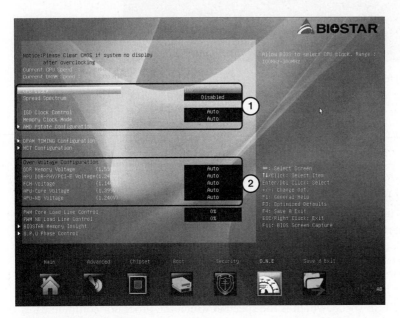

1. Clock adjustment options
2. Voltage adjustments

FIGURE 3-71   CPU Configuration Dialog Used for Viewing and Changing Clock and Bus Speeds for Overclocking

Integrated Graphics Processing Unit (GPU)

Integrating the GPU into the processor makes possible faster video processing, easier access to memory, and lower-cost systems. Intel's Core i3, i5, and i7 CPUs and AMD's A-series advanced processing units (APUs) are the first processors to have integrated GPUs. The newer series from AMD, Ryzen 5 and Ryzen 7, as well as Intel i9, continue to improve on GPU processing.

Intel uses three different names to refer to its processor-integrated graphics:

- HD Graphics refers to base-level 3D graphics in any given processor family. Specific features vary by processor family.

- Intel Iris Plus Graphics 655, formerly code named Coffee Lake, and Intel UHD Graphics 615, formerly code named Amber Lake, were released in 2018.

- Intel UHD Graphics 630, formerly code named Coffee Lake, was released in 2018 It is similar to HD Graphics but was rebranded to reflect a newer eighth generation of GPUs.

There are several families of CPUs, and information about their GPUs can be found at http://www.intel.com.

The GPU-Z reporting app from TechPowerUp (www.techpowerup.com) can be used to display information about discrete or integrated GPUs. Figure 3-72 displays information about the HD Graphics 4000 GPU built into an Intel Core i3-2770U processor and the Radeon HD 6520G built into an AMD A6-3420M processor.

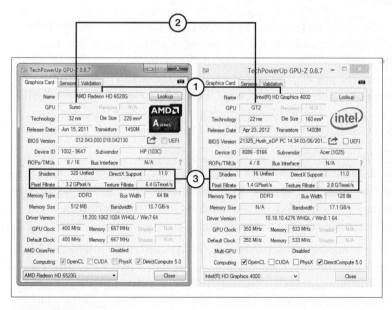

1. **GPU model number**
2. **GPU family**
3. **DirectX version and 3D features**

FIGURE 3-72   GPU-Z Reports on Intel and AMD Processors with Integrated GPUs

AMD, which also manufactures Radeon GPUs for video cards, integrates Radeon GPU features into its line of APUs, which integrate the CPU and GPU:

- APUs in the Llano and Trinity series use Radeon HD 6xxxD, 7xxxD, and 8xxxD graphics using stream processor technology for 3D graphics. These support OpenGL 4.1 or better and OpenCL 1.1 or better.

- Radeon R7 graphics in the 7000 series use Compute Cores, which permit both CPU and GPU cores to access the same memory. These support OpenGL 4.3 and OpenCL 1.2.

- Radeon R5 graphics in the 7000 series feature fewer Compute Cores and run more slowly than R7 but are otherwise similar.

For more information about APU specifications, see http://www.amd.com.

Although the fastest CPU integrated graphics are suitable for casual gaming as well as general office use, high-performance graphics cards are still recommended for 3D gaming. If a high-performance card is installed, the GPU must be disabled in the BIOS.

Processor Compatibility

Intel and AMD, the two main manufacturers of desktop CPUs, use different form factors for attaching the processor to the motherboard. Differences in how the CPUs physically attach and how they work internally means one brand's CPU is not compatible with the other brand's motherboard. Because Intel and AMD use different socket types on their motherboards, CPUs from Intel will not fit an AMD form factor and vice versa. Independent manufacturers of motherboards, such as ASUS and ASRock, make several different boards that support CPUs from both companies.

Intel uses a Land Grid Array (LGA) form factor for CPUs. The pins that connect the CPU to the motherboard are mounted on the motherboard's socket. Because of the grid protruding from the socket, careful handling of the motherboard is essential; damage to any pin can ruin the motherboard.

AMD, on the other hand, uses a Pin Grid Array (PGA) form factor, where the contact pins that insert into the socket are mounted to the CPU itself. Of course, careful handling of the CPU is important here as well. When an AMD chip is installed, the pins and the socket should be carefully aligned, and then the CPU must be gently dropped into the socket without any force applied by hand. The CPU is locked into place using a zero insertion force (ZIF) lever that acts as a retention arm that holds the chip in place. Figure 3-73 shows an AMD CPU with a PGA.

FIGURE 3-73   An AMD CPU with PGA (Left) and an Intel CPU with LGA (Right)
(Images © S.Rimkuss, Shutterstock and © RMIKKA, Shutterstock)

AMD and Intel CPUs are also fundamentally different from one generation to
the next. The CPU form factor must match the socket form factor when building
a PC or when changing out a motherboard or CPU. For example, Intel's Core i7
CPU uses an LGA 1151, meaning that it has 1,151 pins, and the newer Core i9
uses an LGA 2066, with 2,066 pins. Because of the pin difference, each CPU needs
a different motherboard. Similar differences occur between AMD generations.

CPUs have evolved over time, and each generation of CPU, whether Intel or
AMD, can make different demands of a motherboard. For example, earlier CPUs
could support 32-bit processing but not 64-bit processing. When 64-bit CPUs
became available, they would not work on motherboards designed for 32-bit,
since those motherboards could not support the additional RAM capabilities and
other features. Current CPUs have graphics features that were not available on
the previous generation, and the chipsets may need to be enhanced as well.

When upgrading a system, it is wise to start with the speed and features you
want from a CPU and then shop for a motherboard that supports it. Checking
with the manufacturer is the only way to know for sure if a new version of CPU
will work with the current motherboard's chipset.

Cooling Mechanisms

A CPU is one of the most expensive components in any computer, and keeping
it cool is important. The basic requirements for proper CPU cooling include the
use of an appropriate active heat sink (which includes a fan) and the application of
an appropriate thermal material (grease, paste, or a pre-applied thermal or phase-
change compound). Advanced systems sometimes use liquid cooling instead.

Fans

A traditional active heat sinks includes a cooling fan that rests on top of the heat sink and pulls air past the heat sink in a vertical direction (see Figure 3-74). However, many aftermarket heat sinks use other designs (see Figure 3-75).

FIGURE 3-74   Stock (Original Equipment) Active Heat Sinks Made for AMD (Left) and Intel (Right) Processors

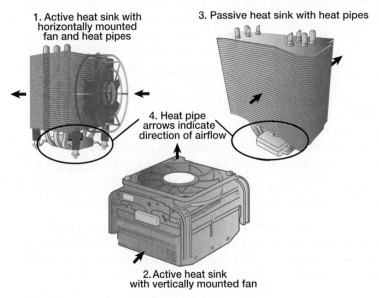

FIGURE 3-75   Typical Third-Party Active and Passive Heat Sinks

Fanless/Passive Heat Sinks

A passive heat sink does not include a fan but has more fins than an active heat sink to help dissipate heat. One typical use for fanless heat sinks is on low-power processors that are soldered in place on Mini-ITX or similar small form factor motherboard designs, such as the one shown in Figure 3-76.

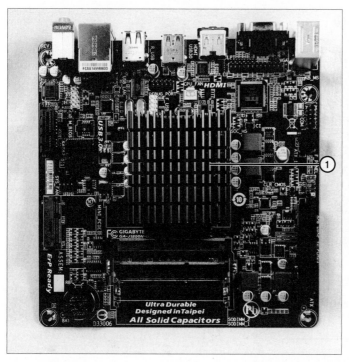

1. Passive heat sink

FIGURE 3-76   A Low-Power Mini-ITX Motherboard Designed for Home Theater and Media Streaming

Heat Sink

Every processor requires a heat sink. A **_heat sink_** is a finned metal device that radiates heat away from the processor. In almost all cases, an active heat sink (a heat sink with a fan) is required for adequate cooling. But if a system case (chassis) is specially designed to move air directly over the processor, then a fan-less passive heat sink can be used instead.

Although aluminum has been the most common material used for heat sinks, copper has better thermal transfer properties, and many designs mix copper and aluminum components. (Figure 3-77 in the next section shows two examples of heat sinks.)

Phase-Change Material/Thermal Paste

Before installing a heat sink bundled with a processor, remove the protective cover over the pre-applied thermal material (also known as *phase-change material*) on the heat sink. When the heat sink is installed on the processor, this material helps ensure good contact between the CPU and the heat sink to maximize heat transfer away from the CPU. Figure 3-77 illustrates pre-applied thermal material on the bottom of typical Intel and AMD active heat sinks.

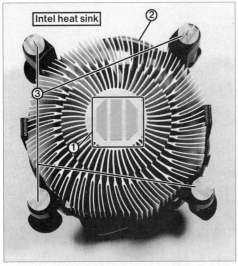

1. Preapplied thermal compound
2. Power cable for fan
3. Locking pins for mounting heat sink to
   motherboard

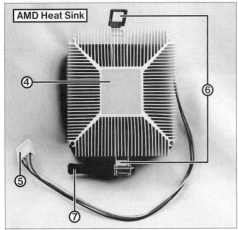

4. Preapplied thermal compound
5. Power connector for fan
6. Clamping mechanism for mounting heat sink to
   frame
7. Clamping lever
AMD Heat Sink

FIGURE 3-77 Bottom View of OEM (Original Equipment Manufacturer) Active Heat Sinks Made for Intel and AMD Processors

TIP When you remove a heat sink, keep in mind that the thermal compound acts as an adhesive. Make sure you have loosened the locking mechanism before you remove the heat sink. You may need to exert some force to remove it from the processor.

If you need to remove and reapply a heat sink, be sure to remove all residue from both the processor and heat sink using isopropyl alcohol and apply new thermal paste or other thermal transfer material to the top of the CPU.

Liquid-Based Cooling

Liquid-based cooling systems for processors, motherboard chipsets, and GPUs are available. Some are integrated into a custom case, whereas others can be retrofitted into an existing system that has openings for cooling fans.

A liquid cooling system involves attaching a liquid cooling unit instead of an active heat sink to the processor and other supported components. A pump moves the liquid (which might be water or a special solution, depending on the cooling system) through the computer to a heat exchanger, which uses a fan to cool the warm liquid before it is sent back to the processor. Liquid cooling systems are designed primarily for high-performance systems, especially overclocked systems. It's essential that only approved cooling liquids and hoses be used in these systems (check with cooling system vendors for details); unauthorized liquids or hoses could leak and corrode system components.

Figure 3-78 illustrates a typical liquid cooling system compared to a typical Intel OEM heat sink.

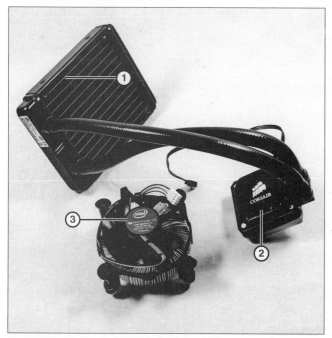

1. Radiator
2. Cooler for processor
3. Intel OEM active heat sink (for comparison)

FIGURE 3-78   A Typical Liquid Cooling System and Active Heat Sink

Expansion Cards

Most new CPUs come with integrated video, and for everyday use, that is sufficient. But for users of graphics applications or gamers, they will likely find a benefit in upgrading to an onboard graphics card that has dedicated memory space for graphics.

The more integrated graphics processors are called upon, the more memory that is used for processing and the more heat that is generated by the CPU. A good video card has a separate processing chip and a cooling system that takes the load of the CPU and frees up space for the CPU to run more efficiently.

Installing Video Cards

The installation process for a *video card* includes three phases:

Step 1.   Configuring the BIOS for the video card being installed

Step 2.   Physically installing the video card

Step 3.   Installing drivers for the video card

Figure 3-79 illustrates a typical high-performance video card that uses an AMD GPU.

1. **Exhaust panel for fans**
2. **Cooling fans**
3. **PCIe x16 connector**
4. **PCIe 6-pin power connector**
5. **Connector for CrossFire multi-GPU cable**

FIGURE 3-79 A PCIe x16 Video Card Designed for Multi-GPU (CrossFire) Support

BIOS Configuration for Video Cards

Video cards interact differently depending on the motherboard and BIOS settings. When adding a card, it may be necessary to enter BIOS to disable the onboard video, and some other systems allow both video systems to interact for better efficiency. These are the basic steps for BIOS configuration for video cards:

Step 1.   Check and adjust the *primary VGA BIOS* setting (for the *primary graphics adapter*) as needed:

Step 2.   Choose **PCIE** or **PCIE > PCI** if you use a PCIe video card. On some systems, the term *NB PCIe video slot* is used for PCIe.

Step 3.   Choose **PCI** or **PCI > PCIE** if you use a PCI video card.

For onboard video (integrated graphics), see the manufacturer's recommendation. (Onboard video can use PCI or PCI Express buses built into the motherboard.) On some recent systems, Auto is the default setting.

If the installed video card and driver are not working well but the screen is still visible, remove the card and use Device Manager's Driver Rollback feature to restore the previous driver.

Removing Drivers for an Old Video Card or Onboard Video

Although all video cards created since the beginning of the 1990s are based on VGA, virtually all of them use unique chipsets that require special software drivers to control acceleration features (faster onscreen video), color depth, and resolution. So, whenever you change video cards, you must change video driver software as well. Otherwise, your operating system will drop into a low-resolution mode and might give you an error message because the driver doesn't match the video card.

To delete an old video driver in Windows, open **Control Panel > Device Manager** and delete the listing for the current video card. Select **Uninstall a Program** in Control Panel and then uninstall the driver or configuration apps used by the current video card.

It is not necessary to delete old drivers in macOS or Linux.

Removing the Old Video Card

Follow these steps to remove an old video card (if present):

Step 1.   Shut down the computer and disconnect it from AC power.

Step 2.   Turn off the display.

Step 3.   Disconnect the data cable attached to the video card.

Step 4.   Open the case.

Step 5.   Disconnect any power cables running to the video card (see Figure 3-80).

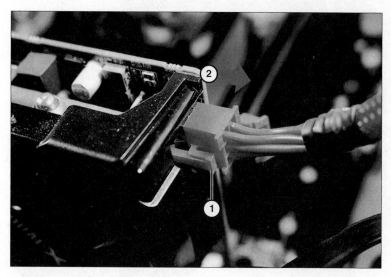

1. **Push locking tab in**
2. **Pull power cable away from card**

FIGURE 3-80   Removing the PCIe Power Cable from a Video Card

Step 6.   Remove SLI (NVIDIA) or CrossFire (AMD) cables connected to any card(s) you are removing (see Figure 3-81).

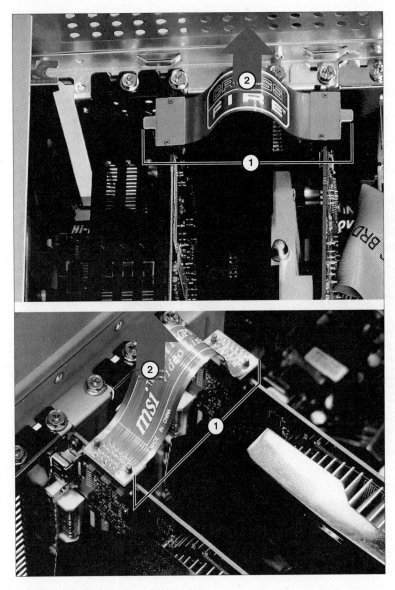

1. **Lift up ends of connector cable to release**
2. **Lift connector cable out of system**

FIGURE 3-81   SLI and CrossFire Cables, Which Should Be Removed Before Removing Video Cards for Replacement

Step 7.   Remove the old video card(s) by removing the screw holding a card bracket in place and releasing the card-retention mechanism that holds video card in place (see Figure 3-82). Repeat for each video card.

NOTE Card-retention mechanisms vary widely from motherboard to motherboard. In addition to the design shown in Figure 3-82, some use a lever that can be pushed to one side to release the lock; others use a knob that is pulled out to release the lock.

1. **Push down on locking tab**
2. **Pull up on card**
3. **Card connectors now visible**

FIGURE 3-82 Releasing the Card-Retention Mechanism Before Removing a PCIe x16 Video Card

To complete a CrossFire or SLI installation, use the configuration apps supplied with the video card drivers to enable CrossFire or SLI and select specific 3D performance settings.

Video Card Physical Installation

Follow these steps to install the new video card:

Step 1. Insert the new video card into a PCIe x16 slot. If the motherboard has two or more PCIe x16 slots, use the slot closest to the port cluster for the primary (or only) card.

Step 2.   Lock the card into position with the card retention mechanism and with the screw for the card bracket.

Step 3.   If the card uses power, connect the appropriate PCIe power connector to the card (refer to Figure 3-80).

Step 4.   If the card is running in multi-GPU mode and uses SLI or CrossFire, connect the appropriate bridge cable between the new card and a compatible existing (or new) card in the system (refer to Figure 3-81).

Step 5.   Reattach the data cable from the display to the new video card.

Driver Installation

Driver installation takes place when the system is restarted:

Step 1.   Turn on the display.

Step 2.   Reconnect power to the system and turn on the computer.

Step 3.   Provide video drivers as requested; you might need to run an installer program for the drivers. If you are installing the card under Linux, check with the card vendor for downloadable Linux drivers for your distribution.

Step 4.   If the monitor is not detected as a Plug and Play monitor but as a default monitor, install a driver for the monitor.

NOTE   A driver disc might have been packed with the monitor, or you might need to download a driver from the monitor vendor's website. If you do not install a driver for a monitor identified as a default monitor, you will not be able to choose from the full range of resolutions and refresh rates the monitor actually supports.

Installing Sound Cards

A sound card converts the digital sound signal into an analog sound experience preferred by the human ear. For most users, the onboard sound card that is integrated into the motherboard is fine, but some users want high-fidelity sound for home theaters and music mixing. Purchasing an internal sound card that is more powerful and has more input/output options makes sense for professionals who work with sound.

Installing a sound card is similar to installing a video card. Before installing a sound card, be sure to disable onboard audio with the system BIOS setup program and uninstall any proprietary mixer or configuration apps used by onboard audio.

To install a sound card, follow these steps:

Step 1. Shut down the computer and disconnect it from AC power.

Step 2. Open the case to gain access to the PC's expansion slots.

Step 3. Select an empty PCIe or PCI expansion slot that is appropriate for the form factor of the sound card to be installed.

Step 4. Remove the corresponding bracket from the back of the case.

Step 5. Insert the card into the slot (see Figure 3-83).

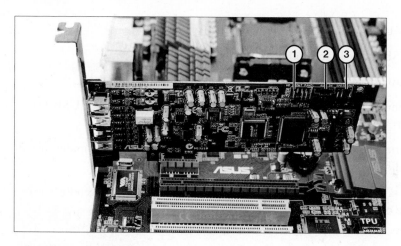

1. Front panel audio header
2. Aux in (from optical drive)
3. SPDIF out digital audio header

FIGURE 3-83   A Typical PCIe Sound Card with 5:1 Surround Audio After Being Inserted into an Expansion Slot

Step 6. Secure the card bracket into place, using the screw or locking mechanism you removed or released in Step 4.

Step 7. Connect any header cables as needed (refer to Figure 3-83).

Step 8. Connect speakers, microphone, and line-in and line-out cables as needed to support your audio or home theater subsystem.

Step 9. Close the system.

Step 10. Reconnect AC power and restart the system.

Step 11.   Install the driver files provided with the sound card or install updated versions provided by the vendor.

Step 12.   If not already installed in Step 11, install the mixer and configuration utilities provided with the new sound card.

External USB Audio Sound Cards

An external USB sound card can allow for higher-quality sound and multiple adapter input/output jacks. These sound cards really look more like USB attached devices than cards, but they perform the same task as cards (for an example, see Sewelldirect.com). You can also add surround audio with a USB-based audio device. This is a good solution for laptops and for systems with limited or no expansion slots.

Installing a USB Audio Sound Card

To install a USB audio device, follow these steps:

Step 1.   Turn off the computer.

Step 2.   Connect the USB audio device to the computer's USB 2.0 or USB 3.0 port.

Step 3.   Turn on the computer and then turn on the device. The computer installs audio drivers automatically.

Step 4.   Install additional or updated drivers downloaded from the vendor's website or provided with the device, if needed.

Configuring a Sound Card with Windows 10

To configure a sound card, onboard audio, or USB audio with Windows:

Step 1.   Type **Sound settings** in the search box.

Step 2.   Select the **Sounds** icon in Control Panel.

Step 3.   Select the **Playback** tab and adjust the settings.

Step 4.   Select the **Recording** tab and adjust the settings.

Step 5.   To specify sounds to play during Windows events (startup, shutdown, errors, and program events), use the Sounds tab.

Step 6.   Click **Apply** and then click **OK** to accept changes.

If the sound card or onboard audio includes proprietary management or configuration programs, run them from the Start menu.

Configuring a Sound Card with macOS

To configure a sound card, onboard audio, or USB audio with macOS:

Step 1. Open the Apple menu.

Step 2. Open **System Preferences**.

Step 3. Select the **Sound** icon.

Step 4. Select the **Output** tab.

Step 5. Select the device to use for sound output.

Step 6. Adjust the balance and volume and then close the window.

Configuring a Sound Card with Linux

To configure a sound card, onboard audio, or USB audio with Linux (Ubuntu 14.x):

Step 1. Open **System Settings**.

Step 2. Open **Sound**.

Step 3. Select the **Output** tab.

Step 4. Select the device to use for sound output.

Step 5. Adjust the balance and volume.

Step 6. Select the speaker mode (stereo or surround options).

Step 7. Click **Test Sound** to verify proper operation.

Step 8. Close the window to save the changes.

Installing Network Cards

Although most computers include a 10/100/1000 Ethernet port or a Wireless Ethernet (WiFi) adapter, you sometimes need to install a network card (network interface card [NIC]) into a computer that you want to add to a network.

To install a Plug and Play (PnP) network card, follow these steps:

Step 1. Shut down the computer, disconnect it from AC power, and remove the case cover.

Step 2. Locate an available expansion slot that matches the network card's design. (Most use PCIe, but some servers and workstations might use PCI-X, and some older desktop systems might use PCI.)

Step 3.   Remove the slot cover and insert the card into the slot. Secure the card in the slot.

Step 4.   Reconnect power to the system, restart the system, and provide drivers when requested by the system.

Step 5.   If prompted to install network drivers and clients, insert the operating system disc.

Step 6.   Connect the network cable to the card.

Step 7.   Test for connectivity (check LED lights, use a command such as ping, and so on), and then close the computer case.

If there are no available slots, or if you need to add (or upgrade) network connectivity on a laptop, use a USB to Ethernet or USB to wireless adapter. Although USB network adapters are also PnP devices, you may need to install the drivers provided with the USB network adapter before you attach the adapter to your computer. After the driver software is installed, the device is recognized as soon as you plug it into a working USB port.

NOTE   If you are using a wireless USB adapter, you can improve signal strength by using an extension cable between the adapter and the USB port on the computer. Using an extension cable enables you to move the adapter as needed to pick up a stronger signal.

Most USB network adapters are bus powered. For best results, they should be attached to a USB port built into your computer or to a self-powered hub. Most recent adapters support USB 3.1 Gen 2 (10Gbps), which provides support for 100BASE-TX (Fast Ethernet 100Mbps) and 1000BASE-T (Gigabit Ethernet, 1000Mbps) signal speeds. A USB 2.0 port (480Mbps) is adequate for Fast Ethernet but does not run fast enough for Gigabit Ethernet. USB 4, which is planned for release in 2019, is set to offer a variety of speeds (depending on the device) up to 40Gbps.

Installing USB Cards

Adding a USB 3.2 card is a quick way to upgrade a system with a spare PCIe slot but no USB 3.2 ports so it can connect to external storage devices at full speed. Here's how:

Step 1.   Shut down the computer, disconnect it from AC power, and remove the case cover.

Step 2.   Locate an available PCIe x1 or wider expansion slot.

Step 3.   Remove the slot cover and insert the card into the slot. Secure the card in the slot.

Step 4.   Connect power to the card. Some cards use a Berg connector, while others use a Molex connector (see Figure 3-84).

Step 5.   Reconnect power to the system, restart the system, and provide drivers when requested by the system.

Step 6.   Connect a USB device to the card.

Step 7.   After verifying that the device works, close the case.

1. **Molex power connector**
2. **Molex power cable**
3. **USB 3.0 ports**
4. **PCIe x1 slot**

FIGURE 3-84   Preparing to Connect a Molex Power Connector to a Four-Port USB 3.0 PCIe Card

SATA and eSATA

The vast majority of desktop and laptop computers in use rely on the Serial ATA (SATA) interface to connect to internal hard disk drives, SSDs, and optical drives. The external version of SATA, eSATA, is not as common, but has been widely used by high-performance Windows and Linux-based desktop computers for external hard drives.

Both SATA and eSATA interfaces carry data digitally using high-speed serial transmission but vary in speeds and connection details. For speed differences, see Table 3-25.

Table 3-25   SATA and eSATA Drive Interface Overview

Interface	Location	Interface Speeds	Also Known As	Drive Types Supported
eSATA	External	1.5Gbps, 3Gbps, and 6Gbps		Hard disk drives, SSDs
SATA1	Internal	1.5Gbps	SATA 1.5Gbps and SATA Revision 1.0	Hard disk drives, optical (DVD, BD media) drives, RAID arrays, SSDs (Can be converted to eSATA via header cable.)
SATA2	Internal	3Gbps	SATA 3Gbps SATA Revision 2.0	Hard disk drives, optical (DVD, BD media) drives, RAID arrays, SSD (Can be converted to eSATA via header cable.)
SATA3	Internal	6Gbps	SATA 6Gbps Revision 3.0	Hard disk drives, RAID arrays, SSDs; backward compatible with SATA1, SATA2 (Can be converted to eSATA via header cable.)

Low-performance and older high-performance desktop motherboards feature top-facing SATA cable headers (see Figure 3-85). However, many recent high-performance motherboards have switched to front-facing SATA cable headers (see Figure 3-86).

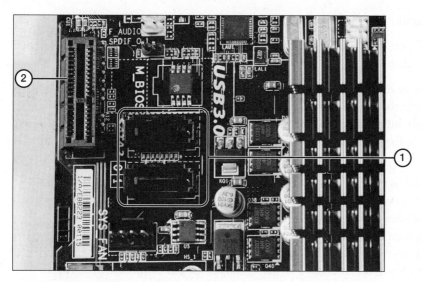

1. SATA host adapters
2. PCIe x1 slot

FIGURE 3-85   A Pair of SATA Ports from a Mini-ITX Motherboard

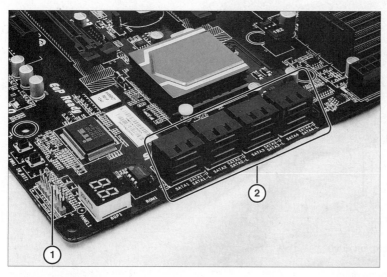

1. Front panel headers
2. SATA host adapters

FIGURE 3-86   A Motherboard That Features Eight Front-Mounted SATA Ports

SATA Configuration and Cabling

Refer to Figure 3-84 to compare the power and data connectors and cables used by typical SATA drives.

A SATA drive has a one-to-one connection to the corresponding SATA interface on the motherboard. Drive jumpers on SATA drives, when present, are used to reduce drive interface speed from the default to the next lower speed (from 6Gbps to 3Gbps or from 3Gbps to 1.5Gbps). See the specific drive's documentation for details.

SATA 1.5Gbps (*SATA1*) and 3Gbps (*SATA2*) drives and interfaces use the same cabling. However, SATA 6Gbps (*SATA3*) drives and interfaces use an improved version with heavier shielding for greater reliability. Cables made for SATA 6Gbps are typically marked as such and can also be used with slower SATA drives and interfaces. All SATA data cables use an L-shaped 7-pin connector, and all SATA power cables use a larger L-shaped 15-pin connector, as shown in Figure 3-87.

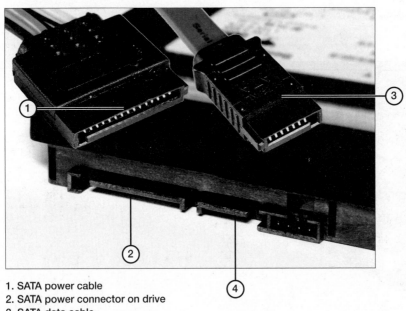

1. SATA power cable
2. SATA power connector on drive
3. SATA data cable
4. SATA data connector on drive

FIGURE 3-87   The Power and Data Cables and Connectors on SATA Drives

NOTE   SATA Express, also known as SATAe or Serial ATA Revision 3.2, was announced in 2014. It uses the PCI Express (PCIe) bus to achieve data transfer rates up to 16Gbps.

SATA data cables are available with straight-through connectors on both ends or with a right-angle connector on one end for easier connection to SATA drives. Some cables, either straight-through or right-angle, include a metal clip to help lock the drive into place.

eSATA cable headers convert standard SATA headers into eSATA ports available from the rear of the system.

See Figure 3-88 for examples of these cables.

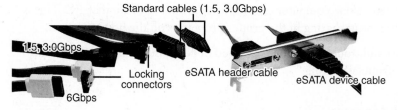

FIGURE 3-88   SATA and eSATA Data Cables

The SATA and eSATA drive interfaces are also designed to support hot swapping but must be configured for AHCI mode (also known as native mode) in the system BIOS or UEFI firmware. If the interface is configured for IDE mode (also known as emulation mode), the drive connected to it cannot be hot swapped and will also lose access to advanced SATA and eSATA features such as native command queuing (NCQ). RAID mode supports AHCI features along with allowing two or more drives to be used as a logical unit.

CAUTION   If internal SATA hard disks are configured to support hot swapping (configured as AHCI devices in the system BIOS/UEFI; it might also be necessary to enable hot swapping as an additional option), they also show up when you open the Safely Remove Hardware and Eject Media dialog in the Notification area of Windows. Do not select these drives for removal.

Peripheral Types

220-1001: Objective 3.6: Explain the purposes and uses of various peripheral types.

Many types of peripheral devices have been developed to perform specific tasks with a computer. Some are designed to input data, and others are designed to output data from the computer. This section describes the most common input and output devices that a technician should be able to install and operate. Some may be obvious, but others may not be.

Printer

Standalone or networked, printers enable the printing of paper documents from applications. Laser printers are common in businesses, and inkjet printers are common for home use.

A printer on a standalone computer can share the printer with another PC. This is done by enabling print sharing in the printer properties on the host computer.

Printer support and troubleshooting is covered in depth in Chapter 5, "Hardware and Network Troubleshooting."

ADF and Flatbed Scanners

Automatic document feeder (ADF) scanners, also known as "sheet fed" scanners, and flatbed scanners are used to create digital documents from printed documents. An ADF scanner can process a stack of several documents automatically, whereas a flatbed scanner can process one sheet at a time.

Some scanners use OCR technology, which scans to a .pdf file, which then becomes searchable data.

Scanners for documents and photos are available in the following form factors:

- Almost every multifunction print/scan/fax/copy device includes a flatbed scanner with resolution up to 2,400dpi. Most of these also include a sheet feeder for easier scanning of multiple pages.

- Scanners made for photos typically support resolutions up to 4,800dpi or greater. Some include a diffuser or clear glass lid light source with negative or transparency holders for use in scanning negatives and slides. Some of these can scan negatives as large as 8×10 inches.

- Scanners made for travel scan a single sheet at a time and might weigh as little as 1 pound. These typically have resolutions up to 600dpi.

All of these scanners plug into a USB port; some can also use WiFi. A driver is typically installed before the scanner is connected. Drivers are available for Windows and macOS, and portable models also support Android and iOS. Some scanner vendors also provide Linux drivers.

Software included with a scanner varies, but scanners for Windows and macOS typically include page-recognition software and some type of photo editing or organizing app.

Barcode and QR Scanners

Barcode readers and QR scanners are used in a variety of point-of-sale (POS) retail, library, industrial, medical, and other environments to track inventory.

A barcode reader uses one of the following technologies:

- Pen-based readers use a pen-shaped device that includes a light source and photo diode in the tip. The point of the pen is dragged across the barcode to read the varying thicknesses and positions of the bars in the barcode and translate them into a digitized code that is transmitted to the POS or inventory system.

- Laser scanners are commonly used in grocery and big-box stores. They use a horizontal-mounted or vertical-mounted prism or mirror and laser beam protected by a transparent glass cover to read barcodes.

- CCD or CMOS readers use a hand-held gun-shaped device to hold an array of light sensors mounted in a row. The reader emits light that is reflected off the barcode and is detected by the light sensors.

- Camera-based readers contain many rows of CCD sensors that generate an image of the sensor that is processed to decode the barcode information.

Wired barcode readers typically interface through the USB port. See the documentation for a reader to determine whether to install the driver before or after connecting the reader. Many barcode readers use Bluetooth to make a wireless connection between the reader and the computer or other data-acquisition device. In such cases, you need a Bluetooth receiver in your PC, and the device needs to be paired with the computer or POS system.

Quick Response (QR) codes are a special type of barcode that are two dimensional and can be read by a scanner on a mobile phone. They were first invented by Toyota to track car production and then gained widespread use as cell phones proliferated.

Monitors

Monitors are used to display the output of data and video information. Some monitors use touchscreen technology that enables both input and output from the monitor.

Generally speaking, any monitor can work with just about any computer, but the connections need to match. If they do not match, you need to purchase a video converter (that can translate the signals) or a new video card; otherwise, a different monitor may be necessary.

VR Headset

Virtual reality (VR) has several medical, engineering, and construction uses as well as an increasing presence in the world of gaming. It allows surgeons to practice difficult procedures before an operation, and it allows engineers to walk through buildings before construction. For gamers it offers an enhanced environment for multiplayer gaming.

The immersion effect provided by a VR experience is usually delivered via a head-mounted device (HMD) that covers the eyes, closing off the external world. Inside the mask, two LED panels—one for each eye—are located inside the HMD. The visual feed to these panels is adjusted to create the 3D effect. Some models have additional lenses to enhance the experience. The HMD can monitor head movements, and a special gaming glove can add hand inputs, so the user can move around in the 3D environment.

The quality of the 3D experience can vary greatly, depending on the power of the computer generating the image. An array of 3D headsets are available for devices ranging from cell phones and game consoles all the way up to powerful gaming PCs.

Optical Drive Types

Most laptops are shipped without optical drives—such as CD/DVD/BD drives. For times when one is necessary, external optical drives are a good solution. They connect via USB and usually self-load drivers. This option allows computers to share drives that are less necessary than they were just a few years ago and prevents the addition of precious weight to laptops.

Mouse

A computer mouse is a wireless or wired device that moves the cursor on a display screen, allowing the user to interact with the computer. There are several features on some mice that allow for scrolling and browsing the Web. Wireless mice use Bluetooth to connect to the computer.

Windows, macOS, and Linux include mouse drivers. To install a USB mouse, simply plug it in, and the operating system installs the drivers needed. Mice are part of the human interface device (HID) category in Device Manager, and Windows installs HID drivers after the mouse is connected.

To install a wireless mouse, plug the receiver into a USB port and follow the directions to pair the mouse and receiver. Receivers that can control multiple devices, such as Logitech's Unifying receiver, might require you to install additional software to enable pairing of multiple devices with a single receiver.

Mouse alternatives, such as touchscreens, trackballs, and touchpads, are considered mouse devices because they install and are configured the same way.

NOTE   Some systems running Windows and Linux have PS/2 mouse and/or keyboard ports. To install a PS/2 mouse or keyboard, be sure to shut down the system and remove power before connecting the mouse or keyboard. PS/2 devices, unlike USB devices, are not hot-swappable devices.

If a mouse uses Bluetooth, it needs to be paired with the computer's Bluetooth receiver.

Pairing a Bluetooth Mouse (Windows)

To pair a Bluetooth mouse computer from the desktop:

Step 1.   Click the **Bluetooth** icon in the taskbar.

Step 2.   Click **Open Settings**.

Step 3.   Enable **Discovery**.

Step 4.   Enable **Allow Bluetooth Devices to Connect to This Computer** (see Figure 3-89).

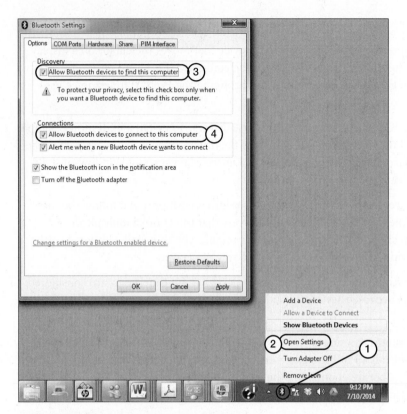

1. Click Bluetooth icon to start pairing process
2. Click to open Settings dialog.
3. Must be enabled to allow a new Bluetooth device to find this computer
4. Must be enabled to enable Bluetooth devices to connect to this computer

FIGURE 3-89   Enabling Discovery of and Connections to Bluetooth Devices

Step 5.   Open the **Bluetooth** icon in the taskbar and click **Add a Device**.

Step 6.   Press the **Connect** button on the mouse.

Step 7.   Select the mouse from the list of Bluetooth devices and click **Next** (see Figure 3-90).

Step 8.   After the mouse is detected and the drivers have been installed, click **Close**.

Step 9.   To prevent connections from unauthorized Bluetooth devices, disable discovery until the next time you want to add a Bluetooth device.

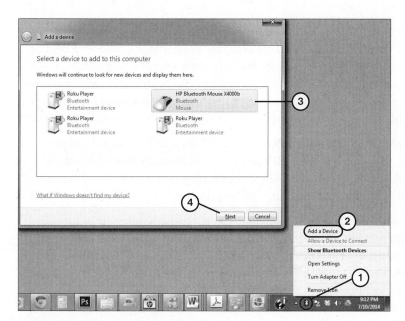

1. Click Bluetooth icon to continue pairing process.
2. Click to add a device.
3. Click the device to pair with the computer.
4. Click Next.

FIGURE 3-90   Selecting a Device to Pair

NOTE   In Windows 10, Bluetooth devices can be easily managed by typing **Bluetooth** in the search box.

Keyboard

Using a keyboard is the most common way to interact with a computer. Like a mouse, it can be wired or Bluetooth wireless. There are many kinds of keyboards designed for use in different environments and for use on different devices.

Windows, macOS, and Linux include keyboard drivers. To install a USB keyboard, simply plug it in, and the operating system installs the drivers needed. Keyboards are part of the human interface device (HID) category in Device Manager, and Windows installs HID drivers after a keyboard is connected.

To install a wireless keyboard, plug the receiver into a USB port and follow the directions to pair the keyboard and receiver. The instructions for pairing a Bluetooth keyboard are similar to those for pairing a mouse, except that the user is prompted to enter a code on the keyboard during the pairing process.

Touchpad

Touchpads (also known as trackpads) are available as externally connecting devices so users can experience the same interaction on a computer as is available with some laptops. They perform most of the functions of a mouse, with finger motions across the pad guiding the cursor. Some touchpads allow multitouch actions for resizing images and other functions. Touchpads connect via USB and self-install the drivers.

Touchpads are built into almost all laptops and the keyboards on many tablets. Touchpads are also available as standalone devices or integrated into keyboards. Touchpads and keyboards that include touchpads plug in through the USB port and are recognized as mice by the built-in Windows drivers.

If a touchpad or a keyboard with an integrated touchpad is wireless, it is normally recognized automatically. If the touchpad or keyboard has additional keys or buttons, it might be necessary to install proprietary drivers to enable the additional keys or buttons. Proprietary drivers are also necessary to enable multitouch gestures (using two or more fingers).

Signature Pad

Signature pads are used in banking, medical, retail, and other environments where signature verification is required. Instead of signing a paper, the user or customer uses a stylus (touch pen) to sign a small signature screen. The signature is captured via OCR to make a legal document. Some have touchpad overlays that allow signature with a finger. Most signature pads use a USB interface.

Game Controllers

Game controllers are usually handheld devices used to control the interaction with a game on the computer. They can include joysticks, keyboards, mice, or controllers controlled by feet for exercise or in-flight games. Some use a visual interaction with an optical sensor on the computer to determine the location of the controller.

Game pads and joysticks plug into a computer's USB port. In most cases, Windows installs compatible drivers automatically as soon as a game pad or joystick is plugged in. However, if a controller does not work, it might be necessary to manually select the correct driver from the controller's properties sheet in Device Manager. If a controller uses Bluetooth, pair it with the receiver in your system.

macOS has varied support for game pads and joysticks. With some controllers, you can install vendor-supplied macOS drivers. If a controller uses Bluetooth, pair it with your system. For more information, see http://www.cnet.com/how-to/how-to-connect-game-controllers-to-your-mac/.

Game pads and joysticks on Linux are supported by the "Joystick" interface and the newer "evdev" interface. If a specific driver is not available, go to https://wiki.archlinux.org/index.php/Gamepad to learn how to configure your controller.

Camera/Webcam

Cameras on computers are used to allow for visual interaction between users. Most laptops and notepads and phones have cameras built into the devices, and for desktops, an external camera can use a USB connection to bring images to the PC.

A webcam is a simple digital camera capable of taking video or still images for transmission over the Internet. Unlike digital cameras, webcams don't include storage capabilities.

Virtually all webcams plug into a USB port or use wireless technology. Webcams are generally used in live chat situations, such as with Skype and FaceTime, or other IM clients. Some offer autofocus and zoom features for better image clarity, and most have built-in microphones.

Before connecting a webcam, you typically need to install driver and configuration software. Obtain the most up-to-date drivers from the vendor's website.

After a webcam is installed, use its setup menu to adjust white balance, exposure, gain, and other options (see Figure 3-91). If you plan to use the webcam's microphone, disable other microphones in your computer's audio mixer application.

Before using the webcam for IM or phone calls, make sure the appropriate application is configured to use the webcam.

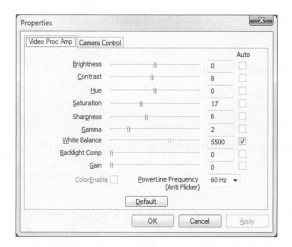

FIGURE 3-91   A Typical Webcam Properties Sheet Being Used to Configure the Camera's Video Processor

Microphone

A microphone plugs into the 3.5mm mini-jack microphone jack. The jack connects the mic to the integrated motherboard audio or to a sound card mounted on the motherboard. The most common microphones used on PCs include those built into headsets or those that use stands.

In Windows, microphone volume is controlled by the Windows Sound applet's mixer control. Open the Recording tab to adjust volume, to mute or unmute the microphone, or to adjust microphone boost.

In macOS, open **System Preferences > Sound > Input** to find the microphone volume control. In Linux, open **System Settings > Sound >Input** to find the microphone volume control.

NOTE   The microphone jack is monaural, whereas the line-in jack supports stereo. Be sure to use the line-in jack to record from a stereo audio source.

To install a microphone on a PC with a sound card or integrated audio, follow this procedure:

Step 1.   Connect the microphone to the microphone jack, which is marked with a pink ring or a microphone icon.

Step 2.   If you see a dialog that asks you to confirm the device you have plugged into the microphone jack, select **Microphone** from the list of devices.

Step 3.   If the microphone has an on/off switch, make sure the microphone is turned on.

To verify that the microphone is working in Windows:

Step 1.   Open the **Sounds** icon in Control Panel.

Step 2.   Click the **Recording** tab.

Step 3.   Make sure the microphone you installed is enabled and selected as the default device.

Step 4.   Click **Configure**.

Step 5.   In the Speech Recognition menu that opens, click **Set Up Microphone**.

Step 6. Select the microphone type and click **Next**.

Step 7. Adjust the microphone position and click **Next**.

Step 8. Read the onscreen text when prompted and click **Next** when finished.

Step 9. Click **Finish**. Close the Speech Recognition dialog to return to the Sounds dialog.

TIP If the volume displayed in Step 8 is too low or too high, click **Properties** in the Sounds dialog. Click the **Levels** tab, adjust **Microphone Boost** to the midpoint (10.0dB), and retry Steps 4 through 9. If the volume is still too low or too high, adjust the volume on the Levels tab.

Speakers

You can connect speakers to a computer in several ways:

- 3.5mm speaker mini-jack
- SPDIF digital audio port
- Proprietary sound card header cable
- HDMI digital A/V port
- USB surround audio external device

The default setting for audio mixers is to use speakers connected to analog 3.5mm audio jacks. To use a digital speaker or audio output in Windows:

Step 1. Click or tap **Hardware and Sound**.

Step 2. In the Sound category, click or tap **Manage Audio Devices**.

Step 3. Click or tap a playback device on the Playback tab (see Figure 3-92).

Step 4. To make the selected device your default, click or tap **Set Default**.

Step 5. Click **Apply** and then click **OK** to use your new selection.

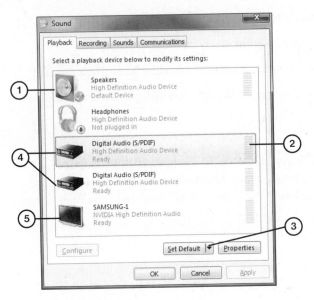

1. Current default
2. Selected device
3. Click or tap to set selected device as default
4. Two SPDIF outputs (coaxial and optical)
5. HDMI A/V connection to HDTV

FIGURE 3-92   Selecting a Digital Audio Output (SPDIF) on a PC

Headset

A computer headset enables the user to both speak and listen to a session on the Web. A headset has both a microphone and headphones (either a single earpiece or double) and connects to a computer either wirelessly or with a USB connection. Some older headsets have two jacks—one for a microphone and one for the speaker.

Projector

Classrooms and conference rooms are natural places for use of LCD or overhead projectors. In those environments, projectors may have dedicated computers, but it should be able to readily connect a laptop as well.

While an older computer may have a VGA port, that analog display connector, introduced in 1987, is definitely a legacy port. When shopping for a display, you should consider displays that support one or more of the following digital display connectors: DVI-D, HDMI, or DisplayPort. Some projectors also support USB connectors.

Using an analog display connector requires a digital-to-analog conversion in the computer and an analog-to-digital conversion at the display or projector, which can introduce display quality problems, limits resolution, and prevents the playback of protected digital content (Blu-ray, premium movie channels, and so on) at full resolution. To make sure you can play back protected digital content with your computer, make sure the video card and display/projector support HDCP (high-bandwidth digital copy protection).

Brightness/Lumens

The brightness of an LCD display is measured in candelas per square meter (cd/m^2), sometimes referred to as "nits." The higher this value, the brighter the display. Typical values for LCD panels range from 250 cd/m^2 to 350 cd/m^2.

The brightness of a projector is measured in lumens. The higher the value, the brighter the output. To use a projector in a normally lit room, look for a projector with a rating of 3,000 lumens or higher, as in most portable and conference room projectors.

Projector support and troubleshooting are discussed in further detail in Chapter 5.

External Storage Drives

External storage is commonly in the form of a USB thumb drive or an eSATA hard drive. See the section "Storage Devices," earlier in this chapter.

KVM

A keyboard-video-mouse (KVM) switch enables a single keyboard, display, and mouse to support two or more computers. KVM switches are popular in server rooms and are also useful in tech support environments.

The simplest *KVM switch* is a box with input connectors for USB or PS/2 mouse and keyboard and VGA or other display and two or more sets of cables leading to the corresponding I/O ports and video ports on the computers that will be hosted. Some KVM switches also support audio. With this type of KVM switch, a special key combination or a push button on the switch is used to switch between computers.

KVM switches for server rooms and data centers are known as *local remote KVM* and typically use CAT5 or higher-quality cables to run to special interface devices on each server.

To install a KVM switch:

Step 1.   Shut down the computers and display.

Step 2.   Connect the keyboard and mouse and other shared connectors (such as speakers) to the KVM switch.

Step 3.   Connect the KVM switch to the computers.

Step 4.   Start the computers.

Step 5.   Install drivers, if necessary.

Be sure to use the correct key combinations to switch between computers and to emulate other keyboards (for example, if a Windows keyboard is used with an macOS computer). In some situations, a firmware upgrade for the switch might be needed. Follow the instructions provided with the switch to perform a successful upgrade.

Magnetic Reader/Chip Reader

The move toward cashless transactions in recent years has required more security from point-of-purchase sales devices. Most of the world has been using chip card readers for many years, but the transition to them in the United States has been fairly recent. A chip adds a layer of authentication not provided by a magnetic stripe, which was easily copied and fraudulently sold on black markets. For the foreseeable future, the devices at check stands and the mobile Square type devices will be able to accept both strip and card chip payments, depending on requirements of the bank backing the cards.

NFC/Tap Pay Device

Near field communication (*NFC*) enables two devices to wirelessly talk to each other when they're close together. One increasingly popular way NFC is being used is with mobile payments, through systems such as Apple Pay, Samsung Pay, and Android Pay (Google Pay). Users, having matched the app with a credit or debit card, simply open the Wallet app when the cashier is ready and tap the device. Payments are authenticated and secure.

An example of the POS devices that use this NFC technology is Square, which makes a few different models of card readers and NFC systems (see www.square.com). These attach to a computer or mobile device via Bluetooth or with a micro USB cable.

Smart Card Reader

A smart card reader plugs into a USB port. Once a smart card reader has been installed, it works the same as a built-in smart card reader for controlling access to corporate networks or other restricted resources.

Smart card readers are supported by Windows, macOS, and popular Linux distributions. A driver is typically installed automatically when a smart card reader is connected.

Power Supplies

220-1001: Objective 3.7: Summarize power supply types and features.

Power supplies vary widely in features and ratings, and when building a custom configuration or updating a system to perform a specific task, the power supply is a critical factor in the success of that system.

The *power supply* is so named because it converts power from high-voltage alternating current (*AC*) to low-voltage direct current (*DC*). There are lots of wire coils and other components inside the power supply that do the work, and during the conversion process, a great deal of heat is produced. Most power supplies include one or two fans to dissipate the heat created by the operation of the power supply; however, a few power supplies designed for silent operation use passive heat sink technology instead of fans. On power supplies that include fans, fans also help to cool the rest of the computer. Figure 3-93 shows a typical desktop computer's power supply.

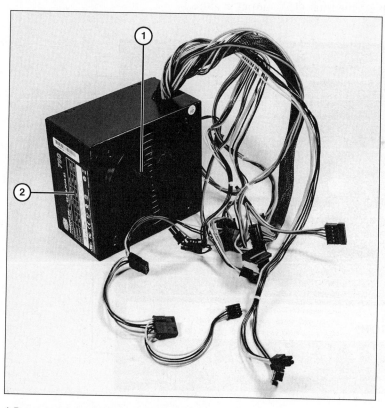

1. **Power supply intake fan (faces into system)**
2. **Specification and safety information label**

FIGURE 3-93 A Typical ATX Power Supply

Power Supply Ratings

Power supply capacity is rated in watts, and the more watts a power supply provides, the more devices it can safely power.

You can use the label attached to a power supply, as shown in Figure 3-94, to determine its wattage rating and see important safety reminders.

A power supply with two separate +12V rails is a dual-rail design. Some high-performance power supplies feature more than two +12V outputs, such as the 650-watt model shown in Figure 3-94. Another term for two or more +12V outputs is *split rail*.

NOTE   Power supplies with two or more separate +12V power sources are common today to provide adequate power for CPUs (which use voltage regulators on the motherboard or in the CPU itself to reduce +12V power to the power level needed) and other devices, such as PCIe video cards, fans, and drives. Add together the values of the +12V rails to get the total +12V output in amps.

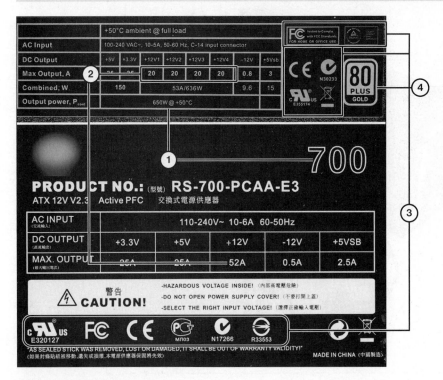

1. Rated maximum output (watts)
2. +12V amperage
3. Safety approvals
4. 80 PLUS Gold rating

FIGURE 3-94   Typical Power Supply Labels

115V vs. 220V Multivoltage Power Supplies

Most power supplies are designed to handle two different voltage ranges:

- 115–120V/60Hz

- 220–240V/50Hz

Power supplies that support these ranges are known as ***dual voltage*** power supplies. Standard North American power is now 115–120V/60Hz-cycle AC. (The previous standard was 110V.) The power used in European and Asian countries is typically 230–240V/50Hz AC (previously 220V).

How can you tell whether a power supply meets minimum safety standards? Look for the appropriate safety certification mark for your country or locale. For example, in the United States and Canada, the backward UR logo is used to indicate that the power supply has the UL and UL Canada safety certifications as a component. (The familiar circled UL logo is used for finished products only.) Both power supplies shown in Figure 3-94 meet U.S. and other nations' safety standards.

CAUTION   Power supplies that do not bear the UL or other certification marks should not be used, as their safety is unknown.

Typically, power supplies in recent tower case (upright case) machines use 500-watt or larger power supplies, reflecting the greater number of drives and cards that can be installed in these computers. Power supplies used in smaller desktop computers have typical ratings of around 220 to 300 watts. The power supply rating is found on the top or side of the power supply, along with safety rating information and amperage levels produced by the power supply's different DC outputs.

Some older power supplies have a slider switch with two markings: 115 (for North American 110–120V/60HzAC) and 230 (for European and Asian 220–240V/50Hz AC). Figure 3-95 shows a slider switch set for correct North American voltage. If a power supply is set to the wrong input voltage, the system will not work. Setting a power supply for 230V with 110–120V current is harmless; however, feeding 220–240V into a power supply set for 115V will destroy the power supply and possibly other onboard hardware.

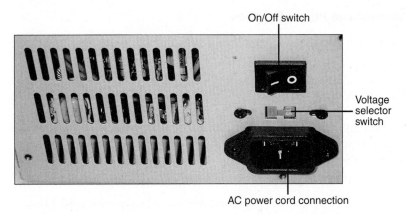

FIGURE 3-95   An Older Power Supply's Sliding Voltage Switch Set for Correct North American Voltage (115V)

NOTE   Note that most recent power supplies for desktop and laptop computers can automatically determine the correct voltage level and cycle rate. These are referred to as *autoswitching* power supplies, and they lack the voltage/cycle selection switch shown in Figure 3-95.

The on/off switch shown in Figure 3-95 controls the flow of current into the power supply. It is not the system power switch, which is located on the front or top of desktop systems and is connected to the motherboard. When you press the system power switch, the motherboard signals the power supply to provide power.

CAUTION   Unless the power supply is disconnected from AC current or is turned off, a small amount of power can still be flowing through the system even when it is not running. Do not install or remove components or perform other types of service to the inside of a PC unless you disconnect the AC power cord or turn off the power supply. Wait a few seconds afterward to ensure that the power is completely off. A desktop motherboard may have indicator lights that turn off when the power has completely drained from the system.

Power Supply Form Factors and Connectors

When shopping for a power supply, it is necessary to make sure it can connect to your motherboard. While almost all power supplies sold today have a 24-pin connector, you may encounter a legacy 20-pin connector used by older mother-boards in the ATX family. The 24-pin is used by recent ATX/microATX/Mini-ITX motherboards requiring the ATX12V 2.2 power supply standard.

Most motherboards use power supplies that feature several additional connectors to supply added power, as follows (see Figure 3-96):

- Some high-wattage power supplies with 20-pin connectors might also include a 20-pin to 24-pin adapter. Some 24-pin power supplies include a split connector to support either 24-pin or 20-pin motherboard power connectors (refer to Figure 3-97).

- The four-wire square ATX12V connector provides additional 12V power to the motherboard. This connector is sometimes referred to as a "P4" or "Pentium 4" connector.

- Most recent power supplies use the 4/8 pin +12V (EPS12V) connector (see Figure 3-98) instead of the ATX12V power connector. The EPS12V lead is split into two 4-wire square connectors to be compatible with motherboards that use either ATX12V or EPS12V power leads.

- Some very old motherboards use a 6-wire AUX connector to provide additional power.

ATX12V secondary   AUX secondary   ATX primary (20-pin)   ATX12V 2.2 primary (24-pin)

FIGURE 3-96 20-Pin ATX and 24-Pin ATX Power Connectors Compared to 4-pin ATX12V and 6-Wire AUX Power Connectors

Figure 3-97 shows both sides of a convertible 24-pin/20-pin ATX power supply connector.

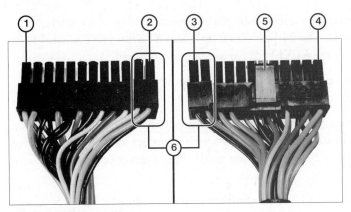

1. Pin 1 (+3.3V, orange wire)
2. Pin 12 (+3.3V, orange wire)
3. Pin 24 (ground wire, black)
4. Pin 13 (+3.3V, orange wire)
5. Retaining clip
6. Used only on motherboards that use a 24-pin ATX power supply

FIGURE 3-97   Both Sides of a 24-pin ATX Power Supply Cable (Also Compatible with 20-Pin Motherboards)

The power supply also powers various peripherals, such as:

- Hard disks and CD/DVD/BD optical drives

- Case fans that do not plug into the motherboard and that use a 4-pin Molex power connector

- An L-shaped 15-pin thinline power connector for Serial ATA (SATA) hard disks

- A PCI Express 6-pin or 8-pin power cable (PCIe 6/8-pin) for high-performance PCI Express x16 video cards that require additional 12V power

Figure 3-98 illustrates these power connectors as well as the EPS12V motherboard power connector.

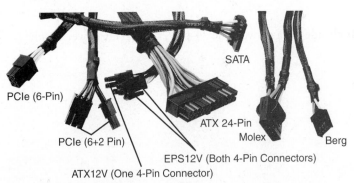

FIGURE 3-98   Power Supply Connectors for Peripherals and Modern Motherboards

Table 3-26 lists the power levels carried by each connector type.

Table 3-26 Power Levels for Different Connector Types

Connector	+5V	+12V	+3.3V	Notes
Molex	Yes	Yes	No	Used today primarily for case fans that do not connect to the motherboard or that can be adapted to SATA drives
Berg	Yes	Yes	No	Some add-on cards use this connector for power
SATA	Yes	Yes	Optional	Use Molex to SATA power connector if power supply lacks adequate SATA connectors
PCIe 6-pin	No	Yes	No	Midrange PCIe video cards
PCIe 8-pin	No	Yes	No	High-performance PCIe video cards
ATX12V	No	Yes	No	Most recent and current motherboards except those using EPS12V
EPS12V	No	Yes	No	Split into two ATX12V-compatible sections

If your power supply doesn't have enough connectors, you can add Y-splitters to divide one power lead into two, but these splitters can short out and can also reduce the efficiency of the power supply. You can also convert a standard Molex connector into a SATA connector with the appropriate adapter.

Standard power supply wires are color-coded thus:

Red: +5V

Yellow: +12V

Orange: +3.3V

Black: Ground (earth)

Purple: +5V (standby)

Green: PS-On

Gray: Power good

White: No connection (24-pin); –5V (20-pin)

Blue: –12V

Some power supplies (see Figure 3-99) use modular connections so that you can customize the power supply connections needed for your hardware. An advantage of such a power supply is that the cables can detach from the power supply, and cable management is much easier.

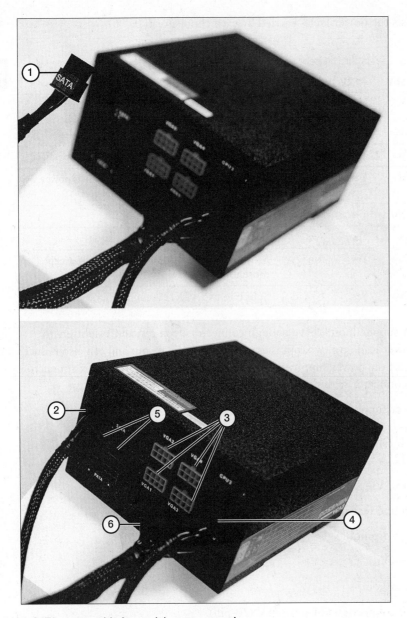

1. SATA power cable for modular power supply
2. SATA power cable after connection
3. PCIe power ports
4. EPS12V power cable
5. Additional SATA power ports
6. Motherboard main power cable

FIGURE 3-99   A Modular Power Supply with Cables You Can Attach to Customize Support for Your System's Needs

If your wattage calculations or your tests agree that it's time to replace a power supply, make sure the replacement meets the following criteria:

- Has the same power supply connectors and the same pinout as the original

- Has the same form factor (shape, size, and switch location) as the original

- Has the same or higher wattage rating as the original; a higher wattage rating is highly desirable

- Supports any special features required by your CPU, video card, and motherboard, such as SLI support (support for PCIe connectors to power two or more high-performance PCIe video cards), high levels of +12V power (ATX12V v2.2 4-pin or EPS12V 8-pin power connectors), and so on

TIP   To ensure form factor connector compatibility, consider removing the old power supply and taking it with you if you plan to buy a replacement at retail. If you are buying a replacement online, measure the dimensions of your existing power supply to ensure that a new one will fit properly in the system. So-called "EPX" power supplies are longer than ATX power supplies and won't fit into smaller cases.

Wattage vs. Amperage

The power supply label shown at the top of Figure 3-94 is rated at 650 watts, while the power supply label shown at the bottom of Figure 3-94 is rated at 700 watts. Take a closer look at the amperage ratings, though, and it becomes clear that the 650-watt power supply provides much more of the +12V power needed by processors and motors.

The 650-watt power supply provides a total of 80A on the +12V lines (20A each on four +12V lines). The 700-watt power supply provides only 52A on its +12V line. The 700-watt power supply provides no information about the temperature or load factor at which its rating is calculated, while the 650-watt power supply indicates that its calculations are made at 50 degrees Celsius (about 122 degrees Fahrenheit) at full load. Despite the rating difference, it's clear that the 650-watt power supply shown in Figure 3-94 provides more useful power than the 700-watt power supply in the same figure.

When replacing a power supply, make sure the new one is robust enough to handle any extra work from upgrades in the past or planned upgrades in the future. Power supplies are best in the middle of their wattage range, and a PC that is underpowered can have many problems that are difficult to diagnose. The power supply is no place to scrimp on budget.

To determine the **wattage rating** needed for a replacement power supply, add up the wattage ratings for everything connected to your computer that uses the power supply, including the motherboard, processor, memory, cards, drives, and bus-powered USB devices. Include any external devices that are used on occasion. If the total wattage used exceeds 70% of the wattage rating of your power supply, you should upgrade to a larger power supply. Check the vendor spec sheets for wattage ratings.

If you have **amperage ratings** instead of wattage ratings, multiply the amperage by the volts to determine wattage and then start adding. If a device uses two or three different voltage levels, be sure to carry out this calculation for each voltage level and add up the figures to determine the wattage requirement for the device. Review Figure 3-94 and the "Wattage vs. Amperage" sidebar earlier in this chapter for a reminder of the importance of +12V amperage.

Table 3-27 provides calculations for typical compact desktop and high-performance desktop systems, based on the eXtreme Outer Vision online calculator at https:// outervision.com.

Table 3-27   Calculating Power Supply Requirements

Components	MicroATX System with Integrated Video	Full-Size ATX System with SLI (Dual Graphics Cards)
CPU	AMD A8-7650K (4 core, 3.3GHz with 4MB cache)	Intel Core i7-5930K (6 core, 3.7GHz with 15MB cache)
RAM Size/Type	2 × 4GB DDR3	2 × 8GB DDR4
Rewritable DVD drive	Yes	Yes
Blu-ray	No	Yes
SATA hard disk	5400RPM	7200RPM
SSD	No	M.2
Case fans	2 × 120mm	2 × 140mm
Liquid cooling	No	Corsair Hydro H75
GPU	Integrated into CPU	NVIDIA GeForce GTX TITAN Z SLI
PCIe card	0	High-end sound card TV tuner (cable) card
USB 2.0 device	1	2
Estimated wattage	224 watts	1239 watts
Recommended power supply size (80% efficiency assumed)	400 watts	1600 watts

Custom Components

220-1001: Objective 3.8: Given a scenario, select and configure appropriate components for a custom PC configuration to meet the customer specifications or needs.

Either as new builds or as upgrades to existing computers, you will need to be able to work on custom PC configurations for some of your clients. From choosing the right motherboard, CPU, and memory size to selecting the right peripherals, power supply, and display, desktop computers offer an amazing variety of options. The A+ 220-1001 exam objectives provide guidelines for seven configurations for graphics, A/V editing, virtualization, gaming, network-attached storage devices, thick clients, and thin clients.

This section covers the requirements for these systems as well as how to select the correct options for each one.

Graphic/CAD/CAM Design Workstation

A workstation optimized for graphics or CAD/CAM (computer-aided drafting/computer-aided manufacturing) design needs the maximum performance available at the time of purchase. Because of the heavy demands that 3D CAD rendering or RAW photo editing place on the workstation, premium components, while expensive, are necessary. Table 3-28 lists the major features needed for this type of computer, along with examples and notes.

Table 3-28 Graphic/CAD/CAM Design Workstation Features

Features	Benefits	Recommendations and Example Products	Notes
SSD with multicore processor	Fast rendering of 3D or 2D graphics	4.0GHz or faster, six cores or more, large cache (8MB or more total cache), 64-bit support Intel Core i97 Extreme Edition AMD Ryzen 7	Fastest multicore CPUs available from Intel or AMD.
High-end video	Faster rendering of 3D or 2D graphics on applications that support GPU acceleration (AutoCAD, Photoshop CC, and others)	PCIe CAD/CAM or 3D cards with 2GB or more RAM optimized for OpenGL 4.x, DirectX 11 or 12, support for two or more displays AMD RadeonPro (CAD, CAM, CGI, Photoshop) NVIDIA Quadro series (CAD, CAM, CGI)	Fastest GPUs available from AMD or NVIDIA. More GPU RAM provides faster performance when rendering large 3D objects. FirePro and Quadro cards use drivers optimized for CAD/CAM/CGI.

Features	Benefits	Recommendations and Example Products	Notes
Maximum RAM	Reduces swapping to disk during editing or rendering	16GB or more DDR3 or DDR4 Use matched memory modules running in multichannel configurations	System should be running 64-bit version of the operating system.

Although the A+ 220-1001 exam objectives do not recommend specific motherboard configurations for these custom PC configurations, you should specify systems with adequate support for high-performance memory, processors, and video for the graphic/CAD/CAM design workstation or audio/video editing workstation. A typical high-performance motherboard suitable as a foundation for these configurations is shown in Figure 3-100.

1. **M.2 SSD**
2. **DDR4 memory sockets**
3. **PCIe video card slots for NVIDIA SLI or AMD CrossFire**

FIGURE 3-100   A High-Performance System That Features a Fast SSD Using the M.2 Form Factor, DDR4 Memory, and Three PCIe Video Card Slots

Audio/Video Editing Workstation

An audio/video editing workstation has many component features in common with the graphic/CAD/CAM design workstation detailed in the previous section. In fact, the recommendations in Table 3-28 for hard drives and displays are suitable for either type of workstation, and the CPU suggestions in Table 3-28 are also suitable for this type of workstation. Table 3-29 lists the major features needed for this type of computer and why they're important.

Table 3-29 Audio/Video Editing Workstation Features

Features	Benefits	Recommendations	Notes
Multicore processor	Fast rendering of 3D or 2D graphics	4.0GHz or faster, six cores or more, large cache (8MB or more total cache), 64-bit support Intel Core i9 Extreme Edition AMD Radeon series	Fastest multicore CPUs available from Intel or AMD.
Maximum RAM	Reduces swapping to disk during editing or rendering	16GB or more DDR3 or DDR4 Use matched memory modules running in multichannel configurations	Especially important for motion graphics editing.
Specialized audio card	Higher sampling rates and higher signal-to-noise ratios for better audio quality	24-bit, 192KHz or better audio performance; upgradable Op-amp (operational amplifier) sockets; PCIe interface Sound Blaster ZxR ASUS, Xonar H6, Essence ST, Essence STX	PCIe interface is preferred because it is faster than PCI. Upgradable Op-amp sockets allow customization of audio characteristics.
Specialized video card	Faster performance when rendering video	AMD FirePro W-series, AMD Radeon R9 NVIDIA Quadro M series	Fastest GPUs on market. HDMI, DisplayPort, or DVI interfaces.
Large, fast hard drive, SSD if possible.	Faster writes during saves, faster retrieval of source material during media editing and creation	Maximum performance: SATA Express or M.2 SSD drive Good performance: SSD SATA 6Gbps large enough for Windows and applications (128GB–512GB) and separate SATA 6Gbps or USB 3.0 data drive or SATA hybrid drive 4TB or larger SATA 6Gbps or USB 3.0 drives from Seagate, WD, Toshiba, HGTS	If an SSD is used as the main drive, use a fast hard disk drive or hybrid drive for temporary files.
Dual monitors	Editing software menus and playback can be on separate screens Can render and edit while using secondary display for other applications	27-inch or larger from many vendors	HDMI or DisplayPort interfaces recommended; DVI acceptable; avoid VGA-only displays.

Figure 3-101 shows a high-end video card with its own cooling system.

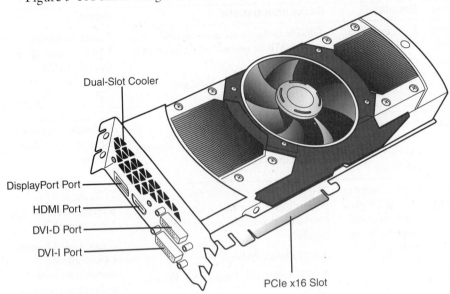

FIGURE 3-101   A High-Performance Video Card That Uses the NVIDIA TITAN Z GPU and Is Suitable for Video and Photo Editing and Gaming

Virtualization Workstation

AMD, Intel, Microsoft, and third-party vendors provide various tools to help determine details about a processor, including whether a system supports hardware-assisted virtualization:

- **AMD Virtualization Technology and Microsoft Hyper-V System Compatibility Check Utility:** Available from https://www.amd.com/en/support

- **CPU-Z:** Available from https://www.cpuid.com

- **Intel Processor Identification Utility:** Available from www.intel.com

- **Microsoft Windows Hardware-Assisted Virtualization Detection Tool:** Available from the Download Center at www.microsoft.com

- **Gibson Research Corporation's SecurAble:** Available from www.grc.com

A virtualization workstation is intended to be a host for two or more operating systems running at the same time in separate virtual machines (VMs). To ensure adequate resources for each VM, the configuration shown in Table 3-30 emphasizes maximum RAM and CPU cores. These guidelines are general and point to minimum recommendations. Requirements will vary depending on how many machines will be running and how much work they will be doing.

Table 3-30 Virtualization Workstation Features

Features	Benefits	Recommendations	Notes
Maximum RAM	By increasing RAM well above the recommended level for a system running a single operating system, you help ensure sufficient RAM for each VM in use.	16GB or more RAM (64-bit system)	Systems running 32-bit versions of Windows cannot use more than 4GB of RAM.
Maximum CPU cores	Multiple VMs use more execution threads than a single operating system, so a multicore CPU helps VMs perform better.	3.0GHz or faster, six to eight cores or more, large cache (8MB or more total cache), 64-bit support Intel Core i9 Extreme Edition, AMD Ryzen Threadripper	Fastest and most powerful Intel or AMD CPU. System needs support for hardware-assisted virtualization in processor and BIOS/UEFI for best performance (see Figure 3-102).

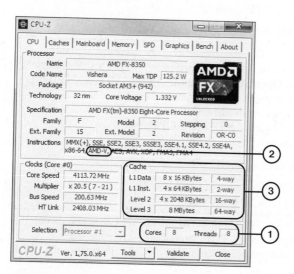

1. Processor cores
2. AMD-V virtualization support
3. Cache sizes

FIGURE 3-102 An AMD FX-8350 That Has Eight Processor Cores, Supports AMD-V (Hardware-Assisted Virtualization), and Has a Large Amount of L2 and L3 Cache

Gaming PC

Gaming is a major force driving development of high-quality PC components. Gaming is the largest entertainment industry, and gamers are knowledgeable and serious consumers who want the best available technology. Manufacturers know this well and spend enormous resources improving gaming-class components.

The configuration covered in Table 3-31 is similar to others previously detailed but adds high-end cooling systems. Gamers frequently overclock their CPUs to enhance performance, and doing so necessitates mitigating extra heat from the CPU.

Table 3-31   Gaming PC Features

Features	Benefits	Recommendations	Notes
SSD	No moving parts; uses flash memory, so much faster performance than HDD	Intel D3-S4610 series; M.2 2280 series Samsung 860 Pro series	2TB SSD available in both M.2 and SATA SSD; Samsung available up to 4TB.
Powerful processor	High performance for maximum frame rates, 3D rendering, and audio performance on games where CPU performance is most significant factor	4.0GHz or faster, six cores or more, large cache (8MB or more total cache), 64-bit support Intel Core i7 Extreme Edition, Core i7 "Haswell-E" AMD FX-9000 series	Although multicore CPUs are also the fastest CPUs available from Intel and AMD, many games are not yet optimized for multicore processors.
High-end video/ specialized GPU	High performance for maximum frame rates in 3D rendering where GPU performance is most significant factor	PCIe 3D cards with 2GB or more RAM optimized for OpenGL 4.x, DirectX 11, support for two or more displays with SLI (NVIDIA) or CrossFire (AMD) multi-GPU support AMD Radeon R9 NVIDIA GeForce GTX 980 Ti, TITAN Z, TITAN X	Fastest available GPUs available from AMD and NVIDIA.
Better sound card	5.1 or 7.1 surround audio for realistic, high-performance 3D audio rendering	24-bit, 96KHz or better audio performance; PCIe interface; hardware acceleration Sound Blaster X-Fi Extreme Gamer Sound Blaster Recon3D series Sound Blaster Fatal1ty series ASUS Xonar DG Azuntech X-Fi Forte	PCIe sound cards provide faster performance than PCI sound cards. Connect to 5.1 or 7.1 surround audio speakers or headsets for 3D audio effects.

Features	Benefits	Recommendations	Notes
High-end cooling	Overclocking is common to reach highest system speeds; overclocked systems can overheat if OEM cooling is not supplemented or replaced by more powerful cooling solutions	Heat-pipe-based CPU cooler for fan or liquid cooling (see Figure 3-103); heat sinks on RAM (see Figure 3-104); dual-slot video card with high-performance cooler; all optional fan bays on chassis equipped with fans See www.FrostyTech.com for reviews of numerous heat-pipe CPU cooling products See www.frozencpu.com for numerous cooling products for CPUs (liquid and heat-pipe), GPUs, and RAM modules	Be sure to verify compatibility with CPU, clearance around CPU socket, and power requirements for a particular system.

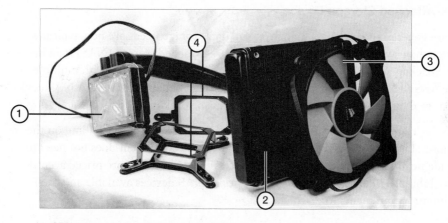

1. CPU water block with thermal material
2. Radiator
3. Cooling fan
4. Water block lockdown mechanisms

FIGURE 3-103   A High-Performance CPU Cooling System

FIGURE 3-104   DDR4 Desktop Memory Module with Aluminum Heatsinks (Image © scanrail, 123rf.com)

Network-Attached Storage Device

We are generating more data than ever, and data storage needs are now typically greater than a workstation can handle. Network-attached storage (NAS) is an in-house backup and storage solution that consists of a storage server with multiple drive bays that hold large hard drives that are accessible on a network. A NAS device can store data from all of your devices for access or backup.

NAS devices come in a variety of sizes and a variety of features, depending on the purpose of the NAS. A NAS for home storage for entertainment does not need to provide nearly as much space as a business-class NAS, and they are priced accordingly. Table 3-32 depicts the three basic types of NAS devices available and the minimum requirements for each class.

Table 3-32   NAS Requirements

Feature	Personal	Home Media Streaming	Business
Number of hard drive disks	1 SSD	2 SSDs	2–8 SSDs
Network medium	Wired/wireless	Wired	Wired/Gigabit NIC
Connection	SATA/Ethernet/USB 3.0	Ethernet/USB 3.0	Ethernet/USB 3.0
RAM	8GB	16GB	32GB ECC
Processor	Multicore 64-bit	Multicore 64-bit	Multicore 64-bit
RAID	Not required	Recommended	Yes
Gigabit NIC	Not required	Recommended	Yes

One type of data being generated and stored at unprecedented rates is media. Movies for entertainment and video from home surveillance systems are generating content daily. Personal storage backup can allow for fast access to media and file sharing without relying on cloud connections, which is especially important in areas with high Internet costs.

RAID can be an important feature with a NAS and is considered essential on business-class systems. But remember that RAID was designed for mechanical hard drives and may not be as necessary if data is simply being backed up for personal use.

As cloud sharing is becoming more common, some people question the continued importance of NAS systems. But the consensus is that while cloud storage is here to stay, NAS devices make an excellent choice as a hybrid partner to cloud storage, offering the advantage of faster access without Web access costs. NAS devices allow an easy way to follow the 3-2-1 rule of backing up data: *Keep 3 copies of your data, on 2 different storage media, with 1 of them off-site.*

Standard Thick Client/Thin Client

Thin and thick client computing are covered in both Objectives 3.8 and 3.9 for the A+ Core 1 exam. For clarity, both requirements and installation are covered in the next section.

Common Devices

220-1001: Objective 3.9: Given a scenario, install and configure common devices.

As noted previously, this section covers thin and thick client information to satisfy both Objectives 3.8 and 3.9 for the A+ Core 1 exam. This section also covers configurations for touchpads, touchscreens, and common application and device settings.

Desktop: Standard Thick Client/Thin Client Requirements

In a client/server topology, the client may be doing some processing, a lot of processing, or hardly any processing, depending on the needs of the users in the network. If considerable processing is demanded of the client, it is considered a thick client and needs to be more robust than a thin client.

Thick Client

Almost any computer you can purchase at a retail store qualifies as a standard thick client. The requirements are simple, as you can see in Table 3-33.

Table 3-33 Standard Thick Client Features

Feature	Benefits	Implementation	Notes
Desktop applications	Perform a broad range of office procedures (word processing, spreadsheets, presentations, database, email, and calendaring)	Current versions of Microsoft Office, including PowerPoint and Access Current versions of OpenOffice or Corel WordPerfect Office	For maximum compatibility with other office apps and data sources, install office apps with all options enabled.
Meets recommended requirements for selected OS	Good performance with basic office tasks	Intel Core i7 or i9, AMD Ryzen-series processors running at 4GHz or faster with 4GB of RAM in a 64-bit OS	Some older systems might require memory upgrades to meet recommended requirements.
Account settings	Local access or domain account access	Local login	

Thin Client

A thin client is the most basic type of system configuration, as Table 3-34 indicates.

Table 3-34 Thin Client Features

Feature	Benefits	Implementation	Notes
Basic applications	Perform basic office procedures (web browsing, word processing, spreadsheets)	Current version of Edge, Firefox, Chrome, or other web browser Current versions of Microsoft Office Word and Excel or OpenOffice	For maximum compatibility with other office apps and data sources, install office apps with all options enabled.
Meets minimum requirements for using selected OS	Runs OS at basic performance levels	Intel i5, i7, or i9 series; AMD Ryzen series running at 4GHz or faster with 4GB of RAM (64-bit OS)	Some older systems might require memory upgrades to meet minimum requirements for desired OS.

Feature	Benefits	Implementation	Notes
Network connectivity	Fast network connection because server handles most computational tasks	Wired: Gigabit Ethernet or faster Wireless: Wireless-AC	Routers and switches must also support Gigabit Ethernet or Wireless-AC standards.
Account settings	Secure authentication	Managed by network administrator	Normal security rules apply.

Laptop/Common Mobile Devices

Optimizing features on a laptop makes it possible for a user to have an enhanced and often customized experience. While the default settings on the following features will work, customization may provide a better computing experience.

Touchpad Configuration

Touchpads (also known as trackpads) are built into almost all laptops and the keyboards on many tablets. Touchpads and keyboards that include touchpads plug in through the USB port and are recognized as mice by the built-in Windows drivers. If a touchpad or keyboard with integrated touchpad is wireless, it is normally recognized automatically. If a touchpad or keyboard has additional keys or buttons, it might be necessary to install proprietary drivers to enable the additional keys or buttons. Proprietary drivers are also necessary to enable multitouch gestures (using two or more fingers).

To customize the settings on a touchpad in Window 10, open Windows Settings and click (or tap) on the **Devices** icon to open the Bluetooth & Other Devices window. Then select **Touchpad** from the left column. Figure 3-105 shows the touchpad settings. On the right are a sensitivity adjustment and a video demonstration for using the touchpad to select items, scroll, zoom, and other options.

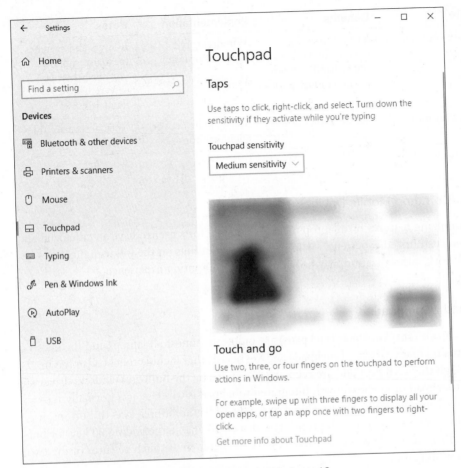

FIGURE 3-105   The Touchpad Settings Menu in Windows 10

On a Mac, access the settings by clicking the **Apple** icon in the top-left corner of the screen and selecting **System Preferences**. The Apple trackpad opens with different settings and customization options for pointing and clicking, scroll and zoom options, and other gestures.

Touchscreen Configuration

Touchscreens often require that a calibration algorithm be run during device setup. This way, the device and the user can learn to interact; a user needs to learn how sensitive the touchscreen is to his or her touch. A touchscreen can easily be recalibrated if it is not responding properly. To do this:

Step 1.   Open Control Panel and select **Tablet PC Settings**. (If this option is not available, check that the drivers are present.)

Step 2.   Click the **Calibrate** button and then choose your option for calibrating the screen for pen or touch input.

Step 3.   Follow the instructions to perform the calibration.

Step 4.   If you are happy with the settings, click **Yes** to save the settings.

Application Installations/Configurations

When installing and configuring applications, minor housekeeping always must be done to make sure the application is safely installed and able to fully and securely function. The many types of applications have different requirements and procedures. But a few basic steps apply to all applications:

Step 1.   Determine if the PC has enough resources to efficiently run the application. If so, download the installation file from a reliable source. Use common sense and be wary of potential virus-infected applications from unknown sources.

Step 2.   Find the .exe file for the downloaded application (typically in the Downloads folder).

Step 3.   Double-click the .exe file to run the Setup program and see a dialog box asking for storage and shortcut preferences. If prompted to choose between an automatic install or a custom install, opting for the auto install is usually a good choice unless there are specific settings to be altered.

Step 4.   Follow the instructions to complete the install and then reboot if necessary.

NOTE   If installing from a USB drive or an optical drive, simply locate the .exe file on the drive and follow the preceding steps.

Synchronization Settings

Synchronization is the matching up of files, email, and other types of data between one computer and another, with mobile devices, or with cloud storage and cloud applications to be used. We use synchronization to bring files in line with each other and to force devices to coordinate their data.

NOTE   Synchronization is covered in depth in Chapter 1.

Account Setup and Settings

When installing applications, setup and settings issues include updating passwords and other account settings, such as payment information for subscription services, depending on the functionality of the applications. For example, financial management applications may require changing settings with other vendor accounts as well.

Wireless Settings

Account and setting configuration may also apply to wireless settings. Some applications may require the transfer of important personal or payment data, and ensuring that the data is securely sent and received is essential. In addition, wireless settings such as those for firewalls or access controls may need to be configured. Wireless settings and configurations are covered in depth in Chapter 2, "Networking."

SOHO Multifunction Devices

220-1001: Objective 3.10: Given a scenario, configure SOHO multifunction devices/printers and settings.

When performing technical support in a small office/home office (SOHO) environment, a technician needs to keep machines and devices up and functioning so staff can continue to be productive. IT personnel are often called to support printing machines, many of which are multifunction devices that incorporate copy, scan, and fax features. (Although many have claimed that faxing is an outdated technology, it is still commonly used and considered more secure than email.)

Multifunction devices output hard-copy versions of files such as documents and photos that are stored on the computer. Most office printers are laser printers, but in a SOHO setting, one will find inkjet, thermal, impact, and virtual (software) technologies for document output. Printers and multifunction devices can connect to a computer's USB or parallel port via Bluetooth, WiFi, cellular wireless networks, or directly to a wired Ethernet network.

This section focuses on laser, inkjet, thermal, and impact printers. Virtual printing techniques such as printing to a file, PDF, XPS, and image are also covered.

Generally, Windows 8 and 10 behave the same when it comes to printers. So whenever Windows is mentioned in this section, the information applies to modern Windows versions unless otherwise stated. This section also deals with printer issues for macOS, Linux, iOS, and Android operating systems.

Configuring a Printer or Multifunction Device

Typical configuration options for printers or multifunction devices include:

- **Duplex (double-sided) printing:** This option may be available on single-sided printers as well as true duplex (both sides of paper) printers. With a single-side printer, the duplex setting is used to determine how to position the paper for printing the second side.

- **Collate setting:** This setting is used when printing two or more copies of a document that has two or more pages. When the Collate setting is enabled, the printer prints each copy of page 1 before printing page 2, and so on. This is useful when creating print jobs for binding, stapling, or punching but is slower than uncollated print jobs.

- **Orientation:** Portrait (long side up) or landscape (short side up) may be selected automatically in some printer drivers based on the orientation of the document to be printed. If not selected automatically, choose the correct orientation. Use Print Preview to help determine the setting needed.

- **Print quality:** Different quality settings are available, depending on the type of printer:

  - With laser printers and multifunction devices, you might be able to select the desired resolution (dots per inch [DPI]). Higher DPI levels produce smoother text output and more finely detailed graphics but require more printer RAM. As an alternative, some drivers have options to enable smoother text printing or adjust page compression.

  - Inkjet printers, instead of specific resolutions, use quality settings such as High, Standard, Fast (Canon); Draft, Text, Text and Image, Photo, and Best Photo (Epson); and Draft, Normal, Best (HP). Each setting optimizes the size of the ink droplet and paper coverage for the best results with the specified paper.

Device Sharing Options

Printer and multifunction devices can be shared between two or more computers by using USB, Serial, or Ethernet.

Serial (RS-232) and USB sharing involve using switch boxes that can be manually switched between devices or that can automatically detect print jobs and switch to the active computer. Serial switch boxes are obsolete for most tasks, and USB switch boxes are limited by the number of computers that can share a printer (typically two or four).

Both serial and USB printer sharing are also limited by relatively short cable runs and lack of management capabilities. Most wired printer/multifunction device sharing now uses Ethernet.

Integrated Ethernet Print/Multifunction Device Sharing

Most recent printers and multifunction devices include software with an integrated print server with support for Ethernet network printing. To configure them for sharing:

Step 1. Connect the printer or multifunction device to the network via an Ethernet (RJ-45) cable.

Step 2. Configure the printer or multifunction device to use Ethernet.

Step 3. Name the printer so it can be located on the network.

Step 4. Specify whether the printer or device will get an IP address from a DHCP router.

Step 5. If you need to configure the printer's or device's IP address manually, determine which IP addresses on the network are not in use by DHCP and manually assign the printer or device to one of those addresses.

Step 6. Record the configuration information for reuse. Some printers and devices might print the information at the end of the setup process.

Figure 3-106 shows some print server setup dialogs from a typical small office printer with wireless Ethernet support.

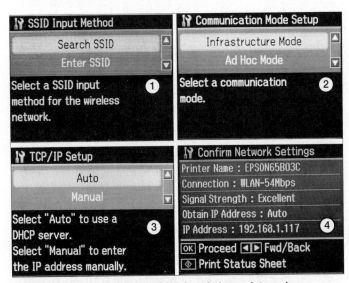

1. Selecting how to locate the SSID for wireless print serving
2. Selecting the network mode for the wireless print server
3. Specifying where to get an IP address (wired/wireless)
4. Confirming network settings

FIGURE 3-106   Configuring a Printer as an Ethernet or Wireless Ethernet Print Server

A multifunction device has an Ethernet port that takes on a network IP address. To print to a network printer or device, you may need to install a network printer driver instead of the normal printer driver on the computer that will use the printer or multifunction device. To learn more about TCP/IP and DHCP, see Chapter 2.

Wireless Device Sharing Options

The two major network protocols used for wireless device sharing are Bluetooth and 802.11 (WiFi). Bluetooth is suitable for very short-range sharing among a few devices, while 802.11-based print sharing supports a much larger number of guest devices over much longer ranges.

Bluetooth

Most printers with built-in Bluetooth support are portable or receipt printers.

Printers lacking Bluetooth support can use special Bluetooth adapters to connect with computers or mobile devices that use Bluetooth. Check with the printer device vendor for models that are compatible with a specific printer.

Before a computer or mobile device can connect to a printer or multifunction device using Bluetooth, both the computer/mobile device and the printer/multifunction device must have Bluetooth transceivers. Bluetooth support is common among laptop and mobile devices and can be added with a USB dongle to computers lacking Bluetooth support.

After enabling Bluetooth on the printer and computer, you must configure both for pairing and pair them before print jobs can be sent. For details, see Chapter 2.

802.11(a, b, g, n, ac)

Most new printers and multifunction devices include some level of 802.11 (WiFi) support. The configuration process is typically similar to that used for wired Ethernet, with the added step of specifying the wireless network's SSID and encryption key (if used). When this configuration is complete, all devices on the network with the proper print driver can use the multifunction device.

Infrastructure vs. Ad Hoc

If you want to use wireless Ethernet (WiFi) printers or multifunction devices but don't use WiFi networking with a wireless router, configure the printers/devices to work in ad hoc mode. In ad hoc mode, each device is connected directly to other devices: No router is used.

Infrastructure mode supports WPA2 encryption, while ad hoc mode supports only WEP encryption, making it unsuitable for secure networking.

Ad Hoc Wireless Network Support in Windows

Ad hoc wireless networking is supported in Windows 8/8.1 through the Network and Sharing Center. It is also available in Windows 8/8.1 from the command line using Netsh, but it has been removed in Windows 10.

Ad Hoc Wireless Network Support in macOS

macOS supports ad hoc wireless networking through the WiFi Status icon on the Finder menu. macOS refers to this feature as "computer-to-computer" networking (see Figure 3-107). When you enable this feature, your computer cannot connect to other WiFi networks at the same time.

1. Select the least-used wireless channel
2. Click to create network

FIGURE 3-107 Creating a Computer-to-Computer (Ad Hoc) Wireless Network with macOS

Ad Hoc Wireless Networking Support in Linux

Ad hoc wireless networking in Linux is sometimes referred to as an *IBSS* (independent basic service set) network. Depending on the distro, this can be set up by turning on the wireless hotspot service in the network settings or by using the command line utilities iw and ip. NetworkManager (https://wiki.gnome.org/Projects/NetworkManager) can be installed on distros that lack easy network management.

Wireless Hosted Networking

As a replacement for ad hoc mode, Windows 7 introduced wireless hosted networking, which is also available in Windows 8/8.1/10. With wireless hosted networking, you can create a WiFi network hotspot that is detectable and usable by WiFi-enabled printers and other computers and devices.

To create an unsecured wireless hosted network, open a command prompt and enter this command:

netsh wlan start *hostednetwork*

replacing ***hostednetwork*** with the name of your network.

Check the Network and Sharing Center to ensure that your new network is available.

Set up your printer or multifunction device to use the same network name. To print, have each user connect to that network. A printer or multifunction device can use only one network at a time, but computers can connect to this network and to other networks (including wireless networks) at the same time.

Cloud and Remote Printing

With ***cloud printing***, you no longer need to be at your office or home office to make a printout. With ***remote printing***, you can print a document stored on your host with your remote printer.

Cloud and remote printing require the following:

- A printer or multifunction device that can be accessed from the cloud or remotely via the Web.

- An app that supports remote or cloud printing. The printer settings are loaded into the app, and the cloud-based document is downloaded and printed from the mobile device.

Using Public and Shared Devices

Sharing printers on a network used to require both the printer and the user to be on the same local network, but recent print-sharing technologies have made shared printing available beyond physical access to a printer.

Public cloud printing devices are available in some office supply stores, schools, and other business centers located in hotels and airports. The customer can submit print jobs via email, web interfacing, mobile apps, or special print drivers. Thus, public cloud printing is available to any type of computer or device that has Internet access. To receive the print job from the printer, the user must provide the credentials needed, such as a retrieval code or account code. Google Cloud Print is an example of a service that allows printing to a Web-enabled computer from anywhere on the Web, including using phones.

Thanks to public cloud printing services, it may be no longer necessary to have a printer you might use only occasionally. For example, a person working remotely from home (or any user for that matter) may have very little use for a printer or may not use it enough to be worth the cost. When the rare print job is required, the user can send the document to an account at a neighborhood Office Depot or similar business and go there and print from professional machines by entering the code on the keypad.

Another wireless printing solution is AirPrint, an Apple proprietary technology that enables a user to discover an AirPrint-enabled printer and print documents or pictures without setting up a local network. AirPrint uses software called Bonjour, which comes built into macOS and iOS systems. Bonjour finds the AirPrint printer, and the document can be sent. Bonjour is also available for Windows 8 and 10, and a user with Bonjour installed on a Windows machine can print to an AirPrint-enabled printer. Another option is having a non-AirPrint printer connected to a computer with Bonjour; this allows any user using Bonjour to direct a print job to the networked computer.

Using Apps

Smartphones and tablets running Android or Apple iOS operating systems typically install apps from their respective app stores to make cloud or remote printing possible.

Connect older printers and multifunction devices that do not have built-in Google Cloud Print support to a computer running Google Chrome and enable its Google Cloud Print feature to enable cloud printing. The Google Print Connector can be used to enable multiple printers in businesses or schools to be used with Google Cloud Print.

Maintaining Data Privacy

When a document is sent to a printer, a special print file is created by the print spooler. To prevent unauthorized users from opening the print file and extracting information from it, two methods can be used: user authentication and hard drive caching.

Using User Authentication

User authentication (which matches print jobs to the IP address of the computer or device requesting the print job) can be enabled at the printer itself or by security settings used on Active Directory–enabled networks.

When user authentication is enabled in the printer (a common feature on enterprise-level print or multifunction devices), the user must provide the appropriate identification during the print process. On a macOS system, this can be done through the

Job Log portion of the printer submenu (the same menu that includes sections for layout, print settings, and so on). On a Windows system, the printer driver or the network might prompt for this information.

Using Hard Drive Caching

On a system running Windows, print spool files are normally stored on the system hard drive at C:\Windows\system32\spool\PRINTERS. If a different location is desired, make sure the location is not shared on the network to avoid access from unauthorized users.

The default location of the print spool files can be changed by selecting the printer or multifunction device in Devices and Printers, opening the Print Server properties dialog, clicking **Advanced**, clicking **Change Advanced Settings**, and specifying a different location.

Print Technologies

220-1001: Objective 3.11: Given a scenario, install and maintain various print technologies.

Printing has long been one of the most common issues confronting help desk technicians. While print technologies have in many ways become simpler over time, knowledge of printer types and the ability to perform printer maintenance remain in high demand.

Laser Printers

A laser printer is a page printer that stores the entire contents of a page to be printed in its memory before printing it. By contrast, inkjet, thermal, and impact printers print a page as a series of narrow bands.

The major components of a laser printer include:

- *Imaging drum*: Applies the page image to the transfer belt or roller; frequently combined with the toner supply in a toner cartridge.
- *Developer*: Pulls toner from the toner supply and sends it to the imaging drum.
- *Fuser assembly*: Fuses the page image to the paper.
- *Transfer belt (transfer roller)*: Transfers the page image from the drum to the page.
- *Pickup rollers*: Picks up paper.

- *Paper separation pad* (**separate pad**): Enables pickup rollers to pick up only one sheet of paper at a time.

- *Duplexing assembly* (**optional**): Switches paper from the front to the back side so that the printer can print on both sides of the paper.

The following sections take a closer look at how these and other components work together to make laser printing possible.

Toner Cartridges

Most monochrome laser printers use toner cartridges that combine the imaging drum and the developer along with a supply of black toner. This provides you with an efficient and easy way to replace the laser printer items with the greatest potential to wear out.

Depending on the model, a new toner cartridge might also require that you change a wiper used to remove excess toner during the fusing cycle. This is normally packaged with the toner cartridge.

When installing a toner cartridge, be sure to follow the directions for cleaning areas near the toner cartridge. Depending on the make and model of the laser printer, this can involve cleaning the mirror that reflects the laser beam, cleaning up stray toner, or cleaning the charging corona wire or conditioning rollers inside the printer. If you need to clean the charging corona wire (also called the *primary corona wire* on some models), the laser printer will contain a special tool for this purpose. The printer instruction manual will show you how to clean the item.

Keep the cartridge closed; it is sensitive to light, and leaving it out of the printer in room light can damage the enclosed imaging drum's surface.

CAUTION When you change a toner cartridge, take care to avoid getting toner on your face, hands, or clothing. It can leave a messy residue that's hard to clean. For information about cleaning up toner spills and taking precautions against inhaling toner, see Chapter 9.

Laser Imaging Process

A laser printer is an example of a page printer. A page printer does not start printing until the entire page is received. At that point, the page is transferred to the print mechanism, which pulls the paper through the printer as the page is transferred from the printer to the paper.

TIP   To master this section, make sure you:

- Memorize the seven steps involved in laser printer imaging.
- Master the details of each step and their sequence.
- Be prepared to answer troubleshooting questions based on these steps.

The laser printing process often is referred to as the electrophotographic (EP) process.

Before the seven-step laser printing process can take place, the following events must occur:

- Because laser printers are page based, a printer must receive an entire page before it can start printing.
- After the page has been received, the printer pulls a sheet of paper into the printer with its feed rollers.

After the paper has been fed into the print mechanism, a series of seven steps takes place, which results in a printed page: processing, charging, exposing (also known as writing), developing, transferring, fusing, and cleaning.

The following section describes this process in more detail. Steps 1–7 are identified in Figure 3-108.

TIP   Make sure you know this exact order of the laser printer imaging process for the exam:

Step 1.   Processing

Step 2.   Charging

Step 3.   Exposing

Step 4.   Developing

Step 5.   Transferring

Step 6.   Fusing

Step 7.   Cleaning

Also make sure you know the parts that make up a laser printer:

- Imaging drum
- Developer
- Fuser assembly

- Transfer belt
- Transfer roller
- Pickup rollers
- Separate pads
- Duplexing assembly

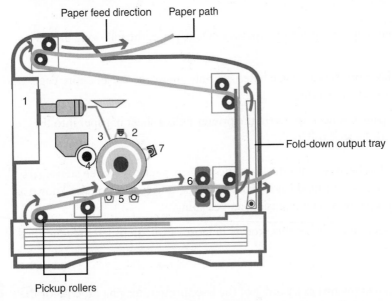

FIGURE 3-108   A Conceptual Drawing of a Typical Laser Printing Process

Step 1: Processing

The printer's raster image *processing* engine receives the page, font, text, and graphics data from the printer driver, creates a page image, and stores it in memory. Depending on the amount of information on the page compared to the amount of memory in the printer, the printer might need to compress the page image to store it. If there is not enough memory to store the page image, a memory error is triggered.

Step 2: Charging

During the *charging* process, the cylinder-shaped imaging drum receives an electrostatic charge of –600VDC (DC voltage) from a conditioning roller. (Older printers used a primary corona wire.) The smooth surface of the drum retains this charge uniformly over its entire surface. The drum is photosensitive and retains this charge only while kept in darkness.

Step 3: Exposing

During the *exposing* process, a moving mirror moves the laser beam across the surface of the drum. As it moves, the laser beam temporarily records the image of the page to be printed on the surface of the drum by reducing the voltage of the charge applied by the charger corona to –100VDC. Instead of using a laser beam, an LED printer activates its LED array to record the image on the page.

Step 4: Developing

During the *developing* process, the drum has toner applied to it from the developer; because the toner is electrostatic and is also at –600VDC, the toner stays on only the portions of the drum that have been reduced in voltage to create the image. It is not attracted to the rest of the drum because the toner and the drum are at the same voltage, and like charges repel each other. This "like charges repel" phenomenon is similar to two like poles of magnets repelling each other.

Step 5: Transferring

During the *transferring* process, while the sheet is being fed into the printer, it receives an electrostatic charge of +600VDC from a corona wire or roller; this enables it to attract toner from the drum, which is negatively charged (see Step 3). As the drum's surface moves close to the charged paper, the toner adhering to the drum is attracted to the electrostatically charged paper to create the printed page.

As the paper continues to move through the printer, its charge is canceled by a static eliminator strip, so the paper itself isn't attracted to the drum.

Step 6: Fusing

During the *fusing* process, the printed sheet of paper is pulled through fuser rollers, using high temperatures (approximately 350 degrees Fahrenheit) to heat the toner and press it into the paper. The printed image is slightly raised above the surface of the paper.

The paper is ejected into the paper tray, and the drum must be prepared for another page.

Step 7: Cleaning

To prepare the drum for a new page, the image of the preceding page placed on the drum by the laser or LED array (see Step 3) is removed by a discharge lamp. During the *cleaning* process, toner that is not adhering to the surface of the drum is scraped from the drum's surface for reuse.

Color Laser Printing Differences

Color laser printers differ from monochrome laser printers in two important ways: They include four different colors of toner (cyan, magenta, yellow, and black), and the imaging drum is separate from the toner. Thus, instead of waste toner being reused as in a monochrome laser printer that has a toner cartridge with an integrated imaging drum, waste toner in a color printer is sent to a separate waste toner container.

Color laser printers use the same basic process as monochrome lasers, but some use a transfer belt instead of an imaging drum. The use of a transfer belt enables all four colors (cyan, magenta, yellow, and black) to be placed on the paper at the same time, enabling color print speeds comparable to monochrome print speeds. When a transfer belt is used, the conditioning and transferring processes are performed on the transfer belt (see Figure 3-109).

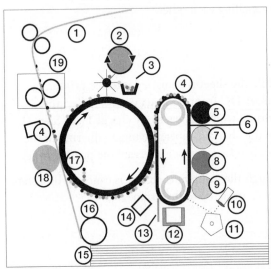

1. Paper path
2. Cleaning unit
3. Waste toner
4. Toner particles
5. Black toner
6. OPC belt
7. Yellow toner
8. Magenta toner
9. Cyan toner
10. Laser
11. Laser mirror
12. Charger
13. Cleaning blade
14. Erase lamp
15. Paper in paper tray
16. Paper pickup
17. Imaging drum
18. Transfer roller
19. Fusing rollers

FIGURE 3-109   The Printing Process in a Typical Color Laser Printer That Uses a Transfer Belt

Laser Media Types

Laser printers use standard smooth-finish printer or copier paper. It is important to use labels and transparency media especially designed for laser printers, as other types of media might jam the printer or become distorted because of the high heat used in the laser printing process.

Labels made for copiers are not suitable for laser printers because they can come off the backing and stick to the printer's internal components.

Laser Maintenance

The major elements in laser printer maintenance include replacing toner, applying maintenance kits, calibration (color lasers only), and cleaning.

Replacing Toner Cartridges

If a laser printer's toner cartridge also includes the imaging drum, replacing the toner cartridge also involves replacing the imaging drum. Because the imaging drum's surface can become damaged, leaving marks on print output, changing the toner cartridge is helpful in improving print quality.

Applying Maintenance Kits

Many HP and other laser printers feature components that should be replaced at periodic intervals. These components often include fuser assemblies, air filters, transfer rollers, pickup rollers, other types of rollers, and separation pads (separate pads). These components wear out over time and can usually be purchased as a maintenance kit as well as separately.

A printer that uses a maintenance kit will display a message or an error code such as "Perform printer maintenance" or "Perform user maintenance" when the printer reaches the recommended page count for maintenance kit replacement. Depending upon the printer model and whether it is used for color or monochrome printing, the recommended page count could be at as few as 50,000 pages or as much as 300,000 pages or more.

After a fuser assembly or full maintenance kit is installed in a laser printer, the page count must be reset; otherwise, you will not know when to perform recommended maintenance again. Typically, the page count is reset by pressing a specified combination of buttons on the printer's control panel.

NOTE If the printer is under service contract or being charged on a per-page (or per-click) basis, it is not recommended to reset the paper count after servicing. However, most laser printers print the page count when you perform a self-test.

Calibration

Color laser printers should be calibrated if print quality declines. The printer *calibration* process on a color laser printer adjusts image density settings to make up for changes caused by environmental differences or aging print cartridges.

Some color laser printers perform automatic calibration, but you can also force the printer to perform calibration on an as-needed basis. See the instruction manual for your printer for details.

> **NOTE**   *Print quality* is affected by many factors, such as the print resolution for graphics; the higher the dpi, the sharper and better the print quality, while using an economy printing mode that uses less toner reduces print quality. A damaged imaging drum or dirty rollers can leave marks on the paper that detract from print quality. If a color laser printer requires four passes to print in color and the colors are not properly lined up (a process known as color registration), print quality is affected.

Cleaning

Because laser printers use fine-grained powdered toner, keeping the inside of a laser printer clean is an important step in periodic maintenance. If you want to use a vacuum cleaner to pick up loose toner, be sure to use a vacuum cleaner that is designed to pick up toner, as toner particles are so small they will pass through conventional bags and filters. If you prefer to use a damp cloth, be sure to turn off the laser printer and disconnect it from power first.

To keep the paper path and rollers clean, use cleaning sheets made for laser printers, as follows:

Step 1.   Insert the sheet into the manual feed tray on the laser printer.

Step 2.   Create a short document with Notepad, WordPad, or some other text editor and then print it on the sheet.

As the sheet passes through the printer, it cleans the rollers. If a specialized cleaning sheet is not available, you can also use transparency film designed for laser printers. Some laser printers use a special software program to print a cleaning pattern onto plain paper.

> **NOTE**   Be sure to know how to maintain a laser printer for the 220-1001 exam: replacing toner, applying a maintenance kit, calibration, and cleaning.

> **CAUTION**   Never use transparency media not designed for laser printers in a laser printer. Copier or inkjet media isn't designed to handle the high heat of a laser printer and can melt or warp and possibly damage the printer.

Inkjet Printers

Inkjet printers are the most popular type of printer in small office/home office (SOHO) use. Their print quality can rival that of laser printers, and virtually all inkjet printers in use today are able to print both color and black text and photographs.

From a tightly spaced group of nozzles, inkjet printers spray controlled dots of ink onto the paper to form characters and graphics. On a typical 5,760×1,440dpi (dots per inch) printer, the number of nozzles can be as high as 180 for black ink and more than 50 per color (cyan, magenta, and yellow). The tiny ink droplet size and high nozzle density enable inkjet printers to perform the seemingly impossible at resolutions as high as 1,200dpi or higher: fully formed characters from what is actually a high-resolution, non-impact, dot-matrix technology.

Inkjet printers are character/line printers. This means they print one line at a time of single characters or graphics up to the limit of the print head matrix. Inkjet printers are functionally fully formed character printers because their inkjet matrix of small droplets forming the image is so carefully controlled that individual dots are not visible. Larger characters are created by printing a portion of the characters across the page, advancing the page to allow the print head to print another portion of the characters, and so on until the entire line of characters is printed. Thus, an inkjet printer is both a character printer and a line printer because it must connect lines of printing to build large characters. Some inkjet printers require realignment after each ink cartridge/print head change to make sure that vertical lines formed by multiple print head passes stay straight; this realignment may be automatic or may require the user to start the process. With other models, alignment can be performed through a utility provided as part of the printer driver when print quality declines due to misalignment.

Inkjet Components

The essential components in the inkjet printing process include ink cartridges, print head, roller, paper feeder, duplexing assembly, carriage, and belt.

NOTE Make sure you know this list of components for the 220-1001 exam.

Some inkjet printers use external ink tanks for longer ink life between refills.

Figure 3-110 shows how many of these components look in a typical printer.

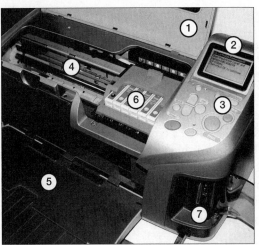

1. Dust cover
2. LCD instruction panel
3. Control panel
4. Printhead drive belt
5. Output tray
6. Ink cartridges
7. Flash memory card reader

FIGURE 3-110   A Typical Inkjet Printer with Its Cover Open

Inkjet Printing Process

Inkjet printers use ink cartridges filled with liquid ink for printing. Some older inkjet printers use a large tank of black ink and a second tank with separate compartments for each color (typically cyan, magenta, and yellow; some models feature light versions of some of these colors for better photo-printing quality). However, almost all inkjet printers produced for a number of years have used a separate cartridge for each color. This improves print economy for the user because only one color at a time needs to be replaced. With a multicolor cartridge, the entire cartridge needs to be replaced, even when only one of the colors runs out.

NOTE   Inkjet printers are sometimes referred to as CMYK devices because of the four ink colors used on most models: cyan, magenta, yellow, and black.

The carriage and belt mechanism move the print head back and forth to place ink droplets as the paper passes through the printer. Depending on the printer, the print head might be incorporated into the ink tank; it might be a separate, user-replaceable item; or it might be built into the printer.

Some inkjet printers feature an extra-wide (more nozzles) print head or a dual print head for very speedy black printing. Some models enable the user to replace either the ink cartridge only or an assembly comprising the print head and a replaceable ink cartridge.

NOTE   On an inkjet printer, print quality settings are typically good, better, best or text, text and image, photo, and best photo and are selected in the printer settings dialog. However, clogged nozzles (leading to ink dropouts), mismatch of paper type setting to actual paper used, and dirty rollers reduce actual print quality.

An inkjet printer is only as good as its print head and ink cartridges. Clogged or damaged print heads or ink cartridges render a printer useless. If an inkjet printer fails after its warranty expires, you should check service costs carefully before repairing the unit. Failed inkjet printers are often "throwaway" models and can be replaced, rather than repaired, even during the warranty period.

CAUTION   Inkjet printers should never be turned off by using the power switch on a surge protector; doing so prevents the printer from self-capping its ink cartridges, which is a major cause of service calls and printer failures. Cleaning the print head—either with the printer's own cleaning feature, using a cleaning utility built into the printer driver, or with a moistened cleaning sheet—will restore most printers to service. Always use the printer's own power switch, which enables the printer to protect the ink cartridges and perform other periodic tasks (such as self-cleaning) properly.

Inkjet printers use two major methods to create the ink dots that make up the page. Most inkjet printers heat the ink to boiling and create a tiny bubble of ink that is allowed to escape through the print head onto the paper. This is the origin of the name BubbleJet for the Canon line of inkjet printers. Printers using this method feature either ink cartridges that include the print head or print heads with removable ink cartridge inserts. In case of a severely clogged print head, you can simply replace the ink cartridge if the ink cartridge incorporates the print head.

Another popular method uses a piezoelectric crystal to distribute the ink through the print head. This method makes achieving high resolutions easier; the Epson printers using this method were the first to achieve 5,760×1,440dpi resolutions. This method also provides a longer print head life because the ink is not heated and cooled. However, the print heads are built into the printer, making a severely clogged print head harder to clean. Both types of inkjet printers are sometimes referred to as *drop-on-demand printers*.

The inkjet print process works as follows:

Step 1.   The paper or media in a feed tray is pulled into position by a roller mechanism.

Step 2.   The print head is suspended on a carriage over the paper and is moved across the paper by a belt. As the print head moves across the paper, it places black and color ink droplets as directed by the printer driver.

Step 3.   At the end of the line, the paper or media is advanced, and the print head either reverses direction and continues to print (often referred to as Hi-Speed mode) or returns to the left margin before printing continues.

Step 4.   After the page is completed, the media is ejected.

Inkjet Media Types

Inkjet printers can use the same types of paper and labels that laser printers can use. However, inkjet printers can also use special matte or glossy-coated paper and business card stock for presentation or photo-realistic images. Transparency stock must be designed specifically for inkjet use. Because of improvements in media and print design, old inkjet photo paper should be recycled rather than used, as older paper types have very slow drying times compared to recent types.

When printing, it's important to select the correct media type in the printer driver to avoid banding, overuse of ink, and other poor-quality results.

Inkjet Maintenance

Ink cartridge replacement, calibration, nozzle check, head cleaning, and jam clearing are the major elements in maintaining an inkjet printer.

NOTE   Make sure you know the elements of inkjet maintenance—ink cartridge replacement, calibration, nozzle check, head cleaning, and jam clearing—for the 220-1001 exam.

Replacing Ink Cartridges

Use the printing preferences or printer properties dialog (which varies by printer and operating system) to determine when it's time to purchase additional ink or replace the ink cartridges (see Figure 3-111).

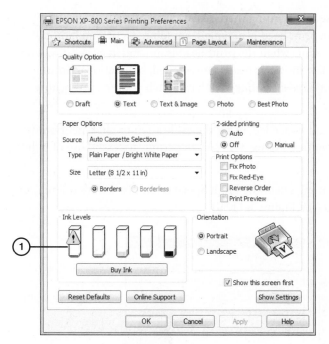

1. Warning of critically low ink level

FIGURE 3-111   A Printer with Low Ink Levels, with the ! Indicating a Cartridge That Is Nearly Empty

NOTE   Most inkjet printers stop printing when one color runs out, even if that color is not being used in the current print job. Some printers offer to use a mixture of photo black and colors if the normal black ink runs low during a print job.

Some printers run automatic nozzle cleaning or calibration routines when you change ink cartridges. If the ink cartridge includes a print head, whenever you change the ink cartridge, you also change the print head. Consequently, replacing ink cartridges is the single best maintenance step you can perform on an inkjet printer.

Calibration

Inkjet printers might require or recommend some type of printer calibration, most typically print head alignment. This process involves printing one or more sheets of paper and selecting the print setting that produces straight lines. Some printers perform this step automatically, and others require user intervention to determine the best setting.

Some inkjet printers can use two printing methods: unidirectional, in which the printer prints only when the print head is moving from left to right, and bidirectional, in which the printer prints when the print head is moving in either direction (left to right or right to left). If the print head is misaligned, bidirectional printing (sometimes referred to as *high-speed printing*) will have much poorer print quality than unidirectional printing.

Be sure to align the print head as needed, using the calibration or alignment utility provided in the printer driver (see Figure 3-112A), to permit successful use of bidirectional printing.

To enable bidirectional printing, select the High Speed option (when it's offered) in the Print Preferences menu (see Figure 3-112B).

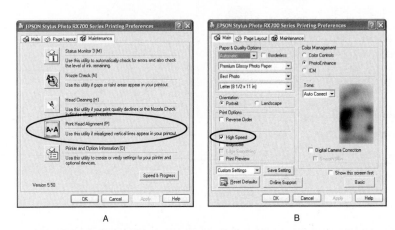

FIGURE 3-112   Aligning the Print Head (A) Helps Produce Better-Quality High-Speed (Bidirectional) Printing (B)

NOTE   With some printers, it might be necessary to realign the print head after changing ink cartridges. Some of these printers perform this task automatically; however, with others, it might be an optional utility that you can run on an as-needed basis.

Nozzle Check and Head Cleaning

Periodically, especially if a printer has not been used for a while or has been used only for monochrome printing, it's a good idea to use the nozzle check routine to verify that all the print heads' nozzles are working correctly.

The nozzle check or pattern check routine prints a pattern that uses all of the nozzles in all of the print heads and displays the pattern's correct appearance. Compare the printout to the onscreen display, and if you see gaps or missing colors, activate the head cleaning routine (see Figure 3-113). Repeat these steps until the nozzle check printout matches the screen display. Keep in mind that performing a nozzle check uses ink.

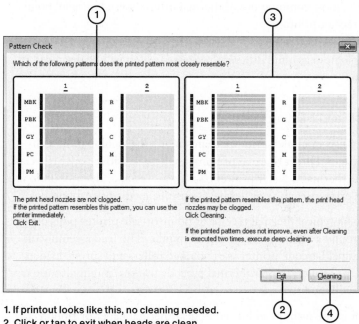

1. If printout looks like this, no cleaning needed.
2. Click or tap to exit when heads are clean.
3. If printout has streaks, run cleaning routine.
4. Click or tap to start head cleaning routine.

FIGURE 3-113   The Pattern Check (Nozzle Check) Dialog from a Canon Inkjet Printer Driver's Maintenance Tab

Depending on the printer, these options might be located in the printer preferences maintenance section, a toolbox dialog, or someplace like the printer's onboard menu. See your printer's documentation for details.

CAUTION   When using a Windows-provided printer driver, some printer options might not be available. Installing the latest available driver from the printer's manufacturer is a good practice.

Thermal Printers

A thermal printer uses heat transfer to create text and graphics on the paper. Thermal printers are available using three different technologies:

Dye sublimation for high quality printing

Thermal wax transfer, similar to laser quality

Direct thermal, the most common use of thermal printing, used in retail point-of-sale (POS) receipt printing

Each of these technologies has quite different processes which will be discussed in the following sections.

Thermal Feed Assembly and Heating Element

Thermal printers can use an impact print mechanism or a dye-sublimation technology to transfer images. Direct thermal printers use heat-sensitive paper (special thermal paper), while thermal transfer printers use a wax, resin, or dye ribbon to create the image. Some printers can use either heat-sensitive media or a ribbon.

The feed assembly on a typical thermal receipt or point-of-sale printer pulls paper from a roll wound around a center plastic spool or spindle. The feed assembly on a typical desktop thermal barcode printer uses notched rollers and spring-loaded sprockets to advance roll paper. Larger thermal barcode printers might also use fan-fold media as well as roll media.

The heating element in the print head is used to heat thermal paper or ribbons to make the image. Printers that use ribbons are thermal transfer printers, and printers that use thermal paper are known as direct thermal printers.

Thermal Printer Ribbons

Thermal transfer printers use wax or resin-based ribbons, which are often bundled with paper made especially for the printer. Dye-sublimation (dye-sub) printers use dye-based film ribbons technology to print continuous-tone photographs. Examples of consumer-grade dye-sublimation printers include Kodak Printer Docks and Canon's Selphy CP series; these printers print 4×6-inch photos. Many vendors also sell larger-format dye-sublimation printers for use in photo labs and professional photography studios.

Figure 3-114 illustrates a typical dye-sublimation ribbon for a Canon Selphy CP printer.

FIGURE 3-114   A Dye-Sublimation Ribbon for a 4-by-6-Inch Photo Printer (Canon Selphy CP)

Thermal Print Process

Although thermal transfer, direct thermal printing, and dye sublimation all involve heating the elements in a print head to a particular temperature to transfer the image, there are some differences in operation. The basic process of thermal printing works like this:

Step 1.   The print head has a matrix of dots that can be heated in various combinations to create text and graphics.

Step 2.   The print head transfers text and graphics directly to heat-sensitive thermal paper in direct thermal printing or to a ribbon that melts onto the paper in thermal transfer printing.

Step 3.   If a multicolor ribbon is used on a thermal transfer or dye-sublimation printer, each ribbon is moved past the print head to print the appropriate color. In the case of dye-sublimation printers, the paper is moved back into position to enable the next color to be printed.

Step 4.   When all colors have been printed, the paper is ejected.

Figure 3-115 compares direct thermal and thermal transfer printing technologies.

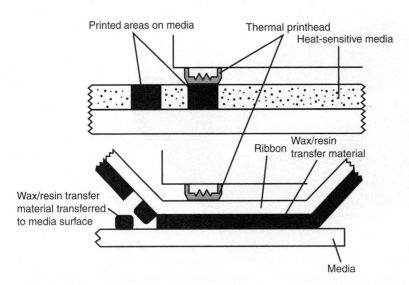

FIGURE 3-115   Direct Thermal (Top) and Thermal Transfer (Bottom) Printing Technologies

Thermal Paper and Media

Direct thermal printers use special thermal (heat-sensitized) paper, and thermal transfer printers might use either standard copy paper or glossy photo paper, depending on their intended use.

If a printer uses direct thermal printing, heat-sensitive paper with characteristics matching the printer's design specifications must be used. For portable printers using direct thermal printing such as the Brother PocketJet series, the usual source for such paper is the printer vendor or its authorized resellers. If the direct thermal printer is used for barcodes or point-of-sale (POS) transactions, you can get suitable paper or label stock from barcode or POS equipment suppliers and resellers.

Thermal transfer ribbons are available in three categories: wax (for paper; smooth paper produces the best results), wax/resin (synthetics), and resin (glossy hard films such as polyester). Choose the appropriate ribbon type for the material you will be printing on.

Dye-sublimation photo printers in the consumer space use special media kits that include both a ribbon and suitable photo paper stocks. Larger-format dye-sublimation printers are designed to print on standard-size and special-format roll and sheet dye-sublimation paper stocks, available separately from the ink or ribbon.

Thermal Maintenance

The elements of thermal printer maintenance include replacing the paper when it runs out, cleaning the heating element as directed, and removing debris from the

heating element, rollers, or other components, as needed. For the 220-1001 exam, be sure to know the steps for thermal printer maintenance:

- Replace paper
- Clean heating element
- Remove debris

Cleaning Heating Elements

Because the heating element in a thermal printer is the equivalent of the print head in impact or inkjet printers, it must be kept clean in order to provide maximum print quality. Many vendors recommend cleaning the print head after each roll of thermal transfer ribbon.

Some thermal transfer ribbons for POS and warehouse printers include special cleaning materials at the beginning of the roll. Some thermal printer vendors also supply special cleaning film you can use to remove dust, debris, and coating residue from print heads.

You can also use isopropyl alcohol to clean print heads. It is available in wipes, pens, pads, and swabs from various vendors. The ribbon must be removed before using isopropyl alcohol. When isopropyl alcohol is used in cleaning, it is essential to wait until the printer dries out before reinstalling the ribbon.

Removing Debris

Debris from torn paper, solid ink flakes, and label coatings can build up on rollers and other components as well as on the print head. Use isopropyl alcohol wipes or other cleaning materials as recommended by the printer supplier to clean up debris for better print quality and longer print life.

Impact Printers

An impact printer is so named because it uses a mechanical print head that presses against an inked ribbon to print characters and graphics. Impact printers are the oldest printer technology, and they are primarily used today in industrial and point-of-sale applications.

Dot-matrix printers, the most common form of impact printers, are so named because they create the appearance of fully formed characters from dots placed on the page.

> **NOTE**   For the 220-1001 exam, be sure to know the basic elements of impact printing:
>
> - Print head
> - Ribbon
> - Tractor feed
> - Impact paper

Impact Components and Print Process

Impact dot-matrix printers have a number of parts moving in coordination with each other during the printing process:

Step 1.   The paper is moved past the print head vertically by pull or push tractors or by a platen.

Step 2.   The print head moves across the paper horizontally, propelled along the print head carriage by a drive belt, printing as it moves from left to right. Bidirectional printing prints in both directions but is often disabled for high-quality printing because it can be difficult to align the printing precisely.

Step 3.   As the print head moves, the pins in the print head are moving in and out against an inked printer ribbon as the print head travels across the paper to form the text or create graphics.

Step 4.   The ribbon is also moving to reduce wear during the printing process.

These steps are repeated for each line until the page is printed. Figure 3-116 illustrates a typical impact dot-matrix printer. The model pictured is a wide-carriage version, but its features are typical of models using either standard or wide-carriage paper.

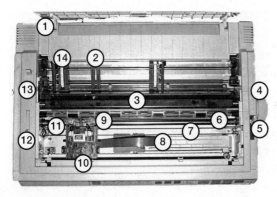

1. Rear cover (top cover removed, not shown)
2. Paper supports for tractor-feed paper path
3. Platen for using single sheets of paper
4. Manual paper advance knob
5. Paper bail lifter
6. Paper bail
7. Timing/drive belt
8. Printhead signal control cable
9. Printhead with heat sink
10. Ribbon holder
11. Printhead support rod
12. Head gap adjustment
13. Tractor/friction-feed selector lever
14. Tractor feed

FIGURE 3-116   Components of a Typical Impact Printer

Impact Print Heads

The most common types of print heads include 9-pin, 18-pin (two columns of 9 pins each), and 24-pin (which produces near letter quality, or NLQ, printing when used in best quality mode).

Figure 3-117 shows actual print samples from a typical 9-pin printer's draft mode, a typical 24-pin printer's draft mode, and the near letter quality (NLQ) mode of the same 24-pin printer.

```
RN_clients.html.Z ──────────────9-pin printer draft mode
RN_loc_cal.html.Z
RN_loc_doc.html.Z
RN_loc_uucp.html.Z

This is a test of switching──24-pin printer draft mode

Congratulations!──────────24-pin printer NLQ mode

If you can read this inform
Panasonic KX-P1624.

The information below descr
```

FIGURE 3-117   Actual Print Samples Illustrating the Differences in 24-Pin and 9-Pin Impact Printers

NOTE   The print samples shown in Figure 3-117 are taken from printers that use 8.5×11-inch or wider paper sizes. The print head design and print quality vary greatly on printers that use smaller paper sizes in point-of-sale applications.

Impact Printer Ribbons

Printer ribbons for impact printers use various types of cartridge designs. Some span the entire width of the paper, and others snap over the print head. Figure 3-118 shows two types of ribbons for impact printers.

FIGURE 3-118   Typical Ribbons for Impact Printers

Impact Printer Paper Types

Impact printers use plain uncoated paper or labels in various widths and sizes. Impact printers designed for point-of-sale receipt printing might use roll paper or larger sizes of paper. When larger sizes of paper are used, these printers typically use a tractor feed mechanism to pull or push the paper past the print head. Tractor-fed printer paper and labels have fixed or removable sprocket holes on both sides of the paper. This type of media is often called "impact," "dot-matrix," "continuous feed," or "pin-feed" paper or labels. Media with standard perforations can be difficult to separate from the paper edge after printing but is less likely to separate prior to use than micro-perforated media.

Multipart forms are frequently used with impact printers used in POS systems. Be sure to adjust the head gap appropriately to avoid print head or ribbon damage.

Impact Printer Maintenance

The keys to successful maintenance of an impact printer include replacing the ribbon, replacing the print head, and replacing the paper.

> **NOTE** For the 220-1001 exam, be sure to know the basic elements of impact printer maintenance:
>
> - Replace ribbon.
> - Replace print head.
> - Replace paper.

Replacing the Ribbon

Keeping the ribbon fresh is important not because when the ribbon is worn, the quality of printing goes down. It is also important because the ribbon on an impact dot-matrix printer lubricates the pins in the print head and protects the print head from impact damage. In addition to replacing the ribbon when print quality is no longer acceptable, be sure to immediately discard a ribbon that develops cuts or snags, as these can snag a print head pin and break or bend the pin.

Replacing the Print Head

If you replace ribbons when needed, you minimize the chances of needing to replace the print head. However, if a print head suffers damage to one or more pins, you must replace it. Damaged pins might snag the ribbon, and if a pin breaks, it will leave a gap in the characters output by the printer.

Replacing Paper

When you replace paper, be sure to check continuous-feed (tractor-fed) paper for problems with torn sprocket holes, separated tear-offs, and damaged sheets. Tear off any problem pages and use only good paper from the stack in your printer.

Be sure tractor feeders are properly adjusted, and if the printer can be run as either a push tractor (allowing zero-tear paper feed) or a pull tractor, be sure the printer is properly configured for the feed type.

Check the head gap carefully: Be sure to adjust it if you need to run multipart forms, thick labels, or envelopes. An incorrect head gap can lead to ribbon and print head damage.

Virtual Printers

The term *virtual printer* applies to any utility that is used as a printer by an app but creates a file instead of a printout. There are three major categories of virtual printers:

- Print to file
- Print to PDF or XPS
- Print to image

Print to File

Print to file is used to create a file that can be copied to a specific printer for output. This type of file contains not only the text and graphics but also specific printer control sequences and font references for the targeted printer.

> **CAUTION**   To avoid problems with print output, make sure you use fonts in your document that are also available to the target printer. If the printer doesn't have the same fonts as the system used to create the file, font substitutions will take place.

To print to a file in Microsoft Windows:

Step 1.   Open the **Print** dialog.

Step 2.   Select the printer.

Step 3.   Check the **Print to File** box.

Step 4.   Click **Print**.

Step 5.   You are typically prompted for a file location. If not, check your Documents folder to locate the file after printing. The file is stored with the .prn file extension.

Print to file is intended for use primarily with printers using the parallel (LPT) port and is not available with all apps. The printer that will be used to output the PRN file must be configured as the default port. However, by sharing a USB printer, it is possible to copy a print file to a USB printer.

> **NOTE**   For more information about printing to a file, see https://filext.com/faq/print_from_prn_file.html.

As an alternative, use Print to PDF (Portable Document Format) or XPS. With these options, it is not necessary to be concerned about font matching.

With macOS, use the Print dialog and select PostScript for output to a PostScript printer.

Print to PDF or XPS

Most Windows apps can save files directly to PDF (Adobe Acrobat/Adobe Reader) format. For apps that don't support direct saving to PDF, you can install a print to PDF virtual printer. Some versions of Windows include this capability, or it can be added by installing Adobe Acrobat or most third-party PDF reading or editing apps.

Print to PDF or XPS in Windows

When you print to PDF using a Windows app, you are prompted to specify the destination for the file. However, most other PDF options (compression, metadata support, and others) are not available. Use the Save to PDF option, when offered, to control these settings.

Current versions of Windows include the Microsoft XPS Document Writer virtual printer. Select this printer if you want to create an XPS (XML Paper Specification) document. When you select this option, you can optionally enable the opening of your XPS file after it is saved.

Print to PDF in macOS

With macOS, use the Print dialog and open the PDF menu to select the type and destination for the PDF file:

- **Save as PDF:** With this option, you can add title, author, subject, and keywords metadata. Use the Security Options button to set up password restrictions for opening, copying content, or printing the document.

- **Fax PDF:** Sends the PDF to your fax device.

- **Mail PDF:** Creates a new email message and attaches your PDF.

- **Save as PDF-X:** Creates a PDF-X file (used by professional print shops).

- **Save PDF to iPhoto:** Imports your PDF into iPhoto.

- **Save PDF to Web Receipts:** Saves your PDF to your Web Receipts folder.

Print to PDF in Linux

To print to PDF in Linux, install CUPS-PDF (the CUPS printer driver for PDF). Restart your system (if necessary), and PDF will show up in your list of printers.

Print to Image

Some virtual printer apps are designed to convert documents directly into common bitmap graphics formats such as TIFF, JPEG, BMP, and others. Some of these apps can also create PDF files.

Print to Image for Windows

Some of the Print to Image apps available for Windows include:

- **Print&Share:** www.printandshare.info

- **Raster Image Printer and TIFF Image Printer:** www.peernet.com

- **Universal Document Converter:** www.print-driver.com

Print to Image for macOS

The print subsystem in macOS can be used to create many types of bitmap images. A freeware app that makes this easy is Spool Pilot for Mac: www.colorpilot.com/spool.html.

3D Printers

3D printing is the common term given to what is technically known as *additive manufacturing* (*AM*). There are two basic types of 3D printing:

- **Fused deposition modeling (FDM):** This is the focus of this section.

- **Stereolithography:** This is a more industrial process involving photopolymer resins and lasers that is beyond the scope of the A+ exam.

3D printing is a relatively old technology, but key patents have expired and made it available to new markets. New ideas for products are being developed at a rapid rate. Small FDM machines are now common for hobbyists and small shops that need plastic components designed or manufactured on-site. Setting up and maintaining small 3D machines will be skills increasingly in demand of IT technicians.

As with other printers mentioned earlier in this section, you should know the basic process and parts of a 3D printer. The physical process of using an FDM printer can be compared to the process of using a household glue gun: A hard material is pushed into a heating chamber, and the melted material is carefully directed through a nozzle, where it will cool and become part of another object. FDM is, of course, much more complex due to software for 3D design and the mechanics of moving the nozzle precisely.

In the FDM printing process, an object is created by adding layers of material to form a complete object. The most common material is a strand of *plastic filament* that is fed from a spool to a moving printer head. The printer head heats the plastic and thinly layers it on the printing platform in cross sections that eventually build up into the 3D object that has been designed on the computer. This process is carried out on a 3D printer using these four components:

- **Filament:** This is the (usually) plastic material that is fed from a spool, though many different materials can be used. The two most common types of filament are polylactic acid (PLA) and acrylonitrile butadiene (ABS). The filament is the "ink" of an FDM printer and is available in various colors.

- **Extruder:** The extruder takes in the plastic filament and melts it.

- **Nozzle:** The nozzle is a small spray hole that emits the melted filament.

- **Bed:** The bed is the platform on which the object is created.

The process of FDM is essentially:

Step 1.   Design an object using computer-aided design (CAD) software. CAD software comes in a wide array of sophistication, and the processing demands on the computer can require enhanced GPUs.

Step 2.   Convert the model to an STL (printing code) format.

Step 3.   Set the print speed. (Slower speeds mean higher-quality printing. If you print too fast, melted filament won't set properly, so start at midrange settings.)

Step 4.   Ensure that the correct temperature is chosen, as different filaments (and even colors) can have variable melting points.

Step 5.   Print.

Figure 3-119 shows a 3D printer with yellow filament being used to print a bowl.

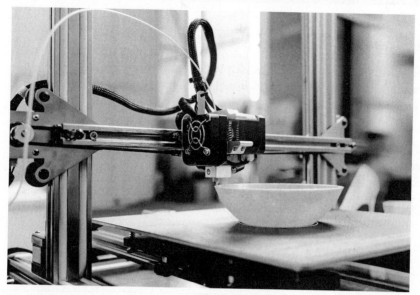

FIGURE 3-119   3D Printing

Maintaining 3D Printers

As with all other printers, cleaning and lubrication are the essential maintenance tasks for performance. But special attention needs to be given in a few areas:

- Lubrications need to be heat resistant, or they may melt and become part of the printed object.

- Different brushes are needed to clean different parts; stiff brass brushes are good for cleaning the outside of nozzles, for example.

- Cleaning the filament between print jobs is important to ensure that the next job starts with filament that is clean and at the correct temperature.

Exam Preparation Tasks

Review All the Key Topics

Review the most important topics in the chapter, noted with the Key Topic icon in the outer margin of the page. Table 3-35 lists these key topics and the page number on which each is found.

Table 3-35   Key Topics for Chapter 3

Key Topic Element	Description	Page Number
Table 3-2	Categories and Uses for TP Cabling	165
Figure 3-2	T568B (Left) and T568A (Right) Wire Pairs and an Assembled T568B Cable	168
Figure 3-3	SC, LC, and ST Fiber-Optic Cable Connectors Compared	170
Table 3-3	Video Connector Types Overview	174
Figure 3-7	DB15M (Cable) and DB15F (Port) Connectors Used for VGA Video Signals	175
Figure 3-8	HDMI Cable Connectors Compared to DVI and DisplayPort Cable Connectors	176
Figure 3-9	HDMI, DVI, and VGA Ports on the Rear of Two Typical PCIe Video Cards	177
Figure 3-11	DVI-I Video Port and DVI-D Video Cable	179
Table 3-5	USB Standards Overview	184
Table 3-6	Network Connector Types	193
Figure 3-25	DDR2 SODIMM and DIMM Modules Compared to DDR3 SODIMM and DIMM Modules	196
Table 3-8	RAM Comparison	197
Figure 3-26	DDR, DDR2, DDR3, and DDR4 DIMM Desktop Memory Modules with Different Notch Locations	198
Section	Installing Memory	202
Figure 3-28	A DDR3 DIMM Partly Inserted (Top) and Fully Inserted (Bottom)	204
Section	DVD Recordable and Rewritable Standards	207
Table 3-9	Comparison of the Three Hard Drive Types	214
Table 3-10	Hard Disk Spin Rate Comparison	216

Key Topic Element	Description	Page Number
Figure 3-34	Front (Left) and Rear (Right) Internal Optical, Desktop and Mobile Internal Hard Disks, and Mobile Internal SSD Drives	216
Section	Flash Drives	217
Table 3-12	Comparisons of Common RAID Levels	222
Table 3-13	ATX Motherboard Family Comparison	229
Figure 3-44	A Typical Late-Model ATX Motherboard	230
Figure 3-45	A Typical Late-Model microATX (mATX) Motherboard	231
Figure 3-46	A Typical Mini-ITX (mITX) Motherboard Optimized for Home Theater	232
Figure 3-47	ATX, microATX, and Mini-ITX Motherboard Component Layouts Compared	233
Section	PCI-X Slots	234
Figure 3-49	PCI Express Compared to PCI Slots	235
Figure 3-51	An Example of How a Right-Angle Riser Card Enables Tall Cards to Fit in a Low-Profile Case (Such as a Small Form Factor or 1U/2U Rack-Mount Chassis)	238
Table 3-15	CPU Manufacturers, Sockets, and Code Names Quick Reference	239
Section	Land Grid Array Sockets	240
Section	mPGA Sockets	248
Figure 3-56	Front/Top-Panel Audio, Music CD, and SPDIF Bracket Headers on a Typical Motherboard	252
Figure 3-57	A Typical Two-Row Front/Top-Panel Connector	253
Figure 3-58	Individual Front-Panel Cables Connected via an Extender to a Motherboard	253
Section	BIOS/UEFI Configuration	254
Paragraph	Accessing the BIOS Setup Program	255
Table 3-24	Major CMOS/BIOS/UEFI Settings	257
Figure 3-62	Boot Sequence and Other Boot Settings in the UEFI/BIOS Features Menu	260
Figure 3-63	A Typical Boot Menu Configured to Permit Booting from a CD/DVD or USB Flash Drive Before the Hard Drive	261
Section	Firmware Updates	261

Complete the Tables and Lists from Memory

Print a copy of Appendix C, "Memory Tables" (found online), or at least the section for this chapter, and complete the tables and lists from memory. Appendix D, "Answers to Memory Tables," also online, includes completed tables and lists to check your work.

Define Key Terms

Define the following key terms from this chapter and check your answers in the glossary.

Ethernet, CAT5e, CAT6, plenum, UTP, STP, 568B, 568A, fiber-optic cabling, coaxial cabling, BNC connector, F connector, VGA, SVGA, High-Definition Multimedia Interface (HDMI), mini-HDMI, DisplayPort, Lightning, Thunderbolt, USB, USB-C, USB 2.0, USB 3.0, USB 3.1 Gen 1, USB 3.1 Gen 2, Serial, SATA, IDE, SCSI, RJ-11, RJ-45, RS-232, BNC, RG-59, RG-6, DB9, Molex, RAM, SDRAM, SDR SDRAM, DDR SDRAM, DDR2, DDR3, DDR4, DIMM, SODIMM, single channel, dual channel, triple channel, parity checking, error-correcting code (ECC), CD-ROM, CD-RW, DVD-ROM, DVD-RW, DVD-RW DL, Blu-ray, BD-R, BD-RE, hard drive, SSD, M.2, MLC, SLC, Non-Volatile Memory Express (NVMe), spin rate, hybrid drive, flash memory, RAID, RAID Level 0 (RAID 0), striping, RAID Level 1 (RAID 1), mirroring, RAID Level 5 (RAID 5), RAID Level 1+0 (RAID 10), hot-swappable drive, ATX, mATX, mITX, miniPCIe, expansion slot, PCI, PCI Express (PCIe), riser card, Land Grid Array (LGA), IDE, Basic Input/Output System (BIOS), power-on self-test (POST), intrusion detection/notification, TPM (Trusted Platform Module), LoJack, Secure Boot, single-core processor, multicore processor, virtualization support, hardware-assisted virtualization, hyperthreading, bus speeds, overclocking, heat sink, video card, primary VGA BIOS, primary graphics adapter, SATA1, SATA2, SATA3, KVM switch, NFC, power supply, AC, DC, dual voltage, wattage rating, amperage rating, cloud printing, remote printing, imaging drum, developer, fuser assembly, transfer belt (transfer roller), pickup rollers, paper separation pad, duplexing assembly, processing, charging, exposing, developing, transferring, fusing, cleaning, calibration (printers), print quality, inkjet printer

Answer Review Questions

1. Identify the port and connector shown in the following display. Choose from the following options:

   a. ATX power supply cable and connector

   b. ATX12V power supply cable and connector

   c. EPS12V power supply cable and connector

   d. USB 3.0 cable and connector

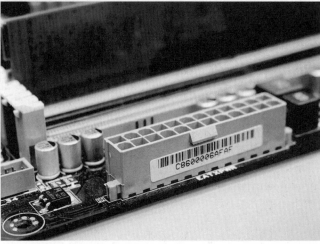

2. Your client has just connected a computer to a receiver for better music playback, but there is no audio coming from the receiver. After checking the SPDIF
cable connection and the output setting on the receiver and verifying that audio
is not muted on the computer, which of the following is the most likely cause?

   a. SPDIF audio is not selected as the default output.

   b. The VGA cable is loose.

   c. The microphone is disconnected.

   d. There is interference from the smart card reader.

3. Which of the following loses its contents when you shut down the computer?

   a. Hard disk drive

   b. USB flash drive

   c. RAM

   d. ROM

4. Identify the type of RAM in the following figure.

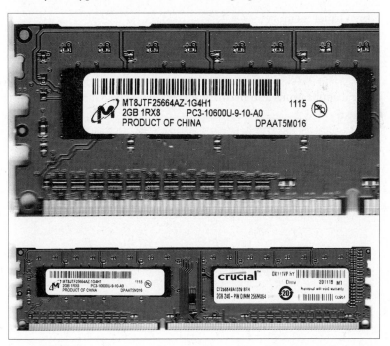

   a. DDR

   b. DDR2

   c. DDR3

   d. DDR4

5. What kind of support is provided by a system that uses matched pairs of memory modules?

   a. ECC

   b. Dual-channel

   c. Buffered

   d. SDRAM

6. Which two methods are used to protect the reliability of memory? (Choose two.)

   a. Parity checking

   b. System checking

   c. ECC (error-correcting code)

   d. Smart checking

7. Most types of desktop memory modules use which kind of memory?

   a. Unbuffered non-ECC memory

   b. Virtual memory

   c. SODIMM module

   d. ECC memory

8. Critical applications and network servers use a special type of memory. What is it called?

   a. ECC memory

   b. Unbuffered memory

   c. Static memory

   d. Crucial memory

9. Identify the type of memory layout this module uses.

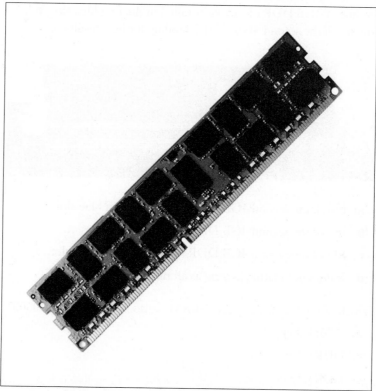

    a. With ECC, with register (or buffer)

    b. With ECC, no register (or buffer)

    c. No ECC, with register (or buffer)

    d. No ECC, no register (or buffer)

10. To correctly install a DIMM module, what should you do? (Choose all that apply.)

    a. Line up the module connectors with the socket.

    b. Verify that the locking tabs on the socket are swiveled to the outside (open) position.

    c. Verify that the module is lined up correctly with the socket and then push the module straight down until the locks on each end of the socket snap into place at the top corners of the module.

    d. None of these options is correct.

11. You have a dual-channel motherboard. You have two identical 4GB DDR3 modules and two identical 2GB DDR3 modules. In the following diagram, one module of 4GB DDR3 is being installed in the first blue slot. Where should you install the second 4GB DDR3 module for best results?

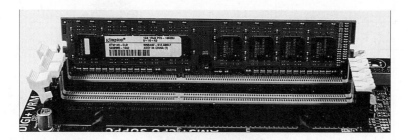

   a. Install the second 4GB DDR3 in the second blue slot.

   b. Install the second 4GB DDR3 in the first black slot.

   c. Install the second 4GB DDR3 in the second black slot.

   d. It does not matter, as long as all the modules are DDR3.

12. Which of the following types of RAM is also known as PC3-10600?

   a. DDR3-800

   b. DDR3-1066

   c. DDR3-1333

   d. DDR3-1600

13. Write the type of storage media (optical, magnetic, or flash) that corresponds with each description.

Description	Storage Media
Records information in tracks and sectors containing 512 bytes each	
Stores data in a continuous spiral	
Used on memory cards	
Records information in a series of lands and pits	
Uses laser light to read data	
Records information in concentric circles	
Information is recorded from the center outward	
Stores data on double-sided platters	
Information is recorded from the outer edge inward	
Used in solid-state drives	

14. Your client is considering purchasing a tablet with eMMC storage. Which one of the following statements is correct?

    a. The tablet will have faster data access than if it is used in SSD.

    b. eMMC is supplied in microSD cards that can be removed.

    c. The tablet cannot use USB devices.

    d. The tablet will have slower data access than if it used an SSD.

15. You want to prepare a series of presentations and copy them onto DVDs. You also want to be able to update the presentations as new information becomes available, so you want to choose a medium that can be erased and reused. Which of the following should you choose?

    a. DVD-R

    b. DVD+R

    c. DVD-RW

    d. DVD-DL

16. Your client has requested a hard disk upgrade for a laptop with the following parameters: 1TB and lowest power consumption. Which of the following factors will a matching drive have? (Choose all that apply.)

    a. 3.5-inch form factor

    b. 5400RPM

    c. 7200RPM

    d. 2.5-inch form factor

17. Match each letter in this figure with the correct cable or port name.

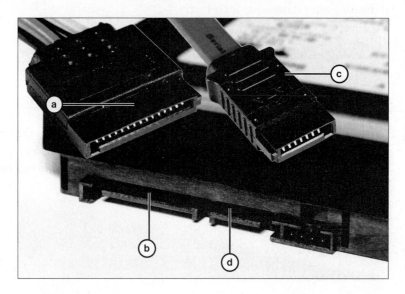

Component	Letter
i. SATA data port	
ii. SATA data cable	
iii. SATA power port	
iv. SATA power cable	

18. A user has requested a RAID array that balances high performance with data safety. Which of the following would you recommend?

    a. RAID 1

    b. RAID 10

    c. RAID 5

    d. RAID 0

19. Which of the following is the most common motherboard form factor used in desktop computers today?

    a. ATX

    b. microATX

    c. ITX

    d. Mini-ITX

20. Which motherboard form factor is commonly used in a home theater system?

    a. ATX

    b. microATX

    c. ITX

    d. Mini-ITX

21. In this figure, match each motherboard diagram with the form factor that it represents.

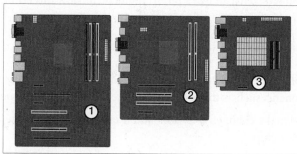

A. Mini-ITX
B. ATX
C. microATX

22. In the following figure, select the numbers that indicate power connectors. (Choose two.)

23. Refer to the figure for question 22. Which numbers identify the RAM slots? (Choose two.)

24. True or false: DDR2 and DDR3 memory modules are compatible with each other and may be used interchangeably in the same RAM slots on a motherboard.

25. Most motherboards have one connector for the CPU fan and one or more connectors for the system fans that circulate air inside the case.

   a. The CPU fan has an extra pin for fan timing

   b. The system fans have an extra pin to regulate air flow direction

   c. The CPU fan has an extra pin to control fan speed

   d. The system fan has an extra pin to control fan speed

26. Which of the following statements best describes how to make changes to the bus speeds of components such as the processor, chipset interconnect, or memory?

   a. You would make changes to POST and then save those changes on the BIOS/UEFI chip.

   b. You would download the changes you want to make from the manufacturer's website and then save the changes to the BIOS/UEFI chip.

   c. You would make changes to the BIOS settings and then save those changes on the CMOS chip.

   d. You would make all desired changes and save those changes to the South Bridge chipset.

27. Identify the component that uses the connector shown in the following figure.

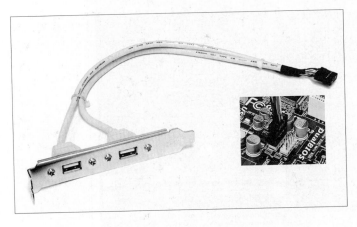

   a. PCIe

   b. PCI-X

    c. USB 2.0

    d. USB 3.0

    e. SATA

28. Identify the component that uses the connector shown in the following figure.

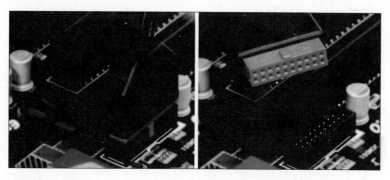

    a. PCIe

    b. PCI-X

    c. USB 2.0

    d. USB 3.0

    e. SATA

29. The CMOS chip allows the user to save and store changes made to the BIOS configurations. Which of the following statements best describes how to clear the CMOS settings and revert to the original BIOS configurations?

    a. Place a jumper block over the CMOS jumper pins.

    b. Write a new program for the CMOS chip.

    c. Download a new program from the manufacturer and flash it to the CMOS chip.

    d. Edit the South Bridge programming to change the CMOS settings.

30. You have noticed that your computer's clock has begun to lose time. You have reset the clock repeatedly, but it still continues to lose time. Which component is most likely at fault?

    a. One of the PCI slots

    b. The CMOS battery

    c. An incorrect entry in the BIOS configurations

    d. An incompatible RAM module

31. When designing and building a new customized PC to be used for graphic design, audiovisual editing, 3D game development, or virtualization, which of the following will probably need to be upgraded?

   a. CPU

   b. RAM

   c. Sound and display

   d. Cooling system

   e. All of the above

32. Which of the following statements best describes the function of a computer's power supply?

   a. To provide DC power from the wall outlet to the computer

   b. To convert DC power to AC power

   c. To convert AC power to DC power

   d. To provide AC power from the wall outlet to the computer

33. Refer to the following figure, depicting two different power supplies, and complete the chart.

	Total Watts (W)	Number of +12V Rails (R)	Amp Output from +12V Rails (Amp)
Power Supply A			
Power Supply B			

34. Which one of the following USB devices is most likely to need additional drivers installed in order to operate?

   a. Keyboard

   b. Mouse

   c. Touchpad

   d. Scanner

35. Your client has just upgraded to a touchscreen display for a desktop computer running Windows 8.1. The display functions work fine, but the touch functions have not worked since the display was set up. Which of the following should be performed first?

   a. Disconnect the mouse to see if it is interfering with the touchscreen.

   b. Reboot the computer.

   c. Make sure the USB cable from the display is plugged in.

   d. Connect all USB devices to a USB hub.

36. Place the steps in the laser printing imaging process in the correct order on the right side of the table.

Charging	1	
Cleaning	2	
Developing	3	
Exposing	4	
Fusing	5	
Processing	6	
Transferring	7	

37. True or false: During the charging step in the laser printing imaging process, the drum receives an electrostatic charge of –600V. Because the drum is photosensitive, it retains its charge only if it is kept in the dark.

38. A laser printer uses which of the following processes?

   a. Line-by-line printing

   b. Impact plus heat transfer

   c. Impact against an inked ribbon

   d. Whole-page printing

39. How do inkjet printers create characters and graphics?

   a. By spraying tiny dots of ink onto the page

   b. By fusing fine grains of toner into the page

   c. By using a thermal transfer ribbon

   d. By using an ink impregnated ribbon

40. Which acronym refers to the colors used by an inkjet printer?

   a. CMYB

   b. CMYK

   c. RBG

   d. RBGY

41. In the following figure, which kind of problem does the right half of the screen demonstrate?

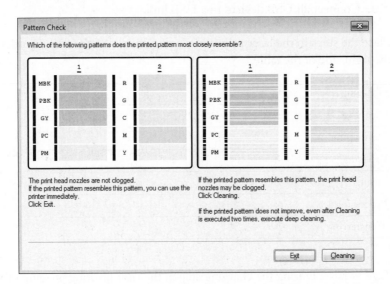

   a. The drum of a laser printer has old toner clinging to it and needs to be cleaned.

   b. The ribbon on an impact printer is old and is wearing out.

   c. The heating mechanism of a thermal printer is not getting hot enough.

   d. The print heads on an inkjet printer are clogged or faulty.

42. Thermal printers use which of the following?

   a. A non-impact matrix of dots that can be heated and used in various combinations to create an image

   b. Toner to create an image and heated rollers to fix the toner to the paper

   c. Closely grouped nozzles of heated ink to produce an image

   d. An ink impregnated ribbon to create an image, followed by heated rollers to set the image

43. Which type of printer typically uses multipart forms?

   a. Laser printer

   b. Impact printer

   c. Inkjet printer

   d. Thermal printer

44. What is the name of the open source printing system used by Linux?

   a. PRT

   b. LPT

   c. XPS

   d. CUPS

45. You have just bought a new printer and are about to install it. Which of the following statements describes the best way to be sure that your drivers are up to date?

   a. Use the installation disc that shipped with the printer.

   b. Use Windows Update to automatically select the best drivers.

   c. Go to the vendor's website to select drivers.

   d. Connect the printer to the computer and allow it to auto install.

46. Which of the following is not a typical print configuration setting for a printer or multifunction device?

   a. Selecting duplex printing

   b. Configuring collating

   c. Choosing a cover page

   d. Changing the orientation of the page

47. Which type of encryption is supported by a printer in ad hoc mode?

    a. WEP

    b. WPA

    c. WPA2

    d. NIC

This chapter covers the two A+ 220-1001 exam objectives related to virtualization and cloud computing. These objectives may comprise 12% of the exam questions:

- **Core 1 (220-1001): Objective 4.1:** Compare and contrast cloud computing concepts.

- **Core 1 (220-1001): Objective 4.2:** Given a scenario, set up and configure client-side virtualization.

## CHAPTER 4

Virtualization and Cloud Computing

Cloud computing involves using remote servers in the Internet "cloud" to store, manage, and process data rather than using local servers or a personal computer. Cloud servers usually reside in large server farms where powerful servers host thousands of virtual machines.

Remember that a computer is made up of hardware components that process software instructions. Virtual computing technology creates and runs multiple instances of software operating systems—such as desktops, servers, and even networks—on a single piece of hardware. Multiple software systems sharing the resources of one hardware system is known as *virtualization*. It is very common for a single laptop, desktop, or server to be used to run two or more different operating systems, such as Linux and Windows 10, at the same time. Figure 4-1 depicts several different servers virtually running on one robust hardware machine.

Cloud computing involves using virtual machines in commercial data centers to relieve customers of the expense of maintaining a network center. Cloud-based systems allow customers to pay for only the services and capacity they use, which allows businesses to grow their technology capacity as they need it and avoid high up-front costs.

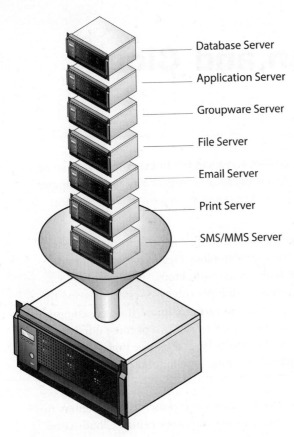

Database Server

Application Server

Groupware Server

File Server

Email Server

Print Server

SMS/MMS Server

FIGURE 4-1   One Hardware Machine Running Several Virtual Servers (Image © Zern Liew. Shutterstock)

"Do I Know This Already?" Quiz

The "Do I Know This Already?" quiz allows you to assess whether you should read the entire chapter. Table 4-1 lists the major headings in this chapter and the "Do I Know This Already?" quiz questions covering the material in those headings so you can assess your knowledge of these specific areas. The answers to the "Do I Know This Already?" quiz appear in Appendix A, "Answers to the 'Do I Know This Already?' Quizzes and Review Question Sections."

Table 4-1   "Do I Know This Already?" Section-to-Question Mapping

Foundation Topics Section	Questions
Common Cloud Models	1–5
Client-Side Virtualization Overview	5–10

CAUTION   The goal of self-assessment is to gauge your mastery of the topics in this chapter. If you do not know the answer to a question or are only partially sure of the answer, you should mark that question as wrong for purposes of the self-assessment. Giving yourself credit for an answer you correctly guess skews your self-assessment results and might provide you with a false sense of security.

1. Which cloud computing model allows companies to access software when they need it but avoid the expense of maintaining the software when they do not need it?

   a. Resource pooling

   b. Rapid elasticity

   c. On-demand

   d. Hybrid

2. You have been asked to arrange for your team to develop software in a cloud environment. Which of the following services will you seek as a solution?

   a. PaaS

   b. SaaS

   c. IaaS

   d. None of the above

3. A company requires high security and high reliability for its network services. What type of cloud environment is likely to meet these requirements?

   a. Public cloud

   b. External cloud

   c. Internal cloud

   d. Infrastructure as a Service

4. How are most cloud customers billed for their services?

   a. Hourly rate

   b. Daily rate

   c. Weekly subscription

   d. Monthly subscription

5. What term describes a cloud provider's ability to rapidly scale up and scale back computing resources as needed?

   a. Rapid elasticity

   b. Flex data services

   c. Virtual data flexing

   d. Expansive data services

6. Which two of the following are used to create and run a VM? (Choose two.)

   a. Hypervisor

   b. VMM

   c. Emulator

   d. Virtual sphere

7. Which of the following is a reproduction of an operating system?

   a. Virtual machine

   b. VMware Fusion

   c. Emulator

   d. Hyper-V

8. Which operating systems can be guests on a VM?

   a. Windows

   b. Linux

   c. Unix

   d. None of the above

   e. All of the above

9. Which of the following is true?

   a. A 32-bit system can host a 64-bit VM.

   b. A VMM can create only one operating system per hardware device.

   c. A 64-bit system can host a 32-bit system.

   d. Only one VM can run at a time on a workstation with one display.

10. Which of the following is true of the BIOS/UEFI when creating a VM?

   a. Hypervisors create their own BIOS/UEFI settings.

   b. The BIOS/UEFI firmware must support VMs.

   c. All BIOS/UEFI firmware supports VMs.

   d. A separate hard disk must be installed for each VM.

Foundation Topics

Common Cloud Models

- **220-1001: Objective 4.1:** Compare and contrast cloud computing concepts.

The *cloud* refers to any type of computing—including program execution, storage, or services—that takes place remotely. Understanding these basic concepts is important for technicians, who will increasingly be asked to manage software or data in the cloud. Some of those functions are described in the following sections.

IaaS

Infrastructure as a Service (*IaaS*) enables customers to purchase access to data center infrastructure such as storage, network, and networking services. In this model, the cloud provider covers the costs and work involved in equipment, firewall configurations, and other maintenance. Thousands of companies are realizing that they can reduce the costs of their network infrastructure by outsourcing storage and computing services to a cloud provider. These include new startup companies that lack the capital resources to buy and manage equipment as they grow and established companies that want to reduce the costs related to backup and storage of their networks.

One of the key features of IaaS is the flexibility it offers to customers who can now just use the virtual resources they need when they need them and not pay for them when they don't need them.

IaaS puts users in charge of all the software used in a project, from applications and data to the operating system. IaaS vendors supply the hardware and network support tools.

Amazon first introduced cloud services in 2006, and the field of cloud providers continues to grow. At press time, the three largest cloud providers were:

- Amazon Web Services (AWS)
- Microsoft Azure
- IBM

SaaS

Software as a Service (*SaaS*) refers to software that is hosted on servers and accessed through a web browser. Because SaaS processing is performed at the server, a thin client, smartphone, or tablet is sufficient to run the software. A browser-based service that does not require a user to download application code to use the service is an example of SaaS.

Perhaps the best-known SaaS is Google Mail (Gmail). Gmail servers provide the Gmail service to anyone who has a web browser. Other examples of SaaS include:

- **Google Docs:** Word processing, spreadsheets, presentations, and forms (www.google.com/intl/en/docs/about/)

- **Microsoft Office 365:** Word processing, spreadsheets, presentations, calendar, collaboration, and email (www.office.com)

- **FreshBooks:** Small business accounting (www.freshbooks.com)

- **Salesforce:** Customer relationship management (www.salesforce.com)

- **Basecamp:** Project management (https://basecamp.com)

SaaS is designed for organizations that need to use a service rather than develop or deploy one. Figure 4-2 illustrates the word processor in Google Docs.

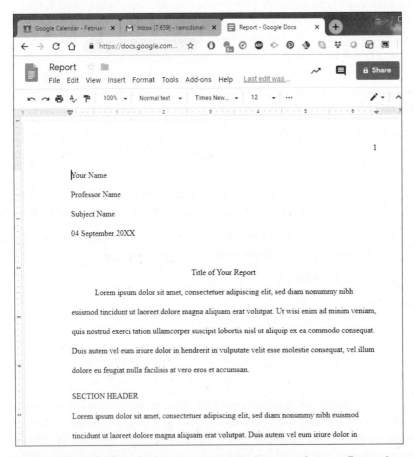

FIGURE 4-2 Using the Google Docs Word Processor to Create a Report from a Template with Random Text as Placeholders

PaaS

Platform as a Service (*PaaS*) enables vendors to develop and deploy application software in a cloud environment. A developer using PaaS can concentrate on software features instead of possible issues with server hardware and operating systems.

Some of the major PaaS vendors include:

- **Oracle Cloud:** https://cloud.oracle.com
- **Google Cloud Platform:** https://cloud.google.com
- **Microsoft Azure:** https://azure.microsoft.com
- **Salesforce Platform:** www.salesforce.com

Many vendors provide many services across multiple platforms.

NOTE Microsoft Azure is listed in both the PaaS and IaaS categories because it can be used in either role, depending on the services purchased by a user.

Some of the considerations in selecting a PaaS vendor include:

- **Language and server-side support:** Make sure the vendor you select supports the languages you use for development and the server-side technologies your apps depend on. Most major PaaS vendors support languages such as Java, Ruby, PHP, and Python, but server-side technology support varies a great deal.

- **Integration with existing investments:** Some PaaS vendor products can integrate with existing apps and data, meaning cloud platforms can work with existing resources instead of requiring them to be replaced them entirely.

- **Costs:** Most PaaS vendors use pricing by the hour, but some price by the month. Be sure your pre-commitment cost estimations take into account the software tools and services you need, as pricing can vary according to the tools or services bundled.

Public vs. Private vs. Hybrid vs. Community

There are four general types of cloud computing. Each type can have variables in its implementation, depending on customer needs. They are:

Key
Topic

- *Public cloud computing* is available to any organization that signs up or pays for it. The connection between services and organizations is the public Internet.

- *Private cloud computing* is available only to authorized users in divisions or departments of a single company. The company owns and manages the cloud behind its corporate firewall, and its employees maintain the equipment. Private cloud computing is considered to be more secure than public cloud computing.

- *Hybrid cloud computing* combines features of public and private cloud computing. A typical hybrid installation includes dedicated and cloud-based servers and high-speed interconnections with load balancing to move workloads between the environments as needed.

- *Community cloud computing* is a type of hybrid cloud computing that is used by different organizations that are working together. The organizations work together to build the community cloud and share its costs. This is a model that works well for organizations that are working together temporarily on a single goal or project and then can dissolve the cloud when the project is finished.

Shared Resources

Sharing equipment or data on a network to save costs is the overall reason to implement cloud computing. But the way clouds are designed and implemented can vary according to the customer's needs. There are two main ways to share devices and data over the Internet: using an internal cloud or an external cloud.

Internal Cloud

Internal and external clouds are defined by the ownership of the cloud's resources. With an internal cloud, a company may need the flexibility of cloud services but also have security and guaranteed availability requirements that prevent the company from accessing cloud services outside its own network. An internal cloud is similar to a private cloud, described above, but is built and owned inside the organization. With an internal cloud, the company gets the virtualization services and flexibility of a commercial cloud but with the security and reliability that comes from existing within the company's network infrastructure. While the cost of an internal cloud maybe higher than outsourcing to commercial services, there is still reduced cost in sharing resources internally.

External Cloud

An external cloud is a cloud solution that exists outside an organization's physical boundaries. It can be private, public, or community based, as long as it is not located on an organization's property.

Rapid Elasticity

Rapid elasticity refers to the ability to rapidly scale up and scale back cloud computing resources as needed. For example, selling high-demand concert tickets in pre-cloud days often resulted in crashing servers and disappointed customers. With the rapid elasticity of the cloud, high-demand events can quickly expand capacity for online sales and not leave customers unserved when they try to buy.

On-Demand

On-demand is a shortened term for *on-demand self-services*. On-demand self-services from SaaS providers such as Salesforce.com, Gmail, and others are available to customers when they need them but do not need to be maintained by the customer when they are not needed.

Resource Pooling

Resource pooling refers to the dynamic combination of a service provider's resources (servers, storage, network connections, and so on) to meet the needs of multiple organizations as demand increases or decreases.

Measured Service

Measured service refers to how cloud services are monitored for quality and effectiveness. Measuring service metrics can help drive decisions about what services to adopt and how to calculate pricing of services.

Metered Service

Cloud computing services are purchased by organizations much as utilities such as gas and water services and are based on usage. Cloud computing services are usually calculated on an hourly basis. Outsourcing by the hour can mean immense savings for customers, and this feature is what has driven the high growth of cloud services.

Off-site Email Applications

Traditional network operations host their services on-site (also known as on premises), behind locked doors and firewalls. Email and other applications can be tightly controlled. In this on-site model, the company absorbs all the costs of purchasing, powering, and maintaining the server equipment. On-site hosted email and other applications are accessed through the company's local area network (LAN).

Most companies and institutions have adopted, or at least investigated, the newer model of off-site hosting for email and other services that are accessed on the Web. Off-site hosting is a type of cloud computing. Paying Google or another vendor to manage email—and the growing mountain of data that it generates—is significantly less expensive than keeping the equipment and technicians in-house. The benefit of lower overhead does, however, have at least a perceived cost of less control over security of the company's private data.

Cloud File Storage Services

With cloud-based synchronization, apps on a mobile device send data to the cloud, where it is downloaded by other mobile apps, by web browsers, or by programs running on Windows or macOS computers. Examples of providers that enable cloud-based synchronization include:

- Dropbox (www.dropbox.com)
- Apple iCloud (www.apple.com/icloud)
- Microsoft OneDrive (https://onedrive.live.com)
- Google Drive (www.google.com)

Data that is synced via cloud-based synchronization is encrypted and secured by passwords and usernames. Mutual authentication is used by each side of the connection to verify its identity to the other side.

Mutual Authentication for Multiple Services (SSO)

Apple, Microsoft, and Google allow mutual authentication for multiple services (also known as SSO, or Single Sign-On) to enable a single login to provide access to multiple services. For example, a single Microsoft account login provides access to Outlook email, the Microsoft Store, and OneDrive. A single Apple login provides access to iTunes, iCloud, and other services. A single Google login provides access to Gmail, Android services, and other services.

Virtual Application Streaming/Cloud-Based Applications

Virtual application streaming of cloud-based applications allows users to have more device options for the applications they use. This is because most applications that were traditionally run on a local desktop or laptop used too many hard drive and RAM resources to be available on tablets and cell phones.

Virtual application streaming solves this problem by storing and running the application in the cloud and delivering the results to the user on any device. This not only enables mobile devices to use bigger applications but also saves resources on laptops and desktops because most people store large applications but use only a small percentage of the functions on applications they run.

To implement virtual application streaming, a client purchases a license and downloads a small app that identifies the person as a user. The application is presented to the user as if it were locally installed, but only the essentials are brought down to the device.

For cell phones and tablets that have very little storage and RAM available, the results and saved files can all be saved to the cloud. For subscribers on laptops and desktops with more resources available, the frequently used parts of the application can be downloaded and kept for faster access, while other features can be stored in the cloud until needed, and users' work can be stored locally, if they desire.

Examples of cloud-based applications saving resources are mentioned in the earlier section "SaaS."

Virtual Desktop

Virtual desktop refers to a user's interface to a computer that is hosted in the cloud. When a company uses a vendor's virtual desktop infrastructure (VDI), users can use minimally powered devices with an Internet connection and work as if processing were happening locally.

Virtual desktop is also known as *thin client networking* because the processing is centralized, and only mouse and keyboard inputs are sent across the Internet.

Virtual NIC

When a VM has an operating system installed, it appears and can behave like any other computer on a network. In order to interact with other machines, it needs to have a **virtual network interface card** (**NIC**) installed so that it can have a physical MAC address and an IP address. The virtual NIC behaves almost exactly like a physical NIC, but the administrator can use the virtual machine manager (VMM) to assign a specific MAC address. This is different from physical NICs with MAC addresses that are assigned at the manufacturer.

If administrators want the VM to communicate with other machines, they can create a path, or bridge, between the virtual NIC and the physical NIC on the VMM hardware. This allows the VM to communicate like any other machine in the LAN.

Client-Side Virtualization Overview

220-1001: Objective 4.2: Given a scenario, set up and configure client-side virtualization.

Microsoft (Hyper-V) and third-party vendors, such as Oracle (VirtualBox), VMware (VMware Workstation, VMware Fusion), and Parallels (Parallels Desktop), have offered virtualization solutions for some time. Virtualization enables a single computer to run two or more operating systems at the same time, using the same hardware resources.

To understand virtualization, make sure you understand these terms:

- *Virtual machine manager (VMM)*: A VMM (often also called the *hypervisor*) is software that creates and manages virtual machines. It is a specialized operating system that uses minimal hardware resources so that memory and processing are available for the VMs it creates. (Later in this section, you will learn the differences between a VMM and a hypervisor.)

- *Virtual machine (VM)*: A VM is a machine created by a hypervisor/VMM that runs like any other computer. It usually needs an operating system installed on it to become functional. A VM uses the VMM/hypervisor for access to memory, CPU, network, video, and other resources.

- *Emulation*: Emulation involves software-based reproduction of various operating systems but without the functionality and resource use of virtualization.

When creating a VM, a VMM/hypervisor sets aside memory space that provides access to virtualized storage, ports, video, and other hardware, as well as a hard disk image file known as a virtual hard disk (VHD and the newer VHDX). When the VM is created, the user specifies the type of operating system that will be installed.

After the VM starts, the user can install the operating system from an .iso image file or from physical media. After the operating system is installed, the virtualized hardware set up by the VMM is detected and used by the VM.

The VMM/hypervisor can start and stop the VM and modify the virtual hardware the VM has access to. For example, the VMM can adjust the amount of RAM used by the VM, change the virtual network adapter used by the VM, and specify what type of network access the VM has. If a VM malfunctions, it can be stopped and restarted without affecting the host device.

There are two ways that a computer can run a different operating system:

- **Virtualization:** In virtualization, the physical resources (for example, RAM, disk space, CPU cycles) are divided between VMs that can run independently of each other. An operating system is loaded into each VM.

■ **Emulation:** In emulation, a full reproduction of a different operating system and different hardware is created by an emulation app, which is then used to run software made for that operating system. Some switch and router emulators have been created to provide training and testing without requiring expensive physical equipment. Other emulators have been created to enable modern PCs to run legacy video games created for systems such as the Atari 2600.

There are several categories of virtualization: host/guest, hypervisor, server-hosted, and client-side virtualization.

Host/Guest Virtualization

In host/guest virtualization, a PC or workstation runs a standard operating system and a VMM that runs inside the operating system; each VM is a guest operating system. Connections to hardware (networking, display, printing, and so on) are passed from the guest operating system to the virtualization program to the host computer's operating system.

Figure 4-3 illustrates Oracle VM VirtualBox, a popular free host virtualizer. Other examples include Windows Virtual PC from Microsoft (for Windows 7), Microsoft Hyper-V (for Windows 8 and later), and VMware Workstation Player.

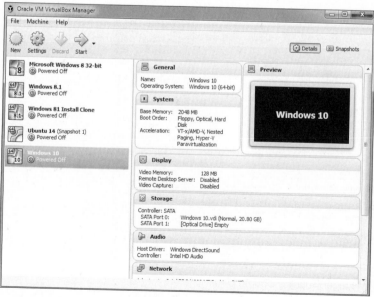

FIGURE 4-3 Oracle VM VirtualBox Manager Preparing to Start a VM

This type of virtualization is often used for client-side virtualization. However, client-side virtualization can also be centrally managed from the standpoint of the creation and management of VM images, although the images are being run locally.

Purpose of Virtual Machines

With VMs, the savings compared to running two or more physical workstations can be significant in terms of space, cooling, and peripheral hardware.

Virtual machines enable help desktop and support specialists to run older operating systems without changing computers and without rebooting their systems. Virtual machines enable a single PC to run 32-bit and 64-bit versions of the same operating system so that applications that run better in 32-bit mode can be run without the need for a separate computer. For example, in Figure 4-3, a 32-bit version of Windows 8 is virtualized.

The virtual machines on a computer can perform different tasks at the same time, enabling more work to be done with less hardware investment.

Figure 4-4 illustrates Microsoft Hyper-V Manager after creating a VM running Ubuntu Linux.

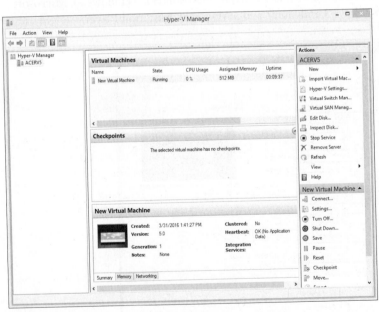

FIGURE 4-4   Hyper-V Manager Running Ubuntu Linux

By running virtual machines on servers, fewer physical servers are required to perform the same tasks, which leads to continuing cost savings, easier scaling to suit the workload, and easier disaster recovery.

System images can be centrally created, modified, and managed for easier installation. Because the VMM acts as a translator between the VM and the actual computer hardware, there are fewer problems due to differences in system hardware.

Resource Requirements

A workstation that will be used for virtualization needs to be designed with fast multicore processors and as much RAM as possible, given the limitations of the motherboard and VMM (or host operating system). For this reason, it's better to use 64-bit processors and a 64-bit-compatible VMM (and host operating system if hosted virtualization, rather than a hypervisor, is being used). 64-bit operating systems or VMMs are not subject to the 4GB RAM limit imposed by 32-bit architecture.

Processors selected for a virtualization system should also feature hardware-assisted virtualization. The system BIOS/UEFI firmware must also support this feature and must be enabled in the system BIOS/UEFI firmware. Otherwise, VMs will run much more slowly, and some VMMs will not be supported.

If several VMs will be run at the same time on a workstation, the use of two or more displays is highly recommended.

Although a VM is are created using an actual operating system rather than a reproduction of one, the physical hardware that will be used for the VMM must meet or exceed the minimum requirements for the VMM. Here are some examples:

- VMware Workstation Player 15 is a simplified version of VMware. It requires a 1.3GHz or faster 64-bit processor, Intel CPU with VT-x support (enabled in BIOS/UEFI firmware) or AMD CPU with segment-limit support in long mode, and 2GB minimum (with 4GB or more recommended).

- Hyper-V requires a 64-bit CPU with Data Execution Prevention (DEP) and hardware virtualization (enabled in BIOS/UEFI firmware), second-level address translation (SLAT), and a minimum of 4GB of RAM (with more recommended).

NOTE SLAT (second-level address translation), also known as *nested paging*, reduces the overhead required to map virtual to physical addresses. By reducing overhead, more virtual machines can be run at the same time on a server.

Emulator Requirements

Because an emulator must simulate an entire operating system and the hardware originally used with the operating system, it requires much more RAM and a faster processor than the original hardware being emulated. For example, the Atari 2600 uses a 1.19MHz 8-bit 6507 processor (a simplified version of the 6502 used by Apple, Atari 400/800/XL, and Commodore 64 home computers) and has 128 bytes of RAM. By contrast, the Windows version of the popular Stella emulator for Atari 2600 requires a 32-bit or 64-bit processor on Windows XP or later (which requires a CPU running at 233MHz or faster).

Checking for BIOS/UEFI and Processor Support for Virtualization

Most VMMs or hypervisors require that hardware virtualization be enabled in BIOS/UEFI firmware. To determine whether this feature is already enabled, download and run the Microsoft Hardware-Assisted Virtualization Detection Tool from www.microsoft.com/en-us/download/details.aspx?id=592.

Security Requirements

Virtual networks require the same attention to security details as physical networks. Because a single physical computer can house two or more VMs, knowing which computers in an organization are using VMs is a vital first step in securing a virtualized environment. Some of the issues to consider include:

- **Monitoring network traffic:** When multiple VMs running on a single physical workstation or server communicate with each other, the hypervisor must monitor the traffic unless it is routed to the physical network and then back to the other VM. A feature known as extensible switch modules enables the operating system to monitor network traffic between VMs.

- **Backing up VMs:** Virtualized storage needs to be backed up with tools made especially for VMs. A VM backup needs to include configuration files and virtual disks to ensure that the VM can be restored wherever needed. Most VMMs and hypervisors include a feature known as *virtual machine checkpoints* (or virtual machine snapshots). A checkpoint saves the state, data, and hardware configuration of a VM while it is running.

- **Updates and patches:** Updates and patches need to be kept current, and antivirus software needs to be installed and updated because the host machine cannot scan the VMs for viruses.

- **Security:** A VMM that enables sandboxing (isolation) of each VM and that provides physical partitioning of resources provides better security against attacks.

- **Best security practices for VMMs and VMs:** Operating systems and apps in VMs must be kept up-to-date and need to use firewalls and anti-malware to protect the VM. VMMs also need to be kept up-to-date, and remote administration should be secured by using a VPN. Connections between the VMs such as clipboards or file sharing should be limited to only those that are necessary.

Network Requirements

Network requirements differ between VMMs and hypervisors. Building on the earlier discussion of virtual NICs, note that Microsoft Hyper-V requires the creation of an external virtual network switch for each physical NIC or adapter. It supports up to four legacy NICs and up to eight VMBus NICs. With Oracle VM VirtualBox and with VMware, a physical wired network adapter is connected as a NAT (network address translation) device.

With these VMMs and most others, wireless network adapters on the host must be bridged to the virtualized wired network adapter to permit the virtual machine to use the wireless adapter. In other words, the wireless adapter is visible and works as a wired adapter inside the virtual machine.

An *authentication server* is used to examine and verify or deny credentials to a user attempting to log into secured networks.

Hypervisor

The machines that create and manage virtual machines are called *hypervisors*. A *hypervisor* that has VMs running on it is considered a host, and the VMs are considered "guest" machines.

Type 1 hypervisor-based virtualization is sometimes referred to as *bare-metal virtualization*. The hypervisor itself uses few computer resources (for example, memory, CPU), but more computer resources can be made available to each VM. Web-hosting companies and companies that offer cloud computing solutions use Type 1 hypervisors for virtual servers and thin client virtualization.

A Type 2 hypervisor is created on a running operating system. For example, a user running macOS can load VMware Fusion onto a laptop to create a VM. Then the user can install Linux or Windows on the virtual machine. The benefit is that the user then has access to two operating systems on one machine. The laptop's resources support both machines.

With a Type 2 hypervisor, guests are one level removed from the hardware and therefore run less efficiently than do guests on Type 1 hypervisors.

Turning a hypervisor on or off is a fairly straightforward process. Search for "Turn Windows features on or off" or access the Windows Features via **Control Panel > Programs > Programs and Features** and then select **Turn Windows Features on or off** from the menu on the left, as depicted in Figure 4-5.

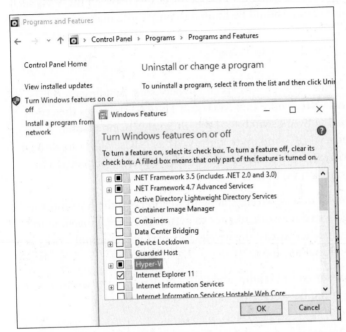

FIGURE 4-5   Enabling Hyper-V in Windows 10

Exam Preparation Tasks

Review All the Key Topics

Review the most important topics in the chapter, noted with the Key Topic icon in the outer margin of the page. Table 4-2 lists these key topics and the page number on which each is found.

Table 4-2 Key Topics for Chapter 4

Key Topic Element	Description	Page Number
Section	Common Cloud Models	391
List	General types of cloud computing	393
Section	Virtual Desktop	397
Section	Client-Side Virtualization Overview	398

Define Key Terms

Define the following key terms from this chapter, and check your answers in the glossary.

virtualization, cloud computing, IaaS, SaaS, PaaS, public cloud computing, private cloud computing, hybrid cloud computing, community cloud computing, rapid elasticity, on-demand, resource pooling, virtual network interface card (NIC), virtual machine manager (VMM), hypervisor, virtual machine (VM), emulation, authentication server

Answer Review Questions

1. Match each of the following cloud-based models to its description.

Model	Description
a. SaaS	
b. IaaS	
c. PaaS	

   1. Provides access to storage, network services, virtualization, and servers

   2. Gives application developers the opportunity to develop and deploy software in a cloud environment

   3. Enables software to be hosted on remote servers and accessed through web browsers

2. Which of the following are characteristics of a virtual machine? (Choose all that apply.)

   a. A user can access multiple guest operating systems without rebooting.

   b. 32-bit and 64-bit operating systems may be installed on different virtual machines on a single host machine.

   c. Multiple virtual machines use the same hardware as the host computer.

   d. Running multiple guest operating systems is more expensive than running those same operating systems as host systems.

3. Which of the following are advantages of cloud computing? (Choose all that apply.)

   a. Rapid elasticity

   b. DHCP services

   c. Resource pooling

   d. Measured service

4. What is the name of the program that acts as the translator between the host machine and its virtual machines?

   a. Virtual machine server

   b. Virtualization machine manager

   c. Virtual host manager

   d. Virtualized guest server

5. The Windows 10 VM is selected in the following figure. Assuming that the host system has 8GB (8,192MB) of RAM, can you determine how much RAM will be available to the host system when the Windows 10 VM is running?

a. 8192MB

b. 2048MB

c. 6144MB

d. Impossible to determine from the image

6. Which of the following best describes sandboxing as it relates to a virtual machine?

a. It is a type of hybrid cloud computing.

b. It is a type of firewall between the host server and the outside world.

c. It is a backup for virtual machines.

d. It is the isolation of VMs within the host system for better security.

7. A VMM that runs directly on the hardware rather than inside the operating system is known as which of the following?

a. Hypervisor

b. Thin-client virtualization

c. Client-side host/guest virtualization

d. DEP (Data Execution Prevention)

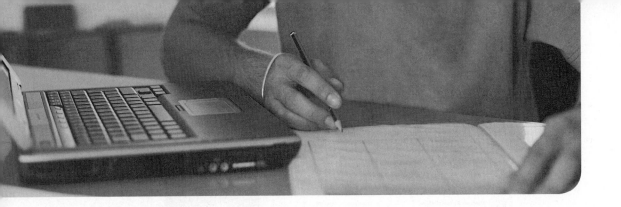

This chapter covers the seven A+ 220-1001 exam objectives related to troubleshooting common problems with motherboards, RAM, CPUs, and power; hard drives and RAID arrays; video, projector, and display issues; mobile device issues while adhering to the appropriate procedures; printers; and wired and wireless network problems. These objectives may comprise 27 percent of the exam questions:

- **Core 1 (220-1001): Objective 5.1:** Given a scenario, use the best practice methodology to resolve problems.

- **Core 1 (220-1001): Objective 5.2:** Given a scenario, troubleshoot common problems related to motherboards, RAM, CPUs, and power.

- **Core 1 (220-1001): Objective 5.3:** Given a scenario, troubleshoot hard drives and RAID arrays.

- **Core 1 (220-1001): Objective 5.4:** Given a scenario, troubleshoot common video, projector, and display issues.

- **Core 1 (220-1001): Objective 5.5:** Given a scenario, trouble-shoot common mobile device issues while adhering to the appropriate procedures.

- **Core 1 (220-1001): Objective 5.6:** Given a scenario, troubleshoot printers.

- **Core 1 (220-1001): Objective 5.7:** Given a scenario, troubleshoot common wired and wireless network problems.

## CHAPTER 5

Hardware and Network Troubleshooting

Chapter 3, "Hardware," introduces hardware components that make up computers, printers, networks, and mobile devices. In this chapter, you learn specific troubleshooting methods for these devices as well as the networks they may inhabit.

"Do I Know This Already?" Quiz

The "Do I Know This Already?" quiz allows you to assess whether you should read the entire chapter. Table 5-1 lists the major headings in this chapter and the "Do I Know This Already?" quiz questions covering the material in those headings so you can assess your knowledge of these specific areas. The answers to the "Do I Know This Already?" quiz appear in Appendix A, "Answers to the 'Do I Know This Already?' Quizzes and Review Question Sections."

Table 5-1 "Do I Know This Already?" Foundation Topics Section-to-Question Mapping

Foundations Topics Section	Questions
Troubleshooting Motherboard, RAM, CPU, and Power Issues	1–5
Troubleshooting Windows STOP Errors (BSOD)	6–8
Recommended Tools	9
Troubleshooting Hard Drives and RAID Arrays	10–13
Troubleshooting Video, Projector, and Display Issues	14
Network Troubleshooting	15–17
Mobile Device Troubleshooting	18–19
Printer Troubleshooting	20

> **CAUTION**   The goal of self-assessment is to gauge your mastery of the topics in this chapter. If you do not know the answer to a question or are only partially sure of the answer, you should mark that question as wrong for purposes of the self-assessment. Giving yourself credit for an answer you correctly guess skews your self-assessment results and might provide you with a false sense of security.

1. Which of the following is not one of the six steps of the CompTIA trouble-shooting theory?

   a. Establish a theory of probable cause.

   b. Check all cables and link lights.

   c. Document findings, actions, and outcomes.

   d. Test the theory to determine the cause.

2. At which step in the troubleshooting methodology might system logs be most helpful to a technician?

   a. Step 1

   b. Step 3

   c. Step 5

   d. Step 6

3. Which is not a system error commonly identified by beep codes?

   a. Memory

   b. Processor or motherboard

   c. Video

   d. Overclocking

4. When a computer boots and then displays the incorrect time and/or date, what are two possible causes? (Choose two.)

   a. The CPU is overclocked.

   b. The CMOS chip is bad.

   c. The battery is depleted.

   d. The BIOS license has expired.

5. You touch the power supply inside the computer, and it is too hot to hold. Before removing the cover at the workstation, you observed that the user's cubicle is more cluttered than most. You observed the following four issues. Which two of them may be responsible for the hot power supply? (Choose two.)

   a. Drinks and food are spread around and left open on the tower next to the desk.

   b. A sweater is hanging down from a hook behind the tower.

   c. Cables are pulled tight from repositioning the monitor.

   d. Crumbs are on the floor and mixing with dust bunnies.

6. Which two of the following might a BSOD indicate? (Choose two.)

   a. Network cables not properly connected during boot

   b. Registry errors

   c. OS license expired

   d. Defective hardware

7. What can be done to isolate the cause of a BSOD? (Choose two.)

   a. Wait 20 seconds and try again.

   b. Remove a newly added component.

   c. Note the error code and research it on line.

   d. Unplug the power for one minute.

8. You have a client running Microsoft Word on macOS. When he tried to print, a spinning pin wheel stopped everything. Choose a likely cause and a likely quick remedy from the following options.

   a. Caused by printer failure; reboot printer

   b. Microsoft Word out of date; reboot and update version

   c. RAM not available to process application demand; force-quit the application and reopen after closing unused applications

   d. System crash; unplug and remove battery for two minutes to allow data to reset

9. Which tool in an IT professional's toolkit can test the DC voltage inside a computer and the AC voltage of the outlet?

   a. Multimeter

   b. Loopback plugs

   c. Power supply tester

   d. POST card/USB

10. If you have determined that you need to upgrade a PC by replacing a SATA HDD with an SSD, which form factor is not a feasible replacement?

   a. mSATA SSD

   b. SATA HDD

   c. PCIe card

   d. m.2 SSD

11. Which of the following is not monitored by S.M.A.R.T.?

   a. Slow spin-up

   b. Drive temperature

   c. Printer retry errors

   d. Bad sectors

12. Which command can be used to find errors on a hard drive.?

   a. DSKERR

   b. DISKPART

   c. CHKDSK

   d. ERRDSK

13. You are working on a hard drive that is nearly full, and you suspect files are stored in fragments around the hard drive. Which one of the following can help you determine whether defragmentation is a plausible solution for this client?

   a. Use the Disk Storage Update tool.

   b. Run DEFRAG at the command prompt.

   c. Run CHKDSK.

   d. Click the Analyze button in the disk optimization window.

14. You are asked to assist with a projector in a conference room where the presenter is having trouble getting the computer image to show on the screen. Which of the following is not a commonly known issue with projection?

   a. Overheated device

   b. Screen set too far from projector

   c. Lens cap not removed

   d. Source setting on projector

15. Which is an example of an IPv4 APIPA/link local address?

   a. 192.168.15.1

   b. 10.1.15.6

     c. 169.254.3.3

     d. 172.16.53.1

16. If a printer has a static address that happens to be in the DHCP range of the network, what is a potential network problem?

     a. No problem as the router can handle both static and DHCP addresses

     b. DHCP being disabled and router handling only static IP addresses

     c. IP address conflict

     d. Intermittent network connectivity during print jobs

17. What can be the result of EMI and/or RFI on a network segment? (Choose two.)

     a. Slow file transfer speeds

     b. IP address conflicts

     c. Intermittent connectivity

     d. Slowing fiber optic transmission

18. What is the minimum amperage required to charge a smartphone?

     a. 100mA

     b. 1A

     c. .5A

     d. 1000mA

19. If a device is plugged into an adapter and has no power, which is a possible step to take to alleviate the problem?

     a. Ensure that the adapter is set to the proper DC voltage.

     b. Make sure the AC outlet is working.

     c. Use a multimeter to test DC voltage from the adapter.

     d. All of these steps are correct.

20. You have been called to check on a printer in an office. You find a paper jam and fix it. Where do you look to resume the printing process and print jobs that were unable to print?

     a. The sending workstation's RAM

     b. The print queue

     c. The printer's hard drive.

     d. The printer's virtual memory.

Foundation Topics

Troubleshooting Methodology

220-1001 Objective 5.1: Given a scenario, use best practice methodology to resolve problems.

The term *methodology* often confuses people. In the IT world, it means a collection of systematic approaches to solving the technical problems we encounter. Since computers and mobile devices are complex, any given problem could have multiple symptoms and several possible causes. To solve computer and mobile device problems, technicians need a proven and effective troubleshooting approach. CompTIA has traditionally defined a basic six-step theory as a best practice approach. As Table 5-2 indicates, the steps help you find the source of a problem, find the solution, and help prevent recurrences.

> **NOTE** Always consider corporate policies, procedures, and impacts before implementing changes.

Table 5-2 The Six-Step CompTIA Troubleshooting Methodology

Step	Description
Step 1	**Identify the problem.** ■ Question the user and identify user changes to the computer and perform backups before making further changes. ■ Inquire regarding environmental or infrastructure changes that may have occurred. ■ Review system application logs for clues to possible system errors.
Step 2	**Establish a theory of probable cause (question the obvious).** ■ If necessary, conduct external or internal research based on symptoms.
Step 3	**Test the theory to determine the cause.** ■ Once the theory is confirmed, determine the next steps to resolve the problem. ■ If the theory is not confirmed, establish a new theory or escalate the issue.
Step 4	**Establish a plan of action to resolve the problem and implement the solution.**
Step 5	**Verify full system functionality and, if applicable, implement preventive measures.**
Step 6	**Document findings, actions, and outcomes.**

As you attempt to troubleshoot computer issues, think in terms of this six-step process. Plug the problem directly into these steps. If you test a theory in Step 3, and the theory is disproven, return to Step 2 and develop another theory. Continue in this manner until you have found a theory that points to the problem. After you solve the problem and verify functionality (Steps 4 and 5), be sure to document what happened (Step 6) so you can more quickly solve a similar problem in the future.

Troubleshooting Motherboard, RAM, CPU, and Power Issues

220-1001: Objective 5.2: Given a scenario, troubleshoot common problems related to motherboards, RAM, CPUs, and power.

Many system problems are caused by bad motherboards, RAM, CPUs, and power. In the following sections, you learn about common symptoms for these problems and the most likely causes. Use this information as you track down real-life issues in your company's and clients' systems.

Unexpected Shutdowns

Typical causes for unexpected shutdowns include:

- **Dead short caused by loose screws, slot covers, or cards:** Shut down the system and secure all metal components.

- **CPU overheating:** Check fan speed for CPU heat sink; clean fan if it is dirty; replace fan if it has failed or is turning too slowly; and check power management settings and CPU drivers in the operating system to make sure that thermal throttling is working.

- **Power supply overheating:** Check the power supply fan and clean it if possible; replace the power supply with a higher wattage–rated unit if problem persists.

- **Power supply failure:** Test the power supply to verify proper operation.

System Lockups

System lockups are typically caused by the corruption of memory contents. Follow these steps to diagnose system lockups:

Step 1.   Shut down the system, remove and reinstall memory, and remove dust from the modules, the sockets, cooling vents, and fans. If the problem persists, memory might be overheating.

Step 2.   Check the specifications for memory; the memory installed might not be the correct type for the motherboard and processor. If memory is incorrect for the CPU or motherboard, replace it with correct-specification memory. On some systems, you can see memory specifications in the system BIOS (see Figure 5-1), or you can run diagnostic apps such as SiSoftware Sandra or the Crucial.com memory advisor. If two or more modules are installed, they should have matching clock speed and timing specifications.

Step 3.   If memory has been overclocked, reset the memory to factory specifications by using the Auto or SPD options in the system BIOS setup.

Step 4.   Add additional system cooling.

> **NOTE**   All references to BIOS in this chapter apply to both traditional BIOS and UEFI firmware, except where noted otherwise.

If you run the processor or memory at speeds faster than those recommended, a process called **overclocking**, you could cause components to overheat and the system to crash. If your system crashes after overclocking, return the settings to standard values and restart the system. If the system is now stable, don't overclock it until you can add adequate cooling to the system. Overclocking is not recommended for business uses or for beginners.

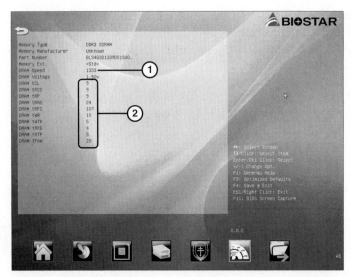

1. Memory speed (frequency)
2. Memory timings. The first four values shown can be written as 9-9-9-24.

FIGURE 5-1   Viewing Memory Speed and Timings for a Selected Module in a Typical UEFI BIOS

CAUTION   Overclocking generates excess heat, which can cause damage to components. To make matters worse, one method overclockers use to improve system stability is to slightly increase the voltage going to the processor core (Vcore) or to the memory modules, which further increases heat.

Don't even think about overclocking unless you study overclocking-oriented websites such as www.overclockers.com or publications such as MaximumPC/PCGamer (www.pcgamer.com/hardware). A careful perusal of these and other resources will tell you that successful overclocking requires a lot of time, a fair amount of cash, a lot of tolerance for damaged components, frequent rebooting, crashes, voided warranties, and so on.

NOTE   Some motherboards come with a basic type of overclocking that only increases CPU frequency by a maximum of 10 percent (for example, Intel's TurboBoost and AMD's Turbo Core technologies). While built-in overclocking is relatively safe, it should still be approached with caution.

POST Code Beeps

POST code beeps are used by many BIOS versions to indicate either fatal or serious errors. Beep codes vary by the BIOS maker. Although some vendors create their own BIOS chips and firmware, most major brands of computers and virtually all "clones" use a *BIOS* made by one of the following vendors: American Megatrends (AMI), Phoenix Technologies, IBM, Award Software (now owned by Phoenix Technologies), or Insyde Software.

As you might expect, the beep codes and philosophies used by these companies vary a great deal. AMI, for example, uses beep codes for more than 10 fatal errors. It also uses 8 beeps to indicate a defective or missing video card. Phoenix uses beep codes for both defects and normal procedures (but has no beep code for a video problem), and the Award BIOS has only a single beep code (one long, two short), indicating a problem with video. Insyde BIOS uses beep codes for errors, but these codes vary widely from model to model.

NOTE   Some vendors have switched from beep codes to blink codes with the advent of UEFI BIOS firmware. Check the documentation for the system or motherboard to determine if beep, blink, or other reporting methods are used to indicate POST problems.

Because beep codes do not report all possible problems during the startup process, you can't rely exclusively on beep codes to help you detect and solve system problems. Also, beep codes can be heard only on systems with built-in speakers.

TIP To add a wired speaker to a desktop computer, plug it into the speaker jack in the front-panel header pins.

The most common beep codes you're likely to encounter are listed in Table 5-3.

Table 5-3   Common System Errors and Their Beep Codes

Problem	Phoenix BIOS	Award BIOS	AMI BIOS	IBM BIOS
Memory	Beep sequences: 1-3-4-1 1-3-4-3 1-4-1-1	Beeping (other than 2 long, 1 short)	1 or 3 or 11 beeps 1 long, 3 short beeps	(None)
Video	(None)	2 long, 1 short beep	8 beeps 1 long, 8 short beeps	1 long, 3 short beeps, or 1 beep
Processor or motherboard	Beep sequence: 1-2-2-3	High-frequency beeps Repeating high/low beeps	5 beeps or 9 beeps	1 long, 1 short beep

For additional beep codes and other BIOS support, see the following manufacturer resources:

- **AMI BIOS:** https://ami.com

- **Phoenix BIOS:** https://www.phoenix.com

- **IBM, Dell, Acer, and other brands**: www.bioscentral.com and https://www.wimsbios.com

NOTE Don't mix up your boops and beeps! Many systems play a single short boop (usually a bit different in tone than a beep) when the system boots successfully. This is normal.

POST Error Messages

Most BIOS versions do an excellent job of displaying POST error messages indicating what the problem with the system is. These messages can indicate problems with memory, keyboards, hard drives, and other components. For example, if the CMOS memory used to store system setup information is corrupt (possibly because of a battery failure or because the CMOS memory has been cleared), systems display a message such as the following:

- **System CMOS Checksum Bad–Run Setup:** Phoenix BIOS

- **CMOS Checksum Invalid:** AMI BIOS

- **CMOS CHECKSUM INVALID–RUN SCU:** Insyde BIOS

- **CMOS Checksum Error–Defaults Loaded:** Award BIOS

Some systems document these messages in their manuals, or you can go to the BIOS vendors' websites or the third-party sites listed earlier in this chapter for more information.

NOTE Keep in mind that the system almost always stops after the first error, so if a system has more than one serious or fatal error, the first problem might stop the boot process before the video card has been initialized to display error messages.

Blank Screen on Bootup

A ***blank screen on bootup*** can be caused by a variety of video configurations or cabling problems, some of which can be caused by motherboard issues:

- If you have only one display, plugging the video cable into an inactive video port on a system will cause a blank screen. For example, some systems deactivate onboard video when you install a video card. If onboard video offers DVI and HDMI ports, typically only one can be selected (usually with motherboard jumpers).

- If a display with two or more inputs (for example, DVI and HDMI or DVI and VGA) is not configured to use the correct cable, the display will be blank. Use the display's push button controls to select the correct signal input.

- If a DVI or VGA cable is not tightly attached to the video port or display, the screen might be blank. Secure the cable.

- If an HDMI, miniHDMI, DisplayPort, or miniDisplayPort cable is not completely plugged into the video port or display, the screen might be blank. Completely insert the cable into the port.

■ If input cables and display input settings check out but the screen is still blank, shine a flashlight on the screen to see if any text or graphics are visible. If you can see text or graphics with the flashlight, the backlight on the display has failed. On an LCD-CCFL, check the inverter first. Inverter failures are much more common than backlight failures, and inverters are relatively easy to replace. On an LED display, check the LED driver board first. Keep in mind that LCD and LED display modules for laptops or complete displays for desktops are far less expensive today than they used to be, and it might make sense to replace the entire display assembly.

Figure 5-2 shows a typical inverter for an LCD-CCFL display in an all-in-one computer.

1. LCD-CCFL inverter
2. SODIMM memory modules
3. 2.5-inch hard disk in removable drive cage

FIGURE 5-2   An All-in-One Computer with the Back Open for Servicing

BIOS Time and Setting Resets

Problems with BIOS time and settings resets are typically caused by problems with either the CMOS battery on the motherboard or the CMOS chip.

If date and time settings or other BIOS settings reset to system defaults or display CMOS corrupted errors, replace the CMOS battery and reset the BIOS settings to correct values. A CMOS battery (usually a CR2032 on recent systems) will work properly for about three years before it needs to be replaced. Figure 5-3 illustrates a typical CR2032 CMOS battery on a recent motherboard.

If replacing the battery does not solve the problem, the CMOS chip on the motherboard might be damaged. The CMOS chip is a surface-mounted chip that cannot be replaced, so if it is bad, the motherboard must be replaced.

If other settings, such as BIOS passwords, have been lost or corrupted, the CMOS contents can be cleared by using a jumper on the motherboard. Depending on the motherboard, the jumper might be labeled JBAT (as in Figure 5-3), CLRTC, or CLR_CMOS. See the motherboard/system documentation for details. Turn off the system, move the jumper block, leave it in place for a few seconds, and then move it back to the normal position. The jumper is often, but not always, near the CMOS battery.

1. CR2032 battery for maintaining CMOS contents
2. JBAT jumper for clearing CMOS contents

FIGURE 5-3   It Might Be Necessary to Remove Cards or Cables to Access the CMOS Battery on Some Systems

Attempts to Boot to Incorrect Device

The boot sequence listed in BIOS settings determines which drives can be used to start the computer and in what order. If a nonbootable drive is in the boot sequence, the system will not start. For example, if a USB drive is listed first, and a nonbootable USB drive is plugged in, the system will not start.

Change the boot order to list the location where the operating system is installed (such as the system hard drive) and restart the computer.

Continuous Reboots

Continuous reboots can be caused by problems with the power supply or by a Windows or other operating system configuration setting:

- **Power Good voltage is too high or too low:** When the Power Good line to the motherboard carries a voltage that is too high or too low, the processor resets, shutting down the system and rebooting it. Test the power supply voltage levels; replace the power supply if Power Good tests out of specifications. See the "Multimeter" section, later in this chapter, for details.

- **Windows configuration setting for dealing with STOP errors (blue screen of death, or BSOD, errors):** If Windows is configured to reboot when a STOP error occurs, the system will continuously reboot until the error is resolved. To leave a STOP error message onscreen until you decide to restart the system, clear the Automatically Restart check box in the System Failure setting in the Startup and Recovery section of Advanced System Properties, as illustrated in Figure 5-4. This is accessed via **Control Panel > System, > Advanced System** settings. Under **Startup and Recovery**, select **Settings**.

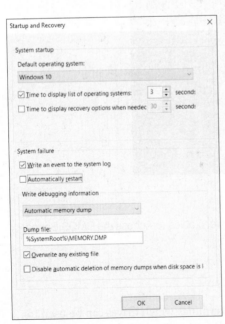

FIGURE 5-4   Note That the Automatically Restart Box Under System Failure Has Been Unchecked

No Power

No power when you turn on the system can be caused by several issues.

Power Supply Failure

A power supply that has stopped working prevents the system from starting. Use a multimeter or a power supply tester to determine if a power supply has failed. For more details, see the "Multimeter" and "Power Supply Tester" sections, later in this chapter.

Incorrect Front Panel Wiring Connections to the Motherboard

The power switch is wired to the motherboard, which in turn signals the power supply to start. If the power lead is plugged in to the wrong pins on the motherboard or has been disconnected from the motherboard, the system will not start, and you will not see an error message.

Check the markings on the front panel connectors, the motherboard, or the motherboard/system manual to determine the correct pinouts and installation.

Loose or Missing Power Leads from Power Supply

Make sure both the ATX and ATX12V or EPS12V power leads from the power supply are connected firmly to the motherboard. The connectors lock into place.

Surge Suppressor or UPS Failure

If the surge suppressor or uninterruptible power supply (UPS) unit connected to the computer has failed, the computer cannot start. Replace the defective surge suppressor or UPS unit or replace the battery in the UPS unit.

Overheating

Got an overheated power supply? Not sure? If you touch the power supply case, and it's too hot to touch, it's overheated. Overheated power supplies can cause system failure and possible component damage, and they can be due to any of the following causes:

- Overloading
- Fan failure
- Inadequate airflow outside the system
- Inadequate airflow inside the system
- Dirt and dust

Use the following sections to figure out the possible effects of these problems in any given situation.

Overloading

An overloaded power supply is caused by connecting devices that draw more power (in watts) than the power supply is designed to handle. Consider upgrading the hard drive when you add more card-based devices to expansion slots, use more bus-powered USB and Thunderbolt devices, and install more internal drives in a system. This will reduce the odds of having an overloaded power supply, which can cause various performance problems.

If a power supply fails or overheats, check the causes listed in the following sections before determining whether you should replace the power supply. If you determine that you should replace the power supply, purchase a unit that has a higher wattage rating and a higher +12V rating.

Fan Failure

The fan or fans inside the power supply cool it and are partly responsible for cooling the rest of the computer. If fans fail, the power supply and the entire computer are at risk of damage. Fans also might stop turning as a symptom of other power problems.

A fan that stops immediately after the power comes on usually indicates incorrect input voltage or a short circuit. If you turn off the system and turn it back on again under these conditions, the fan will stop each time.

To determine whether a fan has failed, listen to the unit; it should make less noise if the fan has failed. You can also see the fan blades spinning rapidly on a power supply fan that is working correctly. If the blades aren't turning or if they are turning very slowly, the fan has failed or is too clogged with dust to operate correctly.

To determine whether case fans have failed, look at them through the front or rear of the system, or, if they are connected to the motherboard, use the system monitoring feature in the system BIOS to check fan speed. Figure 5-5 illustrates a typical example.

NOTE   If a fan has failed because of a short circuit or incorrect input voltage, you will not see any picture onscreen because the system cannot operate.

If the system starts normally but the fan stops turning later, this indicates a true fan failure instead of a power problem.

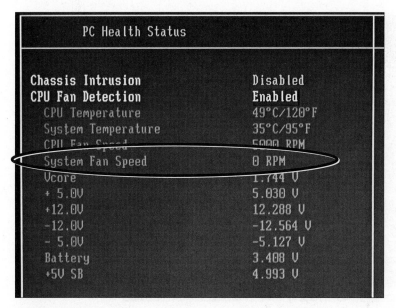

FIGURE 5-5 The System Fan (Case Fan) Has Either Failed or Was Never Connected to the Motherboard Power/Monitor Header

Inadequate Airflow Outside the System

The power supply's capability to cool the system depends in part on free airflow space outside the system. If the computer is kept in a confined area (such as a closet or security cabinet) without adequate ventilation, power supply failures due to over-heating are likely.

Even systems in ordinary office environments can have airflow problems; make sure that several inches of free air space exist behind the fan outputs for any computer.

Inadequate Airflow Inside the System

As you have seen in previous chapters, the interior of the typical computer is a messy place. Data cables (particularly wide ribbon cables on older systems), drive power cables, header cables, and expansion cards can create small air dams that block air-flow between the heat sources—such as the motherboard, CPU, drives, and memory modules—and the fans in the power supply and the case. Figure 5-6 illustrates a typical system with a lot of cable clutter, which can interfere with airflow.

FIGURE 5-6   A Cluttered System with Many Unsecured Cables Blocking Airflow

Although the use of SATA drives and the elimination of internal floppy drives mean that the wide ribbon cables used on the old PATA and floppy drives are no longer used, disorganized systems can still cause overheating. You can do the following to improve airflow inside a computer:

- Use cable ties to secure excess ribbon cable and power connectors out of the way of the fans and the power supply.

- Replace any missing slot covers.

- Make sure that case fans and CPU fans are working correctly.

Figure 5-7 illustrates a different system that uses cable management (using cable ties, bundling cables between the drive bays and outer case wall, and routing cables behind the motherboard) to improve airflow.

FIGURE 5-7   A System with Good Airflow Due to Good Cable Management

Dirt and Dust

Most power supplies, except for a few of the early ATX power supplies, use a cooling technique called ***negative pressure***; with this technique, the power supply fan works like a weak vacuum cleaner, pulling air through vents in the case, past the components, and out through the fan. Vacuum cleaners are used to remove dust, dirt, cat hairs, and so on from living rooms and offices, and the power supply's weak impression of a vacuum cleaner works the same way.

When you open a system for any kind of maintenance, look for the following:

- Dirt, dust, hair, and gunk clogging the case vents
- A thin layer of dust on the motherboard and expansion slots
- Dirt and dust on the power supply vent and fans

For the most thorough check, be sure to remove the computer's front panel. You never know what you'll find inside a PC that hasn't been cleaned out for a year or two. As you can see in Figure 5-8, you might discover a system with almost completely clogged air vents. A system in this condition could fail catastrophically at almost any time.

1. Front-mounted USB ports
2. Clogged air intakes
3. Retaining clips for the front of the case

FIGURE 5-8   A System with Extremely Dirty Air Vents

Use a vacuum cleaner specially designed for computer use or compressed air to remove dirt and dust from inside the system. If using compressed air, be sure to spread newspapers around the system to catch the dirt and dust. If possible, remove the computer from the computer room so the dust is not spread to other equipment.

Installing/Replacing Case Fans

If an overheating system has failed fans or empty fan bays, replace the failed fans or add new ones. To replace a fan:

Step 1.   After removing all power to the system and opening the case, locate any failed fans.

Step 2.   Disconnect the fan from the motherboard or the power supply.

Step 3.   Remove the fan from the case. A fan is held in place by four screws inserted from the outside of the case.

Step 4.   (Start here to add a new fan.) Determine the size of fan needed (typical sizes are 120mm, 140mm, and 200mm) and hold the fan inside the case as you attach screws to the fan from the outside.

Step 5.   Connect the fan to a system fan header (use the same one as before if you are replacing a fan) on the motherboard. If there isn't an available system fan header, use a Molex power supply connector or a splitter if you don't have an unused Molex connector.

Loud Noise

Computers usually run quietly, but if you hear a loud noise coming from the power supply, it's a sure sign of problems. A whirring, screeching, rattling, or thump-ing noise while the system is on usually indicates a fan failure. If a fan built into a component such as a heat sink or power supply is failing, replace the component immediately.

Intermittent Device Failure

Intermittent failures of USB bus-powered devices (mice, keyboard, USB flash drives, portable USB hard drives) usually happen because these devices draw power from the system's power supply via the USB port. These types of failures, especially for devices with low power draws such as mice and keyboards, can be an early sign of an overloaded power supply. Replace the power supply with a higher-rated unit.

Intermittent failures of other USB external devices or of internal devices can be caused by damaged data cables, power supplies or connectors, or ports.

To troubleshoot these problems:

Step 1.   Shut down the device (and the computer, if the device is internal) and replace the data cable with a known-working replacement. If a USB device is plugged into a front-mounted USB port or a USB port on a card bracket, check the USB header cable connections to the motherboard.

Step 2.   Turn on the device or computer.

Step 3.   Test the device over time. If the device works correctly, the problem is solved.

Step 4.   If Step 1–3 didn't resolve the problem, use the original data cable and try plugging it into a different internal or external port. Repeat Steps 2–3.

Step 5.   Try Steps 1–4 again, but this time use a replacement power connector or AC adapter.

Step 6.   When you find the defective component, the problem stops. If the problem is not resolved with different data cables, connectors, or power supplies/AC adapters, the device itself needs to be replaced.

Fans Spin—No Power to Other Devices

 A fan connected directly to a power supply will run as soon as the system is turned on, but if a fan spins and a computer never displays any startup messages, this could indicate a variety of problems. Check the following:

- Make sure the main ATX and 12V ATX or EPS power leads are securely connected to the appropriate sockets.

- Make sure the CPU and memory modules are securely installed in the appropriate sockets.

Indicator Lights

 Indicator lights on the front or top of most desktop computers display power and hard drive activity. If these lights go out but the system is otherwise working properly, check the motherboard connection for the indicator lights.

Smoke or Burning Smells

If you can see smoke or smell a burning odor with a chemical overtone coming from the power supply's outside vent, your power supply has died. This odor can linger for weeks. Sadly, when a power supply blows up like this, it can also destroy the motherboard, bus-powered USB devices connected to the computer, and other components.

Smoke or a burning smell inside the system can also be caused by failing capacitors. The capacitors are cylindrical components near the CPU socket on the motherboard or inside the power supply. If capacitors fail or other components burn up, replace the component.

Step-by-Step Power Supply Troubleshooting

Use the procedure outlined next to find the actual cause of a dead system. If one of the test procedures in the following list corrects the problem, the item that was changed is the cause of the problem. Power supplies have a built-in safety feature that shuts down the unit immediately in case of short circuit.

The following steps are designed to determine whether a power problem is caused by a short circuit or another problem:

Step 1. Smell the power supply's outside vent. If you can detect a burning odor, the power supply has failed. Replace it.

Step 2. Check the AC power to the system; a loose or disconnected power cord, a disconnected surge protector, a surge protector that has been turned off, or a dead AC wall socket will prevent a system from receiving power. If the wall socket has no power, reset the circuit breaker in the electrical service box for the location.

Step 3. Check the AC voltage switch on the power supply; it should be set to 115V for North America. If the switch is set to 230V, turn off the power, reset the switch, and restart the system. Note that many desktop computer power supplies no longer require a switch selection because they are autoswitching.

NOTE The A+ objectives list AC voltage as 115V or 220V. AC power is supplied at slightly different voltages in different parts of the world. The normal range of voltage is 100 to 120 volts or 200 to 240 volts. Some dual-voltage power supplies can accept either, and such a supply may have either a selector switch on the back or may be able to automatically recognize the appropriate setting.

> **CAUTION**   If your area uses 230V and the power supply is set to 115V, you need a new power supply and possibly other components because they've been damaged or destroyed by 100 percent overvoltage.

Step 4.   If the system is older and uses a PS/2 mouse or keyboard, check the connectors; a loose keyboard connector could cause a short circuit.

Step 5.   Turn off the system, disconnect power, and open the system. Verify that the power leads are properly connected to the motherboard. Connect loose power leads, reconnect power, and restart the computer.

Step 6.   Check for loose screws or other components, such as loose slot covers, modem speakers, or other metal items that can cause short circuit. Correct them and retest.

Step 7.   Remove all expansion cards and disconnect power to all drives; restart the system and use a power supply tester or a multimeter to test power to the motherboard. For more details, see the "Multimeter" section, later in this chapter.

Step 8.   If the power tests within accepted limits with all peripherals disconnected, reinstall one card at a time and check the power. If the power tests within accepted limits, reattach one drive at a time and check the power.

Step 9.   If a defective card or drive has a dead short, reattaching the defective card or drive should stop the system immediately upon power-up. Replace the card or drive and retest.

Step 10.   Check the Power Good line at the power supply motherboard connector with a multimeter or a power supply tester.

An unreliable power supply can impact every aspect of PC performance. This is a long list of possible problems and solutions, but chances are you will track down the source of the problem before you reach the end of it.

Distended Capacitors

Capacitors, sometimes referred to as "caps," are used as part of the voltage step-down circuits that provide power to the processor. From 2002 to 2007, many motherboards were built using faulty capacitors that became distended and leaked, causing system failure and sometimes physical damage to the motherboard.

Figure 5-9 illustrates a motherboard with ***distended capacitors***.

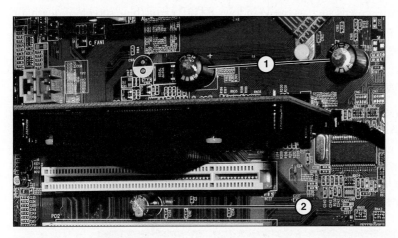

1. Distended, leaking capacitors
2. Capacitor in good working order

FIGURE 5-9   A System with at Least Two Faulty Capacitors

Some of these systems might still be in service, and the faulty capacitors can be replaced.

> **NOTE**   For a detailed step-by-step tutorial on replacing bad capacitors, visit www.itsacon.net/computers/hardware/replacing-bad-motherboard-capacitors/.

Newer systems typically use solid capacitors (see Figure 5-10). These capacitors are much more reliable than older capacitors.

1. Solid capacitors

FIGURE 5-10   A Typical Recent Motherboard with Solid Capacitors

Proprietary Crash Screens (BSOD/Pin Wheel)

Proprietary crash screens such as the Windows STOP error (blue screen of death, or BSOD) or the macOS pin wheel can be caused by operating system, application, or hardware errors.

Troubleshooting Windows STOP Errors (BSOD)

STOP errors (also known as blue screen of death, or *BSOD*, errors) can occur either during startup or after a system is running. The BSOD nickname is used because the background is normally blue (or sometimes black), with the error message in white text. STOP errors in Windows 7 resemble the example shown in Figure 5-11. The STOP error is listed by name and number. The Windows 8 and Windows 10 STOP errors are very similar and are depicted in Figure 5-12.

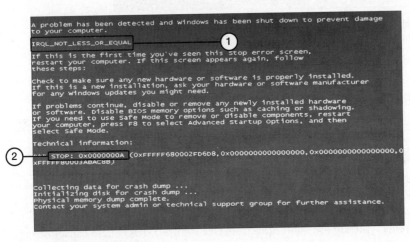

1. STOP error message
2. STOP error number

FIGURE 5-11   A Windows 7 STOP Error

In Windows 8/8.1/10, STOP errors now look like the example shown in Figure 5-12. In these versions of Windows, the STOP error is listed by name.

NOTE   Regardless of when a STOP/BSOD error occurs, the system is halted by default. If the computer does not restart on its own, you must turn off the system and turn it back on. But before you do that, record the error message text and other information so that you can research the problem if it reoccurs. For more information, see the next section, "Causes of BSOD Errors."

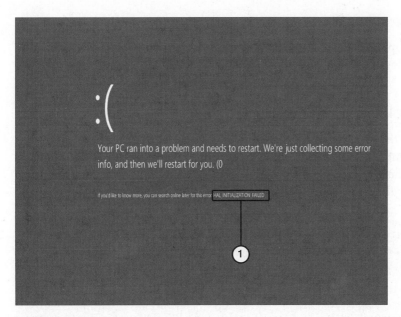

1. STOP error message

FIGURE 5-12   A Windows 8 and Windows 10 STOP Error

NOTE   Regardless of when a STOP/BSOD error occurs, your system is halted by default. If the computer does not restart on its own, you must turn off the system and turn it back on. But before you do that, record the error message text and other information so that you can research the problem if it reoccurs. For more information, see the next section, "Causes of BSOD Errors."

Causes of BSOD Errors

BSOD errors can be caused by any of the following:

- **Incompatible or defective hardware or software:** Start the system in Safe mode and uninstall the last hardware or software installed. Acquire updates before you reinstall the hardware or software. Exchange or test memory. Run SFC/scannow to check for problems with system files.

- **Registry problems:** Select Last Known Good Configuration (Windows 7) and see whether the system will start. System Restore can also be used to revert the system and registry to an earlier state.

- **Viruses:** Scan for viruses and remove any that are discovered.

- **Miscellaneous causes:** Check the Windows Event Viewer and check the System log. Research the BSOD with the Microsoft Support website.

Researching BSOD Causes and Solutions

To determine the exact cause of a STOP error, note the number or name of the error (for example, STOP 0x0000007B, HAL INITIALIZATION FAILED) and look it up at the Microsoft support website: http://support.microsoft.com. When you search for the error, be sure to specify the version of Windows in use.

NOTE   STOP errors are often referred to with a shortened version of the error code or by name. For example, the shortened version of a 0x0000007B error is 0x7B.

TIP   Unfortunately, you can't take a screen capture of a BSOD for printing because a BSOD completely shuts down Windows. In this situation, a digital camera or smartphone can be used for recording the exact error message.

The solution might involve one or more of the following changes to your system:

- Changing the system registry. Sometimes an automated registry repair tool can be downloaded to perform these changes for you. Whether you make the changes manually or automatically, back up the registry first!

- Removing a newly added component. For example, in the case of the error shown in Figure 5-11, removing a recently added memory module solved the problem.

- Replacing components such as memory.

- Upgrading an application.

- Downloading and installing a hotfix for your operating system.

On some systems, auto restart is enabled for STOP/BSOD errors, so the error messages shown in the Figures 5.11 and 5.12 appear for only a moment before the computer restarts. For solutions, see the "Continuous Reboots" section, earlier in this chapter.

NOTE Microsoft Windows 7, 8.1, and 10 have a tool called Windows Trouble-shooter that is available to help resolve Windows problems. Each Windows version provides slightly different access to Troubleshooter. In Windows 7, go to **Control Panel > Troubleshooting**. In Windows 8.1, search for Troubleshooting in Settings. In Windows 10, go to **Settings> Update and Security > Troubleshoot**.

The official name for the macOS *pin wheel* is the *spinning wait cursor* (see Figure 5-13).

1. OS X spinning wait cursor (pin wheel)

FIGURE 5-13   The Pin Wheel in macOS

The pin wheel appears most often when an application or macOS itself has become unresponsive. For this reason, it is sometimes referred to as the "pin wheel of death." This is usually caused by an application failing but it may also indicate that the system is locked up and needs a hard reboot. If the problem is an application failure, it can usually be resolved by force-quitting the application (see the solutions list below).

You may also hear the spinning pin wheel referred to as the spinning rainbow or "beachball of death."

The following are some causes of macOS unresponsiveness:

- **Lack of system RAM:** If a macOS device frequently displays the pin wheel and the device's RAM can be upgraded, do so.

- **Less than 10 percent free space on the macOS system drive:** Free space is used as a swapfile to substitute for RAM. Remove unwanted apps and save data to external or cloud storage to free up space. Some experts suggest keeping at least 20 percent of the macOS system drive free.

- **Damaged application:** Run Disk Utility using the Verify Disk Permissions option (in OS X versions prior to El Capitan).

The following are some solutions for macOS unresponsiveness:

- Use the Force Quit command to terminate an application that won't respond. It's available from the Apple menu or by pressing **Cmd+Option+Esc**. Select the app and click **Force Quit**.

- If a particular application causes unresponsiveness, open the ~Library/Preferences folder, find the .plist file for the app, and drag it to the trash. The .plist file will be rebuilt.

- Use Activity Monitor to view CPU, memory, energy, disk, and networking performance stats. The Activity Monitor is similar to the Windows Task Manager. You can use the Spotlight feature on a Mac to locate Activity Monitor in the Applications folder.

- Upgrade to the latest macOS version and keep it updated.

- A forced restart is performed by pressing and holding the **Cmd+Ctrl** buttons while pressing the power button. Press **Cmd+Ctrl+Eject** buttons to quit all apps and restart.

Log Entries and Error Messages

Logs on a device are records kept to track the history of what has happened on the device. They record the tasks the computer has performed, people who have logged in or out, applications opened, and so on. Error messages tell when something went wrong (for example, a device failure or authentication rejection). These are very helpful when an IT professional is trying to isolate and solve a problem on a system.

To access logs and error messages, go to **Control Panel > Administrative Tools > Event Viewer**. Figure 5-13 shows the Event Viewer with the System log selected. Note the many types of logs available in the different applications and system functions. In the System window note the "Warning" with a yellow triangle, indicating something that failed (in this case, DNS requests).

Take time to click through different folders of events recorded on your PC to become familiar with the vast amount of information available. This much information can be difficult to handle, and tools are available to help search and filter the information down to a manageable amount. Those tools can be explored in the right pane of the Event Viewer window, as shown in Figure 5-14.

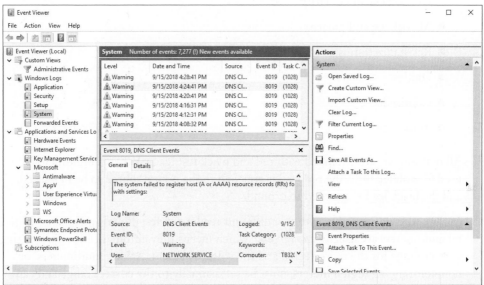

FIGURE 5-14   Windows (10) Event Viewer

Recommended Tools

To diagnose problems with motherboards, RAM, CPUs, and power, use the following tools:

- Multimeter
- Power supply tester
- Loopback plugs
- POST card/USB

Multimeter

A ***multimeter*** is one of the most flexible test devices available. When set for DC voltage, it can be used to test computer power supplies and AC adapters. When set for continuity (CONT), it can be used as a cable tester. It can also be used to test ohm (resistance) and ampere (amp, current) levels.

Multimeters are designed to perform many different types of electrical tests, including the following:

- DC voltage and polarity

- AC voltage and polarity

- Resistance (ohms)

- Diodes

- Continuity

- Amperage

All multimeters are equipped with red and black test leads. When a multimeter is used for voltage tests, the red lead is attached to the power source to be measured, and the black lead is attached to ground.

Multimeters are available with two different readout styles: digital and analog. Digital multimeters are usually *autoranging*, which means they automatically adjust to the correct range for the test selected and the voltage present. Analog multimeters, or non-autoranging digital meters, must be set manually to the correct range and can be damaged more easily by overvoltage. Figure 5-15 compares typical analog and digital multimeters.

FIGURE 5-15 Typical Analog (Left) and Digital (Right) Multimeters

Table 5-4 summarizes the tests you can perform with a multimeter.

Table 5-4   Using a Multimeter

Test to Perform	Multimeter Setting	Probe Positions	Procedure
AC voltage (wall outlet)	AC	Red to hot, black to ground.	Read voltage from meter; should be near 110V–120V in North America.
DC voltage (power supply outputs to motherboard, drives, batteries)	DC	Red to hot, black to ground.	Read voltage from meter; compare to default values.
Continuity (cables, fuses)	CONT	Red to lead at one end of cable; black to corresponding lead at other end.	No CONT signal indicates bad cable or bad fuse.
		For a straight-through cable, check the same pin at each end. For other types of cables, consult a cable pinout to select the correct leads.	Double-check leads and retest to be sure.
Resistance (ohms)	Ohms	Connect one lead to each end of resistor.	Check reading; compare to rating for resistor. A fuse should have no resistance.
Amperage (ammeter)	Ammeter	Red probe to positive lead of circuit (power disconnected!); black lead to negative lead running through component to be tested.	Check reading; compare to rating for component tested.

You can use a multimeter to find out whether a power supply is properly converting AC power to DC power. Here's how: Measure the DC power going from the power supply to the motherboard. A power supply that does not meet the measurement standards listed in Table 5-5 should be replaced.

Table 5-5 Acceptable Voltage Levels

Rated DC Volts	Acceptable Range
+5.0	+4.8–5.2
–5.0	–4.8–5.2
–12.0	–11.4–12.6
+12.0	+11.4–12.6
+3.3	+3.14–3.5
Power Good	+3.0–6.0

If the system monitor functions in the system BIOS do not display voltage levels or if a display is not available, you can take the voltage measurements directly from the power supply connection to the motherboard after the computer is turned on. Both 20-pin and 24-pin (ATX) power connectors are designed to be back-probed, as shown in Figure 5-16; you can run the red probe through the top of the power connector to take a reading (and the black probe uses the power supply enclosure or metal case frame for ground).

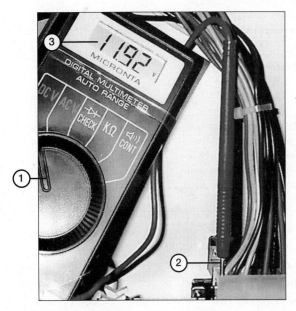

1. Multimeter set to measure DC voltage
2. Red probe inserted into +12V DC (yellow power line) connector
3. DC voltage readout

FIGURE 5-16 Testing the +12V Line on an ATX Power Supply and Finding the Voltage Level (+11.92V) Well Within Limits

Use the power supply pinouts in Figure 5-17 to determine which lines to check.

ATX 20-pin power connector (top view)

11	+3.3v	Orange		Orange	+3.3v	1
12	-12v	Blue		Orange	+3.3v	2
13	Ground	Black		Black	Ground	3
14	PS-On	Green		Red	+5v	4
15	Ground	Black		Black	Ground	5
16	Ground	Black		Red	+5v	6
17	Ground	Black		Black	Ground	7
18	-5v	White		Gray	Power Good	8
19	+5v	Red		Purple	+5v Standby	9
20	+5v	Red		Yellow	+12v	10

ATX version 2.2 24-pin power connector (top view)

13	+3.3v	Orange		Orange	+3.3v	1
14	-12v	Blue		Orange	+3.3v	2
15	Ground	Black		Black	Ground	3
16	PS-On	Green		Red	+5v	4
17	Ground	Black		Black	Ground	5
18	Ground	Black		Red	+5v	6
19	Ground	Black		Black	Ground	7
20	NC	White		Gray	Power Good	8
21	+5v	Red		Purple	+5v Standby	9
22	+5v	Red		Yellow	+12v	10
23	+5v	Red		Yellow	+12v	11
24	Ground	Black		Orange	+3.3v	12

FIGURE 5-17   Pinout for Standard ATX 20-Pin and 24-Pin Power Connectors

Some motherboards bring these same voltage levels to a more convenient location on the motherboard for testing.

If a power supply fails any of these measurements, replace it and retest the new unit.

Power Supply Tester

You can use a ***power supply tester*** to determine if a power supply is working. The power supply does not need to be removed from the computer for testing. However, the 24-pin (or, on older systems, 20-pin) ATX power supply cable and the 4-pin ATX12V or 8-pin EPS12V connectors must be disconnected from the motherboard for testing. The power supply must also be plugged into a working AC outlet or surge suppressor.

Figure 5-17 illustrates two types of power supply testers. One tester is a simple go/no-go tester. When you plug it into a power supply's 20-pin or 24-pin motherboard connector, the power supply starts if it is working, and the green LED turns on. If the power supply doesn't work, the green LED stays off.

The second tester has its own power switch and checks the major voltage levels, including Power Good, when you turn it on. The display turns a light blue if the power supply tests okay; however, if any voltage level is out of range, the display turns red, as in Figure 5-18.

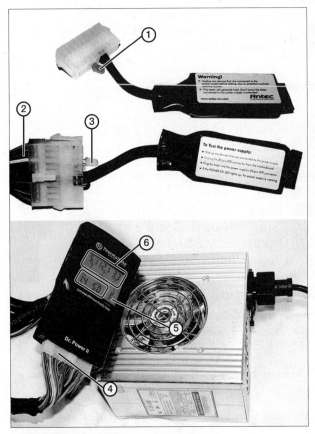

1. Green LED turns on if the power supply works
2. Power supply connected to tester
3. Power supply works – green LED is on
4. Power supply plugged into Dr. Power II tester
5. The power good line has failed, so the power supply is defective
6. All other voltage levels are OK

FIGURE 5-18   A Simple Power Supply Tester (Top) Compared to a Deluxe Model That Tests Voltages and Can Also Test Other Components

Troubleshooting Hard Drives and RAID Arrays

220-1001: Objective 5.3: Given a scenario, troubleshoot hard drives and RAID arrays.

Problems with mass storage devices are among the most frightening to a business or an individual. The tips and techniques in this section can help solve problems and make data recovery possible.

This section discusses both traditional mechanical hard disk drives (HDDs) and solid-state drives (SSDs). Remember that SSDs are nonvolatile storage media on solid-state chips put into HDD form factors. A newer version of SSD, called m.2 SSD, is a surface-mounted drive that requires a different form factor designed for m.2 chips. Because of the specific form factor, they are not interchangeable with SSDs. Figure 5-19 shows SSDs on the left and m.2 SSDs on the right. For more information on hard drives and SSDs, see Chapter 3.

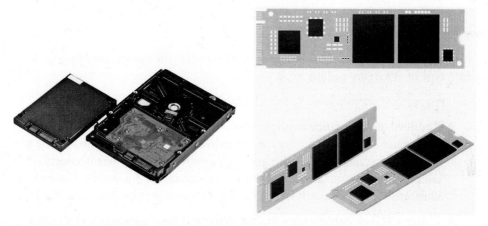

FIGURE 5-19   SSDs (Left) and Surface-Mounted m.2 SSDs (Right)

Read/Write Failure

Read/write failures can take place for a number of reasons, including the following:

- **Physical damage to the drive:** Dropping any magnetic storage drive can cause damage to read/write heads and platters. The drive may start to make noise or might not spin up at all.

- **Damaged cables:** SATA cables are often included with new motherboards and are inexpensive to purchase. Swapping cables is an easy first step that often solves problems.

- **Damaged SATA host adapter on motherboard:** Most late-model motherboards have several *SATA* ports; if swapping a SATA cable doesn't solve a problem, use the original cable in a different SATA port on the motherboard.

- **Overheated hard disk:** The faster a hard disk turns (that is, the higher the RPM), the more likely it is that overheating will take place, especially if airflow is restricted. To prevent overheating, install a cooling fan in front of the 3.5-inch drive bays used for a hard disk(s) and make sure it pulls air into the PC. If you have two or more drives stacked on top of each other with limited airflow, move drives to other drive bays to improve airflow.

- **Overheated CPU or chipset:** Overheated CPU, chipset, or other components can cause read/write failures. Double-check case fans, the power supply fan, and the CPU's and chipset's heat sinks. Remove dust and dirt from air intakes and fans. Remove loose or failed heat sinks, remove old thermal grease, and reassemble them with properly applied thermal grease.

Slow Performance

Although SATA drives can manifest slow performance, the causes and solutions for each type of drive vary widely.

To improve slow performance with SATA hard disks, look for these problems:

- **Reduced-performance configuration of 3Gbps or 6Gbps drives:** Some 3Gbps and 6Gbps SATA drives are jumpered to run at the next slower rate to enable compatibility with older host adapters. Remove the speed-reduction jumper when it is not needed; see drive documentation for details. Figure 5-20 illustrates a jumper on a 3Gbps drive that limits its performance to 1.5Gbps.

- **Using a 3Gbps cable with a 6Gbps drive and host adapter:** SATA cables made for 6Gbps drives can also be used with slower speeds.

- **SATA host adapter configured for IDE or emulation mode:** SATA host adapters can be configured by the system BIOS (conventional or UEFI) to run in IDE (emulation) mode, RAID mode, or AHCI mode. Use AHCI mode to enable full performance because this mode supports native command queuing (NCQ) and other advanced features.

- **SATA host adapter configured to run at reduced speed:** SATA host adapters on some systems can be configured to run at different speeds, such as 6.0Gbps, 3.0Gbps, or Auto. Select **6.0Gbps** when using a 6.0Gbps drive and cabling. To enable the drive and host adapter to auto-negotiate the correct speed, select **Auto**.

1. **Drive is jumpered to run at 1.5Gbps**
2. **Configuration pins for other settings**

FIGURE 5-20   To Run This Drive at Its Designed 3.0Gbps Interface Speed, Remove the Jumper

NOTE   Some SATA drives use a configuration jumper to permit Power-Up in Standby (PUIS) mode. Before removing a jumper block from a SATA hard disk, check the drive's documentation at the vendor's website. Some drives are marked with incorrect jumper block legends.

To improve slow performance with SSDs, look for the following issues:

- **Connecting the drive to a slow SATA host adapter:** Early SSDs were designed for 3Gbps SATA interfaces, but most recent models support the faster 6Gbps interface. When using an SSD on a system with a mixture of 3Gbps and 6Gbps SATA ports, be sure to use the 6Gbps ports.

- **The partition may be misaligned:** Windows automatically creates the first partition on an SSD so that it is on a page boundary to provide maximum performance. However, if you do not use the entire SSD for a single partition, additional partitions might be misaligned (starting in the middle of a page rather than on a page boundary). Misaligned partitions cause slow read/write/reallocate performance. Instead of using Disk Management to create additional partitions, use the command-line program DISKPART and specify Align=1024 as part of the Create partition command. See https://docs.microsoft.com/en-us/previous-versions/windows/it-pro/windows-vista/cc766465(v=ws.10) for the complete syntax.

- **The TRIM command is not enabled for the drive:** If the drive does not support TRIM, you must periodically run a utility provided by the drive vendor to reallocate deleted drive sectors. If the drive supports TRIM and you are using it with Windows 7/8/8.1/10, Windows needs to be optimized for use with SSDs.

■ **Not optimizing the operating system for use with SSDs:** Although Windows 7, 8/8.1, and 10 are designed to disable SuperFetch, defragment, and other services that can slow down SSD performance, Windows does not always detect an SSD as an SSD. Use the SSD Tweaker utility (www.elpamsoft.com) to configure Windows for maximum performance with SSDs.

TIP   Rather than enabling TRIM in real time, Linux users should run the command fstrim periodically and use the Ext4 file system. For details, see https://wiki.archlinux. org/index.php/Solid_State_Drives.

Loud Clicking Noise

Magnetic hard disk drives are generally quiet. Loud noises coming from a drive can have at least two causes:

■ **A loud clicking noise is typically caused by repeated rereads of defective disk surfaces by the hard disk drive heads:** This is typically a sign of a failing drive. Replace the hard disk immediately after making a backup copy.

■ **Humming noises can be caused by rapid head movement on a normally functioning hard disk:** This noise can be reduced or eliminated by enabling Automatic Acoustic Management (AAM), a feature of most recent hard disks. Some vendors provide a downloadable acoustic management tool, which can reduce head speed to reduce noise and may reduce drive performance as a result.

NOTE   A softer clicking noise is typical of hard disks when the system is in Sleep mode. By changing the hard disk drive's power management settings, this noise can be eliminated. To learn more, see http://disablehddapm.blogspot.com/2011/12/disabling-hard-disk-drive-advanced.html.

Failure to Boot

The primary hard drive is almost always the boot drive. *Failure to boot* can be caused by:

■ **Boot sequence does not specify system hard disk, or lists system hard disk after other drives with nonbootable media:** Use the Boot Sequence dialog in the system BIOS to configure the hard disk as either the first boot device or the second boot device, after the optical drive or USB. If a USB flash drive is listed as the first boot device and the system is started with a nonbootable USB flash drive connected, the system boot process will stop and display a boot error.

- **CMOS settings have been corrupted and system cannot find a bootable drive:** Reconfigure the CMOS settings, specify the system drive as a boot drive, and restart the system. Replace the battery if the settings continue to be corrupted.

- **The BCD (boot configuration data) store used by Windows to control disk booting has been corrupted:** To learn how to fix this problem, go to https://docs.microsoft.com/en-us/previous-versions/windows/it-pro/windows-vista/cc709667(v%3dws.10).

Drive Not Recognized

A *drive not recognized* issue can involve problems with cabling, power, BIOS settings, or hard disk failure. If the hard disk is running (you can usually hear faint sounds from a working hard disk), check the following:

- **Bus-powered USB hard disk not recognized:** A bus-powered USB 2.0 or USB 3.0/3.1 hard disk needs 500mA of power to run (and some hard disks temporarily use more power to spin up). Some computers don't provide enough power in their root hubs (built-in USB ports) to support a bus-powered hard disk, and bus-powered hubs can provide only 100mA of power per port. Connect the drive to another port on a different root hub (each pair of USB ports is a root hub) or a self-powered USB hub, or use a Y-cable to pull power from two USB ports. Figure 5-21 illustrates a USB 3.0/3.1 Y-cable.

- **USB or Thunderbolt drive not recognized:** If the data cable between the drive and the port is loose, the drive will not be recognized. Reconnect the cable to both the drive and the port, and the drive should be recognized. If the drive is connected to a front-mounted port, make sure the port header is securely connected to the motherboard.

- **SATA Hard Disk or SSD drive not recognized:** Loose or missing power or data cables cause this problem. Shut down the computer, disconnect it from AC power, and reconnect power and data cables. If you use Y-splitters or converters to provide power to some drives, keep in mind that these can fail. See Figure 5-22.

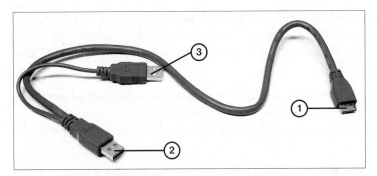

1. mini-USB 3.0 connector to drive
2. USB 3.0 connector (data and power)
3. USB 3.0 Y-connector (power only)

FIGURE 5-21   USB 3.0/3.1 Y-Cable Provides Bus Power from Two USB Ports

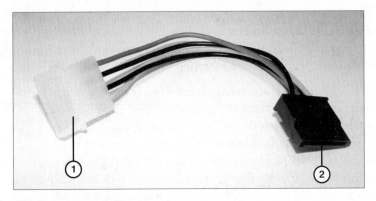

1. Molex power connector
2. SATA power connector

FIGURE 5-22   A Molex-to-SATA Power Converter Cable Is a Potential Point of Failure

OS Not Found

An *OS not found* (operating system not found) error during boot can be caused by:

- **Nonbootable disk in USB Drive:** If a USB drive is listed before the hard disk in the boot sequence and it contains a nonbootable disk, the computer displays an error message that it couldn't find the operating system. Remove the USB flash drive and restart.

- **Boot sequence doesn't list hard disk:** Restart the computer, start the BIOS setup procedure, and make sure the hard disk is listed as a bootable drive and is listed before options such as network boot.

- **Incorrect installation of another operating system:** Windows automatically sets up its own boot manager for access to more than one Windows version if you install the older version of Windows first, followed by the later version. However, if you install a newer version first and install an older version later or install a non-Windows OS later, you cannot access the newer Windows version unless you install a custom boot manager.

NOTE For more information about solving boot problems involving operating system issues, see Chapter 6, "Operating Systems."

RAID Not Found

RAID not found problems can result from the following:

- **RAID function disabled in system BIOS:** Reconfigure SATA ports used for RAID as RAID and restart the system.

- **Power or data cables to RAID drives disconnected:** Reconnect cables to RAID drive(s) and restart the system.

NOTE Some motherboards offer RAID support from the chipset as well as a separate RAID controller chip. Be sure to identify which SATA ports are controlled by the chipset versus a separate RAID controller chip and connect drives accordingly.

RAID Stops Working

A RAID failure is caused by the failure of one or more of the disk drives in the RAID array. Take the following steps if a single drive failure occurs:

- **RAID 0:** Determine which drive has failed. Replace it and follow the vendor's recommendations to re-create the array. Restore the latest backup. Any data that has not been backed up is lost.

- **RAID 1, RAID 10, and RAID 5:** Determine which drive has failed. Replace it. Follow the procedures provided by the RAID vendor to rebuild the array.

If both drives have failed in a RAID 0 or RAID 1 array, you must rebuild the array with new drives and restore the latest backup. Any data that has not been backed up is lost.

If two or more drives have failed in a RAID 10 or RAID 5 array, your recovery options might vary according to the exact configuration of the array. See the RAID vendor's procedures for details and recovery options.

Proprietary Crash Screens (BSOD/Pin Wheel)

See the section "Troubleshooting Windows STOP Errors (BSOD)," earlier in this chapter.

S.M.A.R.T. Errors

Both Serial ATA (SATA) hard disks and older Parallel ATA (PATA or ATA/IDE) hard disks support a detect-warning feature known as Self-Monitoring, Analysis, and Reporting Technology (*S.M.A.R.T*), which is also referred to as SMART. S.M.A.R.T. monitors internal hard disks and warns of impending failure. Typical items monitored include:

- Drive temperature
- Read retries
- Slow spin up
- Too many bad sectors

Typical S.M.A.R.T. warnings include:

- Hard disk failure is imminent
- A hard drive in your system reports that it may fail
- Smart failure imminent, back up your data

When S.M.A.R.T. errors are displayed, back up the system immediately. Then, to determine if the drive is actually bad or if the message was a false positive, download and run the disk testing software provided by your system or drive vendor. The long or complete tests detect surface problems and might also swap defective sectors for good sectors.

When Should You Check S.M.A.R.T. Attributes?

Under normal operating conditions, you should test your hard disks every month by using a program such as CHKDSK (included in Windows) or a vendor-supplied hard disk utility and review the S.M.A.R.T. attributes for errors. On a portable or laptop hard disk, I recommend checking twice a month because these drives are in greater danger of being physically damaged or overheating.

Although third-party S.M.A.R.T. attribute testing apps are available from many sources, drive manufacturers recommend using their own apps, as they are more reliable in interpreting test results and warning of immediate problems.

Troubleshooting Video, Projector, and Display Issues

220-1001: Objective 5.4: Given a scenario, troubleshoot common video, projector, and display issues.

Desktop, laptop, and mobile devices each have screens that can vary significantly. Use the following sections to learn how to diagnose and fix problems with various display types.

VGA Mode

A Windows system starts in *VGA mode* if *Low-resolution mode* or *Safe mode* has been selected at startup or if the correct drivers are not available. Check the following:

- **Make sure correct chipset (motherboard/system) drivers have been installed:** Many business desktops and most laptops use CPU-integrated graphics. Until chipset drivers are installed, these are used as ordinary VGA GPUs. Download the latest system or motherboard drivers from the vendor.

- **If the system is being upgraded from integrated graphics to a separate video card, be sure to install the new drivers after the card is installed:** Download the latest graphics from the card vendor or GPU vendor: www.amd.com (Radeon, Fire GL) or www.nvidia.com (GeForce, Quadro).

- **If the system is being upgraded by replacing an existing video card with a new video card with a different manufacturer's chipset, be sure to uninstall the current video card drivers and support apps from Device Manager and Programs and Features:** Install the new drivers after the new card is installed.

Until the new card's drivers are installed, the card will function as a VGA card (that is, with no 3D acceleration, limited video modes).

No Image on Screen

The possible causes and solutions for no image on screen vary according to the computer and display type.

Laptop/Tablet/Convertible 2-in-1

With a laptop or tablet, the most likely cause for no image on the built-in screen is a failure of the LCD-CCFL, LCD-LED, or OLED display, particularly if there is no external display plugged in.

If an external display is plugged in, the computer might be configured to use the external display only. To quickly determine if the built-in display is working, turn off the external display, shut down the computer, and unplug the display from the computer's video port. Turn the computer back on and see if the built-in display now works. If it does, configure the built-in display as primary and the external display as a mirror or as an extended desktop.

Desktop Computer

If an external display has no image on the screen when it is the only display, check power, display cables, and the input setting on the display. If these check out, use a flashlight to determine if there is any image onscreen. If you see one, the LCD-CCFL backlight has failed. If you don't see any image, the display has failed.

If a secondary or additional display or projector has no image, set the display properties for extended desktop or mirror, as desired.

Projector

Check the lens cap or shutter and make sure it is open. (This might seem obvious, but always remember to check the obvious.) Check the image source selection. Make sure the computer source is configured to use the projector as an extended desktop or mirror of the primary display. Check power and video cables.

Overheat Shutdown

Projectors shut down when they overheat. To avoid overheat shutdown, check the following:

- Clean or replace filters when recommended. Projectors with filters usually display a message onscreen when it is time to clean or replace the filter.

- Make sure the projector has adequate ventilation.

- Check air intakes and exhaust ports for dust and dirt and clean as necessary.

- Use lower brightness setting on projectors to reduce heat.

- Be sure to allow the projector to cool down completely before removing it from power.

A video card (GPU) that overheats will usually display screen artifacts before shutting down.

Dead Pixels

Dead pixels (black pixels) typically result from manufacturing defects in an LCD screen. Check with the manufacturer of the panel or laptop to determine the number of dead pixels that are needed to qualify for screen replacement.

Some "dead" pixels are actually stuck on (bright) or off (dark). There are a variety of ways to solve this problem, including the following:

- Navigate to the JScreenFix website (www.jscreenfix.com) and start the pixel fixer app. Drag the app window to the area of your screen with the pixel problem and leave it over the area for up to 10 minutes. JScreenFix uses HTML5 and JavaScript controls in the web browser. It works with any LCD or OLED device, including mobile devices.

- Gently massage the stuck pixel with a stylus or another object with a blunt, narrow end. See https://www.wikihow.com/Fix-a-Stuck-Pixel-on-an-LCD-Monitor for illustrations.

- For Windows systems, download and run the UDPixel utility (http://udpix.free.fr/index.php). Requires .NET Framework 2.0, which can be added to Windows 7/8/8.1/10 through Control Panel's Add/Remove Windows Features.

Artifacts

Display or screen ***artifacts*** (distorted shapes, colors, pixelated images, scrambled text, or lines through an image) can be caused by an overheated GPU or projector, overclocked GPU, overcompressed graphics, overcompressed video, and low-resolution video or image enlarged to a higher-resolution display.

To solve overheating problems with a projector, see the section "Overheat Shutdown," earlier in this chapter. To solve overheating problems with a GPU (video card):

- Check the card's cooling fan.

- Check the CPU heat sink/fan with CPU-integrated video.

- Disable overclocking and return the card/system to normal clock speeds.

Incorrect Color Patterns

Incorrect color patterns on a projector can have several causes, so try the following:

- Check the signal type in the projector menu and change it if incorrect.
- If one LCD panel (red, green, or blue) is failing in an LCD projector, replace the panel. Panels often fail due to the impact of ultraviolet light causing excessive heat and breaking down organic compounds used in the process.
- On a DLP projector, check the LED light sources (red, green, or blue) or dichroic mirrors.
- Clean the projector LCD panels if odd-colored specks are visible.
- If a laptop has been serviced or upgraded, the LCD ribbon connector to the motherboard might have been damaged. If an external display works correctly, check the LCD ribbon cable inside the laptop.
- Check a VGA cable for bent or broken pins. (However, some pins are not present by default.) Check all video cables for cracked outer casings and loose or damaged connectors.

Dim Image

A *dim image* can be caused by settings issues or by equipment failure. Check the following:

- Check the screen brightness control on a display or projector.
- If a display management program is being run (which is common on Intel, NVIDIA, and AMD 3D GPU drivers), check its settings.
- On a laptop, tablet, or mobile device, check the built-in screen brightness setting.
- On a projector, check the projector bulb. A bulb may become milky, which reduces light output, near the end of its service life.
- On a device that uses a CCFL backlight, check the inverter. A failing inverter can cause a dim display before the inverter fails. The inverter can be replaced separately from the LCD panel or backlight.

Flickering Image

A *flickering image* can have many causes:

- Before looking at hardware replacements, be sure to try updating the GPU (video card) or chipset drivers.

- On displays using an LCD-CCFL backlight, flickering could be caused by a failing inverter or a failing backlight. Inverters are relatively inexpensive and can sometimes be replaced without a complete teardown. Backlights cost more, and it may make more sense to buy a replacement LCD screen or retire a computer or display.

- On any type of LCD display (CCFL or LED backlight), loose internal cables can cause flickering. A two-in-one convertible device (tablet/laptop) may have a hinge problem that can lead to flicker.

- On desktop computers, check the power connector to the PCIe card (if it uses a separate power cable) and the power supply itself. If the problem happens after the computer has been running for a while, it could indicate a heat-related problem.

Distorted Image

A **distorted image** can have several causes and solutions, including the following:

- If image tearing or distortion occurs in 3D games only, change video drivers. In most cases, the newest video driver is recommended, but in a few cases with certain games, the best short-term fix might be to install an older driver. Check driver versions with Device Manager's properties sheet or the proprietary app installed by your GPU or video card maker.

- Distortion with DisplayPort connections can be caused by problems with the way some DisplayPort cables and connectors are manufactured. If you can use a different connection (DVI or HDMI) between a system and a display and the problem is no longer present, replace the DisplayPort cable.

Distorted Geometry

Distorted geometry (pincushion, barrel, and other types) common with CRT displays are not present on LCD or LED displays. However, other factors can cause issues:

- If a projector lens is tilted upward or downward toward the screen, keystoning (non-parallel sides on the projected image) is the result (see Figure 5-23). Most projectors have keystone correction options in their display menus or control panels.

1. Normal projected image
2. Horizontal distortion (right side of screen closer to projector)
3. Keystone distortion (bottom of screen closer to projector)

FIGURE 5-23   Simulations of Normal, Keystoning, and Horizontal Distortions with Projectors

- If a projector is not at a 90-degree angle to the projection screen, the image will be larger on one side than the other, as Figure 5-23 shows. Some projectors have adjustments for this problem. When working with one that does not, adjust the projector or screen position until the image is the same size across the screen.

- When the projector is tilted or is not at a 90-degree angle to the screen, parts of the picture might also be out of focus.

- Curved screen HDTVs have subtle geometric distortions that increase at greater off-axis viewing angles. Place seating closer to the middle of the display.

- When viewing 4:3 aspect ratio content on a widescreen display (16:9 or similar), using the zoom option on the HDTV to fill the screen can distort the edges of the image. Try different zoom options or advise the user that the best picture is at the original aspect ratio.

Burn-in

Burn-in, the persistent display of a "ghost" image onscreen that was displayed previously, even after the current screen contents have changed, can affect both LCD and plasma displays.

LCD Displays

With LCD displays, stuck pixels are the usual cause of burn-in. Programs that run constantly changing patterns across the area, such as the previously mentioned JScreenFix or UDPixel, can be used to fix this problem.

Another solution is to create an all-white image using a graphics program, set it as the screen saver, and turn down the display brightness. Leave the screen saver running about as long as the original image was onscreen.

To avoid image persistence with IPS displays (the most common type of LCD display in use, offering wide viewing angles), Apple recommends using display sleep to turn off the display when idle. To eliminate a persistent image, enable the screen saver to come on before display sleep and run it as long as the persistent image was originally onscreen. For more information, see https://support.apple.com/en-us/HT202580.

Plasma Displays

Plasma displays use phosphors, which can wear unevenly over time. This was also the cause of burn-in on CRT displays. To avoid either temporary or permanent image persistence, try the following:

- For customers who watch mainly 4:3 ratio TV or movie content, advise periodically switching to full-screen (zoomed) mode to avoid black bar persistence on the sides of the image.

- Use the screen clean (screen washing) option available on some plasma HDTVs. This puts a constantly changing display across the entire screen.

TIP   For plasma and LCD display/HDTV users, there are many YouTube videos that can be played to help fix image retention. To play these on an HDTV, go to the YouTube app and search for "image retention fix."

Oversized Images and Icons

Oversized images and icons in Windows can be caused by booting in Limited-resolution (VGA) mode. On Windows 7, selecting this mode from the special startup (F8) options menu sets the display for 640×480 resolution. Many apps cannot be used at this resolution, and menus and icons are enormous (see Figure 5-24). To fix, restart the system and select normal resolutions from the Display properties sheet in the Control Panel.

1. Start menu occupies more than half the screen
2. To see all running apps, use the vertical scroll on the taskbar
3. Enormous icons

FIGURE 5-24   Windows 7 After Starting in Limited-Resolution (640×480) Mode

NOTE   In Windows 8/8.1/10, the Limited-resolution option chooses the lowest resolution available on the display's Resolution slider in the Control Panel. When using the Change the Size of All Items option in **Display > Resolution > Make Text Larger or Smaller**, 100 percent is the default setting. If a custom size that is too large is selected (such as 200 percent; see Figure 5-25), the effect is the same as if a very low resolution were selected. To fix, select **Smaller** (see Figure 5-26), log off the user, and log the user back in again. For Windows 10, select **Settings > Display**, as shown in Figure 5-27.

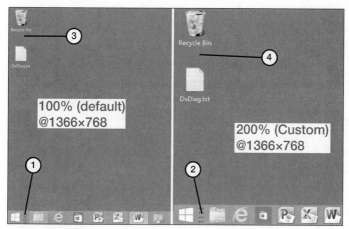

1. Normal taskbar
2. Enlarged taskbar
3. Normal icon size
4. Enlarged icon size

FIGURE 5-25   Windows 8.1 Desktop at Normal (Left) and 200 Percent (Right) Magnifications

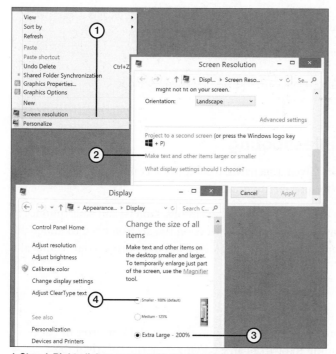

1. Step 1. Right-click or press and hold on desktop and select Screen Resolution
2. Step 2. Click or tap Make text and other items larger or smaller
3. Current percentage
4. Step 3. Select 100%. Log out and log back in again to finish

FIGURE 5-26   Resetting a Custom Item Size Setting in Windows 8.1

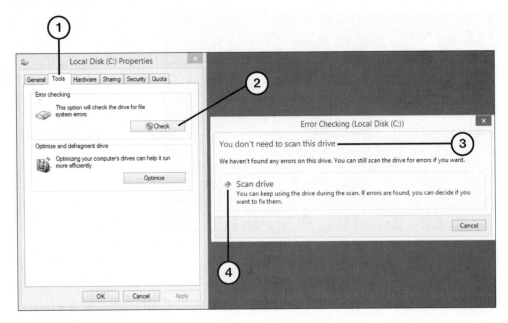

1. **Tools tab**
2. **Click or tap to check drive**
3. **Drive status**
4. **Click or tap to scan drive**

FIGURE 5-27   Display Settings Highlighted in Windows 10 Display Settings

Mobile Device Troubleshooting

220-1001: Objective 5.5: Given a scenario, troubleshoot common mobile device issues while adhering to the appropriate procedures.

With more organizations than ever before using laptops, tablets, and smartphones, it's important to know how to troubleshoot devices on the go. You need to understand the following concepts for the 220-1001 exam and to improve your technical skills.

No Display

On a laptop, no display can be caused by the failure of the LCD inverter or backlight, a damaged cable leading to or from an LCD inverter, the failure of the LED control board, the failure of the display panel, the failure of the onboard display circuit, or the laptop being toggled to use an external display only with an Function key.

First, try toggling the laptop to use the internal display. If that doesn't help, connect it to a monitor or projector. If the external display works, the problem might be with the cable to the LCD inverter or the LCD inverter or the LCD-CCFL backlight on an LED display, or the problem could be with the cable to the LED control board, the LED control board, or the LED backlight. If the external display doesn't work, the motherboard needs to be repaired or replaced.

On a tablet or smartphone, the usual cause is that the unit is out of power. Connect it to a suitable charging connection, wait about 10 minutes, and try to power it up. If there's still no display, have the unit serviced.

Dim Display

On any device, the first step in dealing with a dim display is to check the brightness settings. Smartphones and tablets typically use auto brightness. Disable it and try adjusting the brightness manually. Also, check the charge level. Many devices set the screen to a very dim setting right before shutting down in a last-ditch attempt to stretch battery life. If the screen doesn't return to normal brightness after being connected to AC power, service it.

If a laptop has a dim display not caused by user settings, the most likely cause is the failure of the fluorescent backlight inverter. If the screen flashes for a moment and then becomes dim at startup, the inverter is almost always the cause. Replace it.

If a smartphone or tablet has a dim display that won't respond to user settings, try performing a hard reset (power down, wait a few moments, and then power up again. Also, make sure the ambient light sensor is working and is not being blocked by the case.

If the display dims after the device has been turned on for several minutes and left unattended, the most typical cause is a power management setting. Adjust power management settings as desired.

Flickering Display

On a laptop with an LCD-CCFL backlight, a flickering display is almost always caused by a dying backlight. You can replace it, but it's easier to swap the complete screen assembly for a remanufactured unit. If the unit has been opened, the problem could also be a damaged LCD ribbon cable to the motherboard.

On an Android smartphone, there are some troubleshooting steps to try before deciding to reset the device to factory defaults:

Step 1.   Restart the device.

Step 2.   See if an app is causing the problem.

Step 3.   Turn off Developer Options (if running) by choosing **Home > Settings > More > Developer Options** and turning off the options.

Step 4.   Test the affected part of your screen.

See https://support.google.com/nexus/answer/7666942?hl=en for more information.

On an iOS 9 iPhone 6s Plus or 6 Plus, the flickering is usually caused by dropped frames during graphically intense calculations. To fix it:

Step 1.   Choose **Settings > General > Accessibility > Increase Contrast > Reduce Transparency**.

Step 2.   Turn on **Reduced Transparency**.

Some apps will have less appealing backgrounds when this option is enabled.

In IOS 10 and later, Display Accommodations can easily adjust brightness and colors that may impact how data is displayed to a color-sensitive user. Choose **Settings > General > Accessibility > Display Accommodations**. From this page, colors can be inverted or adjusted, and auto-brightness can be enabled or disabled.

Sticking Keys

Sticking keys on a laptop or tablet usually indicate a problem with the keyboard. It is not always necessary to replace the entire keyboard. Several online vendors offer individual key replacements for laptops. If more than one or two keys are sticking, it may be most cost-effective to replace the entire keyboard.

If a tablet uses a removable keyboard, the keyboard can be replaced if keys are not available.

Intermittent Wireless

Some tablets and smartphones may have intermittent wireless if the WiFi signal is very weak. Switch to a cellular data connection (if available) until a stronger WiFi signal is available.

Change the angle of your laptop or two-in-one device screen or turn the entire unit to help improve WiFi reception, as these units have their antennas in the screen.

Use the signal strength indicator to find the strongest wireless signal that can be used. In a public setting, there might be two or more open networks to choose from.

Battery Not Charging

To fix battery not charging issues on a tablet or smartphone:

- Make sure the charger is rated for the tablet or smartphone. Chargers are rated in amperage (1A = 1000mA). A minimum of 500mA is needed to charge a smartphone (but 1A is much faster), and a minimum of 2.1A is needed to charge a tablet.

- Check the charging port on the device. Pocket lint can make for a faulty connection on a phone. Laptop charging ports are also susceptible to dust and debris.

- If the charger has a toggle for iOS and non-iOS devices, choose the correct setting for your device.

- If you use a USB port on a laptop or desktop computer, enable USB fast charging if it is available on the computer and be sure to use that port.

- You can't charge a smartphone from an unpowered USB hub; it has only 100mA available per port.

- Ordinary USB ports cannot charge a device when the computer is asleep.

If you have checked these issues with no success, replace the cable. If a known-working cable doesn't help, replace the battery or have the unit serviced.

On a laptop, if the system works when plugged into AC power but not on battery power, check the following:

- Make sure the battery is installed properly.

- Wipe off any corrosion or dirt on the battery and laptop battery contacts.

- Determine whether the battery can hold a charge. Make sure the battery is properly installed and the AC adapter has proper DC voltage output levels. Leave the system plugged in for the recommended amount of time needed to charge the battery; then try to run the system on battery power. If the battery cannot run the system, or if the system runs out of battery power in less than an hour, replace the battery. If replacing the battery does not solve the problem, the laptop needs to be serviced or replaced.

- If the battery is hot after being charged or has a warped exterior, replace it.

Ghost Cursor/Pointer Drift

A *ghost cursor* is usually caused by mouse movement too fast for the screen refresh rate. To make the mouse pointer easier to see, adjust the mouse properties to slow down mouse acceleration, use a larger mouse pointer, or enable visibility options (pointer trails) or press the **Ctrl** key to display the mouse location.

Pointer drift can be caused by accidentally swiping or pressing on the device's touchpad or by a problem with the device's integrated pointing stick. If using a mouse, disable the touchpad or change its sensitivity settings to ignore accidental touches.

No Power

If a laptop has no power when plugged into an AC outlet, verify that the battery is not the problem. Remove it. Also try the following:

- Make sure the laptop is plugged in to a working AC outlet. Check the outlet with an outlet tester. Use a voltmeter or a multimeter set to AC voltage to determine whether the output is within acceptable limits.

- Make sure the AC power cord running from the AC outlet to the external AC adapter "power brick" is plugged in completely to the outlet and the adapter. If the power cord or plug is damaged, replace the cord.

- To determine whether the adapter is outputting the correct DC voltage, use a voltmeter or multimeter set to DC voltage to test the voltage coming from the adapter and compare it to the nominal output values marked on the adapter. As Figure 5-28 illustrates, it might be necessary to use a bent paperclip to enable an accurate voltage reading. A value of ±5 percent is acceptable.

1. Nominal output voltage
2. AC adapter tip polarity
3. Positive (red) lead from multimeter
4. Negative (black) lead from multimeter
5. Measured DC voltage output
6. Bent paperclip inserted into adapter tip
7. Multimeter mode selector

FIGURE 5-28   Checking the Output Voltage from a Laptop's AC Adapter

Num Lock Indicator Lights

Some laptops with embedded keypads don't start up with the keypad enabled (Num Lock on). Check the BIOS to see if this option can be enabled.

If *Num Lock indicator lights* will not come on, there might be a problem with the keyboard.

No Wireless Connectivity

Most laptops have a push button, pressure-sensitive touch button, or Fn key combination to enable or disable WiFi networking. If there is no wireless connectivity, press the button or Fn key combination to enable the connection. Most laptops display an indicator light when the connection is enabled.

Late-model laptops, tablets, and smartphones have an Airplane mode that disables all onboard radios (WiFi, Bluetooth, and cellular) when enabled. Turn off Airplane mode and try the connection again. WiFi can also be disabled separately from Airplane mode. Check the Settings menu and enable WiFi if necessary.

If the connection fails, check the WiFi connection in the notification area. You might need to reconnect manually. If there is no WiFi connection indication, open the Device Manager and check the Network Adapters category. If the WiFi adapter is not listed, rescan for hardware changes.

If the WiFi adapter cannot be located by Device Manager, shut down the system, disconnect it from all power sources, and open the access panel to the WiFi card. If the card is loose, reconnect it and retry the connection after restoring power and restarting the computer. If the WiFi antenna wires are loose, tighten them.

No Bluetooth Connectivity

Most laptops with built-in Bluetooth have a push button, pressure-sensitive touch button, or a Fn key combination to enable or disable Bluetooth networking. Here's how to diagnose problems with no Bluetooth connectivity:

Step 1. If there is no connection, press the button or Fn key combination to enable the connection. Most laptops display an indicator light when the connection is enabled.

Step 2. If the connection fails, verify that a Bluetooth adapter is installed and enabled. If the Bluetooth adapter is accessible from the outside of the unit, you can physically verify proper connection. Also check Windows Device Manager, Linux Hardware, or macOS System Information. If the

Bluetooth adapter is not listed, restart the computer and verify that the Bluetooth adapter is enabled in system BIOS setup.

Step 3. If the Bluetooth adapter is installed, use the Bluetooth configuration utility provided by the computer vendor (or device vendor, in the case of a USB Bluetooth adapter) to set up the adapter to connect to other devices.

Step 4. If the adapter is already set up to connect to other devices, check the Bluetooth settings on those devices.

On a tablet or smartphone, also check Airplane mode (see the preceding section, "No Wireless Connectivity," for details).

Cannot Display to External Monitor

To display to an external monitor or projector, use the appropriate keyboard Fn key combination after connecting the display or projector; see documentation for your device for details. If the system cannot display to an external monitor:

- Check the cabling between the computer and the external display.

- Make sure the display is set to the correct input.

- Try a different display to determine if the problem is the mobile device or the external monitor.

Touchscreen Non-Responsive

The most common reason for a touchscreen non-responsive problem is dust, dirt, and grease on the surface. Use an antistatic wipe or spray designed for touchscreens to clean it.

Dry hands may not work well with touchscreens. Gloves without special fingertips can't use a touchscreen.

To determine if the touchscreen has failed, try a stylus made for the touchscreen. Reset the device and retry. If the touchscreen is still not responsive, have the unit serviced.

Apps Not Loading

To solve problems with apps not loading, check the following:

- Check available storage space. If your system is almost out of space, apps can't run. Uninstall apps you never use.

- If you have adequate free storage space, the device might not have enough free RAM. Close some apps.

- For a web-enabled app, make sure the device has a good Internet connection.

Slow Performance

To fix slow performance:

- Remove the case and close apps to help cool an overheating unit.

- Check the power management settings. If a laptop is plugged into AC power, I recommend using the High Performance power setting in Windows.

- Close apps that are running but not in use.

- Don't charge the phone while running a bunch of apps.

Unable to Decrypt Email

Mobile devices and email providers use varying methods to encrypt and decrypt messages between users. As noted in Chapter 1, "Mobile Devices," S/MIME is a protocol supported by Apple and Outlook. Users obtain a digital certificate that will verify the identity of the recipient. For information on this and other email encryption techniques, visit https://www.comparitech.com/blog/vpn-privacy/how-to-encrypt-email/.

Missing or out-of-date security certificates on devices can cause problems with decrypting email. Update security certificates to solve this problem.

Extremely Short Battery Life

Although Li-ion batteries do not have the memory effect that plagued old NiCd batteries, various factors can still cause extremely short battery life. Check the following:

- Don't overcharge a device's battery.

- For best results, don't wait until a device is almost out of power to charge it.

- Adjust screen brightness to the lowest level that is comfortable to use.

- On iOS devices, turn off background app refresh.

- Upgrade to the latest OS or OS updates available for your device.

- Use a phone battery helper app to manage charging but don't run other apps while the device is charging.

- Close apps from the iOS App Switcher.

- Shut down an iOS device weekly with the slider switch.

- On devices that use AMOLED displays, switch to black wallpaper (theme) to save power.

- Extreme cold can quickly sap a device's battery, so be sure the user takes in climate considerations and keeps the device as warm as possible in cold climate use.

Overheating

Mobile device *overheating* can have several causes. Try the following:

- On a laptop, make sure the intake and exhaust fan ports aren't being blocked during use. Despite the name, a lap is not a suitable place for a computer because clothing can block airflow.

- Adjust power settings, especially when on battery power.

- Make sure CPU power management drivers are installed (check Device Manager under System Devices).

- On a tablet or smartphone, shut down unnecessary apps and keep in mind that HD video playback can stress the processor. Some protective cases can cause smartphones to overheat.

Frozen System

A *frozen system* is usually caused by a malfunctioning app. Sometimes going to the lock screen for a few seconds helps a mobile app start responding. If that doesn't work, shut down the system, wait a minute, and then restart it. Check for updates for the app and device.

No Sound from Speakers

No sound from speakers can have several causes:

- With wired speakers, keep in mind that the case might prevent 3.5mm mini-jack connector from making a good connection. It may be necessary to remove the case to make a good connection.

- With Bluetooth speakers, make sure Bluetooth is turned on. Check device pairing.

- Check the volume or mute controls on the mobile device. Apple iPhones have a sliding switch to mute them as well as software controls. The side button on an iPad can be configured to lock the screen or mute speaker output. Check the volume control on the keyboard or OS on macOS and Windows devices.

GPS Not Functioning

If the GPS not functioning, Airplane mode may be turned on. If Airplane mode is on, the GPS is shut down as well. Turn off Airplane mode, and the GPS may come back on. If not, turn on the GPS in the **Settings > Location** menu.

Swollen Battery

A swollen battery is most likely due to overcharging. In addition to replacing the battery, check the AC adapter to make sure it is putting out the correct voltage.

Mobile Device Disassembly Process

Disassembling mobile devices can be challenging even for experienced technicians. Follow these guidelines to ensure successful disassembly and reassembly when you upgrade or service a laptop, convertible two-in-one, tablet, or smartphone.

Document and Label Cable and Screw Locations

A typical laptop may have 100 or more screws of varying sizes. A smartphone could have a dozen or more. Be sure to document and label cable and screw locations: As each screw is removed, note its location and size.

A digital camera or smartphone camera is a good tool, as you can use it to photograph the device and the screws as they are removed.

Figure 5-29 shows a few of the different screws removed from a typical laptop.

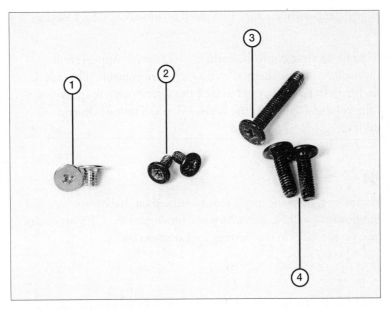

1. Hard disk mounting screws
2. Subassembly mounting screws
3. Keyboard mounting screw
4. Case cover screws

FIGURE 5-29   Typical Laptop Screws and Their Uses

TIP   If you have a service manual for the device, note the screw sizes and positions listed for each component. Use it to create a checklist as you disassemble a device.

Organize Parts

There are many ways to organize parts:

- Use a plastic divided-compartment lidded tray from a hardware store to keep screws and bolts organized. As you put each set of screws into a compartment, add a label to indicate which subassembly they go to.

- Place static-sensitive materials (CPU, RAM, etc.) in antistatic bags.

- Use antistatic bubble wrap for larger components, such as motherboards.

- Use boxes to protect case and trim components.

TIP   If you have a service manual for the device, label components by the subassembly and page number in the manual.

Refer to Manufacturer Resources

Before you start to disassemble a device, make sure you have the information you need to refer to *manufacturer resources*:

- Get the manufacturer's service manual, if it is available.

- For the easiest time in searching, check the underside of a laptop or tablet to find the actual service number or catalog number (not the marketing model number).

Most manufacturers make this information readily available. Some third-party websites also provide service manuals, but don't use these resources unless you can't download the service manual directly from the manufacturer's website.

CAUTION   YouTube has many videos on tablet, smartphone, and laptop disassembly. Also, there are many unofficial teardown documents online. They can be helpful in the absence of manufacturer-supplied documentation, but be careful! Some might advocate potentially dangerous methods for disassembling a device.

Use Appropriate Hand Tools

For an easier time disassembling mobile devices, use appropriate hand tools. They are smaller and differ in other ways from those needed for a desktop computer. For example, Apple now uses the five-point Pentalobe screw for external screws in its smartphones, although some models use the standard Phillips head for internal screws.

Although some users advocate using guitar picks or even playing cards for opening tight enclosures on smartphones, special tools work better. Figure 5-30 illustrates one of many specialty toolkits on the market for working on mobile devices.

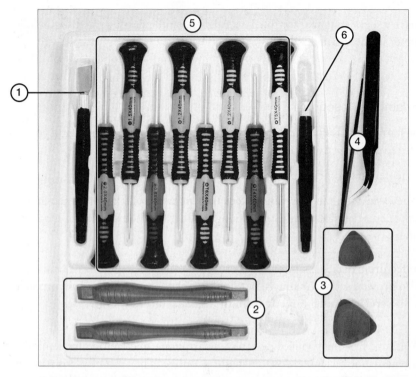

1. Scraper
2. Pry bars
3. Triangle paddles
4. Tweezers
5. Screwdrivers (Phillips, straight-blade, Torx, and 5-point/Pentalobe)
6. Precision cutting knife

FIGURE 5-30   A Typical Mobile Device Toolkit

Printer Troubleshooting

220-1001: Objective 5.6: Given a scenario, troubleshoot printers.

For the 220-1001 exam, be sure you understand how to deal with the symptoms and how to use the tools listed in the following sections.

Streaks

Streaks and smudges can have many causes, depending on the type of printer in use.

Laser Printer

Randomized streaks in printed output, such as uneven printing or blank spots, are usually caused by low toner. As a temporary workaround, remove the toner cartridge and gently shake it to redistribute the toner. Install a new toner cartridge as quickly as possible.

Long vertical streaks that repeat on each page are usually caused by damage to the imaging drum. Replace the drum or toner cartridge if it includes the drum.

Inkjet Printer

Smudged print output from an inkjet printer can be caused by dirty printheads or paper rollers, incorrect head gap settings, and incorrect resolution and media settings.

If you see smudges only when printing on heavy paper stock, card stock, labels, or envelopes, check the head gap setting; use the default setting for paper up to 24-pound rating; and use the wider gap for labels, card stock, and envelopes.

Clean the printhead. If the cleaning process doesn't result in acceptable results, remove the printhead (if possible) and clean it. If the printhead is built in to the printer or if the paper-feed rollers or platen have ink smudges, use a cleaning sheet to clean the paper-feed rollers, platen, and printhead.

Check the Printer Properties setting in the operating system to ensure that the correct resolution and paper options are set for the paper in use. Horizontal streaks in inkjet output are usually caused by trying to print on glossy photo paper using plain paper setting.

Unlike laser output—which can be handled as soon as the page is ejected—inkjet output, particularly from older printers, printed to old paper stocks made for older printers, or output on transparencies or glossy photo paper, often requires time to dry. For best results, use paper specially designed for inkjet printers. Paper should be stored in a cool, dry environment; damp paper also will result in smudged printing.

Thermal Printers

Streaky output in thermal transfer printers can have several causes, including media and print head problems.

If the coating on the media is poor quality, replace the media. If preprinted ink on the media is sticking to the printhead, replace the media with media printed using heat-resistant ink.

If the heating element is dirty, clean the heating element.

Smeared output (primarily when printing bar codes) can be caused by incorrect print head energy settings, a print speed that is too high, and using a 90-degree or 270-degree orientation.

With direct thermal printers, check for improperly stored paper or an incorrect setting in the printer driver. If the printer can be used in either direct or thermal transfer modes, an incorrect driver setting can cause print quality problems of various types.

Impact Printers

Streaky output in dot-matrix impact printers is usually caused by a dried-out ribbon. If the ribbon has an auxiliary ink reservoir, activate it. Otherwise, replace the ribbon.

Faded Prints

Faded prints also have many possible causes, depending on the printer.

Laser Printers

If the printing is even, the printer might be set for an economy mode or a similar mode that uses less toner. Adjust the printer properties to use normal print modes for final drafts.

For a color laser printer, also check the toner levels or the operation of the toner belt.

Inkjet Printers

The print nozzles might be clogged, or some colors may be out of ink. This is a common problem for inkjet printers that have not been used in a few weeks. It is a good idea to print something using all the inks every week or so. Clean the nozzles and use the nozzle check utility to verify proper operation. Replace any cartridges that are out of ink.

Thermal Printers

A faded image can result from installing a thermal transfer ribbon backward. Remove the ribbon, verify proper loading, and reinstall.

If the ribbon is installed correctly but there is still a problem, the ribbon might not be compatible with the media. Check the media settings in the printer configuration to verify.

Impact Printers

If the print is evenly faded, the ribbon is dried out. Replace the ribbon to achieve better print quality and protect the printhead. If the print appears more faded on the top of each line than on the bottom, the head gap is set too wide for the paper type in use. Adjust the head gap to the correct width to improve printing and protect the printhead from damage.

Ghost Images

Laser printers that display ***ghost images*** of part or all of the previous page on a new printout might have problems with the toner cartridge, imaging drum wiper blade, or fusing unit. To determine the cause of the ghosting, measure the distance between the top of the page and the ghost image and consult the service manual for the printer. Clean or replace the defective component.

Toner Not Fused to the Paper

The fuser in a laser printer is supposed to heat the paper to fuse the toner to the paper; fuser failure results in ***toner*** not fused to the paper. If the printed output from a laser printer can be wiped or blown off the paper after the printout emerges from the laser printer, the fuser needs to be repaired or replaced.

Creased Paper

Creased paper is usually caused by incorrect adjustment of the paper guides for feeding pages. If the paper guide is not set to the actual paper width, the paper might move horizontally during the feed process and become creased. Adjust the paper guides to the correct width for the paper or media in use.

Paper Not Feeding

The causes of paper not feeding can vary by printer type:

- With an inkjet, laser, or impact printer running single-sheet paper, check the paper's positioning in the paper tray. Remove the paper, fan it, and replace it. If the problem continues, check for paper jams. If there are no paper jams, the pickup rollers might be worn out.

- With a printer that uses continuous-feed paper (impact or thermal), check the tension of the feeder rollers or the position and operation of the tractor-feed mechanism.

Paper Jam

A *paper jam* can have a variety of causes, depending on the printer type. Use the following sections to solve paper jams.

Paper Path Issues

The more turns the paper must pass through during the printing process, the greater the chance of paper jams. Curved paper paths are typical of some inkjet and many laser printers as well as dot-matrix printers using push tractors: The paper is pulled from the front of the printer, pulled through and around a series of rollers inside the printer during the print process, and then ejected through the front or top of the printer onto a paper tray. Because the cross-section of this paper path resembles a *C*, this is sometimes referred to as a C-shaped paper path.

Some printers, especially those with bottom-mounted paper trays, have more complex paper paths that resemble an *S*.

A straight-through paper path is a typical option on laser printers with a curved paper path. Printers with this feature have a rear paper output tray that can be lowered for use to override the normal top paper output tray. Some printers also have a front paper tray. Use both front and rear trays for a true straight-through path; this is recommended for printing on envelopes, labels, or card stock. Inkjet printers with input paper trays at the rear of the printer and an output tray at the front also use this method or a variation in which the paper path resembles a flattened V.

Paper Loading, Paper Type, and Media Thickness Issues

Paper jams can be caused by incorrect paper-loading procedures, an overloaded input tray, or use of paper or card stock that is thicker than the recommended type for the printer. If the printer jams, open the exit cover or front cover or remove the paper tray(s) as needed to clear the jam.

Media Caught Inside the Printer

If paper, labels, envelopes, or transparencies come apart or tear inside a printer, you must remove all debris to avoid additional paper jams. Don't try to use creased media because it increases the likelihood of a paper jam. However, if paper jams continue to happen, check the paper feed or paper tray operation.

Avoid using paper with damaged edges or damp paper, which can cause paper jams and lead to poor-quality printing.

TIP   When you insert a stack of sheet paper into any type of printer, be sure to fan the pages before you insert the paper into the tray to prevent sticking.

No Connectivity

A loose printer or network cable can cause connectivity issues, as can a router or switch failure. If a shared printer is connected to a computer, determine whether the computer can connect to the network. If not, the problem is network related. If the printer can connect to the network, the problem is related to the printer, printer port, or printer cable.

If the printer has an integrated network connection or connects to a print-sharing device on the network, check the network settings on the printer or device.

If the printer uses wireless networking, check the settings for SSID or ad hoc networking. Move the printer closer to the router. Add a wireless repeater. Replace Wireless-N or Wireless-G routers with Wireless-AC routers to boost network connection reliability to G, N, and AC devices and printers.

Garbled Characters on Paper

Garbled characters on paper (that is, gibberish printing) can occur for several reasons. Check the printer driver first: If the printer driver files are corrupted or the incorrect printer driver has been selected for a printer, gibberish printing is a likely result.

If you can use a printer in an emulation mode or change it to use a different printer language with a personality module or DIMM (for example, a special Postscript DIMM can be used in some PCL-language laser printers), be sure you have correctly configured the printer and the printer driver or installed a new printer driver.

A parallel printer cable that fails can also cause this type of problem.

Vertical Lines on Page

Vertical lines on pages printed with a laser printer can be caused by debris stuck to the imaging drum, surface damage to the imaging drum, or dirty components in the printer (fuser, paper rollers, charging rollers, and so on). To determine which component is the cause, compare the distance between marks on the paper with the circumference of each component. The printer's manual will provide this information.

Replace the imaging drum (which is part of the toner cartridge on many printer models) if the drum is at fault. Clean other components if they're at fault and retest.

Vertical lines on a page printed with an inkjet printer are usually caused by ink on a feed roller. Clean the feed rollers, and if the problem persists, there might be a problem with a leaky ink cartridge.

Vertical lines in thermal printer output can be caused by a dirty heating element or by the failure of part of the heating element. Angled streaks can be caused by a creased ribbon. To solve this problem, adjust the ribbon feed mechanism.

Vertical lines on impact printer output usually indicate dirt on the paper. Replace the paper.

Backed-Up Print Queue

The Windows print spooler switches to offline mode if the printer goes offline, is turned off, or has stopped for some other reason (such as a paper jam or loss of connection to the network). Print jobs are sent to the print queue, but a backed-up print queue fills up until the print jobs are dealt with. After the printer goes online, you can release the print jobs. You can also kill all print jobs or kill selected print jobs.

To access the print queue, open the Printer icon in the notification area or go to Printers or Devices and Printers and open the printer icon.

Releasing a Print Queue

To release print jobs stored in the queue in offline mode after the printer is available, use one of these methods:

Step 1.   Open the print queue.

Step 2.   Open the **Printer** menu.

Step 3.   Click the **Use Printer Offline** toggle. The print jobs go to the printer.

Clearing Select Print Jobs or All Print Jobs in a Queue

You might need to clear a print queue for a variety of reasons:

■ The wrong options are selected for the installed paper.

- Gibberish printing occurs because of a problem with the printer driver, cable, or port.

- You decide not to print the queued documents.

You can clear selected print jobs or all print jobs in a queue. To discard a print job in the print queue, follow these steps:

Step 1.   Open the print queue.

Step 2.   Right-click the print job you want to discard.

Step 3.   Select **Cancel Print**. The print job is discarded.

To discard all print jobs in the queue, follow these steps:

Step 1.   Open the print queue.

Step 2.   Right-click **Printer**.

Step 3.   Click **Cancel All Documents** (or a similar option, depending on the Windows version) to discard all print jobs.

Low Memory Errors

If you send to a laser printer a page that requires more memory than the laser printer contains, the printer tries to print the page but stops after the printer's memory is full. The printer displays *low memory errors* (either with an error message or by blinking error status lights), at which point you must manually eject the page. Only a portion of the page is printed.

If the page requires an amount of memory close to the maximum in the laser printer, most laser printers have techniques for compressing the data going to the printer. Although this technique means that more pages can be printed successfully, compressing the data can slow down the print process.

You can try three options if the pages you need to print require too much memory:

- Reduce the resolution of the print job. Most laser printers today have a standard resolution of 600dpi or 1,200dpi. Reducing the graphics resolution to the next lower figure (from 1,200 to 600dpi or from 600dpi to 300dpi) will reduce the memory requirement for printing the page by a factor of four. The option, when present, could be located on various tabs of the printer's properties sheet. See Figure 5-31 for a typical example.

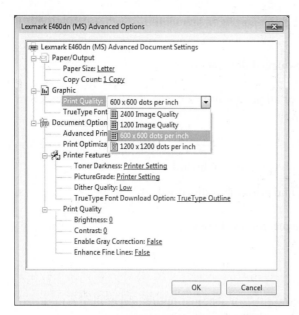

FIGURE 5-31 The **Layout > Advanced > Graphics > Print Quality** Dialog in Windows 7 for a Lexmark Laser Printer Enables You to Adjust the Graphics Resolution; Text Quality Is Not Affected by This Option

- Eliminate or reduce the size of graphics on the page.
- Convert color photos to black-and-white photos before placing them in a desktop publishing document or printing them directly from the file. This can actually enhance the output quality from a monochrome laser printer as well as reduce the memory requirement for pages with photos.

These options are temporary workarounds that might be unsatisfactory for permanent use. The best solution to out-of-memory problems with a printer, as with a computer, is to add more RAM.

NOTE If you reduce the graphics resolution, text resolution stays the same, so a document that is not designed for reproduction or mass distribution will still have acceptable quality. However, graphics resolutions of 600 dots per inch (dpi) or less produce poor-quality photo output.

Access Denied

If you get an *Access Denied* message when trying to print to a network printer, make sure your account has been granted access to the printer or to the computer hosting the networked printer.

Printer Will Not Print

If a printer will not print:

- Check that the correct printer is selected. Some networks have several printers, and the job may be printing at another location.

- If a laser printer produces a blank page immediately after the toner cartridge has been changed, remove the toner cartridge and make sure the tape that holds the toner in place has been removed; without toner, the printer can't print.

- If the printer produces a blank page after printing thousands of pages, the toner probably is exhausted. Replace the toner cartridge.

- If you send a print job to a printer that has specified hours of activity, the print job will not be released to the printer until the printer is ready for it.

- If you set up a printer manually and the wrong printer port is specified, the printer won't print.

- Check the cable connecting the printer to the device (USB) or network (Ethernet). Check wireless or wired network connections.

- To print from a mobile device, install the print app for the printer brand/model from the device's app store.

Color Prints in Wrong Print Color

If a printer uses the wrong colors for color prints, the most likely cause on a color inkjet printer is a clogged printhead. On a color laser, check for low color toner or an empty color toner cartridge.

Inkjet manufactures such as Epson and Cannon may have a Windows interface for managing many printer functions. For Epson inkjet printers on Windows systems, use the Maintenance tab of the printing preferences sheet (see Figure 5-32) to check ink levels, clean and align print heads, and check nozzles for clogs.

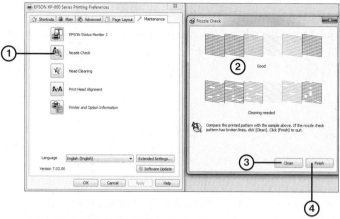

1. Click to start Nozzle Check
2. Compare printout with these examples
3. Click to clean print heads
4. Click when Nozzle Check results are satisfactory

FIGURE 5-32   Using the Nozzle Check Option on an Epson Inkjet Printer

For Canon inkjet printers on Windows systems, use the Maintenance tab of the printing preferences sheet (see Figure 5-33) to clean and align print heads, check nozzles for clogs, clean the bottom plate and rollers, and configure ink usage.

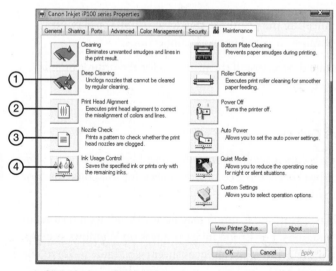

1. Click to clean print heads
2. Click to deep clean print heads
3. Click to align print heads
4. Click to run Nozzle Check

FIGURE 5-33   The Maintenance Tab for a Canon Inkjet Printer Driver

If the print colors are close but not exactly what is wanted on a color photograph or a document with colored graphics or text, you need to set up color management on the printer and the display(s) used to edit the document.

Unable to Install Printer

The unable to install printer issue is caused by not having sufficient privileges; you need administrator (elevated) access to uninstall a printer. If you are installing a printer in Windows, provide the administrator password when prompted by User Account Control. In Linux, get root access with **sudo** and provide a password when prompted.

Error Codes

Printers with LCD or LED panels display error codes or error messages for diagnosis of problems such as paper jams, low ink, or low toner. Error codes vary by printer manufacturer. To diagnose a printer that has only status lights, use the printer's documentation to determine the codes being displayed. To determine the meaning of a specific error code and the appropriate solution, check the printer manual and printer vendor's website.

HP LaserJet printers use numerical error codes to describe printing problems. A good resource for both numerical and text-based error codes for HP LaserJet printers is the HP LaserJet Error Codes page at PrinterTechs.com. Lexmark error codes are available at support.lexmark.com.

Printing Blank Pages

If a printer is printing blank pages, check the following:

- If a new toner cartridge has just been installed in a laser printer, make sure the tape was removed from the toner cartridge.

- The printer might be feeding two or more sheets at a time. Remove the paper, fan it to ensure the paper is not sticking together, reinsert the paper into the printer tray, and retry the print job.

- If the printer is networked, check the network print server configuration. Many network printers are configured to eject a blank page between print jobs for privacy.

- With some printers, you start a print job that uses the rear paper slot before you insert paper. Paper placed in the rear paper slot before the print job starts might be ejected.

No Image on Printer Display

If the there is no image on a printer display, press a button to "wake up" the display. Make sure the printer is turned on.

If you are printing directly from a memory card and no pictures are visible, the pictures on the memory card might be the wrong file format. Printers cannot print RAW-format files but can print JPEG files.

If the display is a plug-in type, the display interface cable might be loose. Turn off the printer, unplug and reconnect the cable, and turn on the printer again.

Failed Jobs in Print Logs

It is possible to track print jobs on a network by enabling print logs in Windows 10. With this feature enabled, a print job on a network can be tracked in the print services section of the Event Viewer.

To enable the logging service, search for the Event Viewer and open it. In the left pane, expand the **Application and Services Logs > Microsoft > Windows > PrintService**. To enable print logs, right-click **Operational** and from the context menu select **Properties**. Then check the **Enable Logging** box. Figure 5-34 depicts the process.

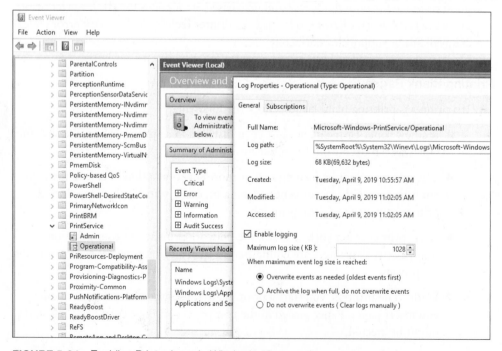

FIGURE 5-34   Enabling Printer Logs in Windows 10

Once operational, the logs can be used to evaluate errors. Figure 5-35 shows an example of an error in a print log. The highlighted error indicates a problem with the print spooler.

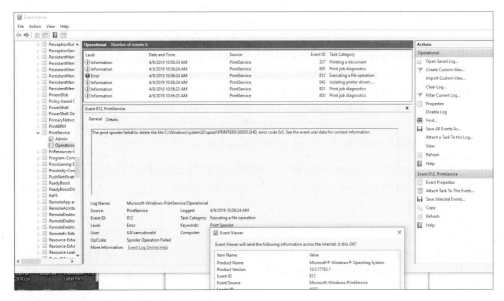

FIGURE 5-35   Print Log Error

Third-party print server software usually has a print logging feature that can assist with troubleshooting. Check with the developers' instructions for the best way to track jobs in the application.

Network Troubleshooting

220-1001: Objective 5.7: Given a scenario, troubleshoot common wired and wireless network problems.

Most computing devices an IT professional encounters are connected to a network. The common network issues discussed in the following sections are essential knowledge for an IT professional. Understanding the problems and solutions in the following sections is important for the 220-1001 exam and to aid in your ongoing work.

No Connectivity

For *no connectivity* errors:

- Check the power supply going to the hub, switch, wireless access point, or router. Reset the device.

- Isolate the problem. If only the users connected to a new switch that is connected to an existing switch lose their network connection, check the connection between the existing switch and the new one. Most switches have an uplink port that is used to connect an additional switch. You can either use the uplink port or the regular port next to the uplink port but not both. Connect the computer using the port next to the uplink port to another port to make the uplink port available for connecting the new hub or switch.

- If the uplink port appears to be connected properly, check the cable. Uplink ports perform the crossover for the user, enabling you to use an ordinary network cable to add a hub or switch.

TIP   If you use a crossover cable, you must connect the new hub or switch through a regular port, not through the uplink port.

APIPA/Link Local Address

An *APIPA/link local address* (IPv4 169.254.x.x range) is assigned to a computer if the DHCP server (which assigns IP addresses) cannot be reached. This is one cause of limited connectivity.

Check the device that provides DHCP service (usually a router on a SOHO network). If that device is working properly, restart the computer and check the IP address after the computer restarts. If the problem persists, check for a bad cable or inability to connect to a wireless network.

TIP   You can usually reset the NIC without a reboot by right-clicking on the interface, selecting Disable, and then reenabling the NIC.

The yellow ! symbol next to the network icon in the Windows taskbar (see Figure 5-36) indicates that the network has *limited connectivity* in Windows 7 (the Internet cannot be reached), also called *local connectivity*. In Windows 10, a red X appearing on the taskbar next to the network icon (see Figure 5-37) also indicates limited connectivity.

1. Click up arrow to see hidden notifications
2. Wired network connection has limited connectivity

FIGURE 5-36   Connection Problem (Windows 7)

FIGURE 5-37   Connection Problem (Windows 10 Taskbar)

Before attempting the following fixes, check connectivity on other devices on the network. If all devices can't connect:

- To diagnose this problem with Windows 7, open the Network and Sharing Center and click the red X in the Internet Connection dialog to launch the Internet troubleshooter. Use the troubleshooter and follow its recommendations.

- With Windows 8/8.1, use Search to locate and start the Internet troubleshooter. Use the troubleshooter and follow its recommendations.

- In Windows 10, click the network icon in the taskbar to open the Network Status window. If not connected, a "troubleshoot" button appears. Click it to start the Internet troubleshooter. Use the troubleshooter and follow its recommendations.

- For connection problems with any OS, turn off the broadband modem or access device, wait about a minute, and then turn it back on. Then turn off the router, wait about a minute, and turn it on again. If the problem was with the broadband modem/access device, this should solve the problem. If it doesn't, contact the ISP as the problem might be on the ISP network.

- If only one device is affected, disconnect from the wireless network and reconnect to it. For a wired network, restart the computer.

Intermittent Connectivity

Intermittent connectivity can be caused by:

- **Dead spots (poor signal) on a wireless network:** Relocate the wireless router.

- **Too many networks using the same channel:** Use a wireless network scanning device or app to see local wireless networks and their channels. Reconfigure the network to use a channel with less traffic.

- **EMI or RFI interference with the wired network:** Alarm systems, elevators, fluorescent lights, and motors can interfere with networks running UTP. Switch to STP cable or relocate cables away from interference.

- **Defective network cable, such as cracked outer jacket or broken locking tab:** Replace cable.

- **Problems with the ISP's Internet service:** Contact the ISP after troubleshooting the local network if the problem persists.

IP Conflict

An *IP conflict* results if two devices on a network have the same IP address. This commonly occurs when a DHCP server assigns an address that has already been assigned manually to a device on the network or when an administrator mistakenly assigns an address that is already in use. Configure devices with manual IP addresses to use a different range of addresses than those used by the DHCP server.

Slow Transfer Speeds

Significant drops in network performance and slow transfer speeds can be traced to a variety of causes, including:

- **Damage to cables, connectors, hubs, switches, and routers:** Check cables for damage.

- **Connecting high-speed NICs to low-speed switches:** When using Gigabit Ethernet switches and routers, confirm that all devices on the network (switches, router, cables, and NICs) meet Gigabit Ethernet standards (CAT 5e or 6, 6a, 7 cable) and are configured to use Gigabit Ethernet.

Fast local connections but sluggish Internet connections can be caused by too much demand for the Internet connection (may be due to multiple downloads or streaming services) or Internet congestion outside the home or office.

- **RFI/EMI interference with wireless networks:** Check wireless phones and microwave ovens to see if their use interferes with the network. Move the router away from interference sources. Switch to a wireless 802.11ac router and NICs and use the 5GHz band to avoid most of this type of interference.

Low RF Signal

A *low RF signal* on a wireless network can be caused by:

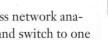

- **Interference from other wireless networks:** Use a wireless network analyzer to determine the least-used channels for the network and switch to one of those channels.

- **Concrete or masonry walls in the building:** If it is not possible to relocate the router, add repeaters. In residential construction, consider using powerline repeaters.

- **Improper antenna positioning on the router or NICs with adjustable antennas:** Follow manufacturer recommendations.

- **The router or NICs do not support MU-MOMO antennas:** Multiuser Multiple Input Multiple Output (MU-MIMO) enables a router to make MIMO connections to multiple users at the same time. MU-MIMO requires routers and client device support, but it can be implemented on client devices that have only a single antenna each. These devices are increasingly common, and prices are falling. With so many wireless devices in homes and businesses competing for wireless bandwidth, a MU-MIMO solution could inexpensively double the speed of downstream traffic on a network.

NOTE   MU-MIMO enables a router to make MIMO connections to multiple users at the same time. MU-MIMO requires routers and client device support, but it can be implemented on client devices that have only a single antenna. As firmware and drivers updates become available to enable MU-MIMO on routers and client devices, MU-MIMO will become more common. To learn more, see www.techhive.com/article/2928725/how-mu-mimo-wi-fi-works.html.

SSID Not Found

If the SSID is configured not to broadcast its name, users can still connect to it. When an SSID is listed as a hidden network in the list of wireless networks in

Windows, users must supply the SSID as well as an encryption key to make the connection.

If an SSID not found error is displayed (either by name or as a hidden network), reboot the router. If rebooting the router does not help, open its configuration web page from your router and verify that it is configured as a router. (Most SOHO routers use the IP address 192.168.1.1.) Change and save the configuration and then try the connection again.

Exam Preparation Tasks

As mentioned in the section "How to Use This Book" in the Introduction, you have a couple choices for exam preparation: the exercises here, Chapter 10, "Final Preparation," and the exam simulation questions in the Pearson Test Prep Software Online.

Review All the Key Topics

Review the most important topics in the chapter, noted with the Key Topic icon in the outer margin of the page. Table 5-6 lists these key topics and the page number on which each is found.

Table 5-6 Key Topics for Chapter 5

Key Topic Element	Description	Page Number
Table 5-2	The Six-Step CompTIA Troubleshooting Methodology	414
List	Causes of unexpected shutdowns	415
List	Diagnosing system lockups	415
Table 5-3	Common System Errors and Their Beep Codes	418
List	Resolving blank screen on bootup issues	419
List	Resolving continuous reboot issues	422
List	Causes of system overheating	423
Steps	Troubleshooting intermittent failures of USB-powered devices	430
Steps	Resolving fan spinning errors	430
Section	Resolving indicator light issues	430
Section	Investigating smoke or burning smells	431

Complete the Tables and Lists from Memory

Print a copy of Appendix C, "Memory Tables" (found on the website for this book), or at least the section for this chapter, and complete the tables and lists from memory. Appendix D, "Answer Key to Memory Tables," also on the website for this book, includes completed tables and lists to check your work.

Define Key Terms

Define the following key terms from this chapter and check your answers in the glossary:

system lockup, overclocking, POST code beeps, BIOS, blank screen on bootup, continuous reboots, negative pressure, distended capacitor, STOP errors, BSOD, pin wheel, multimeter, power supply tester, read/write failure, SATA, failure to boot, drive not recognized, OS not found, S.M.A.R.T., VGA mode, low-resolution mode, Safe mode, dead pixels, artifacts, incorrect color patterns, dim image, flickering image, distorted image, distorted geometry, ghost cursor, pointer drift, Num Lock indicator lights, overheating, frozen system, manufacturer resources, streaks, faded prints, ghost image, toner, creased paper, paper jam, garbled characters, vertical lines, low-memory errors, Access Denied, no connectivity, APIPA/link local address, limited connectivity, local connectivity, intermittent connectivity, IP conflict, low RF signal

Answer Review Questions

1. Your system has begun shutting down suddenly and unexpectedly. Which of the following best describes how to determine whether the cause of these shutdowns is due to the CPU overheating?

   a. Check the CPU temperature in the Device Manager.

   b. Check the CPU temperature in the System Properties.

   c. Check the CPU temperature in Computer Management.

   d. Check the CPU temperature in the system BIOS/UEFI firmware.

2. Which of the following best describes the usual cause of a checksum error?

   a. A failing CMOS battery

   b. A corrupt BIOS or UEFI

   c. An error within the system's arithmetic calculator

   d. Overheating due to overclocking

3. Which of the following is usually checked by POST? (Choose all that apply.)

   a. Memory

   b. Keyboard

   c. Mouse

   d. Hard drives

4. When the date and time on your computer are running slowly and losing time, which of the following statements best describes the most likely cause and the most effective course of action?

   a. There is a fault in the BIOS settings, and you should flash the BIOS.

   b. The CPU is running slowly, and you should check the CPU and its fan to see if dust is clogging it and slowing it down.

   c. At least one of the memory modules may be faulty, and you should check the memory information in the BIOS and replace any failing modules.

   d. The CMOS battery is failing, and you should replace the battery.

5. Which component is indicated in the following figure?

   a. CPU

   b. CMOS battery

   c. Capacitor

   d. BIOS chip

6. If your system is experiencing frequent STOP errors and is automatically rebooting each time, where would you go to change the configuration setting to stop the automatic reboot process?

   a. System Properties, Advanced tab, Startup and Recovery

   b. Drive Properties, Tools tab

   c. Administrative Tools, Disk Management

   d. BIOS, Boot tab, Automatic Reboot

7. Which voltage is used by most personal computers in North America?

   a. 115V

   b. 190V

   c. 230V

   d. 400V

8. Identify the motherboard components indicated in the following figure.

   a. CMOS batteries

   b. Resistors

   c. Jumpers

   d. Capacitors

9. Which of the following tools is used to test AC or DC voltage, continuity, resistance, and amperage?

   a. Loopback plug

   b. PING

   c. Multimeter

   d. Tone generator

10. Which of the following voltage levels should be produced by a healthy power supply? (Choose all that apply.)

    a. +3.3

    b. −3.3

    c. +5.0

    d. −5.0

    e. +8.3

    f. −8.3

    g. +12.0

    h. −12.0

11. You are called to an employee workstation, where it is reported that the network connectivity has failed. At some point in the process, you decide to replace the workstation Ethernet cable with one in your bag that you know to be good. Which step does this demonstrate in the best practice methodology to resolve problems?

    a. Identify the problem.

    b. Establish a theory of probable cause.

    c. Test the theory to determine the cause.

    d. Establish a plan of action.

12. You have received a support call from an employee whose mouse does not work on booting. When you ask the user if the monitor is on and if the keyboard is also disabled, which step does this demonstrate in the best practice methodology to resolve problems?

    a. Identify the problem.

    b. Establish a theory of probable cause.

    c. Test the theory to determine the cause.

    d. Establish a plan of action.

13. What is the purpose of the jumper shown in the following figure?

    a. It protects the prongs inside the connector.

    b. It moves the SATA drive to the first position in the boot sequence.

    c. It is used by RAID to configure a mirrored array.

    d. It slows SATA drive performance.

14. Which of the following statements best describes how to change the boot sequence?

   a. Edit the BIOS and save the changes in CMOS.

   b. Change the jumper settings on the SATA drive to make it the bootable drive.

   c. Reconfigure settings for the RAID array to make a RAID drive the bootable drive.

   d. Use the Disk Management utility in Administrative Tools.

15. S.M.A.R.T. detects and reports errors for which of the following?

   a. CPUs

   b. DDR memory

   c. SATA and PATA hard drives

   d. Expansion cards

16. You have been asked to replace a switch in a wiring closet with an upgraded switch. Unexpectedly, it takes you about two hours using a tone generator to determine where the cables map to in the old switch before you can uninstall it. Which step in the best practice methodology to resolve problems is missing from this scenario and may have saved two hours?

   a. The first

   b. The third

   c. The fifth

   d. The last

17. Which command can be issued at a command prompt to generate output in the following format?

   server: fbks.alaska.edu

   a. **nslookup fbks.alaska.edu**

   b. **ping 181.27.135.135**

   c. **nslookup 181.27.135.135**

   d. **tracert 181.27.135.135**

18. When booting your system in Safe mode, which of the following statements best describes how the display will load?

    a. The display will load in VGA mode.

    b. The display will load using the last known good configuration.

    c. The display will load using the resolution selected when entering Safe mode.

    d. The display will degauss before entering Safe mode.

19. A flickering image on an LCD display might be caused by the failure of which components? (Choose two.)

    a. Backlight

    b. Cathode ray tube

    c. Reflector

    d. Inverter

20. Burn-in refers to which of the following?

    a. The process of recording a CD or DVD

    b. The process of preparing a hard drive for formatting for a clean installation

    c. A persistent ghost image on the display screen

    d. The damaged areas in a plasma display

21. Your client reports that computers on the network cannot connect to the Internet but can connect to each other. You determine that each of the computers affected has been assigned an APIPA address. At Step 2 of the best practice methodology to resolve problems, where would you look next to solve the problem?

    a. DNS

    b. DHCP

    c. Proxy

    d. Router

22. Which step of the best practice methodology to resolve problems is out of order?

   a. Establish a theory of probable cause.

   b. Establish a plan of action to resolve the problem and implement a solution.

   c. Test the theory to determine the cause.

   d. Verify full system functionality.

23. Which of the following does not apply to the first step of the best practice methodology to resolve problems?

   a. Inquiring regarding environmental changes

   b. Inquiring regarding infrastructure changes

   c. Performing backups

   d. Documenting outcomes

24. When your tablet or smartphone does not get a clear cellular signal, which of the following steps could improve the signal? (Choose two.)

   a. Turn off WiFi.

   b. Change the angle of your screen.

   c. Reset your cellular settings to a faster 802.11 specification.

   d. Use the slider switch on an iOS device to fine-tune reception.

25. Which of the following steps could help increase the battery life on your mobile devices? (Choose two.)

   a. Don't overcharge.

   b. On iOS, turn on the background app refresh.

   c. Use the iOS slider switch to shut down weekly.

   d. Wait until almost out of power before recharging a device.

26. Vertical streaks extending down each page printed by a laser printer usually indicate which of the following problems?

   a. Low toner

   b. A dirty print ribbon

   c. Damaged ink nozzles

   d. Damage to the imaging drum

27. Smudged print from an inkjet printer could be caused by which of the following?

    a. Dirty printheads or rollers

    b. Failure of the fuser to reach a high enough temperature

    c. Photosensitive drum not being properly charged

    d. Toner cartridge needing to be replaced

28. If toner can be brushed off the page after printing, which component of a laser printer is malfunctioning?

    a. Print drum

    b. Fuser

    c. Paper feed rollers

    d. Corona

29. If a document requires the maximum amount of memory that is available to a laser printer, the printer might attempt to compress the document. Which of the following statements best describes the result of this compression on the final print page?

    a. Some text could be lost.

    b. The printed text may be cloudy.

    c. The print process will be slower.

    d. Some pictures could be deleted.

30. Which of the following print tools is used to manage and maintain print jobs?

    a. Print spooler

    b. Fuser

    c. Printheads

    d. XPS Document Writer

This chapter covers the nine A+ 220-1002 exam objectives related to operating systems with a focus on the features; tools; versions; command line tools; and configuration and installation of Microsoft Windows as well as macOS and Linux operating systems. These objectives may comprise 27% of the exam questions:

- **Core 2 (220-1002): Objective 1.1:** Compare and contrast common operating system types and their purposes.

- **Core 2 (220-1002): Objective 1.2:** Compare and contrast features of Microsoft Windows versions.

- **Core 2 (220-1002): Objective 1.3:** Summarize general OS installation considerations and upgrade methods.

- **Core 2 (220-1002): Objective 1.4:** Given a scenario, use appropriate Microsoft command line tools.

- **Core 2 (220-1002): Objective 1.5:** Given a scenario, use Microsoft operating system features and tools.

- **Core 2 (220-1002): Objective 1.6:** Given a scenario, use Microsoft Windows Control Panel utilities.

- **Core 2 (220-1002): Objective 1.7:** Summarize application installation and configuration concepts.

- **Core 2 (220-1002): Objective 1.8:** Given a scenario, configure Microsoft Windows networking on a client/desktop.

- **Core 2 (220-1002): Objective 1.9:** Given a scenario, use features and tools of the macOS per rest of book and Linux client/desktop operating systems.

## CHAPTER 6

Operating Systems

Each new Windows version brings changes to features and appearances, but all the versions use similar installation methods. In this chapter, you are introduced to the differences in appearance and features as well as the many options available for installing Windows on individual systems and for deployment to multiple computers. The chapter also covers some of the important macOS and Linux features and tools.

"Do I Know This Already?" Quiz

The "Do I Know This Already?" quiz allows you to assess whether you should read the entire chapter. Table 6-1 lists the major headings in this chapter and the "Do I Know This Already?" quiz questions covering the material in those headings so you can assess your knowledge of these specific areas. The answers to the "Do I Know This Already?" quiz appear in Appendix A, "Answers to the 'Do I Know This Already?' Quizzes and Review Question Sections."

Table 6-1   "Do I Know This Already?" Section-to-Question Mapping

Foundation Topics Section	Questions
Common Operating Systems	1
Microsoft Windows Versions	2
OS Installation and Upgrade Methods	3
Command Line Tools	4
Operating System Features and Tools	5
Control Panel Utilities	6
Summary of Installation and Configuration Concepts	7
Networking Microsoft Windows	8
macOS and Linux	9–10

CAUTION   The goal of self-assessment is to gauge your mastery of the topics in this chapter. If you do not know the answer to a question or are only partially sure of the answer, you should mark that question as wrong for purposes of the self-assessment. Giving yourself credit for an answer you correctly guess skews your self-assessment results and might provide you with a false sense of security.

1. Which is true of FAT32?

    a. It uses file permissions.

    b. It has a max file size of 8GB.

    c. Corrupt files can be repaired.

    d. It works in macOS computers.

2. Which versions of Windows use charms? (Choose all that apply.)

    a. 7

    b. 8

    c. 8.1

    d. 10

3. Which operation requires the help of a utility such as Microsoft Deployment Toolkit?

    a. Network installation

    b. Multi-boot installation

    c. Unattended installation

    d. Clean installation

4. What is the name of the mode you enter when you run the command prompt as an administrator?

    a. Supervisor mode

    b. Elevated mode

    c. Power mode

    d. Action mode

5. Which of the following is not a Microsoft administrative tool?

    a. Performance Monitor

    b. RAM Optimizer

    c. Task Scheduler

    d. Print Management

6. Which of the following are Control Panel utilities? (Choose all that apply.)

    a. System

    b. Folder Options

    c. Devices and Printers

    d. User Accounts

7. What is the name of the process that involves making a shared folder accessible by selecting a drive letter on a client computer?

    a. Tunneling

    b. Share pointing

    c. Mapping

    d. Navigating

8. Which two tasks are configured in the network card properties settings? (Choose two.)

    a. Half duplex or full duplex

    b. Wake-on-LAN

    c. Firewall exceptions

    d. VPN access

9. When an app is not working and cannot be closed properly, what commands can you use to end the app in macOS and in Linux? (Choose one for each operating system.)

    a. terminate

    b. Force Quit

    c. kill

    d. expire

10. What is Time Machine?

    a. A clocking utility that is new in Windows 10

    b. A backup utility in Linux

    c. A macOS backup utility

    d. A backup utility that is new to Windows 10

Foundation Topics

Common Operating Systems

220-1002: Objective 1.1: Compare and contrast common operating system types and their purposes.

All computing devices have some type of operating system to allow for the physical interaction of the logical processes of computers. Some operating systems are very specific and narrow in their purpose, and some, like Windows, are extremely large and encompass many purposes into their design. The CompTIA A+ exam focuses on workstation and mobile phone operating systems.

32-Bit vs. 64-Bit File Systems

A key purpose of operating systems is to keep track of all the files that are used on a computer. A file system describes how data and drives are organized. In Windows, the file system you choose for a hard drive affects the following:

- The rules for how large a logical drive (drive letter) can be and whether the hard drive can be used as one big drive letter or several smaller drive letters or whether it must be multiple drive letters

- The efficiency of data storage (The less wasted space, the better)

- The security of a system against tampering

- Whether a drive can be accessed by more than one operating system

The term *file system* is a general term for how an operating system stores various types of files. Windows supports three different file systems for hard drives and USB flash drives: FAT32, NTFS, and exFAT. For CD storage, it uses CDFS.

FAT32

FAT32 was introduced in 1995 and has the following characteristics:

- It has a 32-bit file allocation table, which allows for 268,435,456 entries (2^{32}) per drive. An entry can be a folder or an allocation unit used by a file.

- The root directory can be located anywhere on the drive and can have an unlimited number of entries, which is a big improvement over FAT.

- FAT32 uses an 8KB allocation unit size for drives as large as 16GB.

- The maximum logical partition size allowed is 2TB (that is, more than 2 trillion bytes).

NOTE   Windows can't create a FAT32 partition larger than 32GB. However, if a larger partition already exists, Windows can use it.

FAT32 does have some limitations in that it can only support individual files up to 4GB in size, it can't use file permissions, and it doesn't support journaling systems that can fix file corruption issues. These three limitations moved the industry beyond FAT32, though it is still possible to use FAT32 to format hard drives.

Because the limitations do not apply to most USB flash and SD cards, FAT32 is still used to format flash memory cards and USB flash drives for use in not only workstations but media players, smart TVs, printers, cameras, and anything else that has a USB port. FAT32 is still compatible with macOS and Linux as well, so FAT32 is far from legacy. Even as the capacity of USB flash drives is increasing and 4GB files will need to be supported, FAT32 will likely stay around to support other devices.

NOTE   In a 32-bit machine, the maximum amount of memory that can be used is around 4GB. On a 64-bit machine, the maximum amount of memory is 2^{64} bytes.

exFAT (FAT64)

exFAT (also known as FAT64) is a file system designed to enable mobile personal storage media to be used seamlessly on mobile and desktop computers. exFAT is designed to be as simple as FAT32 but with many improvements in capacity and scalability.

exFAT is also called FAT64 because it supports 64-bit addressing. exFAT's main features include:

- It supports volumes (drive letters) larger than 32GB. 512TB is the recommended maximum volume size, but the theoretical volume size is 64ZB (zettabytes; 1ZB = 1 billion terabytes).

- The recommended and maximum file sizes increase to 512TB and 64ZB, respectively.

■ Improvements in file system structure enable better performance with flash media and for movie recording.

■ It supports Universal Time Coordinate (UTC) date stamps.

■ exFAT support is included in Windows 7, 8/8.1, and 10.

Figure 6-1 illustrates exFAT as a formatting option for a USB thumb drive in Windows 8.1.

FIGURE 6-1   File System Formatting Options for a 16GB USB Thumb Drive in Windows 8.1, Including FAT32, NTFS, and exFAT

Workstation Operating Systems

Operating systems can be classified as ***open source***, which refers to software that is effectively free to download and modify, and ***closed source***, which refers to software that cannot be modified without express permission and licensing. Other terms used to describe closed source software are "vendor specific," which means only one company has access to the source code, and "proprietary," which means the software is owned and patented and can only be used with permission and usually by paying a licensing fee.

Windows

Microsoft's Windows is a closed source product, and is the most widely used OS in the world. In the 1980s, when businesses transitioned into the digital age using

IBM-compatible PCs, Microsoft usually provided the OS, which was known as the Disk Operating System, or DOS. DOS is a command line OS, which means commands are entered as strings of text. DOS has since that time been replaced with Windows, which uses a graphical user interface (GUI) to allow commands to be entered with the click of a mouse.

In 1985 and 1990, early versions of Windows were introduced, but Windows as we know it today took off with the introduction of Windows 95 in 1995. XP and Vista followed, and they were eventually replaced with Windows 7, 8, 8.1, and Windows 10. Windows 7, 8/8.1, and 10 are the Windows versions covered on the CompTIA A+ 220-1002 exam.

Apple Macintosh OS

Apple's macOS is the OS for Apple desktop products. Like Windows, macOS is closed source, and only some components are open to developers. macOS was released in 2016 and designed to integrate with devices using the iOS operating system, such as the iPhone, Apple TV, and Apple Watch. As of this printing, the latest version of macOS is Mojave, which replaces High Sierra. Figure 6-2 shows the Mojave desktop.

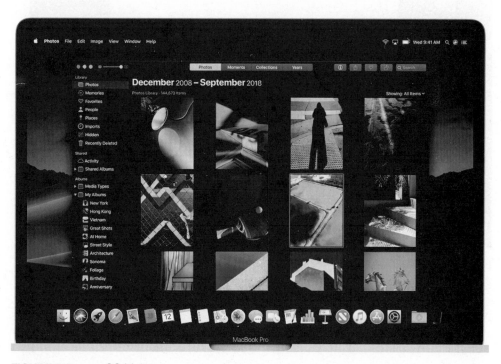

FIGURE 6-2   macOS Mojave

Linux

Linux was derived from the UNIX operating system (used on mainframe computers predating PCs). It is named for Linus Torvalds, who developed Linux in 1991. Linux is an open-source OS, which means the source code is free. Many companies, such as Red Hat, modify Linux source code and then charge individuals and organizations to support the modifications.

Because Linux is open source, it is available free on the web in the form of distros (distributions). Linux is available as command line distros and others as GUI distros. Popular distros of Linux are Ubuntu, Mint, Kali, and Red Hat.

Figure 6-3 shows a Linux Mint desktop environment.

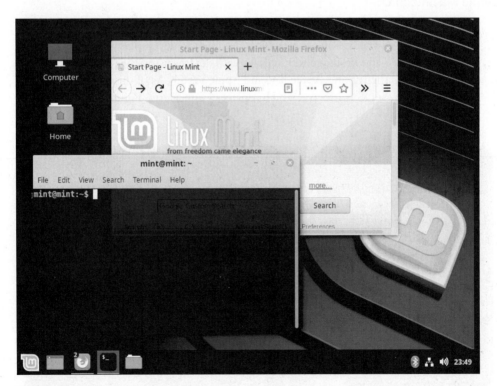

FIGURE 6-3   Mint Desktop

Cell Phone/Tablet Operating Systems

Smartphones use typically either Android or iOS operating systems, although a few use Windows Mobile.

Some differences between Android and iOS smartphones include:

- Operating system updates are provided by the wireless carrier for Android phones.

- Wireless carriers provide network-specific updates for iPhones (iOS), but Apple provides OS updates.

Microsoft Windows

Microsoft used Windows Mobile to support its last release of a Windows phone in 2016. A year later, Microsoft left the phone market and retired Windows 10 Mobile; it ended support for the mobile OS in late 2019.

Microsoft's tablets, such as the Surface Pro, run Windows 10 and have most of the functionality of a laptop.

Android

Android, which is an operating system based on the Linux kernel, is an example of open source software. Used mostly on smartphones and tablet computers, Android is developed by the Open Handset Alliance, a group directed by Google. Google releases the Android OS code as open source, allowing developers to modify it and freely create applications for it. Google also commissioned the Android Open Source Project (AOSP), whose mission is to maintain and further develop Android. Figure 6-4 shows the Android open source OS and related apps.

FIGURE 6-4   Android v8.0.0 OS Home Screen on a Samsung Smartphone

Android OS versions have cute names such as Ice Cream Sandwich (version 4.0), Jelly Bean (versions 4.1 through 4.3), KitKat (version 4.4), and Lollipop (versions 5.0 and 5.1). Pie (version 9) replaced Oreo (version 8) in 2019. Newer versions are constantly being developed.

To determine the current version in use on a device, start at the Home screen (that is, the main screen that boots up by default). Tap the **Menu** button and then tap **Settings**. Scroll to the bottom and tap the **About Phone** (or **About**) option. Then tap **Software Information** or a similar option. You can then see the version of Android. Figure 6-5 shows a smartphone using version 8.0.0 (Oreo).

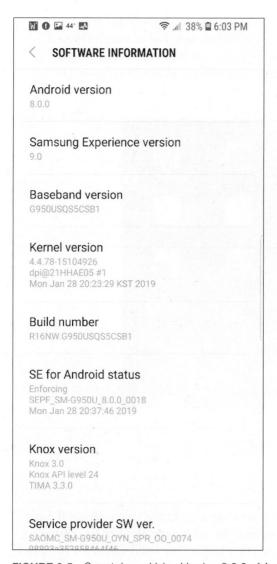

FIGURE 6-5   Smartphone Using Version 8.0.0 of Android

Unlike other mobile operating systems, Android's licensing agreements allow for a great deal of customization of the finished product. Thus, Android smartphones and tablets from different vendors are likely to have different user interfaces and features.

iOS

Apple's *iOS* is an example of closed source software.

Obviously known as the iPhone Operating System, it is now simply referred to as iOS, since it is used on the iPod Touch, iPhone, and iPad as well. It is based on macOS (used on Mac desktops and laptops), and it therefore has its roots in UNIX. Figure 6-6 shows the Home screen of an iPad mini 2 running iOS version 9.0.1.

1. iOS OS update available
2. App updates available
3. Battery charge level

FIGURE 6-6   iPad mini 2 Home Screen

To find out the version of iOS a device is running, go to the Home screen and tap **Settings > General > About**. You can then see the version number. For example, Figure 6-7 shows an iPhone running version 12.1.2. The build number is 16C101, which was the public release of version 12.1.2.

Unlike Android, iOS is not open source. Only Apple hardware uses this operating system.

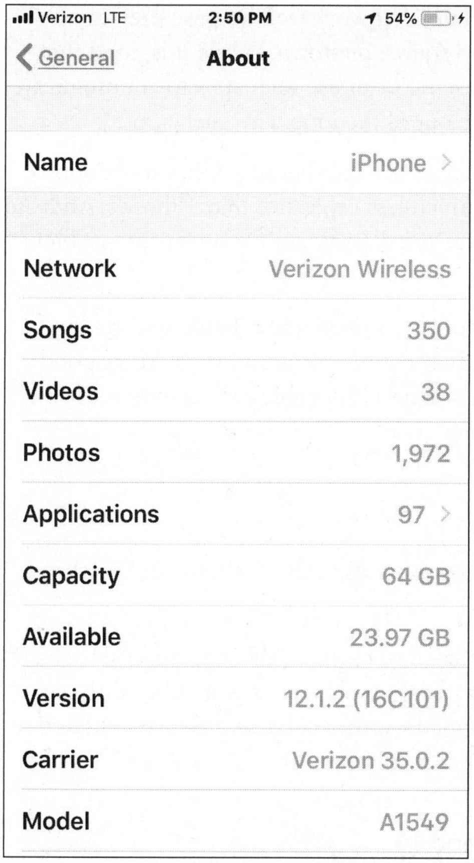

▪▪ll Verizon LTE	2:50 PM	✦ 54% ▭ ✦

‹ General **About**

Name	iPhone ›

Network	Verizon Wireless
Songs	350
Videos	38
Photos	1,972
Applications	97 ›
Capacity	64 GB
Available	23.97 GB
Version	12.1.2 (16C101)
Carrier	Verizon 35.0.2
Model	A1549

FIGURE 6-7   iPhone Using Version 12.1.2 of iOS

Chrome OS

A more recent entrant to the OS market is Google's *Chrome* OS. Chrome, which is based on Linux, is installed on Chromebooks, which are an inexpensive laptop option. Chrome OS is open source and is chiefly designed to run Web-based applications.

Vendor-Specific Limitations/Compatibility Concerns

Nearly 100% of smartphones in the United States use either Android or iOS. Each OS has loyal users, and the debate over which is better has proponents on both sides. Both are good systems, but there are several considerations in choosing between the vendor-specific Apple iOS and the open source Android OS.

One can argue that because Apple has control of iOS, it can better control the quality and safety of Apple products. Also, Apple can develop better applications, such as iMessage, Find My Friends, and FaceTime, that work well because they can be designed around the advantages of a closed source platform. While it is good that those in a family or an organization who use iOS can use such apps to communicate and share data easily, non-iPhone users are out of the loop with such apps.

One can also argue that Android has certain advantages because it has more apps available, and Android devices tend to be much less expensive than iPhones. Android allows third-party apps, but some people see third-party apps as a security problem rather than as an advantage.

The good news is that both iOS and Android are robust and reliable systems, and the best choice depends on the users and their communication needs. More good news is that some apps are coming on the market that enable easy communication and sharing between Android and iOS users.

Microsoft Windows Versions

220-1002: Objective 1.2: Compare and contrast features of Microsoft Windows versions.

Each incremental Windows version is designed to enhance the user experience as well as improve security and performance. Most versions are compatible with past versions, but occasionally features are dropped—either because they are outdated or have been improved and replaced with other features.

Comparing Microsoft Windows 7, 8/8.1, and 10

Windows 7, 8/8.1, and 10 have many features in common, particularly system management features in the Control Panel. However, from the standpoint of user features, there are many differences. Table 6-2 summarizes these features.

Table 6-2   Feature Comparisons for Windows 7, 8, 8.1, and 10

Feature Category/Feature	Windows Version			
	10	8.1	8	7
BranchCache	Yes	Yes	Yes	Yes
Media Center	No	Yes	Yes	Yes
EFS	Yes	Yes	Yes	Yes
Windows Aero	No	No	No	Yes
Sidebar	No	No	No	No
Gadgets	No	No	No	Yes
Start menu	No	No	No	Yes

Feature Category/Feature	Windows Version			
	10	8.1	8	7
Start screen	Yes	Yes	Yes	No
Pinning apps and files	Yes	Yes*	Yes*	Yes
Charms	No	Yes	Yes	No
Multi-monitor task bars	Yes	Yes	Yes	No
Live sign-in (Microsoft accounts for OneDrive, Office 365, and other subscriptions)	Yes	Yes	Yes	No**
Local account	Yes	Yes	Yes	Yes
User Account Control	Yes	Yes	Yes	Yes
Defender antivirus (Microsoft Security Essentials in 7)	Yes	Yes	Yes	Yes
BitLocker full disk encryption	Yes	Yes	Yes	Yes
Windows Firewall (Windows Defender in 10)	Yes	Yes	Yes	Yes
Action Center	Yes	Yes	Yes	Yes
Security Center Service	Yes	No	No	No
Control Panel	Yes	Yes	Yes	Yes
Administrative Tools	Yes	Yes	Yes	Yes
Settings	Yes	Yes	Yes	No
PowerShell	Yes	Yes	Yes	Yes
Event Viewer	Yes	Yes	Yes	Yes
Image Backup	Yes	Yes	Yes	Yes
File Backup	Yes	Yes	Yes	Yes
Shadow Copy	Yes	No	No	Yes
System Restore	Yes	Yes	Yes	Yes
Refresh and Reset (Refresh only in 10)	Yes	Yes	Yes	No
OneDrive (formerly SkyDrive)	Yes	Yes	Yes	Yes
ReadyBoost flash memory disk caching	Yes	Yes	Yes	Yes
Compatibility mode	Yes	Yes	Yes	Yes
Virtual XP mode	No	No	No	Yes
Side-by-side apps	Yes	Yes	Yes	No
Windows Easy Transfer	No	No	Yes	Yes
Windows (App) Store	Yes	Yes	Yes	No

* Apps and files can be pinned to the Start screen or the desktop taskbar.

** System login uses a local account, but access to OneDrive requires a Microsoft account (formerly known as Live sign-in).

The following are a few Windows features noted by the CompTIA objectives:

- BitLocker is a data encryption utility that encrypts hard drives for added security. It encrypts all data, including personal and system files. A companion program, BitLocker To Go, encrypts removable disks and USB drives. BitLocker and BitLocker To Go are covered in Chapter 7, "Security."

- Encrypting File System (EFS) is also offered on all Windows systems. Whereas BitLocker encrypts an entire drives, EFS has the capability of encrypting individual files. EFS is discussed further in Chapter 7.

- Windows Media Center, which was discontinued in Windows 10, plays DVDs, music, and slide shows, and it can stream from online services such as Netflix.

- BranchCache is software designed to allow efficient use of bandwidth for remote clients and offices. BranchCache caches the most commonly requested data on a client computer so that bandwidth is not wasted on repetitive data requests.

OS Installation and Upgrade Methods

220-1002: Objective 1.3: Summarize general OS installation considerations and upgrade methods.

Boot Methods

The boot process involves loading the necessary OS files into RAM so the computer becomes functional. The OS can be stored on the local hard drive, but it can also be stored on a CD/DVD, on an external USB or eSATA drive, or on another computer on the network. Wherever it is stored, the computer needs to be told where to go to find the OS files. This is done in the BIOS/UEFI's Boot Order settings. When booting, the PC looks in the preferred place for files and loads them into RAM, and the computer then becomes operational. If the PC can't find the files in the boot order, it moves on to the second place, and then keeps looking until it finds an OS. Figure 6-8 shows the boot order in typical BIOS. Keep in mind, though, that each vendor's boot order screen looks slightly different.

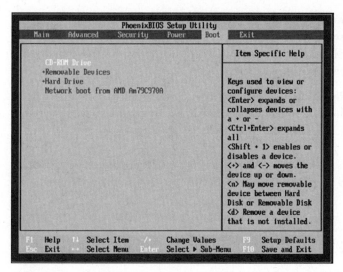

FIGURE 6-8   BIOS Boot Order Menu

There are many methods to boot a system during the installation process:

- **Optical disc (CD-ROM/DVD/Blu-ray):** Use this method to install Windows to an individual PC and to create a master PC from which disk images can be created.

- **Network/PXE boot (Preboot Execution Environment):** Use this method to install Windows to one or more systems that have working network connections. To use this method, network adapters must be configured to boot using the PXE boot ROM to a network location that contains an operating system image.

NOTE   *Netboot* is a network boot technology developed by Apple. Netboot uses Boot Server Discovery Protocol (BSDP) to locate and install operating system files.

- **USB/eSATA boot (booting from USB thumb drive):** Use this method when installing from a DVD isn't feasible, such as installing Windows to a computer that lacks a DVD drive. The Windows USB/DVD Download Tool available from https://www.microsoft.com/en-us/download/windows-usb-dvd-download-tool can create a bootable USB drive from a Windows ISO (.iso) image you have downloaded. If necessary, change the boot order in the system BIOS or UEFI firmware to permit booting from USB.

- **Internal hard drive (HDD/SSD):** This is the most common place for OS files to reside. Once the OS is installed, it is important to change the boot order in BIOS/UEFI so that the computer looks here first for files and doesn't try to reinstall from the external source.

- **Partition on the internal hard disk drive or SSD:** Similar to the internal hard drive above, but a designated partition, or section on the drive reserved for booting.

With each of these types of drives, the Windows installation files could be extracted or, with Windows 7 or later, the ISO file could be used as an installation source.

Installation Types

Windows can be installed in a variety of ways. The most common methods are:

- As an in-place upgrade to an existing version

- As a clean install to an empty hard drive or to the same partition as the current version

- As a multi-boot, which means installing to unused disk space (a new partition) to enable a choice between the current version and the new version, as needed

- As a repair installation to fix problems with the current installation

- With the recovery partition (which resets the system to its original installed state)

- Refresh and Reset in Windows 8/8.1 (but removed from Windows 10, as discussed in the following note)

> **NOTE**   Refresh and Reset were removed from Windows 10, where the Reset Your PC feature offers a simpler reset that includes the option for keeping personal files.

> **NOTE**   Refresh and Reset may be listed as "Refresh/Reset" or "Refresh and Restore" or "Refresh/Restore" on the 220-1002 exam.

The preceding installation options typically use the original distribution media or preinstalled recovery files.

Large-scale or customized installations might use the following methods:

- Unattended installation

- Remote network installation

- Image deployment

These installation options typically require the creation of an image file.

Unattended Installation

In an attended installation, information must be provided at various points during the process. To perform an unattended installation, create the appropriate type of answer file for the installation type. Microsoft currently offers the Microsoft Deployment Toolkit (MDT) for automated installation of Windows 7, Windows 8.1, Windows 10, and Windows Server 2008 R2 and newer versions. The MDT creates and updates the Unattend.xml file (used to provide answers during the process) automatically during the deployment. Download the MDT from the Microsoft website: https://docs.microsoft.com/en-us/sccm/mdt/.

Windows 7 uses the Windows System Image Manager to create the Unattend.xml file.

In-Place Upgrade Installation

To perform an in-place upgrade installation of Windows, start the installation process from within the existing version of Windows. It is possible to upgrade directly from Windows 7 to Windows 8, from Windows 8 to 8.1, and from Windows 8/8.1 to Windows 10. These in-place upgrades do not delete previous installations, which means the user can retain apps and settings as well as personal files. Other upgrade paths, such as from Windows 7 to Windows 8.1, enable the user to keep personal files but not apps or settings.

The exact upgrade paths between Windows versions vary according to the Windows edition currently in use. You can upgrade to the equivalent or better edition of Windows but not a lower edition. For example, you can upgrade from Windows 7 Professional or Ultimate to Windows 8 Pro but not to Windows 8 Home or from Windows 8 Pro to Windows 8.1 Pro but not to Home. The 32-bit versions can upgrade to 32-bit versions only; 64-bit versions can upgrade to 64-bit versions only.

Clean Install

Before starting a clean install process, check the following:

- Make sure the drive for installation is placed before the hard drive in the boot sequence. The system needs to boot from the Windows distribution media if you are installing to an empty hard drive. You can perform a clean install of Windows from within an older version of Windows if you want to replace the older installation.

- If you will be installing to a drive that might require additional drivers (SATA, RAID, or third-party host adapters on the motherboard or in an expansion slot), have the drivers available on any type of removable media supported by the system.

- If you are installing from optical media, from a disk image (ISO or VXD), or within a virtual machine (VM), after restarting the system with the CD or DVD media or image file in place, press a key when prompted to boot.

During the installation process, be prepared to confirm, enter, select, or provide the following settings, information, media, or options when prompted:

- **Custom installation:** Choose this option if performing a "clean boot" installation to an unused portion of the hard drive or wiping out the existing installation rather than upgrading it.

- **Edition of Windows you are installing:** If the incorrect version is entered, the installation cannot be activated.

- **Location (home, work/office, or public):** The location information is used to configure Windows Firewall.

- **Network settings:** These settings are normally detected automatically for a wired connection. If your connection is wireless, make sure the SSID and password (encryption key) are available.

- **Partition location, partition type, and file system:** See the section "Partitioning Overview," later in this chapter, for details.

- **Password and password hint:** Windows prompts for a password, but only Windows 7 and newer versions also prompt for a password hint.

- **Product key:** Some installations allow skipping this temporarily, but it must be provided it before you can activate Windows.

- **Time, date, language, and region:** See the section "Time/Date/Language/Region Settings," later in this chapter, for details.

- **Time zone, time, and date:** These settings are normally detected automatically but can be manually set here.

- **Username and company name:** The company name is optional.

- **Workgroup or domain name:** A group of computers with common access to files and centralized administration and authentication.

> **NOTE**   The settings in this list are in alphabetical order. Operating systems prompt for this information at different points in the installation process.

At the end of the process, remove the distribution media, and Windows is ready to download the latest updates and service packs.

Multiboot Installation

A multiboot installation of Windows enables a choice between two or more operating systems when you start your computer. Windows 7, Windows 8/8.1, and Windows 10 all support multiboot installations. To use the multiboot support that is built in to Windows, follow these rules:

- **Install the oldest version of Windows first:** For example, if you want to multiboot Windows 8.1 and Windows 10, install Windows 8.1 first.

- **Install Windows on a separate disk partition from the previous operating systems and prepare that partition as a primary partition:** For example, to install Windows 7 and Windows 8.1 to multiboot on a 2TB hard drive, first install Windows 7 to a primary partition that uses only a portion of the disk, and leave the rest of the drive unassigned. When installing Windows 8.1, create a new primary partition on the remainder of the drive and install to that partition.

- **To install multiple editions of Windows for multibooting, ensure that each installation is on its own primary partition:** It is possible to have up to four primary partitions on a hard drive.

- **The Windows multiboot support does not cover non-Windows operating systems such as Linux:** Use a third-part boot manager if you want to multiboot Windows and non-Windows operating systems or if you are installing an older version of Windows to multiboot on a system that already has a newer Windows version installed.

TIP If access is needed to older Windows versions or non-Windows operating systems, use virtualization to avoid rebooting between versions.

Repair Installation

If a Windows operating system installation becomes corrupt, use a repair installation to restore working files and Registry entries without losing existing programs or information. Repair installations are available in Windows 7/8/8.1/10. Make a backup copy of your data files (stored in \Users*Username* for each user of your PC) before performing a repair installation in case of problems.

NOTE The repair installation process is also known as an *in-place upgrade*.

To perform a *repair installation* of Windows 10 with a USB flash drive (which needs to be created before you start this process):

Step 1. Boot the computer normally and sign into the Administrator account. Disable any third-party security software to avoid interruptions of the upgrade.

Step 2. Insert the flash drive and run **setup.exe** to start the setup.

Step 3. When prompted, download and install updates.

Step 4. Accept the end-user licensing agreement. The updates begin.

Step 5. When the updates are ready, click **Install** when prompted.

Step 6. Choose to keep personal files if that is the preference.

Step 7. Let the Windows 10 Setup process run and repair Windows.

The remainder of the installation proceeds as with a normal installation.

Remote Network Installation

A remote network installation (which involves installing Windows from a network drive) begins by starting the computer with a network client and logging on to the server to start the process. To automate the process, Windows 7, 8/8.1, and 10 can all be installed from a network drive automatically by using Windows Deployment Services. Windows Deployment Services is included in newer Windows Server operating systems.

Server-based programs work along with the Microsoft Development Toolkit or Windows System Image Manager program. These programs are used to create an answer file that provides the responses needed for the installation.

Image Deployment

An ***image deployment*** is the process of installing Windows from a disk image of another installation. This process is also called *disk cloning*. You can create a disk image by using a variety of tools, including Acronis True Image (www.acronis.com) and Seagate DiscWizard (which is based in part on Acronis True Image, available from www.seagate.com).

NOTE   It is possible to burn a disc image file, which often has either an .iso or .img filename extension, to a USB flash or recordable CD or DVD by using Windows Disc Image Burner in Windows 7/8/8.1/10.

However, if deploying a disk image to multiple computers, rather than as a backup of a single computer, consider these special issues:

- **Hardware differences:** Traditional image cloning methods, such as those using Acronis True Image, were designed for restoration to identical hardware (that is, the same motherboard, the same mass storage host adapters, the same BIOS configuration, the same Hardware Abstraction Layer [HAL], and the same Ntoskrnl.exe [NT kernel] file). For organizations that have different types and models of computers, this poses a problem.

- **Same security identifier:** A cloned system is identical in every way to the original, including having the same security identifier (SID). This can cause conflicts in a network.

To overcome these problems, use cloning programs designed to capture an image that can be deployed to different types of computers (laptops, desktops, and tablets) with different hardware and software.

For Windows 10, use the System Preparation Tool (Sysprep) to prepare the image for installation over many computers. Sysprep will load files and restart the PC. If you select Generalize in Sysprep, Windows removes unique PC information, including the SID. When the install completes and the computer is restarted, a new SID is generated.

Figure 6-9 shows the Sysprep window and the option to generalize the installation. Note the option to reboot at the end of the process.

FIGURE 6-9 Starting the Sysprep Tool on a Windows 8.1 System

All cloning tools can work with a target drive that is the same size or larger than the original cloned system drive. Some can also work with a smaller drive; check documentation for details.

CAUTION Do not use disk cloning to make illegal copies of Windows. Use disk-cloning software legally to make a backup copy of your installation, and if duplicating the installation on another PC, make sure to clone a system created with a volume license for Windows and make sure that you do not exceed the number of systems covered by that license; alternatively, make sure to use the correct license number (product key) for each duplicate system. For more information about Windows licensing, see https://www.microsoft.com/en-us/licensing/default.aspx.

Recovery Partition

When upgrading Windows or doing a clean install with Windows Setup, a recovery partition is created. The recovery partition is a space that holds the Windows Recovery Environment (WinRE), which can repair some common boot errors. WinRE is built into Windows 10 versions for desktop editions.

Refresh/Restore

If a PC is underperforming or appears to be somehow infected by a virus, it may be a good idea to reset the PC back to the factory default settings. Resetting a PC in Windows 8 and 10 is a straightforward process. Go to **Settings > Recovery** and click **Get Started** Under Reset This PC. When you click Get Started, you get two choices: Keep My Files and Remove Everything. Keep My Files is for a minor reset; it allows personal files to be kept while removing apps and any settings that have been changed. Remove Everything performs a major reset, removing all files; before you choose this option, you need to back up personal files. Figure 6-10 shows the Recovery page along with the window that appears when you click Get Started.

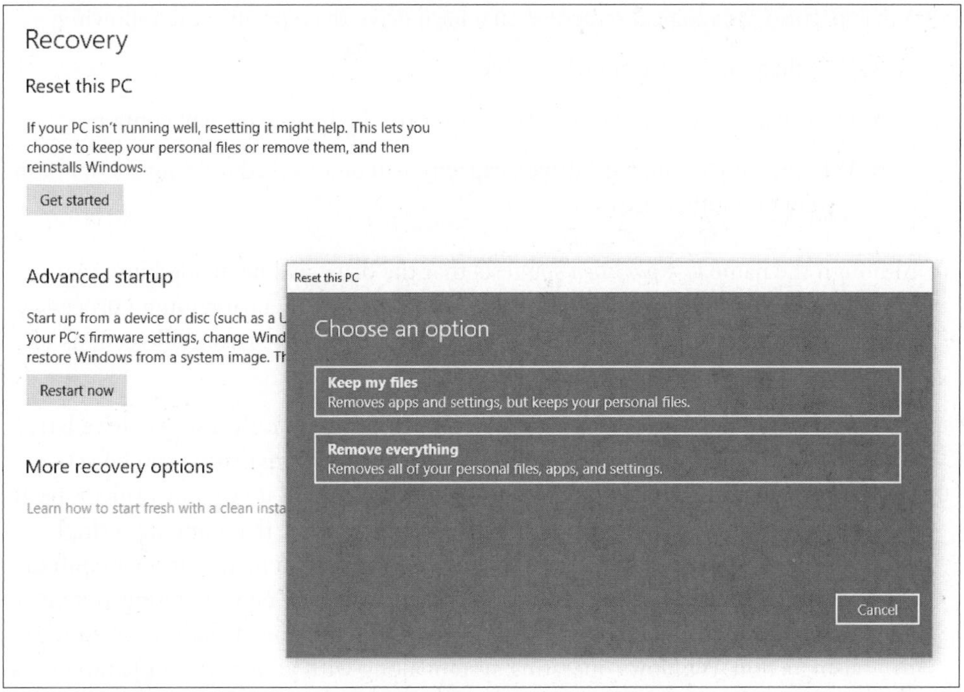

FIGURE 6-10 The Recovery Window and the Reset This PC Window

Partitioning Methods

Whether Windows is being installed to an empty hard drive or to a hard drive that has unassigned space (for multibooting), at least one new hard drive partition must be created. To do this successfully, you need to understand the differences between:

- Master Boot Record (MBR) and GUID Partition Table (GPT) partition tables

- Primary and extended partitions

- Extended partitions and logical disk drives

- Dynamic and basic disks

Partitioning Overview

A hard drive cannot be used until it is prepared for use. There are two steps involved in preparing a hard drive:

Step 1. Create partitions.

Step 2. Format partitions (and assign drive letters).

A disk partition is a logical structure on a hard drive that specifies the following:

- Whether the drive can be bootable

- How many drive letters (one, two, or more) the hard drive will contain

- Whether any of the hard drive's capacity will be reserved for a future operating system or another use

Although the name *disk partition* suggests that the drive will be divided into two or more logical sections, every hard drive must go through a partitioning process, even if you want to use the entire hard drive as a single drive letter. All versions of Windows support two major types of disk partitions:

- **Primary partition:** A *primary partition* can contain only a single drive letter and can be made active (bootable). Only one primary partition can be active. Although a single physical drive using MBR can hold up to four primary partitions, only one primary partition is needed on a drive that contains a single operating system. If installing a new operating system in a multiboot configuration with your current operating system, install the new operating system to a different disk partition than is used for the previous Windows version. If using a non-Windows operating system along with your current operating system, it should be installed into its own primary partition. A drive partitioned using GPT can have up to 128 primary partitions.

NOTE Depending on the layout and contents of your current disk partitions, you might be able to shrink the size of existing partitions with Windows Disk Management to make room for a new primary partition, or you might need to use third-party software such as Acronis Disk Director or EaseUS Partition Master.

- **Extended partition:** An *extended partition* differs from a primary partition in two important ways:

  - An extended partition doesn't get a drive letter but can contain one or more logical drives, each of which is assigned a drive letter.

  - Neither an extended partition nor any drive it contains can be bootable.

Only one extended partition can be stored on each physical drive. Extended partitions are used only with MBR drives.

MBR vs. GPT Partition Types

Master Boot Record (MBR) partitions are supported by classic ROM BIOS as well as UEFI firmware. MBR supports a maximum drive size of 2TB and up to four primary partitions.

A **GPT** (GUID Partition Table) supports drives up to 256TB and up to 128 primary partitions. GPT is also more reliable than MBR because it protects the partition table with replication and cyclic redundancy check (CRC) of the partition table's contents. GPT also provides a standard way for system vendors to create additional partitions. GPT partition tables are supported by UEFI firmware.

To boot from a GPT drive, the system must have a 64-bit version of Windows 7/8/8.1/10. (Newer Windows Server versions also support GPT.) 32-bit versions of Windows can use GPT drives for data.

Disk Preparation Using MBR

If a drive will be used by a single operating system using an MBR partition table, one of these three ways of partitioning the drive will be used:

- **Primary partition occupies 100% of the physical drive's capacity:** This is typically the way the hard drive on a system sold at retail is used and is also the default for disk preparation with Windows. This option is suitable for the only drive in a system or an additional drive that can be used to boot a system but should not be used for additional drives in a system that will be used for data storage.

- **Primary partition occupies a portion of the physical drive's capacity, and the remainder of the drive is occupied by an extended partition:** This enables the operating system to be stored on the primary partition and the applications and data to be stored on one or more separate logical drives (that is, drive letters created inside the extended partition). This is a common setup for laptops but requires the partitioning process to be performed with different settings than the defaults. This configuration is suitable for the only drive or for the first drive in a multiple-drive system.

- **Extended partition occupies 100% of the physical drive's capacity:** The drive letters on the extended partition can be used to store applications or data but not for the operating system. An extended partition cannot be made active (bootable). This configuration is suitable for additional hard drives in a system (not the first drive); an extended partition can contain only one logical drive or multiple logical drives.

You can also leave some unpartitioned space on the hard drive for use later, either for another operating system or for another drive letter.

After a disk is partitioned, the drive letters must be formatted using a supported file system.

Partitioning Using GPT

GPT partitioning creates one or more primary partitions. There are no extended partitions or logical drives on a GPT drive; each partition can be assigned a drive letter. However, only one partition can be active.

Dynamic and Basic Disks

Windows supports two types of disks: *basic* and *dynamic*. A dynamic disk is more versatile than a basic disk because it can span two physical drives into a single logical drive, create striped or mirrored arrays, and adjust the size of a partition. However, during installation, Windows creates only basic disks. Only basic disks can be bootable.

Creating Partitions During Windows 7/8/8.1/10 Installation

When installing Windows 7/8/8.1/10 to an empty hard drive, there is a prompt for a location. To use all the space in the disk, make sure that the desired disk and partition is highlighted and click **Next** (see Figure 6-11).

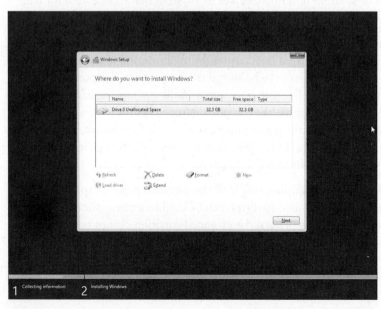

FIGURE 6-11　Example of Using an Entire Disk for a Windows 8.1 Installation

To use only part of the space, click **Drive Options (Advanced)**, click **New**, specify the partition size, and click **Apply**. Windows displays a message that it is creating an additional partition. Click **OK** to clear the message. A system-reserved partition is created, followed by the partition size you selected, which will be used by Windows, and the unused (unallocated) space (see Figure 6-12).

To use an existing partition, highlight the desired partition and click **Next**. Be careful: Whatever partition is selected for the installation will be formatted, and all data on that partition will be erased.

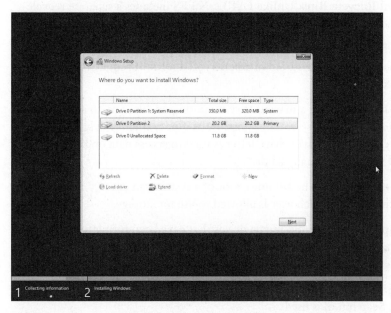

FIGURE 6-12   The Installation Dialog After Specifying Only Part of the Partition Size

File System Types/Formatting

What exactly is a file system? A *file system* determines how data and drives are organized, but it is also a general term for how an operating system stores various types of files. As discussed earlier in this chapter, Windows supports three different file systems for hard drives and USB flash drives: FAT32, NTFS, and exFAT.

NOTE   *CDFS* (Compact Disc File System) is the file system used for CD media.

NTFS

The *New Technology File System* (*NTFS*) is the native file system of Windows 7/8/8.1/10. NTFS has many differences from FAT32, including:

- **Access control:** Different levels of access control, by group or user, can be configured for both folders and individual files.

- **Built-in compression:** Individual files, folders, or an entire drive can be compressed without the use of third-party software.

- **Individual Recycle Bins:** Unlike FAT32, NTFS includes a separate recycle bin for each user.

- **Support for the Encrypting File System (EFS):** *Encrypting File System (EFS)* enables data to be stored in an encrypted form. It requires no password and no access to files!

- **Support for mounting a drive:** Drive mounting enables you to address a removable-media drive's contents, possibly as if its contents are stored on your hard drive. The hard drive's drive letter is used to access data on both the hard drive and the removable media drive.

- **Disk quota support:** The administrator of a system can enforce rules about how much disk space each user is allowed to use for storage.

- **Hot-swapping:** Removable-media drives that have been formatted with NTFS (such as USB) can be connected or removed while the operating system is running.

- **Indexing:** The indexing service helps users locate information more quickly when the Search tool is used.

Follow these steps to determine what file system was used to prepare a Windows hard drive:

Step 1.   Open Windows Explorer or File Explorer.

Step 2.   Right-click the drive letter in the Explorer window and select **Properties**.

The properties sheet for the drive lists NTFS for a drive prepared with NTFS and FAT32 for a drive prepared with FAT32 (see Figure 6-13).

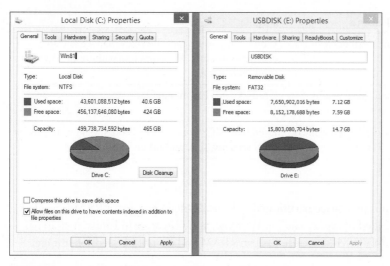

FIGURE 6-13   A Hard Drive Formatted with NTFS Version 5 (Left) and a Flash Memory Drive Formatted with FAT32 (Right)

During installation, Windows 7/8/8.1/10 automatically formats the partitions created by the partition process with NTFS.

exFAT, FAT32, and NTFS are common Windows files systems. Table 6-3 briefly describes these and other file systems that perform the same tasks as these but on different operating systems.

Table 6-3   File System Format Comparison

System Type	Full Name	Details
exFAT	Extended File Allocation Table	Microsoft file system used for flash drives larger than 32GB and files larger than 4GB.
FAT32	File Allocation Table	Format for USB flash drives holding files smaller than 4GB, game consoles, and so on. Works with all operating systems.
NTFS	New Technology File System	Windows default formatting for hard drives. Supports sharing and journaling.
CDFS	Compact Disc File System	Windows legacy format for CDs for storage. Supported by Windows and Linux.
NFS	Network File System	Works independently of the operating system, allowing network user access. It appears local but is a common network drive. Open source.
ext3	Third Extended File System	Linux version of NTFS. Allows journaling of changes to minimize damage if crash occurs. Supports a maximum of 32,000 subdirectories.

System Type	Full Name	Details
ext4	Fourth extended file system	Linux. Supports larger file sizes than ext3. Can disable journaling. Supports a maximum of 64,000 subdirectories.
HFS	Hierarchical File System	Used like NTFS on macOS.
HFS Plus	Extended Hierarchical File System	Used like NTFS on macOS Lion and later. Improves HFS security, size, and other features.

Swap Partition

A swap partition is disk space partitioned to be available in case extra RAM is needed. This feature is called *virtual memory* in Windows and *swap space* in Linux. A swap partition is specially formatted to be used as extra RAM and cannot be used for storage.

Quick Formatting vs. Full Formatting

Quick formatting is an option with all versions of Windows discussed here. With new hard drives or existing drives that are known to be error free, you can use the quick format option to quickly clear the areas of the hard drive that store data location records. With the full format option, Windows must rewrite the disk structures across the entire disk surface. This can take several minutes with today's large hard drives.

NOTE   If concerned about the condition of a used hard drive that is being reused with Windows, use Windows CHKDSK if the drive has been formatted to check its state. The drive vendor's disk diagnostic utility program also verifies the condition of a drive.

Configuring Windows During/After Installation

Some configuration settings for Windows are made during installation and others afterward. The following sections describe the major issues to keep in mind.

Loading Alternative Drivers

If Windows does not detect hard drives during installation, *an alternative third-party driver must be provided*. The most likely situations in which this could occur include when third-party SATA or RAID onboard or add-on card host adapters are used in Windows 7/8/8.1/10.

In Windows 7/8/8.1/10, device drivers are added using the same screen that is used for partitioning and clicking **Load Driver** (refer to Figures 6-11 and 6-12). Device drivers can be installed from CD, DVD, or USB flash drive.

If you click **Load Driver** and cannot supply a proper driver for Windows or if the computer cannot read the media where the driver is stored, you must exit the installation program.

Workgroup vs. Domain Setup

During the installation process, Windows can connect to either a workgroup (the default setting) or to a network managed by a domain controller. Domain controllers are typically used in large networks at workplaces or schools. Home networks and small-office networks use workgroups, and computers running Windows 7 or newer might also belong to a homegroup. During a manual installation, the user is prompted to supply network information. The appropriate network login information should be inserted into automatic setup scripts.

Time/Date/Language/Region Settings

On a new installation, Windows prompts for time, date, language, and region settings early in the installation process. However, in the case of a repair ("in-place upgrade") installation, the settings from the previous Windows installation are used.

Installing Drivers, Software, and Updates

After Windows is installed, it should be updated with the latest drivers, hotfixes, and service packs. For individual PCs, the easiest way to perform these steps is to set up Windows Update for automatic updates.

However, if installing Windows for the first time and if the system or motherboard was supplied with a driver disc, perform driver installation first before running Windows Update. Windows updates can also be performed manually.

Using the Factory Recovery Partition

Most vendors no longer provide a full installation DVD/CD of Windows for computers that have Windows preinstalled. Instead, the ***factory recovery partition*** (a disk partition containing a special recovery image of the Windows installation) is provided. Typically, you are prompted to burn the restore image to one or more DVDs or CDs or a USB flash drive.

NOTE   A factory recovery disc is also known as a *system restoration disc*. Such a version of Windows isn't a standalone copy of Windows; that is, it can't be used to install Windows on another PC (unless the PC is identical to the one for which the disc was made).

Typically, there are limited choices for restoring a damaged installation with a recovery disc or recovery files on a disk partition. Typical options include:

- Reformatting the hard drive and restoring it to just-shipped condition (which causes the loss of all data and programs installed after the system was first used)

- Reinstalling Windows only

- Reinstalling support files or additional software

After running the factory recovery disc to restore your system to its original factory condition, activate the Windows installation again.

CAUTION   You might need the Windows product key or your system's serial number to run the recovery disc program. Keep this information handy. Most systems with preinstalled Windows have a sticker with the Windows license key (product key) somewhere on the system case.

Properly Formatted Boot Drive with Correct Partition

Starting with a new drive or a cleanly formatted drive using the disk setup utility will help you create a reliable drive with correct partitions. Using an old drive is possible, but it should be cleaned of old files first.

Hardware and Application Prerequisites and Compatibility

Before attempting to install any version of any OS, it is important to be sure that the hardware and applications that will be used will work with (that is, are compatible with) the OS. This section briefly describes the process manufacturers use to ensure compliance and the steps PC techs take to make sure products comply.

Prerequisites

When doing a clean install, it is important to make sure your hardware meets the prerequisites for working with the software—usually a minimal amount of RAM and a certain level of processing power. The prerequisites, however, are minimums; not having enough processing power and not having enough RAM are the most common causes of performance issues. Be sure to exceed the minimums so that the OS can smoothly operate.

The following list is a summary of the current requirements for Windows 10:

- **Processor:** 1GHz (gigahertz) or faster processor or System on a Chip (SoC)

- **RAM:** 1GB (gigabyte) for 32-bit OS or 2GB for 64-bit OS

- **Hard drive space:** 16GB for 32-bit OS or 32GB for 64-bit OS

- **Graphics card:** DirectX 9 or later with WDDM 1.0 driver

- **Display:** 800×600

- **Internet Connection:** Internet connectivity to perform updates and to take advantage of some features

Anything below these recommendations will likely result in a difficult install and poor performance. Upgrading to these standards or above is highly recommended.

Windows Compatibility Program

Manufacturers have an interest in making sure their products will be usable by the world's largest OS audience, so they design their products to comply with the Windows Compatibility Program standards. This allows them to test their hardware and software products to ensure that they will work when the customer buys and installs them.

Hardware and Application Compatibility

For a consumer, the easiest way to check for compatibility with a Windows OS is to consult Microsoft. For many years, Microsoft has maintained the Hardware Compatibility List (HCL), also called the Windows Compatibility Product List, Windows Catalogue, or Windows Logo'd Product List (Windows 7). The HCL provides information about manufactures and drivers that can be used (or not used) with Windows. With Windows 10, most previous equipment should run. The Microsoft Hardware Compatibility Checker matches compatible products for Windows and macOS (see https://www.microsoft.com/accessories/en-us/support/compatibility).

Most popular manufacturers submit drivers to Windows to allow for plug-and-play capability, but drivers usually need to be updated at some point in the device life cycle. Whenever installing a device or an application, it is wise to check with the manufacturer's website for the latest update.

A program is written to work on a certain OS, and with each OS upgrade comes the possibility that a program will running poorly or not at all. If running programs written for previous versions of Windows, the compatibility with Windows 10 can be checked with the Compatibility Troubleshooter tool. In Windows Explorer, right-click the program to be run and select **Properties**. Select the **Compatibility** tab, check **Run This Program in Compatibility Mode**, and select the OS previously used.

Another option in Windows 10 is to type **Run Programs** in the search bar and then select **Run Programs Created for Previous Versions of Windows**.

Command Line Tools

220-1002: Objective 1.4: Given a scenario, use appropriate Microsoft command line tools.

Windows has a number of command line tools for system operation and management. While it also has many administrative tools that offer graphical interfaces for managing performance and troubleshooting, mastery of these commands will make the common tasks much more efficient.

Starting a Command Prompt Session with CMD.EXE

Although most computer users don't use the command prompt often, technicians use it to:

- Recover data from systems that can't boot normally
- Reinstall lost or corrupted system files
- Print file listings (which can't be done in Windows Explorer, File Explorer, This PC, or Computer)
- Copy, move, and delete data
- Display or configure certain operating system settings

You can start a command prompt session in Windows by clicking the **Command Prompt** option in the **Start** menu. However, other methods can be faster.

In Windows 8/8.1 (and also 10), press **Windows+X** and then click or tap **Command Prompt** to run in standard mode. Click or tap **Command Prompt (Admin)** to run in elevated mode (that is, run as administrator). See Figure 6-14.

1. Windows key+X

2. Select the command prompt mode desired

FIGURE 6-14 Starting a Command Prompt from the Windows+X Menu in Windows 8/8.1

Figure 6-15 shows a typical command prompt session in Windows 10.

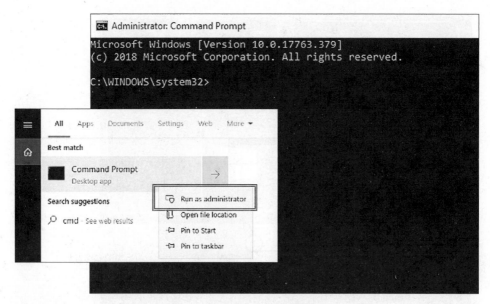

FIGURE 6-15   Windows 10 Command Prompt Window

Figure 6-16 shows the **help** command being used to view a list of command prompt commands.

TIP   To get help for any command prompt function or program, type the command name followed by /?. For example, type **DIR /?** to see help for the DIR command.

```
C:\Windows\system32\cmd.exe

C:\Users\Marcus>help
For more information on a specific command, type HELP command-name
ASSOC        Displays or modifies file extension associations.
ATTRIB       Displays or changes file attributes.
BREAK        Sets or clears extended CTRL+C checking.
BCDEDIT      Sets properties in boot database to control boot loading.
CACLS        Displays or modifies access control lists (ACLs) of files.
CALL         Calls one batch program from another.
CD           Displays the name of or changes the current directory.
CHCP         Displays or sets the active code page number.
CHDIR        Displays the name of or changes the current directory.
CHKDSK       Checks a disk and displays a status report.
CHKNTFS      Displays or modifies the checking of disk at boot time.
CLS          Clears the screen.
CMD          Starts a new instance of the Windows command interpreter.
COLOR        Sets the default console foreground and background colors.
COMP         Compares the contents of two files or sets of files.
COMPACT      Displays or alters the compression of files on NTFS partitions.
CONVERT      Converts FAT volumes to NTFS.  You cannot convert the
             current drive.
COPY         Copies one or more files to another location.
DATE         Displays or sets the date.
DEL          Deletes one or more files.
DIR          Displays a list of files and subdirectories in a directory.
DISKCOMP     Compares the contents of two floppy disks.
DISKCOPY     Copies the contents of one floppy disk to another.
DISKPART     Displays or configures Disk Partition properties.
DOSKEY       Edits command lines, recalls Windows commands, and
             creates macros.
DRIVERQUERY  Displays current device driver status and properties.
ECHO         Displays messages, or turns command echoing on or off.
ENDLOCAL     Ends localization of environment changes in a batch file.
ERASE        Deletes one or more files.
EXIT         Quits the CMD.EXE program (command interpreter).
```

FIGURE 6-16   Using the **help** Command to View a List of Command Prompt Commands

Commands Available with Standard Privileges vs. Administrative Privileges

Most of the commands shown in Table 6-4 can be run with **standard privileges** (by any user). However, some commands can be run only with **administrative privileges** in what is known as *elevated mode* or *administrative mode*. Elevated commands can make more operational changes to the PC than can basic commands.

To run an elevated command, mouse over an application, such as the Command Prompt shortcut (as shown in Figure 6-17), and select **Run as Administrator**. The Administrator Command Prompt window opens.

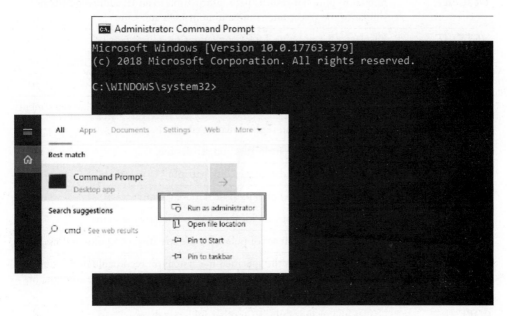

FIGURE 6-17   Selecting Run as Administrator Allows Elevated Commands

Windows Commands

Table 6-4 lists the basic commands and their uses. Commands are listed here in all caps, but Windows allows you to enter them in lowercase, uppercase, or mixed case. Open a command prompt and try out these commands as a preparation for the exam. They are described further after the table.

Table 6-4   Windows Command Prompt Commands

Command	Use
DIR	Displays list of the current folder's files and subfolders
CD (CHDIR)	Changes the working directory
CD ..	Navigates to the previous directory
IPCONFIG	Displays TCP/IP network information on the device
PING	Sends IP packets to check network connectivity
TRACERT	Similar to ping but returns path information to an IP address destination; similar to the traceroute command in macOS and Linux
NETSTAT	Displays a list of active TCP connections on a local network
NSLOOKUP	Gathers the network's Domain Name System (DNS) information
SHUTDOWN	Shuts down the computer
DISM	Services images; stands for Deployment Image Servicing and Management
*SFC**	Scans system files and replaces damaged or missing files
*CHKDSK**	Scans specified drive for errors and repairs them
*DISKPART**	Creates, removes, and manages disk partitions
TASKKILL	Stops specified task(s) on a local or remote computer
GPUPDATE	Refreshes group policy on local or Active Directory systems
GPRESULT	Displays the resultant set of policy for the specified computer and user
FORMAT	Creates or re-creates the specified file system on recordable or rewritable storage (magnetic, flash, or optical media) and overwrites the contents of the drive
COPY	Copies one or more files to another folder or drive
XCOPY	Copies one or more files and folders to another folder or drive
ROBOCOPY	Copies or moves files/folders; can be configured via various optional GUIs
NET USE	Connects to shared folders; similar to mapping a network drive
NET USER	Manages user accounts (add, remove, change)
[Command]/?	Displays help for the specified command

* This command must be run in elevated mode (administrative mode or run as administrator).

> **NOTE**   In this chapter and throughout this book, "Windows" refers to Windows 7 and 8/8.1/10. Specific Windows versions are listed only if a command is not available or has different syntax in different versions of Windows.

FORMAT

In Windows, the FORMAT command is used primarily to create or re-create the specified file system on recordable or rewritable storage (magnetic, flash, or optical media). In the process, the contents of the drive are overwritten.

FORMAT appears to "destroy" the previous contents of magnetic storage (such as a hard disk), but if FORMAT is used on a hard disk by mistake, third-party data recovery programs can be used to retrieve data from the drive. This is possible because most of the disk surface is not changed by FORMAT when a quick format option is selected.

Windows overwrites the entire surface of a disk with zeros if the quick FORMAT option is not selected. If the Quick Format or Safe Format option is used, the contents of the disk are marked for deletion but can be retrieved with third-party data recovery software.

NOTE The hard-disk format process performed by the FORMAT command (which creates the file system) is sometimes referred to as a *standard format* to distinguish it from the *low-level format* used by hard drive manufacturers to set up magnetic structures on the hard drive.

Using FORMAT with USB Flash and Removable-Media Drives

Although USB flash memory drives and removable-media drives are preformatted at the factory, FORMAT is still useful as a means to erase the contents of a disk quickly, especially if it contains many files or folders. It also places new sector markings across the disk.

Formatting Drives with Windows Explorer and File Explorer

Use Windows File Explorer/This PC (8/8.1/10) to format all types of drives. Right-click the drive you want to format and select **Format**. The Format options for Windows appear, as shown in Figure 6-18. The Format tool is also available in Disk Management.

Windows also offers the exFAT (FAT64) file system option for hard disks and high-capacity flash drives. Windows 7 does not offer the compression option on the Format menu, but if you want to compress a drive after formatting it, you can do so from the General tab of the drive's properties sheet.

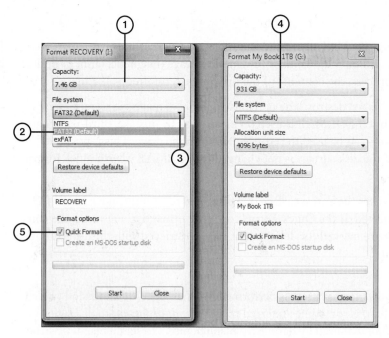

1. Flash drive capacity
2. FAT32 is default file system
3. Click or tap to see other file system options (NTFS, exFAT)
4. Hard disk capacity
5. Click or tap to clear checkbox for Quick format

FIGURE 6-18   The Format Menu for a Flash Drive (Left) and for a Hard Disk (Right)

Using FORMAT from the Command Prompt

The FORMAT command overwrites the current contents of the target drive unless the **/Q** (Quick Format) option is used. When **/Q** is used, only the file allocation table and root folder are overwritten. To retrieve data from a drive that has been formatted, you must use third-party data-recovery software.

FORMAT includes a variety of options for use with hard disks, removable media and optical drives, and USB flash memory drives. The most useful examples include:

- **FORMAT F: /FS:exFAT** formats drive F: using the exFAT file system.

- **FORMAT F: /Q** performs a quick format on drive F:.

To see the additional options for FORMAT, use **FORMAT /?.**

Note that the FAT and FAT32 file systems impose the following restrictions on the number of clusters on a volume:

- **FAT:** Number of clusters ≤ 65,526

- **FAT32:** 65,526 < Number of clusters < 4,177,918

FORMAT immediately stops processing if it decides that the preceding requirements cannot be met using the specified cluster size. NTFS compression is not supported for allocation unit sizes above 4,096.

COPY

The COPY command copies files from one drive and folder to another folder and drive. The folder specified by COPY must already exist on the target drive. COPY does not work with files that have the system or hidden file attributes; to copy these files, use XCOPY or ROBOCOPY instead.

The syntax for COPY in Windows is:

COPY [/D] [/V] [/N] [/Y | /-Y] [/Z] [/L] [/A | /B] source [/A | /B]

[+ *source* [/A | /B] [+ ...]] [*destination* [/A | /B]]

Examples include:

- **COPY *.* F:** copies all files in the current folder to the current folder on the F: drive.

- **COPY *.TXT C:\Users*Username*** copies all .txt files in the current folder to the *Username* folder on the C: drive.

- **COPY C:\WINDOWS\TEMP*.BAK** copies all *.bak files in the \Windows\Temp folder on drive C: to the current folder.

- **COPY C:\WINDOWS*.BMP D:** copies all .bmp files in the \Windows folder on drive C: to the current folder on drive D:.

To see a list of all the options for COPY, use **COPY /?**.

XCOPY

The XCOPY command can be used in place of COPY in most cases and has the following advantages:

- **Provides faster operation on a group of files:** XCOPY reads the specified files into conventional RAM before copying them to their destination.

- **Creates folders as needed:** If you specify the destination folder name in the XCOPY command line, the destination folder will be created if needed.

- **Operates as backup utility:** Can be used to change the archive bit from on to off on files to allow XCOPY to be used in place of commercial backup programs.

- **Copies files changed or created on or after a specified date:** This is useful when using XCOPY as a substitute for commercial backup programs.

XCOPY can be used to "clone" an entire drive's contents to another drive. For example, the following copies the entire contents of the D: drive to the H: drive:

XCOPY D:\ H:\ /H /S /E /K /C /R

This command copies all files from drive D:'s root folder (root directory) and sub-folders to drive H:'s root folder and subfolder, including system and hidden files, empty folders and subfolders, and file attributes. This process continues even if errors are detected, and it overwrites read-only files.

To see a list of all the options for XCOPY, use **XCOPY /?**.

ROBOCOPY

ROBOCOPY is a robust file-copying Windows utility that can be used in place of XCOPY. ROBOCOPY has several advantages over XCOPY, including the capability to tolerate pauses in network connections, to mirror the contents of the source and destination folders by removing files as well as copying files, to perform multi-threaded copies for faster copying on multicore PCs, to log copy processes, and to list or copy files matching specified criteria including minimum file size.

The syntax for ROBOCOPY for Windows is available from https://technet.microsoft.com/en-us/library/cc733145.aspx. Let's look at two examples of what you can do with ROBOCOPY.

To copy files in *sourcefolder* that are at least 16MB (16,777,216 bytes) in size to *targetfolder*:

ROBOCOPY C:*SOURCEFOLDER* D:*TARGETFOLDER* /MIN:16777216

Add the **/L** option to the end of this command to list the files that would be copied.

To mirror a local folder to a network folder with tweaks for more reliable operation and omit hidden files (/XA:H), use:

ROBOCOPY \\SOURCESERVER\SHARE \\DESTINATIONSERVER
SHARE /MIR /FFT /Z /XA:H /W:5

/FFT uses the two-second rule for comparing files, which can prevent recopying of files that are unchanged but that have a time stamp that's off by a second or two from the destination's version; /W:5 changes the wait time between retries from the default of 30 seconds to 5 seconds.

These examples were adapted from the excellent TechNet Wiki posting "Robocopy and a Few Examples," available at https://social.technet.microsoft.com/wiki/ contents/articles/1073.robocopy-and-a-few-examples.aspx.

As you can see from these examples, ROBOCOPY uses much different syntax than XCOPY and, for those who used ROBOCOPY in Windows XP or older versions, keep in mind that ROBOCOPY has had syntax changes over its different versions. For these reasons, you might prefer to run it by means of a GUI, such as the ROBOCOPY GUI available at https://docs.microsoft.com/en-us/previous-versions/ technet-magazine/cc160891(v=msdn.10) or third-party GUIs available online.

DISKPART

DISKPART is a disk management program included in Windows. It can be used to perform disk partitioning and management commands that are not included in Computer Management's Disk Management module.

When you run DISKPART, a new window opens with a DISKPART> prompt. Only DISKPART commands can be entered in this window. For a full list of DISKPART commands, use **DISKPART /?**.

Figure 6-19 demonstrates two DISKPART commands: SELECT DISK *X* and DETAIL DISK. In this example, DISKPART shows that the selected disk drive is the boot drive, contains the pagefile, and is used to store crashdump information.

FIGURE 6-19   Using DISKPART to Determine Details About the Selected Disk

SFC

System File Checker (SFC) is a Windows utility that checks protected system files (files such as .dll, .sys, .ocx, and .exe files, as well as some font files used by the Windows desktop) and replaces incorrect versions or missing files with the correct files.

Use SFC to fix problems with Internet Explorer or other built-in Windows programs caused by the installation of obsolete Windows system files, user error, deliberate erasure, virus or Trojan horse infections, and similar problems.

To run SFC, open the command prompt in elevated mode (that is, run as administrator) and type **SFC** with the appropriate switch. A typical option is SFC /scannow, which scans all protected files immediately (see Figure 6-20).

FIGURE 6-20   SFC /scannow Reports That Corrupt Files Were Repaired (Windows 7)

Another option is SFC /scanonce, which scans all protected files at the next boot. If SFC finds that some files are missing and replacement files are not available on your system, you are prompted to reinsert your Windows distribution disc so that the files can be copied to the DLL cache. Other options include /scanboot, which scans all protected files every time the system starts; /revert, which returns the scan setting to the default; and /purgecache and /cachesize=x, which enable a user to delete the file cache and modify its size.

If errors are detected, they are logged in the CBS.log file, found in %WinDir%\Logs\CBS\.

To read the contents of CBS.log, you can use the **findstr** command, which sends the details to a separate file called sfcdetails.txt.

For more information about using SFC and findstr, and to learn how to replace corrupted system files manually if SFC is not able to do it, see https://support.microsoft.com/en-us/kb/929833.

CHKDSK

CHKDSK is a command line tool for checking disk drives (other than optical drives) for errors and optionally repairing those errors. It must be run in elevated mode (that is, run as administrator). Note that some commands differ depending on the file system (FAT/FAT32 or NTFS) of the target drive. The syntax of the CHKDSK command is as follows:

CHKDSK [*volume*[[*path*]*filename*]]] [/F] [/V] [/R] [/X] [/I] [/C] [/L[:size]] [/B]

Consider these examples:

- **CHKDSK /F** scans for and fixes errors on the current drive.

- **CHKDSK F: /F** scans for and fixes errors on drive F:.

If CHKDSK /F is run on the system drive, the following message appears:

The type of the file system is NTFS.

Cannot lock current drive.

Chkdsk cannot run because the volume is in use by another

process. Would you like to schedule this volume to be

checked the next time the system restarts? (Y/N)

If you answer **Y**, CHKDSK runs before the Windows desktop appears and displays a message in the notification area about the condition of the drive. If CHKDSK /F is run on a non-system drive, it runs immediately.

For a complete list of CHKDSK options, use **CHKDSK /?**.

GPUPDATE

GPUPDATE is used to update the group policy on a local or remote computer. Its syntax is as follows:

GPUPDATE [**/Target:{***Computer* | *User*}] [**/Force**] [**/Wait:<***value***>**]

[**/Logoff**] [**/Boot**] [**/Sync**]

You could, for example, use this command to refresh the group policy on a specified computer called *AccountingPC* and reboot that computer after the processing is complete:

GPUPDATE /target:accountingpc /boot

For a complete list of options for the GPUDATE command, use **GPUPDATE /?**.

GPRESULT

Use GPRESULT to display the current policy for a specified user and computer. Its syntax is as follows:

GPRESULT [/S system [/U *username* [/P [*password*]]]] [/SCOPE scope]
[/USER *targetusername*] [/R | /V | /Z] [(/X | /H) <*filename*> [/F]]

For a complete list of options for the GPRESULT command, use **GPRESULT /?**.

Consider these examples:

- **GPRESULT /R** displays summary data.

- **GPRESULT /H GPReport.html** saves report as GPReport.html.

- **GPRESULT /USER *targetusername* /V** provides verbose information for the specified username.

Operating System Features and Tools

220-1002: Objective 1.5: Given a scenario, use Microsoft operating system features and tools.

Many administrative Windows tools provide graphical interfaces for managing performance and troubleshooting. Mastery of these tools make common tasks much more efficient.

Microsoft Administrative Tools

Windows offers a number of administrative tools and features designed to help you manage operations and users. The following sections discuss many of these components, including:

- Computer Management

- Local Security Policy

- Performance Monitor

- Services

- System Configuration

- Task Scheduler

- Component Services

- Print Management

- Windows Memory Diagnostic

- Windows Defender Firewall with Advanced Security
- Event Viewer

The following tools are administrative tools but are found under Computer Management (Windows 10):

- Device Manager
- Local Users and Groups
- Data Sources
- User Account Management

NOTE   User Account Management is discussed in depth in Chapter 7.

To start any of the administrative tools:

Step 1.   Open **Control Panel**.

Step 2.   Open the **System and Security** category.

Step 3.   Click or tap **Administrative Tools**.

Step 4.   Click or tap the tool you want to use.

NOTE   For Windows 10, the simplest way to access any of these tools is type its name in the search window.

Computer Management: Microsoft Management Console (MMC)

Instead of hunting around for different utilities in different places in Windows, it's simpler to use the Computer Management console window because it has most of the tools you need in one organized window system. How you open Computer Management depends on the Windows version.

In Windows 7, use one of the following:

- Click **Start**, right-click **Computer/My Computer**, and select **Manage**.
- Navigate to **Start > All Programs > Administrative Tools > Computer Management**.
- Open the **Run** prompt (**Windows+R**) and type **compmgmt.msc**.

In Windows 8/8.1/10: Press **Windows+X** and select **Computer Management** from the menu. In Computer Management, select **Event Viewer > Device Manager > Local Users and Groups > Services > Disk Management**. If you select **Disk Management** in the left pane, you see display volume and disk information in the right pane.

Computer Management is an example of the ***Microsoft Management Console*** (***MMC***), which is a blank console that uses various snap-in console windows. MMC saves the consoles you snap in and remembers the last place you were working, which makes it a valuable and time-saving tool.

To open the MMC, click the Search box (Windows 7) or press **Windows+R**, select **Run** (Windows 8/8.1/10), and type **MMC**. A new blank MMC appears. Then, to add the console windows, go to **File > Add/Remove Snap-in** (or press **Ctrl+M**). From there, click the **Add** button to select the desired console, such as Computer Management, Performance Logs and Alerts, or ActiveX Controls.

When you're finished using it, save the MMC and consider adding it as a shortcut within the desktop or in the Quick Launch area and maybe add a keyboard shortcut to open it. The MMC remembers all the console windows added and starts you at the location used when the program was closed. MMC version 3.0 is used with Windows 7/8/8.1/10.

Local Security Policy

Local Security Policy is a Microsoft Management Console snap-in you can use to view and set security policies for the local system or a system on a workgroup network. To select a setting for a policy, open the category in the left pane, scroll to the policy in the right pane, and select the setting desired.

For example, to set up an account lockout policy, expand Account Policies and click Account Lockout Policy in the left pane. In the right pane, select a value for Account Lockout Threshold to specify the number of invalid login attempts allowed. Then specify a lockout duration and other settings, as desired.

Performance Monitor

The Windows ***Performance Monitor*** can be used for real-time performance monitoring or to record performance over time.

To access Performance Monitor in Windows 7/8/8.1, open the **Run** prompt, type **perfmon.exe**, and press **Enter**. In Windows 10, search for Performance Monitor (just type **perfmon**) in the search box and then click the **Performance Monitor** node.

Many different types of performance factors can be measured. You can measure objects, including physical devices, such as the processor and memory, and software, such as protocols and services. These objects are measured with counters. For example, a common counter for the processor is % Processor Time.

To see whether additional RAM is needed in a system, for example, select the object called Paging File; then select the counters % Usage and Pages/Sec, as described in the following steps:

Step 1.   Click the **+** sign or right-click in the table beneath the graph and select **Add Counters**.

Step 2.   Select **Paging File** as the performance object and then choose **% Usage**.

Step 3.   Click **Add**.

Step 4.   Select **Memory** as the performance object and then choose **Pages/Sec** from the drop-down menu.

Step 5.   Click **Add**.

Step 6.   Click **OK** and then run normal applications for this computer.

If the Performance Monitor/System Monitor indicates that the Paging File % Usage counter is consistently near 100% or the Memory Pages/Sec counter is consistently higher than 5, add RAM to improve performance. Figure 6-21 shows an example of inadequate memory in Windows 7's Performance Monitor.

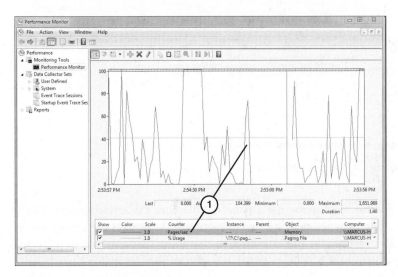

1. **High memory pages/sec levels**

FIGURE 6-21   A Windows 7 System That Needs More RAM for the Programs It Is Running, as Indicated by the High Levels of the Memory Pages/Sec Counters

Services (Services.msc)

Many of the core functions of Windows are implemented as services, including features such as the print spooler, wireless network configuration, DHCP client service, and many more. Services can be run automatically or manually and are controlled through the Services node of the Computer Management Console.

You can also access the Services dialog (shown in Figure 6-22) from the Services applet in Control Panel's Administrative Tools folder or by running **Services.msc** from the Run dialog. The Services dialog lists each service by name; and provides a description, status message, and startup type; and indicates whether the service is for a local system or network service.

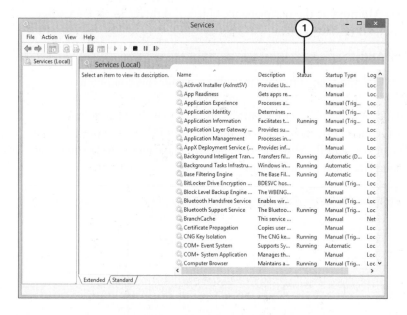

1. Use the Status column to determine if a service is running

FIGURE 6-22   The Services Dialog in Windows 8.1

To view the properties for a particular service, double-click the service listing. The General tab of the properties sheet, shown in Figure 6-23, displays the service name, description, path to executable file, startup type, and status. You can also stop, pause, or resume a service from this dialog, as well as from the Services dialog.

Use the Log On tab if you need to configure the service to run for a specific user, the Recovery tab to specify what to do if the service fails, and the Dependencies tab to see what other services work with the specified service.

If a system cannot perform a task that uses a service, go to the Services dialog and restart the service. If a service prevents another task from running (for example, if a third-party wireless network client does not run because the Windows WLAN Autoconfig service is running), go to the Services dialog and stop the service.

FIGURE 6-23   Viewing the General Tab for the Print Spooler Service

System Configuration Utility

Use the *System Configuration* utility (*MSCONFIG.exe*) to configure how Windows starts, to choose startup programs and services, and to change the boot procedure. System Configuration is discussed in detail later in this chapter, in the section "MSCONFIG."

Task Scheduler

Windows uses *Task Scheduler* to run a task on a specified schedule.

To create a basic task in Windows, follow this procedure:

Step 1.   Open **Control Panel** in Small Icons or Large Icons mode.

Step 2.   Open the **Administrative Tools** folder.

Step 3.   Double-click **Task Scheduler**.

> **NOTE**   You can also run Task Scheduler from the Run or Search box by entering **taskschd.msc**.

Step 4.   Click **Create Basic Task** in the Actions menu.

Step 5.   Enter a name and a description for the task and click **Next**.

Step 6.   Select an interval (for example, daily, weekly, monthly, one-time only, when my computer starts, when I log on, or when a specific event is logged) and click **Next**.

Step 7.   Specify when to start the task and the recurrence and whether to synchronize across time zones and then click **Next**.

Step 8.   Specify to start a program (or send an email or display a message) and click **Next**.

Step 9.   Select a program or script to run, add options (arguments), and specify where to start the program or script. Click **Next**.

Step 10.   Review the settings for the task (see Figure 6-24) and click **Finish**.

The task is saved in the Task Scheduler library (see Figure 6-25). Tasks can be edited or deleted in this folder as needed.

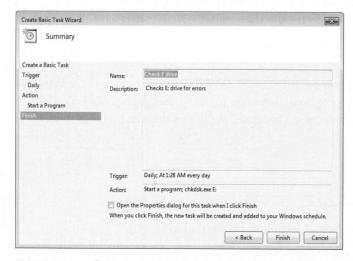

FIGURE 6-24   Reviewing a Disk Check Task Created with the Windows 7 Task Scheduler

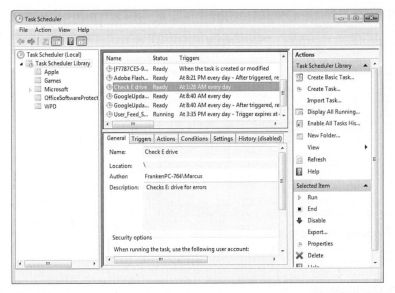

FIGURE 6-25   The Windows 7 Task Scheduler Library After a New Task Is Added

Component Services

Developers and administrators use the ***Component Services*** MMC snap-in to manage the Component Object Model (COM), COM+ applications, and the Distributed Transaction Coordinator (DTC).

Data Sources (ODBC)

The ODBC Data Source Administrator is used to list and manage data sources and drivers. 64-bit versions of Windows include both 64-bit and 32-bit versions. Data sources are listed by user, system, and file, and the Data Source Administrator also lists drivers and provides options for tracing and pooling data sources.

Print Management

Print Management is a utility for managing printers connected to the computer or on a network. To start Print Management, open the Administrative Tools folder in Control Panel and double-click **Print Management**. The Print Management console opens (see Figure 6-26). From it, you can view print servers and connected printers, manage jobs, manage printer ports and forms, and perform other tasks.

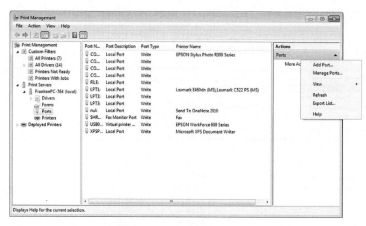

FIGURE 6-26   The Windows Print Management Console

Windows Memory Diagnostics

The *Windows Memory Diagnostics* tool tests system and cache memory before the Windows desktop is loaded. The user can select the type of test and number of test repetitions to perform (see Figure 6-27). The results are displayed in a pop-up message from the taskbar after the Windows desktop reloads.

To launch the Windows Memory Diagnostics tool in Windows 10, type **Windows memory diagnostics** and select the link. It can also be started by pressing **Windows+R** and typing **mdsched.exe**. A reboot is required to perform the test.

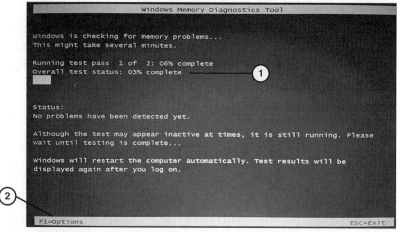

1. Test status
2. Press the F1 key to change test options

FIGURE 6-27   Windows Memory Diagnostics Testing a System Running Windows 8.1

Windows Firewall

Windows Firewall is a security application that is included in Windows. It has improved with each OS version and in Windows 10 is called Windows Defender Firewall. It can block unwanted traffic going into or out of the computer. Figure 6-28 depicts how settings are configured in the default and advanced modes.

NOTE Windows Defender is discussed in more detail in Chapter 7.

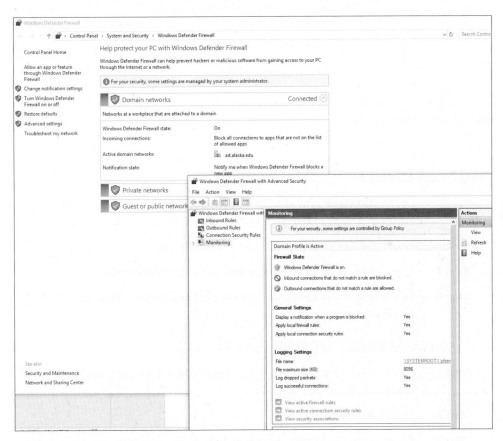

FIGURE 6-28   Windows Defender Firewall

Event Viewer

The *Event Viewer* allows an administrator to track and log event logins, security actions, crashes, and other events that have happened in the computer. Figure 6-29 shows an example of the events tracked in the Event Viewer for Windows 10.

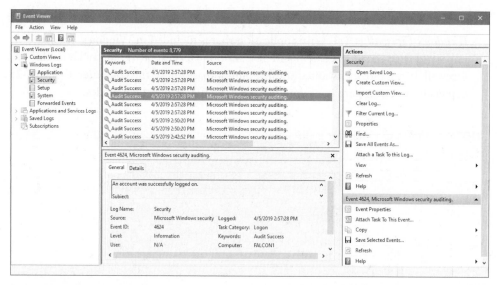

FIGURE 6-29   Event Viewer

Using Device Manager

Windows ***Device Manager*** is used to display installed device categories and specific installed devices, as well as to troubleshoot problems with devices.

To start Device Manager in Windows 7, follow these steps:

Step 1.   Click **Start**, right-click **Computer**, and select **Properties**.

Step 2.   In the System window that appears, click the **Device Manager** link on the left side, under Tasks.

To start Device Manager in Windows 8/8.1/10

Step 1.   Open the charms menu and click **Search** (8/8.1) or click the Search window (10).

Step 2.   Search for **Device Manager**.

Step 3.   Click or tap the **Device Manager** link.

Alternatively:

Step 1.   Press **Windows+X**.

Step 2.   Click or tap **Device Manager**.

To view the devices in a specific category, click the plus (+) sign next to the category name, as shown in Figure 6-30. If a particular category contains a device with problems, the category automatically opens when you start Device Manager.

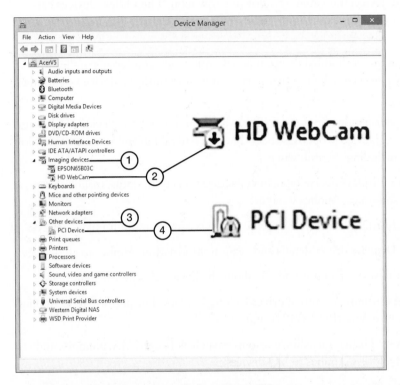

1. Imaging devices category has a device with a problem
2. The HD webcam has been disabled
3. Other devices category is used for unidentified devices
4. An unidentified device

FIGURE 6-30   Device Manager with Selected Categories Expanded

NOTE   Different systems have different categories listed in Device Manager because Device Manager lists only categories for installed hardware. For example, the system shown in Figure 6-30 is a laptop, so it has a Batteries category.

If a computer has devices that are malfunctioning in a way that Device Manager can detect, or if it has devices that are disabled, they are displayed as soon as you open Device Manager. For example, in Figure 6-30, the Imaging Devices category lists a disabled device, indicated by a down-arrow icon. The Other Devices category lists a device that cannot run, indicated by an exclamation point (!) in a yellow triangle.

If a malfunctioning or disabled device is an I/O port, such as a serial, parallel, or USB port, any device attached to that port cannot work until the device is working properly.

To see more information about a specific device, double-click the device to open its properties sheet. Device properties sheets have a General tab and some combination of other tabs, including the following:

- **General:** Displays device type, manufacturer, location, status, troubleshoot button, and usage. Applies to all devices.

- **Properties:** Displays device-specific settings. Applies to multimedia devices.

- **Driver:** Displays driver details and version information. Applies to all devices.

- **Details:** Displays technical details about the device. Applies to all devices.

- **Policies:** Optimizes external drives for quick removal or performance. Applies to USB, FireWire (IEEE 1394), and eSATA drives.

- **Resources:** Displays hardware resources such as IRQ, DMA, memory, and I/O port address. Applies to I/O devices.

- **Volumes:** Displays drive information such as status, type, and capacity. Click **Populate** to retrieve information. Applies to hard disk drives.

- **Power:** Displays the power available per port. Applies to USB root hubs and generic hubs.

- **Power Management:** Specifies device-specific power management settings. Applies to USB, network, keyboard, and mouse devices.

Figure 6-31 illustrates some of these tabs.

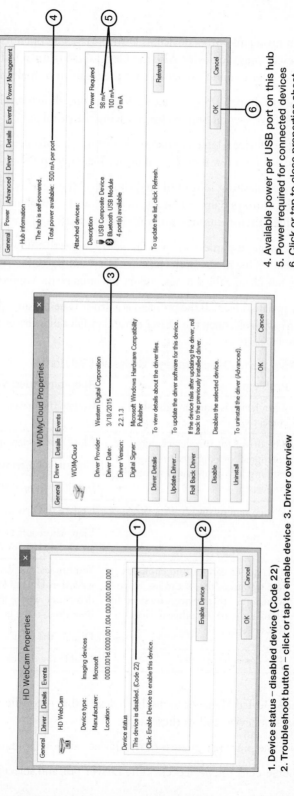

FIGURE 6-31 Selected Device Manager tabs: The General Tab for a Disabled Device (A); the Driver Tab for a Network Storage Device (B); and the Power Tab for a USB Hub (C)

1. **Device status – disabled device (Code 22)**
2. **Troubleshoot button – click or tap to enable device**   3. **Driver overview**

4. **Available power per USB port on this hub**
5. **Power required for connected devices**
6. **Click or tap to close properties sheet**

To troubleshoot problems with a device in Device Manager, open its properties sheet by double-clicking the device. Use the General tab (shown in Figure 6-31) to display the device's status and to troubleshoot the disabled or malfunctioning device.

When you have a malfunctioning device such as the one shown on the left in Figure 6-31, you have several options for resolving the problem:

- Look up the Device Manager code to determine the problem and its solution. (See Table 6-5 for a few examples of device manager codes and solutions.)

- Click the troubleshoot button (if any) shown on the device's General Properties tab; the button's name and usage depend on the problem. Table 6-5 lists a few examples, their meanings, and the solution button (if any).

- Manually change resources (primarily in older systems that don't use ACPI power management). If the nature of the problem is a resource conflict, you can click the Resources tab, change the settings, and try to eliminate the conflict.

- Manually update drivers. If the problem is a driver issue but an Update Driver button isn't available, open the Driver tab and install a new driver for the device.

Table 6-5   Examples of Some Device Manager Codes and Solutions

Code Number	Problem	Recommended Solution
1	This device is not configured correctly.	Update the driver.
3	The driver for this device might be corrupted, or your system might be running low on memory or other resources.	Close some open applications. Uninstall and reinstall the driver. Install additional RAM.
10	Device cannot start.	Update the driver. View Microsoft Help and Support article 943104 for more information.
12	This device cannot find enough free resources that it can use. If you want to use this device, you need to disable one of the other devices on this system.	You can use the Troubleshooting wizard in Device Manager to determine where the conflict is and then disable the conflicting device. Disable the device.
22	The device is disabled.	Enable the device.

You can also use Device Manager to disable a device that is conflicting with another device. To disable a device, follow these steps:

Step 1.   Click the plus (+) sign next to the device category containing the device.

Step 2.   Double-click the device, click the **Driver** tab, and select **Disable**.

Depending on the device, you might need to physically remove it from the system to resolve a conflict. To use Device Manager to remove a device, follow these steps:

Step 1.   Click the plus (**+**) sign next to the device category containing the device.

Step 2.   Double-click the device and select **Uninstall**.

Step 3.   Shut down the system and remove the physical device.

Or:

Step 1.   Double-click the device and select **Properties**.

Step 2.   Click the **Driver** tab and click the **Uninstall** button.

Step 3.   Shut down the system and remove the physical device.

If a device malfunctions after a driver update, roll back the driver. Click the **Roll Back Driver** button on the Driver tab to return to the preceding driver version.

MSCONFIG

The Microsoft System Configuration utility, MSCONFIG, enables you to selec-
tively disable programs and services that run at startup. If your computer is unstable, runs more slowly than usual, or has problems starting up or shutting down, using MSCONFIG can help you determine whether a program or service running when the system starts is at fault. To start MSCONFIG in Windows 7:

Step 1.   Click **Start** to open the Windows Desktop Search pane.

Step 2.   Type **MSCONFIG** and press **Enter**.

To start MSCONFIG in Windows 8/8.1/10:

Step 1.   Press **Windows+X**.

Step 2.   Click or tap **Run**.

Step 3.   Type **MSCONFIG** and press **Enter**.

Every version of MSCONFIG has a multitabbed interface used to control startup options. The General tab (see Figure 6-32) enables you to select from Normal, Diagnostic (clean boot), or Selective Startup. (You choose which items and services to load.) Use the Boot tab (see Figure 6-33) to specify how to boot a Windows system.

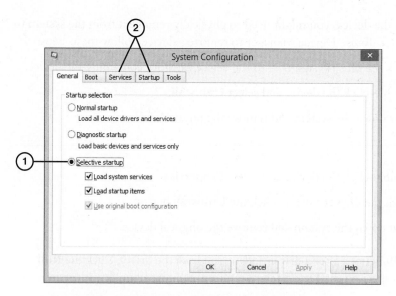

1. Select if you want to disable some services or startup programs.
2. Configure startup services and programs with these tabs.

FIGURE 6-32   MSCONFIG's General Tab (Windows 8.1)

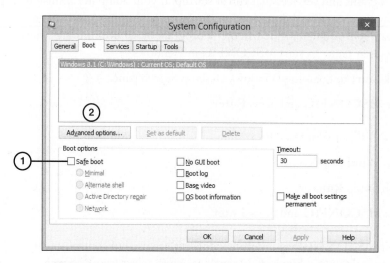

1. Click or tap and select options if you want to start in Safe Mode or use other special startup options.
2. Installed operating systems. If you are using the Windows boot loader, the additional operating systems installed are shown here.

FIGURE 6-33   MSCONFIG's Boot Tab (Windows 8.1)

Use the Services tab to disable or reenable system services. Use the Startup tab to disable or reenable startup programs. Use the Tools tab to launch System Restore, Computer Management, and other management tasks.

Figure 6-34 shows the System Configuration dialog's Tools tab in Windows 10. Note that many of the tools listed in this section are accessible from this utility.

FIGURE 6-34   System Configuration Utility (MSCONFIG) Tools Tab in Windows 10

TIP   When you select a tool from the Tools tab, MSCONFIG displays the command line needed to run it. Add any options desired before starting the tool.

Task Manager

The *Task Manager* utility provides a useful real-time look into the inner workings of Windows and the programs that are running. There are several ways to display Task Manager, including:

- Right-click the taskbar and select **Task Manager**.
- Press **Ctrl+Shift+Esc**.
- Open the Run or Search box and type **taskmgr**.
- Press **Ctrl+Alt+Del** and select **Task Manager** from the Windows Security dialog.

In Windows 7, Task Manager opens to the Applications tab, shown in Figure 6-35.

1. To kill a task that is not responding, select it and then click or tap the End Task button.

FIGURE 6-35   The Windows Task Manager's Applications Tab in Windows 7

The Windows 7 Task Manager includes the following tabs:

- **Applications:** Shows running applications.

- **Processes:** Displays program components in memory.

- **Performance:** Displays CPU, memory, pagefile, and caching stats.

- **Networking:** Lists network utilization by adapter in use.

- **Users:** Lists current users.

- **Services:** Lists services and their status.

Use the Applications tab to determine whether a program has stopped responding; you can shut down these programs by using the **End Task** button.

Use the Processes tab to see which processes are consuming the most memory. Use this dialog along with the System Configuration utility (MSCONFIG) to determine whether you are loading unnecessary startup applications; MSCONFIG can disable them to free up memory. If you are unable to shut down a program from the Applications tab, you can also shut down its processes from the Processes tab, but this is not recommended unless the program cannot be shut down in any other way.

Use the Performance tab to determine whether you need to install more RAM memory or need to increase the computer's paging file size. Use the Networking tab to monitor the performance of the computer's connection to the network. Use the Services tab to see the services currently running on a system.

In Windows 8/8.1/10, Task Manager uses a new design that lists only running programs when you start it (see Figure 6-36). Click or tap **More Details** to see details about those programs and additional tabs (see Figure 6-37).

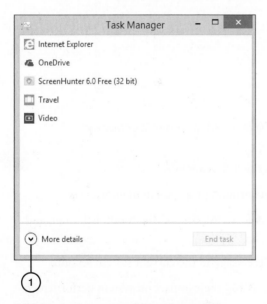

1. Click or tap to see more information and tabs.

FIGURE 6-36   The Windows Task Manager's Opening Dialog in Windows 8.1

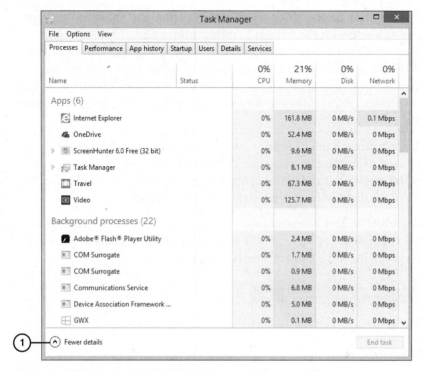

1. Click or tap to return to simplified dialog.

FIGURE 6-37   The More Details View of the Windows 8.1 Version of Task Manager

The Windows 8/8.1 Task Manager has the following tabs:

- **Processes:** Displays apps and background processes in memory.

- **Performance:** Displays CPU, memory, disk drives, Bluetooth, Ethernet, and WiFi stats.

- **App history:** Displays app resource usage in the current system session.

- **Startup:** Displays startup programs and their impact on system performance.

- **Users:** Lists current users.

- **Details:** Displays PID, status, username, CPU, and memory usage by app or service.

- **Services:** Lists services and their status.

To open Task Manager in Windows 10, enter **Task Manager** in the search box. Task Manager in Windows 10 is similar to Task Manager in previous Windows versions.

One of the most common uses of Task Manager is to end programs that are malfunctioning. To end a program, click on the Processes tab and select the process of the nonresponsive program. Figure 6-38 depicts a list of processes. By right-clicking on a process, you get options to stop and start the app.

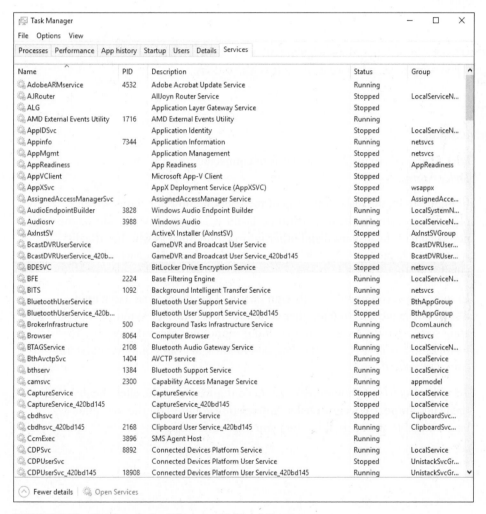

FIGURE 6-38   Services in the Windows 10 Task Manager

Disk Management

The ***Disk Management*** snap-in of the MMC is a GUI-based application for analyzing and configuring hard drives. Try some of the configurations listed in the following sections on a test computer with one or two drives of unpartitioned space. Disk Management is also accessible by right-clicking on the **Windows** icon (start) and selecting **Disk Management** from the menu that appears.

> **CAUTION**   Some operations wipe out all drive contents. Make sure you back up any data you want to keep before trying any of these tasks.

Drive Status

Disk Management displays the status of connected drives with ***Drive Status***.

In Figure 6-39, the disks at the top of the window and their status are displayed. For example, the C: partition is healthy. This window also shows the percentage of the disk used and other information, such as whether the disk is currently being formatted, whether it's basic or dynamic, or whether it has failed.

In some cases, you might see "foreign" status. This means that a dynamic disk has been moved from another computer (with another Windows operating system) to the local computer, and it cannot be accessed properly. To fix this and enable access to the disk, add the disk to your computer's system configuration.

To add a disk to your computer's system configuration, right-click the disk and then click **Import Foreign Disks**. Any existing volumes on the foreign disk become visible and accessible when you import the disk.

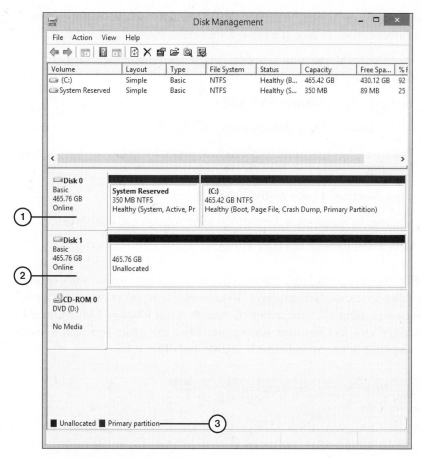

1. A disk with two primary partitions
2. A disk with no partitions
3. Disk status color key (changes as other disk types are added or created)

FIGURE 6-39 Using Disk Management (Windows 8.1)

Mounting a Drive

You can use Disk Management to mount drives. A ***mounted drive*** is a drive that is mapped to an empty folder within a volume that has been formatted as NTFS. Instead of using drive letters, mounted drives use drive paths. This is a good solution for when you need more than 26 drives in a computer because you are not limited to the letters in the alphabet. Mounted drives can also provide more space for temporary files and can enable you to move folders to different drives if space runs low on the current drive. To mount a drive, follow these steps:

Step 1. Right-click the partition or volume you want to mount and select **Change Drive Letters and Paths**.

Step 2. In the displayed window, click **Add**.

Step 3. Click **Mount** in the following empty NTFS folder.

Step 4. Browse to the empty folder to which you want to mount the volume and click **OK**.

Step 5. Click **Next** (see Figure 6-40).

Step 6. Choose the appropriate drive partitioning settings and click **Next**.

Step 7. Review the settings and click **Finish**.

Figure 6-40 shows that a hard disk partition has been mounted within a folder on the system hard drive called MountPoint. To remove the mount point, go back to Disk Management, right-click the mounted volume, select **Change Drive Letters and Paths**, and then select **Remove**. Keep in mind that the folder you want to use as a mount point must be empty and must be within an NTFS volume.

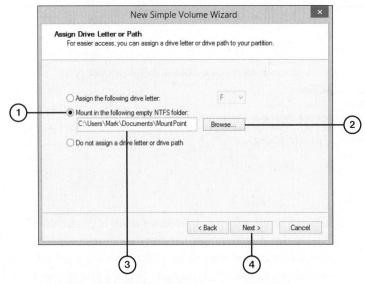

1. The selected drive will be mounted in an empty NTFS folder
2. Click or tap to browse for the folder
3. After selecting the folder, it appears here
4. Click or tap to continue

FIGURE 6-40 Assigning a Partition as a Mounted Drive

Initializing a Disk

When a new drive is connected, the OS may prompt to *initialize* it. If prompted by the Initialize Disk dialog, select the disk and choose the partition style to use (MBR for drives under 2.1TB and GPT for larger drives). Afterward, an unformatted drive will appear as Unallocated in Disk Management.

NOTE   An MBR drive can have up to four primary partitions. A GPT drive can have more than four primary partitions. A GPT partition must be used for drives over 2.1TB in size.

Creating a New Simple Volume

When a new simple volume is created, a drive is added. A new simple volume can occupy a portion or all of the space on an unallocated disk. Follow these steps to create a new simple volume:

Step 1.   Right-click unallocated space on a drive. (With a new drive, the entire drive is listed as unallocated.)

Step 2.   Select **New Simple Volume**.

Step 3.   Click **Next**.

Step 4.   To use the entire space for a volume (drive letter), click **Next**. To use only part of the space, specify the amount of space to use (in megabytes) and then click **Next**.

Step 5.   Select the drive letter to install and click **Next**. (You can also select the option to not assign a drive letter or to mount the drive in an empty NTFS folder on an existing drive.)

Step 6.   Specify the file system (NTFS is the default), the volume name, and whether to use a quick format or prepare the drive as compressed. Click **Next**.

Step 7.   Review all options and click **Finish** (see Figure 6-41).

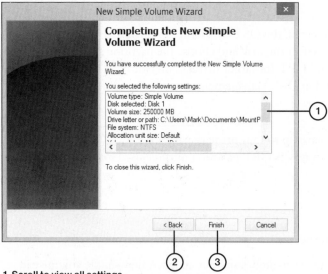

1. Scroll to view all settings
2. Click or tap to return to previous screens to make changes
3. Click or tap to prepare drive with listed settings

FIGURE 6-41   Creating a New Simple Volume (Windows 8.1)

Extending Partitions

Windows enables you to *extend* the size of a partition (volume) with the Disk Management utility. It's highly recommended that you back up your data before attempting this operation. Then follow these steps:

Step 1.   Right-click the volume to be extended.

Step 2.   Select **Extend Volume**. (Remember that a volume is any section of the hard drive with a drive letter.)

Step 3.   Click **Next** and select how much space you'd like to add to the partition.

Step 4.   Click **Finish** at the summary screen.

A reboot is not required, and this process should finish fairly quickly. This process can also be done by using the DISKPART command.

Splitting Partitions

To *split* a single partition into two or more partitions using Disk Management, follow this procedure:

Step 1. Shrink the existing partition to make room for an additional partition (as described in the next section). If you are unable to shrink the partition sufficiently, back up some of the information in the partition and try again.

Step 2. Create one or more new partitions in the unallocated space created in step 1.

Shrinking Partitions

To free up space on a drive in order to install another operating system, it is possible to *shrink* a partition. As with extending a volume, you should back up data before starting. Then follow these steps:

Step 1. Right-click the volume to be shrunk.

Step 2. Select **Shrink Volume**.

Step 3. Select the amount of space you'd like to use for the partition.

Step 4. Click **Shrink**.

The free space created by this process is listed as unallocated.

Assigning/Changing Drive Letters

If a volume was created without a drive letter being assigned, use Change Drive Letters and Paths. Here's how:

Step 1. Right-click the partition or volume and select **Change Drive Letters and Paths**.

Step 2. In the window that appears, click **Add**.

Step 3. Make sure **Assign the Following Drive Letter** is selected. The next available drive letter is listed. (If a different drive letter is preferred, use the pull-down menu to choose the drive letter desired.)

Step 4. Click **OK**. The drive is now referred to by the selected drive letter.

To change the drive letter of a connected drive (for example, so that a USB drive can use the same drive letter on different computers), follow this procedure:

Step 1. Right-click the partition or volume to be changed and select **Change Drive Letters and Paths**.

Step 2. When the current drive letter assignment is shown, click **Change**.

Step 3. Use the pull-down menu to choose the preferred drive letter.

Step 4. Click **OK**.

Step 5. Click **Yes** to change the drive letter. The drive is now referred to by the selected drive letter.

Adding Arrays

Disk Management supports basic disks, which can be bootable, and dynamic disks. Although dynamic disks can't be used as boot disks, they can be used in the following types of drive arrays:

- **Spanned:** The capacity of all disks is added together. This is equivalent to a just a bunch of disks (JBOD) hardware array and requires at least two disks.

- **Striped:** Data is written across all drives to enhance speed. This is equivalent to a RAID 0 hardware array and requires two disks.

- **Mirrored:** Copies of data are written to all disks at the same time to enhance data security. If one drive fails, data is still safe, and the array can be rebuilt. This is equivalent to a RAID 1 hardware array and requires two disks.

- **RAID 5:** Data and recovery information is written across all disks to enable recovery if one disk in the array fails. This is equivalent to RAID 5 hardware array and requires at least three disks.

To create any of these arrays, follow these steps:

Step 1. Make sure the disks to be used in the *drive array* have been backed up. Any disk in an array has its previous information overwritten.

Step 2. Right-click the first drive to add to the array and select the array type.

Step 3. Click **Next** to continue.

Step 4. Select the next drive to add to the array and click **Add**.

Step 5. If creating a RAID 5 array, repeat step 3 until the desired number of disks are added to the array.

Step 6. Click **Next** to continue.

Step 7. Assign a drive letter or mount point. Click **Next**.

Step 8. Select the option to format the volume and name it. Click **Next**.

Step 9. Review settings. Click **Finish**.

Step 10. Click **Yes** to convert the drives to dynamic disks (required for arrays). The array is created.

Figure 6-42 shows how two 500GB drives appear in mirrored, spanned, and striped arrays.

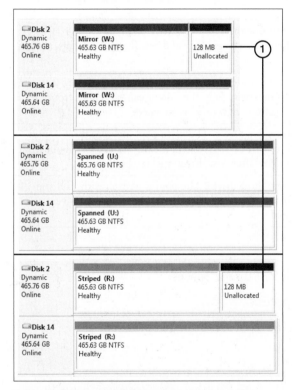

1. The first drive selected in an array has a small unallocated portion of the disk.

FIGURE 6-42   Mirrored, Spanned, and Striped Disk Arrays

NOTE   Windows Disk Management's disk arrays are slower than some hardware RAID arrays; the difference in performance depends on the hardware RAID host adapter in the comparison. However, these arrays can be set up with standard non-RAID SATA host adapters.

Storage Spaces

Windows 8/8.1/10 include *Storage Spaces*, which provides a way to use multiple hard disks or SSDs for redundant storage. Drives work in a similar fashion to RAID in that they are backed up and, in case of drive failure, are protected. Storage Spaces can be used to expand storage by adding additional drives. Table 6-6 provides an overview of the options available. Notice that the options are similar to the options available with RAID.

Table 6-6   Storage Spaces Overview

Configuration	Use
Simple	Requires at least one drive. The capacity of all drives is grouped together and used as a single logical drive. If any drive fails, all data is lost.
Two-way mirror	Requires at least two drives. Each drive has a copy of the information. If one drive fails, the mirror can be rebuilt from the surviving drive after a new drive is attached.
Three-way mirror	Requires at least five drives. The drive pool includes three copies of the data. If one or two drives fail, the mirror can be rebuilt from the surviving drive after new drives are attached.
Parity	Requires at least three drives. The pool is written with data and parity information. If a single drive fails, the surviving drives can rebuild the pool.

To use Storage Spaces:

Step 1.   Open Search and search for **Storage Spaces**.

Step 2.   Click or tap **Storage Spaces**.

Step 3.   Click or tap **Create a New Pool and Storage Space**.

Step 4.   Select the drive(s) to use.

> **CAUTION**   When using a drive for a storage pool, all existing files on the drive are deleted, bypassing the Recycle Bin. Make sure to back up any files that need to be kept before assigning a drive to a storage pool.

Step 5.   Click **Create Pool**.

Step 6.   When Storage Spaces displays a recommended layout, make any changes desired and then click or tap **Create Storage Space** (see Figure 6-43).

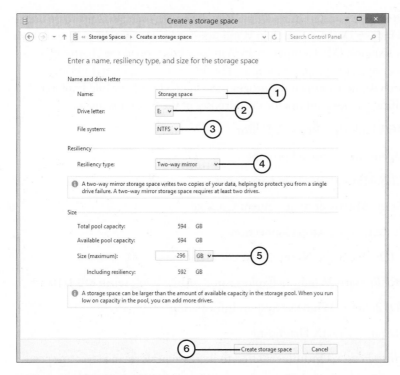

1. **Enter name for logical drive**
2. **Select drive letter desired**
3. **Select NTFS (default) or ReFS file system**
4. **Select resiliency type**
5. **Maximum size; can be reduced**
6. **Click or tap to create storage space**

FIGURE 6-43   Creating a Two-Way Mirror in Storage Spaces

After the storage space is created, the Manage Storage Spaces dialog displays the new storage space.

The Storage Spaces storage pool is assigned a drive letter and shows up in File Explorer and Disk Management as a normal drive. If a drive fails, warnings are displayed in Action Center. Click the link to open Storage Spaces. Take the recommended action to bring the pool back to health.

Use Storage Spaces to manage the drives in a drive pool. As far as Disk Management is concerned, a drive pool is recognized as only a single drive.

System Utilities

Windows includes a variety of command line utilities known as *system utilities* that are used for system management. As discussed earlier in this chapter, a command line utility is a program you can start by using the Run dialog. You can also start these utilities by using Windows Desktop Search in Windows 7 or by opening the program's icon from Windows Explorer (My Computer). In Windows 8/8.1, open the charms menu and use Search or open the program's icon in This PC or File Explorer. In Windows 10, use the Search window or open the program's icon in This PC or File Explorer. The most significant system utilities for the purposes of the A+ exams include:

- **REGEDIT**: Launches Registry Editor

- **CMD**: Opens the command prompt

- **SERVICES.MSC**: Shows Windows Services

- **MMC**: Starts Microsoft Management Console

- **MSTSC**: Remote Desktop Connection

- **NOTEPAD**: Opens the Notepad text editor/viewer

- **EXPLORER**: Starts Windows Explorer in 7 or File Explorer in 8/8.1/10

- **MSINFO32**: Starts Windows System Information

- **DxDiag**: Starts DirectX Diagnostic

- **Disk Defragmenter/Optimizer:** Used to increase performance (access speed) by rearranging files stored on a disk to occupy contiguous locations

- **System Restore**: Allows the PC to reset to a previous configuration

- **MSCONFIG:** Starts the System Configuration utility

The following sections cover these utilities in more detail.

> **NOTE**   SERVICES.MSC is discussed earlier in this chapter, in the "Services (Services.MSC)" section. MMC is discussed earlier in this chapter, in the "Computer Management Console (MMC)" section.

Using REGEDIT

Under most normal circumstances, the Registry does not need to be edited or even viewed. However, Registry editing might be necessary under the following circumstances:

- To view a system setting that cannot be viewed through other interfaces.

- To add, modify (by changing values or data), or remove a Registry key that cannot be changed through normal Windows menus or application settings.

This might be necessary, for example, to remove traces of a program or hardware device that was not uninstalled properly or to allow a new device or program to be installed.

■ To back up the Registry to a file.

To start REGEDIT, open the Run or Windows Desktop Search window, type **REGEDIT**, and press **Enter**. Changes made using REGEDIT are automatically saved upon exit. However, it may be necessary to log off and log back on or restart the system for changes to take effect.

CAUTION   The Registry should never be edited unless a backup copy has been made first because there is no Undo option for individual edits, and there is no way to discard all changes when exiting REGEDIT.

Editing the Windows Registry can be difficult because Registry keys can be expressed in decimal, hexadecimal, or text. When editing the Registry, be sure to carefully follow the instructions provided by a vendor.

Figure 6-44 shows the Registry (which is same in all versions of Windows) with a modification being made to the MenuShowDelay Registry key, which isn't accessible within normal Windows display menus.

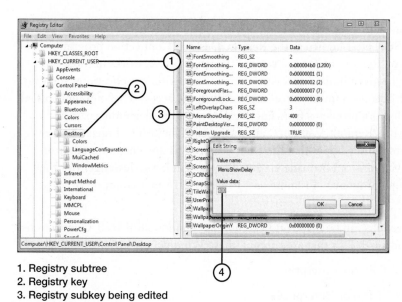

1. Registry subtree
2. Registry key
3. Registry subkey being edited
4. Enter new value here

FIGURE 6-44   Using REGEDIT (Windows 7)

Always back up the Registry before editing it. Follow these steps to back up part or all of the Registry to a text file:

Step 1.   Start **REGEDIT**.

Step 2.   To make a partial backup, highlight the section of the Registry to be backed up.

Step 3.   Click **File** and select **Export**.

Step 4.   Select a location to store the Registry backup.

Step 5.   Enter a name for the backup.

Step 6.   Click **All** to back up the entire Registry. Click **Selected Branch** to back up only the Registry branch you selected in step 2.

Step 7.   Click **Save**.

Command

In old versions of Windows, command.com is the 16-bit command interpreter, and CMD.EXE is a 32-bit or 64-bit command interpreter. However, in current Windows versions, running Command actually runs CMD.EXE.

MSTSC

To facilitate connections to remote computers and allow full remote control, Microsoft uses MSTSC, better known as the Remote Desktop Connection program, which is based on Remote Desktop Protocol (RDP). MSTSC works in three ways. First, users can be given limited access to a remote computer's applications, such as Word or Excel. Second, administrators can be given full access to a computer so that they can troubleshoot problems from another location. Third, another part of the program, known as Remote Assistance, allows a user to invite a technician to view his or her desktop in the hopes that the technician can fix any encountered problems. These invitations can be made via email or by Windows Messenger or other instant-messaging programs. A remote user needs to have an account on the host computer.

MSTSC connections can be made on PCs running Windows 8/8.1/10. Connections can only be made with PCs that are running these Windows operating systems:

- Windows 10 Pro or Enterprise

- Windows 8.1 Pro or Enterprise

- Windows 8 Pro or Enterprise

- Windows 7 Enterprise, Professional, or Ultimate

NOTE   Home editions of Windows 7/8/8.1/10 can use Remote Assistance. The check box for Remote Assistance is on the same Remote tab used to configure Remote Desktop.

Configuring Remote Settings on the Host Computer

To set up a computer's ***remote settings*** options to receive remote connections:

Step 1.   Open the System properties sheet in Control Panel.

Step 2.   Click or tap **Remote**.

Step 3.   Click or tap the empty **Allow Remote Connections to This Computer** check box.

Step 4.   Specify which users can connect and whether a connection must use Network Level Authentication (NLA).

Step 5.   Click **OK**.

Starting MSTSC and Connecting to a Remote Computer

To run MSTSC in Windows 7:

Step 1.   Click **Start** to open the Windows Desktop Search pane.

Step 2.   Type **MSTSC** and press **Enter**.

To run MSTSC in Windows 8/8.1:

Step 1.   Press **Windows+X**.

Step 2.   Click **Run**.

Step 3.   Type **MSTSC** and press **Enter**.

NOTE   In Windows 10, search for Remote Desktop.

To connect to the remote computer:

Step 1.   Enter the name or IP address of the remote computer.

Step 2.   Click **Connect**.

Step 3.   Select or enter the account name and enter the account password. The connection starts.

To see options for saving a connection or using a saved connection, click **Show Options**. The available options are shown in Figure 6-45.

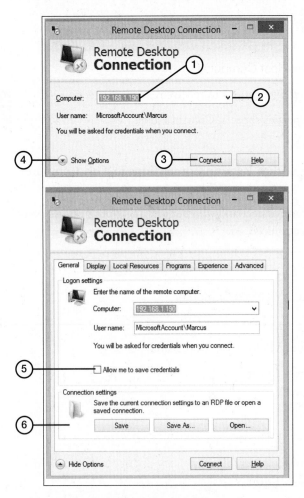

1. Enter IP address of remote computer
2. Open menu to look up a previously added remote computer
3. Click or tap to connect
4. Click or tap to show options
5. Click or tap to save credentials
6. Use these buttons to save or open connection settings

FIGURE 6-45   Making a Remote Desktop Connection in Windows

NOTE   If you are having trouble connecting to a system remotely using a remote program such as Remote Desktop Connection or helping someone by using Remote Assistance, RDP port 3389 may be blocked at the firewall and need to be allowed/open for you to connect.

Notepad

Notepad is a simple plain-text editor that has several uses in system management:

- Creating batch files and scripts. When saving a batch file or script, use quotes around the filename and extension (for example, "myscript.scr" or "mybatch.bat").

- Viewing text-based reports.

- Editing HTML files.

Notepad is the default program for opening .txt (plain-text) files.

To open a text file with a different extension in Notepad:

Step 1.   Right-click the file in Windows Explorer or File Explorer.

Step 2.   Select **Open With**.

Step 3.   Choose **Notepad**.

Explorer

Windows Explorer is the file management utility in Windows 7. In Windows 8/8.1/10, it is called File Explorer. This section uses Explorer to discuss common features.

Windows can use Explorer to view both local drive/network and Internet content. By default, Explorer doesn't display hidden and system files unless the View options are changed. (See the section "Folder Options," later in this chapter, for details.)

Windows Explorer (Windows 7)

Windows Explorer in Windows 7 provides a scrolling pane with access to libraries, local and network locations, and homegroup computers (see Figure 6-46).

Windows 7 groups shortcuts to a wide variety of locations in its left pane. The Favorites section includes shortcuts to the current user's desktop, downloads folder, and recently visited objects (folders and libraries). The Libraries section includes shortcuts to the current user's Documents, Music, Pictures, and Videos libraries. If the computer is part of a homegroup network (a network type introduced in Windows 7 and supported in Windows 8/8.1 but discontinued in Windows 10), the Homegroup section lists other computers in the homegroup. The Computer section lists all connected drives. The Network section lists all computers on the network. The right pane lists the contents of the current location. Common tasks are shown in a menu strip above the panes.

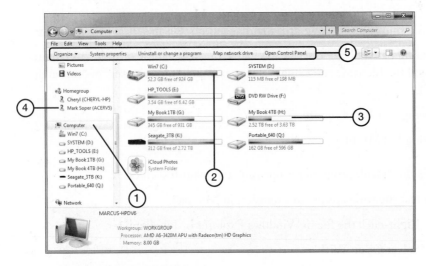

1. Selected object (Computer)
2. Red capacity indicator = 10% or less free space
3. Blue capacity indicator = more than 10% free space
4. Computers/users in homegroup
5. Common tasks

FIGURE 6-46   The Computer View Using Tiles in Windows 7's Windows Explorer

File Explorer (Windows 8/8.1/10)

File Explorer (see Figure 6-47) can be started in any of the following ways in Windows 8/8.1:

- Open the charms menu, search for **Explorer**, and tap or click **File Explorer**.
- Tap or click the **Desktop** tile and click or tap the **File Explorer** icon on the taskbar.
- Press **Windows+X** and click or tap **File Explorer**.

NOTE   In Windows 10, you can press **Windows+X** or open the **Start** menu and click the **File Explorer** icon to start File Explorer.

1. Default object selected when File Explorer opens
2. Folders view
3. DVD R/W Drives and devices view
4. Computer tab

FIGURE 6-47   Windows 8.1 File Explorer's This PC (Default) View

Windows 8/8.1/10's File Explorer opens to the This PC view, which combines the Computer and Libraries views from Windows 7. It offers a multi-tabbed ribbon menu for working with files, computer settings (default tab), and view options.

Displaying Drives, Files, and Folders

Explorer offers the following viewing options:

- **Small icons :** Shows small icons in rows across the Explorer window.

- **List:** Shows small icons arranged in columns.

- **Medium icons, large icons, and extra large icons:** Show different-sized thumbnails of supported file types.

- **Details:** Shows the file or folder name, date modified, type, and size. Right-click or press and hold the header to select additional details to display.

- **Tiles:** Displays the capacity of USB drives, hard disk drives, and SSDs.

Windows 7/8/8.1/10 also include the following:

- **Content:** Lists medium icons (thumbnails) along with a file's most recent modified date and size.

Libraries (Windows 7/8/8.1/10)

Windows Explorer in Windows 7 provides a scrolling pane with access to libraries, local and network locations, and homegroup computers. With Windows Explorer in Windows 7, the default view shows libraries. A library includes the contents of the current user's Documents, Music, Pictures, or Videos folder and also includes the contents of the corresponding Public folder and can display the contents of any other local or network folder the user adds to the library. In Figure 6-48, the Pictures library has been expanded in the left pane to reveal two additional folders that have been added. In any Windows Explorer view in Windows 7, click **Organize** to display file, folder, and layout options and to view properties for the currently selected object.

Windows 8/8.1/10 also include library support. To display libraries in Windows 8/8.1/10, click or tap the **View** tab, click or tap **Options**, and check the **Show Libraries** check box.

1. Click to expand view
2. Additional folders added to Pictures library by user

FIGURE 6-48   The Default Libraries View in Windows 7's Windows Explorer

MSINFO32 (System Information)

MSINFO32, also known as System Information, displays a great deal of information about the computer hardware and Windows installation in a system. The System Summary (see Figure 6-49) provides basic information about the Windows installation and hardware configuration. Simply click a subnode (left pane) for more detailed information about system hardware, components, or software environment. To dig deeper, open the nodes in the left pane. Figure 6-50 shows loaded program modules listed.

Use the **Find What** window to locate specific information. Use the **File** menu to save a report or to export it as a text file.

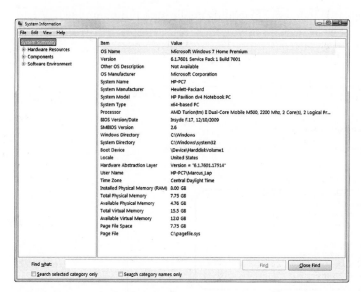

FIGURE 6-49   MSINFO32 System Summary

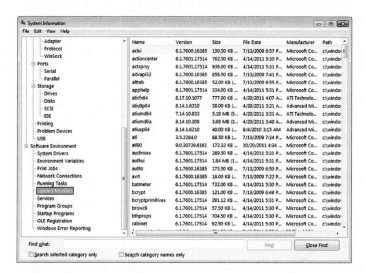

FIGURE 6-50   MSINFO32 Loaded Program Modules Display (Right Pane)

DxDiag (DirectX Diagnostics)

DxDiag displays and troubleshoots DirectX components in Windows. Use it to determine the version of DirectX on your system and to test DirectX components (see Figure 6-51).

> **NOTE**   DirectX is Microsoft Windows's 3D gaming application programming interface (API).

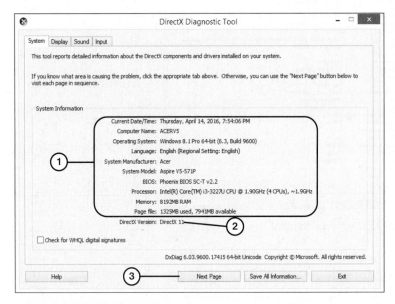

1. Device and Windows information
2. DirectX major version installed
3. Click to view next tab

FIGURE 6-51   DxDiag's System Tab, Which Displays the DirectX Version Installed, Windows Version, and Computer Hardware Features

> **NOTE**   If DxDiag finds problems with the system, you should download updated drivers for any problematic devices.

Disk Defragmenter/Optimize Drives

Defragging a hard disk drive can help improve system performance, especially if the drive is frequently changed. With heavy use, the data on a disk can be spread around the drive, which slows down access. Defragmentation is the process of reorganizing the data into contiguous blocks. Defragmenting SSD storage is not as necessary as on HDDs, but Windows can still defrag SSDs on a schedule with the Optimize Drives app in Windows 10, where defragmentation is set by default and can also be scheduled. Figure 6-52 shows the Optimize Drives app in Windows 10.

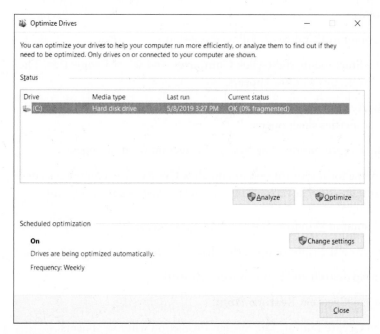

FIGURE 6-52   The Optimize Drives App in Windows 10

System Restore

System Restore enables you to fix problems caused by a defective hardware or software installation by resetting the computer's configuration to the way it was at a specified earlier time. The configuration is stored in a file called a *restore point*. The driver or software files installed stay on the system, and so does the data you created, but Registry changes made by the hardware or software are reversed, so your system works the way it did before the installation. Restore points can be created by the user with System Restore and are also created automatically by the system before new hardware or software is installed. Restore points in Windows 7 also store older versions of data files created by the Windows Shadow Copy service. Windows 8/8.1 and 10 use File History to store older versions of data files.

> **TIP**   Before you make changes to your system configuration, create a restore point so that you can easily reverse the changes if they are not satisfactory.

Creating a Restore Point

To create a restore point in Windows 7, follow these steps:

Step 1.   Open the **Start** menu, right-click **Computer**, and select **Properties**. The System Properties window appears.

Step 2.   Click the **System Protection** task, and the System Protection tab on the System properties sheet opens.

Step 3.   Click the **Create** button. The System Protection window appears.

Step 4.   Type a name for the restore point and click **Create**. The computer's current hardware and software configuration is stored as a restore point.

To create a restore point in Windows 8/8.1, follow these steps:

Step 1.   Swipe in from the right to open the charms menu.

Step 2.   Click or tap **Search** and enter **System Restore**.

Step 3.   Click or tap **Create a Restore Point**.

Step 4.   Click the **Create** button. The System Protection window appears.

Step 5.   Type a name for the restore point and click **Create**. The computer's current hardware and software configuration is stored as a restore point.

To create a restore point in Windows 10, follow these steps:

Step 1.   Click or tap **Search** and enter **System Restore**.

Step 2.   Click or tap the **Create** button.

Step 3.   Type a name for the restore point and click **Create**. The computer's current hardware and software configuration is stored as a restore point.

Restoring Your System to an Earlier Condition

Follow these steps to restore your system to an earlier condition:

Step 1.   Open the **System Protection** tab again and this time click the **System Restore** button. The Restore System Files and Settings window appears.

Step 2.   Click **Next**, and you see the window Restore Your Computer to the State It Was in Before the Selected Event.

Step 3.   Select a restore point to restore to and click **Next**. (You can also select the box **Show More Restore Points** to display a list of older restore points.)

Step 4.   Click **Finish** on the Confirm Your Restore Point page. The system initiates the restore and automatically restarts.

You can also undo a system restore that does not repair the problem.

If you cannot boot the system directly into Windows, you can run System Restore from the Windows Recovery Environment.

Configuring System Restore Options

If System Restore is not available, it might be turned off. You can enable or disable System Restore on any volume from the System Properties window's System Protection tab. Click or tap **Configure** to add or remove a drive from the list of drives protected by System Restore, to change the amount of disk space to reserve for System Restore, or to delete all restore points.

What to Try Before Using System Restore

Be aware that System Restore is not necessarily the first step you should try when troubleshooting a computer. Simply restarting the computer has been known to "fix" all kinds of issues. It's also a good idea to try the Last Known Good Configuration. You can access this within the Windows Advanced Boot Options menu by pressing **F8** (Windows 7) or using the special startup options (Windows 8/8.1/10) when the computer first boots. Also, if System Restore doesn't seem to work in normal mode, attempt to use it in Safe mode (which is an option in the Windows Advanced Boot Options menu). You'll learn more about these options in the next section.

NOTE   Be wary of using System Restore if you're fighting a computer virus or malware infection. If you (or the system) create a restore point while the system is infected, you could re-infect the system if you later revert the system to that restore point. To prevent re-infection, most antivirus vendors recommend that you disable System Restore (which eliminates stored restore points) before removing computer viruses. To disable System Restore in Windows 8/10, open System Restore and click **Create a Restore Point**. Then select a drive and click **Configure**. Change **Restore Settings** to **Disable System Protection** and click **OK**.

Windows Update

Windows 10 periodically checks for the latest updates and security features and installs them automatically to keep a device running smoothly and securely. To update quickly, select **Check for Updates Now** and then select **Check for Updates**. Or click the **Start** button, go to **Settings > Update & Security > Windows Update**, and select **Check for Updates**.

As shown in Figure 6-53, the Windows 10 Windows Update page provides options to edit the update schedule and view the update history.

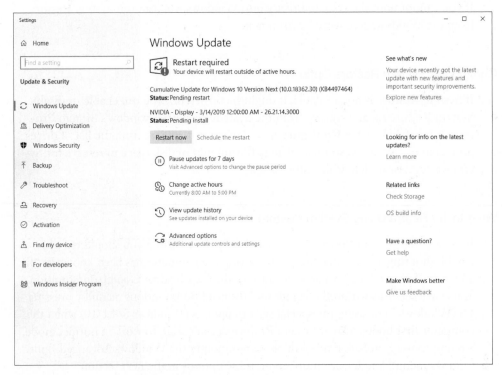

FIGURE 6-53   Windows 10 Update Menu

Safe Mode

Safe mode and other advanced boot options can be used when the system won't boot normally. To enter Safe mode in Windows 7, press **F8** repeatedly when starting the system until you see the Advanced Boot Options menu and then select **Safe Mode**. With Windows 8/8.1/10, getting to the Advanced Boot Options menu takes more steps. Press the Power button on the login screen, hold down the **Shift** key, and click/tap **Restart**. Select **Troubleshoot > Advanced Options > Startup Settings > Restart**.

The Windows 8/8.1 startup settings menu (see Figure 6-54) includes a couple of new features but otherwise looks similar to that of Windows 7.

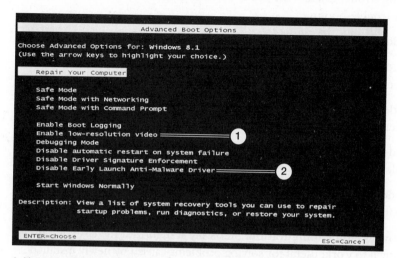

1. Uses lowest resolution of primary display instead of 640×480
2. New in Windows 8/8.1

FIGURE 6-54   The Windows 8.1 Advanced Boot Options Menu, Featuring Safe Mode and Other Special Startup Options

The Windows 10 Startup Settings menu has similar options to the Windows 8.1 version but is more graphical (see Figure 6-55).

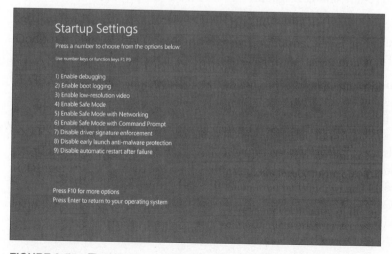

FIGURE 6-55   The Windows 10 Startup Settings Menu, Which Has the Same Options as the Windows 8.1 Version but in a Different Order and Selectable by Number

Here's what the Windows 10 Startup Settings options do:

- **Debugging Mode:** Enables the use of a debug program to examine the system kernel for troubleshooting.

- **Enable Boot Logging:** Creates an ntbtlog.txt file.

- **Enable Low-Resolution Video:** Uses a standard VGA driver in place of a GPU-specific display driver but uses all other drivers as normal.

- **Safe Mode:** Starts the system with a minimal set of drivers; can be used to start System Restore or to load Windows GUI for diagnostics.

- **Safe Mode with Networking:** Starts the system with a minimal set of drivers and enables network support.

- **Safe Mode with Command Prompt:** Starts the system with a minimal set of drivers but loads the command prompt instead of the Windows GUI.

- **Last Known Good Configuration:** Starts the system with the last configuration known to work; useful for solving problems caused by newly installed hardware or software.

- **Disable Driver Signature Enforcement:** Allows drivers containing improper signatures to be installed.

- **Disable Automatic Restart on System Failure:** Prevents Windows from automatically restarting if a STOP (BSOD) error causes Windows to fail. Choose this option only if Windows is stuck in a loop in which Windows fails, attempts to restart, and fails again.

- **Disable Early Launch Anti-malware Protection:** Helps when a legitimate driver is mistaken for malware by Windows 8/8.1/10's Early Launch Anti-Malware Protection feature.

- **Start Windows Normally:** Boots to regular Windows. This option is listed in case a user inadvertently presses **F8** but does not want to use any of the advanced boot options.

If Windows fails to start properly and then restarts automatically, it normally displays the Windows Error Recovery screen, which offers the following options: Safe Mode, Safe Mode with Networking, Safe Mode with Command Prompt, Last Known Good Configuration, and Start Windows Normally. This truncated version of the Advanced Boot Options menu indicates that Windows has acknowledged some sort of error or improper shutdown.

Control Panel Utilities

220-1002: Objective 1.6: Given a scenario, use Microsoft Windows Control Panel utilities.

The Control Panel is the major starting point for adjusting the hardware and user interface settings in Windows. Although Windows 8/8.1 includes PC Settings and Windows 10 includes Settings, many configurations in those versions of Windows are performed through the Control Panel.

> **NOTE** Just as there are often different ways to access information in the Windows OS, this section repeats some content from other chapters but in the context of the Control Panel. This repetition is done to help readers who are tracking the CompTIA A+ Core 2 objectives, which themselves have elements of redundancy.

Starting Control Panel

To start Control Panel in Windows 8/8.1, press **Windows+X** and then click or tap **Control Panel**. On a touchscreen, open the charms menu (Windows 8/8.1), search for **Control Panel**, and then tap **Control Panel**.

To start Control Panel in Windows 10, type **Control Panel** in the search box and then select the **Control Panel** link.

Shortcuts to Control Panel Functions

Some Control Panel functions can be accessed through properties sheets. Here are some examples:

- Right-click **Computer/This PC** and select **Properties** to open the System properties sheet.

- Right-click **Taskbar** and select **Properties** to open the Taskbar and Start Menu Properties sheet.

- Right-click **Desktop** in Windows 7/8/8.1 and choose one of the following options: **Personalize**, **Screen Resolution**, or **Gadgets** (Windows 7 only).

- Right-click **Network** and select **Properties** to open the Network and Sharing Center dialog.

Internet Options

Access the Internet Options menu via the Network and Internet Options link in the Control Panel (Windows 10). Figure 6-56 shows the Internet Properties dialog that appears, with the Security tab selected. Note that these choices differ from the options available in the Network and Sharing Center.

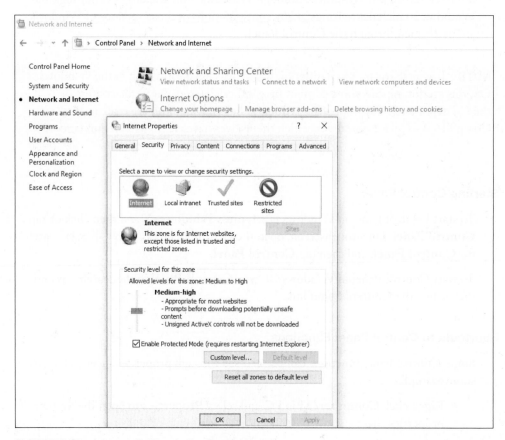

FIGURE 6-56   Internet Options in the Control Panel

The Internet Properties dialog accessed from the Control Panel has seven tabs. The tabs and their uses are listed in Table 6-7.

Table 6-7   Internet Properties Dialog Tabs

Tab	Function
General	Set the home page; set tab settings; delete browsing history, cookies, temporary files, and saved passwords; change appearance; and configure accessibility settings
Security	Configure security zones
Privacy	Select privacy settings for the current zone, location settings, pop-up blocker, and InPrivate browsing settings
Content	Set options for family safety, SSL certificate management, AutoComplete, and feeds
Connections	Set options for VPNs, dial-up, LAN connections, and proxy servers
Programs	Select the default web browser, manage add-ons, select the default HTML editor, and set the default apps for email and other Internet services
Advanced	Enable/disable accelerated graphics; configure accessibility settings, browsing settings, HTTP settings, international settings, multimedia settings, and security settings; and reset Internet Explorer to the default settings

Display/Display Settings

Depending on the version of Windows you use, there may be several different Control Panel applets to use to configure Display settings. Table 6-8 provides a reference to these.

Table 6-8   Configuring Display Settings in Windows 7 and Widows 8/8.1/10

Display Setting	Control Panel Setting/Tab	
	Windows 7	Windows 8/8.1, 10
Resolution (Higher resolution provides a sharper display, with smaller items—more of which fit on the screen)	Screen Resolution	Screen Resolution
Color depth (Maximum number of colors that can be displayed)	Display Advanced/List Monitor	N/A (32-bit color used for all modes)
Screen saver (Blanks screen or generates active images after a certain time)	Personalization	Personalization
Background (Wallpaper or an image on the computer desktop)	Personalization	Personalization
Theme (Combination of desktop background pictures and colors that are in visual harmony)	Personalization	Personalization
Windows color (Backgrounds)	Personalization	Personalization
Add additional displays	Screen Resolution	Screen Resolution
Refresh rate	Advanced Settings/ Monitor	Advanced Settings/ Monitor

User Accounts

From the Control Panel, if you select Accounts (Windows 8/8.1/10), you can manage the user account and access to other users. Figure 6-57 shows the Windows 10 account options from the Control Panel.

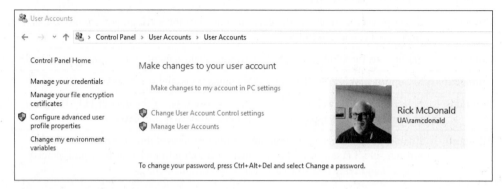

FIGURE 6-57   User Accounts in the Control Panel

Folder Options

The Folder Options properties sheet affects how Explorer:

- Displays file and folder information (View tab)
- Selects folders to index for searching (Search tab)
- Opens folders (General options tab)

You can open Folder Options in the Control Panel or open it from the Options menu in Explorer.

By default, Explorer hides the following file information:

- File extensions for registered file types; for example, a file called letter.docx displays as letter because Microsoft Word is associated with .docx files
- The full path to the current folder
- Files or folders with hidden or system attributes, such as the AppData folder
- The Windows folder

Concealing this information is intended to make it harder for users to "break" Windows, but having this information hidden also makes management and troubleshooting more difficult.

As an alternative to using the Folder Options applet in Control Panel, you can use this procedure in Windows 8/8.1/10:

Step 1.   Open **File Explorer**.

Step 2.   Click or tap the **View** tab.

Step 3.   Select the options you want (see Figure 6-58). The following changes are recommended for experienced end users:

■ Enable the Display the Full Path in the Title Bar option.
(In Windows 7, this works only if you are using the Classic theme.)

■ To see all file extensions, disable the Hide Extensions for Known File Types option.

■ If you are maintaining or troubleshooting a system, change the following:

■ To view hidden files, enable the Show Hidden Files, Folders, and Drives setting.

■ Disable the Hide Protected Operating System Files setting.

Step 4.   Click **OK** to close the Folder Options window.

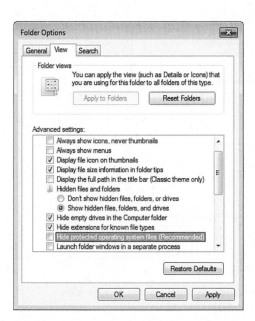

FIGURE 6-58   The View Tab of the Folder Options Dialog in Windows 7 with Recommended Options Set

System

Use the System properties sheet to view:

- Windows version

- Edition (32-bit or 64-bit)

- Processor model number and clock speed

- Windows Experience Index (WEI) (Windows 7 only)

Figure 6-59 shows the System properties sheet for Windows 8.1. Figure 6-60 shows the System properties sheet for Windows 10.

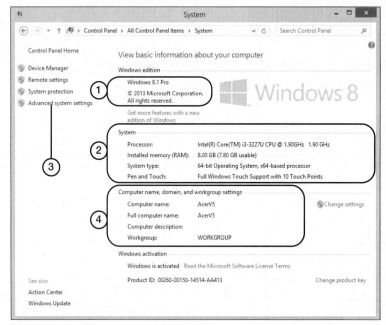

1. Windows edition
2. Processor, RAM, system type, pen/touch support
3. Click to open advanced system settings
4. Network and computer name settings

FIGURE 6-59   System Properties Sheet for a Windows 8.1 System with a Touchscreen

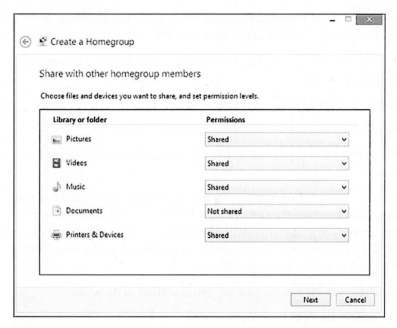

FIGURE 6-60   System Properties Sheet for a Windows 10 System

Selecting **Change Settings** in the System properties sheet for Windows 10 brings up the System applet, which allows you to change the following:

- Computer name
- Workgroup name
- Domain name
- System protection settings (System Restore)
- Hardware profiles
- Remote settings
- Performance and virtual memory settings

Performance (Virtual Memory) Settings

If a system is short on memory, it can borrow hard disk space and use it as virtual memory. The penalty for this type of borrowing is performance: Virtual memory is much slower than real RAM memory. However, it is possible to adjust how the system uses virtual memory to achieve better performance.

When additional RAM is added to a computer running Windows, it is automatically used first before the paging file.

The performance of the *paging file* can be improved by:

- Setting its minimum and maximum sizes to the same amount.

- Moving the paging file to a physical disk (or disk partition) that is not used as much as others.

- Using a striped volume for the paging file. A striped volume is an identical area of disk space stored on two or more dynamic disks referred to using a single drive letter. Create a striped volume with the Windows Disk Management tool. If a RAID 0 (striped) disk array is available, use it instead of a striped volume for even better paging file performance.

- Creating multiple paging files on multiple physical disks in the system.

- Moving the paging file away from the boot drive.

To adjust the location and size of the paging file in Windows, follow these steps:

Step 1.   In the System Properties window, click or tap **Advanced System Settings** under Tasks.

Step 2.   Click or tap the **Settings** button in the Performance box.

Step 3.   Click or tap the **Advanced** tab and then click or tap the **Change** button.

Step 4.   Clear or tap the **Automatically Manage Paging File Size** check box.

Step 5.   Click or tap the **Custom Size** radio button.

Step 6.   Specify the initial and maximum sizes you want to use for the paging file and its location (see Figure 6-61). Click or tap **Set** and then click or tap **OK** to finish.

Step 7.   If you make any changes to size or location, restart the computer so that the changes take effect.

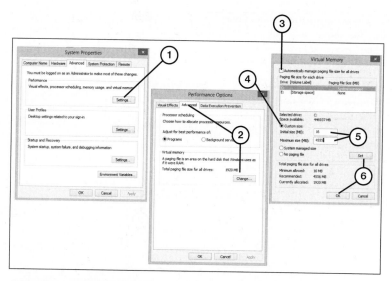

1. Opening the Settings menu
2. Opening the Virtual Memory menu
3. Clear this box to set virtual memory size manually
4. Click or tap to set a custom size
5. Enter the minimum and maximum sizes
6. Click or tap Set, then OK

FIGURE 6-61   Changing Virtual Memory Settings (Windows 8.1)

Windows Firewall Settings

Windows Firewall provides protection against unwanted inbound connections and can also be configured to filter outbound connections. Use one of the following methods to open Windows Firewall:

- Click or tap the **Windows Firewall** link in the Network and Sharing Center.

- Search for **Windows Firewall** and start it.

When Windows Firewall starts, it displays Firewall settings for the current connection (see Figure 6-62).

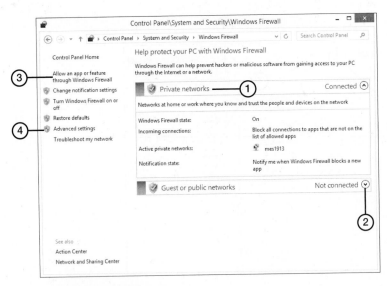

1. Connected network type
2. Click or tap to view settings
3. Click or tap to set up a firewall exception
4. Click or tap to set up an outbound rule or to open a UDP or TCP port

FIGURE 6-62   Viewing the Firewall Settings for the Current Connection (Private Networks) in Windows 8.1

To change notification settings or turn the firewall on or off, click or tap the **Change Notification Settings** or **Turn Windows Firewall On or Off** links in the left pane. Either selection opens the Customize dialog (see Figure 6-63). In this dialog, the default settings are the same:

- Windows Firewall is turned on.

- The user is notified when Firewall blocks a new app.

- To block all incoming connections on a public network, click or tap the first check box in the Public Network Settings section.

The Customize dialog can also be used to turn off or turn on Windows Firewall (refer to Figure 6-62):

- If malware or user error has turned off Windows Firewall and no other firewall is present, click or tap **Turn On Windows Firewall** in both sections.

- If the computer uses a third-party firewall, click or tap **Turn Off Windows Firewall** in both sections.

- If an app's installer recommends or requires that firewalls be turned off, turn off Windows Firewall and then turn it on again after the app installation process is complete.

The Action Center reports which firewall is in use on a particular computer.

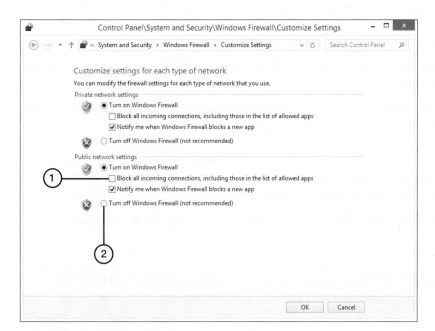

1. Blocks all incoming connections on public networks
2. Turns off Windows Firewall

FIGURE 6-63   Customizing Firewall Settings in Windows 8.1

Power Options

You can manage power options from the Control Panel Power Options applet. If a Power options icon is available in the notification area of the Windows taskbar, use it to view the current power option setting and, if desired, select a different one.

Hibernate

You can select Hibernate as an option from the shutdown menu in Windows 7. Hibernate creates a special disk file (hiberfil.sys) that records open apps, memory contents, and the apps' positions onscreen. In effect, it "pauses" the system so you can return to right where you left off.

In Windows 8/8.1/10, Hibernate is not a listed option for the shutdown menu. However, it can be added by modifying a power plan by selecting the **Change What the Buttons Do** link under Power Options.

To awaken a system from hibernation, press the power button on the computer. If the system has a password set for access, you are prompted to enter the password to restart the system.

Power Plans

Windows offers three standard *power plans* (see Figure 6-64):

- **Balanced:** Default plan; balances performance with energy consumption
- **High Performance:** Fastest CPU performance, brightest screen, and shortest battery life
- **Power Saver:** Reduces CPU performance and screen brightness more than the Balanced plan for longest battery life

Desktop computers hide Power Saver by default; laptop computers hide High Performance by default. To show or hide these other plans, click **Show/Hide Additional Plans (#2 in Figure 6-64)**.

Windows 10 adds the additional option Ultimate Performance for high-end computers.

NOTE   Some portable device vendors might offer additional plans in systems with Windows preinstalled. Tablets offer only the Balanced power plan.

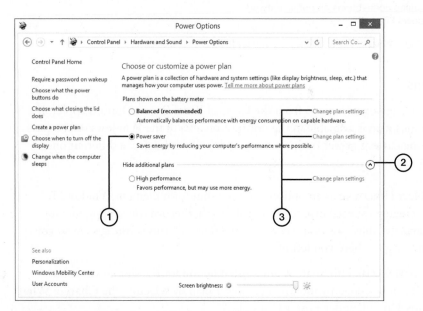

1. Current power plan
2. Click or tap to display/hide additional power plans
3. Click or tap to change plan settings

FIGURE 6-64   Standard Power Plans in Windows 8.1

To change a plan, click or tap **Change Plan Settings**. You can change the display of and sleep settings for each plan. To change additional settings, click or tap **Change Advanced Power Settings**. You can change power settings for:

- Hard-disk shutoff timing
- Desktop backgrounds
- Wireless adapters
- Sleep timings
- Hibernation options
- USB ports and devices
- Power buttons and lid
- PCI Express devices
- CPU performance and cooling
- Display shutoff timings
- Multimedia idle time and screen quality
- Internet Explorer JavaScript timing frequency

To create a new power plan, click **Create a Power Plan** in the Power Options dialog. Then, in the Create a Power Plan dialog, follow these steps:

Step 1.   Select a plan to use as the basis for your plan.

Step 2.   Enter a plan name and click **Next**.

Step 3.   Specify timings for the display and sleep and then click **Create**.

To change additional settings, click **Change Plan Settings**, select the custom plan, and change other settings. See Figure 6-65.

FIGURE 6-65   Editing a Custom Power Plan in Windows 7

Sleep/Suspend/Standby

Sleep/Suspend mode is also supported in Windows 7/8/8.1/10. If the system does not correctly enter Sleep/Standby mode, there might be a problem with startup programs interfering with this mode. Use **MSCONFIG** to disable startup programs selectively until you discover the offending app.

With most laptops and many desktops, you can put the computer into sleep mode by pressing a special sleep key or by pressing the power key and releasing it right away. To change how the sleep or power key works, modify your power plan.

NOTE   For Sleep/Standby mode to work correctly, the system needs to support the S3 power setting in the system BIOS.

Additional Control Panel Utilities

Table 6-9 lists a few additional essential links in the Control Panel and briefly describes where to look for them. The table is based on Windows 10. The Control Panel is similar in all versions, but there are slight path link differences. It is highly recommended that you explore the links in the table as you prepare for the A+ exams.

Table 6-9   Control Panel Utilities

Control Panel Utility	Panel Link Location (Windows 10)	Description
Credential Manager	User Accounts	View/Change user logon information (usernames and passwords) for networks and websites
Programs and Features	Programs	Install/uninstall programs; enable/disable Windows features; run programs made for earlier versions of Windows
Homegroup	Network and Internet	Windows 7/8 only
Devices and Printers	Hardware and Sound	Manage webcams, scanners, printers/faxes, and so on and print jobs
Sound	Hardware and Sound	Manage sound events and recording and playback settings
Troubleshooting	System and Security (at bottom of page)	Link to Windows Program Compatibility Troubleshooter app; run the app and select the program causing problems

Control Panel Utility	Panel Link Location (Windows 10)	Description
Network and Sharing Center	Network and Internet	Network preferences, sharing, and status changes (This is a common link for PC techs doing troubleshooting.)
Device Manager	Hardware and Sound	Add/remove devices; check status and roll back device drivers
BitLocker	System and Security	Encrypt drives for enhanced security
Sync Center	Control Panel > Sync Center	Manage synchronization activity and settings and initialize a sync; sync files between the current computer and network folders

Summary of Installation and Configuration Concepts

220-1002: Objective 1.7: Summarize application installation and configuration concepts.

This section provides a basic review of configuration concepts studied in Core 2 and later in this book. There will likely be questions about this material on the A+ exam. Be sure to review this section before taking the A+ exam.

Table 6-10 describes the installation process, from choosing proper hardware and software, through the installation process, to refinement and service. The different parts of the process are discussed in different chapters of this book, but the table brings them together so you can view this information not as discrete steps but as a workflow for a quality installation. It is very likely that you will see questions from each phase of this process on the A+ exam.

Table 6-10   Installation and Configuration Concepts

Concept	Requirements	Chapter/Section(s) Where This Is Covered in Detail
System requirements for hard drive space and RAM	Make sure the physical hardware can handle the work required of the software	Chapters 3 and 5
	Check the OS and applications requirements to make sure there is enough drive space to store the data and enough RAM installed to open and run the software	
	If possible, exceed the minimum requirements. Future downloads and updates will consume more drive space and RAM	

Concept	Requirements	Chapter/Section(s) Where This Is Covered in Detail
OS requirements for compatibility	Make sure the software version selected will run with the operating system. Make sure the operating system updates have not impacted the use of the software.	Chapter 8
Methods of installation and deployment (local or network based)	Be familiar with using image files on USB flash drives, external drives, or CD/DVDs on local installs Understand the basics of a network-based installation process	Chapter 6
Local user permissions Folder/file access for installation	Understand what is involved in setting up local user permissions and getting a workstation to work in an organization's domain. Know how to grant and restrict access to files and folders for different users.	Chapter 7
Security considerations	Understand the threats and vulnerabilities in a network and how to mitigate them. Be able to describe how end-user education is fundamental to an organization's security and overall success.	Chapter 7

Networking Microsoft Windows

220-1002: Objective 1.8: Given a scenario, configure Microsoft Windows networking on a client/desktop.

Windows networking includes three different types of networks, remote control and assistance options, a built-in firewall, and much more. The following sections can help you master networking concepts.

Homegroup vs. Workgroup

Windows 7, 8/8.1, and 10 support two different types of SOHO networks: *workgroups* and *homegroups*. The following sections describe how they differ from each other.

Workgroup Networking

Windows 8/8.1, and 10 all support workgroup networks. In a workgroup network:

- All computers can share folders and devices with other computers in a peer-to-peer arrangement. File and printer sharing (which is configured by default) is required for any computer that will share resources.

- All computers must be part of the same local network or subnet. For example, computers in the IP address range 192.168.1.100–192.168.1.120 with the subnet 255.255.255.0 can share resources with each other but not with computers in the IP address range 192.168.2.100–192.168.2.120.

- The workgroup does not have a password; however, each computer must have a user account for each user who will access that computer (unless password-protected sharing is disabled). For example, a computer can have an account for Mark and an account for Mary, and another computer could have an account for Mark and an account for Jerry. Mark might be able to connect to both computers, but Mary and Jerry might be able to connect to only one computer. In this situation, Mark could use one of the computers and log in via the network to another computer.

The workgroup is identified through the Computer Name section of the System properties sheet.

Creating a Workgroup

To create a workgroup in Windows:

Step 1. Configure all devices in the workgroup to use the same range of IP addresses and the same subnet. If the devices obtain their IP addresses from a router, this step has already been done for you.

Step 2. Confirm that each device has a unique computer name. The name is generated automatically when Windows is installed on a device. To verify the name, open the System properties sheet from the Control Panel or by right-clicking **Computer** (see Figure 6-66). In Windows 8/8.1, you can also open the charms menu, click or tap **Settings**, and click or tap **PC Info** to see the information.

Step 3. Confirm that each device is in the same workgroup. (The default workgroup name is WORKGROUP.)

TIP To add a bit of extra security to your workgroup, use the **Change Settings** link shown in Figure 6-66 to change the workgroup name for all computers in the workgroup.

Most computers are already in the default WORKGROUP workgroup as soon as Windows is installed. However, configuring file and printer sharing must be done manually.

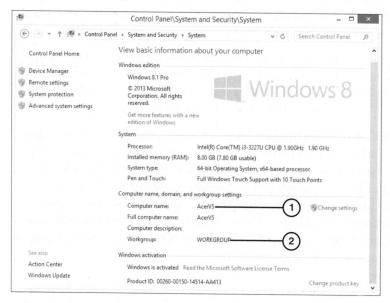

1. Computer name
2. Workgroup name

FIGURE 6-66   Viewing the Computer Name and Workgroup Name with Windows 8.1's System Properties Sheet

HomeGroup Networking

Starting with Windows 7, Microsoft introduced HomeGroup networking as a new way to do SOHO networking. In October 2018, however, HomeGroup was removed from Windows 10 (Version 1803). While homegroups set up in Windows 10 before the HomeGroup option was removed from that version still work, the following information refers to Windows 7/8/8.1. More information on sharing is covered in Chapter 7.

NOTE   Microsoft uses the term *HomeGroup* to refer to its particular networking technology and *homegroup* or *homegroups* to refer to networks that use HomeGroup technology.

Homegroups can coexist with workgroups, but HomeGroup networking enables easier security and sharing than workgroup networking does:

- Although one user on one computer creates a homegroup, all computers that join a homegroup can share folders and devices with other homegroup computers in a peer-to-peer arrangement. When a user on a computer joins a homegroup, the user selects what to share by using a simple check box dialog.

- A single password is used for security for all homegroup shares. The password is generated automatically when a homegroup is created and is used only when a computer/user joins a homegroup.

- If a computer has two or more user accounts, each user can choose whether to join a homegroup. For example, Kevin on CornerDeskPC can join a homegroup created by Cathy on HallwayPC, but Paul on CornerDeskPC has the option to join the homegroup, or not, as desired.

- When custom file or device shares are created, a single share enables all members of a homegroup to access the device or file share. Contrast this to workgroup networking, in which each computer must have a user account for every remote user or must disable password-protected file sharing, in which case there is no security.

To create a homegroup in Windows 7/8/8.1, use this procedure:

Step 1.   Open the Control Panel.

Step 2.   Click or tap **Network and Internet**.

Step 3.   Click or tap **HomeGroup**.

Step 4.   Click or tap **Create a Homegroup**.

Step 5.   Click **Next**.

Step 6.   Select the items (folders, libraries, or printers) you want to share (see Figure 6-67). (In Windows 7, the wizard uses check boxes rather than drop-downs.)

Step 7.   When the homegroup password appears, write it down or print it. Each user who wants to join the homegroup must provide it when prompted.

Step 8.   Click or tap **Finish**.

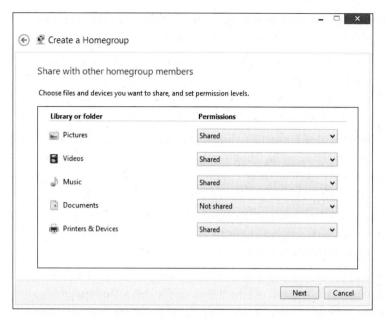

FIGURE 6-67 Selecting Folders and Resources to Share with the Homegroup Wizard in Windows 8.1

If a network includes only Windows 7, 8, and 8.1 computers (in any combination), a homegroup can be created. However, if the network will also be shared with Windows, macOS, or Linux clients, workgroup file and printer sharing settings must also be configured to enable those users to share resources.

One significant limitation to either type of networking is that no more than 10 computers at a time can connect to a workgroup or homegroup computer.

Domain Setup

Larger networks, including networks with users in multiple locations, use domain networking. Some of the special features of domain networking include:

- Shared resources (files, folders, printers, and devices) and user accounts are stored on servers. An Active Directory server is used to authenticate users, and other servers can be used for print, file, email, and other services.

- User accounts are not tied to a particular computer. A user on a domain can use any computer or computers on the domain and have access to their files and shared resources.

- Resources available to a particular user can be limited by group policy. For example, group policy settings can prevent a user from connecting a USB flash drive.

- Group policy can also be used to limit configuration settings that are available to a user. For example, group policy can be used to turn off AutoPlay for removable-media devices.

- Different local networks with hundreds to thousands of users can be part of a single domain.

The *domain setup* for a computer is performed from the Computer Name section of the System properties sheet. To join a domain:

Step 1.   Open the System properties sheet.

Step 2.   Click or tap **Change Settings**.

Step 3.   On the Computer Name tab, click or tap **Network ID**.

Step 4.   Confirm that **This Computer Is Part of a Business Network** is selected. Click or tap **Next**.

Step 5.   Confirm that **My Company Uses a Network with a Domain** is selected. Click or tap **Next**.

Step 6.   Review the information needed to connect to a domain and click **Next**.

Step 7.   Enter the username, password, and domain name and click **Next**.

Step 8.   Click **OK** on the Welcome to the Domain message.

Network Shares

A shared folder or drive can be accessed by other computers on the network. Shares can be provided in three ways:

- On a client/server-based network or on a peer-to-peer network with peer servers that support user/group permissions, shares are protected by lists of authorized users or groups. Windows 7, 8/8.1, and 10 support user/group access control.

- A workgroup network can offer unlimited sharing (full control or read-only) for any user who connects to a system if password-protected sharing is disabled. (This is not recommended.)

- A homegroup network offers read-only access for any shared resource to any homegroup user. However, individual folders can be configured for read/write (full control) access for any homegroup user.

A *network share* can be accessed by either its mapped drive letters or its folder names in File Explorer (Windows 8/8.1/10).

When user/group-based permissions are used, only members who belong to a specific group or who are listed separately on the access list for a particular share can access that share. After users log on to the network, they have access to all shares they've been authorized to use without the need to provide additional passwords. Access levels include full and read-only and, on NTFS drives, other access levels, such as write, create, and delete.

Administrative Shares

Administrative shares are hidden shares that can be identified by a $ at the end of the share name. These shares cannot be seen by standard users when browsing to the computer over the network; they are meant for administrative use. All the shared folders that include administrative shares can be found by navigating to **Computer Management > System Tools > Shared Folders > Shares**. Note that every volume within the hard drive (C: or D:, for example) has an administrative share; for example, C$ is the administrative share for the C: drive. Although it is possible to remove these by editing the Registry, this is not recommended because it might cause other networking issues. You should be aware that only administrators should have access to these shares.

Sharing a Folder

To share a folder with Windows 7/8/8.1/10, follow these steps:

Step 1.   Ensure that file sharing is enabled by opening the Control Panel and double-clicking the **Network and Sharing Center** icon. To access this dialog in Windows 7/8/8.1, click **Change Advanced Sharing Settings** after opening the Network and Sharing Center.

Step 2.   Open Windows Explorer/File Explorer and click **Computer/This PC**.

Step 3.   In the Computer/This PC window, navigate to a folder that you want to share.

Step 4.   Right-click the folder that you want to share and choose **Share With**.

Step 5.   If password-protected sharing is enabled, click **Selected People** and select which users will have access to the shared folder and select their permission levels. To allow all users, select the **Everyone** group within the list of users.

Step 6.   When finished configuring permissions, click **Share** and then click **Done**.

Joining a Homegroup and Custom File Sharing

When joining a homegroup in Windows 7/8/8.1, joining the homegroup and configuring default sharing settings is a simple process:

Step 1.   In the Network and Internet window, click **HomeGroup**.

Step 2.   Click **Join Now**.

Step 3.   Click **Next**.

Step 4.   Select the items you want to share.

Step 5.   Click **Next**.

Step 6.   Type the homegroup password.

Step 7.   Click **Next**.

Step 8.   Click **Finish**.

At this point, items shared through the homegroup are shared as read-only. To set up custom access for a particular folder:

Step 1.   In the Computer/This PC window, navigate to a folder that you want to share.

Step 2.   Right-click the folder that you want to share and choose **Share With**. The File Sharing window appears.

Step 3.   In Windows 7, choose from **Homegroup (Read)**, **Homegroup (Read/ Write)**, **Nobody** (turns off sharing), or **Specific People (Choose from Accounts on Your System)**. In Windows 8/8.1/10, choose from **Homegroup (View)**, **Homegroup (View/Edit)**, **Stop Sharing**, and **Specific People (Choose from Accounts on Your System)**.

Step 4.   When you are done configuring permissions, click **Share** and then click **Done**.

> **TIP** If you use a third-party firewall, consult the documentation or Help files for the appropriate setting to use homegroups.

Mapped Drive Letters

Windows enables shared folders and shared drives to be mapped to drive letters on clients. In Windows Explorer/File Explorer/Computer/This PC, these mapped drive letters show up in the list along with the local drive letters. A shared resource can be accessed either through Network (using the share name) or through a mapped drive letter.

Drive mapping has the following benefits:

- A shared folder mapped as a drive can be referred to by the drive name instead of by using a long Universal Naming Convention (UNC) path. (See the sidebar "Universal Naming Convention (UNC)," later in this chapter, for details.)

- When using MS-DOS programs, keep in mind that using mapped drives is the only way for those programs to access shared folders.

Mapping drives is a rather straightforward procedure:

Step 1.   Open the Network view in Windows Explorer/File Explorer.

Step 2.   Right-click the shared folder in Network view and select **Map Network Drive**.

Step 3.   Select a drive letter from the list of available drive letters; only drive letters not used by local drives are listed. Drive letters already in use for other shared folders display the UNC name of the shared folder.

Step 4.   Click the **Reconnect at Login** box if you want to use the mapped drive every time you connect to the network. This option should be used only if the server will be available at all times; otherwise, the client will receive error messages when it tries to access the shared resource.

Step 5.   Click the **Connect Using Different Credentials** box if you want to use a different username/password to connect to the shared resource. See Figure 6-68.

Step 6.   Click **Finish**.

NOTE   You can browse for any shared folder by its UNC name by starting the Map Network Drive process from the Tools menu in Computer (Windows 7) or by clicking This PC (Windows 8/8.1/10) and selecting **Map Network Drive** from the Computer ribbon menu.

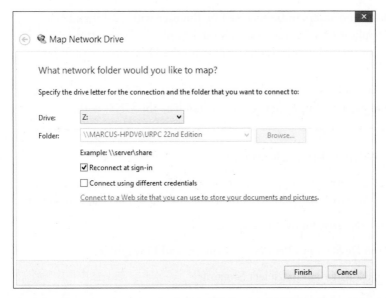

FIGURE 6-68   The Map Network Drive Dialog for Creating a Temporary or Permanent Drive Mapping

Universal Naming Convention (UNC)

The Universal Naming Convention (UNC) is designed to enable users to access network resources such as folders or printers without mapping drive letters to network drives or specifying the type of device that stores the file or hosts the printer. A UNC name has the following structure in Windows:

`\\servername\share name\path\filename`

A typical UNC path to a document would resemble:

`\\Tiger1\O\NetDocuments\his_doc.docx`

A typical UNC path to a shared printer on the same system would resemble:

`\\Tiger1\Printername`

What does this mean in plain English?

- **\\Tiger1** is the server.
- **\O** is the share name.
- **\NetDocuments** is the path.
- **his_doc.docx** is the document.
- **\Printername** is the printer.

UNC enables files and printers to be accessed by the user with 32-bit and 64-bit Windows applications. Because a maximum of only 23 drive letters can be mapped, UNC enables network resources beyond the D–Z limits to still be accessed.

To display the UNC path to a shared folder with Windows, right-click the share and select **Properties**. The Target field in the dialog lists the UNC path.

Printer Sharing vs. Network Printer Mapping

Printers connected to network computers can be shared or printers can be connected directly to a network with Ethernet or wireless Ethernet (WiFi) connections.

To perform *printer sharing*, follow these steps:

Step 1. Open the Devices and Printers or Printers and Faxes folder.

Step 2. Right-click a printer and select **Sharing**.

Step 3. Select **Share This Printer** and specify a share name.

Step 4. Click **Additional Drivers** to select additional drivers to install for other operating systems that will use the printer on the network. Supply driver media when prompted.

A printer connected to a computer in a homegroup is shared with other homegroup users through the Homegroup wizard.

Whether a printer has its own IP address or is connected to a computer as a shared printer, use this procedure to install it on a system in a process called *network printer mapping*:

Step 1. Open Devices and Printers (Windows 7/8/8.1/10) in the Control Panel.

Step 2. Click or tap **Add a Printer** (or **Add Printer**).

Step 3. Click or tap **Add a Network**, **Wireless**, or **Bluetooth**. Windows tries to search for a printer automatically. To bypass this, click **The Printer I Want Isn't Listed**.

Step 4. To find a printer on an Active Directory (domain-based) network, choose **Find a Printer in the Directory, Based on Location or Features**. To find a printer by name (*server**printername*), choose **Select a Shared Printer by Name**. To find a printer by its URL or IP address, choose **Add a Printer Using a TCP/IP Address or Hostname**. Click **Next**.

Step 5. After the printer is selected, specify whether you want to use the new printer as the default printer. Click **Next**.

Step 6. Specify whether you want to print a test page. Printing a test page allows you to verify whether the correct print driver has been installed.

Step 7. Click **Finish** to complete the setup process. Provide the Windows CD or printer setup disc if required to complete the process.

Establish Networking Connections

The Network and Sharing Center includes a Set Up a New Connection or Network wizard for the following connection types:

- Virtual private networking
- Dialup networking
- Broadband

> **NOTE** Windows 10 also supports these connection types. To create connections, click or tap **Start** > **Settings** > **Network & Internet** and select the connection type to create.

VPN Connections

A VPN connection creates a secure tunnel over a public network, such as the Internet, between two computers. To configure a new VPN connection:

Step 1. In the Set Up a Connection or Network dialog, click or tap **Connect to a Workplace** and click or tap **Next** (see Figure 6-69).

FIGURE 6-69   Starting the VPN Connection Creation Process in Windows 8.1

Step 2.   Click or tap **Use My Internet Connection** (VPN).

Step 3.   In Windows 8/8.1, enter the Internet address (IP address, website) and the destination name, select options such as **Use a Smart Card** and **Remember My Credentials** as desired, and click **Create** (see Figure 6-70). In Windows 7, enter the Internet address (IP address, website) and the destination name, and select options such as **Use a Smart Card** and **Remember My Credentials** as desired. To make the connection later, click **Don't Connect Now**. Click **Next** and then click **Close**.

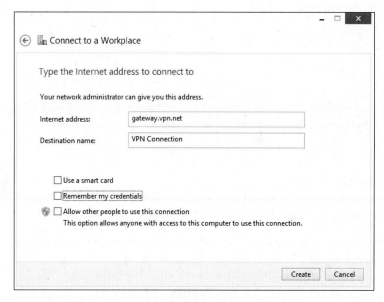

FIGURE 6-70   Setting Up a VPN Connection's Address and Destination in Windows 8.1

Step 4.   In Windows 8/8.1, to display the VPN connection, click the network connection icon in the taskbar or from the charms menu. Windows prompts the user for credentials when the connection is started. In Windows 7, enter the username, password, and domain. Click **Create**. The VPN connection is available from the Connections menu that appears when the user clicks the network connection icon in the taskbar.

Dial-up Connections

A dial-up connection is a network connection between two computers via phone lines. Windows can create two types of dial-up connections on systems with analog modems:

- Dial-up networking connections to an ISP

- Direct dial-in connections to a corporate computer

To configure a new dial-up connection to an ISP:

Step 1. In the Set Up a Connection or Network dialog, click or tap **Connect to the Internet** and click **Next** (refer to Figure 6-69).

Step 2. Click or tap **Dial-up** and click or tap **Next**.

Step 3. Enter the ISP's dial-up phone number, username, and password. Check the **Remember This Password** box if the user doesn't want to enter the password again. Name the connection and click **Connect**.

The connection is stored along with other wired and wireless connections.

To configure a new direct dial-in connection to a corporate computer:

Step 1. In the Set Up a Connection or Network dialog, click or tap **Connect to a Workplace** and click or tap **Next**.

Step 2. Click or tap **Dial Directly** and click or tap **Next**.

Step 3. Enter the remote computer's dial-up phone number and destination name. Select options as desired. To connect now, click or tap **Next**. To set up the connection for later, check the **Don't Connect** box.

Step 4. Enter the username and password. Enter the domain. Check the **Remember This Password** box if the user doesn't want to enter the password again. Click or tap **Connect** or **Create**.

The connection is stored along with other network connections (see Figure 6-71).

FIGURE 6-71   VPN, Dial-up ISP, and Direct Dial-in Connections Listed Along with Wireless Connections

Wireless Connections

A wireless connection can be configured when the user clicks on the SSID from the taskbar or Settings menu. However, if you use the Wireless Connection option in the Network and Sharing Center, more options can be specified, including WPA2-Personal and WPA2-Enterprise security types:

Step 1.   In the Set Up a Connection or Network dialog, click or tap **Connect to a Wireless Network** and click or tap **Next**.

Step 2.   Enter the network name. Select the Security type and enter the security key. To start the connection automatically, check the **Start This Connection Automatically** box (see Figure 6-72). Click or tap **Next**.

Step 3.   Click or tap **Close**. The connection is added to the list of connections.

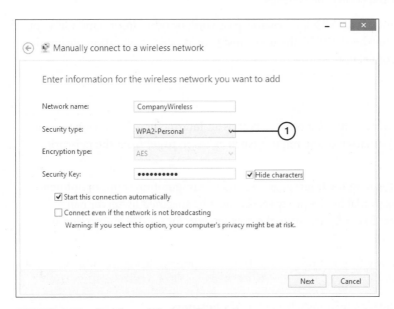

FIGURE 6-72   Creating a Wireless Connection

Wired Connections

Use the option to configure a **wired** connection if setting up a point-to-point protocol over Ethernet (PPPoE) connection. This type of connection is used by cable or DSL ISPs that require the user to log in to the connection:

Step 1.   In the Set Up a Connection or Network dialog, click or tap **Connect to the Internet** and click or tap **Next**.

Step 2.   Click or tap **Broadband (PPPoE)** and click or tap **Next**.

Step 3.   Enter the username and password. Enter the domain. Check the **Remember This Password** box if the user doesn't want to enter the password again. Click or tap **Connect**.

The connection is stored along with other network connections.

WWAN (Cellular) Connections

A WWAN (cellular) connection shows up in the list of network connections after a SIM card is installed and activated by a mobile provider. To use this type of connection, select it from the list of network connections displayed when selecting the network icon in the taskbar or Settings.

If the access point name (APN), username, password, or other information has not yet been stored for the WWAN, the user must provide this information during the first use of the connection.

Proxy Settings

A corporate network may use a proxy server as an intermediary between a network client and the destination of the request (such as a web page) from the network client.

If a proxy server is used for Internet access and a configuration script or automatic detection are not available, the proxy server must be specified by server name and port number. To configure manual *proxy settings* for a LAN connection in Windows:

Step 1.   Open the Internet properties (Internet options) dialog from the Control Panel.

Step 2.   On the Connections tab, click **LAN Settings**.

Step 3.   In the Local Area Network (LAN) Settings window, choose the appropriate option under Proxy Server. If a single proxy server address and port number is used for all types of traffic, click the **Use a Proxy Server** check box and enter the address and port number provided by the network administrator. However, if different proxy servers or ports will be used, click the **Use a Proxy Server** check box and click the **Advanced** button.

Step 4.   Specify the correct server and port number to use (see Figure 6-73).

Step 5.   Click **OK** to save changes in each dialog until you return to the browser display.

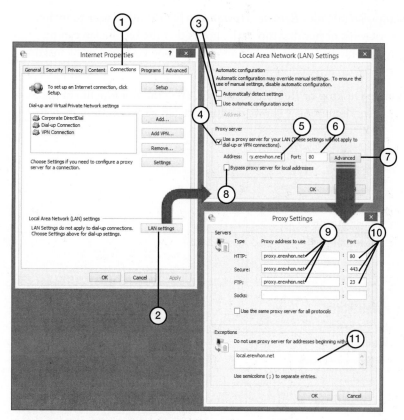

1. The Connections tab of Internet properties
2. Click or tap **LAN settings** to continue
3. If automatic detection or proxy scripts are not used, clear these checkboxes
4. Click this checkbox to add manual proxy server information
5. Proxy server address
6. Proxy server port number
7. To specify different proxy servers or port numbers, click or tap **Advanced**
8. To exclude all local addresses from proxy filtering, check the **Bypass Proxy server...** box.
9. Enter the name for each proxy server by traffic type
10. Enter the port number for each proxy server
11. Enter any exceptions here

FIGURE 6-73   Setting Up Proxy Servers Manually

Remote Desktop Connection and Remote Assistance

To facilitate connections to remote computers and allow full remote control, Microsoft uses the Remote Desktop Connection program, which is based on Remote Desktop Protocol (RDP).

Remote Desktop also includes *Remote Assistance*, which allows a user to invite a technician to view his or her desktop in the hopes that the technician can fix any encountered problems. These invitations can be made via email or by instant messenger.

To enable Remote Desktop or Remote Assistance, open the Remote tab of the System properties sheet. Figure 6-74 shows the Remote tab with both remote features enabled.

FIGURE 6-74   Configuring Windows for Remote Assistance and Remote Desktop

Click or tap the **Advanced** button to specify how long an invitation remains valid and whether to accept connections only from Windows or newer versions (which is recommended for improved security).

The msra.exe program is used to send and receive Remote Assistance invitations (see Figure 6-75). To run msra, open it from the command line or search for it.

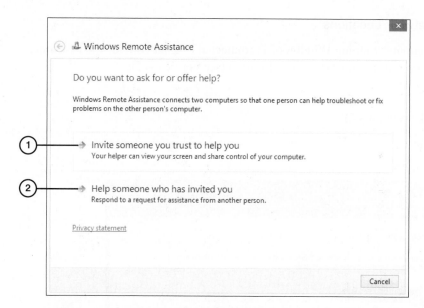

1. Click or tap to send an invitation to get help
2. Click or tap to help someone who sent an invitation

FIGURE 6-75   The Dialog That Appears When msra.exe Runs

An invitation file and a separate password (see Figure 6-76) must be used by the helper to gain access to the system making the Remote Access request.

FIGURE 6-76   A Password to Provide Along with the Invitation to Get Help

Home vs. Work vs. Public Network Settings

In Windows, the settings Home, Work, Public, and Private refer to network locations. Selecting the right network location affects how Windows Firewall configures protection and the networking features available to a particular PC.

Windows 7 Network Locations

When a computer running Windows 7 is connected to a network for the first time, Windows prompts the user to select a location (see Figure 6-77):

- Home
- Work (Windows 7)
- Public

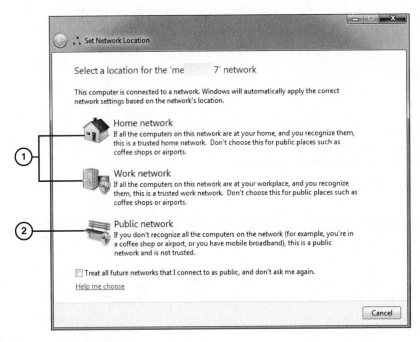

1. Private networks
2. Public network

FIGURE 6-77 Network Location Dialog (Windows 7)

By choosing **Home** or **Work (Office)**, you can configure the network connection as private. If this computer is connected to a secure wireless network or a wired network, it is visible only to devices connected to the network. The computer is discoverable, so file and printer sharing and media streaming work.

You can choose **Home** to make Windows HomeGroup networking available.

Choose **Public** for non-secured networks (such as in a hotel, coffee shop, library, or other public location). This option turns off network discovery, so the computer is not visible to other computers using the network.

If the location is set incorrectly, click the link below the current network location setting in the Network and Sharing Center (see Figure 6-78) and choose the correct location. **Close** the window to complete the process.

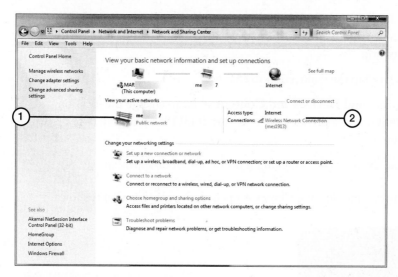

1. Public network location is incorrect
2. No access to homegroup

FIGURE 6-78   Network and Sharing Center Displays the Network Type for the Current Connection

Windows 8/8.1 Network Locations

When a computer running Windows 8/8.1 is connected to a network for the first time, Windows prompts the user to select a location. In Windows 8, the dialog has two options:

- Yes, Turn on Sharing and Connect to Devices (for home or work networks)

- No, Don't Turn on Sharing or Connect to Devices (for networks in public places)

The Windows 8.1 version of this dialog looks like the dialog in Figure 6-79.

As in Windows 7, the Network and Sharing Center in Windows 8.1 displays the current network connection and location. However, if the network location needs to be changed, the user must open the Network dialog from PC Settings:

Step 1.   Sweep in from the right to open the charms menu.

Step 2.   Click or tap **Settings**.

Step 3.   Click or tap the active network connection icon in the Settings pane. If no network connection is active, click or tap **Change PC Settings, Network**.

Step 4.   Click or tap the connection to change.

Step 5.   Use the **Find Devices and Content** slider to change the location. Turn it on for a private network. Turn it off for a public network (see Figure 6-80).

Step 6.   Close the menu (by dragging it down until it disappears).

When the Network and Sharing Center is opened, the new location is shown.

1. Click or tap to enable private networking and support for homegroup networks

FIGURE 6-79   Selecting a Network Type for a New Network Connection in Windows 8.1

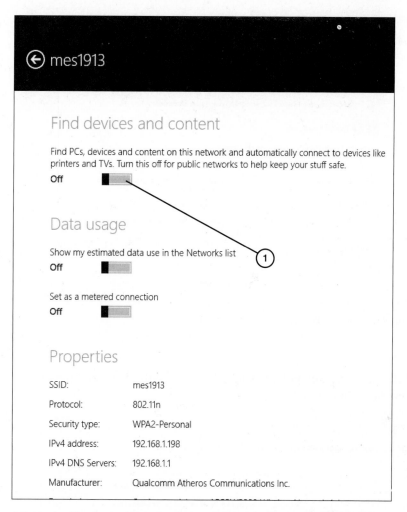

1. Correct setting for a public network; drag right to turn On for a private network

FIGURE 6-80 Changing the Network Settings for the Current Connection in Windows 8.1

In Windows 10, setting up a network is more streamlined and wizard driven than in earlier versions. Each of the three possible options begins a dialog process for establishing a connection. Figure 6-81 shows the Windows 10 Set Up a New Connection link in the Control Panel.

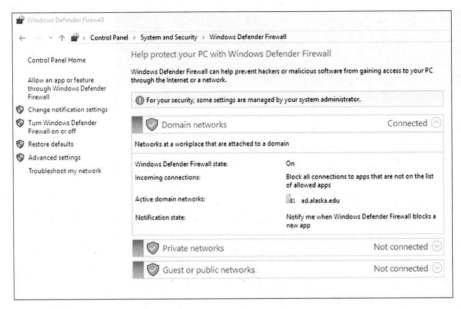

FIGURE 6-81   Setting Up a New Connection in Windows 10

Firewall Settings

In Windows 10, select **System and Security** from the Control Panel to bring up the settings option shown in Figure 6-82.

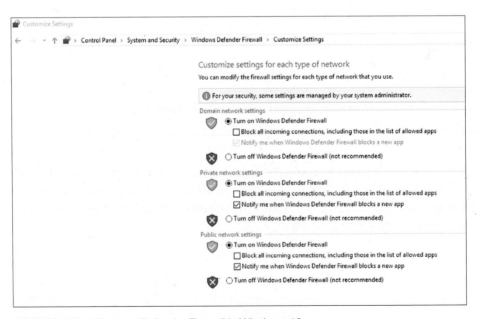

FIGURE 6-82   Windows Defender Firewall in Windows 10

In Windows 10, choose the link **Turn Windows Defender Firewall On or Off** from the left menu of the Windows Defender Firewall page. The link brings up the options for turning off Windows defender, as shown in Figure 6-83.

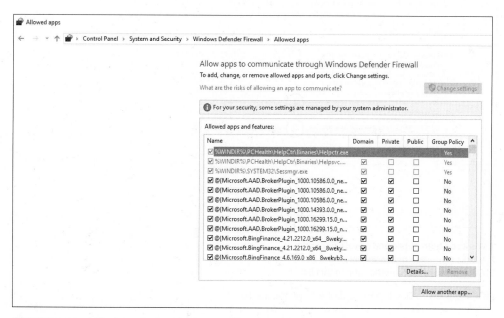

FIGURE 6-83   Windows Defender Firewall: Enable/Disable Menu

Exceptions and Configuration

Windows Firewall can be configured to permit specified applications to pass through the firewall, to open specific ports needed by applications, or to block all traffic. Whenever possible, it's easier to permit traffic by application rather than by UDP or TCP port numbers. Each application or port that is opened is called an *exception*.

Windows Firewall sets up exceptions automatically when an app is blocked and the user allows the app to access the network or Internet.

In Windows 10, choose the link **Allow App or Feature Through Windows Defender Firewall** from the left menu of the Windows Defender Firewall page (refer to Figure 6-81). The link brings up options for allowing apps, as shown in Figure 6-84.

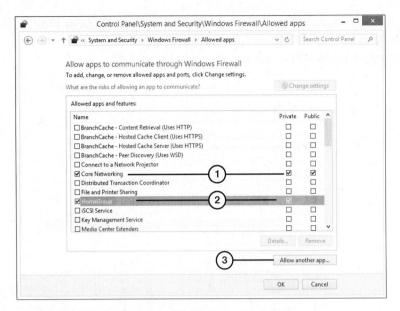

1. Works on both public and private networks
2. Works on private networks only
3. Click or tap to add another app to this list

FIGURE 6-84 Allowing Exceptions in Windows 10

In Windows 7/8/8.1,Windows Firewall includes several configuration settings. To change firewall settings for an app or a feature, click or tap the **Allow an App or Feature Through Windows Firewall** link (refer to upper left of Figure 6-81).

To change the setting for a listed app or feature, click or tap the **Change Settings** button. Click or tap an empty check box to permit the app through the firewall; click a filled check box to block the app. Click or tap **Details** to learn more about the app. To remove an app from the list, click or tap **Remove**. Note that separate settings are available for private and public networks.

To browse for another app to add to the list, click the **Allow Another App** button and then click **Browse**. After the app and network type are selected, Windows Firewall puts the app on the list of allowed apps and features.

In Windows 7/8/8.1, click or tap **Advanced Settings** (refer to Figure 6-82) to open the dialog shown in Figure 6-85. Use this mode to set up rules for inbound or outbound traffic, to block or permit specific UDP or TCP port numbers, and to configure monitoring.

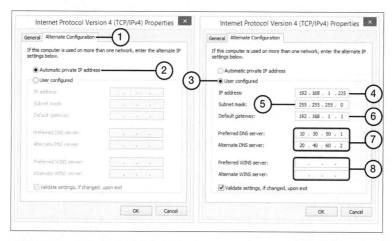

1. Click or tap Alternate Configuration
2. Default setting assigns an APIPA if a DHCP server is not available
3. Click or tap to set up manual IP configuration
4. Enter a unique IP address on the network
5. Enter the same subnet mask as other computers on the network
6. Enter the default gateway for your network
7. Enter the DNS servers you prefer
8. Leave these blank unless your network has WINS servers

FIGURE 6-85   Setting Up New Exceptions in Windows 8.1's Firewall

Configuring an Alternative IP Address in Windows

An *alternative IP address* enables a system to stay on the network if the DHCP server fails or if the system is sometimes on a different network than normal. To view or change the settings on the Alternate Configuration tab for a network adapter (see Figure 6-86), follow these steps:

Step 1.   Open the Network and Sharing Center.

Step 2.   Click or tap **Change Adapter Settings**.

Step 3.   Click or tap the connection to change.

Step 4.   Click or tap **Change Settings of This Connection**.

Step 5.   Click or tap **Internet Protocol Version 4 (TCP/IPv4)**.

Step 6.   Click or tap **Properties**.

Step 7.   Click or tap **Alternate Configuration**.

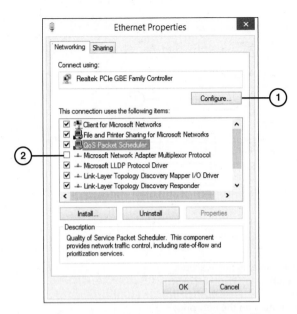

1. Click or tap to configure network adapter settings
2. Checked items are installed and active

FIGURE 6-86   Using the Alternate Configuration Tab to Set Up a Different IP Configuration for Use on Another Network or When No DHCP Server Is Available

The Alternate Configuration tab is used to set up a different TCP/IPv4 configuration for use when a DHCP server is not available or when a different set of user-configured settings is needed, as when a laptop is being used at a secondary location. By default, Automatic Private IP Addressing (APIPA) is used when no DHCP server is in use. APIPA assigns each system a unique IP address in the 169.254.x.x range. APIPA enables a network to perform LAN connections when the DHCP server is not available, but systems using APIPA cannot connect to the Internet. Linux and macOS use the term *IPv4 Link-local*.

NOTE   In IPv6, every device is assigned a link-local address using the prefix fe80::/64, even if a DHCP server is running or a manual IPv6 address has been assigned.

Network Card Properties

Although most wired network adapters (network cards or NICs) work well using the default settings, some network configurations might require changes to default settings. The following sections describe network card properties and how to change them.

To access the properties listed in the upcoming sections, follow this procedure:

Step 1.   Open the Network and Sharing Center.

Step 2.   Click or tap **Change Adapter Settings**.

Step 3.   Click or tap a wired connection.

Step 4.   Click or tap **Change Settings of This Connection**.

Step 5.   Click or tap **Configure** (see Figure 6-87).

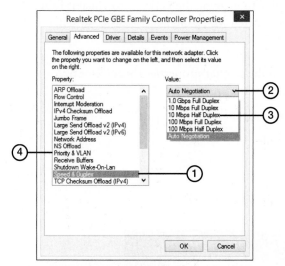

1. Click or tap Speed & Duplex
2. Open menu to view options
3. Select a manual setting if Auto doesn't provide expected performance
4. Click or tap to make sure Priority & VLAN are enabled for use with QoS

FIGURE 6-87   Configuring a Gigabit Ethernet Adapter in Windows 8.1

Half Duplex/Full Duplex/Auto

Half duplex/full duplex/auto are settings that determine how a network card communicates with the rest of the network. If the hardware in use on an Ethernet, Fast Ethernet, or Gigabit Ethernet network permits, you can configure the network to run in full-duplex mode. Full-duplex mode enables the adapter to send and receive data at the same time, which doubles network speed compared to the default half-duplex mode (where the card sends and receives in separate operations).

To achieve full-duplex performance on a UTP-based Ethernet network, the network adapters on a network must all support full-duplex mode and must be configured to use full-duplex mode with the device's setup program or properties sheet, and a switch must be used in place of a hub.

The default Auto Negotiation setting (see Figure 6-88 in the next section) allows the adapter to determine the best setting, but it can be overridden if necessary.

Speed

Ethernet adapters can run at more than one speed, but the speed available is limited by the slowest network hardware. For example, if network clients have Gigabit Ethernet (10/100/1000Mbps) adapters, but the network switch is a Fast Ethernet (10/100Mbps) device, the network will run at Fast Ethernet speeds. If network cabling is CAT5e or faster, it is possible to upgrade the network to Gigabit Ethernet speeds by replacing the Fast Ethernet switch with a Gigabit Ethernet switch.

To change duplex and speed settings:

Step 1.   Click or tap **Configure** on the adapter properties sheet (refer to Figure 6-88).

Step 2.   Click or tap the **Advanced** tab.

Step 3.   Click or tap **Speed & Duplex**.

Step 4.   Select the value desired.

Step 5.   Click **OK** when done.

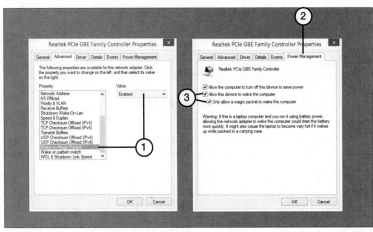

1. Wake on Magic Packet enabled
2. Click or tap Power Management tab
3. Check Allow this device to wake the computer and Only allow a magic packet to wake the computer

FIGURE 6-88   Viewing Speed & Duplex Settings for a Gigabit Ethernet Adapter

Wake-on-LAN

Wake-on-LAN (WOL or WoL) enables a computer connected to a wired network to be awakened from sleep mode via a special "magic packet" signal delivered by the network. Wake-on-LAN can be used to awaken a computer for updates, backup, or other tasks, as needed, and allow it to run in low-power mode when not in use.

The successful configuration of Wake-on-LAN requires changes to the default settings of a computer's BIOS or UEFI firmware, network adapter, Windows services, firewall settings, and router port forwarding. The changes to a network adapter's default setting include:

- Open the **Advanced** tab in the properties sheet for the network adapter and enable **Wake on Magic Packet**.

- Open the **Power Management** tab for the network adapter and check the boxes for **Allow This Device to Wake the Computer** and **Only Allow a Magic Packet to Wake the Computer**.

Figure 6-89 shows these tabs on a system running Windows 8.1.

The following additional changes in system configuration are needed to make Wake-on-LAN work properly:

- Enable Wake-on-LAN in the system BIOS or UEFI firmware and save changes. Some systems might not have a BIOS/UEFI firmware option for WOL, but it might be supported automatically.

- Open the Control Panel's Windows Features dialog (in Programs and Features) and turn on **Simple TCP/IP Services**.

- Open Computer Management's Services dialog, start Simple TCP/IP Services, and configure it to run automatically.

- Ensure that UDP port 9 (recommended) or port 7 (if UDP port 9 doesn't work properly) is open in your firewall. If you use Windows Firewall, start it in Advanced mode and set up a new inbound rule.

- Configure your router to forward UDP port 9 (or UDP 7) to the computers that need WOL services.

```
markesoper@markesoper-VirtualBox: /etc
markesoper@markesoper-VirtualBox:/etc$ crontab -l    ──────── 1
# Edit this file to introduce tasks to be run by cron.
#
# Each task to run has to be defined through a single line
# indicating with different fields when the task will be run
# and what command to run for the task
#
# To define the time you can provide concrete values for
# minute (m), hour (h), day of month (dom), month (mon),
# and day of week (dow) or use '*' in these fields (for 'any').#
# Notice that tasks will be started based on the cron's system
# daemon's notion of time and timezones.
#
# Output of the crontab jobs (including errors) is sent through
# email to the user the crontab file belongs to (unless redirected).
#
# For example, you can run a backup of all your user accounts
# at 5 a.m every week with:
# 0 5 * * 1 tar -zcf /var/backups/home.tgz /home/    ──────── 2
#
# For more information see the manual pages of crontab(5) and cron(8)
#
# m h  dom mon dow   command
markesoper@markesoper-VirtualBox:/etc$
```

3

1. Use crontab –l to view and create tasks to be run by cron
2. Backup task to be run by cron
3. Pound sign is equivalent to REM (remark) statement. Remove it from a line that has a command you want to run

FIGURE 6-89   Configuring Wake-on-LAN Settings on a Typical Ethernet Adapter

QoS (Quality of Service)

Quality of service (**QoS**) enables a computer connected to a wired network to optimize real-time streaming traffic, such as VoIP, streaming video, or streaming music services. QoS is installed by default in Windows. To verify that it is installed and enabled, open the properties sheet for the Ethernet or wireless adapter and click the **Networking** tab. Ensure that **QoS Packet Scheduler** is checked (refer to Figure 6-87).

To enable QoS to perform properly, make sure that **Priority & VLAN** (also called **QoS Packet Tagging**) is enabled on the Advanced tab.

TIP   Additional QoS optimization can be performed by using group policy settings. See https://www.biztechmagazine.com/article/2010/03/boost-network-performance-windows-7-qos for more information.

BIOS (On-board NIC)

The BIOS in an on-board NIC can be used to boot the computer if it is configured as a bootable device in the BIOS or UEFI firmware setup. Enable this setting to obtain an installable OS image from the network.

macOS and Linux

220-1002: Objective 1.9: Given a scenario, use features and tools of the Mac OS and Linux client/desktop operating systems.

Although macOS and Linux operating systems are far less common than Windows on organizational desktops, macOS is very popular in educational markets, and Linux runs many of the world's servers. To be a well-rounded computer technician, you need to understand how these operating systems differ from Windows and from each other and be able to perform basic commands and maintenance procedures.

Best Practices

To maintain any computer system, you should follow best practices related to:

- Scheduled backups
- Scheduled disk maintenance
- System updates/App Store
- Patch management
- Driver/firmware updates
- Antivirus/antimalware updates

The following sections discuss best practices in these areas for macOS and Linux.

Scheduled Backups

Scheduled backups help prevent major data loss in case of system failure, accident, or loss. Backups can be used to safeguard:

- Contacts
- Email
- Media files (photos, videos, and music)
- Documents

The default backup app in macOS is ***Time Machine***. Linux includes several utilities that can be used for backups. These include the command line tar and rsync utilities. Others, including the grsync (GUI for rsync) and duplicity (command line and GUI available as Déjà Dup), are available from the repository for a Linux distribution or from the vendors.

> **NOTE**   The BackupYourSystem page on Ubuntu Linux Help (https://help.ubuntu.com/community/BackupYourSystem) provides a long list of command line and GUI-based backup tools that also work with other Linux distros.

Scheduled backups should be run at times when the system is idle, such as overnight and on weekends.

Backup Types

A full backup backs up the entire contents of the computer or selected drive to another local or network location. A backup program may create a compressed file to store backed-up information. With this type of backup, the backup program must run a restore utility to make the files usable again. Another type of backup program simply copies backup files to a different location, where they can be opened by the operating system.

Most backup programs can also run an incremental backup, which backs up only the files that have been created or changed after the last full backup.

Backup features to look for include:

- **Compression:** Reduces the amount of file space and often the amount of time needed to make a backup.

- **Support for incremental as well as full backups:** Good backup practice calls for periodic full backups followed by backups of files changed since the last full backup (incremental backups).

- **Local and network backup destinations:** Some backup utilities might require additional configuration before a network backup can be performed.

For more details about how to perform a backup, see the "Backup/Time Machine" section, later in this chapter.

Scheduled Disk Maintenance

macOS does not require the user to schedule disk maintenance, as routine issues are fixed automatically by the operating system. In Linux, automated tasks of all types, including disk maintenance, can be set up and run by the cron utility. The crontab utility displays cron scripts by system or by user.

Figure 6-90 illustrates a crontab that contains a command to back up user accounts at 5:00 AM daily.

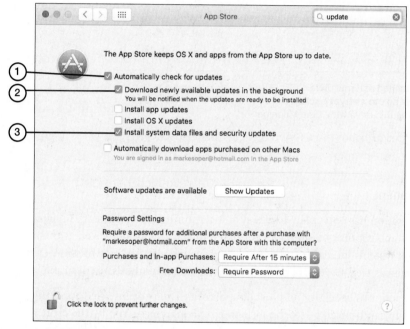

1. Automatic check for updates enabled
2. Automatic download of updates enabled; you decide when to install them
3. System data files and security updates are installed automatically

FIGURE 6-90 Crontab with cron Script for Daily Backup in Linux

System Updates/App Store

Linux distributions include a command line system update tool such as dnf (Red Hat, Fedora) or apt-get (Debian, Ubuntu). Use these tools to update Linux, install apps, and maintain the list of apps (packages) known to the OS. For more information about using apt-get, see the section "apt-get," later in this chapter.

If a Linux installation includes GNOME or KDE, it might include an update feature.

macOS has a variety of options for system updates in the App Store section of System Preferences (see Figure 6-91). The App Store can be configured to automatically check for updates for apps and macOS, automatically install updates, and download apps installed on other macOS devices under the same user account.

Key Topic

1. Newly-attached external drive
2. Check this box to encrypt backup drive
3. Click to use this drive with Time Machine

FIGURE 6-91   Configuring the macOS App Store to Update macOS and Apps

Patch Management

If an organization has only a few Linux systems, running manual system updates with yum or apt-get may be sufficient for patch management. However, as the number of Linux systems increases and when Linux systems are used for mission-critical functions such as web servers, better patch management methods are desirable.

If you use a script to check for and install updates to Linux or installed apps, the crontab utility can be used to set the task on a schedule that is run by the cron utility.

Driver/Firmware Updates

In macOS, driver and firmware updates are delivered automatically through the App Store. Most Linux distros include driver updates as part of the distribution; they can also be retrieved manually by using the apt-get command.

Antivirus/Anti-malware Updates

It's widely believed that Linux and macOS are immune to viruses and malware. Although Linux and macOS are not targeted nearly as much as Windows, an unprotected Linux or macOS computer can be used as an infection vector for Windows machines that connect to it.

ClamAV (http://www.clamav.net) is an open source antivirus app available for both macOS and Linux. Scans and updates can be automated with cron, and a GUI front end known as ClamTK is available. Well-known antivirus software usually has Linux and macOS versions as well as Windows versions.

Antivirus/anti-malware apps for Linux and macOS should be updated at least daily.

Tools

Linux and macOS include a variety of applications for system maintenance, referred to here as "tools." The sections that follow discuss:

- Backup (Time Machine in macOS)
- Restore/Snapshot
- Image (Backup) Recovery
- Disk Maintenance Utilities
- Shell/Terminal
- Screen Sharing
- Force Quit (macOS)

Backup/Time Machine

Some Linux distros already have a backup utility installed, while others do not. macOS includes the Time Machine backup utility. Both Linux and macOS must have their backup utilities configured and running to be useful in the event that data is lost.

Configuring Time Machine

macOS includes Time Machine, an automatic backup utility that creates daily backups and maintains weekly and monthly versions. To enable and configure Time Machine:

Step 1.   Connect a suitable external disk to a macOS system.

Step 2.   When prompted, click **Use as Backup Disk**. You can also check the **Encrypt Backup Disk** box to protect the backup (see Figure 6-92).

Step 3.   If you selected the option to encrypt your backup in step 2, enter a password, confirm it, and enter a password hint. Click **Encrypt Disk** (see Figure 6-93).

Step 4.   Make sure Time Machine is turned on (see Figure 6-94). After the selected disk is encrypted, the backup starts.

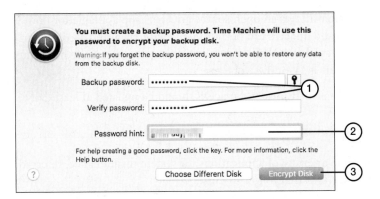

1. Create and confirm password for encrypted Time Machine drive
2. Enter a password hint
3. Click to start encryption of Time Machine drive

FIGURE 6-92   Selecting an External Disk for Use with Time Machine

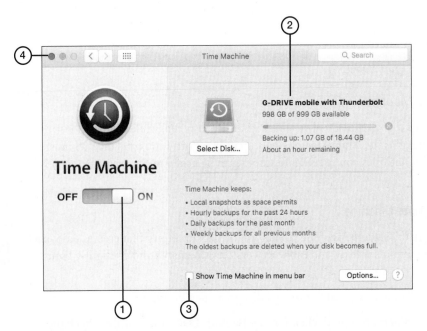

1. Time Machine turned on
2. Progress bar and backup disk information
3. Check box to put Time Machine on menu bar at top of screen
4. Click to close (Red) or minimize (Yellow) Time Machine menu

FIGURE 6-93   Encrypting the Time Machine Disk

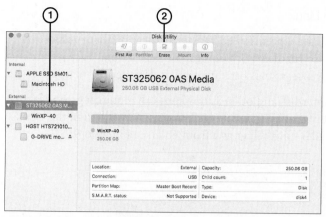

1. Click drive to erase
2. Click Erase to start process

FIGURE 6-94   Creating a Backup with Time Machine

Time Machine is designed to back up user files automatically. However, to create a disk image that can be restored in case of disaster, use Disk Utility.

Using Disk Utility in macOS

Disk Utility can be started by pressing the **Cmd+Spacebar** keys and searching for Disk Utility, from Launchpad, or from Finder. To start Disk Utility at startup, press and hold **Cmd+R** until it starts.

Disk Utility, shown in Figure 6-95, can be used to create blank disk images that can be used as containers for other files, including image backups. It can also be used to erase non-macOS drives and prepare them for use with macOS.

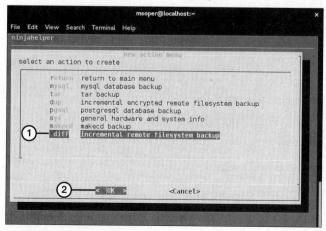

1. Select a backup job to create
2. Press OK to continue

FIGURE 6-95   Preparing to Erase a Disk for Reuse with Disk Utility

Configuring a Backup App in Linux

The Ubuntu distributions have a preinstalled backup application that runs weekly and can also be configured to run daily. Backups can be kept as long as space permits or for at least six months or a year. This backup utility is designed for new users.

Backup utilities based on tar, rdiff, and other Linux apps can require a great deal of scripting. One backup utility that helps create backup scripts by filling in the blanks is backupninja, which includes ninjahelper as a front end (see Figure 6-96).

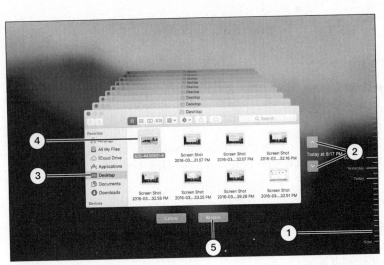

1. Time Machine backup stored locally
2. Select backup to view
3. Select backup location
4. Click file(s) to restore
5. Click to restore selected files

FIGURE 6-96   Creating a Backup Job with backupninja's ninjahelper

Restore/Snapshot

When a file is deleted from a macOS system or when a different version of an existing file is needed, you can restore a file from a Time Machine backup:

Step 1.   Open a **Finder** window where the restored file belongs. (Skip this step to restore to the Desktop.)

Step 2.   Open **Time Machine** from **Dock**.

Step 3.   Scroll through the backups shown to find the file(s) to restore.

Step 4.   Select the file(s) to restore and click **Restore** (see Figure 6-97).

The file is restored to its original location.

When Time Machine is enabled on a macOS laptop, backups known as snapshots are stored on the laptop's system drive as well as on the Time Machine external drive. Backups can also be restored from snapshots.

To restore a file from a Linux backup, see the documentation for the backup app being used.

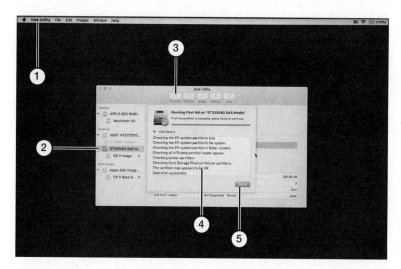

1. Menu bar
2. Selected drive
3. Click First Aid to test drive
4. Results
5. Click Done to complete process

FIGURE 6-97   Preparing to Restore a File with Time Machine

Image Recovery

macOS offers several *image recovery* options:

- After you create an image with Disk Utility, the image can be restored by using **Edit > Restore**.

- Disk Utility can also be used to reinstall macOS. If the Recovery System is available from the Startup drive, the latest edition of macOS is reinstalled. However, if the Recovery System has been deleted or is not available, you must use Internet Recovery. Internet Recovery installs the same edition of macOS originally installed on your system. You can then update it to the latest edition.

To recover an image with a Linux backup utility, see the utility's documentation for details.

Disk Maintenance Utilities

macOS's Disk Utility app includes options for repairing drives with First Aid. First Aid (see Figure 6-98) can repair problems with the file system, partitions, and other issues.

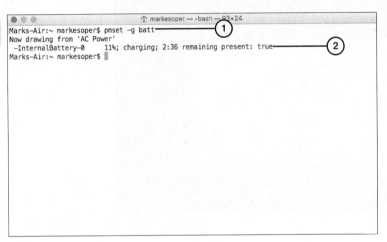

1. **Command**
2. **Result**

FIGURE 6-98   macOS's First Aid After a Successful Disk Test

Some useful disk maintenance commands for the Linux Terminal mode include:

- **df -h:** Lists files and free space in a computer
- **>directory path/filename:** Removes the contents of the specified file without removing the file itself
- **ls -lsr | tail -5:** Finds the five largest files in the current directory

Shell/Terminal

macOS and Linux both include *shell/terminal* apps that open a command line environment. The Linux Terminal utility is used to run commands, scripts, and programs without a GUI (see "Basic Linux Commands," later in this chapter). macOS also has a Terminal utility that supports many of the same commands. Figure 6-99 illustrates the macOS Terminal utility running pmset -g batt to display battery charge percentage in the Terminal command line.

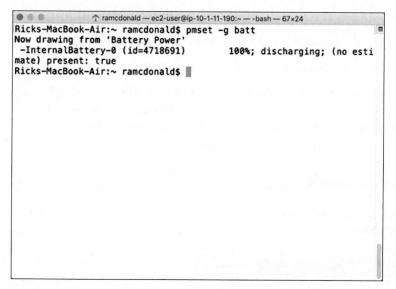

FIGURE 6-99   macOS's Terminal in Action

Screen Sharing

macOS includes support for ***Screen Sharing***, which enables local users on the network or remote users running virtual network computing (VNC) to control the screen for training or troubleshooting (see Figure 6-100). Screen Sharing and other types of sharing (file, printer, Internet, Bluetooth, and remote apps) are configured through the Sharing section of System Preferences.

Linux also supports screen sharing, sometimes using the term *VNC* or *Remote Desktop Viewer*. To see if a Linux installation has screen sharing, search for **VNC** or **Remote**.

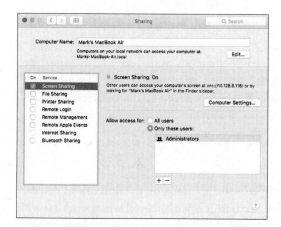

FIGURE 6-100   Configuring Screen Sharing in macOS

Force Quit

The *Force Quit* feature in macOS enables the user to shut down a malfunctioning app.

To open the Force Quit application from the keyboard, press **Cmd+Option+Esc**.

Force Quit can also be started from the menu bar: Open the Apple menu and select **Force Quit**. You can also point at the app's icon in the Dock (at the bottom of the screen) and right-click or click and hold it to bring up a menu with Quit as an option. From the Force Quit menu, select the app to stop (see Figure 6-101).

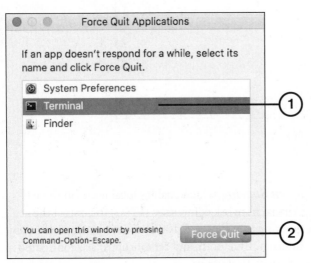

1. Select an app to force quit

2. Click Force Quit to close it

FIGURE 6-101   Using Force Quit in macOS

Features

Although macOS can run many of the same commands from Terminal as Linux, it isn't Linux, and it has many features that have no Linux counterpart. The following sections provide an introduction to macOS basics that should help PC techs work comfortably around the macOS laptops and desktops that are often found in the more creative parts of a company's IT infrastructure.

Multiple Desktops/Mission Control

Mission Control (see Figure 6-102) displays all apps open on the desktop so you can copy or move them between different desktops. It is very helpful when working with multiple displays. It is also possible to navigate between desktops with multi-finger swipes on trackpads.

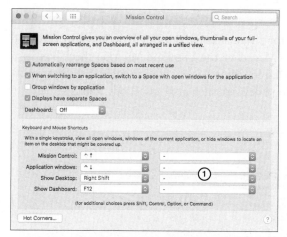

1. Keyboard and mouse shortcuts for viewing Mission Control, Dashboard, application windows, and the Desktop

FIGURE 6-102   Configuring Keyboard and Mouse Shortcuts in Mission Control

Spotlight

Spotlight is the macOS search tool for files, apps, photos, web results, dictionary entries, news, movie listings, and more. Open Spotlight by pressing the **Cmd+Spacebar** and then type in keywords to search the entire machine. A similar search feature is available on iPads and iPhones. Figure 6-103 show a search for the word **dashboard** and the response.

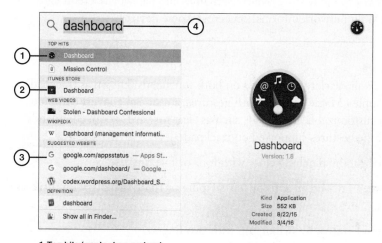

1. Top hits (content on system)
2. iTunes matches
3. Web content matches
4. Search term

FIGURE 6-103   Searching for "dashboard" Finds Matches on This Computer, in iTunes, and on the Internet

iCloud

macOS uses *iCloud* cloud storage for photo sharing, document and data storage, and Find My Mac. To turn on Find My Mac, click the Use Find My Mac check box, as shown in Figure 6-104. When iCloud for Photos is enabled, it enables the user to see a photo stream from other iCloud devices, such as iPads, iPods, and iPhones.

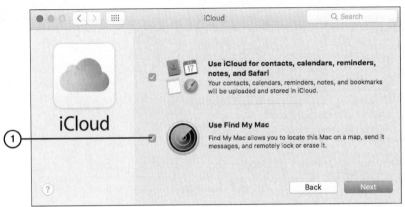

1. Enable Find My Mac when you open iCloud for the first time

FIGURE 6-104   Using Find My Mac in iCloud

Keychain

Use iCloud *Keychain* to safely store Safari usernames and passwords, credit card information, and WiFi network information across Apple devices.

Gestures

macOS supports a wide variety of *gestures* on both touchpads (known as trackpads on macOS) and Apple's Magic Mouse. With gestures, a user can convert common touch patterns to customizable commands such as "fast forward" zoom commands. Here are some of the gestures supported on trackpads:

- Open Launchpad by pinching close with four or five fingers.

- Switch between full-screen apps by left-swiping or right-swiping with three or four fingers.

- Open Mission Control by swiping up with two fingers.

Open **Trackpad** in the System Preferences folder for more gestures and options.

The Magic Mouse has a touch-sensitive cover, so it can also be used with gestures:

- Hold down the **Ctrl** key and scroll with one finger to make items onscreen larger.

- Switch between apps by left-swiping or right-swiping with two fingers.

Open **Mouse** in the System Preferences folder for more gestures and options.

Finder

Finder is macOS's file manager. Figure 6-105 shows Finder displaying the contents of the Applications folder and preparing to perform an operation on the App Store folder.

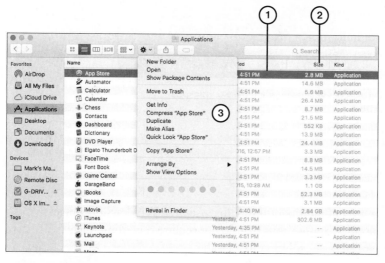

1. Selected folder.
2. Size of all apps in the selected folder
3. Options for the selected folder

FIGURE 6-105   Using Finder to Work with the Applications Folder

Remote Disc

Recent Apple models do not have optical disks. **Remote Disc** enables access to files from a CD or DVD on another computer on a network. To share a CD or DVD from a Windows system, install DVD or CD Sharing Update 1.0 for Windows from the Apple website.

Dock

macOS uses the ***Dock*** (see Figure 6-106) to display and switch between running apps along the bottom of the display. It is possible to adjust the magnification of the selected app.

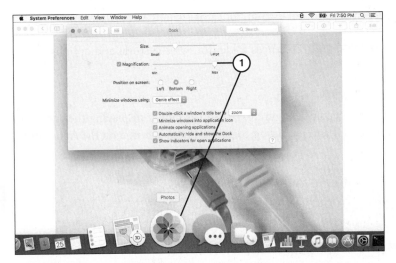

1. Configures the zooming effect as you move your mouse or trackpad pointer along the apps in Dock.

FIGURE 6-106   Adjusting the Dock's Settings

Boot Camp

Boot Camp is the macOS multiboot utility for installing Windows on a macOS computer. Virtualization applications that do not require rebooting, such as VMware Fusion for Mac, are an easier solution to consider.

Basic Linux Commands

With more and more Linux systems showing up on corporate networks, and with macOS being based in part on Linux, it's important for computer technicians to understand basic Linux commands. The following sections review the commands that may appear on the A+ exam.

To use these commands, open a Terminal session. Some commands must be run as root user. (To run commands as root, log in as root or use **sudo**.)

> **NOTE**   There are many additional options for these commands. Linux distributions ("distros") contain a manual (manpages) with options for each command. To view or print a command's manpage, use the command **man**. To learn more, see www.linfo.org/man.html. To view manpages for Ubuntu (one of the most popular distros) online, see http://manpages.ubuntu.com.

ls

ls is the macOS and Linux equivalent to the Windows command **DIR**. Use **ls -l** to list the contents of a directory (folder), including permissions and other information (see Figure 6-107).

1. Directories are listed in blue
2. Press the up-arrow key to repeat the last command; press it again to repeat the previous one, and so on

FIGURE 6-107   Using **ls -l** in Fedora 23 Workstation

grep

Use *grep* to perform text searches. The grep command line specifies what to search for and where to search.

grep can be used to find a specified word in one or more specified files. grep normally searches for exact matches (Linux and macOS are case-sensitive), but it can be configured to ignore case with -i.

grep supports recursive searching—that is, searching in all files in directories (folders) beneath the current directory.

Figure 6-108 shows grep being used to search for the word *model* in the /proc/ cpuinfo directory (folder).

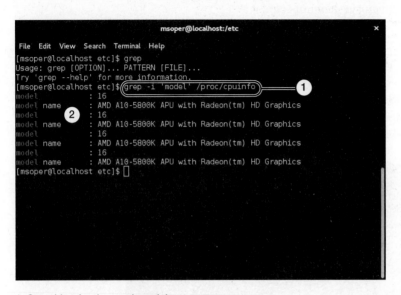

1. Searching for the word *model*
2. Matches

FIGURE 6-108   Searching for Specific Text in a Folder by Using **grep**

cd

Use *cd* to change directories (folders). The syntax is different from the Windows command line in that Linux uses the / slash, whereas Windows uses the \ slash.

Use **cd /etc** to change to the /etc folder.

Use **cd ..** to move up one level.

shutdown

Use *shutdown* to shut down the system. Figure 6-109 shows shutdown used along with options to specify when to shut down and to broadcast a warning message. Note that the sudo command is used with this command because shutdown requires root access.

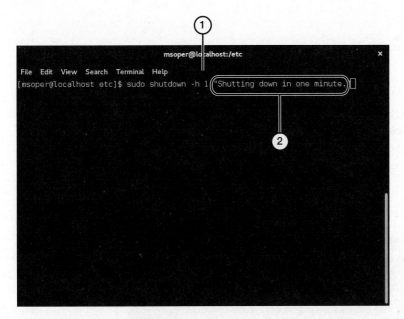

1. One minute (1) to shutdown
2. Message broadcast to all systems logged in to this computer

FIGURE 6-109   Preparing to Shut Down a System

pwd vs. passwd

The pwd and passwd commands are often confused. Keep in mind:

- *pwd*: Displays the name of the current/working directory.

- *passwd*: Starts the password change process.

mv

Use *mv* to move files to a specified location, as in this example:

mv thisfile.ext destination-folder

cp

Use *cp* to copy files to a specified location (using the syntax **cp** *filename /folder/ subfolder*) or to a different name in the same folder (for example, **cp -i origfile copiedfile**). Use the -i option to be prompted in case the command would overwrite a file.

rm

Use *rm* to remove (delete) files from the system (rm filename).

chmod

Use *chmod* to change permissions of files and directories using the syntax **chmod** *permissions filename*. In Figure 6-110, **chmod** is used to change permissions on the file test. The numbers that are used stand for different permissions. To learn more about these values, see the Chmod Calculator at https://chmod-calculator.com. Also note in Figure 110 that the command ls -l is used to display file permissions and the filename.

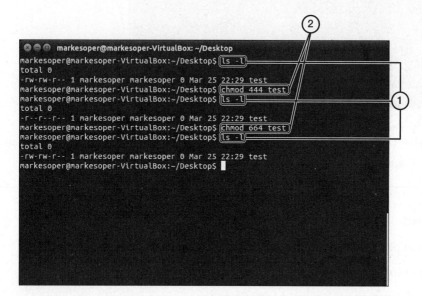

1. Using the `ls -l` command to see the file permissions changes made with `chmod`
2. Changing file permissions with `chmod`

FIGURE 6-110   Changing Permissions for the File *Test* Using Ubuntu

chown

Use *chown* to change file ownership using the syntax **sudo chown** *newowner filename*.

iwconfig/ifconfig

Use *iwconfig* to display wireless network connections (Linux only).

Use *ifconfig* to display wired network connections (Linux). In macOS, this command also displays wireless network settings.

ps

Use the *ps* command to list the currently running processes (see Figure 6-111).

1. Current processes listed by name and PID

FIGURE 6-111   Listing Processes for the Current User with **ps**

su/sudo

Use *sudo* to run a command as another user. It is most commonly used by a user to run a command as root.

Use *su* to switch between accounts. Entering **su** without specifying options changes to root and prompts for root password.

apt-get

Use *apt-get* to install or manage APT (Advanced Packaging Tool) software packages, which are common in Debian-based distributions such as Ubuntu (see Figure 6-112). The apt-get command must be used with **sudo**. Use this syntax: **sudo apt-get** *function appname*.

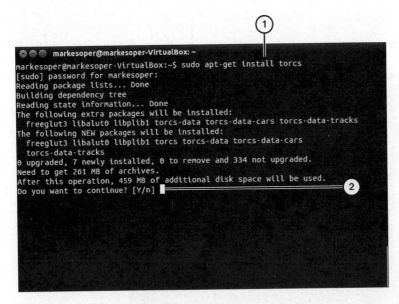

1. The function to perform is install
2. Answer Y to continue

FIGURE 6-112   Installing torcs (The Open Racing Car Simulator) with **apt-get** on Ubuntu

vi

The *vi* command starts the **vi** text editor. For syntax switches, see https://www.computerhope.com/unix/uvi.htm. Note that many Linux distros have easier-to-use text editors installed.

dd

Use *dd* to perform a block file copy and to convert between formats. This command must be run as superuser (root) and can be used to back up or restore a hard disk or partition. For details, see https://linoxide.com/linux-command/linux-dd-command-create-1gb-file/.

kill

The *kill* command is similar to Force Quit in macOS. To terminate an app in Linux, enter **top** to see a list of process IDs (PIDs) and the apps they represent. Press **q** to quit. To kill an app by specifying its PID, enter the command **kill *xxx*** (where *xxx* is the PID).

Figure 6-113 illustrates this process.

1. General output from top
2. Processes listed by PID
3. Command to `kill` PID 11496 (terminal)

FIGURE 6-113   Running **kill** from a Terminal Session in Linux (Fedora 23 Workstation)

Exam Preparation Tasks

As mentioned in the section "How to Use This Book" in the Introduction, you have a couple of choices for exam preparation: the exercises here, Chapter 10, "Final Preparation," and the exam simulation questions in the Pearson Test Prep Software Online.

Review All the Key Topics

Review the most important topics in the chapter, noted with the Key Topic icon in the outer margin of the page. Table 6-11 lists these key topics and the page number on which each is found.

Table 6-11   Key Topics for Chapter 6

Key Topic Element	Description	Page Number
List	Impact of file system selection	508
Section	Workstation Operating Systems	510

Key Topic Element	Description	Page Number
Section	Cell Phone/Tablet Operating Systems	513
Table 6-2	Feature Comparisons for Windows 7, 8, 8.1, and 10	518
List	Methods for system booting during installation	521
List	Windows installation types	522
Section	In-Place Upgrade Installation	523
Section	Precautions for clean Windows installations	524
Section	Windows multiboot installation rules	525
List	Windows repair installation	526
List	Disk partition types	530
Section	Creating Partitions During Windows 7/8/8.1/10 Installation	532
Section	NTFS	534
Paragraph	Reasons to use a command prompt session in Windows	540
Section	Command Line Tools	540
Table 6-4	Windows Command Prompt Commands	544
Section	FORMAT	545
Section	COPY	547
Section	XCOPY	547
Section	ROBOCOPY	548
Section	DISKPART	549
Section	SFC	550
Section	CHKDSK	550
Section	GPUPDATE	551
Section	Microsoft Administrative Tools	552
Steps	Creating a task in Windows with Task Scheduler	557
Steps	Using Device Manager	562
Section	MSCONFIG	567
Section	Task Manager	569
Steps	Mounting a drive	575
Steps	Creating a new simple volume	577
Steps	Creating extended partitions	578

Key Topic Element	Description	Page Number
Steps	Splitting partitions	579
Steps	Shrinking partitions	579
Steps	Assigning/changing drive letters	579
Section	Adding Arrays	580
Table 6-6	Storage Spaces Overview	582
Steps	Using storage spaces	582
Section	System Utilities	583
Section	Using REGEDIT	584
Steps	Setting up remote setting options	587
Figure 6-49	MSINFO32 System Summary	593
Section	System Restore	595
List	Windows Startup Settings menu options	600
Table 6-7	Internet Options	603
Table 6-8	Configuring Display Settings in Windows 7 and Widows 8/8.1/10	603
List	Adjusting the location and size of the paging file in Windows	608
Table 6-9	Control Panel Utilities	614
Table 6-10	Installation and Configuration Concepts	615
Section	Homegroup vs. Workgroup	616
Steps	Creating a workgroup with Windows	617
Steps	Creating a homegroup with Windows	619
Steps	Joining a domain	621
Section	Network Shares	621
Steps	Mapping drives	624
Steps	Configuring a new VPN connection	627
Steps	Configuring a new dial-up connection to an ISP	629
Steps	Configuring a new direct dial-in connection to a corporate computer	629
Steps	Configuring a wireless connection	630
Steps	Configuring a wired connection	631
Steps	Configuring manual proxy settings for a LAN connection in Windows	632

Complete the Tables and Lists from Memory

Print a copy of Appendix C, "Memory Tables" (found online), or at least the section for this chapter, and complete the tables and lists from memory. Appendix D, "Answers to Memory Tables," also online, includes completed tables and lists to check your work.

Define Key Terms

Define the following key terms from this chapter and check your answers in the glossary:

file system, FAT32, exFAT, open source, closed source, smartphone, Android, iOS, Chrome, Netboot, in-place upgrade, repair installation, image deployment, primary partition, extended partition, GPT, basic (disk type), dynamic (disk type), CDFS, NTFS, Encrypting File System (EFS), factory recovery partition, DIR, CD (CHDIR), IPCONFIG, PING, TRACERT, NETSTAT, NSLOOKUP, SHUTDOWN, DISM, SFC, CHKDSK, DISKPART, TASK-KILL, GPUPDATE, GPRESULT, FORMAT, COPY, XCOPY, ROBOCOPY, NET USE, NET USER, [Command]/?, standard format, low-level format, MMC, Local Security Policy, Performance Monitor, System Configuration, MSCONFIG, Task Scheduler, Component Services, Print Management, Windows Memory Diagnostics, Windows Firewall, Event Viewer, Device Manager, Task Manager, Disk Management, Drive Status, mounted drive, initialize (drive), extend (partition), split (partition), shrink (partition), Spanned (array), Striped (array), Mirrored (array), RAID 5 (array), drive array, Storage Spaces, REGEDIT, CMD, SERVICES.MSC, MMC, MSTSC, NOTEPAD, EXPLORER, MSINFO32, DxDiag, Disk Defragmenter, System Restore, remote settings, Safe mode, paging file (virtual memory), power plan, Sleep/Suspend, workgroup, homegroup, domain setup, network share, printer sharing, network printer mapping, proxy settings, Remote Assistance, alternative IP address, half duplex/full duplex/auto, Wake-on-LAN, Time Machine, image recovery, shell/terminal, Screen Sharing, Force Quit, Mission Control, Spotlight, iCloud, Keychain, gestures, Remote Disc, Dock, Boot Camp, ls, grep, cd, shutdown, pwd, passwd, mv, cp, rm, chmod, chown, iwconfig, ifconfig, ps, sudo, su, apt-get, vi, dd, kill

Answer Review Questions

1. Which of the following statements best describes a workgroup? (Choose all that apply.)

   a. All the computers in a workgroup must be on the same subnet.

   b. File and printer sharing should be enabled on each computer in a workgroup.

   c. The workgroup should have a password.

   d. Each computer in a workgroup must have a user account for each user.

2. Mark is re-deploying a workstation for a new user in another building. It has been determined that the computer needs to be renamed for management purposes. Which one of the following options will allow him to the make the change?

   a. Open System properties.

   b. Type Msinfo32 at the command line.

   c. Open the System Configuration utility.

   d. Access the drive properties.

3. In the following table, indicate which command should be used to execute each task.

Task	Command
a. Open a command prompt	
b. View all the directories in a specified location	
c. Create a new folder	
d. Remove an empty folder	
e. Remove one or more files	
f. Stop running a specified task	
g. Copy single or multiple files	
h. Scan for errors and repair hard drive	
i. Close command prompt	
j. Create new partitions	
k. Display the help files for a specific command	

1. CHKDSK

2. CMD or COMMAND

3. COMMAND/?

4. DEL

5. DIR

6. DISKPART

7. EXIT

8. MD or MKDIR

9. RD or RMDIR

10. TASKKILL

11. XCOPY, ROBOCOPY

4. Your client wants to create a homegroup, but the homegroup option is not showing up in the Network and Sharing Center. Which of the following statements best describes the most likely cause?

    a. The network location is set to Public.

    b. The network adapter is configured to use half-duplex mode.

    c. A workgroup has already been configured.

    d. An alternative IP configuration is not complete.

5. Your network adapter is disabled. How will this be indicated in the Windows Device Manager?

    a. The device will not be listed.

    b. An ! will be displayed over the device icon.

    c. A down-arrow icon will be displayed over the device icon.

    d. A ? will be displayed over the device icon.

6. A client reports that the system is starting up very slowly. Which of the following utilities is best for determining what's going on?

    a. Devices and Printers

    b. Programs and Features

    c. System Protection

    d. System Configuration

7. Which of the following steps is necessary to turning on file sharing?

    a. Opening the Firewall application

    b. Opening the System properties

    c. Opening the Network and Sharing Center

    d. Opening the System Configuration utility

8. You have created a shared folder on a network server. You have assigned a letter designation to the folder and made it available to all members of the Research department. This folder now appears as a drive letter on each user's computer. Which type of folder have you created?

   a. Administrative share

   b. Homegroup share

   c. Mapped network drive

   d. VPN

9. In the following table, write the command used to open the respective utilities.

Utility	Command
a. The Registry	
b. System Information	
c. System Configuration	
d. Microsoft Management Console	

   1. MMC
   2. MSCONFIG
   3. MSINFO32
   4. REGEDIT

10. Which of the following utilities is used to create a VPN?

    a. Network and Sharing Center

    b. Internet Options

    c. System properties

    d. Windows Firewall

11. Which of the following utilities would you use to see the items that are set to run automatically at a particular time?

    a. Task Scheduler

    b. Services

    c. Device Manager

    d. Performance

12. A client wants a RAID array installed, but the system doesn't have hardware RAID onboard. Which of the following Windows utilities is used to create a RAID array?

    a. Disk Management

    b. RAID BIOS utility

    c. CHKDSK

    d. MSCONFIG

13. Antonio is using his laptop in a restaurant and has set his network profile to Public. Which of the following will not be available to him? (Choose all that apply.)

    a. File and printer sharing

    b. Access to the homegroup

    c. Network discovery

    d. Media streaming

14. Which of the following statements best describes a firewall?

    a. A firewall is a specially constructed barrier in the server room that is meant to limit the spread of fire.

    b. A firewall is a fire suppression technology that uses plenum grade cabling in ducts and ceiling spaces.

    c. A firewall is a proxy server with a VPN connection.

    d. A firewall is software or hardware that controls the flow of information between a computer and the Internet or another network.

15. Which of the following can be configured as exceptions in Windows Firewall? (Choose all that apply.)

    a. Applications that are to be allowed through the firewall

    b. Ports and port numbers to be opened

    c. The IP address to be used

    d. The Subnet mask to be used

16. Setting an alternative configuration for the IP address allows you to set up a secondary IP address in case there is no DHCP server available. By default, Automatic Private IP Addressing is used for the alternative configuration. Which of the following addresses might you expect to see if the default alternate address is used?

   a. 10.196.74.12

   b. 192.168.200.24

   c. 169.254.21.3

   d. 172.16.10.5

17. Which of the following is the backup utility for the macOS operating system?

   a. Tar

   b. Crontab

   c. Time Machine

   d. File History

18. What is the purpose of Disk Utility in macOS?

   a. It prepares a disk to be used for storing image backups and other files.

   b. It manages the network connection to the Internet.

   c. It ejects a disk.

   d. It manages remote storage in the cloud.

19. In the macOS or Linux Terminal, which of the following is used to force quit an app by using its PID number?

   a. **kill**

   b. **Ctrl+Alt+Del**

   c. **end**

   d. **fq**

20. What is the function of the tar command in Linux operating systems?

   a. Compression

   b. IP addressing

   c. Encryption

   d. Backup

21. Screen sharing, file sharing, and printer sharing are configured through which macOS utility?

    a. Control Panel

    b. System Preferences

    c. The Sharing app

    d. Display

22. Which role does Mission Control play in macOS?

    a. It displays all open apps on multiple desktops.

    b. It installs an operating system on a virtual machine.

    c. It manages the flow of incoming and outgoing data across a network.

    d. It manages the flow of data through a firewall.

23. Which of the following macOS apps is used for sharing photos and documents and for data storage?

    a. Time Machine

    b. iCloud

    c. Apple Assist

    d. Spotlight

24. What is the name of the file manager used by macOS?

    a. Explorer

    b. Search

    c. Finder

    d. File Explorer

25. Which of the following refers to the row of icons of currently running apps at the bottom of the display screen in macOS?

    a. Taskbar

    b. Menu bar

    c. Finder

    d. Dock

26. Match the following Linux user commands with their descriptions.

   a. su

   b. iwconfig

   c. cd

   d. ls

   e. chmod

   f. ps

   g. rm

   h. grep

   i. pwd

   j. vi

   k. chown

Answer Options (in alphabetical order):

   1. Change file ownership

   2. Change folders

   3. Change permissions

   4. Delete files or folders

   5. Display wireless network connections

   6. List currently running processes

   7. Perform text/word searches

   8. Print (display) working directory

   9. Run commands as a different user (usually root)

  10. Show contents of a directory or folder

  11. Start text editor

This chapter covers the 10 A+ 220-1002 exam objectives related to security. These objectives may comprise 24 percent of the exam questions:

- **Core 2 (220-1002): Objective 2.1:** Summarize the importance of physical security measures.

- **Core 2 (220-1002): Objective 2.2:** Explain logical security concepts.

- **Core 2 (220-1002): Objective 2.3:** Compare and contrast wireless security protocols and authentication methods.

- **Core 2 (220-1002): Objective 2.4:** Given a scenario, detect, remove, and prevent malware using appropriate tools and methods.

- **Core 2 (220-1002): Objective 2.5:** Compare and contrast social engineering, threats, and vulnerabilities.

- **Core 2 (220-1002): Objective 2.6:** Compare and contrast the differences of basic Microsoft Windows OS security settings.

- **Core 2 (220-1002): Objective 2.7:** Given a scenario, implement security best practices to secure a workstation.

- **Core 2 (220-1002): Objective 2.8:** Given a scenario, implement methods for securing mobile devices.

- **Core 2 (220-1002): Objective 2.9:** Given a scenario, implement appropriate data destruction and disposal methods.

- **Core 2 (220-1002): Objective 2.10:** Given a scenario, configure security on SOHO wireless and wired networks.

## CHAPTER 7

Security

The most important asset most companies own is their data. Data has become so important to business success that it is what most thieves seek. Because of the interconnected nature of the Internet, a security breach of a single device or network can lead to data theft, including the theft of client financial data that can greatly affect the lives of millions. Large-scale data breaches have brought large companies to bankruptcy, so data security is among the top concerns of business leadership. In this chapter, you learn about the multifaceted threats to security in the modern computing environment and how to mitigate them through the study of these CompTIA A+ Core 2 objectives. This chapter covers the following topics:

- **Physical security measures:** Physical security practices and their implementation.

- **Logical security concepts:** Software-based security measures.

- **Wireless security protocols and authentication:** Types of wireless security and authentication.

- **Malware removal and prevention:** Methods and protocols for detection and prevention.

- **Social engineering threats and vulnerabilities:** The various types of threats.

- **Microsoft Windows OS security settings:** The important Microsoft security settings.

- **Security best practices to secure a workstation:** Implementation of best practices.

- **Securing mobile devices:** Implementation methods for securing devices.

- **Data destruction and disposal:** Methods and techniques for safely and securely disposing of hardware.

- **Configuring security on SOHO networks:** Methods for configuring SOHO security.

"Do I Know This Already?" Quiz

The "Do I Know This Already?" quiz allows you to assess whether you should read the entire chapter. Table 7-1 lists the major headings in this chapter and the "Do I Know This Already?" quiz questions covering the material in those headings so you can assess your knowledge of these specific areas. The answers to the "Do I Know This Already?" quiz appear in Appendix A, "Answers to the 'Do I Know This Already?' Quizzes and Review Question Sections."

Table 7-1   "Do I Know This Already?" Section-to-Question Mapping

Foundation Topics Section	Questions
Physical Security Measures	1
Logical Security Concepts	2
Wireless Security Protocols and Authentication	3–4
Social Engineering Threats and Vulnerabilities	5
Microsoft Windows OS Security Settings	6
Security Best Practices to Secure a Workstation	7
Securing Mobile Devices	8
Data Destruction and Disposal	9
Configuring Security on SOHO Networks	10

CAUTION   The goal of self-assessment is to gauge your mastery of the topics in this chapter. If you do not know the answer to a question or are only partially sure of the answer, you should mark that question as wrong for purposes of the self-assessment. Giving yourself credit for an answer you correctly guess skews your self-assessment results and might provide you with a false sense of security.

1. What kind of security breach is a mantrap designed to foil?

    a. Biometric

    b. Tailgating

    c. Sleeping guard

    d. Shoulder surfing

2. Say that you have been asked to improve security by adding a system to examine network packets to determine whether they should be forwarded or blocked. What is the function you would be most likely to add?

    a. MAC address filtering

    b. MAC address cloning

    c. Software firewall

    d. Multifactor authentication

3. Which of the following is the most secure wireless protocol in use today?

    a. WEP

    b. WEP3

    c. TKIP

    d. WPA2

4. A user has unwittingly downloaded malware while also downloading a free application on a gaming site. What general term describes the unintentionally downloaded file?

    a. Worm

    b. Trojan

    c. Ransomware

    d. Botnet

5. Several computers on a network have been commandeered to launch an attack on a server on the Web. Which term best describes this situation?

    a. Phishing

    b. DoS

    c. Spoofing

    d. DDoS

6. Which setting allows the user the most privileges on a Windows network?

    a. Modify

    b. Read and Execute

    c. Ultimate Use

    d. Write

7. Which is the best example of a strong password?

    a. dr0wssap

    b. Password9

    c. Pa5SwoRd5

    d. pA55wrds

8. Which of the following is not an example of biometric authentication?

    a. Entering a password and answering a secret question

    b. Apple FACE ID

    c. Windows Hello

    d. Touch ID

9. Which method erases storage media but leaves the device intact?

    a. Data shredding

    b. Degaussing

    c. BitLocking

    d. Incineration

10. To help hide the identity of a wireless router, what should be changed from the default setting?

    a. Private IP address

    b. MAC address filter

    c. IP default gateway

    d. Service set identifier

Foundation Topics

Physical Security Measures

220-1002: Objective 2.1: Summarize the importance of physical security measures.

Physical security of IT equipment is a fundamental first factor in a secure network. As mentioned earlier, data is typically the most valuable asset in a company, and leaving it in an unlocked area is dangerous in two ways. First, computer equipment is valuable, and a thief may want it for its face value, not caring about the valuable data it may contain or harm its release may do to customers. Second, an unlocked door is an invitation for someone to install sniffing equipment and gain access to company network assets well beyond the physical room left unattended. In the realm of physical security, there are several measures an IT professional must understand and practice.

Mantrap

Some secure areas include what is known as a *mantrap*, which is an area with two locking doors. A person might get past a first door by way of tailgating but might have difficulty getting past the second door, especially if there is a guard in between the two doors. A mantrap essentially slows down the entry process in hopes that people sneaking in behind others will be thwarted before gaining entry to the secure area. If the person doesn't have proper authentication, he will be stranded in the mantrap until authorities arrive.

Badge Reader

Badge readers are devices that can interpret the data on a certain type of ID. While photo IDs are still best assessed by humans, other types of IDs add extra security that can be read by badge readers.

ID badges and readers can use a variety of physical security methods, including the following:

- **Photos:** If the bearer of the card doesn't look like the person on the card, the bearer might be using someone else's card and should be detained.

- **Barcodes and magnetic strips:** The codes embedded on these cards enable the cards to carry a range of information about the bearers and can limit individuals' access to only authorized areas of buildings. These cards can be read quickly by a barcode scanner or swipe device.

■ **RFID technology:** Like barcoded badges, cards with radio-frequency identification (RFID) chips can be used to open only doors that are matched to the RFID chip. They can also track movement within a building and provide other access data required by a security officer.

To prevent undetected tampering, ID badges should be coated with a tamper-evident outer layer.

Smart Card

A smart card is a credit card–sized card that contains stored information and might also contain a simple microprocessor or an RFID chip. Smart cards can be used to store identification information for use in security applications and to store values for use in prepaid telephone or debit card services, hotel guest room access, and many other functions. Smart cards are available in contact and contactless form factors.

Contactless cards are also known as *proximity cards*. Readers for these cards are usually wall mounted so users can scan their cards within 6 inches of a reader.

A *smart card*–based security system includes smart cards, card readers that are designed to work with smart cards, and a back-end system that contains a database that stores a list of approved smart cards for each secured location. Smart card–based security systems can also be used to secure individual personal computers.

To further enhance security, smart card security systems can also be multifactor, requiring the user to input a PIN or security password as well as provide the smart card at secured checkpoints, such as the entrance to a computer room.

Security Guard

Even the best security plans can be foiled by a determined and skillful thief. The best way to deter a thief is to use a mix of technical barriers and human interaction. Guards can be deployed in different ways. When employees enter the work area in the presence of a guard, it is more likely that best practices will be followed and everyone will scan in and be authenticated. Without a guard, it is more common for people to hold the door for people who are recognized but say they have misplaced their IDs. Knowing that someone is watching carefully keeps honest people honest and those who are dishonest away from the door.

Another way to deploy guards is to have them watch several areas via security cameras that record access into and out of the buildings. While this method is not as effective as posting a guard at each door, it makes it possible for fewer security guards to scan different areas for traffic behaviors that warrant further attention.

Door Lock

Of course, the easiest way to secure an area is to lock doors. While this seems an obvious statement, it is surprisingly common for people to get to unauthorized areas by just wandering in. Some organizations have written policies explaining how, when, and where to lock doors. Aside from main entrances, you should also always lock server rooms, wiring closets, labs, and other technical rooms when not in use.

Physical door locks might seem low tech, but they can't be taken over by hackers. Other precautions to take include documenting who has keys to server rooms and wiring closets and periodically changing locks and keys. Cipher locks that use punch codes also enhance security. Using a combination of these methods provides for greater protection.

Biometric Locks

Biometric security refers to the use of a person's biological information—through fingerprint scanning, retina scanning, or facial recognition, for example—to authenticate potential users of a secure area. The most common type of biometric security system for PCs is fingerprint based, but other methods include voice measurements, facial recognition, and scans of the eye's retina or iris. Newer versions of device security that use fingerprint and facial recognition are Microsoft's Hello (available in Windows 10) and Apple Face ID on newer iPhones.

Tokens

Any physical device that a user must carry to gain access to a specific system can be called a *token*. Examples are smart cards, RFID cards, USB tokens, and key fobs. (Key fob hardware tokens are explained later in this section.)

Laptop and Cable Locks

Most desktops, laptops, and many other mobile devices such as projectors and docking stations feature a security slot. On a laptop, the slot is typically located near a rear corner (see Figure 7-1).

1. Security slot

FIGURE 7-1   A Security Slot on a Laptop

This slot is used with a laptop *cable lock*, such as the one shown in Figure 7-2. Laptop locks use a combination or keyed lock and are designed to lock a laptop (or other secured device) to a fixed location such as a table.

FIGURE 7-2   A Combination Laptop Security Lock

Server Locks

Even with building security in place, it may be necessary to have more granular security in place in areas like server rooms. A data center might contain equipment from several different companies, and non-employees may need access to server areas. Of course, not all threats are external, and some employees who have access to equipment areas should also have access to server equipment in the data center.

Rack-level security involves locking down equipment in a server rack. This can be done with cabinets or cages with secure biometric locks or perhaps keycards that can be changed often. Security cameras are appropriate in data centers as well. Rack cabinets can be quite sophisticated, with alarms that indicate access and improperly closed doors.

Examples of rack level security can be seen at https://tzsmartcabinets.net.

USB Locks

It is possible for someone to remove a USB cable from a computer and insert another USB device (or simply plug into an empty USB port), making it possible for a thief to then move data from the computer. *USB locks* can be used to secure USB cables into the computer and to securely plug empty USB ports. One manufacturer of these specialty port locks is PadJack (http://www.padjack.com/usb-cable-lock-seal/).

Privacy Screen

Privacy issues are important to any company that handles confidential data, and when such data is being used on a workstation screen or mobile device, it needs to be protected from unintentional viewing. Data on a computer screen can be easily protected by installing a *privacy screen*, which is a transparent cover for a PC monitor or laptop display. It reduces the cone of vision, usually to about 30 degrees, so that only the person directly in front of the screen can see the content. Many of these screens are also antiglare, helping to reduce the user's eye strain.

Key Fobs

Key fobs can be used with a variety of security devices. They can contain RFID chips, and many key fobs are used as part of a two-step authentication protocol that works as follows:

- The user carries a key fob that generates a code every 30 to 60 seconds. Every time the code changes on the fob, it is also matched in the authentication server. In some cases, the user must also log into the fob to see the access code for an extra layer of security.

- The user then logs into the system or restricted area, using the randomly generated access code displayed on the key fob's LCD display. The authentication server matches the current code and allows access.

A key fob used in this way is often referred to as a hardware token.

Entry Control Roster

An *entry control roster*, which is a list of individuals or representatives who are authorized to enter a secured area, can be used with a variety of security systems. Potential entrants can be looked up on an entry control roster and granted access if their credentials match those listed. A keypad lock on an entrance to a secure area can store a list of authorized PINs. Only users with recognized PINs can enter the secure area. Logs are usually kept to record who entered and exited a room at different times.

Logical Security Concepts

220-1002: Objective 2.2: Explain logical security concepts.

Because a computer is a combination of physical and logical systems, security practices must address both of these sides of computing. The physical components of security addressed in the previous section are only part of a good security plan and will be ineffective if the security policies stop there. Addressing software (logical) security practices is essential as well.

Active Directory

Active Directory is a Microsoft solution for managing users, computers, and information access in a network. It is based on a database of all resources and users that will be managed within the network. The information in the database determines what people can see and do within the network. Complete understanding of Active Directory is beyond the scope of this course, but every IT support person should know the basics of what it is and how it works. Here are the basics:

- *Login script*: When a user logs onto the network, Active Directory knows who that user is and runs a login script to make the assigned resources available. Examples of login tasks include virus updates, drive mapping, and printer assignments.

- *Domain*: The domain is a computer network or group of computer networks under one administration. Users log into the Active Directory domain to access network resources within the domain.

- *Group Policy*: This is a set of rules and instructions defining what a user or group of users can or cannot do when logged into the domain. You may see the term Group Policy Object (GPO), which is a set of instructions assigned to a group of users or to certain machines on the network.

- *Organizational Unit (OU)*: OUs are logical groups that help organize users and computers so that GPOs can be assigned to them. For example, a team of accountants may be assigned to an OU, and their GPO may give them special access to financial records.

- *Home folder*: This folder, which is accessible to the network administrator, is where the user's data and files are kept locally.

- *Folder redirection*: This allows for the work done by an OU to be saved on a common folder in the domain as directed by the administrator instead of the user. For example, a policy may indicate that all work must be kept in a common folder so all members of a team can see the latest work and updates.

Software Tokens

Like key fobs, mentioned in the previous section for physical security, *software tokens* are part of a multifactor authentication process. The difference is that software tokens exist in software and are commonly stored on devices.

An example of a software token is Google Authenticator, an app that is downloaded to a device and provides a shared secret key. The user logs in with his or her username and password, and the app runs an authenticating algorithm. This multifactor authentication is more secure than earlier versions of software tokens, which could be stolen.

MDM Policies

Organizations that have many mobile devices need to administer them such that all devices and users comply with the security practices in place. This is usually done with a suite of software known as *mobile device management (MDM)*. The MDM marketplace is quite competitive, and several solutions are available from companies such as VMware (AirWatch), Citrix (XenMobile), and SOTI MobiControl. These products push updates and allow an administrator to configure many mobile devices from a central location. Good MDM software secures, monitors, manages, and supports multiple different mobile devices across the enterprise.

Port Security

Disabling ports refers to using a firewall appliance or software firewall to prevent specified UDP or TCP ports from being used by a service, an application, a specific device, or all devices. Turning off unused ports makes it harder for hackers to find stealthy access into a machine.

MAC Address Filtering

Every network adapter, whether it's built into a PC, is an add-on card, or is built into a specialized device such as a media adapter or a networked printer, has a unique identifier known as the media access control address, or *MAC address*. The MAC address (sometimes known as the physical address) is a list of six two-digit hexadecimal numbers. For example, a typical PC MAC address is FA-15-B7-89-6C-24. (MAC addresses are sometimes listed as 12 digits rather than in six groups of 2 digits.)

A MAC address is usually found on a label on the side of a network adapter. If an adapter is already installed, enter **ipconfig /all** at a command prompt to display the MAC address.

Because MAC addresses are unique, it is possible to control access to most wireless networks by allowing only certain addresses in. The practice of allowing only certain devices is sometimes called *whitelisting*. Some routers can also be configured to block a list of specified MAC addresses from accessing the wired network.

MAC address filtering can be a useful way to block casual hackers from gaining access to a small wireless (or wired) network, but it can be troublesome for a large network with many different devices coming into and going out of the system as each needs to be entered separately. MAC address filtering is discussed in further detail in Chapter 2, "Networking."

It is possible to use software to change the MAC address of a network device (a feature sometimes referred to as *MAC address cloning*). Also, MAC addresses are not encrypted and can be detected by software used to hack networks. Thus, MAC address filtering alone should not be relied on to stop serious attacks.

Certificates

Apps can sometimes hold viruses or other bugs that can cause trouble on a network. It is important to be sure all apps installed come from reliable sources and have been approved by the operating system vendor. App stores for iOS, Android, Windows 8 and later, macOS, and many Linux distros are examples of trusted sources of software.

However, not all software for an operating system comes from an app store. Digital *certificates* included in software are used to identify the publisher, and most operating systems display warning messages when an app without a digital certificate is being installed. Some settings block the installation of any app that does not have a digital certificate.

In Windows 10 the Certificate Manager keeps track of and check certificates. Figure 7-3 shows the Windows Certificate Manager with specific certificates listed in the right pane. To access Certificate Manager in Windows 10, click the **Start** button, type **certmgr.msc** in the search field, and press **Enter**.

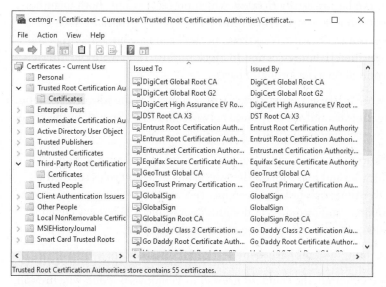

FIGURE 7-3   Certificate Manager

Antivirus/Anti-malware

Just as there is antivirus software for PCs, there is also *antivirus/anti-malware software* for mobile devices. These are third-party applications that need to be paid for, downloaded, and installed to the mobile device. Some common examples of reliable companies offering antivirus and anti-malware products include McAfee, Norton, and Trend, though many companies offer such products.

iOS works a bit differently from the other mobile operating systems. iOS is a tightly controlled operating system. One of the benefits of being a closed-source OS is that it can be more difficult to write viruses for it, making it somewhat more difficult to compromise. But there is no OS that can't be compromised, and as Apple's success has grown, efforts to write viruses for Apple machines have increased. McAfee, Norton, Trend Micro, and others have well-respected iOS protection products.

Firewalls

A *firewall* is a physical device or a software program that examines data packets on a network to determine whether to forward them to their destination or block them. A firewall can be a one-way firewall, which means it is used to protect against inbound threats only, or it can be a *two-way firewall*, which protects against both unauthorized inbound and outbound traffic. Most third-party firewall programs, such as ZoneAlarm, are two-way firewalls. A software firewall can be configured to permit traffic between specified IP addresses and to block traffic to and from the Internet except when permitted on a per-program basis.

A corporate network may use a proxy server with a firewall as the sole direct connection between the Internet and the corporate network and use a firewall in the proxy server to protect the corporate network against threats.

Physical firewalls are specialized computers whose software is designed to quickly analyze network traffic and make forwarding decisions based on rules set by the administrator. Over time, that task has been incorporated more and more into software on the computers and into the OS design. An example is Windows Defender Firewall in Windows 10, which is discussed later in the chapter.

Most current operating systems have some sort of firewall built in:

- As initially configured, the standard firewall in Windows is a one-way firewall. However, it can be configured to work as a two-way firewall. For more information about how it works, see the section "Firewall Settings," later in this chapter.

- macOS includes an application firewall. In OS X 10.6 and newer, the application firewall offers additional customization options.

- Linux, starting with distros based on kernel 2.4.x and later, includes iptables to configure netfilter, its packet-filtering framework. To learn more, see www.netfilter.org. Many distros and third-party Linux apps are available to help make iptables and netfilter easier to configure.

User Authentication/Strong Passwords

Authenticating users means making sure those who are logging in are truly who they say they are. Requiring passwords for user authentication can make systems more secure, but humans have proven pretty lax at voluntarily practicing security. To solve this problem, administrators should mandate strong passwords in their *authentication* settings.

Strong passwords that foil casual hackers have the following characteristics:

- They are at least eight characters long; every character added to this minimum makes the password exponentially safer.

- They include a variety of uppercase and lowercase letters, numbers, and symbols.

- They do not include real names and words.

Multifactor Authentication

The best type of authentication system is one that uses two or more authentication methods. This is known as *multifactor authentication*. An example of this would be a person using a smart card and typing a username and password to gain access to a system. The combination of the password and the physical token makes it very difficult for imposters to gain access to a system.

Directory Permissions

Directory permissions is the term used in macOS and Linux for configuring the access levels a user has to a directory (folder) and individual files. In Windows, the equivalent term is *file and folder permissions*.

In Linux and macOS, directory permissions include:

- Read (opens file but no changes)

- Write (able to read and change file)

- Execute (runs executable file or opens directory)

The chmod command is used in Linux to change directory permissions. In macOS, the Get Info menu's Sharing & Permissions submenu is used to change directory permissions.

In Windows, file and folder permissions on an NTFS drive include:

- Full control

- Modify

- Read & Execute

- List folder contents (applies to folders only)

- Read

- Write

These settings are configured through the Security tab of the file or folder's properties sheet. The chmod command and output are discussed in further detail in Chapter 6, "Operating Systems."

VPN

A *virtual private network (VPN)* is a private and secure network connection that is carried by an insecure public network, such as the Internet. A VPN connection requires a VPN server at the remote site and a VPN client at the client site. VPN traffic between client and server is encrypted and encapsulated into packets suitable for transmission over the network. VPNs can be used in place of leased lines for connections between locations and for telecommuting workers.

The most common types of VPNs use Point-to-Point Tunneling Protocol (PPTP) and Layer 2 Tunneling Protocol (L2TP/IPsec). Tunneling refers to the practice of using encryption to shield traffic between the client and server from other traffic. PPTP uses 128-bit encryption, and L2TP combined with IPsec (L2TP/IPsec) uses 256-bit encryption. VPNs are discussed further in Chapter 2.

DLP

Data loss/leakage prevention (DLP) involves preventing confidential information from being viewed or stolen by unauthorized parties. DLP goes beyond normal digital security methods such as firewalls and antivirus software by observing and analyzing unusual patterns of data access, email, and instant messaging, whether the data is going into or out of an organization's network.

Access Control Lists

Access control lists (ACLs) are lists of permissions or restriction rules for access to an object such as a file or folder. ACLs control which users or groups can perform specific operations on specified files or folders.

Smart Card

Smart cards can be used to enable logins to a network, encrypt or decrypt drives, and provide digital signatures when supported by the network server.

Email Filtering

Email filtering can be used to organize email into folders automatically, but from a security standpoint, its most important function is to block spam and potentially dangerous messages.

Email filtering can be performed at the point of entry to a network with a specialized email filtering server or appliance as well as by enabling the spam and threat detection features that are built into email clients or security software.

Spam or suspicious emails can be discarded or quarantined by the user, and false positives that are actually legitimate messages can be retrieved from the spam folder and placed back into the normal inbox.

Trusted/Untrusted Software Sources

As mentioned previously concerning certificates, app stores for iOS, Android, Windows, macOS, and many Linux distros are examples of trusted sources of software. Apps installed from these sources have been approved by the operating system vendor and awarded certificates.

But not all software for an operating system comes from an app store. Digital certificates included in software are used to identify the publisher, and most operating systems display warning messages when an app without a digital certificate is being installed. Some operating systems block the installation of any app that does not have a digital certificate. It is ultimately up to the user to determine the trustworthiness of a software source.

Principle of Least Privilege

Applying the *principle of least privilege* means giving a user access to only what is required to do his or her job. Most users in a business environment do not need administrative access to computers and should be restricted from functions that could compromise security.

While the principle of least privilege appears to be basic common sense, it should not be taken lightly. When user accounts are created locally on a computer—and especially on a domain—great care should be taken in assigning users to groups. Also, many programs, when installed, ask who can use and make modifications to the program; often the default is "all users." Some technicians just accept the defaults when hastily installing programs without realizing that they are giving users full control of the program. It is an important practice to give clients all they need but limit their access to only what they need.

Wireless Security Protocols and Authentication

220-1002: Objective 2.3: Compare and contrast wireless security protocols and authentication methods.

220-1002 Exam

Wireless security has evolved over the past few years to adapt to the increasingly available tools that can hack into a wireless network. An administrator cannot safely install a wireless network using the default settings. The following sections describe the security options available on a wireless network.

Protocols and Encryption

An encrypted wireless network relies on the exchange of a passphrase between the client and the wireless access point (WAP) or router before the client can connect to the network. There are several standards for encryption:

- **WEP:** *Wired Equivalent Privacy (WEP)* was the original encryption standard for wireless Ethernet (WiFi) networks. WEP encryption has aged, however, and is no longer strong enough to resist attacks from hackers. This is because the encryption keys are short, and some of the transmissions for the handshaking process are unencrypted. WEP encryption should not be considered secure for a wireless network.

- **WPA versions:** As a replacement to WEP, *WiFi Protected Access (WPA)* was developed in 2003. It is available in three strengths:

  - WPA uses the *Temporal Key Integrity Protocol (TKIP)* encryption, which was designed to provide better encryption than WEP.

  - WPA2 was released in 2004 and uses *Advanced Encryption Standard (AES)* encryption. WPA2's AES encryption is much stronger than WPA's; it uses 128-bit blocks and supports variable key lengths of 128, 192, and 256 bits. It allows up to 63 alphanumeric characters (including punctuation marks and other characters) or 64 hexadecimal characters. WPA2 also supports the use of a RADIUS authentication server in corporate environments.

  - WPA3, which was released in January 2018, uses 128-bit encryption (192-bit in an enterprise version) and has a different method for sharing security keys than the other types of encryption. WPA3 is designed to add better privacy and protection against attacks on public WiFi networks. WPA3 is not currently part of the A+ 220-1002 exam objectives, but its use is expanding as new hardware supporting it becomes common.

TKIP and AES encryption are quite different. TKIP is somewhat like WEP in design so that it can operate on legacy hardware lacking computing power. TKIP is no longer considered secure. AES is much more secure and has been adopted by the U.S. government as the encryption standard.

Authentication

There are four different authentication methods for access to a wireless network: single-factor, multifactor, RADIUS, and TACACS. These methods also apply to wired networks.

Single-Factor

Single-factor authentication is basic username and password access to a computer or network. For years, this was sufficient—and it is still used in many environments. But the rise of online banking and shopping drew more advanced hacking methods, and single-factor authentication is now rare in online commerce.

Multifactor

A ***multifactor authentication*** system uses two or more authentication methods and is far more secure than single-factor authentication. An example of this would be a person using a digital code from a fob and typing a username and password to gain access to a system. The combination of the password and the digital token makes it very difficult for imposters to gain access to a system.

As mentioned earlier in the chapter, Google Authenticator is an app that is downloaded to a device and provides a shared secret key. The user can log in with his or her username and password, and the app runs an authenticating algorithm as well. This multifactor authentication is more secure than earlier versions of software tokens, which could be stolen.

RADIUS

Remote Authentication Dial-In User Service (RADIUS) dates back to the days of dial-up modem access to networks in the early 1990s. It has been widely distributed and has been updated over the years and is still in use. A user who wants to access a network or an online service can contact a RADIUS server and enter username and password information when requested. The server authenticates (or declines) the user and advises the network or service to allow the client in (or not).

TACACS

Terminal Access Controller Access Control System (TACACS) solved a problem that occurred as network use expanded in the 1980s. While the name and acronym seem convoluted, it does describe the function and process pretty well. In early network computing, when a user logged into a network, each time he or she accessed a different resource or host on that network, the user had to re-authenticate. Dial-up was slow, and logging in was a time-consuming process. With TACACS, a user who was already authenticated into the network was automatically logged into other resources in the system as well. The user's terminal access was taken care of by the network's access control system.

TACACS in its original form is quite insecure, but it has been updated and re-released in proprietary form by Cisco Systems as TACACS+.

Malware Removal and Prevention

220-1002: Objective 2.4: Given a scenario, detect, remove, and prevent malware using appropriate tools and methods.

Wireless security has evolved over the past few years to adapt to the increasingly available tools that can be used to hack into a wireless network. An administrator cannot safely install a wireless network using the default settings. The following sections describe the security options available on a wireless network.

Malware

Malicious software, or malware, is software designed to infiltrate a computer system and possibly damage it without the user's knowledge or consent. Malware is a broad term used by computer professionals to include viruses, worms, Trojan horses, spyware, rootkits, keyloggers, adware, and other types of undesirable software. The sections that follow describe some types of malware in more detail.

Ransomware

Ransomware uses malware to encrypt the targeted computer's files. The ransom demand might be presented after you call a bogus technical support number displayed by a fake error message coming from the ransomware, or the ransom demand might be displayed onscreen. The ransom must be paid within a specified amount of time, or the files will not be decrypted.

The most famous example of ransomware is the WannaCry virus, which spread throughout the world in 2017. It impacted Windows machines that had not been updated with security patches that would have prevented the spread of the attack.

Trojan

Trojan malware, also known as a Trojan horse, is a malware program disguised as a "gift"—usually popular videos or website links—that trick the user into downloading a virus that might be used to trap keystrokes or transmit sensitive information.

Trojans are aptly named for the famous story of the wooden Trojan horse—an apparent gift that hid invading soldiers and allowed them to sneak inside the city gates of Troy.

Keylogger

Keylogger viruses are especially dangerous because they track keystrokes and can capture usernames and passwords of unwitting users. A keylogger can be delivered via a Trojan horse, phishing, or a fake email attachment that the user opens. One way to foil these attacks is to require multifactor authentication because the second authentication factor changes, rendering the stolen password invalid.

Rootkit

A *rootkit* is a set of hacking tools that makes its way deep into the computer's operating system or applications and sets up shop to take over the computer. Some rootkits do keylogging, some listen for banking information, and more complex ones can take over a computer completely. A rootkit is a complex type of malware that is difficult to detect and remove with standard malware antivirus software. Sometimes wiping the drive and reinstalling the operating system is the only certain solution.

Virus

Just as biological viruses can infect humans and cause all sorts of different illnesses, computer viruses can infect and damage computers. *Virus* is a generic term for any malicious software that can spread to other computers and cause trouble. Some are more malicious than others, but all need to be guarded against with antivirus updates. Most virus attacks are spread with human assistance when users fall prey to phishing and carelessly open attachments. (Phishing is discussed later in the chapter.)

Botnet

One danger in not protecting a computer from virus attacks is that it may be taken over and become a "bot"—or robot on a network of infected computers. Hackers can infect multiple computers to form a *botnet* and then use the infected machines to work together to cause trouble, such as by mounting denial of service attacks or spreading spam. Hackers who install networks of bots sometimes sell access to them to other hackers.

Worm

Worms are different from other viruses in that they are able to self-replicate on computers and push themselves out to other computers. Phishing and other human errors are not required for worms to thrive.

Spyware

Spyware is software that spies on system activities and transmits details of web searches or other activities to remote computers. Getting multiple unwanted pop-up windows when browsing the Internet is a good indicator of spyware. Some of the pop-up windows may show fake security alerts (as shown in Figure 7-4) in the hopes that the user will click on something and then purchase rogue or fake antivirus software or just download more malware. Spyware can possibly cause slow system performance.

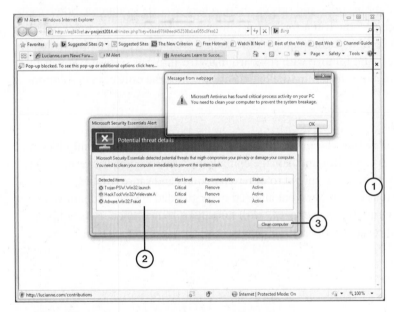

1. The only safe place to click is the close browser button.
2. Fictitious threats.
3. Clicking either of these buttons might launch malware or spyware.

FIGURE 7-4   A Fake Security Alert That Purports to Be from Microsoft

Tools and Methods

The antivirus/anti-malware industry has worked hard to keep pace with the menace of hackers and ever-more-sophisticated viruses. The following sections discuss some of the tools and methods that are used to thwart the hackers.

Antivirus/Anti-malware

Protection against viruses and malware is necessary for every type of computing device, from mobile devices to servers. Computer protection suites that include antivirus, anti-malware, anti-adware, and anti-phishing protection are available from many vendors, but some users prefer a "best of breed" approach and choose the best available product in each category.

Antivirus/anti-malware programs can use some or all of the following techniques to protect users and systems:

- Real-time protection to block infection

- Periodic scans for known and suspected threats

- Automatic updating on a frequent (usually daily) basis

- Renewable subscriptions to obtain updated threat signatures

- Links to virus and threat encyclopedias

- Inoculation of system files

- Permissions-based access to the Internet

- Scanning of downloaded files and sent/received emails

When attempting to protect against viruses and malware, the most important thing to remember is to keep your anti-malware application up to date. The second most important item is to watch out for is unknown data, whether it comes via email, USB flash drive, mobile device, or some other mechanism.

Recovery Console

The ***Recovery Console*** allows you to reset your PC or boot from a recovery disk. If resetting the PC is not sufficient, you can boot from a recovery disk to remove some infected files and restore your original files. Access the recovery tools in Windows 10 by going to **Settings > Update & Security > Recovery**. Figure 7-5 shows the recovery tools page in Windows 10.

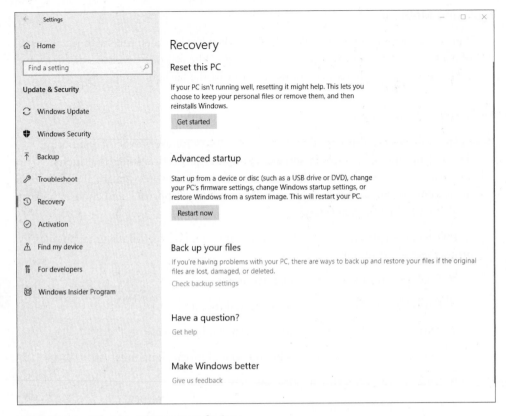

FIGURE 7-5   Windows 10 Recovery Options

Backup/Restore

Troubleshooting an infected PC can be done from a recovery drive. This is a drive that is created and put aside in case it is needed. The drive allows you to boot into a minimal Safe mode that does not install all applications or services. From this mode, you can remove infected files and reboot the computer to normal condition. Figure 7-6 shows the Windows 10 Backup options, which you access by going to **Settings > Update & Security > Backup**.

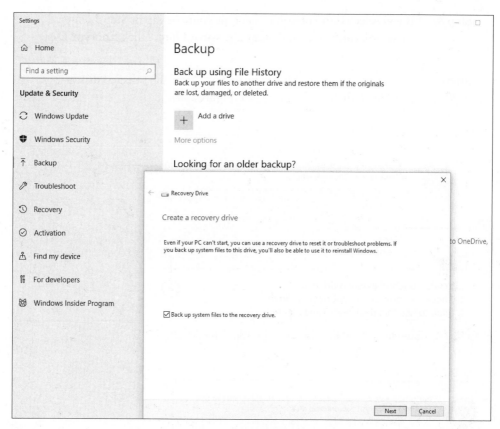

FIGURE 7-6 Tools for Creating a Recovery Drive in Windows 10

Backup/Time Machine

Some Linux distros already have a backup utility installed, and others rely on third-party software. Backing up in Linux can be done by creating a TAR (tape archive) file. macOS includes the Time Machine backup application. Both Linux and macOS must have their backup utilities configured and running in order to be useful in the event that data is lost.

macOS includes Time Machine, a backup utility that can be set up to automatically create daily backups and maintain weekly and monthly versions. To enable and configure Time Machine:

Step 1.   Connect a suitable external disk to a macOS system.

Step 2.   When prompted, click **Use as Backup Disk**. You can also check the Encrypt Backup Disk box to protect the backup (see Figure 7-7).

Step 3.   If you selected the option to encrypt your backup in Step 2, enter a password, confirm it, and enter a password hint. Click **Encrypt Disk** (see Figure 7-8).

Step 4.   Make sure Time Machine is turned on. After the selected disk is encrypted, the backup starts (see Figure 7-9).

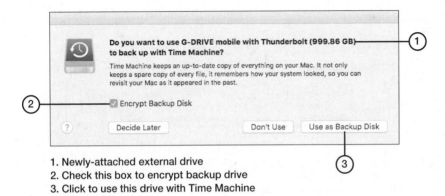

1. Newly-attached external drive
2. Check this box to encrypt backup drive
3. Click to use this drive with Time Machine

FIGURE 7-7   Selecting an External Disk for Use with Time Machine

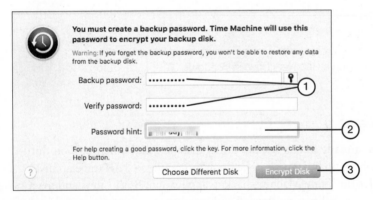

1. Create and confirm password for encrypted Time Machine drive
2. Enter a password hint
3. Click to start encryption of Time Machine drive

FIGURE 7-8   Encrypting the Time Machine Disk

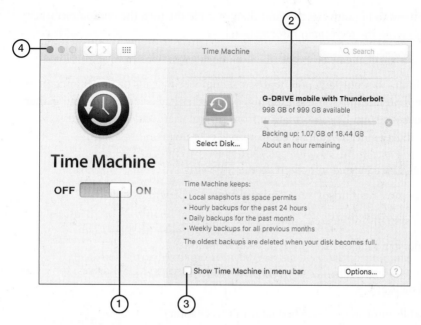

1. Time Machine turned on
2. Progress bar and backup disk information
3. Check box to put Time Machine on menu bar at top of screen
4. Click to close (Red) or minimize (Yellow) Time Machine menu

FIGURE 7-9   Creating a Backup with Time Machine

Time Machine is designed to back up user files automatically. However, to create a disk image that can be restored in case of disaster, use Disk Utility.

User Education/AUP (Acceptable Use Policy)

Regardless of the sophistication of physical or digital security measures, the lack of user education and an *acceptable use policy (AUP)* can lead to security issues. Some elements of a good AUP include the following:

- Have users ask for an ID when approached in person by somebody claiming to be from the help desk, the phone company, or a service company.

- Have users ask for a name and supervisor name when contacted by phone by someone claiming to be from the help desk, the phone company, or a service company.

- Provide contact information for the help desk, phone company, and authorized service companies and ask users to call the authorized contact person to verify that a service call or phone request for information is legitimate.

- Ask users to log into systems and then provide the tech the computer rather than giving the tech login information.

- Have users change passwords immediately after service calls.

- Ask users to report any potential social engineering calls or in-person contacts, even if no information was exchanged. Social engineering experts can gather innocuous-sounding information from several users and use it to create a convincing story to gain access to restricted systems.

Users should be educated in how to do the following:

- Keep antivirus, antispyware, and anti-malware programs updated.

- Scan systems for viruses, spyware, and malware.

- Understand major malware types and techniques.

- Scan removable media drives (such as optical discs and USB drives) for viruses and malware.

- Disable autorun (as described later in this chapter).

- Configure scanning programs for scheduled operation.

- Respond to notifications that viruses, spyware, or malware have been detected.

- Quarantine suspect files.

- Report suspect files to the help desk.

- Remove malware.

- Disable antivirus software when needed (such as during software installations) and know when to reenable antivirus software.

- Avoid opening attachments from unknown senders.

- Use anti-phishing features in web browsers and email clients.

Firewalls

Firewalls are used to prevent unauthorized communication into or out of a device or network. Android does not include a firewall, and third-party apps, such as NetGuard, NetStop Firewall, or AFWall+, must be used to provide protection against unwanted Internet traffic. Google Play offers many free firewall apps.

Apple does not include a firewall because the design of iOS uses a feature called "sandboxing" that runs apps in separate protected space.

Windows 10 has incorporated Windows Defender Firewall into the OS. When it is enabled to default settings, Windows Defender Firewall prevents the most common types of malicious traffic into the computer, and the user can customize the settings as needed. Windows Defender is discussed in much greater detail in Chapter 6.

DNS Configuration

Domain Name Service (DNS) involves a database containing public IP addresses and their associated domain names. The purpose of DNS is to translate domain names used in web page requests into IP addresses. Domain name server functions are included in SOHO routers, and in larger networks, a separate domain name server can be used. Domain name servers communicate with other, larger, domain name servers if the requested addresses are not in their databases.

Hackers like to capture DNS information because it provides links between domain names (such as company.com) and IP addresses. With DNS records, a hacker can create false DNS information that can point victims to fake websites and get them to download malware or viruses. Third-party software can provide DNS Security (DNSSEC) that secures a system's domain name server.

Configuring DNS is covered in Chapter 2, and here we review how the DNS settings are entered when configuring the NIC IPv4 properties. Domain name server addresses can be obtained automatically from the ISP, or they can be statically assigned. Figure 7-10 shows a statically assigned domain name server address and a backup alternative address.

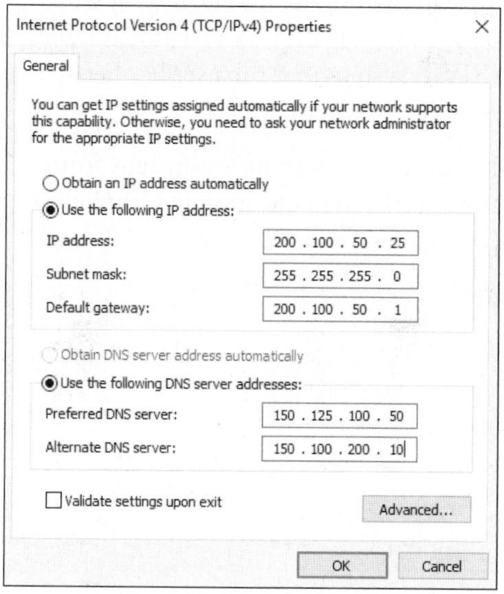

FIGURE 7-10 DNS Addressing Under NIC Properties

Social Engineering Threats and Vulnerabilities

220-1002: Objective 2.5: Compare and contrast social engineering, threats, and vulnerabilities.

Botnets have made hacking so easy that any network can be tested by hackers thousands of times per day. Updated antivirus/anti-malware software and other software does the heavy lifting in protecting networks and devices. But another constant threat to a computer network is users being manipulated or tricked into doing hackers' work for them. This hacking technique is known as social engineering. The following sections describe social engineering and other threats and vulnerabilities to networks.

Social Engineering

Six common *social engineering* techniques that all employees in an organization should know about are phishing, spear phishing, impersonation, shoulder surfing, tailgating, and dumpster diving. The sections that follow describe each of these social engineering techniques.

The key to mitigating these social engineering threats is a combination of ensuring employee awareness, implementing policies and protocols for handling sensitive internal information, and, whenever possible, using cybersecurity tools.

Phishing

Phishing involves creating bogus websites or sending fraudulent emails that trick users into providing personal, bank, or credit card information. A variation, phone phishing, uses an interactive voice response (IVR) system that the user has been tricked into calling to dupe the user into revealing information.

Phishing is a constant threat that can be addressed with awareness warnings from administrators that give examples of the latest threats and education for employees about using judgment to identify suspicious messages.

Figure 7-11 illustrates a typical phishing email.

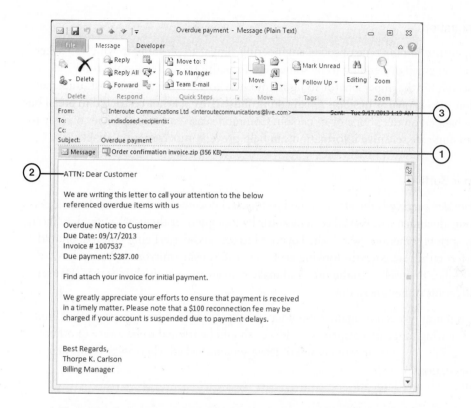

1. Zip archive files are frequently used by malware; open the file and your system is infected
2. Genuine emails from a company you work with will be addressed to a person or account number
3. Live.com is typically used by personal email, not company email

FIGURE 7-11   A Message That Purports to Be About an Overdue Payment but Shows Classic Signs of a Phishing Attack

Spear Phishing

Spear phishing involves sending spoof messages that appear to come from an internal source requesting confidential information, such as payroll or tax information. These attacks typically target a specific person, organization, or business. The best protection against spear phishing is implementing security software that identifies spear phishing mail and educating users about how to handle sensitive information within the organization.

Impersonation

Impersonation is a type of social engineering similar to phishing in which a hacker sends an email pretending to be someone the victim trusts. It can take time and research for the impersonator to figure out how to gain the target's trust. Impersonation, also known as business email compromise (BEC), is not restricted to email but can happen on the phone or in person. Common sense and strict policies on how to communicate sensitive information can help prevent impersonation attacks.

Shoulder Surfing

Shoulder surfing is the attempt to view physical documents on a user's desk or electronic documents displayed on a monitor by looking over the user's shoulder. Shoulder surfers sometimes watch the keyboard to see passwords being entered. Shoulder surfers either act covertly, looking around corners, using mirrors or binoculars, or introduce themselves to the user and make conversation in the hopes that the user will let his or her guard down.

A common protection against shoulder surfing is a special privacy screen that limits the viewing range of a display. Employees should be trained to be aware of others being able to see their screens and to leave screens locked when away from their workstations.

Tailgating

Tailgating occurs when an unauthorized person attempts to accompany an authorized person into a secure area by following that person closely and grabbing the door before it shuts. This is usually done without the authorized person's consent, and sometimes the authorized person is tricked into believing the thief is authorized. If the authorized person is knowingly involved, it is known as *piggybacking*. Mantraps, mentioned earlier, are designed to thwart tailgating.

Dumpster Diving

Going through the trash seeking information about a network—or a person with access to the network—is called *dumpster diving*. This type of activity doesn't have to involve an actual dumpster, of course—just someone searching for any information that will help him or her socially engineer a way into a network. To limit the prospects of a dumpster diver, paper shredders or shredding services should be employed to keep available data limited.

DDoS

A *distributed denial of service (DDoS)* attack occurs when several (up to thousands) of computers have been compromised with special malware that turns them into bots. The bots then get directions from their new master to attack with thousands of requests to a network site. The traffic is so overwhelming that the site is unreachable by normal traffic and is effectively shut down.

DoS

A *denial of service (DoS)* attack involves one computer attacking a specific target with an overwhelming number of service requests. This is very similar to a DDoS attack but without the bots. The messages coming from one source can still take down a network, at great cost to a business.

Zero-Day

When legitimate software is sold and distributed, it may have security vulnerabilities that are unknown. When the flaws are discovered, the users may put out alerts while the software company who made the software creates a patch. Sometimes hackers watch for those alerts and exploit the vulnerabilities before the patch is installed, hence the term *zero day*.

Man-in-the-Middle

A *man-in-the-middle (MiTM)* attack involves the attacker intercepting a connection while fooling the endpoints into thinking they are communicating directly with each other. Essentially, the attacker becomes an unauthorized and undetected proxy or relay point and the attacker uses this position to capture confidential data or transmit altered information to one or both ends of the original connection.

Brute Force

A *brute force attack* involves cracking passwords by calculating and using every possible combination of characters until the correct password is discovered. The longer the password used, and the greater the number of possible characters in a password, the longer brute forcing will take. One way an administrator can block brute forcing is to set authentication systems to lock after a specified number of incorrect passwords are offered. Longer passwords also aid in the fight against brute force attacks.

Dictionary Attacks

Dictionary attacks involve attempting to crack passwords by trying all the words in a list, such as a dictionary. A simple list might include commonly used passwords such as "12345678" and "password." Dictionary attacks can be blocked by locking systems after a specified number of incorrect passwords are offered. Requiring more sophisticated passwords that do not include identifiable information such as birthdays or family names is also a strategy that can be employed.

Rainbow Table

A *rainbow table* is used in an attack in much the same manner as in a brute force attack, but it is more mathematically sophisticated and takes less time. Rainbow tables are precomputed tables that can speed calculations when cracking hashes.

Spoofing

Spoofing is a general term for malware attacks that purport to come from a trustworthy source. Phishing, spear phishing, and rogue antivirus programs are three examples of spoofing.

Non-Compliant Systems

Non-compliant systems are systems that are tagged by a configuration manager application (for example, Microsoft's System Center Configuration Manager) for not having the most up-to-date security patches installed. Systems that don't have the most up-to-date security patches are especially vulnerable to attacks. An example of this would be a user attempting to log on to a corporate network with a personal computer that has not been updated to network standards that comply with the corporations specifications.

Zombie/Botnet

A *zombie*/botnet is a computer on the Internet that has been taken over by a hostile program so it can be used for malware distribution or distributed denial of service (DDoS) or other attacks without notification to the regular users of the computer. Many malware attacks attempt to turn targeted computers into zombies on a hostile botnet.

Microsoft Windows OS Security Settings

220-1002: Objective 2.6: Compare and contrast the differences of basic Microsoft Windows OS security settings.

Microsoft has made several security settings and tools available in the Windows OS. These settings and tools allow users and administrators to control access to files, folders, printers, and physical locations.

The sections that follow discuss the purposes and principles of *access control* through:

- Users and groups
- NTFS vs. share permissions
- Shared files and folders
- System files and folders
- User authentication
- Run as administrator vs. standard user
- BitLocker
- BitLocker To Go
- EFS

Users and Groups

Users in Windows can be assigned to different groups, each with different permissions. The Local Policy settings (for local PCs) and Group Policy settings (for networked PCs connected to a domain controller running Active Directory) can restrict PC features by group or by PC. The 220-1002 exam covers some of the differences between the accounts. There are three standard account levels in Windows:

- **Standard user:** Standard accounts have permission to perform routine tasks. However, these accounts are blocked from performing tasks that involve systemwide changes, such as installing hardware or software, unless they can provide an administrator password when prompted by User Account Control (UAC).

- **Administrator:** Users with an administrator account can perform any and all tasks.

■ **Guest:** The guest account level is the most limited. A guest account cannot install software or hardware or run already-existing applications and cannot access files in shared document folders or the Guest profile. The Guest account is disabled by default. If it is enabled for a user to gain access to the computer, that access should be temporary, and the account should be disabled again when the user no longer requires access.

NOTE   When a user is created using the Users applet in Windows, the user must be assigned a standard or administrator account. Guest accounts are used for visitors.

In Windows versions up to 8.1, the power users account is a specific account type that has more permissions than standard users but fewer than administrators. In those versions, power users have the same rights and permissions as standard users, but a custom security template can be created if the Power Users group needs specific permissions, such as for the operation of legacy programs.

In Windows 10 the Power Users group has been discontinued, but it is available to assign for backward compatibility.

NTFS vs. Share Permissions

Microsoft introduced *New Technology File System (NTFS)* as an improved way to store files on disks over the FAT system of Windows 95. The changes in storage systems allowed for implementing file security in the form of permissions. Permissions control both local and network access to files and can be set for individual users or groups.

Allow vs. Deny

Each permission has two settings: Allow or Deny. Generally, if you want a user to have access to a folder, you add that user to the list and select **Allow** for the appropriate permission. If you don't want to allow a user access, normally you simply don't add the user to a list. In some cases, an administrator must issue an explicit denial if the user is part of a larger group that already has access to a parent folder but needs to be kept out of a particular subfolder.

Moving and Copying Folders and Files

Moving and copying folders and files have different results depending on permissions. For example, when you copy a folder or file to a different volume, the folder or file inherits the permissions of the parent folder it was copied to (the target directory). When you move a folder or file to a different location on the same volume, the folder or file retains its original permissions.

File Attributes

File attributes are used in Windows to indicate how files can be treated. They can be used to specify which files should be backed up, which should be hidden from the normal GUI or command-line file listings, whether a file is compressed or encrypted, and so on, depending on the operating system.

To view file attributes in Windows, right-click a file in File Explorer or Windows Explorer and select **Properties**. To view file attributes from the Windows command line, use the **Attrib** command.

Shared Files and Folders

Shared files and folders have their permissions assigned via the Security tab of the object's properties sheet. Folder and file permissions vary by user type or group and can include the following:

- **Full control:** Complete access to the contents of the file or folder. When Full Control is selected, all of the following are selected and enabled automatically.

- **Modify:** Change file or folder contents.

- **Read & Execute:** Access file or folder contents and run programs.

- **List Folder Contents:** Display folder contents.

- **Read:** Access a file or folder.

- **Write:** Add a new file or folder.

Administrative Shares vs. Local Shares

Local shares are normally configured on a folder or library basis in Windows. However, Windows sets up special *administrative shares* that are available across a network for each local drive. For example, the administrative share for the C: drive on a system called MARK-PC is \\MARK-PC\C$.

To connect to the administrative share, a user must provide a username and password for an account on that system.

Permission Inheritance and Propagation

Permission propagation and inheritance describe how files and folders receive permissions.

If you create a folder, the default action is for the folder to inherit permissions from the parent folder—that is, any permissions that you set in the parent will be inherited by any subfolder of the parent. To view an example of this, locate any folder within an NTFS volume (besides the root folder), right-click it and select **Properties**, access the **Security** tab, and then click the **Advanced** button. In Windows 8/8.1/10, the Advanced Security Settings dialog offers these buttons: Add, Remove, View, and Disable Inheritance.

You can also propagate permission changes to subfolders that are not inheriting from the current folder. To do so, select **Replace All Child Object Permissions with Inheritable Permissions from This Object**. Remember that folders automatically inherit from the parent unless you turn off inheritance, and you can propagate permission entries to subfolders at any time by selecting the **Replace** option.

System Files and Folders

System files and folders are files and folders with the system(s) attribute. They are normally not displayed in File Explorer to help protect them from deletion.

To make these files and folders visible in Windows 10:

Step 1.   Open **File Explorer**.

Step 2.   In the top left select the **View** tab.

Step 3.   Uncheck the boxes that are hidden that need to be viewed.

Figure 7-12 depicts the File Explorer boxes that hide files.

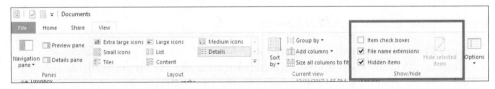

FIGURE 7-12   Showing Hidden Files in Windows 10

User Authentication

Authentication is the process of securely determining that authorized persons accessing computers or network are who they say they are. Windows includes a variety of authentication protocols that can be used on a corporate network, including Kerberos, TLS/SSL, PKU2U, and NTLM.

Apple, Microsoft, and Google use mutual authentication for multiple services (also known as **SSO** or **Single Sign-on**) to enable a single login that provides access to multiple services. For example, a single Microsoft Account login provides access to Outlook email, the Microsoft Store, and OneDrive. To make SSO possible in Windows, client IP addresses are mapped to usernames in Windows Active Directory. Similarly, a single Apple login provides access to iTunes, iCloud, and other services. A single Google login provides access to Gmail, Google Drive, and other services.

BitLocker and BitLocker To Go

To encrypt an entire drive, you need some kind of full disk encryption software. Several options are currently available on the market; one option developed for business-oriented versions of Windows by Microsoft is called **BitLocker**. This software can encrypt the entire disk, which, after completed, is transparent to the user. However, there are some requirements for this, including:

- A **Trusted Platform Module (TPM)** chip, which is a chip residing on the motherboard that actually stores the encrypted keys.

or

- An external USB key to store the encrypted keys. Using BitLocker without a TPM chip requires changes to Group Policy settings.

and

- A hard drive with two volumes, preferably created during the installation of Windows. One volume is for the operating system (most likely C:), and it will be encrypted; the other is the active volume, and it remains unencrypted so that the computer can boot. If a second volume needs to be created, the BitLocker Drive Preparation Tool can be of assistance; it can be downloaded from the Microsoft Download Center.

BitLocker software is based on Advanced Encryption Standard (AES) and uses a 128-bit encryption key.

Since Windows Vista SP1, it has been possible to use BitLocker to encrypt internal hard disk volumes other than the system drive. For example, if a hard disk is partitioned as C: and D: drives, BitLocker can encrypt both drives.

Windows 10 has several enhancements that allow BitLocker to be more user friendly, but the essentials of BitLocker are the same as in Windows 7.

BitLocker To Go

In Windows 7 and later versions, BitLocker functionality is extended to removable drives and external USB drives (including flash drives) with *BitLocker To Go*.

To enable BitLocker on Windows 10, go to the **Control Panel > System and Security > BitLocker Drive Encryption**. For external drives, simply right-click the drive to encrypt and select **Enable BitLocker** to start the encryption process. During the process, you are prompted to specify a password or a smart card for credentials to access the drive's contents.

EFS

Business-oriented editions of Windows include support for *Encrypting File System (EFS)*. EFS can be used to protect sensitive data files and temporary files and can be applied to individual files or folders. (When EFS is applied to folders, all files in an encrypted folder are also encrypted.)

EFS files can be opened only by the user who encrypted them, by an administrator, or by EFS keyholders (users who have been provided with the EFS certificate key for another user's account). Thus, they are protected against access by hackers.

Files encrypted with EFS are listed with green filenames when viewed in Windows Explorer or File Explorer. Only files stored on a drive that uses NTFS can be encrypted.

To encrypt a file in Windows 10, follow this process:

Step 1.   Right-click the file in File Explorer and select **Properties**.

Step 2.   Click the **Advanced** button on the General tab.

Step 3.   Click the empty **Encrypt Contents to Secure Data** check box. Figure 7-13 shows the steps for EFS encryption.

Step 4.   Click **OK**.

Step 5.   Click **Apply**. When prompted, select the option to encrypt the file and parent folder or only the file as desired and click **OK**.

Step 6.   Click **OK** to close the properties sheet.

To decrypt the file, follow the same procedure but clear the **Encrypt Contents to Secure Data** check box in Step 3.

NOTE To enable the recovery of EFS encrypted files in the event that Windows cannot start, you should export the user's EFS certificate key. For details, see the Microsoft TechNet article "Data Recovery and Encrypting File System (EFS)" at https://docs.microsoft.com/en-us/previous-versions/tn-archive/cc512680(v=technet.10).

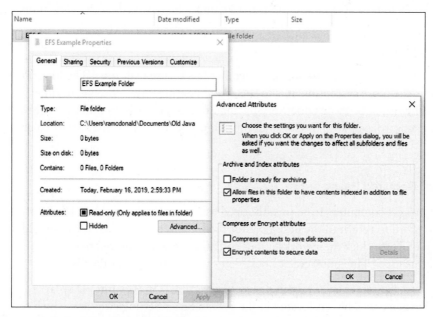

FIGURE 7-13 EFS Encryption Steps

Security Best Practices to Secure a Workstation

220-1002: Objective 2.7: Given a scenario, implement security best practices to secure a workstation.

Secure workstations are the foundation of secure networks. If an outside hacker or thief can access a workstation, the whole network may be compromised. The following sections cover use of passwords, account management, and other methods to make workstations secure.

Password Best Practices

Not all passwords are equally secure, and some are very easy to hack. It is important that administrators use stringent security policy settings to require users to follow strict guidelines for password they use to access the network. The guidelines in the following sections reflect password best practices.

Setting Strong Passwords

Guidelines for setting strong passwords should include requirements for minimum length and a mixture of alphanumeric and symbol characters. Every extra character in a password makes it much harder to hack. Using a password generator can make the creation of strong passwords easier. For example, the Norton Identity Safe Password Generator (https://identitysafe.norton.com/password-generator) offers highly customizable random passwords and can generate multiple passwords at the same time.

Password Expiration

No matter how strong a password is, it becomes less secure over time. The longer it is in use, the more susceptible it is to social engineering, brute forcing, or other attacks. The risk of password discovery by unauthorized users is minimized by the use of a password expiration policy under which passwords expire after a particular length of time and must be reset.

Screensaver Required Password

To help protect computers from unauthorized use, users can be required to enter their password to return to the desktop after the screensaver appears. Users should also be required to lock their workstations so that a logon is required to return to the desktop. (See "Timeout/Screen Lock," later in this chapter, for details.)

In Windows, the screensaver required password setting (**On Resume, Display Logon Screen** check box) is located in the Screen Saver Settings window, which can be accessed from **Settings > Personalization** in Windows 10. In macOS, use the **Desktop & Screen Saver** menu to choose a screen saver and **Security & Privacy** to require a password to unlock the system.

BIOS/UEFI Passwords

BIOS/UEFI passwords prevent unauthorized users from changing settings. Note that they can be removed by resetting the CMOS. Some motherboards feature a jumper block or a push button to reset the CMOS. If this feature is not present, the CMOS can be reset by removing the CMOS battery for several minutes. Configuration of BIOS/UEFI security settings is covered in more detail in Chapter 3, "Hardware."

Requiring Passwords

PC users should be trained to use passwords to secure their user accounts. Administrators can require this through the Local Security Policy and Group Policy in Windows.

Passwords can be set up to require users to do the following:

- Change passwords periodically to keep them fresh and secure.

- Be informed in advance that passwords are about to expire so that users can change passwords early and prevent being locked out at an inconvenient time.

- Enforce a minimum password length to keep passwords strong.

- Require complex passwords that include a mixture of letters, numbers, and special characters.

- Prevent old passwords from being reused continually by tracking past passwords and not allowing them.

- Wait a certain number of minutes after a specified number of unsuccessful logins has taken place before being able to log in again.

To create a password or adjust password settings in Windows 10, go to **Settings > Accounts > Sign-in Options**. To change or enforce password policy settings, go to the following location by using the Group Policy Management Console: **Computer Configuration > Windows Settings > Security Settings > Account Policies > Password Policy**. Figure 7-14 shows the path to these settings.

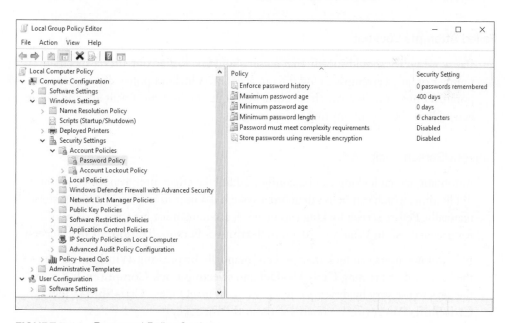

FIGURE 7-14 Password Policy Settings

Account Management

User account settings, when combined with workstation security settings, help prevent unauthorized access to the network. The account management settings described in the sections that follow can enhance security.

Restricting User Permissions

User permissions for standard users prevent systemwide changes, but additional restrictions can be set with Group Policy or Local Security Policy.

Login Time Restrictions

To prevent a user account from being used after hours or before the start of business, login time restrictions can be used to specify when an account can be used.

Disabling Guest Account

The guest account in Windows is a potential security risk, so it should be disabled. If visitors need Internet access, a guest wireless network that doesn't connect to the business network is a good replacement.

Failed Attempts Lockout

Password policy should specify that a user should be locked out after a specified number of failed attempts to log into an account. A lockout policy can also incorporate a timeout policy, which specifies how long the user must wait after an unsuccessful login before attempting to log in again.

Timeout/Screen Lock

Automatic screen locking can be configured to take effect after a specified amount of idle time, which can help safeguard a system if a user forgets to lock the system manually. Before screen locking can be used, accounts must have the screen lock feature enabled. In Windows 10, go to **Settings > Personalization > Lock Screen**.

In Windows, users can lock their screens manually by pressing **Windows+L** on the keyboard or pressing **Ctrl+Alt+Del** and selecting **Lock Computer**. In Linux, the keys to use vary by desktop environment. In macOS, use **Ctrl+Shift+Eject** or **Ctrl+Shift+Power** (for keyboards without the Eject key).

Changing Default Usernames and Passwords

Default usernames and passwords for SOHO routers or other devices or services that have default passwords should be changed. Default usernames and passwords are available in documentation for these devices, so it is easy for an attacker to find the defaults and use them to take over routers or other devices that are still set to the default passwords.

Basic Active Directory Functions

Active Directory (AD) functions occur in the Windows Server environment, not on local workstations. A full discussion of Active Directory is well beyond the scope of the CompTIA A+ exam, but understanding the essentials of user accounts is necessary because user access issues are a common for support personnel. If a support technician has access to Active Directory, basic user account functions can be performed in the Microsoft Management Console (MMC) or by navigating to the Active Directory Users and Computers folder. This second method is used in Figure 7-12, which shows an account being created.

Creating, Deleting, Resetting/Unlocking, and Disabling an Account

To create an account, select **Action > New > User** (or right-click the **Users** folder), as shown in Figure 7-15. Windows opens a dialog where you now enter the new user's account information, as shown in Figure 7-16.

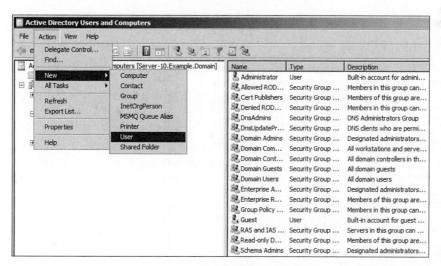

FIGURE 7-15 Creating a New User Account in Active Directory Users and Computers

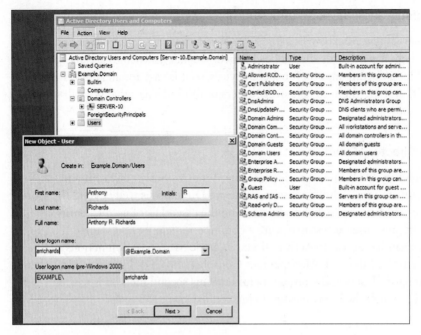

FIGURE 7-16   New User Account

Click the **Next** button, and an initial password dialog box appears. Figure 7-17 shows this dialog for a new account; note that this dialog allows you to set a password and indicate how the password will be managed by Active Directory.

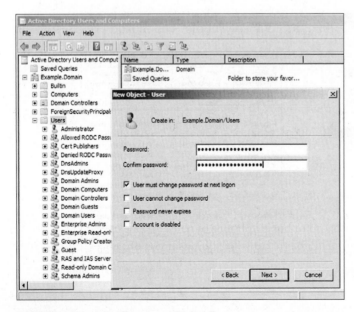

FIGURE 7-17   Initial Password Dialog Box

Click the **Next** button to create the user.

After a user is created, a technician might need to perform a few common tasks:

- **Account deletion:** A technician might need to completely remove a user from Active Directory.

- **Password reset/unlock:** This may need to be done when a user has forgotten a password or failed to authenticate.

- **Disable account:** It is possible to deactivate a user but keep the account and its records.

These tasks can all be performed by right-clicking on a user's name. Note that commands for all three of these functions—Delete, Reset Password, and Disable account—appear in the menu in Figure 7-18.

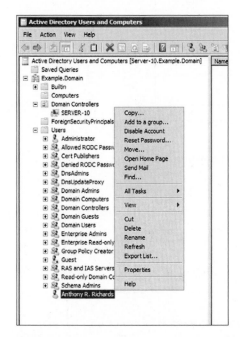

FIGURE 7-18   User options in Active Directory

Disabling Autorun/AutoPlay

Autorun is a feature that enables programs to start automatically when a CD or USB drive or flashcard is connected to a computer. AutoPlay is a similar feature with enhanced options in a Windows environment. Both Autorun and AutoPlay allow the user to be selective in what kinds of programs, updates, and syncs can take place. When you disable autorun, an optical disc or USB drive won't automatically start its autorun application (if it has one), and any embedded malware won't have a chance to infect the system before you scan the media. AutoPlay is a similar feature that pops up a menu of apps to use for the media on an optical drive or USB flash drive.

The easiest way to turn off AutoPlay in Windows 10 is to open the AutoPlay applet in **Settings > Devices > AutoPlay** and toggle the button off. Figure 7-19 shows the AutoPlay Settings window in Windows 10. Figure 7-20 shows how to turn off Auto-Play from the Group Policy settings.

FIGURE 7-19   AutoPlay Settings in Windows 10

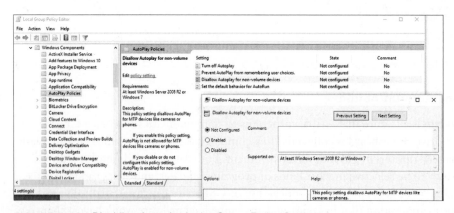

FIGURE 7-20   Disabling Autoplay in the Group Policy Settings

To disable autorun in Windows by using Local Group Policy, complete the following steps:

Step 1. Click **Start** and in the search field type **gpedit.msc** to open the Local Group Policy Editor.

Step 2. Navigate to **Computer Configuration > Administrative Templates > Windows Components > AutoPlay Policies**.

Step 3. Double-click the **Turn Off AutoPlay** setting to display the Turn Off AutoPlay configuration window.

Step 4. Click the **Enabled** radio button and then click **OK** to enable the policy named Turn off AutoPlay.

NOTE Laptops that do presentations might require AutoPlay.

For security reasons, macOS does not support any type of autorun feature, but it is possible to select apps you want to run on startup. To edit this list, select **Apple menu > System Preferences > Users and Groups > Login Items**.

In Linux, you can disable autorun on systems that use the Nautilus file manager by changing the properties on the Media tab to enable **Never Prompt or Start Programs on Media Insertion** and disable **Browse Media When Inserted**.

Using Data Encryption

Data encryption should be used on laptops and other systems that might be used outside the more secure corporate network environment. Laptops containing unencrypted sensitive data have led to many data breaches. To encrypt folders or drives, use the following steps:

Step 1. Right-click the folder or drive to be secured and select **Properties**.

Step 2. Click the **Advanced** button at the bottom of the General tab.

Step 3. In the Advanced Attributes dialog, select the **Encrypt Contents to Secure Data** check box and click **OK**.

These steps are shown in Figure 7-21, where a folder named A+ is being encrypted.

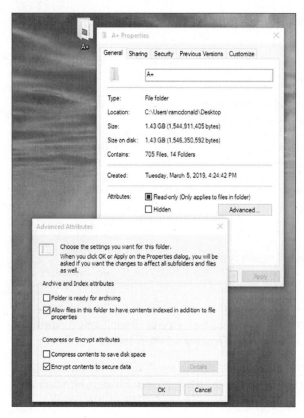

FIGURE 7-21   Encrypting Files or Drives

Patch/Update Management

Patches and updates to operating systems and applications should be managed centrally to prevent systems from falling out of compliance. Microsoft's Windows Server Update Services (WSUS) can be used for OS and application patches and updates for Microsoft products. macOS Server's Software Update service provides the same role for macOS machines. Linux distributions use various programs to manage updates.

Securing Mobile Devices

220-1002: Objective 2.8: Given a scenario, implement methods for securing mobile devices.

Mobile devices have evolved to the point that they can hold as much valuable data as any workstation. Add to this their compact and easy-to-conceal design and the high cost of the devices, and it becomes clear why mobile devices pose a serious security threat. The following sections cover methods and practices that can mitigate mobile device threats.

NOTE   For the 220-1002 exam, be familiar with:

- Screen locks
- Remote wipes
- Locator applications
- Remote backup applications
- Failed login attempt restrictions
- Antivirus/anti-malware
- Patching/OS updates
- Biometric authentication
- Full device encryption
- Multifactor authentication
- Authenticator applications
- Trusted sources vs. untrusted sources
- Firewalls
- Policies and procedures

Screen Locks

The first step in securing a mobile device is setting a numeric passcode or another type of *screen lock*. Such a passcode locks the device, making it inaccessible to everyone except those who know the passcode and experienced hackers. A screen lock can be a pattern that is drawn on the display, a PIN (passcode lock), or a password. A very strong password is usually the strongest form of screen lock. The screen lock setting can be accessed on an Android device by going to **Settings > Security**. On iPhone 6, go to **Settings > Touch ID > Passcode** (requires entering current passcode). On iPhone 7 go to **Settings > General > Passcode**. On iPhone X and later, go to **Settings > FaceID & Passcode**. While the navigation will vary between Android and iPhone versions, the settings here apply to both types of phones unless noted.

You can select how long the phone waits after inactivity to lock; this is usually set to three or five minutes, but in a confidential environment, it may be appropriate to set this to **Immediate**. To enable Auto-Lock, go to **Settings > General > Auto-Lock** and select a number of minutes. If this is set to **Never**, the device will never sleep, negating the security of the passcode and using valuable battery power. The default setting is two minutes. On an iPhone, Auto Lock is under the Display Settings area.

In addition to the default timeout, devices can also be locked by pressing the power button quickly. If configured, the passcode must be supplied whenever a mobile device comes out of a sleep or lock state and whenever it is first booted.

Some devices support other types of screen locking, including *fingerprint lock* (where the user's fingerprint is matched against a list of authorized user fingerprints) and *face lock* (where the user's face is matched against a list of authorized user faces). Windows Hello, a Windows 10 feature supported on some devices, is an example of a face lock. Face ID is the Apple version that is supported on newer versions of iPhone and iPad Pro.

A *swipe lock* app immediately locks a device when the user swipes the display to one side.

The next option on the Security screen is Visible Passwords. If this option is checked, the device shows the current letter of the password being typed by the user. This type of setting is vulnerable to shoulder surfers (people looking over your shoulder to find out your password) and should be deselected so that only asterisks (*) are shown when the user types a password.

There is also a Credential Storage option. By default, secure credentials are dropped after a session is over. (An exception to this rule is a Gmail or other similar login.) However, if Use Secure Credentials is checked, and a user accesses a website or an application that requires a secure certificate, the credentials are stored on the device. A user can set a password here so that only he or she can view or clear credentials or install credentials from a memory card. The use of secure credentials is usually configured only if a user needs access to confidential company information on the Internet.

Passcode locking can be accessed on iPad and iPhone devices by going to **Settings > Passcode** and tapping **Passcode Lock** to display the Passcode Lock screen. Tap **Turn Passcode On** to set a passcode.

Remote Wipes

A lost or missing mobile device is a serious security threat. A hacker can get past passcodes and other screen locks. It's just a matter of time before the hacker has access to the data. So, an organization with confidential information should consider enabling a *remote wipe* program of a device. As long as the mobile device still has access to the Internet, the remote wipe program can be initiated from a desktop computer to delete all the contents of the remote mobile device.

Some devices (such as the iPhone) have a setting that causes the device to be erased after a certain number of incorrect password attempts (10 in the case of the iPhone). There are also third-party apps available for download for most mobile devices that can wipe the data after a specified number of attempts. Some apps configure a device to automatically take a picture after three failed attempts and email the picture to the device owner. Examples of software that can accomplish this include Google Sync, Google Apps Device Policy, Apple's Data Protection, and third-party apps such as Mobile Defense. In some cases, such as with Apple's Data Protection, the command that starts the remote wipe must be issued from an Exchange server or mobile device management (MDM) server. Of course, you should have a backup plan in place as well so that data on the mobile device is backed up to a secure location at regular intervals. This way, if the data needs to be wiped, you know that most or all of the data can be recovered. The type of remote wipe program, backup program, and policies regarding how these are implemented can vary from one organization to the next.

Locator Applications

By installing or enabling a *locator application* or service such as Android Device Manager, Lookout for iOS or Android, or Find My iPhone, a user can track down a lost device. These apps can be operated from any other phone that has a similar app installed as long as the power is on and geolocation is working.

Remote Backup Applications

There are two ways to back up a mobile device: via a USB connection to a desktop or laptop computer or to the cloud by using a *remote backup application*.

Apple's iCloud offers free cloud backup service for a limited amount of data (currently 5GB), with more space available by subscription. iTunes, which can be used for USB-based backup, enables the entire device to be backed up to a hard drive at no additional cost.

Android users have free backup for email, contacts, and other information via Google Cloud. However, backing up photos, music, and other content and documents must either be performed manually via USB or file sync to the cloud, using a service such as Dropbox or another third-party app.

Both iOS and Android users can use popular third-party cloud-based backups that are also supported for macOS and Windows, such as Carbonite (carbonite.com) and iDrive (idrive.com).

Failed Login Attempts Restrictions

Most mobile devices include failed login attempt restrictions. If a person fails to enter the correct passcode after a certain number of attempts, the device locks temporarily, and the person has to wait a certain amount of time before attempting the passcode again. If the person fails to enter the correct passcode again, on most devices the timeout increases. As mentioned earlier, multiple failed logins may result in a remote wipe of the hard drive.

Antivirus/Anti-malware

Just as there is antivirus software for PCs, there is also antivirus/anti-malware software for mobile devices. These are third-party applications that need to be paid for, downloaded, and installed to the mobile device. Some common examples for Android include McAfee's VirusScan Mobile, AVG, Lookout, Dr. Web, and NetQin.

iOS works a bit differently than Android. iOS is a tightly controlled operating system. One of the benefits of being a closed-source OS is that it can be more difficult to write viruses for it, making it somewhat more difficult to compromise. But there is no OS that can't be compromised. For the longest time there was no antivirus software for iOS, but Apple now allows the download of previously unavailable applications and software not authorized by Apple.

Patching/OS Updates

Patching/OS updates help protect mobile devices from the latest vulnerabilities and threats. By default, you are notified automatically about available updates on Android and iOS-based devices. However, you should know where to go to manually update these devices as well:

- For Android, go to **Settings > General > About Device > Software Update** or **Settings > System > About Device > Software Update > Check for Updates**.

- For iOS, go to **Settings > General > Software Update**.

When it comes to large organizations that have many mobile devices, a mobile device management (MDM) suite should be used. McAfee and many other companies have MDM software suites that can take care of pushing updates and configuring many mobile devices from a central location. Decent-quality MDM software secures, monitors, manages, and supports multiple different mobile devices across the enterprise.

Biometric Authentication

Both current and older Android and iOS devices can use *biometric authentication* through the use of add-on fingerprint readers or iris readers.

Recent and current iOS devices have built-in support for fingerprint reading with all Touch ID feature enabled phones and iPad versions.

Face locks, like Microsoft's Windows Hello and Apple's Face ID, are also considered a type of biometric authentication.

Full Device Encryption

With *full device encryption*, your data is not accessible to would-be thieves unless they know the passcode. Apple's iOS devices feature full device encryption that is activated when a passcode is assigned to the device. To learn more about this and other iOS security, Apple provides an iOS Security guide at https://www.apple.com/business/docs/iOS_Security_Guide.pdf.

Android 5 and later supports full disk encryption, and Android 7 and later supports file-based encryption. File-based encryption is encryption on individual files, meaning each file has a separate encryption key, so all the phone resources do not have to be tied up in the encryption process.

Multifactor Authentication

Any authentication method for email, e-banking, or other tasks that requires two forms of authentication is considered multifactor authentication. For example, websites and apps might require authentication of both the account information (name and password) and the device being used to access the account. Typically, this is done by sending an SMS text message or making a robocall to the pre-registered mobile phone of the account holder. The account holder must enter the code received when prompted by the website or app before the app can run or the website opens. Unless the app is deleted or cookies are deleted from the browser, the device is an approved device for that account.

Authenticator Applications

An *authenticator application* is used to receive or generate authentication codes for one or more apps or services.

Google Authenticator from the Google Play app store enables a user to receive or generate multifactor codes with Android, iOS, and BlackBerry devices. It supports options to add or remove trusted computers and devices and works with the Security

Key USB device. There are several other authenticator apps for mobile devices, but before selecting one, be sure to determine which websites and services it supports.

Trusted Sources vs. Untrusted Sources

The Apple Store (apps for iOS), Google Play (Android), and Microsoft Store (Windows 10 Mobile) are trusted sources for apps for mobile devices. Apps downloaded from other locations are considered untrusted and should not be used if at all possible. Jailbreaking the phone is usually required to run untrusted apps, and jailbreaking removes security measures built into the phones.

Firewalls

Android does not include a firewall, so third-party apps must be used to provide protection against unwanted Internet traffic. Google Play offers many free firewall apps for Android.

Apple does not include a firewall because the design of iOS uses a feature called "sandboxing" that runs apps in separate protected space.

Policies and Procedures

Many individually owned mobile devices are now being used on corporate networks. Because these devices were not configured by the corporation, they could potentially present security threats. To prevent security threats, organizations need to address these issues in their policies and procedures.

BYOD vs. Corporate-Owned Devices

Benefits of *bring your own device (BYOD)* policies include:

- No hardware cost to the organization
- Higher usage due to employee satisfaction with their selected device
- Greater productivity

Potential drawbacks include:

- Hidden costs of management and security
- Possibility that some employees will not want to buy their own devices

Profile Security Requirements

Whether an organization uses corporate-owned mobile devices, BYOD, or a mixture, setting and following profile security requirements are very important to achieving increased productivity without incurring significant risks. Issues involved include specifying approved devices and operating system versions, requiring passwords and lock screens, requiring device encryption, support issues, and when and how to remove company information when an employee leaves the organization.

Data Destruction and Disposal

220-1002: Objective 2.9: Given a scenario, implement appropriate data destruction and disposal methods.

Even after computers, mobile devices, and even some types of printers have reached the end of their useful lives, the hard drives inside contain potential security risks. Risks also lie in flash drives, external drives, and optical media. To prevent confidential company or client information from being accessed from a computer or another device that is being disposed of for resale, recycling, or deconstruction for parts, the methods in the following sections should be used.

> **NOTE**   For the 220-1002 exam, the importance of these methods should be well understood.
>
> - Physical destruction methods
> - Recycling or repurposing best practices

Physical Destruction Methods

Physical destruction renders a mass storage device into small pieces that cannot be reconstructed, making the data inside unrecoverable. Methods include the following:

- **Shredder:** Some office-grade shredders can be used to destroy optical media. Electronics recyclers use heavy-duty shredders made for hard disks and mass storage devices to reduce storage devices, tape, or other types of media into small bits.

- **Drill/Hammer:** Remove the hard disks and destroy their platters with a drill, hammer, or other device; then recycle the scrap.

- **Electromagnetic (degaussing):** Other tools such as electromagnetic degaussers and permanent magnet degaussers can also be used to permanently purge information from a disk. The drive is physically intact, but all data, formatting, and control track data is missing. Use this type of physical destruction if you want to use a drive for display purposes.

- **Incineration:** Incineration of tape, floppy, and other types of magnetic and optical media is allowed in some areas and available from various companies.

Data-recycling companies that destroy hard drives or other storage devices can provide a certificate of destruction to prove compliance with local laws or institutional policies.

Recycling or Repurposing Best Practices

As long as the data on a hard drive or other mass storage device can be rendered unrecoverable, it is not necessary to destroy the media itself. The following are some best practices for recycling and repurposing:

- **Low-level format vs. standard format:** The standard format used in operating systems is a quick format. This type of format clears only the root folder. The remainder of the data on the disk can be recovered until it is overwritten. A long format rewrites the disk surface. However, data recovery programs available from many third-party firms can recover data from a formatted drive. A low-level format that creates the physical infrastructure where data will be stored on a disk is performed by the drive manufacturer before the drive is shipped and cannot be performed in the field.

- **Overwrite:** Some disk maintenance programs from mass storage vendors include options to *overwrite* a hard disk's or SSD's data area with zeros. Data recovery programs can often recover data that has been overwritten in this fashion.

- **Drive wipe:** To ensure the complete destruction of retrievable data on a storage device, it must be overwritten with a program that meets or exceeds recognized data-destruction standards, such as the U.S. Department of Defense (DoD) 5220.22-M (which requires 7 passes) or Peter Gutman's 35-pass maximum-security method. These programs, referred to as *drive wipes*, destroy existing data and partition information in such a way as to prevent data recovery or drive forensic analysis. Use this method when maintaining the storage device as a working device is important for repurposing (such as for donation or resale). A variety of commercial and freeware programs can be used for this task, which is also known as disk scrubbing or disk wiping.

Configuring Security on SOHO Networks

220-1002: Objective 2.10: Given a scenario, configure security on SOHO wireless and wired networks.

Both wireless and wired small office/home office (SOHO) networks are important to businesses of all sizes as well as individual users. However, they also represent significant vulnerabilities if they are not properly secured. The following sections explain how the different encryption methods work and the additional steps that must be taken to completely secure a wireless network.

NOTE   For the 220-1002 exam, be familiar with the following tasks:

- Wireless-specific security settings

- Changing default usernames and passwords

- Enabling MAC filtering

- Assigning static IP addresses

- Firewall settings

- Port forwarding/mapping

- Disabling ports

- Content filtering/parental controls

- Updating firmware

- Physical security

Wireless-Specific Security

The default settings for a wireless network should be changed to provide security. The following sections discuss these issues.

Changing Default SSID

The *service set identifier (SSID)* can provide a great deal of useful information to a potential hacker of a wireless network. Every wireless network must have an SSID, and by default, WAPs and wireless routers typically use the manufacturer's name or the device's model number as the default SSID. If a *default SSID* is broadcast by a wireless network, a hacker can look up the documentation for a specific router or the most common models of a particular brand and determine the default IP address range, the default administrator username and password, and other information that would make it easy to attack the network.

To help "hide" the details of your network and location, a replacement SSID for a secure wireless network should not include any of the following:

- Your name

- Your company name

- Your location

- Any other easily identifiable information

An SSID that includes obscure information (such as the name of your first pet) would be a suitable replacement.

Setting Encryption

The importance of setting encryption to the latest possible standards is covered earlier in this chapter, in the section "Wireless Security Protocols and Authentication." The information there applies to SOHO networks as well, as a SOHO may be set up as an extension of a business. In such a case, all security policies from the business should apply at the SOHO extension as well.

Disabling SSID Broadcast

Disabling SSID broadcast is widely believed to be an effective way to prevent a wireless network from being detected and is so regarded by the A+ certification exams. But that is not always enough. Even though disabling SSID broadcast prevents casual bandwidth snoopers from finding your wireless network, Microsoft does not recommend disabling SSID broadcasting as a security measure because there are methods serious hackers can use to discover networks.

Figure 7-22 illustrates a Linksys router configuration dialog in which several of these security recommendations have been implemented.

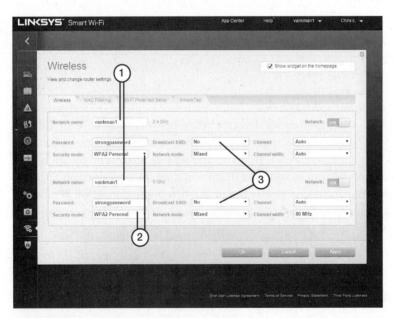

1. User-assigned SSID in place of factory default
2. WPA2 Personal security mode selected
3. SSID broadcast disabled

FIGURE 7-22   Configuring a Router with Alternative SSIDs, WPA2 Encryption Enabled, and SSID Broadcast Disabled

Antenna and Access Point Placement

When configuring and/or troubleshooting wireless connections, think about the wireless access point's (WAP's) location. The placement of the access point plays a big part in a strong signal. Generally, it should be placed in the middle of an office to offer the greatest coverage while reducing the chance of outsiders being able to connect to the device. The antennas on the access point should be set at a 90-degree angle to each other. Keep the device away from any forms of electrical interference, such as other wireless devices, speakers, and any devices that use a lot of electricity.

Radio Power Levels

Some wireless routers and access points have adjustable radio power levels. When they are set too low, clients at the perimeter of the building will not be able to gain access. When they are set too high, computers located in neighboring businesses will be able to attempt access. If a wireless signal is too weak, regardless of the router location and radio power levels, and the router is older, consider replacing it with a new wireless router.

WiFi Protected Setup (WPS)

Using WiFi Protected Setup (WPS) is an easy way to configure a secure wireless network with a SOHO router, provided that all devices on the network support WPS. There are several ways that WPS can be configured. The most common ways include:

- **PIN:** A personal identification number (PIN) marked on the router may be entered into each new device added to the network. This is the default method.

- **Push button:** The router or WAP may have a push button, and each new device may also have a physical push button or (more often) a software push button in the setup program. Both the button on the WAP or router and the button on the other device must be pushed within a short period of time to make the connection.

A security flaw with the PIN method was discovered, and many professionals recommend against WPS on this basis. But it really depends on the features available on the router. Some routers let you disable the PIN and allow the push-button method, but many do not. Some routers allow you to disable WPS altogether. These settings are worth investigating when looking to install or replace a WAP. Figure 7-23 depicts WiFi Protected Setup options.

FIGURE 7-23   WiFi Protected Setup Options

Change Default Usernames and Passwords

As mentioned previously, the documentation for almost all WAPs and wireless routers lists the default administrator password, and the documentation can be readily downloaded in PDF or HTML form from vendor websites. Because an attacker could use this information to "take over" the device, it is essential to change the default to a private password. Most routers use the Administration or Management dialog for the password and other security settings.

> **TIP**   To further secure a router or WAP, configure the device so it can be managed only with a wired Ethernet connection.

Enable MAC Filtering

As mentioned earlier in this chapter, every device on a network has a MAC address. All devices on a SOHO network, including phones and tablets, have MAC addresses as well, and they need to be managed with filtering. Refer to the section "Physical Security Measures," earlier in this chapter, for details about software used to hack networks. MAC filtering is described in more detail in Chapter 2.

Assign Static IP Addresses

The DHCP server built into a router hands out IP addresses to all computers connected to it. This is convenient, but if you want to limit access to the Internet for certain computers or log activity for computers by IP address, the DHCP setting should be disabled, and a static IP address should be assigned to each computer. This way, outside devices will not be assigned IP addresses and be able to access the network.

Firewall Settings

By default, most WAPs and wireless routers use a feature called *Network Address Translation (NAT)* to act as simple firewalls. NAT prevents traffic from the Internet from determining the private IP addresses used by computers on the network. However, many WAPs and wireless routers offer additional firewall features that can be enabled, including:

- Access logs

- Filtering of specific types of traffic

- Enhanced support for VPNs

See the router manufacturer's documentation for more information about advanced security features. Figure 7-24 shows an example of firewall settings.

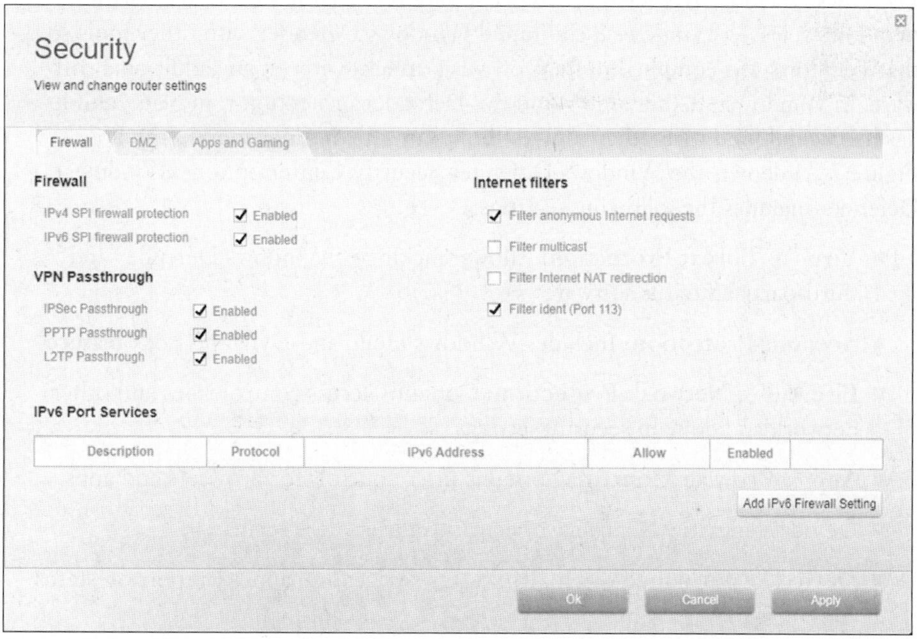

FIGURE 7-24   Firewall Settings

Port Forwarding/Mapping

Use *port forwarding* (also known as *port mapping*) to allow inbound traffic on a particular TCP or UDP port or range to go to a particular IP address rather than to all devices on a network. A basic example would be an FTP server internal to a LAN. The FTP server might have the IP address 192.168.0.250 and have port 21 open and ready to accept file transactions (or a different inbound port could be used). Clients on the Internet that want to connect to the FTP server would have to know the IP address of the router, so the clients might connect with an FTP client using the IP address 68.54.127.95 and port 21. If there is an appropriate port-forwarding rule, the router sees these packets and forwards them to 192.168.0.250:21, or whatever port is chosen. Many ISPs block this type of activity, but port forwarding is a common and important method in larger networks.

Disabling Ports

Blocking TCP and UDP ports, also known as disabling ports, is performed with a firewall app such as Windows Defender Firewall with Advanced Security. Hackers take advantage of unused ports sitting idle on a network, and disabling unnecessary ports makes it harder to access your domain.

Content Filtering/Parental Controls

Windows Defender is Microsoft's anti-spyware tool that has evolved over the Windows releases. Windows 8 combined Windows Defender with other tools so that Windows was equipped to fight off virus attacks without any additional software. In Windows 10, the same Windows Defender protection is in place, and it has been combined with other tools and put into the Settings menu as an app. Figure 7-25 depicts the Windows Defender Security Center options. Windows Defender includes the following sections:

- **Virus & Threat Protection:** Allows tracking of Windows Defender and third-party antivirus software

- **Account Protection:** Includes Windows Hello and Dynamic Lock features

- **Firewall & Network Protection:** Contains access control rules and other network and domain security settings

- **App & Browser Control:** Contains filter controls for browsers and apps

- **Device Security:** Tests device security and sets core security

- **Device Performance & Health:** Scans devices and apps to report on status

- **Family Options:** Provides parental controls and family device management options

Spending time getting to know the settings in the Windows Defender Security Center is a must for any technical support professional.

Apple has parental controls in macOS versions. They can be found by selecting the **Apple menu > System Preferences > Parental Controls**.

Linux distros do not include parental controls, but many third-party apps are available.

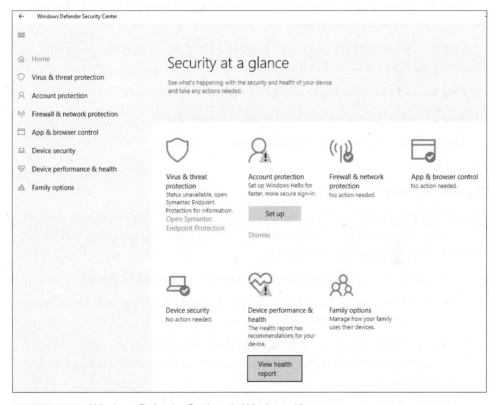

FIGURE 7-25 Windows Defender Settings in Windows 10

Update Firmware

Most SOHO router vendors issue at least one firmware update during the life span of each model of WAP and wireless router. Updates can solve operational problems and might add features that enhance WiFi interoperability, security, and ease of use. To determine whether a WAP or wireless router has a firmware update available, follow these steps:

Step 1.   View the device's configuration dialogs to record the current firmware version. Also note the router's model number and revision from the back or bottom of the device.

Step 2.   Visit the device vendor's website to see whether a newer version of the firmware is available.

Step 3.   Download the firmware update to a PC that can be connected to the device with an Ethernet cable.

Step 4.   Connect the PC to the device with an Ethernet cable.

Step 5.   Navigate to the device's firmware update dialog.

Step 6.   Follow the instructions to update firmware.

Physical Security

In a SOHO network environment, physical security refers to preventing unauthorized use of the network. The same basics of physical security apply in a SOHO network in a large office environment:

- Secure the network equipment in a locked wiring closet or room.

- Disable any unused wall Ethernet jacks by either disabling their switch ports or unplugging the patch panels in the wiring closet.

- Route network cables out of sight, in the walls and above the ceiling. Having them out of sight cuts down on the chances of someone tapping into the network.

- Lock doors when leaving.

- If possible, dedicate a lockable room as a workspace in a home office to protect company devices and other resources from the hazards of daily family life, such as children and pets.

Exam Preparation Tasks

As mentioned in the section "How to Use This Book" in the Introduction, you have a couple choices for exam preparation: the exercises here, Chapter 10, "Final Preparation," and the exam simulation questions in the Pearson Test Prep Software Online.

Review All the Key Topics

Review the most important topics in the chapter, noted with the Key Topic icon in the outer margin of the page. Table 7-2 lists these key topics and the page numbers on which each is found.

Table 7-2   Key Topics for Chapter 7

Key Topic Element	Description	Page Number
List	Active Directory Service basics	694
List	Built-in OS firewalls	698
List	Strong password characteristics	699
Section	Directory Permissions	699
Section	Wireless protocols and encryption types	702
Section	Malware Types	704
List	Antivirus/anti-malware protection techniques	707
Section	Backup/Restore	708
Steps	Enabling/configuring Time Machine	709
List	Characteristics of an acceptable use policy (AUP)	711
Paragraphs	Firewalls/DNS	712
Section	Social Engineering/Attack Types	714
Section	Windows OS Security Settings	719
Section	Shared Files and Folders	721
Paragraph	Single Sign-on (SSO)	723
List	Drive encryption requirements	723
Steps	Encrypting files	724
Section	Password Best Practice	725
Section	Account Management	728

Key Topic Element	Description	Page Number
List	Securing mobile devices	735
List	Physical destruction methods	741
List	Recycling/repurposing best practices	742
Section	Wireless-Specific Security	743
Steps	Updating SOHO router firmware	750
List	Physical security best practices in a SOHO network environment	750

Define Key Terms

Define the following key terms from this chapter and check your answers in the glossary:

mantrap, RFID technology, smart card, biometric security, token, cable lock, USB lock, privacy screen, key fob, entry control roster, Active Directory Service, login script, domain, Group Policy, Organizational Unit (OU), home folder, folder redirection, software token, mobile device management (MDM), MAC address, whitelisting, MAC address filtering, MAC address cloning, certificate, antivirus/anti-malware software, firewall, two-way firewall, authentication, multifactor authentication, directory permissions, file and folder permissions, virtual private network (VPN), data loss/leakage prevention (DLP), access control list, email filtering, principle of least privilege, Wired Equivalent Privacy (WEP), WiFi Protected Access (WPA), Temporal Key Integrity Protocol (TKIP), Advanced Encryption Standard (AES), single-factor authentication, multifactor authentication, Remote Authentication Dial-In User Service (RADIUS), Terminal Access Controller Access Control System (TACACS), ransomware, Trojan, keylogger, rootkit, virus, botnet, worm, spyware, Recovery Console, acceptable use policy (AUP), Domain Name Service (DNS), social engineering, phishing, spear phishing, impersonation, shoulder surfing, tailgating, piggybacking, dumpster diving, distributed denial of service (DDoS), denial of service (DoS), zero day, man-in-the-middle (MiTM), brute force attack, dictionary attack, rainbow table, spoofing, non-compliant systems, zombie, access control, NT File System (NTFS), file attributes, local shares, administrative shares, system files and folders, SSO, Single Sign-on, BitLocker, Trusted Platform Module (TPM), BitLocker To Go, Encrypting File System (EFS), autorun, screen lock, fingerprint lock, face lock, swipe lock, passcode locking, remote wipe, locator application, remote backup application, patching/OS updates, biometric authentication, full device encryption, authenticator application, bring your own device (BYOD), overwrite, drive wipe, service set identifier (SSID), default SSID, Network Address Translation (NAT), port forwarding, port mapping

Answer Review Questions

1. Andre was running late for work and left his security badge in his car. Rather than take the time to return to his car and be late, he waited by the outer door and walked in behind another employee. The other employee was unsure of who Andre was and was irritated with him for following so closely, so she didn't allow Andre to follow her through the inner door to work. He had to return to his car for the badge. What two security concepts were involved in this scenario? (Choose two.)

   a. Security guard

   b. Tailgating

   c. Mantrap

   d. Shoulder surfing

2. Alexa was working her shift in the server room when an alarm went off on a server belonging to a vendor from another company. She was unable to get to the reset button on the server. What likely prevented her from accessing the server whose alarm was going off?

   a. Lack of a key fob

   b. Rack-level security

   c. Lack of authentication

   d. Privacy screen

3. Match the type of malware to its description.

Description	Type of Malware
1. Infects and rewrites files. Replicates automatically with no user intervention.	
2. A method of hiding malware from detection programs.	
3. Tracks web browsing; uses pop-ups to attract a user's attention.	
4. Encrypts target files and then demands payment to unencrypt files.	
5. Infects and rewrites files. Replicates itself if a user executes the file.	

Answer options:

   a. Spyware

   b. Virus

   c. Worm

   d. Rootkit

   e. Ransomware

4. As an IT professional, you should be sure to employ security best practices. Which of the following is not a best practice?

   a. Strong passwords for user accounts

   b. Antivirus/malware protection

   c. Changing the default password on a WAP

   d. WEP encryption

5. Which of the following is generally the most difficult form of security for a malicious hacker to overcome?

   a. Firewall

   b. Encryption

   c. Biometrics

   d. Physical lock and key

6. Biometrics includes the use of which of the following? (Choose all that apply.)

   a. Fingerprint scan

   b. RFID

   c. Retinal scan

   d. Token

7. Which of the following is not a type of token?

   a. Key fob

   b. Cable lock

   c. RFID card

   d. Smart card

8. Which of the following is a program that either blocks or allows data packets to be delivered to network addresses?

   a. DHCP server

   b. Key fob

   c. Firewall

   d. Network server

9. Which of the following is a characteristic of a strong password? (Choose all that apply.)

   a. No more than six characters

   b. Lowercase only

   c. Use of symbols

   d. Use of numbers

10. Mike was called to a workstation that was running slowly. After interviewing the user and asking about recent activity, Mike determined that the user had opened a fake email and reset his password. Which of the following was the user most likely involved in?

    a. Tailgating

    b. Dumpster diving

    c. Phishing

    d. Shoulder surfing

11. Fred determined that encryption was the best solution for keeping his USB flash drive safe while on the road. Which security product would satisfy this need?

    a. Recovery Console

    b. Single Sign-on (SSO)

    c. BitLocker To Go

    d. USB 3 Lockup

12. Ellen, who works at home as an accountant, noticed her wireless network slowing and wondered if neighbors had started using her network for streaming. Which security practices can she employ to ensure that neighbors don't gain access to her network and that her clients' files are protected? (Choose two.)

   a. Change the default IP address on the default gateway.

   b. Change the network name and disable the SSID broadcast.

   c. Use MAC address filtering.

   d. Change the Netflix password.

13. Jen has been tasked with repurposing laptops used by the human resources department. What can she do to make sure important personnel information cannot be compromised?

   a. Overwrite

   b. Low-level format

   c. Standard format

   d. Drive wipe

14. Hiro is able to log into his account at work but can't see the work his team is doing for an advertising client. He didn't have any trouble before he went on vacation. What is a reasonable explanation for this problem?

   a. Share permissions were updated while he was gone.

   b. Hiro was locked out due to inactivity

   c. It took Hiro three tries to log into his computer, and his permissions were suspended after the second attempt.

   d. The boss thought Hiro was leaving the company, so his account was disabled.

15. Victoria was updating a computer from another office and realized she needed to change the UEFI settings. Unfortunately, the UEFI BIOS was password protected, and the motherboard had no reset buttons or jumpers, as she was used to seeing. What should she do?

   a. Scrap the motherboard because control of the BIOS/UEFI is essential.

   b. Unplug the computer overnight.

   c. Remove the CMOS battery, go to lunch, and replace the batter after eating.

   d. Change the CPU jumpers.

This chapter covers the five A+ 220-1002 exam objectives related to troubleshooting Microsoft Windows OS, PC security, malware removal, mobile OS and application operational and security issues, and related topics. These objectives may comprise 26% of the exam questions:

- **Core 2 (220-1002): Objective 3.1:** Given a scenario, troubleshoot Microsoft Windows OS problems.

- **Core 2 (220-1002): Objective 3.2:** Given a scenario, troubleshoot and resolve PC security issues.

- **Core 2 (220-1002): Objective 3.3:** Given a scenario, use best practice procedures for malware removal.

- **Core 2 (220-1002): Objective 3.4:** Given a scenario, troubleshoot mobile OS and application issues.

- **Core 2 (220-1002): Objective 3.5:** Given a scenario, troubleshoot mobile OS and application security issues.

## CHAPTER 8

Software Troubleshooting

Given the widespread use of mobile devices, troubleshooting is now more than just solving problems with computers. However, many of the same principles apply whether solving problems with computers, peripherals, or mobile devices: knowledge of products and operating system functions, understanding of the tools needed to diagnose and repair problems, and a determination to avoid data loss except when unavoidable. This chapter helps you apply these principles.

"Do I Know This Already?" Quiz

The "Do I Know This Already?" quiz allows you to assess whether you should read the entire chapter. Table 8-1 lists the major headings in this chapter and the "Do I Know This Already?" quiz questions covering the material in those headings so you can assess your knowledge of these specific areas. The answers to the "Do I Know This Already?" quiz appear in Appendix A, "Answers to the 'Do I Know This Already?' Quizzes and Review Question Sections."

Table 8-1   "Do I Know This Already?" Section-to-Question Mapping

Foundation Topics Section	Questions
Troubleshooting Microsoft Windows OS Problems	1–3
Troubleshooting PC Security Issues	4–6
Best Practice Procedure for Malware Removal	7
Troubleshoot Mobile OS and Application Issues	8–9
Troubleshoot Mobile OS and Application Security Issues	10–11

CAUTION   The goal of self-assessment is to gauge your mastery of the topics in this chapter. If you do not know the answer to a question or are only partially sure of the answer, you should mark that question as wrong for purposes of the self-assessment. Giving yourself credit for an answer you correctly guess skews your self-assessment results and might provide you with a false sense of security.

1. Kate is experiencing inconsistent Web access; sometimes it is down for a few minutes at a time. She does not lose a connection to her local network but can't browse. What symbol appears on her Windows 10 screen to warn her that her access to the Internet is down?

   a. A red ! on the taskbar

   b. A red ? on the taskbar

   c. A yellow ! on the WiFi icon on the taskbar

   d. A red * on the taskbar

2. Which message indicates that the boot/BCD file on the active partition may be missing?

   a. The Windows Boot Configuration Data file is missing required information

   b. Fixboot

   c. GRUB loader error

   d. failsafeX

3. Which of the following options appears when a macOS machine is booted with **Cmd+R**? (Choose all that apply.)

   a. Disk Utility

   b. Get Help Online

   c. Reinstall macOS

   d. Restore from Time Machine Backup

4. What kind of malware can cause home page settings to change?

   a. Pop-ups

   b. Browser redirection

   c. WannaCry

   d. Rapidly opening windows

5. Which current OS version(s) includes built-in security protections?

   a. macOS

   b. Linux

   c. Neither A nor B

   d. Both A and B

6. What is the main purpose of a bootable antivirus program?

   a. It allows continuous scanning for malware.

   b. It can run scans without an OS.

   c. It checks the BIOS/UEFI for viruses.

   d. It scans the OS as it loads.

7. What is the second step in the best practice procedure for removing malware?

   a. Identify symptoms.

   b. Disable System Restore.

   c. Quarantine infected systems.

   d. Update anti-malware software.

8. Ivan is trying to stream music on his cell phone, and his usual app wouldn't work. What should his *first* step be?

   a. Keep his finger on the app icon until it wiggles and then delete it.

   b. Restart the phone.

   c. Shut down the phone.

   d. Update the app.

9. Lorna likes to stream TV shows on her phone while on the bus. One day her service slows down, and she can't watch her shows. Why would Lorna's phone slow down so much?

   a. Lorna changed her bus route and now goes a different way to work.

   b. Lorna watched so much TV this month that her provider throttled her data rate.

   c. Lorna forgot to pay her bill.

   d. Lorna's phone provider merged with a cable company, and they decided to change her service.

10. Eric is stuck in a system lockout. What likely caused this to happen to him?

   a. His phone was infected with malware.

   b. Eric opened an infected attachment in an email.

   c. Eric didn't pay his phone bill.

   d. Eric forgot his password.

Troubleshooting Microsoft Windows OS Problems

220-1002: Objective 3.1: Given a scenario, troubleshoot Microsoft Windows OS problems.

Troubleshooting is an essential skill for a PC technician. The ability to recognize and remediate OS issues starts with concepts covered in this section.

Slow System Performance

Slow system performance can be caused by many issues in Windows. Table 8-2 list some possible causes and solutions.

Table 8-2   Slow System Performance Causes/Solutions

Windows System Performance Troubleshooting	
Problem	**Solution**
System not configured for maximum performance	To solve this problem, set the Power setting to High Performance using the Power options icon in the notification area or the Power options in Control Panel. This option is not available on tablets.
Drive containing paging file and temporary files is nearly full or badly fragmented	Use Disk Cleanup in the drive properties to remove unwanted files, check the drive for errors, and defragment the drive. If you have more available space on a different drive, use the Advanced tab in the system properties to change the location of the paging file and temp files.
System is overheating and CPU is running at reduced speed	Remove dust and dirt on the CPU and system fans. Check for adequate airflow through the system. Change back to Balanced power setting.
Running low on memory	Add RAM. This fixes many performance problems. Exceed the minimums recommended for the version of Windows in use for better performance.
Sudden performance drop	Check for viruses and malware; this is especially important if performance has suddenly plunged.
Registry errors messages	The program CCleaner is widely used for this task.
General and undiagnosed performance issues	Use the performance troubleshooters in your version of Windows.

Linux: Three Steps to Better Performance	
Performance Optimization	**Solution**
Remove unneeded startup programs	With recent versions of Ubuntu, use the Startup Application manager. With Fedora or other distributions, install GNOME-TWEAK and use its Startup Application manager.
Install more RAM	Exceed the minimums recommended for the version of Linux in use for better performance.
Disable unneeded system services	System services are typically located in the /etc/init.d directory (folder). Depending on your distribution, you might have a control center that can be used to disable system services, or you might need to use the Nautilus file manager, right-click a service, go to **Properties > Permissions**, and deselect **Execute: Allow Executing File as Program**. To determine what a particular service does, look it up in the man pages for your distribution.

macOS: Steps to Better Performance	
Performance Optimization	**Solution**
Try the additional strategies at right to improve system responsiveness.	If your MacBook Pro uses a hard disk, replace it with an SSD.
	Add more RAM.
	Use Disk Utility to remove apps you no longer need.
	Use System Preferences to disable unneeded startup apps.
	Be sure to install macOS updates as they become available.
	Remove unwanted Dashboard programs (widgets).

Limited Connectivity/Local Connectivity

The yellow ! symbol next to the network icon in the Windows 7 taskbar indicates that the network has limited connectivity (that is, the Internet cannot be reached), also called *local connectivity*. In Windows 10 a red X icon appears on the taskbar next to the network icon. (To see what these icons look like, refer to Figures 5-36 and 5-37 in Chapter 5, "Hardware and Network Troubleshooting.")

Before doing anything else, check connectivity on other devices on the network. If all devices can't connect, take these measures:

- To diagnose this problem with Windows 7, open the Network and Sharing Center and click the red X in the Internet connection dialog. Windows launches an Internet troubleshooter. Follow the troubleshooter's recommendations.

- With Windows 8/8.1, use Search to locate and start the Internet troubleshooter. Follow the troubleshooter's recommendations.

- In Windows 10, click the network icon in the taskbar to open the Network Status window. If you are not connected, a Troubleshoot button will appear.

- For connection problems with any OS, turn off the broadband modem or access device, wait about a minute, and then turn it back on. Then turn off the router, wait about a minute, and turn it on again. If the problem was with the broadband modem/access device, this should solve the problem. If this does not solve the problem, contact the ISP as the problem might be on its network.

If only one device is affected, disconnect from a wireless network and reconnect to it. For a wired network, restart the computer.

Failure to Boot

Boot failures (or failure to boot) can be caused by incorrect boot configuration in the BIOS, corrupt or missing boot files, and missing driver files. The solutions for these problems vary depending on the operating system version in use.

Windows Boot Errors

Windows uses the bootmgr and BCD files during the startup process. If these files are corrupted or missing, you see corresponding error messages:

- **BOOTMGR is missing:** This message appears if the bootmgr file is missing or corrupt. This black screen will probably also say **Press Ctrl+Alt+Del to Restart**; however, doing so probably will not fix the issue.

- **The Windows Boot Configuration Data file is missing required information:** This message means that either the Windows Boot Manager (Bootmgr) entry is not present in the *Boot Configuration Data (BCD)* store or that the Boot\BCD file on the active partition is damaged or missing. Additional information you might see on the screen includes **File: \Boot\ BCD**, and **Status: 0xc0000034**.

There are two ways to repair a missing bootmgr file:

- Boot to the System Recovery options and select the **Startup Repair** option. This should automatically repair the system and require you to reboot. To access the options in Windows 7, restart the computer and hold the F8 key before the Windows logo appears. In Win 8/ and 10, locate the Advanced Startup Settings menu.

- Boot to the System Recovery options and select the **Command Prompt** option. Type the **bootrec /fixboot** command, as shown in Figure 8-1.

NOTE   A hard drive's lifespan is not infinite. In some cases, it is not possible to repair this file and unfortunately the hard drive will need to be replaced and the operating system reinstalled.

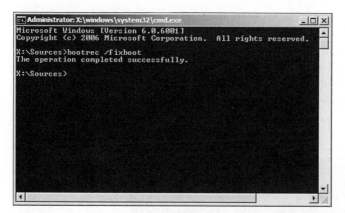

FIGURE 8-1   Repairing BOOTMGR.exe from the Windows Recovery Environment's Command Prompt

For more about these steps, see https://support.microsoft.com/en-us/kb/2622803.

To repair the BCD store, use this short process:

Step 1.   Boot to the System Recovery options and select the **Startup Repair** option. Windows should automatically repair the system and require you to reboot. If not, move on to the second step.

Step 2.   Boot to the System Recovery options and select the **Command Prompt** option. Type **bootrec /rebuildbcd**.

  a. If the Bootrec.exe tool runs successfully, Windows presents you with an installation path for a Windows directory. To add the entry to the BCD store, type **Yes**. A confirmation message appears, indicating that the entry was added successfully. Restart the system.

  b. If the Bootrec.exe tool can't locate any missing Windows installations, you must remove the BCD store and then re-create it. To do this, type the following commands in the order shown here, pressing **Enter** after each command.

```
Bcdedit /export C:\BCD_Backup
ren c:\boot\bcd bcd.old
Bootrec /rebuildbcd
```

NOTE   While Core 2 Objective 3.1 specifically mentions problems with Microsoft Windows OS, a brief discussion of Linux and macOS issues is included here since a technician may be called to an environment that uses more than one OS.

Linux Boot Errors

If Linux won't start normally, hold down the **Shift** key while starting the system. If the GRUB or GRUB2 boot loader appears, select the entry marked **Rescue** or **Recovery** to load a minimal version of Linux. With some distributions, such as Ubuntu, you might need to select **Advanced** (see Figure 8-2) before you can select a recovery option.

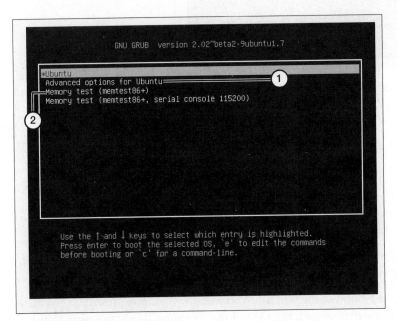

1. Select to see recovery options
2. Select to test RAM

FIGURE 8-2   GRUB2 Bootloader for Ubuntu Offers Memory Diagnostics as Well as Access to Advanced Boot Options

Most distros hide startup commands by default, but when Linux is run in Recovery mode, the screen is full of commands. From the Recovery menu (see Figure 8-3), you might be offered a variety of options to fix your system; the options you see depends on the distribution. If a Linux distribution doesn't have a menu offering these options, you can run most of the options from the command prompt; you might need to use **su** or **sudo** to run them.

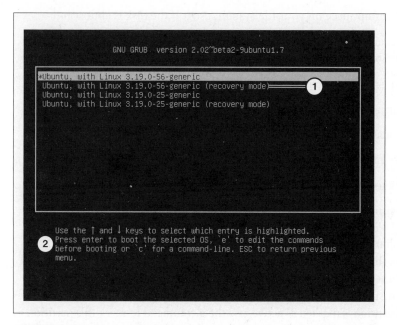

1. **Select to start Linux in recovery mode**
2. **Other options**

FIGURE 8-3   Selecting a Recovery Mode

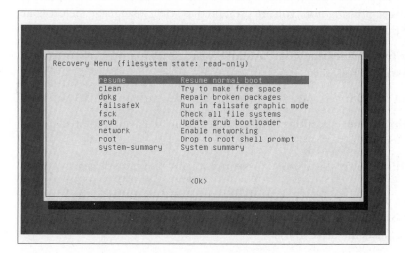

FIGURE 8-4   Recovery Options in Ubuntu

Ubuntu offers the following Recovery Menu options, as shown in Figure 8-4:

- **resume:** Continues the normal boot process.

- **clean:** Frees up space on your file system; use it if the disk is almost full.

- **dpkg:** Repairs broken software; use this if software installation failed and be sure to enable networking first with **network**.

- **failsafex:** Enables system to boot to GUI.

- **fsck:** Repairs file system errors.

- **grub:** Updates grub boot loader.

- **network:** Enables networking, which is turned off in Recovery mode.

- **root:** Opens system in read/write root shell mode (for experts only).

- **system-summary:** Displays information about the system.

Some BIOS will not boot to Linux because Linux partitions don't use the MS-DOS boot flag. To fix the problem, start the system from a Live CD or Live USB drive and open a terminal session. Use the command **sudo fdisk /dev/sda** and view partition table settings by running the **p** (print) command. A bootable partition is marked as **a** (active). If no partition is marked as active, use the **a** command to mark this partition as active, save changes with **w** (write), and restart the system after removing the Live CD.

macOS Boot Errors

To start macOS in special startup modes, press **Cmd+R** as soon as the startup sound plays and continue pressing until you are prompted to select a language. Select your language, and the macOS Utilities menu appears. It includes the following options:

- **Restore from Time Machine Backup:** Select this option if a backup exists and you wish to restore it.

- **Reinstall macOS:** Select this option to install a new version of macOS.

- **Get Help Online:** Select this option to open online help and remote diagnostics options.

- **Disk Utility:** Select this option to repair problems with hard drives.

To boot from a different partition than usual, such as a Boot Camp partition, start up your macOS system and hold down the **Alt** or **Option** key until a list of bootable drives appears. Select the drive to use.

NOTE   Boot Camp is macOS's multiboot support for Windows.

Other Symptoms and Common Solutions.

Other common symptoms and solutions related to A+ Core 2 Objective 3.1 are included in Table 8-3. It is important to understand the problems that can occur and the solutions that can mitigate them.

Table 8-3   Common Symptoms, Causes, and Solutions for a Malfunctioning OS

Symptom	Common Cause(s)	Common Solution(s)
Application crashes	There are several different causes for this, but most common ones are lack of RAM and overheated CPU.	Kill tasks Add RAM Clean airflow vents Reboot Apply application updates Roll back updates if problems started after last update
Blue and black screens, BSOD, and pin wheel	Software conflicts, corrupt OS files. (See Chapter 5 for more details).	Safe boot Check hardware Re-image/reload OS
Printing issues	Several possibilities include drivers, print spoolers, and network connectivity. See the section "Printer Troubleshooting" in Chapter 5 for detailed steps.	Check connections Clear print queue Reboot printer Reprint
Services fail to start	Search for "Local Services" and try right-clicking to restart.	Restart services
Slow bootup	Slow loading of services or drivers. Drivers may be corrupt.	Check boot order Scan for malware Disable/delay startup applications
Slow profile load	Corrupt profile (drives, etc.).	Edit the Registry—cautiously! Microsoft and others have support steps for this, but they involve Registry edits. Be sure you know what you are doing before editing the Registry!

Troubleshooting PC Security Issues

220-1002: Objective 3.2: Given a scenario, troubleshoot and resolve PC security issues.

The following sections help you deal with PC security issues, including common symptoms of malware infections and software tools to help battle malware.

Common Symptoms of Malware Infections

There are many common symptoms of *malware* infections. Table 8-4 describes what to look for. Be sure to know these symptoms for the 220-1002 exam.

Table 8-4   Common Symptoms of Malware Infection

Symptom	Possible Causes
Pop-ups	If the browser has pop-up blocking enabled but pop-ups are showing up anyway, the system might be infected with malware. If many pop-ups are displayed onscreen rapidly and they keep showing up even as they are closed, the system is almost certainly infected and needs to be scanned immediately.
Browser redirection	Browser redirection, also known as *browser hijacking*, takes place when the home page setting for your browser is changed without your permission. Some "free" apps offer to change your browser home page during installation, but you can opt in or opt out of the change. If an app changes your browser home page without notifying you, it could be malware. Scan the system.
Security alerts	Security alerts from Windows Defender or from your OS might indicate malware infection or other problems. Sometimes alerts that pop up without any notification in Defender or the Action Center are attempts to infect your system by tricking you into clicking a phishing link in the pop-up. Scan the system.
Slow performance	Slow performance that isn't caused by running a lot of apps or using very resource-intensive software could be caused by a malware infection. Use Task Manager or the equivalent to see which programs are running. Unfamiliar programs could be malware. Scan the system.
Internet connectivity issues	Internet connectivity problems that do not affect all computers and devices on the network could be caused by malware. Run troubleshooters to repair the problem. If it continues to occur, scan the system.
PC/OS Lockups	Lockups can be caused by many problems. If you have already checked hardware and OS issues but haven't found a cause, scan the system. See the section "Proprietary Crash Screens (BSOD/Pin Wheel)" in Chapter 5 for more information.

Symptom	Possible Causes
Application crashes	Application crashes could be caused by malware, but first repair the app or reinstall it. If it continues to crash, update it. If it continues to crash, scan the system.
OS updates failures	If you are unable to install updates for the OS, make sure the computer has enough free disk space and that the antivirus or anti-malware software is not blocking updates.
Rogue antivirus	Rogue antivirus programs look like legitimate antivirus programs but actually are designed to infect your system or phish users for personal information. Uninstall any such program and scan the computer.
Spam	Unsolicited email can carry malware through attachments or may contain links to purported e-commerce or e-banking websites that are actually phishing sites.
Renamed system files	Malware infections might rename system files (such as msconfig, regedit, and taskmgr) that can help block malware.
Files disappearing	Some malware infections change file attributes to hidden and might also create file shortcuts that are visible.
File permission changes	Some malware infections change file permissions to make the malware harder to remove or to prevent users from running anti-malware apps.
Hijacked email and responses from users regarding email	Hijacked email is almost certainly caused by a malware infection. Receivers of hijacked email might reply to complain about inappropriate content, links, or messages that seem out of character.
Automated replies from unknown sent email	Hijacked email can also trigger automated replies indicating that messages were being rejected. If a user who has previously been able to send messages to a recipient notices that the messages are being rejected ("bouncing"), there could be a malware infection at either end of the connection.
Access denied	If a user sees an "access denied" message when trying to start anti-malware tools, it indicates that file permissions changes are blocking access to the tools.
Invalid certificate (trusted root CA)	Operating systems and browsers use digital certificates to determine the sources of apps and drivers. Certificates that have been obtained fraudulently from a certificate authority can be used to launch malware attacks.
Logs	Windows stores system events, warnings, and errors in various event logs. These events can be viewed from Event Viewer. Event Viewer can be run from the Tools tab in msconfig or from Administrative Tools in the System folder of Control Panel. For more information, see the section "Log Entries and Error Messages" in Chapter 5.

Tools for Preventing/Mitigating Malware

Windows, macOS, and Linux all include tools that can be used to prevent malware attacks or clean up damage, and third-party tools are available to help plug any holes in built-in protection. Table 8-5 discusses these tools and provides Web addresses for more information.

Table 8-5   OS and Third-Party Tools to Prevent and Fight Malware Infections

Tool	How Used and Where to Find More Information
Antivirus software	Antivirus software provides real-time protection against threats from local files, websites, and email. It should also be configured to perform scans at least weekly. Most recent versions of Windows and macOS include security protections, but Linux does not. For a list of third-party providers for Windows, many of whom also support macOS and Linux, see http://windows.microsoft.com/en-US/windows/antivirus-partners.
Anti-malware software	Anti-malware software is normally used to scan for infections that might have been missed by antivirus software. These programs, from vendors such as Malwarebytes (www.malwarebytes.org), typically do not conflict with antivirus software. Anti-malware software called Gatekeeper is built into macOS, and Windows 10 includes anti-malware and antivirus software called Windows Defender.
WinRE/Recovery Console	Windows Recovery Environment (WinRE) can be used when a Windows OS fails to start. The CompTIA A+ objectives refer to the Recovery Console, which is a recovery tool used in XP, even though XP is not part of the exam Objectives. WinRE can be used to try commands in a safe environment to see if they resolve an issue. For more information, see https://support.microsoft.com/en-us/help/4026030/how-to-use-windows-recovery-environment-winre-to-troubleshoot-common-s.
Bootable antivirus programs	Bootable USB flash drives or optical discs (based on WinPE, Live CD, or Live USB) can be used to launch antivirus and anti-malware scans without starting the normal OS. For a list of free bootable antivirus programs, see https://www.lifewire.com/free-bootable-antivirus-tools-2625785.
Terminal	Terminal (macOS and Linux) can be used to change file attributes, delete files, and run backup and repair utilities.
Preinstallation environments	WinPE is the basis for many USB- or disc-based repair tools. It can also be used by itself to run programs on a Windows system from the command line.
Event Viewer	Use the Event Viewer to see what events have taken place in the system, including app crashes, security changes, and more.

Tool	How Used and Where to Find More Information
Refresh/Reset	Windows 8/8.1 includes Refresh (reinstalls Windows and Windows Store apps, removes other apps, leaves user data in place) and Reset (returns system to its as-shipped condition and deletes user data).
	In Windows 8, Reset Your PC removes all files and performs a factory reset.
	Windows 10 offers Refresh and Reset. Reset enables you to keep personal files, if desired.
MSCONFIG/Safe boot	Msconfig can be used to turn off selected startup programs and nonessential system services. The Safe Boot option turns off all startup programs and nonessential system services.

Best Practice Procedure for Malware Removal

220-1002: Objective 3.3: Given a scenario, use best practice procedures for malware removal.

Malware removal will be a common task for a support technician for the foreseeable future. The following steps are best practices that should be followed each time the task is undertaken.

Follow this seven-step procedure to remove malware—and know it well for the A+ exam:

Step 1. **Identify malware symptoms.** Use Table 8-4 to identify symptoms.

Step 2. **Quarantine infected systems.** Disconnect the system from wired and wireless networks and suspect any media that has touched the system as being possibly infected.

Step 3. **Disable System Restore (in Windows).** Disable System Restore at this point so that it doesn't run and create a restore point with infected files before the system is cleaned. Some malware programs have used System Restore to reinfect systems. System Restore is designed to help recover from user error or system crashes, not spread malware.

Step 4. **Remediate the infected systems.** Use a different system to change passwords for network access, e-commerce, and social media. Back up data in case the system must be reformatted. Check backup for malware before reinstalling it. This process involves the following substeps:

   a. Updating anti-malware software: To update anti-malware on a quarantined system, download offline update files on a different system, copy them to a USB flash drive, and install the updates on the quarantined system.

b. Scanning and removal (Safe mode, preinstallation environment): Run scans and remove threats in Safe mode or WinRE. If a quarantined system's antivirus/anti-malware cannot be updated, the apps might be themselves infected or blocked by malware. Download the files needed to create a CD or USB bootable anti-malware disc or USB drive on a different system.

Step 5. **Schedule scans and run updates.** Update anti-malware and antivirus software and run full scans with both. If the infection source is known by name, first use a specific removal tool (if available) and follow it up with full scans. Scan with more than one tool to ensure that the infection is removed.

Step 6. **When the system is clean, enable System Restore without copying infected files.** Manually create a restore point in Windows.

Step 7. **Educate the end user.** Discuss principles of avoiding malware infections with end users. If the infection vector (that is, the way the virus accessed the computer, such as by email, flash drives, or a downloaded app) is known, discuss it specifically. Also provide general guidance for safe computing (for example, avoiding the use of "orphan" USB flash drives, not opening attachments from unknown sources, using real-time antivirus software, scanning systems weekly).

Troubleshoot Mobile OS and Application Issues

220-1002: Objective 3.4: Given a scenario, troubleshoot mobile OS and application issues.

This section describes some of the common mobile OS and application issues you might encounter, including system lockouts and app log errors. The sections that following discuss such issues and possible solutions.

NOTE The following mobile device issues are discussed in Chapter 5:

Mobile Device Issue	Section in Chapter 5 to Review	Page #
System lockup	"System Lockups"	417
Dim display	"Dim Image"	456
Intermittent wireless	"Intermittent Wireless"	464
No wireless connectivity	"No Wireless Connectivity"	467
No Bluetooth connectivity	"No Bluetooth Connectivity"	467

Mobile Device Issue	Section in Chapter 5 to Review	Page #
Cannot broadcast to an external monitor	"Cannot Display to External Monitor"	468
Touchscreen non-responsive	"Touchscreen Non-Responsive"	468
Apps not loading	"Apps Not Loading"	468
Inaccurate touchscreen response	"Common Symptoms"	468
Slow performance	"Slow Performance"	469
Unable to decrypt email	"Unable to Decrypt Email"	469
Extremely short battery life	"Extremely Short Battery Life"	469
Overheating	"Overheating"	470
Frozen system	"Frozen System"	470
No sound from speakers	"No Sound from Speakers"	470

System Lockout

A *system lockout* takes place when you have forgotten your password, PIN code, or pattern code (a shape or pattern drawn on the screen) and make so many attempts to log in that login attempts are blocked.

On an Android phone, make sure you know your Google (Android) login information, which you are prompted to provide if you are locked out. If you can provide this when prompted, you are logged back into your device. Be sure to change the password, PIN code, or pattern code. If you don't have this information, you might need to perform a hard reset on the phone, which wipes out all apps and data.

On an iPhone, if you are locked out, you can use iTunes to restore your device if you have previously used iTunes to back up the device.

App Log Errors

A user may be locked out from an app when the rest of the phone is performing normally. The problem could stem from any of several possibilities, including:

- A recent OS update conflicts with the app.
- The app has an update that needs to be installed.
- App authentication needs to be updated.

Apps on mobile devices usually store logs with information about these errors, but they are not accessible from the phones themselves. Access to the logs requires the use of software developer tools.

In most cases, however, it is likely that a simple update or reset will solve the problem. If you try to update the app and problems persist, you can take two basic steps to address the issue:

Step 1. Completely shut down (not just restart) the phone or device. If this solves the problem, you can stop here.

Step 2. If Step 1 did not solve the problem, follow these four steps:

   a. Delete the app.

   b. Shut down the phone again.

   c. Restart the phone.

   d. Download a fresh version of the app.

Updating an iOS App

Before you uninstall a misbehaving iOS app, try updating it:

Step 1. Open the **App Store** icon and tap the **Update** button for each app you want to update.

Step 2. Tap the icon of the app you want to update and then scroll down and tap **What's New** to see what has been changed.

Repairing an Android App

Before you uninstall an Android app, try these options first:

- If an update is available, update the app. To change update options, open **Google Play > Menu > Settings > Auto-Update Settings**.

- If the app ran well until the latest update, you might be able to roll back the updates. Go to Apps and select the app to be reverted. Access the menu on the upper-right. Choose the **Uninstall Updates** button (when available) to revert to an earlier version.

- For any app, you can tap the **Clear Cache** button to discard information that is retained for reuse. This might improve the app's performance and stability.

- Tap the **Clear Data** button to remove all app settings; the app will then run as if you have just installed it. However, keep in mind that all your app data—game progress, social media passwords, and so on—is lost when you use this option.

Uninstall/Reinstall Apps

To solve problems with corrupt or outdated apps, you can uninstall them and then reinstall them. For Android:

Step 1. Go to **Settings > Device > Applications > Application Manager**.

Step 2. Select an app and tap **Uninstall**.

Step 3. To reinstall the app, go to Google Play and install it again.

For iOS:

Step 1. On the home screen, press and hold any app's icon until the apps all wiggle.

Step 2. Tap the **X** on an app to remove that app. Tap **Delete** to confirm. (On iOS, you can also delete apps by going to **Settings > General > Storage & iCloud Usage > Manage Storage**, selecting an app, and then tapping **Delete**.)

Step 3. To reinstall the app, go to the Apple App Store and install it again.

For Windows 10 Mobile:

Step 1. Press and hold the app's icon and tap **Uninstall**.

Step 2. To reinstall the app, go to the Microsoft Store and install it again.

Soft Reset

A *soft reset*, also known as a *soft restart*, restarts an Android device to help fix problems with the phone or its apps without deleting user data. Depending upon the device, you can use one or more of the following methods:

- Press and hold the power button until you are prompted to turn off the device and then tap **Power Off**. To turn the device back on, press and hold the power button until the device restarts.

- Remove the battery. After a minute or two, reinstall the battery and restart the device.

- Press and hold the power button and volume down button simultaneously until the device restarts.

On an iOS device, some people use the term *hard reset* to refer to a reset that clears the iOS firmware and can help solve problems with unresponsive hardware, botched updates, and other issues but does not erase any data or apps. Apple prefers to use the term *restart* or *forced restart* instead. Here's how to do a restart that simply turns off and re-starts the device:

Step 1.   Press and hold **Sleep/Wake** (on the right side of the iPhone) until the Slide to Power Off slider appears.

Step 2.   Drag the slider to the off position and then wait a few seconds.

Step 3.   Press and hold **Sleep/Wake** until the device displays the Apple logo.

If this doesn't work, try a forced restart that clears the iOS but does not erase data:

- **iPhone 7 or iPhone 7 Plus:** Hold down both the Side and Volume Down buttons for about 10 seconds until the Apple logo is displayed.

- **iPhone 8 or later:** Press and quickly release the Volume Up button and then press and quickly release the Volume Down button. Then press and hold the Side button until you see the Apple logo.

See https://support.apple.com/en-us/HT201559 for more information.

Hard Reset / Erase

The term **hard reset** refers to deleting all the information from a mobile device to reset it to factory condition (or reset to factory default). Apple prefers to use the term *erase*.

To erase an iOS device so it can be given away or sold, go to **Settings > General > Reset > Erase All Content and Settings**. It will ask for a passcode or Apple ID password before erasing. If a passcode is unavailable, check the Apple support page and search for **erase**.

Before doing a hard reset on an Android device:

Step 1.   Back up the device, if possible.

Step 2.   Try a soft reset.

Step 3.   If you must perform a hard reset, make sure the device is charged.

Step 4.   Unplug the device from power.

Step 5.   Turn it off.

Step 6.   Use the appropriate keystroke(s) for your smartphone or tablet and version of Android.

As an example of step 6, with recent Samsung Galaxy smartphones:

Step 1.   Press and hold Volume Up, Home, and Power at the same time.

Step 2.   Release the Power button only when the Galaxy logo is displayed or the phone vibrates.

Step 3.   From the Android system recovery screen, use the volume keys to scroll to **Wipe Data/Factory Reset** and choose this option by pressing the Power button.

Step 4.   When the factory reset is complete, select **Reboot System Now** to restart a phone empty of user data with factory settings only.

Adjust Configurations/Settings

The Settings menus in iOS and Android provide options for removing unwanted apps, checking for updates, and other troubleshooting features. Table 8-6 lists typical settings for Android and the various options available.

Table 8-6   Android Mobile Configuration Settings

Settings Menu	Options
Connections	Configure WiFi, Bluetooth, Airplane mode, mobile hotspot and tethering, NFC, tap and pay, printing, MirrorLink (connect to car), VPN, set default messaging app, network operators
	Check data usage
Device > Sounds and Notifications	Configure sounds, vibration, volume, ringtones, sound quality, do not disturb
Device > Display	Change brightness, font, screen timeout, screen mode, others
Device > Motions and Gestures	Change direct call, mute, others
Device > Applications	Change settings for each application, select default apps, uninstall, force stop, or disable apps
Personal	Configure wallpaper, themes, lock screen, security, privacy and safety, accessibility, accounts, backup and reset, and easy mode
System	Access language and input, battery and power savings modes, storage usage, date and time, help, developer options, and information about the device (software updates)

Table 8-7 lists typical settings for iOS and the options available.

Table 8-7   Apple iOS Mobile Configuration Settings

Setting Menu	Option
General	Set options for Siri, software updates, search, multitasking, lock rotation/mute, auto lock, date and time, keyboard
Main menu	Access Airplane mode, WiFi, Bluetooth, notifications, control center, do not disturb, and settings for individual apps
Display & Brightness	Set brightness, text size, and bold text
Wallpaper	Choose new wallpaper
Sounds	Set volume, event sounds (such as ringtones), lock sounds, and keyboard clicks
Passcode	Create or change the passcode
Battery	View the battery usage and percentage
Privacy	Access location services, contacts, calendars, reminders, photos, Bluetooth sharing, microphone, cameras, HomeKit, motion and fitness, third-party apps (Twitter, Facebook, and so on), diagnostics and usage data sharing, and advertising (to limit ad tracking)

Windows 10 Mobile uses the Settings menu for configuration. It is similar to the Windows 10/Windows 10 Pro versions for desktop and laptop computers.

Troubleshoot Mobile OS and Application Security Issues

220-1002: Objective 3.5: Given a scenario, troubleshoot mobile OS and application security issues.

Mobile devices, due to their limited storage, memory, and reliance on wireless and cellular networking, are subject to many issues that do not affect more robust devices. The following security issues, which may appear on the exam, reflect the challenges of day-to-day mobile use.

Signal Drop/Weak Signal

When you experience signal drop or a weak signal with a WiFi connection, you can scan for other available wireless networks.

When you experience signal drop or a weak signal with a cellular data connection, you can move to a different location, preferably near a window or outside the building, or adjust how you hold the phone. The number of signal bars on the phone can vary greatly in buildings or in mountainous areas.

If cellular connections are good outside the office or home but poor inside, a cellular repeater can help improve performance. If you are considering installing a cell signal repeater, you can determine the exact cellular signal strength in decibels (dB) for a smartphone by dialing into the Field Test mode. For information for iOS and Android phones, see https://www.repeaterstore.com/pages/field-test-mode. Note that a stronger signal is indicated by a lower value.

It's a good idea to check connection speeds with the case on and off the phone to see if the case is affecting performance. Ookla Speedtest is available from Google Play and the App Store to test performance over cellular and WiFi connections.

Power Drain

Power drain is usually caused by the screen brightness being turned up and by having too many apps running at the same time. Dimming screens and closing apps properly will help, but force closing apps that run continuously saves more power. Going into Airplane mode when out of cell range will also keep the phone from searching for a signal.

Slow Data Speeds

Slow data speeds can be caused by a number of factors:

- **No connection to a cellular network:** Check the network indicator at the top of the smartphone or cellular-equipped tablet to determine the network connection type.

- **A weak cellular or WiFi signal:** With WiFi, switch to a stronger SSID signal if possible. With 4G, use a cell tower scanner to locate a stronger cell tower.

- **"Unlimited" data plan speed caps after reaching speed or data limits per billing period:** Some providers that offer "unlimited" data plans drastically reduce speed after a certain level of data is transferred during a billing period. Check data usage and set up a warning to be displayed before you reach this goal or consider switching to a different plan.

Unintended WiFi Connection

Some smartphones connect automatically to available WiFi hotspots; for example, AT&T smartphones can connect automatically to AT&T hotspots. These hotspots are not secure connections and are thus not desirable for secure communications.

To disable this feature, check the WiFi settings on your smartphone. On an AT&T Android phone, for example, go to **Settings > Connections > Wi-Fi > More > Advanced > Disable Auto Connect**.

On an iPhone, go to **Settings > Wi-Fi** and then turn off **Ask to Join Networks**.

To prevent reconnections to a previously used network, select the network and tap **Forget**.

Unintended Bluetooth Pairing

To prevent your device from *pairing* with unknown devices:

- Turn off Bluetooth when you are not using a Bluetooth device.

- When you use a Bluetooth device, make sure your mobile device requests a code from a device attempting to pair with it. You can do this by attempting to pair a Bluetooth-enabled device in your possession with another Bluetooth-enabled device.

Leaked Personal Files/Data

To prevent personal files or data from being discovered in the event that your mobile device is lost:

Step 1. Enable encryption.

Step 2. Enable options to lock and wipe your device in case of loss.

Step 3. Avoid attaching to open WiFi networks.

Step 4. Use a VPN for secure connections if you must use an open WiFi network.

Step 5. Disable WiFi tethering or connection sharing services if not in use.

Data Transmission Over Limit

Exceeding the amount of data included in your cellular plan can be expensive. To avoid unexpected bills, periodically check data usage. On Android, go to **Settings > Connections > Data usage**. Scroll down to see which apps are using the most data. Ensure that **Set Data Limit** is turned on to set a limit and give you a warning to prevent exceeding the limit.

On iOS, go to **Settings > Cellular > Cellular Data Usage**. Use the sliders to disable any apps that should not be using cellular connections. Turn off cellular data if there is no data allowance left in the current period.

If you see unusual amounts of data usage, of the device could be infected with malware.

Unauthorized Account Access

Set up security on your banking or other accounts so that attempts to access it must be authorized by you first. Typically, this is done by specifying an email or messaging number that must be responded to before a new device can be added as an authorized device. Most financial institutions now require two-factor authentication for added security.

Unauthorized Root Access

Android devices are relatively easy to root (that is, to gain root access to) so that users can install different operating systems and continue to use their cellular and data connections. On the other hand, to gain the same sort of access to an iOS device, it must be "jailbroken," which means it may thereafter be blocked from getting updates.

Unauthorized root access can be dangerous, and it is a risk when users download apps that are not from Google Play. These apps do not properly follow the permissions rules and may elevate permissions without the user's knowledge or consent. Running a device in Developer mode (used for software and service development and testing) disables most safeguards. On current versions of Android, it takes several steps to enable Developer mode, so it's difficult to do it accidentally.

Jailbreaking an iOS device or rooting an Android device puts the device and its information at much higher risk than would be the case for a normally functioning device.

Unauthorized Location Tracking

Location tracking features are available in both iOS and Android smartphones.

To prevent iOS from tracking your location by using WiFi connections, go to **Settings > Privacy > Location Services > System Services** and then turn off **Frequent Location**s and clear the history.

To prevent Android from tracking your location by using WiFi connections, go to **Settings > Personal > Privacy and Safety > Location > Locating Method > GPS Only**.

Third-party apps can be used to perform location tracking without the authorization of the device user. These apps, which are legitimate, are marketed to parents and organizations that want to keep track of individuals using their phones. In addition, however, malicious apps can perform unauthorized location tracking; such apps are not legitimate and would have to be purchased from someplace other than Google Play or the App Store.

Unauthorized Camera/Microphone Activation

Third-party apps can use the device's camera or microphone without the authorization of the device user. These apps, which are legitimate, are marketed to parents and organizations that want to keep track of individuals using their phones. In addition, however, malicious apps can perform unauthorized camera/microphone activation; such apps are not legitimate and would have to be purchased from someplace other than Google Play or the App Store.

Some apps can be installed on iOS without physical access to the device: Just the Apple ID and password are needed.

High Resource Utilization

High resource utilization (of cellular data, CPU, memory, or storage) can have many causes. To check cellular data use by app, see the "Data Transmission Over Limit" section, earlier in this chapter.

To reduce CPU, memory, and storage usage:

- Uninstall apps that are not needed.
- Configure apps to receive updates only via WiFi (not cellular data).
- Turn off background updates.

To see real-time resource usage by app for iOS, download the latest version of Xcode from the Apple Developer website and use its Instruments app. Learn more at https://apple.stackexchange.com/questions/71237/how-to-identify-cpu-and-memory-usage-per-process-on-iphone.

To see real-time resource usage by app for Android, use System Monitor from AndroidPit.com. For additional resource monitoring, see https://www.androidpit.com/best-apps-for-monitoring-system-performance-on-your-android-device.

See the next section, "Tools," for methods for detecting and blocking malware and hostile apps and processes.

Tools

Mobile users and techs have a wide variety of software tools available to help boost performance and security. They're covered in the following sections.

Anti-Malware

Both Android and iOS devices can be protected with anti-malware apps—some free and some paid—from the same vendors who protect desktop and laptop systems. Every mobile device should be protected, if for no other reason than that a mobile device can be used as an infection vector for any other device it connects to. Check Google Play and the App Store for anti-malware apps from AVAST, AVG, Kaspersky Labs, Norton, McAfee, Bitdefender, AVIRA, ESET, and many others.

App Scanner

App scanners monitor the permissions and the use of apps. During the installation process for an app, the user sees a long list of permissions the app is being granted. An app scanner can help determine whether an app is safe to use.

Factory Reset/Clean Install

Before retiring a device or to eliminate apps that may put privacy at risk, perform a factory reset on the device. This can be followed by a clean install of desired apps, if desired.

If the device is not encrypted yet, set up a PIN to automatically encrypt the device.

For Android:

Step 1.   Make sure **Back Up My Data** and **Automatic Restore** are enabled.

Step 2.   Go to **Settings > Personal > Backup and reset > Factory Data Reset**.

Step 3.   After reviewing the warnings, click **Reset Device**.

The device is returned to its factory configuration. All data and device updates are removed from the device. To restore the data to the device, using the data backed up to Google in Step 1, follow the steps on the screen.

For iOS:

Step 1.   Install the latest version of iTunes on your host PC or macOS computer.

Step 2.   Start iTunes.

Step 3.   Connect your device to the computer via the charge/sync cable. Trust the device or enter a passcode if prompted.

Step 4.   Select your device.

Step 5.   Back up its contents. Be sure to select **Transfer Purchases** for content purchased from iTunes, back up the Health & Activity data stored on your device in encrypted form, and start your backup.

Step 6. To erase the device, go to **Summary > Restore**.

Step 7. Tap **Restore** again to erase your device and reload it to its original factory condition.

Before you uninstall a misbehaving iOS app, try updating it.

Exam Preparation Tasks

As mentioned in the section "How to Use This Book" in the Introduction, you have a couple of choices for exam preparation: the exercises here, Chapter 10, "Final Preparation," and the exam simulation questions in the Pearson Test Prep Software Online.

Review All the Key Topics

Review the most important topics in the chapter, noted with the Key Topic icon in the outer margin of the page. Table 8-8 lists these key topics and the page number on which each is found.

Table 8-8   Key Topics for Chapter 8

Key Topic Element	Description	Page Number
Table 8-2	Slow System Performance Causes/Solutions	762
Section	Failure to Boot	764
Table 8-3	Common Symptoms, Causes, and Solutions for a Malfunctioning OS	769
Table 8-4	Common Symptoms of Malware Infection	770
Section	Best Practice Procedure for Malware Removal	773
Section	Uninstall/Reinstall Apps	777
Table 8-7	Apple iOS Mobile Configuration Settings	780
Section	Troubleshoot Mobile OS and Application Security Issues	780

Complete the Tables and Lists from Memory

Print a copy of Appendix C, "Memory Tables" (found online), or at least the section for this chapter, and complete the tables and lists from memory. Appendix D, "Answers to Memory Tables," also online, includes completed tables and lists to check your work.

Define Key Terms

Define the following key terms from this chapter and check your answers in the glossary:

Boot Configuration Data (BCD), malware, pop-up, browser redirection, rogue antivirus, spam, invalid certificate, log, antivirus software, anti-malware software, WinRE/Recovery Console, system lockout, soft reset, hard reset, power drain, pairing

Answer Review Questions

1. To answer this three-part question, examine the following figure.

   1a. Which operating system is displaying this message?

   ```
   A problem has been detected and windows has been shut down to prevent damage
   to your computer.

   IRQL_NOT_LESS_OR_EQUAL

   If this is the first time you've seen this Stop error screen,
   restart your computer. If this screen appears again, follow
   these steps:

   Check to make sure any new hardware or software is properly installed.
   If this is a new installation, ask your hardware or software manufacturer
   for any windows updates you might need.

   If problems continue, disable or remove any newly installed hardware
   or software. Disable BIOS memory options such as caching or shadowing.
   If you need to use Safe Mode to remove or disable components, restart
   your computer, press F8 to select Advanced Startup Options, and then
   select Safe Mode.

   Technical information:

   *** STOP: 0x0000000A (0xFFFFF680002FD6D8, 0x0000000000000000, 0x0000000000000000, 0
   xFFFFF80003ABAC8B)

   collecting data for crash dump ...
   Initializing disk for crash dump ...
   Physical memory dump complete.
   Contact your system admin or technical support group for further assistance.
   ```

   a. macOS

   b. Windows 7

   c. Linux

   d. Windows 8.1

   1b. How would go about researching this problem?

   a. Search online for **A problem has been detected**.

   b. Go to Linux.org and search for **IRQ_NOT_LESS_OR_EQUAL**.

   c. Go to Apple.com and search for **IRQ_NOT_LESS_OR_EQUAL**.

   d. Go to Microsoft.com and search for **IRQ_NOT_LESS_OR_EQUAL**.

1c. Which of the following is the most likely solution to the problem?

    a. Install an update to macOS.

    b. Open Device Manager and update a driver.

    c. Use **apt-get** to install a Linux update.

    d. Reinstall the operating system.

2. In the following figure, the screen is displaying a spinning wait cursor, or pin wheel, which indicates that the system is unresponsive. One possible reason for the system being unresponsive could be that there is less than 10% free space left on the system drive. Why would a lack of free space be causing a problem for the system?

1. OS X spinning wait cursor (pin wheel)

    a. The hard drive is running out of space and cannot store any more files.

    b. At least 10% free space is needed for a swap file.

    c. The hard drive does not have enough free space to upgrade to the latest version of the operating system.

    d. The applications need more space in which to run.

3. How would you try to repair a missing or corrupt BOOTMGR file on a Windows system?

    a. Use the System Recovery options.

    b. Use the Advanced Boot options.

    c. Reboot the computer and edit the BIOS startup program.

    d. Download a new BOOTMGR file from the Internet.

4. Which of the following procedures best describes how to access the special startup modes in macOS?

   a. Press **Ctrl+R**.

   b. Press **Cmd+R**.

   c. Press **Ctrl+Alt+Del**.

   d. Press **Alt+F1**.

5. Which of the following could be causes of poor system performance on a Windows computer? (Choose all that apply.)

   a. The drive containing paging and temporary files is nearly full.

   b. Dust and dirt are restricting airflow, and the CPU is overheating.

   c. Too many services are configured to start automatically during startup.

   d. Minimum memory requirements have been met but not exceeded.

6. Put the steps of the malware removal process in order by matching each of the following descriptions to one of the following steps (including the two parts for step 4).

Step	Description
1.	
2.	
3.	
4.	
4a.	
4b.	
5.	
6.	
7.	

   a. Schedule scans and run updates.

   b. Disable System Restore (in Windows).

   c. Update the anti-malware software.

   d. Quarantine the infected systems.

   e. Educate the end user.

   f. Enable System Restore and create a restore point (in Windows).

   g. Identify and research malware symptoms.

   h. Scan and use removal techniques (Safe mode, preinstallation environment).

7. In which of the following locations would you find the log files that Windows creates to describe information, warnings, and errors on your system?

   a. Device Manager

   b. Event Viewer

   c. Finder

   d. Recovery Environment

8. System Restore is used to do which of the following?

   a. Restore the system to its original configuration.

   b. Remove apps that are not from the Microsoft Store and reinstall apps that are from the Microsoft Store.

   c. Use a system image to restore the computer to its original condition.

   d. Create a restore point with which to restore the computer to an earlier point in time.

9. Which Windows utility is used to disable any programs and services that run when the computer boots?

   a. regedit

   b. msconfig

   c. sfc

   d. msinfo32

10. In Windows 8/8.1, which of the following procedures is used to open Safe mode? (Choose two.)

    a. Press **F8** during startup.

    b. Press **Alt+F1** during startup.

    c. Use msconfig and go to the Boot tab.

    d. Reboot, hold down the **Shift** key, and select **Restart**.

11. Match each of the following Advanced Boot options or Startup Settings options with the phrase that describes its function.

Option	When to Use This Option
a. Safe Mode	
b. Boot Logging	
c. Low Resolution	
d. Last Known Good Configuration	
e. Disable Automatic Restart	

Answer options:

1. You want to determine which device or process is stopping startup.
2. You have just installed new hardware or software, and Windows won't start.
3. You have just upgraded a device driver, and Windows won't start.
4. You frequently encounter STOP errors.
5. You have just installed a new video card, and Windows won't start.

12. Which of the following is the best way to stop mobile devices from pairing with unknown Bluetooth devices?

   a. Use encryption on your mobile devices.
   b. Require a device to have the correct code before pairing.
   c. Use a VPN whenever possible.
   d. Disable WiFi tethering.

13. Which of the following problems might occur when you install third-party apps on a mobile device? (Choose all that apply.)

   a. Unexpectedly high resource utilization
   b. Unauthorized root access
   c. Unauthorized location tracking
   d. Unauthorized camera or microphone activation

14. You want to prevent an Android smartphone from tracking the user by using WiFi connections. Which of the following is the correct command sequence to use in this case?

   a. **Settings > Privacy > Location Services > System Services**
   b. **Settings > Network > Wi-Fi > Disabled**
   c. **Settings > Personal > Privacy and Safety > Location > Locating Method > GPS Only**
   d. **Settings > Network > Airplane Mode**

This chapter covers the nine A+ 220-1002 exam objectives related to operational procedures, with a focus on safety, environmental controls, change management, documentation, privacy, and other concepts. Even the best-planned networks experience problems, and an important IT skill is knowing how to recognize trouble and then manage it for minimum network impact. These objectives may comprise 23% of the exam questions:

- **Core 2 (220-1002): Objective 4.1:** Compare and contrast best practices associated with types of documentation.

- **Core 2 (220-1002): Objective 4.2:** Given a scenario, implement basic change management best practices.

- **Core 2 (220-1002): Objective 4.3:** Given a scenario, implement basic disaster prevention and recovery methods.

- **Core 2 (220-1002): Objective 4.4:** Explain common safety procedures.

- **Core 2 (220-1002): Objective 4.5:** Explain environmental impacts and appropriate controls.

- **Core 2 (220-1002): Objective 4.6:** Explain the processes for addressing prohibited content/activity, and privacy, licensing, and policy concepts.

- **Core 2 (220-1002): Objective 4.7:** Given a scenario, use proper communication techniques and professionalism.

- **Core 2 (220-1002): Objective 4.8:** Identify the basics of scripting.

- **Core 2 (220-1002): Objective 4.9:** Given a scenario, use remote access technologies.

## CHAPTER 9

Operational Procedures

The focus of this book until now has been the hardware and software technical skills an A+ certified technician can be expected to have in an IT position. But it is important to always keep in mind that a successful employee in the technical field must also be adept at communication and organizational skills. This chapter focuses on these "soft skills" that often make the difference between an adequate technician and a valuable employee. Scripting and use of remote technologies are covered as well.

"Do I Know This Already?" Quiz

The "Do I Know This Already?" quiz allows you to assess whether you should read the entire chapter. Table 9-1 lists the major headings in this chapter and the "Do I Know This Already?" quiz questions covering the material in those headings so you can assess your knowledge of these specific areas. The answers to the "Do I Know This Already?" quiz appear in Appendix A, "Answers to the 'Do I Know This Already?' Quizzes and Review Question Sections."

Table 9-1 "Do I Know This Already?" Section-to-Question Mapping

Foundation Topics Section	Questions
Best Practices and Documentation	1
Change Management	2
Disaster Prevention and Recovery	3
Explain Common Safety Procedures	4–7
Environmental Impacts and Appropriate Controls	8–10
Addressing Prohibited Content or Activity	11
Communication Techniques and Professionalism	12
Scripting Basics	13–14
Remote Access Technologies	15

CAUTION   The goal of self-assessment is to gauge your mastery of the topics in this chapter. If you do not know the answer to a question or are only partially sure of the answer, you should mark that question as wrong for purposes of the self-assessment. Giving yourself credit for an answer you correctly guess skews your self-assessment results and might provide you with a false sense of security.

1. Jennifer has asked for a document showing the LANs and IP addresses in the building. What kind of document did she request?

   a. IP address directory

   b. Logical topology

   c. Netspace directory

   d. Physical topology

2. Enrique has been asked to attend a meeting to report on how proposed network changes will affect his workgroup. Which term best describes the meeting he will attend?

   a. Scope impact meeting

   b. CIO roundtable

   c. Change management meeting

   d. Disaster prevention meeting

3. A power outage in Centerville took down the network operations center, but all equipment was safe as it could run while it powered down. What device was installed to make this possible?

   a. Circuit breaker

   b. Cloud backup

   c. Surge suppressor

   d. UPS

4. According to building codes, what does every grounded outlet used for computers connect to?

   a. The neutral circuit in the wiring closet

   b. A copper pipe buried underground

   c. The hot wire circuit cutoff

   d. A UPS in the server room

5. Gina was upgrading graphics cards on 10 PCs in a design office. After she removed the old cards, she had to use scissors before installing the new ones. Why would she need scissors in her tech bag?

    a. To trim the plastic tabs off the power connectors

    b. To cut "installed on" tags noting the date to mail back to the manufacturer

    c. To cut the tape on the bubble wrap around the new cards

    d. To open antistatic bags

6. What is the purpose of an ESD strap?

    a. To equalize potential

    b. To seal antistatic bags

    c. To ground PC power supplies while unplugged

    d. To eliminate electromagnetic interference on the fiber lines

7. When a workstation installation creates a tripping hazard, which best practice is not being practiced?

    a. Cable management

    b. Disaster prevention

    c. Acceptable use policy

    d. Self-grounding

8. Eric comes across a box containing a chemical in use in the building that has spilled in the main aisle of the warehouse. What should he do before sweeping it up?

    a. Call 911

    b. Rope off the area and evacuate the building

    c. Consult the chemical hot sheet

    d. Consult the SDS

9. Jacob is upset because he can only use a particular app on three of his four computers. His fourth computer is capable of running it, but he doesn't want to pay more. Which of the following are keeping him from just adding the app to his machine without paying more? (Choose two.)

   a. DRM

   b. GDPR

   c. EULA

   d. PHI

10. Which is not a type of regulated data?

   a. PCI

   b. GDPR

   c. DRM

   d. PII

11. What is the name for a set of procedures that an investigator follows when examining a technology incident?

   a. Incident response

   b. AUP

   c. DRM

   d. EULA

12. Which of the following are examples of appropriately dealing with a customer's confidential and private materials? (Choose two.)

   a. Mary asks a client to move her handbag away from the work area.

   b. Bob turns off his cell phone when talking to customers.

   c. Alexandria is assisting in a doctor's office and asks for insurance files to be removed from the workstation.

   d. Ali refuses an offer to eat lunch in the discounted employee cafeteria.

13. Which programming language is the file extension .sh associated with?

   a. Python

   b. PowerShell

   c. 123 and 48

   d. Linux

14. Which of the following is an example of a string?

   a. 189.3

   b. 27

   c. "5 things I like to eat."

   d. 4*5%

15. Which of these is a proprietary desktop sharing application?

   a. DRM

   b. RDP

   c. EULA

   d. SDS

Foundation Topics

Best Practices and Documentation

220-1002: Objective 4.1: Compare and contrast best practices associated with types of documentation.

A technician must be a good communicator, and one of the most important forms of communication in an IT career is documentation. Any experienced technician can tell stories of how proper documentation could have saved time and money on a job. This section explains how different types of documentation help keep an organization running smoothly long after a technician has left the building.

Network Topology Diagrams

When a technician is called into a building to service a computer or a network of computers, one of the first tasks is to understand how the network is supposed to work. A topology diagram is essentially a map of a network that show how equipment is physically arranged in the building and logically connected as a network.

A physical topology diagram uses representational icons to depict types of equipment such as laptops, PCs, servers, wireless access points, switches, and routers. It may also show how computers and printers are arranged and the physical cables that connect them together. Figure 9-1 shows an example of a basic topology with computers connected on a bus.

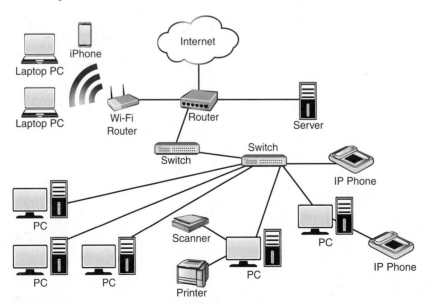

FIGURE 9-1   A Physical Topology Diagram

A physical topology diagram also maps wireless access ports and wiring closets. The diagram may "zoom in" and depict a single room or floor. A technician can use a physical topology diagram to find a device she has been called to service. She can also use it to see what other equipment, such as printers, security cameras, and switches, are in use and where to find them. Physical topologies may also "zoom out" and give the general design of a building, including wiring closets on floors and the point-of-presence (PoP) for connectivity to the ISP. These cut sheets should be posted in secure wiring closets but, for security reasons, not available to the general public.

A logical topology diagram depicts a network's design, including how computers are grouped together into local area networks (LANs). A logical diagram may include a basic map of wiring closets and general areas of the building, but instead of computers, this diagram focuses on network IP addresses. This is beneficial because troubleshooting Internet connectivity is a major part of the IT workday, and knowing which network devices should be on saves time in troubleshooting. Figure 9-2 shows a logical topology diagram of a medical facility.

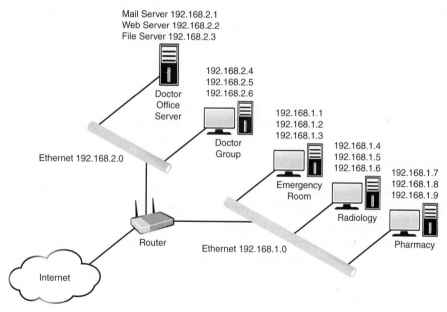

FIGURE 9-2 A Logical Topology Diagram

Knowledge Base and Articles

Reading and research may not be thought of as such, but they are technical skills. Being an IT technician means being in a constant state of learning, and a good technician knows how to find answers to unusual problems. Keeping a library of articles and links to helpful resources is essential.

A *whitepaper* is a type of resource that is common in technical fields. A whitepaper differs from other types of writing in that it focuses on a complex technical topic and tries to make it understandable to the average reader. Companies often publish whitepapers on new technologies or products they are presenting to the public in order to influence decision makers. Knowledge bases may also consist of links to commonly accessed support forums where fellow IT professionals go to seek and give technical support.

The easiest way to access knowledge base articles and whitepapers is to go to the support site for a product or do a search for a topic. An example of a documentation support site is the AWS CloudFormation documentation site, at https://docs.aws.amazon.com/cloudformation/index.html.

Incident Documentation

Documenting problems, or incidents, that happen to a network can be very helpful in keeping a computer network robust. Hard drive failures, for example, may show a pattern of a problem with a certain manufacturer that allows the technicians to anticipate potential points of failure. Similarly, understanding how an incident came about and how a solution was found—as well as who may have had a role in the solution—will be invaluable to technicians the next time an incident occurs.

There are several helpdesk software systems available to help PC technicians track workflow and improve customer service. Examples include Vivantio (https://www.vivantio.com) and HappyFox (https://www.happyfox.com)

Regulatory and Compliance Policy

Compliance with local government regulations is a necessary part of legal and safe electronics and technology work. There are many regulations for workplaces, and they vary in different areas. For example, electronics recycling is subject to local disposal laws, and privacy concerns for client data are increasingly coming under regulatory scrutiny. Construction codes for electrical and ventilation design are also subject to local rules.

Acceptable Use Policy

Chapter 7, "Security," discusses an *acceptable use policy (AUP)* as it pertains to user safety and security procedures. An AUP is designed to keep a network safe from outside intruders. But acceptable use goes further when it comes to computer best practices within a company. Each organization should define what it considers acceptable use of its computing resources within its network. For example, government networks generally are not available for private use, and private email may not be allowed on work computers. Inappropriate use of the Web has been a problem in workplaces since the Internet became common in business.

For legal protection of the company, acceptable use rules need to be established and agreed to (usually with a signature) by users.

Password Policy

Password policy is mostly managed by network administrators, who may require complex passwords that need to be changed regularly. But users also need to understand that technology alone cannot protect a network if users are not careful in keeping their passwords secret. Thieves and hackers trying to access a network use social engineering and phishing to get passwords from unsuspecting workers, and employees need to be trained to protect their information.

Inventory Management

Organizations of all types need to be accountable for the money and other resources they spend on technology. It usually falls to the IT department to receive and document equipment with durable asset tags. The tags are usually customized, with each one including the name of the organization along with a barcode and serial number. They are most often made of a metalized polyester that should last as long as the computer asset is expected to be in use.

An asset tag allows the company to track who is responsible for the equipment and how often it has needed repair. Using a barcode scanner is the most convenient way to keep track of the equipment while it is in use in the company. The IT department is then responsible to document the equipment at the end of its usefulness as it goes out of inventory and is sold, donated, or destroyed.

Change Management

220-1002: Objective 4.2: Given a scenario, implement basic change management best practices.

Change is a constant force in the field of IT, and that force needs to be managed well so that the benefits of change can improve processes in the organization and the potential perils of change can be avoided. For example, if a data manager wants to make changes to a loan management software system in a bank, she must first make sure that the marketing department, which may rely on the loan data, has software that will work with the new system. Otherwise, improving loan management may cause problems for the marketing department.

Change management is the process of preparing for changes in a network, including planning, staffing, organizing, and getting feedback from impacted stakeholders. Change management is studied by IT and business organizations such as ITIL and ISO 20000, which produce change process guidelines for their members.

Documented Business Processes and Practices

Knowing how a company performs its many tasks can help create a map of how the change should be implemented. It cannot be assumed that everyone can do without services while the network is down. Also, there is likely tremendous overlap in network use. For example, changes to the production end of a business may impact other parts unintentionally. An IT manager may believe that an old server is useless, not realizing that it serves as a backup server for another department.

Many parts of an organization use the IT infrastructure in different ways, and it is necessary to have a document that records how it is used. This means creating a record of who uses the network, what parts they use, and how they impact other users.

Purpose of the Change

Clarity in purpose is essential for a successful network change or migration. First, knowing the purpose of the project will help limit the scope of change and keep it from getting larger than necessary. Second, users will be inconvenienced, so they will need to be brought into the process to identify issues and help make the change successful.

Scope the Change

Scope refers to the extent of the impact of a change. Scope must be determined so that all users and managers do not suddenly lose the ability to work when a change is implemented. Scoping a change means creating a detailed plan itemizing things that will stay the same after the change (things needed to perform core functions), things that will go away (old equipment, outdated applications, and so on), and things that have a mixed outcome (meaning there will be some benefit, like efficiency, but some drawback, like layoffs of loyal employees).

Risk Analysis

There is always a level of risk in making changes to a network, and a goal of change management is to identify the risks and mitigate them. Examples of risks that IT managers plan for include delays, lower-than-expected quality, and use of more resources. Once the risks are identified, managers and planners can work to neutralize them.

A change manager may group the several aspects of a change into high-, medium-, and low-risk categories and manage the team resources according to the potential impact on the organization.

Plan for Change

Even small changes to a network need to have a well-planned implementation. Change management puts planning at the forefront and engages IT people and users from across the organization. It is important that all users of a network be aware of changes that will come and understand, based on detailed analysis, how those changes will impact their functions. For example, a software change made to benefit sales or marketing functions may have an adverse effect on how accounting tracks company expenses. Understanding the full impact of a change across the organization is essential, and that knowledge must be brought to the change board members.

End-User Acceptance

The end users of the network will be the final arbiters of success or failure in the change migration. Those planning and implementing the change should be informed, but all users will have a role, so they need to be involved, too. Managers might need to schedule training time, and there may be a learning curve that users will have to accept and endure. The more ownership they can have in the process, the more likely it is that they will tolerate the hardship of the process.

Change Board

The change board (also known as a change advisory board, or CAB) is a group gathered from areas of the organization that will be impacted by the planned changes. The task of the change board is to analyze requests for change (RFCs) and study the benefits and risks of implementing changes. The change manager works under the authority of the change board and gives approval for the work to be done. Members of the change board are usually leadership-level employees who understand the impact that requested changes will have on the work in their respective areas.

Backout Plan

The backout plan is a document that lets the change administrators restore the network to the service level that was present before the change. Sometimes even the best plans can have unintended consequences on a network, or a planned upgrade may fail. When this happens, it is important to have an exact document that tells all the planned steps and logs the configuration codes necessary to get back to normal.

Document Changes

When changes occur, it is important to record what was changed and how it was accomplished. The change documentation can include a backout plan to implement in case there is trouble at a future date. This document needs to be available for anyone who wants to make further changes to the network.

Disaster Prevention and Recovery

220-1002: Objective 4.3: Given a scenario, implement basic disaster prevention and recovery methods.

It has been mentioned many times throughout this book that data is usually the most important asset that a company has to protect. Loss or breach of data can paralyze a company and bring it down. Disasters, by definition, are sudden and cause great damage. They are often nature driven and cannot be avoided. The best an organization can hope for in planning for a disaster is to have a system that can fail well and provide a reasonable path to recovery.

Backup and Recovery

Data is fragile by nature, and many things can go wrong, resulting in corrupt or unusable data on a computer or mobile device. Backing up any computing device is easier than ever, and our increasing reliance on data makes the practice essential even for home users.

Windows, Linux, and macOS have systems in place to make backing up and, if necessary, restoring data a fairly routine process. There are several ways to back up images, including backup to the cloud, using a backup service, and creating a network-attached storage (NAS) system for a network.

There are three levels of data backup, as listed here and described in more detail in the sections that follow:

- **System image:** Making a copy of an entire disk, including the Windows image

- **File-level backup:** Backing up or archiving files such as documents, reports, and pictures

- **Critical application backup:** Applications needed to restore business after a disaster

System Image

A *system image backup* includes everything on the drive—including the operating system (which is the system image). This backup can be used to restore a failed computer if there is a failure. This is a full backup and is also known as a "snapshot" of everything on a drive at a given time. The time of the snapshot becomes the restore point in the recovery process.

After the OS is installed, the data files are recovered. If backup space is an issue, doing a system image backup may not be the best choice since the OS takes up considerable space, and it is likely that there is a copy of the OS that can simply be reinstalled. In recent years, however, storage prices have dropped, and the OS process for backup has been simplified, so backing up with a system image is a more common choice now. Details of the process are discussed in Chapter 8, "Software Troubleshooting."

File-Level Backup

Files are generally the data saved by users when they use applications. File backups can be documents, media files like video or music, or pictures. Keeping just the data takes less space than backing up the applications as well. As with the OS, most applications can be restored from the original disks or downloaded again, and then the files can be recovered. See Chapter 8 for procedural details.

Critical Applications

What files are considered critical varies depending on the organization, but generally they are the first files that will be restored after a disaster to get things running again. This can be accomplished with a system image or with VMs that can be loaded to run quickly.

Backup Testing

Testing backups is important because the worst time to find out your scheduled backups were not working properly is when they are needed to recover data. Testing backups ensures that the needed data is available when a backup is necessary, and it allows IT staff to practice restoration so the skill is in place when it is most needed.

In the days when tape backups were run, it was a time-consuming task to test backups. Thanks to cloud storage, NAS solutions, and virtualization, the process is much easier today.

UPSs and Surge Protectors

The main electrical hazards to computers are surges, brownouts, and blackouts. To combat these dangers, every good wiring closet and server room has a combination of surge suppressors and uninterruptable power supplies, commonly known as UPSs.

An ***uninterruptable power supply (UPS)*** keeps the power to the units in a server room, wiring closet, or other environment clean and allows for time to run and shut down properly in case of power failure. A true UPS is one in which connected devices are always powered by the battery, which uses an inverter to continually convert AC power into DC power. This protects the equipment from the sometimes variable nature of AC power. However, in many cases a unit that is called a UPS actually passes AC power through the unit's integrated surge suppressor until the AC power fails. At that point, the battery takes over. This type of unit is most properly known as a standby power supply (SPS) or line-interactive unit. In practice, both types of battery backup units are known as UPS units.

Surge protectors protect devices from extreme changes in power flow. These are essentially power strips that are plugged into a grounded wall outlet; devices such as PCs or phones are plugged into the protectors. If there is a surge or spike in power, a protector simply breaks the circuit, and the device loses power.

Not all surge protectors are the same, and costs vary greatly. They are rated in joules, which is how the protection level is described. The more joules, the stronger the protection. Some come with phone land line jacks because power spikes can come through phone lines.

Surge protectors are a much cheaper solution than UPSs but can cause problems with equipment constantly booting if the local power is inconsistent. A UPS is a more sound, although more expensive, solution.

> **NOTE**   Surge protectors and surge suppressors are technically different devices, but many technicians use the terms interchangeably. (Suppressors are mentioned in a later section.)

Local Storage vs. Cloud Storage Backups

The easiest way to back up data on workstations is to use an external drive (hard drive or USB flash drive) with a redundant backup on the cloud.

For an external drive backup, mount a USB flash drive (or an external hard drive) and drag the files into the drive window. Unmount/eject the USB drive and store the flash drive. Copy files to a flash drive for backup.

The Windows Backup and File History utilities and Time Machine in macOS easily back up files and system images to external hard drives. With an external hard drive plugged into a USB port, start the backup utility and select the drive. Once the backup is complete, store the drive in a safe, dry environment until the next backup is to be performed. Scheduled backups should be run at times when the system is idle, such as overnight and on weekends. Figure 9-3 shows the first steps of Windows 10 Backup using the File History utility for storing or retrieving files.

FIGURE 9-3   Windows 10 Backup

macOS includes Time Machine, an automatic backup utility that can create hourly backups for 24 hours and that saves those hourly backups as daily backups and maintains weekly and monthly versions. Go to **System Preferences** to enable and configure Time Machine:

Step 1.   Connect a suitable external disk to a macOS system (see Figure 9-4). In this example Rick Bup is an external drive connected via USB.

Step 2.   Click **Backup Disk**.

Step 3.   In the new window that appears, check the **Encrypt Backups** box to protect the backup (see insert of Figure 9-5).

Step 4.   Enter a password, confirm it, and enter a password hint. Click **Encrypt Disk**.

Step 5.   Make sure Time Machine is turned on. After the selected disk is encrypted, the backup starts.

FIGURE 9-4   macOS Time Machine Backup Utility.

FIGURE 9-5   Selecting and Encrypting an External Disk (Rick Bup) in Time Machine

Linux includes several utilities that can be used for backups. These include the command line tar and rsync utilities. Others, including grsync (which is a GUI for rsync), duplicity (which is available as a command line utility and also as a GUI called Déjà Dup), and others are available from the repository for a Linux distribution or from the vendors.

> **NOTE** The BackupYourSystem page on Ubuntu Linux help (https://help.ubuntu.com/community/BackupYourSystem) provides a large list of command line and GUI-based backup tools that also work with other Linux distros.

Cloud Storage and Local Backups

Backing up files or images to the cloud can be managed by a cloud backup service that syncs the drives on a schedule you choose. Common names in the increasingly crowded cloud provider arena are:

- Amazon Drive
- Dropbox
- Google Drive
- OneDrive app in Windows

All of these options provide varying levels of storage space, encryption services, and price points. Each has an introductory level for personal use that provides free or discounted storage space and bigger plans for business-level customers.

All of these services mimic a flash or external drive by mounting a virtual drive on the desktop for accessing files. As with any other drive window on the computer, files can be copied or moved by simply dragging them to or from cloud drive window. User data can also be accessed via the provider's web page. Table 9-2 compares storage of files in the cloud vs. local storage.

Table 9-2 Comparing Cloud vs. Local Storage

Factor	Cloud Storage	Local Storage	Advantage
Media	Web	Tape, CD, USB, hard drives	None
Cost	As-needed subscription	Hardware, utilities, external location costs, and administrative overhead	Cloud
Accessibility	On-demand access to files	Must be physically stored and secured in separate location	Cloud
Safety	Secure but requires Web access	Secure when properly handled	None
Flexibility	Backup any computer or file; restore files on demand	Can only back up local computers; need physical access to restore files	Cloud

As you can see from the table, there are increasing advantages to the cloud, but the benefits of secure local storage have not completely disappeared. Add to this mix the possibility of internal clouds (see Chapter 4, "Virtualization and Cloud Computing"), and the lines become even less clear. A good backup plan is not restricted to either of these options and involves taking advantage of the benefits of each.

Backup Types

There are three main types of data backup:

- **Full:** A full backup backs up the entire contents of the computer or selected drive to another local or network location. Since every file is copied, this backup takes the longest and uses the most storage of the three types.

- **Incremental:** These backups copy only data that has changed since the last backup. If a full backup is performed every Saturday, then an incremental backup could be run each day of the week, recording one day of activity each time. This way, backups are current but a full backup does not have to be run each day.

- **Differential:** These backups record changed data since the last full backup. These backups can be done often to ensure that data backups are very current.

Account Recovery Options

It is easy to lose track of all the accounts people keep in their daily digital lives. As we increase the roles of digital work and recreation into our daily lives with activities such as shopping, banking, TV subscriptions, online storage, medical records, and access to networks where we work, the need for accounts and authentication become more vital. Losing access to an account can result in anything from a mere inconvenience that requires a password recovery process to a disaster if it means being cut off from financial or medical services.

Account recovery can take many forms, depending on the account and who is responsible for its safekeeping. No matter who is responsible, smart account holders know how to get out of trouble before trouble occurs. Having a plan in place to recover your digital life if laptops or phones are lost, stolen, or destroyed will allow you to recover quickly and keep records secure until they are back online.

Most personal accounts from vendors can be recovered in one of several ways:

- Submitting an account email address on the login page and having a password recovery link sent via email

- Having a tech support agent reset an account with a temporary password that must be reset upon login

- Answering secret questions with answers provided during account setup

For example, subscribers to Microsoft online user accounts in Windows 10 can have their accounts shut down if Microsoft sees signs of unusual activity. When an account is disabled, users can sign into their Microsoft account and follow instructions to get a security code. Similarly, a bank may lock down a credit card if it sees unusual purchasing patterns; then, the account holder must contact a bank agent to verify purchases or the bank may contact the customer.

At work, users count on the system administrator to help them get back online. Windows Active Directory and most all other enterprise-level server solutions have administrative tools that can be used to recover user accounts that have been deleted.

Explain Common Safety Procedures

220-1002: Objective 4.4: Explain common safety procedures.

Workplace safety should be the primary concern of every employee at every level in an organization. Most organizations have safety plans and procedures that directly apply to the work performed by a PC technician, who needs to be aware of not only data safety and security but physical safety as well. This section covers basic safety procedures common for a PC technician.

Computer safety involves keeping computers safe from failure and keeping technicians safe while working in a dangerous environment. The concepts in this section are:

- Preventing electrostatic discharge

- Working with electricity safely

- Handling toxic waste

- Protecting personal and physical safety

Equipment Grounding

Construction codes require that every building with electrical service must be grounded. *Grounding* an electrical system means making a direct connection from the building's electrical service to the earth so that dangerous voltage from line surges and lightning strikes will find its way into the earth instead of injuring people, damaging equipment, or causing a fire. Every grounded outlet in a building has a direct connection to a metal grounding electrode that goes several feet into the earth. Using proper grounding outlets provides an element of safety for the user and the computer. Figure 9-6 shows a common grounded outlet. Grounded outlets have three prongs in almost all world areas.

FIGURE 9-6   A Common Grounded Outlet (Image © Jason Kolenda, Shutterstock)

When a grounded outlet is not available, a grounded to ungrounded adapter (see Figure 9-7) can be used for temporary setups if the loop on the adapter can be connected to a working ground (such as a grounding screw or a copper wire wrapped around a metal pipe).

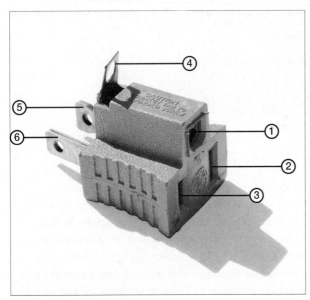

1. Ground connector   4. Ground loop
2. Neutral connector   5. Neutral prong
3. Hot connector   6. Hot prong

FIGURE 9-7   Using a Ground Screw or Wire to Provide a Safe Connection for Grounded Equipment

In the United States, grounded 120V AC electrical outlets have been required by code since 1962. Thus, a more likely issue in residential and office environments is the possibility of an improperly installed grounded outlet: one in which the ground line doesn't connect to a ground.

The easiest way to determine proper building wiring, including grounding, is to use an electrical outlet tester such as the one shown in Figure 9-8.

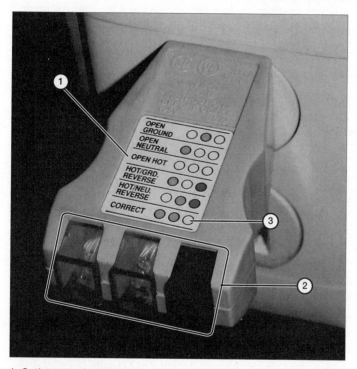

1. Outlet tester legend
2. Test lights
3. Legend indicates wiring is correct

FIGURE 9-8   Using an Electrical Tester to Determine Whether an Outlet Is Properly Wired and Grounded (Earthed)

Component Handling and Storage

During the building, upgrading, repairing, or teardown of electronic and computer equipment, there are many potential opportunities for equipment to be damaged or destroyed by *electrostatic discharge (ESD)*.

ESD is the silent enemy of computer equipment. ESD may be too low for humans to detect but still strong enough to damage electronic components. The human body constantly builds up static electricity—even when sitting at a desk. And the dryer the atmosphere is, the more easily static electricity builds. Table 9-3 shows the ESD potential at different humidity levels and activities.

Table 9-3 ESD by Activity and Relative Humidity

Activity	Relative Humidity		
	55%	**40%**	**10%**
Normal Activities			
Walking on carpet	7500V	15,000V	35,000V
Walking on vinyl floor	3000V	5000V	12,000V
Workbench Repair and Packing Tasks			
Typical worker tasks at an electronics bench	400V	800V	6000V
Removing computer chips from plastic tube	400V	700V	2000V
Removing computer chips from vinyl tray	2000V	4000V	11,500V
Removing computer chips from Styrofoam	3500V	5000V	14,500V
Removing bubble pack from a printed circuit board (motherboard, video card, and so on)	7000V	20,000V	26,500V
Packing motherboards, video cards, or other printed circuit boards in a foam-lined box	5000V	11,000V	21,000V

Equipment can be damaged by ESD of 700V or higher, and Table 9-3 demonstrates that even ordinary activities can cause levels of ESD that are dangerous to components. As humidity decreases, the voltage released during ESD climbs.

Without ESD protection, static electricity will seek to discharge to anything else that has a different electric potential—especially metallic items like circuit boards. Casually picking up an expensive video card can possibly damage it. This damage could cause a complete failure or could cause intermittent issues that would be difficult to troubleshoot. Make things easier for yourself by employing antistatic measures at all times. There are four keys to protection:

- Antistatic bags
- ESD straps
- ESD mats
- Self-grounding

Antistatic Bags

When removing a component from a computer, immediately place it in an antistatic bag and put it off to the side (see Figure 9-9). Parts should never be lying around outside an antistatic bag. Normal bubble wrap bags do not constitute antistatic protection, so make sure to use proper antistatic bags. Some bubble wrap is antistatic and is so labeled.

After an item is placed in an antistatic bag, place it in a protective box to avoid physical impact damage.

1. Antistatic bag
2. microPCIe card inside anti-static bag

FIGURE 9-9 Using an Antistatic Bag to Protect a microPCIe Wireless Network Adapter

ESD Straps

An ESD strap is designed to equalize the electric potential of the user and the device the strap is clipped to, such as the interior of a computer. By equalizing the electric potential, ESD is prevented because ESD is the movement of electricity between two objects with different electric potential.

An ESD strap has two pieces:

- An elastic or hook-and-loop strap with a built-in metal snap backed by a metal plate

- A coiled flexible cable with a matching snap at one end and an alligator clip at the other end. The snap contains a 1 megohm resistor, which can help prevent injury in case of electrical discharge.

To properly use an ESD strap:

Step 1. Place the elastic or hook-and-loop strap around one wrist with the flat metal plate against the skin.

Step 2. Adjust the strap until the metal plate stays in place as you move your wrist.

Step 3. Snap the cable to the strap around your wrist.

Step 4. Open the alligator cable and clamp it to unpainted metal on the object you are servicing.

The strap around the wrist with the metal plate, snap, and cable equalizes electrical potential between you and the object you are servicing to prevent ESD.

Figure 9-10 illustrates a typical ESD strap and suitable locations for attaching it to a computer.

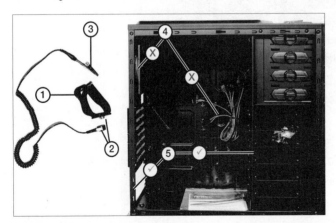

1. Adjustable wrist strap
2. Snap cable to wrist strap
3. Clamp alligator clip to unpainted metal components on the device
   being serviced
4. Not suitable (plastic fan or coated wires)
5. Suitable (metal chassis frame or drive bay frame)
   Green check (indicates suitable locations for strap)
   Red X (not suitable locations)

FIGURE 9-10 Using an ESD Strap to Help Prevent Damaging ESD When Working on Electronics

ESD Mats

The next level of protection for bench repairs and upgrades is to use an ESD mat. An ESD mat can be connected to a device being repaired using one of the following methods:

- A cable with an alligator clip

- A cable with a loop designed to be held in place by a case screw but with the cable snapped to the mat rather than to your wrist

As with an ESD strap, the end of the cable that snaps to the mat has a 1 megohm resistor built into it.

The ESD mat shown in Figure 9-11 is bundled with an ESD strap. Some versions use anti-fatigue material suitable for floor use.

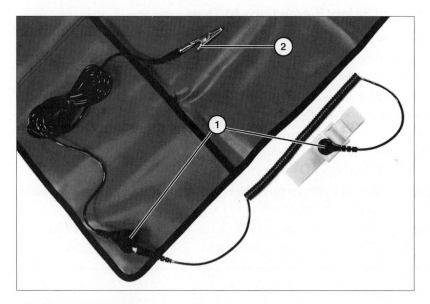

1. Resistors built into cables
2. Attach this clip to equipment being serviced

FIGURE 9-11 Using an ESD Mat for Additional Protection Against Damaging ESD

Self-Grounding

In some instances it may be necessary to work on equipment without any ESD protection. In such cases, self-grounding is a way to protect the equipment being worked on.

Self-grounding involves touching a nearby metal component before touching the device being serviced (for example, touching a metal portion of a chair before picking a component up or opening the device). Before opening a computer, you can self-ground by touching an unpainted portion of the case with both hands before installing or uninstalling a component. Do this every time before touching a component. If no other antistatic options are available, this technique can be used as a last resort.

> **NOTE**   Remember to keep the computer unplugged while working inside it. Disconnect the power or turn off the computer using the power switch (if there is one) before working on the system. You might not know whether the AC outlet is wired properly. By simply disconnecting the power, you eliminate any chance of a shock.

Other ESD and Safety Precautions to Take

When working with electronics, consider these precautions:

- When handling components or cards, hold them by the edge or bracket. Don't touch the chips, contacts, or other circuitry.
- When handling components, stay stationary. Don't shuffle your feet or move any more than necessary while installing or removing the component.
- Remove jewelry and wear protective clothing. In some labs, technicians wear antistatic nylon jumpsuits. For the average person, wearing rubber-soled shoes can also help prevent ESD.
- If possible, work in a non-carpeted area. Carpet is perhaps the leading cause of high electrical potential that leads to ESD.
- Avoid using AC-powered tools near a computer. Use battery-powered devices (such as a multimeter) only when necessary.

Toxic Waste Handling

There are five types of computer-related toxic waste that the CompTIA A+ certification exam addresses for safe handling:

- Batteries
- Toner
- CRT displays
- Cell phones
- Tablets

The following sections provide guidance for ***toxic waste handling***.

Recycling Batteries

Nickel-cadmium (Ni-Cad), nickel-metal hydride (NiMH), and lithium-ion (Li-Ion) batteries for cell phones, computers, and other electronics as well as lead-acid cells used in UPS battery backup units should not be discarded as trash. If not recycled properly, these items will become toxic waste.

There are several ways to recycle these batteries safely to avoid environmental threats:

- For small numbers of rechargeable batteries or devices that contain rechargeable batteries, use a recycling drop-off station (such as a drop-off station at an electronics retailer).

- For large numbers of rechargeable batteries, devices, or UPS devices with batteries, contact an electronics recycler in your area.

- Some batteries can be returned directly to the manufacturer for recycling.

- During storage and transport, make sure battery contacts are prevented from touching each other. Check and follow regulations regarding the shipment of Li-Ion batteries, which pose a potentially high fire and explosion hazard in some environments.

Toner

Toner bottles and cartridges for laser printers and copiers should be recycled instead of discarded. Unlike with batteries, users can actually earn money or credits toward additional purchases by recycling toner bottles and cartridges products at local office-supply stores or toner recycling shops. Although inkjet cartridges are not recognized as toxic waste, they shouldn't be discarded. They can be turned in for credit at office-supply stores or inkjet cartridge remanufacturers. Some manufacturers include a prepaid label in the box containing the ink for easy returns.

After removing the old toner cartridge, use a specially designed toner vacuum to remove loose toner from inside the printer before inserting the new cartridge.

CRT Displays

Although ***cathode ray tube (CRT)*** displays have become much less common in recent years, as long as they exist, they represent significant environmental and personal safety hazards.

CRT displays contain heavy metals, including lead solder on older models, and a CRT can retain potentially dangerous electric charges long after it has been shut down. To avoid these hazards, use an approved electronics recycler for CRT displays. These organizations can safely discharge CRT displays before dismantling and recycle their components.

> **NOTE**   Many electronics recyclers now charge by the pound to recycle CRT monitors and CRT TVs.

LCD-CCFL Displays

Although LCD-CCFL displays are not specifically cited on the CompTIA A+ certification exam as being potentially hazardous, the fluorescent backlights in these units contain toxic mercury. Mercury could be released into the environment if panels are crushed or broken when disposed of as ordinary trash.

LCD-CCFL displays as well as all other types of computers, peripherals, and electronics, should be disposed of through an approved electronics recycler.

Cell Phones and Tablets

As mentioned previously, batteries for cell phones and tablet should be recycled. But before disposing of these devices, be sure any personal or company data is safely deleted and the SIM card is removed. Data to check for includes contacts, messages, downloads, pictures, and voice mails. Browser data should be cleared as well.

Personal Safety

In this section, we discuss methods for keeping a bench tech safe while working on computer and electronics equipment.

Disconnect Power First

Electricity is a hazard to computers and to humans. Approach any encounter with electricity with great caution. Always be sure to disconnect power before repairing a PC.

Remove Jewelry

Remove jewelry of all kinds (rings, necklaces, earrings, and so on) before working on a computer. Do not allow jewelry to come into contact with any components.

Lifting Techniques

Use safe lifting techniques to avoid injury. When lifting a large or heavy item, stand close to the item, squat down to the item by bending the knees, grasp the item firmly, keep the back straight, and slowly lift with the legs, not the back. Be sure not to twist the body and keep the item close to the body to help prevent back injuries. When moving items, it is best to have them stored at waist level so that minimal lifting is necessary. The Occupational Safety and Health Administration (OSHA) has plenty of guidelines and recommendations for physical safety at the workplace; see https://www.osha.gov.

Weight Limitations

Know your weight limitations to avoid injury. Lifting heavy items incorrectly can cause many types of injuries. As a general rule, if an item is heavier than one-quarter of your body weight, you should ask someone else to help. Approach a box and move it slightly to gauge whether help is needed to move it safely. Lifting is among the most common causes of worker injuries.

Electrical Fire Safety

With electrical fire safety, the safest measures are preventive ones. Buildings should be outfitted with smoke detectors and fire extinguishers. The proper type of fire extinguisher for an electrical fire is a Class C extinguisher. CO_2-based BC fire extinguishers are common and relatively safe to humans, but they can cause damage to computers. If equipment needs to be protected more, then an ABC Halotron extinguisher should be used. Server rooms and data centers often are protected by a larger special hazard protection system that uses the FM-200 clean agent system. This clean agent won't cause damage to servers and other expensive equipment and is safe for humans.

If you see an electrical fire, use the proper extinguisher to attempt to put it out. If the fire is too big for you to handle, dial your country's emergency number (911 in the United States). Then evacuate the building. Afterward, you can notify building management, your supervisor, or other facilities people. If the fire involves a live electrical wire, it should be shut off at the source. Do not attempt this with bare hands and make sure that your feet are dry and that you are not standing in any water. Use a wooden stick, board, or rope. If this is not possible, contact the supervisor or building management so they can shut down power at another junction.

If you find an apparently unconscious person underneath a live wire, do not touch the person! Again, attempt to move the live wire with a wooden stick or similar object. Never use anything metal and do not touch anything metal while you are doing it. After moving the wire, call 911 and contact your superiors immediately. While waiting, attempt to administer first aid to the person.

Always follow company policy and local government regulations for handling emergencies.

Cable Management

Cable management is even more important outside a computer than it is inside. Routing power cables and data cables inside a PC is important for providing good airflow for cooling. But cables outside the computer can be a trip hazard. Any external USB cables should be routed in such a way that they won't interfere with the normal activity of employees. More importantly, network cables should be stationary and routed away from walking areas.

Local governments have rules for how networking and telecommunications wires should be installed, and many municipalities require a license to install any of these cables. When running network cables for new computers, check local regulations first and see whether a licensed installer is required for compliance with local government regulations. Make sure that cables do not pose trip hazards and are not run near any electrical devices or wires if at all possible.

Safety Goggles

Wear safety goggles when performing computer repairs, cleaning, or upgrades to avoid eye injuries from dust, dirt, flyaway screws or bolts, solder, or other activities. The U.S. standard for protective work eyewear is ANSI Z87.1-2010. Eye protectors that meet this standard can be rated for non-impact or impact (Z87+) applications, so choose according to the risks involved in your specific application.

In other countries, determine the relevant standards for industrial protection when selecting safety goggles.

Air Filter Mask

If a job being performed requires metal machining, buffing, sanding, soldering, waste processing, recycling, or painting as part or all of your technology-related work, an air filter mask might be required for safety.

The U.S. National Institute for Occupational Safety and Health (NIOSH) standards for particulate filtering respirators include the following filter series:

- **N:** Not resistant to oil
- **R:** Resistant to oil
- **P:** Oil proof

The highest ratings available are P100 (99.97% efficiency against oil and non-oil particulate aerosols; meetings HEPA standards), R95 (95% efficiency against oil and non-oil particulate aerosols), and N95 (95% efficiency against non-oil particulate aerosols). Some filters can also block ozone.

Check the particulate hazard types associated with a task before selecting an R-series or N-series filter, or choose a P100 filter. Some masks can accept any of these filter types.

Compliance with Local Government Regulations

Compliance with local government regulations is a necessary part of legal and safe electronics and technology work. Check with your local municipality for recommended electronics recyclers. Electronics recyclers should have an ISO 14001 certification. ISO 14001 is an international standard describing requirements for an effective environmental management system (EMS). Follow regulations for ventilation and other workplace issues as well.

Environmental Impacts and Appropriate Controls

220-1002: Objective 4.5: Explain environmental impacts and appropriate controls.

220-1002
Exam

IT equipment is not restricted to climate-controlled data centers, and an IT professional must be aware of how different environments can impact the performance of a computer or network.

For the 220-1002 exam, you need to know how and why to control temperature and humidity, what an MSDS is and how to use it, and how to deal with dust and debris when it comes to computers.

> **NOTE** For the 220-1002 exam, prepare to answer questions on these topics:
> - MSDS documentation for handling and disposal
> - Temperature, humidity level awareness, and proper ventilation
> - Power surges, brownouts, and blackouts
> - Protection from airborne particles
> - Dust and debris
> - Compliance with local government regulations

Material Safety Data Sheet (MSDS)

A *safety data sheet (SDS)*, also known as material safety data sheet (MSDS), is a document that gives information about particular substances, such as the toner in a laser printer's toner cartridge. Any product that uses chemicals is required to have an SDS. An SDS includes the following information:

- Proper treatment if a person comes into contact with or ingests the substance

- How to deal with spills

- How to handle and dispose of the substance properly

- How and where to store the substance

> **TIP** SDS personal protection ratings are designed to inform the consumer of the safe way to handle the material.
>
> The recommendations for ratings A–D are as follows:
> - **Rating A:** Safety glasses
> - **Rating B:** Safety glasses and gloves
> - **Rating C:** Safety glasses, gloves, and apron
> - **Rating D:** Face shield, eye protection, gloves, and apron

Most companies have their SDS documents online. For example, accessing https://www8.hp.com/us/en/hp-information/environment/msds-specs.html or searching for "HP SDS" would take you to all the SDS documents for Hewlett-Packard's various inkjet cartridges, toner cartridges, cleaners, digital projector and printer lamps, batteries, and so on. SDS documents are usually in PDF format so be sure to have Adobe Reader or another PDF reader installed.

Generally, substances that contain chemicals should be stored in a cool, dry place, away from sunlight. "Cool" means the lower end of the OSHA guideline, about 68 degrees Fahrenheit (20 degrees Celsius). Often, this is a storage closet away from the general work area and outside the air filtration system. Such a closet is also usually less humid than other parts of the building.

As far as disposal goes, basically, any substance with an MSDS should not be thrown away when you are finished with it. It should usually be recycled according to the procedures documented in the MSDS. This recycling could occur through the local municipality (in the case of batteries) or by returning items directly to the manufacturer or vendor (in the case of ink/toner cartridges).

It's important to know what to do when someone is adversely affected by a product that contains chemicals. A person might have skin irritation from coming into contact with toner particles or a cleaner that was used on a keyboard or mouse. As a technician, it is your job to find out how to help such a person. If you do not have direct access to the MSDS, contact your organization's facilities department or building management. Perhaps the cleaning crew uses a particular cleaning agent that you are not familiar with, and only the facilities department has been given the MSDS for it. It's best to review all MSDS documents and be proactive, but in this case, you probably won't have access to the document. Collaborate with the facilities department to get the affected person the proper first aid and, if necessary, take the person to the emergency room. Finally, remove the affected device (if it is a keyboard or mouse, for example) and replace it with a similar device until you can get the original device cleaned properly.

Temperature, Humidity, and Air

You should be aware of the temperature and humidity measurements in your building. You also should be thinking about airborne particles and proper ventilation. Collectively, OSHA refers to this as "air treatment," and it involves the removal of air contaminants and/or the control of room temperature and humidity. Although there is no specific government policy regarding this, there are recommendations, including a recommended temperature range of 68 to 76 degrees Fahrenheit (20 to 24 degrees Celsius) and a recommended humidity range of between 20% and 60%. Remember that the higher the humidity, the less chance of ESD, but it might get a bit uncomfortable for workers, so a compromise will have to be sought. If the organization uses air handlers to heat, cool, and move the air, it will be somewhat difficult to keep the humidity much higher than 25% to 30%.

Ventilation

An organization should employ the use of local exhaust (to remove contaminants generated by the organization's processes) and introduce an adequate supply of fresh outdoor air through natural or mechanical ventilation. For air treatment, organizations should use filtration devices, electronic cleaners, and possibly chemical treatments activated with charcoal or other sorbents (that is, materials used to absorb unwanted gases). Most filtration systems use charcoal and HEPA filters. These filters should be replaced at regular intervals. Air ducts and dampers should be cleaned regularly, and ductwork insulation should be inspected periodically.

If a considerable level of airborne particles remains, portable air filtration enclosures can be purchased that also use charcoal and HEPA air filters or that possibly utilize ultraviolet light to eliminate particles. These enclosures are commonly found in computer repair facilities due to the amount of dust and debris sitting in computers that are waiting for repair. Some organizations even provide masks or even respirators for their employees.

Compressed Air and Vacuum Systems

A PC workbench may be equipped with a compressed air system and vacuum system. This way, the PC tech can blow out the dust and dirt from a computer and vacuum it up at the same time. Otherwise, it is usually best to take the computer outside when cleaning it (unless it is very windy).

Power Surges, Brownouts, and Blackouts

Reliable power delivery at a consistent level is essential for protecting electronic equipment such as computers and televisions. Even in communities with quality power delivery, power surges and sags endanger computers. An electrical outlet may be properly wired (see the section "Equipment Grounding," earlier in this chapter), but there are other threats to the well-being of computers or other devices connected to the outlet, including:

- Power surges
- Brownouts
- Blackouts

Power Surges and Surge Suppressors

A surge suppressor is designed to block power surges from damaging the equipment plugged into it. Power surges are defined as overvoltage events that last no more than 50ms and that can reach voltage levels as high as 6000V and 3000A.

Surge suppressors are rated in joules to indicate the amount of energy a surge suppressor can absorb before failing. All other factors being equal, the higher the joule rating, the better. However, keep in mind that a unit with multiple metal-oxide varistors (MOVs) on each power lead might provide better protection than a single large MOV.

MOVs absorb power surges and gradually wear out. Although many (but not all) surge suppressors have lights that indicate when protection has failed, only a few models stop providing power in the event that protection fails.

Attention should be paid to how many computers are connected to a surge suppressor. Add the combined wattage or volt-amp ratings of the devices to be plugged into the surge suppressor and compare that to the maximum that the surge suppressor can support. Usually a surge suppressor can handle two basic computers and two monitors. But a high-powered device such as a laser printer should get its own surge suppressor.

Surge suppressors should be replaced every three to five years, or right after an event that damages the MOVs, such as a nearby lightning strike, frequent power flickers, burn marks, or smoke in any outlet on the unit.

Blackouts, Brownouts, and Battery Backup Units

Blackouts (total loss of power) and **brownouts** (sustained voltage drops of as much as half of rated output) stop computers and peripherals from working. Unfortunately, if computers and peripherals lose power in the middle of backups, updates, or reports, files can be corrupted. The solution is to use a battery backup UPS. (As mentioned earlier in this chapter, the term *UPS* means *uninterruptable power supply*.)

Battery backup units are rated in two ways: volt-amps (VA) or watts (W). Different battery backup units with the same wattage rating can vary in terms of the VA rating. However, the usual calculation for comparing W to VA is to assume that VA × .60 = W. Thus, a UPS with a 1000VA rating will provide about 600W of power.

In addition to providing enough power to run connected devices (such as a computer, a display, and USB devices but not a laser printer), a UPS needs to be able to run on battery an appropriate amount of time before being shut down by the UPS—called the run time. Some vendors and third-party websites (for example, www.easycalculation.com/physics/classical-physics/ups-power-requirement.php) provide calculators that use input watts or amperage draws to calculate the UPS size needed. To increase runtime, select a unit with a larger VA or watt rating.

NOTE   Do not use the battery-backed outlets on a UPS for devices such as laser printers. These power-hungry devices can drain the UPS battery quickly or damage the unit. For such devices, use the surge suppressed outlets that are not connected to the battery.

Table 9-4 provides a quick review of what the 220-1002 exam requires you to know about dealing with power surges, blackouts, and brownouts.

Table 9-4   Electrical Conditions and Protective Measures

Type of Electrical Condition	Description	Protective Measure
Power surge	Overvoltage event lasting less than 50ms. Up to 6000V and 3000A.	Surge suppressor
Sag	Momentary voltage drop from 10% to 90% of normal voltage for a few seconds to one minute.	UPS
Brownout	Sustained voltage drop of up to half the normal voltage. Can last for minutes to hours.	UPS
Blackout	Total loss of power for an extended period of time	UPS or generator

Compliance with Local Government Regulations

Compliance with local government regulations is a necessary part of legal and safe electronics and technology work. Check with your local municipality for recommended electronics recycling locations that comply with an ISO 14001 certification. Follow regulations for ventilation and other workplace issues as well.

Addressing Prohibited Content or Activity

220-1002: Objective 4.6: Explain the processes for addressing prohibited content/ activity, and privacy, licensing, and policy concepts.

Network administrators have several challenges in keeping a network safe and secure. While many tools and procedures are utilized to prevent misuse of resources, security incidents are bound to happen. Not all of them come from outside the network. In fact, some of the most perilous threats come from users inside the organization violating security rules or rules of acceptable use.

Managing user content, activity, and privacy is challenging because users and managers do not all understand these concepts in the same way. So it is important for an organization to go through the process of creating a well-defined policy spelling out what is and is not acceptable use and practice and providing information about consequences for not complying with the organization's standards while using its equipment. This section details the process of responding to violation incidents.

For the sake of studying the incident response process, prohibited content and activity can be defined as follows:

■ Any content stored on a company-owned or company-managed computer, mobile device, or network that is contrary to organizational policy

■ Any activity performed or received by a company-owned or company-managed computer, mobile device, or network that is contrary to organizational policy

When someone has been found to have acted inappropriately, having a response and process in place will protect the organization and the users.

Incident Response

Incident response is the set of procedures that any investigator follows when examining a technology incident. The initial response and documentation are important because that information and evidence gathered there will guide the rest of the process.

First Response

When an incident is reported, the responder's first task is to identify exactly what happened. He must first *identify* whether this is a simple problem that needs trouble-shooting or an incident that needs to be escalated. The key to any problem solving is understanding what problem needs to be resolved.

For example, if a person has prohibited content on a computer, this can be considered an incident, and as part of first response, the incident should be escalated to the violator's supervisor, with reporting on exactly what was found. Copyrighted information, malware, inappropriate content, and stolen information could all be considered prohibited.

Once the problem had been identified, it is essential that it be *reported through proper channels*, and then steps must be taken to ensure **data/device preservation**. This often means making a backup of the computer's image using special software. However, depending on the organization's policies, it may be better to leave everything as is and wait for a computer forensics expert or a security analyst. It is important to preserve the scene for that other person so that he or she can collect evidence.

Documentation

It is essential to document everything that is found and anything that happens after the initial report. If the organization doesn't have set reporting formats, then writing down the details and/or taking pictures is appropriate. It is important that any and all information be available to the supervisor. If the first responder is able to fix the problem and no other specialists are required, the **documentation process** can continue through to the completion of the task (and beyond, while monitoring the system). Documentation should include any processes, procedures, and user training that might be necessary to avoid a similar incident in the future.

Chain of Custody

If preserving evidence is required, one way of doing this is to set up a **chain of custody**—the chronological documentation or paper trail of evidence. It should be initiated at the start of any investigation and should include tracking of evidence/documenting process, who had custody of the evidence all the way up to litigation (if necessary), and verification that the evidence has not been modified or tampered with.

NOTE   A PC tech will not normally get too involved with investigations, but the A+ exam covers the basic concepts of first response, documentation, and chain of custody.

Licensing

Software licensing issues of all types can complicate your life as a PC tech. It's important to realize that carelessness with licensing could put your company in financial and legal jeopardy.

Some issues to watch out for include:

- The limitations created by digital rights management (DRM)
- End-user license agreements (EULAs)
- Open source vs. commercial licenses
- Personal license vs. enterprise licenses

DRM

Digital rights management (DRM) is the general term for software or service mechanisms that limit the end user's rights to copy, transfer, or use software or digital media. Some examples of DRM include:

- Restrictions on digital music playback when the music has been burned to an audio CD, such as with Apple iTunes
- Limits on the number of systems that can use an application at the same time, such as Adobe Creative Cloud or Microsoft Office 365

When upgrading a system that is running DRM-based apps, it's important to determine in advance how the upgrade might affect DRM issues. In some cases, moving to a new OS might be transparent to the DRM system, while in other cases, the DRM system might require the user to confirm the license.

When removing from service a system that is running DRM-based apps, it's important to determine in advance how to properly move the DRM-based apps or DRM-limited files to another system. It might be necessary to remove authorization from the system before a new system can be authorized to use the app.

EULA

An *end-user license agreement (EULA)* restricts how an app can be used and what transfer rights are available. If an app was preinstalled on a system, its licensing might not allow for the app to be moved to another system. Be sure to check the EULA for a particular app or for an operating system with bundled apps to determine what can legally be done with the operating system and apps when the original computer is withdrawn from service or upgraded to a new operating system.

Understanding Open Source and Commercial Licenses

According to the Open Source Initiative website (https://opensource.org/osd):

> Generally, *open source* software is software that can be freely accessed, used, changed, and shared (in modified or unmodified form) by anyone. Open source software is made by many people, and distributed under licenses that comply with The Open Source Definition.

Linux operating system distributions (known as "distros") and Linux apps are some of the most well-known examples of open source software.

Open source software can be used for commercial purposes, and it can even be sold. However, open source licenses require that the sellers of open source software not limit the rights of purchasers to use, change, or share the software. The rights obtained when Company A, for example, starts using Software X must be passed on to Company B when Company A sells any version of Software X, and so on. These rights include source code.

NOTE   The Open Source Initiative website offers a variety of OSI-approved licenses that can be used as models for licensing; see https://opensource.org/licenses.

Most commercial software other than open source can be called "closed source." For example, Microsoft Windows, Apple macOS, Adobe Creative Cloud, and Microsoft Office are examples of operating systems and apps that use *commercial licenses*. Unlike an open source license, which permits free use, modification, and sharing of source code, commercial licenses do not cover source code (the actual instructions used to make the software) and limit how licensees can use object code (the program). For example, Adobe Creative Cloud subscriptions can be used on two computers (for example, a work and a home or travel computer) but not at the same time. If a third computer has Adobe Creative Cloud installed, Adobe permits Creative Cloud apps to run on the additional device if the other computers' licenses are deactivated by Creative Cloud.

Personal vs. Enterprise Licenses

Personal licenses are software licenses provided for computers purchased at retail or online stores and downloaded or packaged apps designed for use by individuals. Essentially, these licenses limit the use of the software to one or a very small number of computers in the same household (for example, antivirus utilities designed for up to five Windows, macOS, or mobile devices).

Enterprise licenses can differ from personal software licenses in several ways:

- Software covered by enterprise licenses includes management and security features designed for the enterprise.

- Software covered by enterprise licenses have much different rules for software upgrades than personal-licensed software.

- Software covered by enterprise licenses may be licensed per seat, per device, per processor, or in other ways.

- Some personal software licenses, such as for Microsoft Office Home and Student, are specifically restricted from being used in business.

The company can face serious fines if software licensing terms are not followed. A supervisor should be notified if a technician is asked to violate the terms of a license.

Regulated Data

Four types of data are regulated and must be protected by network administrators. They are listed with the acronym first since that is how they are referred to in the field:

- *PII*: Personally identifiable information, such as a person's name, address, driver's license number, credit card numbers, and Social Security number

- *PCI*: Payment Card Industry standards that are in place to protect credit cardholders' data, including card numbers and address and credit information

- *GDPR*: General Data Protection Regulation, enacted in Europe to protect several types of data, including health, biometrics, genetic, and criminal history

- *PHI*: Protected health information (a part of the HIPAA law), which covers health status as well as payment methods, account numbers, and beneficiaries

Any organization that holds or uses this type of information has responsibility for protecting it from identity thieves. There have been many serious (and very expensive) data breach cases in recent history, and some of them have had crippling effects on the companies that lost data. A computer technician's role in protecting data includes:

- Configuring systems to use secure cloud storage rather than locally stored sensitive information on laptops and mobile devices

- Configuring and using strong encryption on wireless networks and point-of-sale (POS) systems

- Using full-disk encryption such as BitLocker, BitLocker To Go or similar products on laptops and mobile devices that store or access sensitive data

- Configuring hardware and software firewalls to protect sensitive data

- Educating users on methods to remove personally identifiable information from documents, photos, and other files that might be shared or posted online

Of course, it is important to protect users and the organization by keeping up with recent developments in both knowledge and application of these policies and best practices. Understanding them is necessary for the A+ exam.

Communication Techniques and Professionalism

220-1002: Objective 4.7: Given a scenario, use proper communication techniques and professionalism.

Of all the technical skills a PC support technician should have in her toolkit, strong communication skills are among the most enduring and vital. No matter what version of software or generation of hardware is in use, effective written and oral communication are needed to identify and document issues and to train users in how to function in their technical environment. Employers consistently rank communication as the most desirable "soft skill" (as opposed to hard technical skill) they look for when hiring new employees. This section highlights aspects of communication and professionalism expected of a PC support technician.

Use Proper Language

Using proper language is one way to instill confidence in the people you are trying to help. Proper language is whatever is customary and professional in your work environment. Cursing and swearing are never considered acceptable, even if some at work may speak this way. Speak clearly and in a simple, concise, and respectful manner. Use proper English and no slang. Avoid computer jargon and acronyms such as "WPA2" or "TCP/IP" that might confuse the customer.

Maintain a Positive Attitude/Project Confidence

Customers watch technicians while they work on their problems, and they can lose confidence when the tech sounds or looks worried. A bad service tech projects arrogance by rejecting or brushing aside questions and comments, and a good one maintains the attitude that the problem will be solved. A customer is reassured when a technician is confident that by using the right tools and resources, the problem will be solved.

Actively Listen to the Customer

The key to getting information from a customer is *active listening*, a conversational skill that includes making eye contact, taking notes, and encouraging open-ended answers without interrupting. Listen carefully to what someone has to say about a problem he or she is experiencing. What the person says might provide clues about the reason for the problem. Even when a customer admits to being a nontechnical person or even a technophobe, listen carefully.

Be Culturally Sensitive

Nations, organizations, and departments all have cultures—ways of communicating, rituals to follow, and definitions of good manners. Cultural sensitivity helps prevent barriers to good communications. Be sure to use the appropriate honorific titles (Mr., Ms., Mrs., and so on), pick up visual and verbal cues, and use professional titles when applicable (doctor, professor, and so on). When a person has an accent and is hard to understand, concentrate and ask the person to repeat anything that you didn't understand.

Be Punctual

Punctuality is probably the most important ingredient in customer relationships. If you have to be late, contact the customer. You might also consider contacting your supervisor, depending on how late you are. Reliability is always highly valued by clients.

Avoid Distractions

Don't let your cell phone, an event on TV, or the view out the corner office window get between you and a solution. Avoid distractions and/or interruptions when talking with customers. Stay focused on what your customer is telling you, and the solution will be easier to find. Don't talk with other coworkers while interacting with customers. Don't use social media sites or use text messaging for non-work-related issues; when you send a text to ask for help, make sure your customer knows why you are sending a text. Avoid personal interruptions except in an emergency. Respect the customer's time and save personal calls for breaks or when the job is finished. Customers usually pay by the hour, and they deserve every minute of your attention.

Dealing with Difficult Customers or Situations

Solving technology problems is difficult, and customers can make it harder. These tips should help mitigate a difficult situation:

- **No matter how tough the problem (or the customer), avoid arguing with customers and don't be defensive:** The job is to solve the customer's problem, and doing that well sometimes takes a lot of patience.

- **Do not minimize customers' problems:** Problems that seem simple to a technician can be very difficult for a customer. Keep in mind that every person with a broken PC may be losing valuable personal or business data; they may even lose enough data to wipe out a business.

- **No matter how incorrect their actions or how poor their judgment, avoid being judgmental of your customers:** Again, focus on the problem and finding a solution. Forming opinions based on your personal feelings usually has a bad outcome.

- **Clarify customer statements:** Ask the customer open-ended questions to further identify what the issue is and narrow the scope of the problem. Clarify by repeating the problem back to the customer. Restate the issue to verify everyone's understanding of the problem.

- **Don't disclose experiences on social media:** A customer relationship is to be valued, and gossiping on social media tells the customer that you don't value customer privacy.

Set and Meet Expectations/Timeline and Communicate Status with the Customer

Many of the communication skills discussed in this section come together in the process of setting and meeting customer expectations. There are many ways expectations and communication can be strengthened, including the following:

- Coming in the door with a smile and getting right to work on determining the problem sets the tone for the customer's experience. Clearly state what the problem is, what the plan is to fix it, how long it will take, and, if known, any extra costs. Minimizing surprises is always appreciated by clients.

- Create a timeline of the steps and when you expect to meet them; communicate the status with the customer often.

- If applicable, offer different repair/replacement options and allow the customer to select the one that works best in the situation.

- Provide and organize proper documentation of any services and products that are offered. After the job is complete, document the problem, process, and solution.

- Follow up with the customer at a later date to verify continued satisfaction.

Dealing Appropriately with Customers' Confidential and Private Materials

Whether working in the customer's office or at a workbench, remember that the customer's computer information, printouts, and other information is the customer's, and such data needs to be kept private. In many cases, this is not just good practice but the law.

Asking a customer to move confidential materials such as bank statements, accounting information, legal documents, and other top-secret company information to another area will protect you from any suspicion later on. Private materials belonging to the customer personally should also be moved out of the way.

Scripting Basics

220-1002: Objective 4.8: Identify the basics of scripting.

PC technicians are often called upon to work on, configure, and update many computers or other devices at one time, and that can mean repeating the same tasks on each machine. Waiting for long processes to run or updates to install on each machine can take a lot of time, but by writing a script with all of the commands and inputs, the updates can be run automatically, saving valuable time and money.

Programming is a very important technical skill, but it is beyond the scope of the CompTIA A+ exam. However, being able to identify the basics of scripting is important as running scripts as a PC tech or as an administrator is an invaluable asset.

Script File Types

Script files are text files that contain instructions, or commands that a computer will follow to perform a task. They can be straight text commands of an OS or written in a scripting language (which is a limited kind of programming language) that can be run on the computer and interpreted by the operating system. The operating system then performs the commands in the script to complete the tasks. Table 9-5 identifies and briefly describes the six common scripting languages required for the A+ exam. It is important to be able to recognize them by their file extensions.

Table 9-5 Basic Scripting Languages

Extension	Language	Basic Information
.bat	Windows batch file	Batch files are script files that are strictly Windows based. They are text files that contain commands or instructions for the command line interpreter to execute. The instructions in a batch file can only be interpreted by the Windows operating system.
.ps1	PowerShell	Windows PowerShell is a tool to help technicians and network administrators automate support functions through the use of scripts and snippets. Windows 7, 8, and 10 ship with PowerShell.
.vbs	VBScript	VBScript, a scripting language developed by Microsoft, is considered a subset of the Visual Basic programming language. It was designed specifically for use with Microsoft's Internet Explorer. It gives web pages a level of interactivity.
.sh	Linux shell script	A shell script is a text file that contains a sequence of commands for a Linux or UNIX-based system. Shell scripts may not run correctly on a Windows system. Linux has had several shells, and BASH (Bourne-Again Shell) is the most common of them.
.py	Python	Shell is known as Python Interactive Shell. Python is often a good choice for those beginning to learn programming. It is relatively easy to learn, and Python scripts can run on most operating systems.
.js	JavaScript	JavaScript is a programming language that has many uses today. It is valuable for creating scripts because it can be run on any operating system. It is usually written into web pages to create client interactions; JavaScript is read by the browser. Creating and running command line JavaScript requires installing Node.js.

Scripts can be opened and read or edited in basic text editors such as Notepad or in special programming environments that assist with commands and testing of scripts. These are often referred to as "shells," and they are designed to assist in script writing. Figure 9-12 shows a basic "Hello World" script in Windows PowerShell. Note that the file was written in Notepad and saved as scriptdemo.ps1, using the filename extension for PowerShell. The entire text of the script is:

Write host "Hello World"

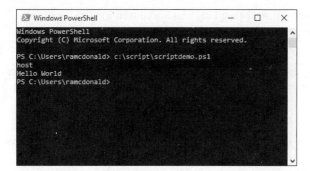

FIGURE 9-12   Basic Script in Windows PowerShell

Basic Script Constructs

A common frustration for people new to scripting is "fat fingering" a script with a wrong character or number and having even this type of small error cause the script to fail. All computer languages follow strict command structures and syntax, and while shells take away some of the burden, syntax still needs to be correct.

Basic Data Types

Scripts are written in coding languages humans recognize, and then the code is interpreted into a machine language that the computer uses to execute the commands. Scripting languages are interpreted by a computer rather than compiled like other programming languages. When writing scripts, coders use different data types to inform the computer about how to process different kinds of data. The basic data types are:

- **Integer:** *Integers* are whole numbers that do not have any fractional part. They can be positive or negative, and zero is considered an integer. Examples of whole numbers are 0, 1, –273, and 1,564.

- **Floating point number:** Floating point (fp) numbers have fractions and may also contain exponents. Decimals can "float" into different positions to make fractional numbers.

- **Character:** A character (char) can be a letter of the alphabet, a symbol, or even a number. These are textual characters, so even if it is a number, say 7, the computer will read it as text and not perform calculations with it. Examples include A, n, 8, and %.

- **Strings:** A *string* is a sequence of characters that are grouped together to represent one data type. A string is usually enclosed in quotation marks so the computer recognizes the parts of the string as a single object. For example, "This is my text string" can be coded as an operational value.

NOTE Integers and strings are noted in Objective 4.8 for the A+ 220-1002 exam.

Data types used can vary by scripting language, but the ones listed here are common to all languages. Scripts can use several types of data; Table 9-6 summarizes the basic types.

Table 9-6 Data Types

Data Type	Description	Examples
Integer	Whole numbers	1, 23, 795
Floating point number	Non-whole numbers	1.5, 88.8, 99.999
Character	Letter or other special character	A, l., &%
String	String or group of characters	"Hello World", "numbers to 250"

Environmental Variables

An *environmental variable* allows a single script to run yet still have sources in various places. For example, if an update of three files is needed, but the files are in different places, the script writer can insert the locations of the files where a variable was identified in the script. An environmental variable makes an object more dynamic.

Variables and Loops

The strict construction of code still allows for *variables*—or parts of the instructions that can change while the script is run. For example, if a script is run to install updates X, Y, and Z, the script can be run three times with the variable first being X, then changing to Y, then changing to Z.

As another example of a script *loop*, say that a lab with 20 computers needs files updated. The script may loop 20 times, once for each computer in the lab. After 20 loops, it stops.

This brief introduction to scripting covers the basics mentioned in the CompTIA A+ objectives, but there is much more to learn. The following links provide more information about scripting in PowerShell, Linux, Python, and JavaScript:

- https://docs.microsoft.com/en-us/powershell/scripting/components/ise/how-to-write-and-run-scripts-in-the-windows-powershell-ise?view=powershell-6

- https://help.ubuntu.com/community/Beginners/BashScripting

- https://www.python.org

- https://www.javascript.com

Remote Access Technologies

220-1002: Objective 4.9: Given a scenario, use remote access technologies.

It is common for a technician to have to access client computers or virtual computers remotely. The machines may be in another part of the network operations center or at the homes of clients working in other parts of the world. Remote access allows a user to see and control what is going on in another computer or device in a different location. Examples of using remote access include:

- A support technician accessing a client's computer to troubleshoot or update a PC

- A network administrator adjusting settings on a server in another part of the network

- A network administrator needing to access a router, switch, firewall, or other network device to manage traffic. (These devices usually do not have keyboards or monitors for input or output.)

A few protocols and applications have long been used for remote access, and third-party applications have become more prevalent. This section describes examples of remote access technology.

RDP

Remote Desktop Protocol (RDP) was developed by Microsoft to allow a user to securely connect to a remote computer in order to perform services or support another user. The protocol allows for encrypted access with screen capture, mouse, and keyboard functions. Common tasks with the remote connections are support and management of remote computers.

RDP is based on a client/server model. The user is the client, and the remote Windows computer enables the RDP server. The remote computer serves a graphic capture of the screen to the support tech. The support tech can manipulate the mouse and keyboard of the remote computer as well. So if a remote worker needs tech support, the technician can instruct the worker to enable RDP server (if it isn't already enabled) and remotely see what is going on. This can greatly reduce the cost of tech services in a company.

RDP is a proprietary Microsoft protocol that is preinstalled on Windows, but macOS and Linux versions of both server and client are available as well. To enable Remote Desktop in Windows 10, go to **Settings > System > Remote Desktop**. Remember that RDP uses port 3389, which needs to be opened in the firewall. RDP is discussed in detail in Chapter 6, "Operating Systems."

NOTE This type of software is known as "thin client" software because only the mouse movement, keyboard activity, and screenshot captures are sent across the network, requiring very low bandwidth. Citrix, working with Microsoft, was the pioneer of thin client software, but many other vendors now compete in the market.

Telnet

Telnet enables a user to make a text-based connection to a remote computer or networking device and use it as if he or she were a user sitting right in front of it.

Windows and Linux contain a command line Telnet program. To open a connection to a remote computer, open a command prompt (Windows) or Terminal session (Linux) and type **telnet** and press the **Enter** key to open the Telnet command prompt.

Another option is to download the Telnet application and open it to configure settings. Telnet can connect via IP connection or a VTY modem connection. Once it is configured, a Telnet session is established as long as the remote computer is configured to accept a Telnet connection and any authentication passwords are correct. Typically, Telnet uses TCP port 23.

macOS includes a menu-driven Telnet program available from Terminal.

NOTE Telnet does not encrypt content, so passwords may be discovered by hackers. Using SSH is a way to overcome the security concerns of Telnet.

SSH

Secure Shell (SSH) allows data to be exchanged between computers on a secured channel. This protocol offers a more secure option than FTP and Telnet. The Secure Shell server uses TCP port 22.

Third-Party Tools

There has been a market for specialized tools or third-party development of terminal services like Telnet and SSH, as well as FTP, for years. Some tools are free, and others have free client software but paid server software; still others are pay only. Often a free 30-day download is available to individuals but not to companies.

Sometimes Windows incorporates third-party tools into the OS, but the options available may vary from those of the third parties that created the tools. For example, PuTTY (https://www.putty.org) is an open source application that provides connectivity software for Telnet and SSH connections.

File Sharing

Several protocols use SSH as a way of making a secure connection. One of these is Secure File Transfer Protocol (SFTP). Regular FTP, which was designed decades ago, before security was a major concern, can be insecure. SFTP combats this by providing file access over a reliable data stream, generated and protected by SSH.

FTP uses two ports during a file transfer session: port 21 to initiate a connection and port 20 to establish a connection to transfer files.

Many large companies use FTP to manage large documents and files that need to be shared to a distributed workforce. SolarWinds's Serv-U (https://www.serv-u.com) is a commercial provider of FTP, and FileZilla (https://sourceforge.net/projects/filezilla/) is an open source FTP application that works for Windows, macOS, and Linux.

Cloud file management is now doing much of the work FTP has performed in the past. Examples of cloud storage providers are Dropbox, Google Drive, Microsoft OneDrive, and Amazon Drive. There is also widening acceptance of cloud-based document sharing, such as Google Docs, where documents are created and edited in a shared cloud environment. Most cloud-based file transfers are faster and easier than FTP, but FTP is in wide use and easy to manage, so technicians will encounter it for the foreseeable future.

Exam Preparation Tasks

As mentioned in the section "How to Use This Book" in the Introduction, you have a couple of choices for exam preparation: the exercises here, Chapter 10, "Final Preparation," and the exam simulation questions in the Pearson Test Prep Software Online.

Review All the Key Topics

Review the most important topics in the chapter, noted with the Key Topic icon in the outer margin of the page. Table 9-7 lists these key topics and the page number on which each is found.

Table 9-7   Key Topics for Chapter 9

Key Topic Element	Description	Page Number
Section	Change Management	801
List	Backup and Recovery	804
Section	Local Storage vs. Cloud Storage Backups	806
Section	Account Recovery Options	810
Section	Equipment Grounding	811
Section	Component Handling and Storage	813
Figure 9-10	Using an ESD Strap to Help Prevent Damaging ESD When Working on Electronics	816
Section	Toxic Waste Handling	818
List	Proper methods for recycling batteries	819
Section	Personal Safety	820
Paragraph	MSDS	824
Section	Blackouts, Brownouts, and Battery Backup Units	827
Section	Incident Response	828
Section	Licensing	830
List	Regulated data	832
Section	Communication Techniques and Professionalism	833
Table 9-5	Basic Scripting Languages	837
Table 9-6	Basic Data Types	839

Complete the Tables and Lists from Memory

Print a copy of Appendix C, "Memory Tables" (found online), or at least the section for this chapter, and complete the tables and lists from memory. Appendix D, "Answers to Memory Tables," also online, includes completed tables and lists to check your work.

Define Key Terms

Define the following key terms from this chapter and check your answers in the glossary:

whitepaper, acceptable use policy (AUP), change management, system image backup, uninterruptable power supply (UPS), surge protector, grounding, electrostatic discharge (ESD), self-grounding, toxic waste handling, cathode ray tube (CRT) display, safety data sheet (SDS), blackout, brownout, data/ device preservation, documentation process, chain of custody, software licensing, digital rights management (DRM), end-user license agreement (EULA), open source, commercial license, personal license, enterprise license, PII, PCI, GDPR, PHI, active listening, integer, string, environmental variable, variable, loop, Remote Desktop Protocol (RDP), Telnet, Secure Shell (SSH)

Answer Review Questions

1. Identify the parts of the plug in the following figure.

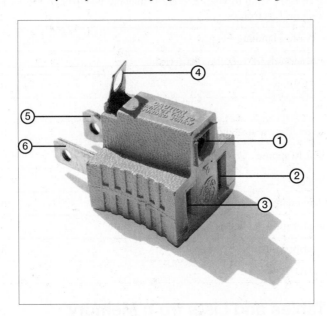

   a. Hot prong

   b. Hot connector

   c. Neutral prong

   d. Neutral connector

   e. Ground loop

   f. Ground connector

2. The object in the following figure is an electrical outlet tester. What does this outlet tester tell you about the outlet into which it is currently plugged?

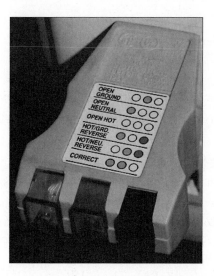

a. The ground wire is faulty.

b. The hot wire is faulty.

c. The neutral wire is faulty.

d. All of the wires are correct.

3. Which of the following statements best defines ESD?

a. Electronic shutdown device

b. Electrostatic discharge

c. Environmentally sustainable development

d. Energy sensitive differential

4. Which of the following can be used as protection against ESD? (Choose all that apply.)

a. An antistatic bag

b. A 3-wire to 2-wire adapter

c. An ESD mat

d. An ESD strap

5. Which of the following increases the likelihood of ESD?

    a. Carpet on the floor

    b. Increasing the humidity of the room

    c. Increasing the room temperature

    d. Rubber-soled shoes

6. Which of the following best describes how to dispose of used batteries?

    a. Open the batteries and very carefully remove their lead cores before recycling.

    b. Recycle batteries in the recycling bin.

    c. Recycle NiMH and Li-Ion in the recycling bin; NiCad batteries can be disposed of in the trash.

    d. Return the batteries to an electronics store for recycling.

7. Which of the following is a hazard posed by a CRT monitor?

    a. A CRT display presents an electrical shock hazard.

    b. A CRT display presents a fire hazard due to overheating.

    c. A CRT display presents a radiation hazard through the CRT display screen.

    d. A CRT display presents a toxic chemical hazard.

8. Which class of fire extinguisher should be used on an electrical fire?

    a. Class A

    b. Class B

    c. Class C

    d. Class D

9. When selecting an air filter mask, which category provides the highest level of protection?

    a. A

    b. N

    c. P

    d. R

10. Which of the following statements best describes an MSDS?

    a. An MSDS provides simultaneous accessibility to multiple data sources.

    b. An MSDS provides safety information concerning storage, spills, and accidental exposure to dangerous chemicals.

    c. An MSDS helps protect computer components from damage due to ESD.

    d. An MSDS is a legal document used to establish chain of custody in legal cases.

11. Which of the following is the term for a short increase in AC voltage?

    a. Blackout

    b. Brownout

    c. Whiteout

    d. Power surge

12. Which of the following best describes the function of a UPS in a technology environment?

    a. A UPS is a battery backup.

    b. A UPS is a rating for system performance.

    c. A UPS is a security program.

    d. A UPS is a package delivery company.

13. Which of the following best describes chain of custody?

    a. Chain of custody is documentation of the ownership of a computer or of computer components.

    b. Chain of custody is documentation of who was in possession of evidence relative to an investigation.

    c. Chain of custody is documentation of how a computer was repaired, such as what was done and who did it.

    d. Chain of custody is documentation of possession of a computer, not related to ownership.

14. Which of the following best describes open source software? (Choose all that apply.)

    a. Open source software can be used for free.

    b. Open source software can be used for commercial purposes.

    c. Open source software can be sold.

    d. Open source software can be modified.

15. As a computer technician, what can you do to help your clients protect their personal information? (Choose all that apply.)

   a. You can advise them to store their sensitive information using cloud storage instead of local storage.

   b. You can advise them to use BitLocker encryption.

   c. You can advise them to store sensitive information on a PC's hard drive rather than with the backup files.

   d. You can advise them to use firewalls to prevent hacker intrusions.

16. Which of the following statements describes the best way to explain a problem to a customer?

   a. Use as much technical vocabulary as possible because this makes you sound knowledgeable and will impress the customer.

   b. Explain as little as possible because the customer probably would not understand the explanation, and it would only confuse him.

   c. Explain the problem in non-technical terms and offer to show the customer what the problem was and how you fixed it.

   d. Ask the customer not to be concerned about the details and assure him that you will take care of the problem.

17. Ellen is working on a workstation in the Accounting department. In an open browser tab she notices a meme with racist comments and graphic pictures. What is the next step Ellen should take?

   a. Finish fixing the problem and warn the user that this content is against the AUP

   b. Call corporate security

   c. Contact her supervisor

   d. Contact the user's supervisor

18. Fatima was helping Mark, a new employee having trouble accessing the network folders he needed for his new assignments. When she asked him to describe the problems, she took notes, did not interrupt, and restated his problem in her own words to make sure she understood. Which customer service skill was Fatima demonstrating?

   a. Presumptive listening

   b. Cultural sensitivity

   c. Active listening

   d. Dealing with a difficult customer

19. Martin, a tech support worker on a macOS helpdesk, took a support call from Sarah, and he soon determined that Sarah's laptop needed a few settings changed. He had Sarah allow him secure access to her desktop, and he was able to control her mouse and make the necessary changes. Which protocol is it likely that Martin and Sarah's computers were using during that help session?

    a. Telnet

    b. RTP

    c. RDP

    d. FTP

20. Jess and Hiroko have to update several computers, and their lab manager has written a basic script to speed up the process. They are given a flash drive with four files on it, but the one they want is written in a shell for Linux machines. Which file extension is likely the one they want to use?

    a. update.js

    b. update.sh

    c. update.py

    d. update.bat

21. When Josh is unable to answer a question about a new type of software coming on the market and how his customer might implement it, what action should he take?

    a. Give the best answer possible with the knowledge he has

    b. Look for a whitepaper online

    c. Send the client to the software developer's web page

    d. Refer the question to his boss

22. When Carla, who works in payroll, got to work one day and realized she no longer had access to employee wellness bonus pay information that was key to her job. Later she found out that the health care provider implemented a new reporting system that separated accounting reports from private wellness records. What is this most likely an example of?

    a. Not getting stakeholder feedback

    b. Poor password management

    c. Domain failure

    d. The knowledge base not being updated

## CHAPTER 10

Final Preparation

In this chapter we demystify the certification preparation process for you. This includes taking a more detailed look at the actual certification exam itself.

This chapter shares some helpful ideas on ensuring that you are ready for the exams. Many people become anxious about taking exams, and our hope is that this chapter will give you the tools to build confidence for exam day.

The first nine chapters of this book cover the technologies, protocols, design concepts, and considerations required to be prepared to pass the CompTIA A+ Core 1 (220-1001) and Core 2 (220-1002) exams. While these chapters supply the detailed information, most people need more preparation than just reading the first nine chapters of this book. This chapter provides a set of tools and a study plan to help you complete your preparation for the exams.

This short chapter has four main sections. The first section lists the CompTIA A+ 220-1001 and 220-1002 exam information and breakdown. The second section shares some important tips to keep in mind to ensure that you are ready for this exam. The third section discusses exam preparation tools that may be useful at this point in the study process. The final section of this chapter lists a suggested study plan to follow once you have completed all the earlier chapters in this book.

NOTE   Note that Appendix C, "Memory Tables," and Appendix D, "Answer Key to Memory Tables," exist as digital appendixes on the website for this book, which you can access by going to www.pearsonITcertification.com/register, registering your book, and entering this book's ISBN: **9780789760517**.

Exam Information

Here are details you should be aware of regarding the two exams that map to this text.

> **Exam ID codes:** 220-1001 (Core 1) and 220-1002 (Core 2)
>
> **Question types:** Multiple-choice, drag-and-drops, and performance-based questions

Number of questions: Maximum of 90 per exam

Time limit: 90 minutes per exam

Required passing score: 220-1001: 675 (on a scale of 100–900); 220-1002: 700 (on a scale of 100–900)

Available languages (subject to change): English, German, Japanese, Portuguese, Simplified Chinese, and Spanish

Exam fee (subject to change): US$219 per exam

CompTIA A+ 220-1001 covers PC hardware and peripherals, mobile device hardware, and networking and troubleshooting of hardware and network connectivity issues.

CompTIA A+ 220-1002 covers installing and configuring operating systems, including Windows, iOS, Android, macOS, and Linux. It also addresses security, the fundamentals of cloud computing, and operational procedures.

CompTIA A+ is the preferred qualifying credential for technical support and IT operational roles. It is about much more than PC repair:

- Candidates are better prepared to troubleshoot and solve problems.

- Technicians understand a wide variety of issues, ranging from networking and operating systems to mobile devices and security.

- A+ supports the ability to connect users to the data they need to do their jobs, regardless of the devices being used.

Successful candidates will have the knowledge required to:

- Assemble components based on customer requirements.

- Install, configure, and maintain PCs, mobile devices, and software for end users.

- Understand the basics of networking and security forensics.

- Properly and safely diagnose, resolve, and document common hardware and software issues.

- Apply troubleshooting skills.

- Provide appropriate customer support.

- Understand the basics of scripting, virtualization, desktop imaging, and deployment.

Core 1 (220-1001) Exam Domains and Objectives

The 220-1001 exam is broken up into five different domains. Here are those domains and the percentage of the exam for each of the domains:

- 1.0 Mobile Devices: 14 percent
- 2.0 Networking: 20 percent
- 3.0 Hardware: 27 percent
- 4.0 Virtualization and Cloud Computing: 12 percent
- 5.0 Hardware and Network Troubleshooting: 27 percent

Here is the breakdown of the exam objectives for these various domains:

Domain 1: Mobile Devices

- **1.1 Given a scenario, install and configure laptop hardware and components.**

    - Hardware/device replacement
      - Keyboard
      - Hard drive
        - SSD vs. hybrid vs. magnetic disk
        - 1.8in vs. 2.5in
      - Memory
      - Smart card reader
      - Optical drive
      - Wireless card/Bluetooth module
      - Cellular card
      - Video card
      - Mini PCIe
      - Screen
      - DC jack
      - Battery
      - Touchpad
      - Plastics/frames
      - Speaker
      - System board
      - CPU

- **1.2 Given a scenario, install components within the display of a laptop.**

    - Types
      - LCD
      - OLED

- WiFi antenna connector/placement
- Webcam
- Microphone
- Inverter
- Digitizer/touchscreen

- **1.3 Given a scenario, use appropriate laptop features.**

  - Special function keys
    - Dual displays
    - Wireless (on/off)
    - Cellular (on/off)
    - Volume settings
    - Screen brightness
    - Bluetooth (on/off)
    - Keyboard backlight
    - Touchpad (on/off)
    - Screen orientation
    - Media options (fast forward/rewind)
    - GPS (on/off)
    - Airplane mode
  - Docking station
  - Port replicator
  - Physical laptop lock and cable lock
  - Rotating/removable screens

- **1.4 Compare and contrast characteristics of various types of other mobile devices.**

  - Tablets
  - Smartphones
  - Wearable technology devices
    - Smart watches
    - Fitness monitors
    - VR/AR headsets
  - E-readers
  - GPS

- **1.5 Given a scenario, connect and configure accessories and ports of other mobile devices.**

  - Connection types
    - Wired
      - Micro-USB/Mini-USB/USB-C
      - Lightning

- Tethering
- Proprietary vendor-specific ports (communication/power)
  - Wireless
    - NFC
    - Bluetooth
    - IR
    - Hotspot
- Accessories
  - Headsets
  - Speakers
  - Game pads
  - Extra battery packs/battery chargers
  - Protective covers/waterproofing
  - Credit card readers
  - Memory/MicroSD

- **1.6 Given a scenario, configure basic mobile device network connectivity and application support.**

  - Wireless/cellular data network (enable/disable)
    - Hotspot
    - Tethering
    - Airplane mode
  - Bluetooth
    - Enable Bluetooth
    - Enable pairing
    - Find a device for pairing
    - Enter the appropriate pin code
    - Test connectivity
  - Corporate and ISP email configuration
    - POP3
    - IMAP
    - Port and SSL settings
    - S/MIME
  - Integrated commercial provider email configuration
    - iCloud
    - Google/Inbox
    - Exchange Online
    - Yahoo
  - PRI updates/PRL updates/baseband updates
  - Radio firmware
  - IMEI vs. IMSI
  - VPN

- **1.7 Given a scenario, use methods to perform mobile device synchronization.**
  - Synchronization methods
    - Synchronize to the cloud
    - Synchronize to the desktop
    - Synchronize to the automobile
  - Types of data to synchronize
    - Contacts
    - Applications
    - Email
    - Pictures
    - Music
    - Videos
    - Calendar
    - Bookmarks
    - Documents
    - Location data
    - Social media data
    - E-books
    - Passwords
  - Mutual authentication for multiple services (SSO)
  - Software requirements to install the application on the PC
  - Connection types to enable synchronization

Domain 2: Networking

- **2.1 Compare and contrast TCP and UDP ports, protocols, and their purposes.**
  - Ports and protocols
    - 21 – FTP
    - 22 – SSH
    - 23 – Telnet
    - 25 – SMTP
    - 53 – DNS
    - 80 – HTTP
    - 110 – POP3
    - 143 – IMAP
    - 443 – HTTPS
    - 3389 – RDP
    - 137-139 – NetBIOS/NetBT
    - 445 – SMB/CIFS

- — 427 – SLP
- — 548 – AFP
- — 67/68 – DHCP
- — 389 – LDAP
- — 161/162 – SNMP
- ■ TCP vs. UDP

- ■ **2.2 Compare and contrast common networking hardware devices.**

  - ■ Routers
  - ■ Switches
    - — Managed
    - — Unmanaged
  - ■ Access points
  - ■ Cloud-based network controller
  - ■ Firewall
  - ■ Network interface card
  - ■ Repeater
  - ■ Hub
  - ■ Cable/DSL modem
  - ■ Bridge
  - ■ Patch panel
  - ■ Power over Ethernet (PoE)
    - — Injectors
    - — Switch
  - ■ Ethernet over Power

- ■ **2.3 Given a scenario, install and configure a basic wired/wireless SOHO network.**

  - ■ Router/switch functionality
  - ■ Access point settings
  - ■ IP addressing
  - ■ NIC configuration
    - — Wired
    - — Wireless
  - ■ End-user device configuration
  - ■ IoT device configuration
    - — Thermostat
    - — Light switches
    - — Security cameras
    - — Door locks
    - — Voice-enabled, smart speaker/digital assistant

- Cable/DSL modem configuration
- Firewall settings
  - DMZ
  - Port forwarding
  - NAT
  - UPnP
  - Whitelist/blacklist
  - MAC filtering
- QoS
- Wireless settings
  - Encryption
  - Channels
  - QoS

- **2.4 Compare and contrast wireless networking protocols**

  - 802.11a
  - 802.11b
  - 802.11g
  - 802.11n
  - 802.11ac
  - Frequencies
    - 2.4Ghz
    - 5Ghz
  - Channels
    - 1–11
  - Bluetooth
  - NFC
  - RFID
  - Zigbee
  - Z-Wave
  - 3G
  - 4G
  - 5G
  - LTE

- **2.5 Summarize the properties and purposes of services provided by networked hosts.**

  - Server roles
    - Web server
    - File server
    - Print server

- DHCP server
- DNS server
- Proxy server
- Mail server
- Authentication server
- syslog
■ Internet appliance
  - UTM
  - IDS
  - IPS
  - End-point management server
■ Legacy/embedded systems

■ **2.6 Explain common network configuration concepts.**

■ IP addressing
  - Static
  - Dynamic
  - APIPA
  - Link local
■ DNS
■ DHCP
  - Reservations
■ IPv4 vs. IPv6
■ Subnet mask
■ Gateway
■ VPN
■ VLAN
■ NAT

■ **2.7 Compare and contrast Internet connection types, network types, and their features.**

■ Internet connection types
  - Cable
  - DSL
  - Dial-up
  - Fiber
  - Satellite
  - ISDN
  - Cellular

- Tethering
  - Mobile hotspot
- Line-of-sight wireless Internet service
- Network types
  - LAN
  - WAN
  - PAN
  - MAN
  - WMN

- **2.8 Given a scenario, use appropriate networking tools.**

  - Crimper
  - Cable stripper
  - Multimeter
  - Tone generator and probe
  - Cable tester
  - Loopback plug
  - Punchdown tool
  - WiFi analyzer

Domain 3: Hardware

- **3.1 Explain basic cable types, features, and their purposes.**

  - Network cables
    - Ethernet
      - Cat 5
      - Cat 5e
      - Cat 6
      - Plenum
      - Shielded twisted pair
      - Unshielded twisted pair
      - 568A/B
    - Fiber
    - Coaxial
    - Speed and transmission limitations
  - Video cables
    - VGA
    - HDMI
    - Mini-HDMI
    - DisplayPort
    - DVI (DVI-D/DVI-I)

- Multipurpose cables
  - Lightning
  - Thunderbolt
  - USB
  - USB-C
  - USB 2.0
  - USB 3.0
- Peripheral cables
  - Serial
- Hard drive cables
  - SATA
  - IDE
  - SCSI
- Adapters
  - DVI to HDMI
  - USB to Ethernet
  - DVI to VGA

- **3.2 Identify common connector types.**

  - RJ-11
  - RJ-45
  - RS-232
  - BNC
  - RG-59
  - RG-6
  - USB
  - Micro-USB
  - Mini-USB
  - USB-C
  - DB-9
  - Lightning
  - SCSI
  - eSATA
  - Molex

- **3.3 Given a scenario, install RAM types.**

  - RAM types
    - SODIMM
    - DDR2
    - DDR3
    - DDR4

- Single channel
- Dual channel
- Triple channel
- Error correcting
- Parity vs. non-parity

■ **3.4 Given a scenario, select, install and configure storage devices.**

- Optical drives
  - CD-ROM/CD-RW
  - DVD-ROM/DVD-RW/DVD-RW DL
  - Blu-ray
  - BD-R
  - BD-RE
- Solid-state drives
  - M2 drives
  - NVME
  - SATA 2.5
- Magnetic hard drives
  - 5,400rpm
  - 7,200rpm
  - 10,000rpm
  - 15,000rpm
  - Sizes:
    - 2.5
    - 3.5
- Hybrid drives
- Flash
  - SD card
  - CompactFlash
  - Micro-SD card
  - Mini-SD card
  - xD
- Configurations
  - RAID 0, 1, 5, 10
  - Hot swappable

■ **3.5 Given a scenario, install and configure motherboards, CPUs, and add-on cards.**

- Motherboard form factor
  - ATX
  - mATX

- ITX
- mITX
■ Motherboard connectors types
  - PCI
  - PCIe
  - Riser card
  - Socket types
  - SATA
  - IDE
  - Front panel connector
  - Internal USB connector
■ BIOS/UEFI settings
  - Boot options
  - Firmware updates
  - Security settings
  - Interface configurations
  - Security
    • Passwords
    • Drive encryption
      ○ TPM
      ○ LoJack
      ○ Secure boot
■ CMOS battery
■ CPU features
  - Single-core
  - Multicore
  - Virtual technology
  - Hyperthreading
  - Speeds
  - Overclocking
  - Integrated GPU
■ Compatibility
  - AMD
  - Intel
■ Cooling mechanism
  - Fans
  - Heat sink
  - Liquid
  - Thermal paste

- Expansion cards
  - Video cards
    - Onboard
    - Add-on card
  - Sound cards
  - Network interface card
  - USB expansion card
  - eSATA card

- **3.6 Explain the purposes and uses of various peripheral types.**

  - Printer
  - ADF/flatbed scanner
  - Barcode scanner/QR scanner
  - Monitors
  - VR headset
  - Optical
  - DVD drive
  - Mouse
  - Keyboard
  - Touchpad
  - Signature pad
  - Game controllers
  - Camera/webcam
  - Microphone
  - Speakers
  - Headset
  - Projector
    - Lumens/brightness
  - External storage drives
  - KVM
  - Magnetic reader/chip reader
  - NFC/tap pay device
  - Smart card reader

- **3.7 Summarize power supply types and features.**

  - Input 115V vs. 220V
  - Output 5V vs. 12V
  - 24-pin motherboard adapter
  - Wattage rating
  - Number of devices/types of devices to be powered

- **3.8 Given a scenario, select and configure appropriate components for a custom PC configuration to meet customer specifications or needs.**

  - Graphic/CAD/CAM design workstation
    - Multicore processor
    - High-end video
    - Maximum RAM
  - Audio/video editing workstation
    - Specialized audio and video card
    - Large, fast hard drive
    - Dual monitors
  - Virtualization workstation
    - Maximum RAM and CPU cores
  - Gaming PC
    - Multicore processor
    - High-end video/specialized GPU
    - High-definition sound card
    - High-end cooling
  - Standard thick client
    - Desktop applications
    - Meets recommended requirements for selected OS
  - Thin client
    - Basic applications
    - Meets minimum requirements for selected OS
    - Network connectivity
  - Network attached storage device
    - Media streaming
    - File sharing
    - Gigabit NIC
    - RAID array

- **3.9 Given a scenario, install and configure common devices.**

  - Desktop
    - Thin client
    - Thick client
    - Account setup/settings
  - Laptop/common mobile devices
    - Touchpad configuration
    - Touchscreen configuration
    - Application installations/configurations
    - Synchronization settings
    - Account setup/settings
    - Wireless settings

■ **3.10 Given a scenario, configure SOHO multifunction devices/printers and settings.**

- ■ Use appropriate drivers for a given operating system
  - — Configuration settings
    - Duplex
    - Collate
    - Orientation
    - Quality
- ■ Device sharing
  - — Wired
    - USB
    - Serial
    - Ethernet
  - — Wireless
    - Bluetooth
    - 802.11(a, b, g, n, ac)
    - Infrastructure vs. ad hoc
  - — Integrated print server (hardware)
  - — Cloud printing/remote printing
- ■ Public/shared devices
  - — Sharing local/networked device via operating system settings
    - TCP/Bonjour/AirPrint
  - — Data privacy
    - User authentication on the device
    - Hard drive caching

■ **3.11 Given a scenario, install and maintain various print technologies.**

- ■ Laser
  - — Imaging drum, fuser assembly, transfer belt, transfer roller, pickup rollers, separate pads, duplexing assembly
  - — Imaging process: processing, charging, exposing, developing, transferring, fusing, and cleaning
  - — Maintenance: Replace toner, apply maintenance kit, calibrate, clean
- ■ Inkjet
  - — Ink cartridge, print head, roller, feeder, duplexing assembly, carriage, and belt
  - — Calibrate
  - — Maintenance: Clean heads, replace cartridges, calibrate, clear jams

- Thermal
  - Feed assembly, heating element
  - Special thermal paper
  - Maintenance: Replace paper, clean heating element, remove debris
- Impact
  - Print head, ribbon, tractor feed
  - Impact paper
  - Maintenance: Replace ribbon, replace print head, replace paper
- Virtual
  - Print to file
  - Print to PDF
  - Print to XPS
  - Print to image
- 3D printers
  - Plastic filament

Domain 4: Virtualization and Cloud Computing

- **4.1 Compare and contrast cloud computing concepts.**

  - Common cloud models
    - IaaS
    - SaaS
    - PaaS
    - Public vs. private vs. hybrid vs. community
  - Shared resources
    - Internal vs. external
  - Rapid elasticity
  - On-demand
  - Resource pooling
  - Measured service
  - Metered
  - Off-site email applications
  - Cloud file storage services
    - Synchronization apps
  - Virtual application streaming/ cloud-based applications
    - Applications for cell phones/tablets
    - Applications for laptops/desktops
  - Virtual desktop
    - Virtual NIC

■ **4.2 Given a scenario, set up and configure client-side virtualization.**

- ■ Purpose of virtual machines
- ■ Resource requirements
- ■ Emulator requirements
- ■ Security requirements
- ■ Network requirements
- ■ Hypervisor

Domain 5: Hardware and Network Troubleshooting

■ **5.1 Given a scenario, use the best practice methodology to resolve problems.**

- ■ Always consider corporate policies, procedures, and impacts before implementing changes

  - — Identify the problem
    - ● Question the user and identify user changes to computer and perform backups before making changes
    - ● Inquire regarding environmental or infrastructure changes
    - ● Review system and application logs
  - — Establish a theory of probable cause (question the obvious)
    - ● If necessary, conduct external or internal research based on symptoms
  - — Test the theory to determine cause
    - ● Once the theory is confirmed, determine the next steps to resolve problem
    - ● If theory is not confirmed re-establish new theory or escalate
  - — Establish a plan of action to resolve the problem and implement the solution
  - — Verify full system functionality and, if applicable, implement preventive measures
  - — Document findings, actions, and outcomes

■ **5.2 Given a scenario, troubleshoot problems related to motherboards, RAM, CPUs, and power.**

- ■ Common symptoms
- ■ Unexpected shutdowns
- ■ System lockups
- ■ POST code beeps
- ■ Blank screen on bootup
- ■ BIOS time and setting resets
- ■ Attempts to boot to incorrect device

- Continuous reboots
- No power
- Overheating
- Loud noise
- Intermittent device failure
- Fans spin – no power to other devices
- Indicator lights
- Smoke
- Burning smell
- Proprietary crash screens (BSOD/pin wheel)
- Distended capacitors
- Log entries and error messages

- **5.3 Given a scenario, troubleshoot hard drives and RAID arrays.**

  - Common symptoms
    - Read/write failure
    - Slow performance
    - Loud clicking noise
    - Failure to boot
    - Drive not recognized
    - OS not found
    - RAID not found
    - RAID stops working
    - Proprietary crash screens (BSOD/pin wheel)
    - S.M.A.R.T. errors

- **5.4 Given a scenario, troubleshoot video, projector, and display issues.**

  - Common symptoms
    - VGA mode
    - No image on screen
    - Overheat shutdown
    - Dead pixels
    - Artifacts
    - Incorrect color patterns
    - Dim image
    - Flickering image
    - Distorted image
    - Distorted geometry
    - Burn-in
    - Oversized images and icons
    - Multiple failed jobs in log

■ **5.5 Given a scenario, troubleshoot common mobile device issues while adhering to the appropriate procedures.**

- ■ Common symptoms
  - — No display
  - — Dim display
  - — Flickering display
  - — Sticking keys
  - — Intermittent wireless
  - — Battery not charging
  - — Ghost cursor/pointer drift
  - — No power
  - — Num lock indicator lights
  - — No wireless connectivity
  - — No Bluetooth connectivity
  - — Cannot display to external monitor
  - — Touchscreen non-responsive
  - — Apps not loading
  - — Slow performance
  - — Unable to decrypt email
  - — Extremely short battery life
  - — Overheating
  - — Frozen system
  - — No sound from speakers
  - — GPS not functioning
  - — Swollen battery
- ■ Disassembling processes for proper reassembly
  - — Document and label cable and screw locations
  - — Organize parts
  - — Refer to manufacturer resources
  - — Use appropriate hand tools

■ **5.6 Given a scenario, troubleshoot printers.**

- ■ Common symptoms
  - — Streaks
  - — Faded prints
  - — Ghost images
  - — Toner not fused to the paper
  - — Creased paper
  - — Paper not feeding
  - — Paper jam

    — No connectivity
    — Garbled characters on paper
    — Vertical lines on page
    — Backed-up print queue
    — Low memory errors
    — Access denied
    — Printer will not print
    — Color prints in wrong print color
    — Unable to install printer
    — Error codes
    — Printing blank pages
    — No image on printer display

- **5.7 Given a scenario, troubleshoot common wired and wireless network problems.**

  - Common symptoms
    - Limited connectivity
    - Unavailable resources
      - Internet
      - Local resources
        - Shares
        - Printers
        - Email
    - No connectivity
    - APIPA/link local address
    - Intermittent connectivity
    - IP conflict
    - Slow transfer speeds
    - Low RF signal
    - SSID not found

Core 2 (220-1002) Exam Domains and Objectives

The 220-1002 exam is broken up into four different domains. Here are those domains and the percentage of the exam for each of the domains:

- 1.0 Operating Systems: 27 percent
- 2.0 Security: 24 percent
- 3.0 Software Troubleshooting: 26 percent
- 4.0 Operational Procedures: 23 percent

Here is the breakdown of the exam objectives for these various domains:

Domain 1: Operating Systems

- **1.1 Compare and contrast common operating system types and their purposes.**

  - 32-bit vs. 64-bit
    - RAM limitations
    - Software compatibility
  - Workstation operating systems
    - Microsoft Windows
    - Apple Macintosh OS
    - Linux
  - Cell phone/tablet operating systems
    - Microsoft Windows
    - Android
    - iOS
    - Chrome OS
  - Vendor-specific limitations
    - End-of-life
    - Update limitations
  - Compatibility concerns between operating systems

- **1.2 Compare and contrast features of Microsoft Windows versions.**

  - Windows 7
  - Windows 8
  - Windows 8.1
  - Windows 10
  - Corporate vs. personal needs
    - Domain access
    - BitLocker
    - Media center
    - BranchCache
    - EFS
  - Desktop styles/user interface

- **1.3 Summarize general OS installation considerations and upgrade methods.**

  - Boot methods
    - USB
    - CD-ROM
    - DVD

- PXE
- Solid state/flash drives
- Netboot
- External/hot-swappable drive
- Internal hard drive (partition)
- Type of installations
  - Unattended installation
  - In-place upgrade
  - Clean install
  - Repair installation
  - Multiboot
  - Remote network installation
  - Image deployment
  - Recovery partition
  - Refresh/restore
- Partitioning
  - Dynamic
  - Basic
  - Primary
  - Extended
  - Logical
  - GPT
- File system types/formatting
  - ExFAT
  - FAT32
  - NTFS
  - CDFS
  - NFS
  - ext3, ext4
  - HFS
  - Swap partition
  - Quick format vs. full format
- Load alternate third-party drivers when necessary
- Workgroup vs. Domain setup
- Time/date/region/language settings
- Driver installation, software, and Windows updates
- Factory recovery partition
- Properly formatted boot drive with the correct partitions/format
- Prerequisites/hardware compatibility
- Application compatibility
- OS compatibility/upgrade path

- **1.4 Given a scenario, use appropriate Microsoft command line tools.**
  - Navigation
    - dir
    - cd
    - ..
  - ipconfig
  - ping
  - tracert
  - netstat
  - nslookup
  - shutdown
  - dism
  - sfc
  - chkdsk
  - diskpart
  - taskkill
  - gpupdate
  - gpresult
  - format
  - copy
  - xcopy
  - robocopy
  - net use
  - net user
  - [command name] /?
  - Commands available with standard privileges vs. administrative privileges

- **1.5 Given a scenario, use Microsoft operating system features and tools.**
  - Administrative
    - Computer Management
    - Device Manager
    - Local Users and Groups
    - Local Security Policy
    - Performance Monitor
    - Services
    - System Configuration
    - Task Scheduler
    - Component Services
    - Data Sources
    - Print Management
    - Windows Memory Diagnostics

- — Windows Firewall
- — Advanced Security
- — Event Viewer
- — User Account Management
- MSConfig
  - — General
  - — Boot
  - — Services
  - — Startup
  - — Tools
- Task Manager
  - — Applications
  - — Processes
  - — Performance
  - — Networking
  - — Users
- Disk Management
  - — Drive status
  - — Mounting
  - — Initializing
  - — Extending partitions
  - — Splitting partitions
  - — Shrink partitions
  - — Assigning/changing drive letters
  - — Adding drives
  - — Adding arrays
  - — Storage spaces
- System utilities
  - — Regedit
  - — Command
  - — Services.msc
  - — MMC
  - — MSTSC
  - — Notepad
  - — Explorer
  - — Msinfo32
  - — DxDiag
  - — Disk Defragmenter
  - — System Restore
  - — Windows Update

- **1.6 Given a scenario, use Microsoft Windows Control Panel utilities.**
  - Internet Options
    - Connections
    - Security
    - General
    - Privacy
    - Programs
    - Advanced
  - Display/Display Settings
    - Resolution
    - Color depth
    - Refresh rate
  - User Accounts
  - Folder Options
    - View hidden files
    - Hide extensions
    - General options
    - View options
  - System
    - Performance (virtual memory)
    - Remote settings
    - System protection
  - Windows Firewall
  - Power Options
    - Hibernate
    - Power plans
    - Sleep/suspend
    - Standby
  - Credential Manager
  - Programs and features
  - HomeGroup
  - Devices and Printers
  - Sound
  - Troubleshooting
  - Network and Sharing Center
  - Device Manager
  - BitLocker
  - Sync Center

■ **1.7 Summarize application installation and configuration concepts.**

- ■ System requirements
  - — Drive space
  - — RAM
- ■ OS requirements
  - — Compatibility
- ■ Methods of installation and deployment
  - — Local (CD/USB)
  - — Network-based
- ■ Local user permissions
  - — Folder/file access for installation
- ■ Security considerations
  - — Impact to device
  - — Impact to network

■ **1.8 Given a scenario, configure Microsoft Windows networking on a client/desktop.**

- ■ HomeGroup vs. Workgroup
- ■ Domain setup
- ■ Network shares/administrative shares/mapping drives
- ■ Printer sharing vs. network printer mapping
- ■ Establish networking connections
  - — VPN
  - — Dial-ups
  - — Wireless
  - — Wired
  - — WWAN (Cellular)
- ■ Proxy settings
- ■ Remote Desktop Connection
- ■ Remote Assistance
- ■ Home vs. Work vs. Public network settings
- ■ Firewall settings
  - — Exceptions
  - — Configuration
  - — Enabling/disabling Windows Firewall
- ■ Configuring an alternative IP address in Windows
  - — IP addressing
  - — Subnet mask
  - — DNS
  - — Gateway

- Network card properties
  - Half duplex/full duplex/auto
  - Speed
  - Wake-on-LAN
  - QoS
  - BIOS (on-board NIC)

- **1.9 Given a scenario, use features and tools of the Mac OS and Linux client/desktop operating systems.**

  - Best practices
    - Scheduled backups
    - Scheduled disk maintenance
    - System updates/App Store
    - Patch management
    - Driver/firmware updates
    - Antivirus/Anti-malware updates
  - Tools
    - Backup/Time Machine
    - Restore/Snapshot
    - Image recovery
    - Disk maintenance utilities
    - Shell/Terminal
    - Screen sharing
    - Force Quit
  - Features
    - Multiple desktops/Mission Control
    - Key Chain
    - Spot Light
    - iCloud
    - Gestures
    - Finder
    - Remote Disc
    - Dock
    - Boot Camp
  - Basic Linux commands
    - ls
    - grep
    - cd
    - shutdown
    - pwd vs. passwd
    - mv
    - cp

— rm
— chmod
— chown
— iwconfig/ifconfig
— ps
— su/sudo
— apt-get
— vi
— dd
— kill

Domain 2: Security

- **2.1 Summarize the importance of physical security measures.**

  - Mantrap
  - Badge reader
  - Smart card
  - Security guard
  - Door lock
  - Biometric locks
  - Hardware tokens
  - Cable locks
  - Server locks
  - USB locks
  - Privacy screen
  - Key fobs
  - Entry control roster

- **2.2 Explain logical security concepts.**

  - Active Directory
    — Login script
    — Domain
    — Group Policy/Updates
    — Organizational Units
    — Home Folder
    — Folder redirection
  - Software tokens
  - MDM policies
  - Port security
  - MAC address filtering

- Certificates
- Antivirus/Anti-malware
- Firewalls
- User authentication/strong passwords
- Multifactor authentication
- Directory permissions
- VPN
- DLP
- Access control lists
- Smart card
- Email filtering
- Trusted/untrusted software sources
- Principle of least privilege

- **2.3 Compare and contrast wireless security protocols and authentication methods.**

  - Protocols and encryption
    - WEP
    - WPA
    - WPA2
    - TKIP
    - AES
  - Authentication
    - Single-factor
    - Multifactor
    - RADIUS
    - TACACS

- **2.4 Given a scenario, detect, remove, and prevent malware using appropriate tools and methods.**

  - Malware
    - Ransomware
    - Trojan
    - Keylogger
    - Rootkit
    - Virus
    - Botnet
    - Worm
    - Spyware

- Tools and methods
  - Antivirus
  - Anti-malware
  - Recovery console
  - Backup/restore
  - End user education
  - Software firewalls
  - DNS configuration

- **2.5 Compare and contrast social engineering, threats, and vulnerabilities.**

  - Social engineering
    - Phishing
    - Spear phishing
    - Impersonation
    - Shoulder surfing
    - Tailgating
    - Dumpster diving
  - DDoS
  - DoS
  - Zero-day
  - Man-in-the-middle
  - Brute force
  - Dictionary
  - Rainbow table
  - Spoofing
  - Non-compliant systems
  - Zombie

- **2.6 Compare and contrast the differences of basic Microsoft Windows OS security settings.**

  - User and groups
    - Administrator
    - Power user
    - Guest
    - Standard user
  - NTFS vs. share permissions
    - Allow vs. deny
    - Moving vs. copying folders and files
    - File attributes

- Shared files and folders
  - Administrative shares vs. local shares
  - Permission propagation
  - Inheritance
- System files and folders
- User authentication
  - Single sign-on
- Run as administrator vs. standard user
- BitLocker
- BitLocker To Go
- EFS

- **2.7 Given a scenario, implement security best practices to secure a workstation.**

  - Password best practices
    - Setting strong passwords
    - Password expiration
    - Screensaver required password
    - BIOS/UEFI passwords
    - Requiring passwords
  - Account management
    - Restricting user permissions
    - Logon time restrictions
    - Disabling guest account
    - Failed attempts lockout
    - Timeout/screen lock
    - Change default admin
    - User account/password
    - Basic Active Directory functions
      - Account creation
      - Account deletion
      - Password reset/unlock account
      - Disable account
  - Disable autorun
  - Data encryption
  - Patch/update management

- **2.8 Given a scenario, implement methods for securing mobile devices.**

  - Screen locks
    - Fingerprint lock
    - Face lock

- — Swipe lock
- — Passcode lock
- Remote wipes
- Locator applications
- Remote backup applications
- Failed login attempts restrictions
- Antivirus/Anti-malware
- Patching/OS updates
- Biometric authentication
- Full device encryption
- Multifactor authentication
- Authenticator applications
- Trusted sources vs. untrusted sources
- Firewalls
- Policies and procedures
  - — BYOD vs. corporate-owned
  - — Profile security requirements

- **2.9 Given a scenario, implement appropriate data destruction and disposal methods.**

  - Physical destruction
    - — Shredder
    - — Drill/hammer
    - — Electromagnetic (Degaussing)
    - — Incineration
    - — Certificate of destruction
  - Recycling or repurposing best practices
    - — Low-level format vs. standard format
    - — Overwrite
    - — Drive wipe

- **2.10 Given a scenario, configure security on SOHO wireless and wired networks.**

  - Wireless-specific
    - — Changing default SSID
    - — Setting encryption
    - — Disabling SSID broadcast
    - — Antenna and access point placement
    - — Radio power levels
    - — WPS

- Change default usernames and passwords
- Enable MAC filtering
- Assign static IP addresses
- Firewall settings
- Port forwarding/mapping
- Disabling ports
- Content filtering/parental controls
- Update firmware
- Physical security

Domain 3: Software Troubleshooting

- **3.1 Given a scenario, troubleshoot Microsoft Windows OS problems.**
  - Common symptoms
    - Slow performance
    - Limited connectivity
    - Failure to boot
    - No OS found
    - Application crashes
    - Blue screens
    - Black screens
    - Printing issues
    - Services fail to start
    - Slow bootup
    - Slow profile load
  - Common solutions
    - Defragment the hard drive
    - Reboot
    - Kill tasks
    - Restart services
    - Update network settings
    - Reimage/reload OS
    - Roll back updates
    - Roll back device drivers
    - Apply updates
    - Repair application
    - Update boot order
    - Disable Windows services/applications
    - Disable application startup
    - Safe boot
    - Rebuild Windows profiles

- **3.2 Given a scenario, troubleshoot and resolve PC security issues**

  - Common symptoms
    - Pop-ups
    - Browser redirection
    - Security alerts
    - Slow performance
    - Internet connectivity issues
    - PC/OS lockup
    - Application crash
    - OS updates failures
    - Rogue antivirus
    - Spam
    - Renamed system files
    - Disappearing files
    - File permission changes
    - Hijacked email
      - Responses from users regarding email
      - Automated replies from unknown sent email
    - Access denied
    - Invalid certificate (trusted root CA)
    - System/application log errors

- **3.3 Given a scenario, use best practice procedures for malware removal.**

  - Identify and research malware symptoms.
  - Quarantine the infected systems.
  - Disable System Restore (in Windows).
  - Remediate the infected systems.
    - Update the anti-malware software.
    - Scan and use removal techniques (safe mode, pre-installation environment).
  - Schedule scans and run updates.
  - Enable System Restore and create a restore point (in Windows).
  - Educate the end user.

- **3.4 Given a scenario, troubleshoot mobile OS and application issues.**

  - Common symptoms
    - Dim display
    - Intermittent wireless
    - No wireless connectivity

- No Bluetooth connectivity
- Cannot broadcast to external monitor
- Touchscreen non-responsive
- Apps not loading
- Slow performance
- Unable to decrypt email
- Extremely short battery life
- Overheating
- Frozen system
- No sound from speakers
- Inaccurate touch screen response
- System lockout
- App log errors

- **3.5 Given a scenario, troubleshoot mobile OS and application security issues.**

  - Common symptoms
    - Signal drop/weak signal
    - Power drain
    - Slow data speeds
    - Unintended WiFi connection
    - Unintended Bluetooth pairing
    - Leaked personal files/data
    - Data transmission over limit
    - Unauthorized account access
    - Unauthorized location tracking
    - Unauthorized camera/microphone activation
    - High resource utilization

Domain 4: Operational Procedures

- **4.1 Compare and contrast best practices associated with types of documentation.**

  - Network topology diagrams
  - Knowledge base/articles
  - Incident documentation
  - Regulatory and compliance policy
  - Acceptable use policy
  - Password policy
  - Inventory management
    - Asset tags
    - Barcodes

- **4.2 Given a scenario, implement basic change management best practices.**
  - Documented business processes
  - Purpose of the change
  - Scope the change
  - Risk analysis
  - Plan for change
  - End-user acceptance
  - Change board
    - Approvals
  - Backout plan
  - Document changes

- **4.3 Given a scenario, implement basic disaster prevention and recovery methods.**
  - Backup and recovery
    - Image level
    - File level
    - Critical applications
  - Backup testing
  - UPS
  - Surge protector
  - Cloud storage vs. local storage backups
  - Account recovery options

- **4.4 Explain common safety procedures.**
  - Equipment grounding
  - Proper component handling and storage
    - Antistatic bags
    - ESD straps
    - ESD mats
    - Self-grounding
  - Toxic waste handling
    - Batteries
    - Toner
    - CRT
    - Cell phones
    - Tablets

- Personal safety
  - Disconnect power before repairing PC
  - Remove jewelry
  - Lifting techniques
  - Weight limitations
  - Electrical fire safety
  - Cable management
  - Safety goggles
  - Air filter mask
- Compliance with government regulations

- **4.5 Explain environmental impacts and appropriate controls.**

  - MSDS documentation for handling and disposal
  - Temperature, humidity level awareness, and proper ventilation
  - Power surges, brownouts, and blackouts
    - Battery backup
    - Surge suppressor
  - Protection from airborne particles
    - Enclosures
    - Air filters/mask
  - Dust and debris
    - Compressed air
    - Vacuums
  - Compliance to government regulations

- **4.6 Explain the processes for addressing prohibited content/activity, and privacy, licensing, and policy concepts.**

  - Incident response
    - First response
      - Identify
      - Report through proper channels
      - Data/device preservation
    - Use of documentation/documentation changes
    - Chain of custody
      - Tracking of evidence/documenting process
  - Licensing/DRM/EULA
    - Open-source vs. commercial license
    - Personal license vs. enterprise licenses

- Regulated data
  - PII
  - PCI
  - GDPR
  - PHI
- Follow all policies and security best practices

- **4.7 Given a scenario, use proper communication techniques and professionalism.**

  - Use proper language and avoid jargon, acronyms, and slang, when applicable
  - Maintain a positive attitude/project confidence
  - Actively listen (taking notes) and avoid interrupting the customer
  - Be culturally sensitive
    - Use appropriate professional titles, when applicable
  - Be on time (if late, contact the customer)
  - Avoid distractions
    - Personal calls
    - Texting/social media sites
    - Talking to coworkers while interacting with customers
    - Personal interruptions
  - Dealing with difficult customers or situations
    - Do not argue with customers and/or be defensive
    - Avoid dismissing customer problems
    - Avoid being judgmental
    - Clarify customer statements (ask open-ended questions to narrow the scope of the problem, restate the issue, or question to verify understanding)
    - Do not disclose experiences via social media outlets
  - Set and meet expectations/timeline and communicate status with the customer
    - Offer different repair/replacement options, if applicable
    - Provide proper documentation on the services provided
    - Follow up with customer/user at a later date to verify satisfaction
  - Deal appropriately with customers' confidential and private materials
    - Located on a computer, desktop, printer, etc.

■ **4.8 Identify the basics of scripting.**

- ■ Script file types
  - — .bat
  - — .ps1
  - — .vbs
  - — .sh
  - — .py
  - — .js
- ■ Environment variables
- ■ Comment syntax
- ■ Basic script constructs
  - — Basic loops
  - — Variables
- ■ Basic data types
  - — Integers
  - — Strings

■ **4.9 Given a scenario, use remote access technologies.**

- ■ RDP
- ■ Telnet
- ■ SSH
- ■ Third-party tools
  - — Screen share feature
  - — File share
- ■ Security considerations of each access method

Getting Ready

Here are some important tips to keep in mind to ensure that you are ready for this rewarding exam:

- ■ **Build and use a study tracker:** Consider using the exam objectives shown in this chapter to build a study tracker. This can be a notebook outlining the objectives, with your notes written out. Using pencil and paper and taking time to think out answers can help your concentration. A study tracker will help ensure that you have not missed anything and that you are confident for your exam. There are other ways, including a sample Study Planner as a website supplement to this book. Whatever works best for you is the right option to use.

- **Think about your time budget for questions in the exam:** When you do the math, you see that you have 1 minute per question. While this does not sound like enough time, realize that many of the questions will be very straightforward, and you will take only 15 to 30 seconds on those. This leaves time for other questions as you take your exam.

- **Watch the clock:** Check in on the time remaining periodically as you are taking the exam. You might even find that you can slow down pretty dramatically if you have built up a nice block of extra time.

- **Consider ear plugs:** Some people are sensitive to noise when concentrating. If you are one of them, ear plugs may help. There might be other test takers in the center with you, and you do not want to be distracted by them.

- **Plan your travel time:** Give yourself extra time to find the center and get checked in. Be sure to arrive early. As you test more at that center, you can certainly start cutting it closer time-wise.

- **Get rest:** Most students report success with getting plenty of rest the night before the exam. All-night cram sessions are not typically successful.

- **Bring in valuables but get ready to lock them up:** The testing center will take your phone, your smart watch, your wallet, and other such items and will provide a secure place for them.

- **Use the restroom before going in:** If you think you will need a break during the test, clarify the rules with the test proctor.

- **Take your time getting settled:** Once you are seated, take a breath and organize your thoughts. Remind yourself that you have worked hard for this opportunity and expect to do well. The 90-minute timer doesn't start until you tell it to after a brief tutorial. The timer starts when you agree to see the first question.

- **Take notes:** You will be given note-taking materials, so take advantage of them. Sketch out lists and mnemonics that you memorized. The note paper can be used for any calculations you need, but it is okay to write notes to yourself before beginning.

- **Practice exam questions are great—so use them:** This text provides many practice exam questions. Be sure to go through them thoroughly. Remember, you shouldn't blindly memorize answers; rather, let the questions really demonstrate where you are weak in your knowledge and then study up on those areas.

Tools for Final Preparation

This section lists some information about the available tools and how to access them.

Pearson Cert Practice Test Engine and Questions on the Website

Register this book to get access to the Pearson IT Certification test engine (software that displays and grades a set of exam-realistic multiple-choice questions). Using the Pearson Cert Practice Test Engine, you can either study by going through the questions in Study mode or take a simulated (timed) A+ exam.

The Pearson Test Prep practice test software comes with two full practice exams. These practice tests are available to you either online or as an offline Windows application. To access the practice exams that were developed with this book, please see the instructions in the card inserted in the sleeve in the back of the book. This card includes a unique access code that enables you to activate your exams in the Pearson Test Prep software.

Accessing the Pearson Test Prep Software Online

The online version of the Pearson Test Prep software can be used on any device with a browser and connectivity to the Internet, including desktop machines, tablets, and smartphones. To start using your practice exams online, simply follow these steps:

Step 1.   Go to http://www.PearsonTestPrep.com.

Step 2.   Select **Pearson IT Certification** as your product group.

Step 3.   Enter the email/password for your account. If you don't have an account on PearsonITCertification.com or CiscoPress.com, you need to establish one by going to PearsonITCertification.com/join.

Step 4.   In the My Products tab, click the **Activate New Product** button.

Step 5.   Enter the access code printed on the insert card in the back of your book to activate your product. The product is now listed in your My Products page.

Step 6.   Click the **Exams** button to launch the exam settings screen and start the exam.

Accessing the Pearson Test Prep Software Offline

If you wish to study offline, you can download and install the Windows version of the Pearson Test Prep software. There is a download link for this software on the book's companion website, or you can just enter this link in your browser:

http://www.pearsonitcertification.com/content/downloads/pcpt/engine.zip

To access the book's companion website and the software, simply follow these steps:

Step 1.   Register your book by going to PearsonITCertification.com/register and entering the ISBN **9780789760517**.

Step 2.   Respond to the challenge questions.

Step 3.   Go to your account page and select the **Registered Products** tab.

Step 4.   Click on the **Access Bonus Content** link under the product listing.

Step 5.   Click the **Install Pearson Test Prep Desktop Version** link under the Practice Exams section of the page to download the software.

Step 6.   When the software finishes downloading, unzip all the files on your computer.

Step 7.   Double-click the application file to start the installation and follow the onscreen instructions to complete the registration.

Step 8.   When the installation is complete, launch the application and click the **Activate Exam** button on the My Products tab.

Step 9.   Click the **Activate a Product** button in the Activate Product Wizard.

Step 10. Enter the unique access code found on the card in the sleeve in the back of your book and click the **Activate** button.

Step 11. Click **Next** and then click the **Finish** button to download the exam data to your application.

Step 12. You can now start using the practice exams by selecting the product and clicking the **Open Exam** button to open the exam settings screen.

Note that the offline and online versions will sync together, so saved exams and grade results recorded on one version will be available to you on the other as well.

Customizing Your Exams

When you are in the exam settings screen, you can choose to take exams in one of three modes:

- Study mode
- Practice Exam mode
- Flash Card mode

Study mode allows you to fully customize your exams and review answers as you are taking the exam. This is typically the mode you use first to assess your knowledge and identify information gaps. Practice Exam mode locks certain customization options, as it presents a realistic exam experience. Use this mode when you are preparing to test your exam readiness. Flash Card mode strips out the answers and presents you with only the question stem. This mode is great for late-stage preparation, when you really want to challenge yourself to provide answers without the benefit of seeing multiple-choice options. This mode will not provide the detailed score reports that the other two modes will, so it should not be used if you are trying to identify knowledge gaps.

In addition to these three modes, you will be able to select the source of your questions. You can choose to take exams that cover all of the chapters, or you can narrow your selection to just a single chapter or the chapters that make up specific parts in the book. All chapters are selected by default. If you want to narrow your focus to individual chapters, simply deselect all the chapters and then select only those on which you wish to focus in the objectives area.

You can also select the exam banks on which to focus. Each exam bank comes complete with a full exam of questions that cover topics in every chapter. You can have the test engine serve up exams from all four banks or just from one individual bank by selecting the desired banks in the exam bank area.

There are several other customizations you can make to your exam from the exam settings screen, such as the time of the exam, the number of questions served up, whether to randomize questions and answers, whether to show the number of correct answers for multiple-answer questions, and whether to serve up only specific types of questions. You can also create custom test banks by selecting only questions that you have marked or questions on which you have added notes.

Updating Your Exams

If you are using the online version of the Pearson Test Prep software, you should always have access to the latest version of the software as well as the exam data. If you are using the Windows desktop version, every time you launch the software, it will check to see if there are any updates to your exam data and automatically download any changes that have been made since the last time you used the software. This requires that you are connected to the Internet at the time you launch the software.

Sometimes, due to many factors, the exam data may not fully download when you activate your exam. If you find that figures or exhibits are missing, you may need to manually update your exams. To update a particular exam you have already activated and downloaded, simply select the **Tools** tab and click the **Update Products** button. Again, this is only an issue with the desktop Windows application. If you wish to check for updates to the Pearson Test Prep exam engine software, Windows desktop version, simply select the **Tools** tab and select the **Update Application** button. This will ensure that you are running the latest version of the software engine.

Premium Edition

In addition to the free practice exam provided on the website, you can purchase additional exams with expanded functionality directly from Pearson IT Certification. The Premium Edition of this title contains an additional two full practice exams and an eBook (in both PDF and ePub format). In addition, the Premium Edition title also has remediation for each question to the specific part of the eBook that relates to that question.

Because you have purchased the print version of this title, you can purchase the Premium Edition at a deep discount. There is a coupon code in the book sleeve that contains a one-time-use code and instructions for where you can purchase the Premium Edition.

To view the premium edition product page, go to www.informit.com/title/9780789760517.

Memory Tables

Like most other Exam Cert Guides, this book purposely organizes information into tables and lists for easier study and review. Rereading these tables and lists can be very useful before the exam. However, it is easy to skim over the tables without paying attention to every detail, especially when you remember having seen the table's contents when reading the chapter.

Instead of just reading the tables in the various chapters, this book's Appendixes C and D give you another review tool. Appendix C lists partially completed versions of many of the tables from the book. You can open Appendix C (a PDF available on the book website after registering) and print the appendix. For review, you can attempt to complete the tables. This exercise can help you focus on the review. It also exercises the memory connectors in your brain, and it prompts you to think about the information from context clues, which forces a little more contemplation about the facts.

Appendix D, also a PDF located on the book website, lists the completed tables so you can check yourself. You can also just refer to the tables as printed in the book.

Chapter-Ending Review Tools

Chapters 1 through 9 each have several features in the "Exam Preparation Tasks" section at the end of the chapter. You might have already worked through these in each chapter. It can also be useful to use these tools again as you make your final preparations for the exam.

Suggested Plan for Final Review/Study

This section lists a suggested study plan from the point at which you finish reading through Chapter 9 until you take the CompTIA A+ 220-1001 and 220-1002 exams. Certainly, you can ignore this plan, use it as is, or just take suggestions from it.

The plan involves four steps:

Step 1.   **Review key topics and "Do I Know This Already?" questions:** You can use the table that lists the key topics in each chapter or just flip the pages, looking for key topics. Also, reviewing the "Do I Know This Already?" questions from the beginning of the chapter can be helpful for review.

Step 2.   **Complete memory tables:** Open Appendix C from the book website and print the entire thing or print the tables by major part. Then complete the tables.

Step 3.   **Review "Review" sections:** Go through the review questions at the end of each chapter to identify areas where you need more study.

Step 4.   **Use the Pearson Cert Practice Test engine to practice:** The Pearson Cert Practice Test engine can be used to study using a bank of unique exam-realistic questions available only with this book.

Summary

The tools and suggestions listed in this chapter have been designed with one goal in mind: to help you develop the skills required to pass the CompTIA A+ 220-1001 and 220-1002 exams. This book has been developed from the beginning to not just tell you the facts but to also help you learn how to apply the facts. No matter what your experience level leading up to when you take the exams, it is our hope that the broad range of preparation tools, and even the structure of the book, helps you pass the exams with ease. We hope you do well on the exams.

Answers to the "Do I Know This Already?" Quizzes and Review Question Sections

"Do I Know This Already?" Quiz Answers

Chapter 1

1. c
2. a, b, c, and d
3. b
4. a
5. c
6. c
7. c
8. c
9. b and c
10. b
11. b, c, and d
12. d
13. c
14. b and c

Chapter 2

1. b
2. c and d
3. a
4. b
5. d
6. c

7. b, c, and e

8. b

9. b

10. c

11. d

12. c

13. a

14. d

15. b

16. c

17. d

18. d

19. b

Chapter 3

1. c

2. b

3. a

4. c

5. c

6. a

7. d

8. a

9. b and d

10. a and c

11. a

12. c

13. c

14. a

15. b

16. d

17. c

18. b
19. b, c, and d
20. c

Chapter 4

1. c
2. a
3. c
4. a
5. a
6. a and b
7. c
8. e
9. c
10. b

Chapter 5

1. b
2. a
3. d
4. b and c
5. b and d
6. b. and d
7. b and c
8. c
9. a
10. d
11. c
12. c
13. d
14. b
15. c

16. c

17. a and c

18. c

19. d

20. b

Chapter 6

1. d

2. b and c

3. c

4. b

5. b

6. a, b, c, and d

7. c

8. a and b

9. b and c

10. c

Chapter 7

1. b

2. c

3. d

4. b

5. d

6. a

7. c

8. a

9. b

10. d

Chapter 8

1. c
2. a
3. a, b, c, and d
4. b
5. a
6. b
7. c
8. d
9. b
10. d

Chapter 9

1. b
2. c
3. d
4. b
5. d
6. a
7. a
8. d
9. a and c
10. c
11. a
12. a and c
13. d
14. c
15. b

Answers and Explanations to Review Questions

Chapter 1

1. **c.** SODIMM stands for small outline DIMM, which is a smaller RAM form factor developed for laptops. The other options listed are for desktops.

2.

Operating System	Application Download Site
a. Android	**2.** Google Play
b. Apple iOS	**3.** App Store
c. Windows 10 Mobile	**1.** Windows Store

3. **c.** An SSD (solid-state drive) is faster than an HDD or an SSHD. While adding RAM may be part of the solution, DIMM is a RAM form factor for desktops, not laptops.

4. **a, d.** Memory speed and timing must match the existing RAM when adding RAM to a machine.

5. **a.** Augmented reality is used to impose images on real-world data. VR is virtual reality, which immerses the user completely into a digital experience. NFC is nearfield communication, which is not used in this game. IR is infrared, which is also not used.

6. **d.** Hailing an Uber has not yet been assigned a common function key. All the others are.

7. **b, c.** Tethering allows two devices to share an Internet connection via a USB cable. A hotspot sets up a smartphone as a temporary SSID that other devices can connect to. IMAP is a protocol for receiving email, and SSL is a method for encrypting email.

8. **a.** Airplane mode turns off the antennas in mobile devices so that they cannot transmit or receive cellular and GPS data while in flight. Bluetooth and WiFi may still be enabled.

9. **d.** Bluetooth uses an 802.11 wireless network for data transmission. Tethering is not a networking standard. WEP is an obsolete wireless encryption standard, not a network standard as such. Ethernet is a wired networking standard.

10. **a, b, c, d.** Bluetooth creates a short-range, low-speed, peer-to-peer network populated by dissimilar devices. This type of network is called a PAN (personal area network).

11. **c, d.** SSL and the more advanced TLS provide encryption for secure communication between an email server and a web browser.

12. **c.** S/MIME Secure/Multipurpose Internet Mail Extension. IMAP and POP3 are mail server settings. NFC is near field communication.

13. **d.** POP3 uses port 110 for incoming mail, IMAP uses port 143 for incoming mail, and SMTP uses port 25 for outgoing mail. Port 53 is used for DNS. Port 80 is used for HTTP.

14. **b.** IMEI identifies a mobile device by assigning it a unique security code that allows the network provider or cell phone company to identify and then disable the device when it is reported lost or stolen. IMSI identifies the owner of the device. SDK assists programmers in developing apps for mobile devices. S/MIME provides encryption support for email.

15. **b.** Synchronization to the cloud, desktop, and automobile are the three methods that the A+ 220-1001 exam expects you to know. Synchronization to the cloud involves using a secure user ID and password and mutual authentication. With synchronization to the desktop, the user must have access to both the mobile device and the computer, and the two devices must be physically connected by a cable. Synchronization to the automobile enables safe and legal use of mobile devices while driving.

Chapter 2

1.

Wired	Fiber	Cable	DSL	ISDN	Dial-up
← Fastest ---------------------------------- Slowest →					
Wireless	Cellular		Fixed line-of-sight		Satellite

2. **a, c, d.** Video, voice, and gaming require real-time streaming, and re-sending data would interrupt the stream. For both email and SMS, data would be re-sent if a message failed.

3. **c.** The browser is likely using HTTPS to transport on port 443. Port 80 is the less-secure HTTP. Port 68 is a DHCP port, and 53 is used for DNS.

4. **a.** The router connects the LAN to other LANs. All other devices work with traffic within the LAN.

5. **b.** VLANs are created in a LAN using advanced switches that allow configuration management.

6.

Device	Definition
Wireless access point	Extends wired LANs into wireless connected space
Router	Allows networks to communicate with each other
Switch	Uses a MAC address to direct data to a specific computer
Modem	Converts digital signals to analog and analog signals to digital
Firewall	Prevents unwanted intrusion from outside the network
Hub	Broadcasts data to all attached computers
Patch panel	Acts as a junction point for network cabling

7. **c.** Cloud-based network controllers allow an administrator to manage a LAN from anywhere on the Web.

8. **d.** TCP/IP is a suite of protocols used for managing traffic on the Internet and is the accepted standard used by all major operating systems.

9. **c.** This is an IPv4 address.

10. **b.** The 255s in the subnet mask indicate the network portion of the address. Therefore, the first two octets identify the network portion of the address, and the last two octets are the host portion.

11. **b.** 255.255.255.0 is the subnet mask for a network with 255 addresses in the last octet.

12. **b, e.** 127.0.0.1 is a diagnostic tool known as the IPv4 loopback address, which is used to test connectivity between a computer and its network. ::1 is the IPv6 counterpart.

13. **b.** This is an example of a Class A private IP address.

14. **d.** APIPA addresses are automatically assigned in the event that the DHCP system is unable to provide IP addresses. As a technician, anytime you see an IP address that begins with 169.254.x.x, you should look for problems with DHCP. APIPA is supported by Microsoft, macOS, and Linux.

15. **d.** Every device that accesses the Internet (every PC, laptop, tablet, smartphone, and so on) must have its own IP address—and no two addresses may be the same. Today, a single family might need a dozen addresses; the world is simply running out of IPv4 addresses. IPv6 provides a huge increase in the number of available IP addresses.

16. **b.** DHCP automatically assigns IP addresses to computers on a network.

17. **c.** DNS resolves domain names to their IP addresses. TCP is an Ethernet protocol, and DHCP assigns addresses to devices on a network. UPnP is an access setting on SOHO routers.

18.

Protocol	IMAP	FTP	HTTP	HTTPS	SMTP	DNS	SSH	POP3
Port	143	21	80	443	25	53	22	110

As an IT technician, you might be called upon to configure ports for a network. The ports in this chart are only a few of the ones you might need to know.

19. **a.** Simple Mail Transfer Protocol (SMTP) is used to send email.

20. **b.** 802.11 includes 802.11a, 802.11b, 802.11g, 802.11n, and 802.11ac wireless network standards.

21. **b.** WPA2 uses stronger encryption than WPA. Both WPA and WPA2 have stronger encryption, use longer passphrases, and have other security improvements compared to WEP.

22. **a.** NAT is a protocol used by a router to change a computer's private IP address used inside a LAN to a public IP address when communicating outside the network. NAT allows the computers on a LAN to remain hidden from the outside world.

23. **d.** This is an Internet of Things (IoT) device. The number of IoT devices talking to each other and sharing data today numbers in the many billions, and that number is expected to grow exponentially.

24. **b.** A crimper is used to attach an RJ-45 or RJ-11 connector to a TP cable.

Chapter 3

1. **a.** The ATX 24-pin power cable and connector provides primary power to the motherboard and connected devices.

2. **a.** SPDIF audio is not selected as the default output. Computers use analog speakers as the default output. You must select SPDIF as the output if you are now connecting to a receiver via the SPDIF (digital audio) port. VGA and microphone cables have no effect on audio output. Smart card readers do not cause interference.

3. **c.** Random access memory (RAM) loses its contents when the computer shuts down. Hard disk drives, USB flash drives, and read-only memory (ROM) are designed to retain their contents even when they are not receiving power.

4. **c.** DDR3. The label identifies this module as PC3, which indicates that it contains DDR3 type RAM.

5. **b.** Dual-channel support requires that the paired memory slots both use memory with identical specifications.

6. **a, c.** Parity memory and ECC have an additional memory chip added for parity. They are both methods used to protect the reliability of memory.

7. **a.** Unbuffered, non-ECC memory is used in most common desktop computers sold in the market. This kind of memory is also used in some servers and workstations.

8. **a.** ECC memory enables the system to correct single-bit errors and notify the user of larger errors.

9. **a.** The memory module in the diagram contains 18 memory chips (2 banks of 8 each, plus a parity or ECC chip) and an additional chip that contains the register (or buffer).

10. **a, b, c.** To correctly insert the memory modules, you should follow all the steps listed. You might also have to use a fair amount of pressure to securely lock these modules in place.

11. **a.** For best results, you should always install identical modules in the same channel. The two 4GB modules should be the same size, speed, latency, and so on, and should be installed in the same channel (in this case, in the two blue slots). The same is true for the two 2GB modules, which should be installed in the two blue slots. The slots on this motherboard are color-coded to indicate the channels. Always check your documentation for the correct orientation of the channels and the type of RAM your motherboard will accept.

12. **c.** DDR3-800 is also known as PC3-6400 (6400MBps peak transfer rate). DDR3-1066 is also known as PC3-8500 (8500MBps peak transfer rate). DDR3-1333 is also known as PC3-10600 (10667MBps peak transfer rate). DDR3-1600 is also known as PC3-12800 (12800MBps peak transfer rate).

13. The storage media types (optical drive, magnetic drive, or flash drive) correspond to the descriptions as follows:

Description	Storage Media
Records information in tracks and sectors containing 512 bytes	Magnetic drive
Stores data in a continuous spiral	Optical drive
Used on memory cards	Flash drive
Records information in a series of lands and pits	Optical drive
Uses laser light to read data	Optical drive
Records information in concentric circles	Magnetic drive
Information is recorded from the center outward	Optical drive
Stores data on double-sided platters	Magnetic drive
Information is recorded from the outer edge inward	Magnetic drive
Used in solid-state drives	Flash drive

14. **d.** The tablet will have slower data access than if it used an SSD. eMMC memory is slower than memory used in SSDs. It is built into tablets and therefore not removable. A tablet's ability to use USB devices is a function of whether it has USB ports, not its built-in storage.

15. **c.** DVD-RW is erasable and rewritable. -R and +R are writable but not erasable and rewritable. -DL (dual layer) uses a second recording layer to record more information but is not erasable.

16. **b, d.** 5400RPM drives are slower but require less energy to run than faster drives. Laptop computers use 2.5-inch or smaller form factor drives.

17.

Component	Letter
i. SATA data port	d
ii. SATA data cable	c
iii. SATA power port	b
iv. SATA power cable	a

18. **b.** RAID 10 includes striping across two drives for faster performance and mirroring of the striped array for data safety.

19. **a.** The ATX form factor has been the most frequently used motherboard in desktop computers for the past 15 years.

20. **d.** Mini-ITX is a small form factor motherboard that is frequently used in home theater systems and gaming computers.

21. **1. b; 2. c; 3. a.**

22. **e, f.** e is the 8-pin EPS12V power connector, and f is the 24-pin ATX power connector.

23. **f** and **g** are RAM slots as noted by the white tabs that lock them in place. **a** and **d** are PCIe slots. **b** and **c** are PCI slots.

24. **False.** DDR2 and DDR3 both have 240-pin designs, but the arrangement and keying of the pins are different, and thus they are not interchangeable.

25. **c.** The CPU fan connector usually has four pins, and the system fan connector usually has three pins. The extra pin in a CPU fan connector is used to control fan speed.

26. **c.** Make any desired changes to the BIOS startup program and then save those changes to the CMOS chip. The BIOS chip is ROM and cannot be edited; the CMOS chip is RAM and may be edited.

27. **c.** The figure displays a USB 2.0 cable and header.

28. **d.** The figure displays a USB 3.0 cable and header.

29. **a.** CMOS is RAM, and RAM is volatile. This means the CMOS chip must have power to maintain its memory. There are two ways to erase the CMOS settings and revert to the default settings in the BIOS: You can remove the CMOS battery or you can place the jumper block over the CMOS jumper pins.

30. **b.** When the computer's clock begins to lose time, the fault frequently lies in a weak CMOS battery.

31. **e.** In a high-end customized system, one or all of these components must be upgraded. The CPU will need as many cores as possible for the fastest processing. More and faster RAM, high-end sound cards, multiple displays, and HDMI might be required for peak performance in some systems. In a gaming computer where overclocking is used, you might choose to use a liquid cooling system. A customized system will probably be comparable in cost to a new system.

32. **c.** The computer's power supply is really a power converter. It converts AC power from the wall outlet to DC power that the computer can use.

33.

	Total Watts (W)	Number of +12V Rails (R)	Amp Output from +12V Rails (Amp)
Power Supply A	650	4	80
Power Supply B	700	1	52

Power Supply A produces 650 watts of power and uses four +12V rails that produce 20 amps each, for a total of 80 amps. Power Supply B produces 700 watts, but it has a single +12V rail that produces only 52 amps. Power Supply A has more usable amperage available to components, so it is the better value. Notice also that Power Supply A was tested at 50 degrees Celsius (122 degrees Fahrenheit) at full load. The Power Supply B label does not tell you how it was tested.

34. **d.** The keyboard, mouse, and touchpad options are incorrect because all use standard input device drivers incorporated into the operating system. A scanner driver is likely not included in the operating system.

35. **c.** Make sure the USB cable from the display is plugged in. The touchscreen digitizer must connect to a USB port, or it will not work. Rebooting the computer could help if the touchscreen had been working but then had stopped. However, in this example, it had never worked. The mouse will not interfere with the touchscreen. A USB hub is necessary when there are more USB devices than ports, but that is not the issue here.

36. Step 1: Processing
    Step 2: Charging
    Step 3: Exposing
    Step 4: Developing
    Step 5: Transferring
    Step 6: Fusing
    Step 7: Cleaning

37. **True.** As long as the drum is kept in the dark, it will retain its charge. During the exposing phase, when the laser writes an image onto the drum, the areas where the laser strikes the drum lose their strong negative charge and become charged at only –100V. This lesser charge allows the toner—also charged at –600V —to stick to only the lower-voltage areas, which contain the image to be printed.

38. **d.** A laser printer stores an entire page in its memory and then prints the entire page at one time. An inkjet printer prints one line at a time. Thermal printers do not use impact printing. A dot-matrix printer is an impact printer; it creates characters by pressing each character onto an inked ribbon and then onto the paper.

39. **a.** Inkjet printers use closely grouped nozzles of ink to spray tiny dots of color onto the paper to form letters, numbers, and graphics.

40. **b.** CMYK refers to cyan, magenta, yellow, black.

41. **d.** The diagram shows the result of a nozzle check for an inkjet printer. If the print head nozzles are clean and are working properly, the test pattern should look like the left half of the screen. If they are clogged and in need of cleaning, the pattern may look similar to the right side of the screen.

42. **a.** Thermal printers use either a dot-matrix or dye-sublimation mechanism. The dot-matrix mechanism has a print head that uses a series of raised dots that can be used to create an image. These dots are heated and used in conjunction with special heat-sensitive paper or ribbon to transfer the image to the paper.

43. **b.** Multipart forms require an impact printer to transfer the image through multiple layers of paper. Laser, inkjet, and thermal printers will only print on the top layer of a multipart form.

44. **d.** CUPS is the open-source printing system used by Linux.

45. **c.** The vendor's website will have the most updated drivers available. The disc that ships with the printer will contain the vendor's drivers, but they might not be the most updated versions. The drivers included in Windows might not support recent printers, and Windows Update in version 8/8.1/10 does not update printer drivers.

46. **c.** Choosing a cover page is a function of the current application (such as a word processor), not part of the printing process.

47. **a.** Ad hoc mode supports only WEP encryption. This type of encryption is not as secure as WPA or WPA2 and is not generally recommended for secure networking. A NIC is a network interface card, not a type of encryption.

Chapter 4

1.

Model	Description
a. SaaS	**3.** Enables software to be hosted on remote servers and accessed through web browsers
b. IaaS	**1.** Provides access to storage, network services, virtualization, and servers
c. PaaS	**2.** Gives application developers the opportunity to develop and deploy software in a cloud environment

2. **a, b, c.** Virtualization allows a single machine to act as though it were several machines. A single operating system may host several virtual guest operating systems and may switch between them without being rebooted. These virtual machines may be both 32- and 64-bit systems. A virtual machine uses the same hardware as the host machine, which enables considerable reduction of capital investment.

3. **a, c, d.** Rapid elasticity is the ability of users to quickly increase or decrease the resources they use. Resource pooling allows a cloud provider's resources to be allocated, divided, and used by many clients simultaneously. Measured service means that the user pays only for the resources used. DHCP is a network service that automatically assigns IP addresses to client computers and is not a service provided by cloud computing.

4. **b.** A virtual machine manager (VMM) manages the interaction of the virtual environment with the host environment.

5. **c.** 6144MB (6GB) is the amount of RAM available to the system after starting a 2GB VM. 2048MB (2GB) is the size of the VM itself. 4096MB (4GB) is incorrect. 128MB is the size of the video memory assigned to the display.

6. **d.** Sandboxing is a security procedure that involves isolating a program, separating it from the main system. A VMM that enables sandboxing (isolation) of each VM and provides physical partitioning of resources provides better security against attacks.

7. **a.** A hypervisor VMM runs directly on the hardware. It is faster and uses fewer resources than host/guest virtualization. Because the hypervisor uses few computer resources (such as memory and CPU), more computer resources can be made available to each VM.

Chapter 5

1. **d.** Reboot the computer and open the BIOS/UEFI menu. Check the BIOS settings for the CPU temperature. As a technician, you should be very familiar with all the diagnostic information that is available in the BIOS.

2. **a.** A checksum error is generated when the CMOS settings have failed, either because they have been erased or because the CMOS battery has failed. If you see a checksum error message, acknowledge it and allow startup to continue. The system then loads using the default BIOS settings.

3. **a, b, d.** POST checks the memory, keyboard, hard drives, and other essential hardware. The mouse is not considered to be essential to the operation of the computer and is not checked by POST. If POST finds any problems, it reports them as error messages during startup.

4. **d.** When the clock and calendar on a computer are no longer able to keep accurate time, this is an indication of a failing CMOS battery.

5. **b.** This is a CMOS battery, which provides a constant source of electricity to the CMOS chip to maintain the CMOS programming.

6. **a.** The automatic reboot option is configured in System Properties on the Advanced tab, under Startup and Recovery.

7. **a.** North America uses 115 volts. Europe and Asia use 230 volts.

8. **d.** These components are capacitors. Capacitors store an electrical charge and can deliver a painful and even dangerous shock if accidentally discharged.

9. **c.** A multimeter is used to test AC or DC voltage, continuity, resistance, and amperage. A loopback plug is used to test ports. PING is a network diagnostics program. A tone generator is used to test network cables.

10. **a, c, d, g, h.** A power supply should produce +3.3, +5.0, −5.0, +12.0, and −12.0 volts.

11. **c.** Having identified the problem as network connectivity and established a theory that a cable is broken, you are testing the theory with a known good cable.

12. **a.** These questions are being asked to determine what problem the user's computer has.

13. **d.** This jumper forces the SATA drive to run at a slower rate to make it compatible with older host adapters.

14. **a.** Reboot the computer and access the BIOS startup program. Reorder the boot sequence and save the changes. Changes made to the BIOS configurations are saved on the CMOS chip.

15. **c.** S.M.A.R.T. refers to Self-Monitoring, Analysis, and Reporting Technology, which is used to detect problems with and warns of failure of internal magnetic hard drives.

16. **d.** Had there been proper documentation of a cable map left by a previous technician, the current technician would have saved time.

17. **c.** The nslookup command resolves an IP address or a domain name. In this fictional example, a domain name was returned after an IP address was submitted.

18. **a.** VGA mode uses low resolution (640×480 on Windows 7, 8, 8.1, and 10) with minimum colors and basic drivers and is used when troubleshooting display problems. A Windows system starts in VGA mode if Low-resolution mode or Safe mode has been selected at startup or if the correct drivers are not available.

19. **a, d.** If an LCD display is flickering, the most likely cause is a failing backlight or inverter.

20. **c.** Burn-in, the persistent display onscreen of a "ghost" image that was displayed previously, even after the current screen contents have changed, can affect both LCD and plasma displays. On an LCD display, it is frequently caused by stuck pixels.

21. **b.** Step 2 of the best practice methodology to resolve problems is to establish a theory of probable cause. A DHCP server is responsible for assigning IP addresses on a network. If valid IP addresses are not available, APIPA (169.254.x.x) addresses will be assigned. If a network is using APIPA addresses, you should add additional valid IP addresses to the DHCP server.

22. **b.** Establishing a plan of action should come after testing the theory to determine the cause (choice c).

23. **d.** Documenting outcomes is the sixth step of the best practice methodology.

24. **a, b.** Some cellular connections do not work well if WiFi is enabled, so if you are having problems getting a clear cellular signal, you should disable your WiFi connection. You should also try rotating your screen because the antenna is located around the periphery of the screen casing. 802.11 is a WiFi specification. The iOS slider switch does not affect reception.

25. **a, c.** You can increase battery life by not overcharging and by shutting down an iOS device weekly with the slider switch.

26. **d.** Vertical streaks that show up on every page printed by a laser printer usually indicate damage to the imaging drum. Low toner might cause uneven printing. A dirty print ribbon could create problems on a thermal printer or an impact printer. Damaged ink nozzles would be a problem on an inkjet printer.

27. **a.** Clogged or dirty printheads and rollers on an inkjet printer can cause smudging of the printed page. Fusers, photosensitive drums, and toner cartridges are components of a laser printer, not of an inkjet printer.

28. **b.** The fuser is responsible for heating the toner and pressing it into the paper. Brittle or flaking toner is indicative of a failing fuser.

29. **c.** Compressing the data in a print job takes time, which may make the print job slower.

30. **a.** The print spooler stores print jobs in a queue and releases the computer to perform other tasks while the spooler manages the print job.

Chapter 6

1. **a, b, d.** All computers in a workgroup must be part of the same local network or subnet, and if they are to share resources, they must use file and printer sharing. Also, each user must have a local user account on each computer in the workgroup. The workgroup does not, however, have a password.

2. **a.** Each computer on the network must have a unique name. This name is usually given automatically during installation, but if you want to check your computer's name or if you want to change it, you should open the System properties. There are several ways to do it. You can open the **Control Panel**, select **System**, and select **Change Settings**. In Windows 7, you can open the **Start** menu, right-click **Computer**, choose **Properties**, and then **Change Settings**. In Windows 8/8.1, you can press **Windows+X**, select **System**, and then select **Change Settings** (or you can open the charms menu, select **Settings**, and then select **PC Info**). In Windows 10, you can search for **rename** and find **View Your PC's Name in Settings**. It is also possible to see the name by right-clicking **Start** and selecting **System**. The PC name will be in the top center, and you have the option to rename.

3.

Task	Command
a. Open a command prompt	2. CMD or COMMAND
b. View all the directories in a specified location	5. DIR
c. Create a new folder	8. MD or MKDIR
d. Remove an empty folder	9. RD or RMDIR
e. Remove one or more files	4. DEL
f. Stop running a specified task	10. TASKKILL
g. Copy single or multiple files	11. XCOPY, ROBOCOPY
h. Scan for errors and repair hard drive	1. CHKDSK
i. Close command prompt	7. EXIT
j. Create new partitions	6. DISKPART
k. Display the help files for a specific command	3. COMMAND /?

4. **a.** Setting a network location to Public stops all sharing. Set the network location to Home in Windows 7 and to Private or Allow Network Discovery and Sharing in Windows 8/8.1/10. Only a Home network will allow you to create or join a homegroup in Windows 7. In Windows 8/8.1/10, use Private as the network (firewall) setting. Note that the use of homegroups has been removed in Windows 10 (Version 1803).

5. **c.** Device Manager contains a list of hardware devices and reports on their condition. From Device Manager, you can update drives and disable or enable or uninstall devices. A disabled device in Device Manager displays a downward-pointing arrow over the device icon.

6. **d.** System Configuration allows you to select the programs and services that run automatically at startup. Devices and Printers provides centralized management of the computer and most of the hardware connected to it. Programs and Features is used to manage programs installed and Windows features available on the computer. System protection is used to configure System Restore.

7. **c.** Open the Network and Sharing Center. In Windows 7/8/8.1/10, click **Change Advanced Sharing Settings**, select the type of network you want to configure, and then select **Turn on File and Printer Sharing**.

8. **c.** You have created a mapped network drive. A mapped network drive is a shared folder or drive on a networked computer that has been assigned a drive letter and mapped to a location on another computer on the network. That share appears to the user as though it is located on the user's own computer.

9.

Utility	Command
a. The Registry	**4.** REGEDIT
b. System Information	**3.** MSINFO32
c. System Configuration	**2.** MSCONFIG
d. Microsoft Management Console	**1.** MMC

10. **a.** A VPN is created in the Network and Sharing Center, under Set Up a New Connection or Network.

11. **a.** Use the Task Scheduler to schedule and view tasks to run at regularly scheduled intervals.

12. **a.** Disk Management allows you to analyze and configure your hard drives. A RAID BIOS utility is available at startup only on systems with hardware RAID, which is not available on this computer. CHKDSK is used to locate and optionally repair problems with files stored on a drive. MSCONFIG is used to adjust boot options.

13. **a, b, c, d.** All of these features are unavailable when you configure a computer for a public network. When on a public network, you do not want other

computers that might be using the network at the same time to be able to see or interact with your computer.

14. **d.** A firewall blocks or allows information to flow into your computer from the Internet or from another network by closing or opening ports. A firewall can prevent hackers and malware from entering your computer, and it can also be used to prevent your computer from sending malware out to other computers.

15. **a, b.** Specific applications that are to be allowed through the firewall and specific ports that are to be opened may be configured as exceptions in Windows Firewall.

16. **c.** 169.254.x.x is an APIPA address. By default, an address within this range will be assigned when there is no DHCP server available or when the DHCP server has run out of IP addresses to assign.

17. **c.** Time Machine is the backup utility for macOS. tar and crontab are commands used to schedule and back up a Linux machine. File History is a file backup program in Windows 8/8.1/10 that can be accessed from the Control Panel.

18. **a.** Disk Utility can be used to create blank disk images that can be used as containers for other files, including image backups. It can also be used to erase non-macOS drives and prepare them for use with macOS. Use **System Preferences > Network** to manage the network connection. Drag the disk icon on the desktop to the Trash, wait for it to change into an Eject symbol, and after the symbol disappears, remove the disk. Use iCloud to manage cloud storage.

19. **a.** To force quit an app from the Terminal in either macOS or Linux, enter **top** to see a list of process IDs (PIDs) and the apps they represent. Press **q** to quit. To kill an app by specifying its PID, enter the command **kill xxx** (where **xxx** is the PID). **Ctrl+Alt+Del** is used in Windows to display options including the Task Manager. end and fq are not valid terminal commands.

20. **d.** Linux includes several utilities that can be used for backups. These include the command line tar and rsync utilities. grsync (GUI for rsync), duplicity (command line and a GUI available as Déjà Dup), and other commands are available from the repository for a Linux distribution or from the vendors. The compress command is used to compress files. The ifconfig command is used to view IP address information. The gpg command is used to encrypt files.

21. **b.** In macOS, screen sharing, file sharing, printer sharing, Internet, Bluetooth, and remote apps are configured through Sharing in System Preferences. Control Panel is a Windows configuration utility. macOS does not have a Sharing app. Display is used to configure display resolution and multiple-monitor settings.

22. **a.** Mission Control allows a user to open and manage applications across multiple displays. Mission Control displays all apps open on the desktop, so you can copy or move them between different desktops. This is very helpful when working with multiple displays.

23. **b.** iCloud allows users to store, share, and back up music, video, picture, and document files in a cloud environment. Time Machine is the macOS backup utility. There are many utilities for macOS that contain the word "assist" or "assistant" (for example, Migration Assistant). Spotlight is the macOS search tool.

24. **c.** The file manager and graphical user interface in the macOS operating systems is known as Finder. In Windows 7, it is Windows Explorer, and in Windows 8/8.1/10 it is File Explorer. Search is a Windows search utility.

25. **d.** The Dock is the utility that macOS uses to display icons of all the currently running apps. The taskbar and menu bar are used by Windows. Finder is the file manager for macOS.

26. **a.** su   **9.** Run commands as a different user (usually root)
    b. iwconfig   **5.** Display wireless network connections
    c. cd   **2.** Change folders
    d. ls   **10.** Show contents of directory or folder
    e. chmod   **3.** Change permissions
    f. ps   **6.** List currently running processes
    g. rm   **4.** Delete files or folders
    h. grep   **7.** Perform text/word searches
    i. pwd   **8.** Print (display) working directory
    j. vi   **11.** Start text editor
    k. chown   **1.** Change file ownership

Chapter 7

1. **b, c.** Andre tailgated into the first door, but the mantrap stopped him from fully entering the building.

2. **b.** Rack-level security can isolate a single server to prevent unauthorized access.

3.

Description	Type of Malware
1. Infects and rewrites files. Replicates automatically with no user intervention.	**c.** Worm
2. A method of hiding malware from detection programs.	**d.** Rootkit
3. Tracks web browsing; uses pop-ups to attract a user's attention.	**a.** Spyware
4. Encrypts target files and then demands payment to unencrypt files.	**e.** Ransomware
5. Infects and rewrites files. Replicates itself if a user executes the file.	**b.** Virus

4. **d.** WEP is considered insecure and should not be used. Options a, b, and c are all considered important security measures.

5. **d.** A physical lock and key might be the most difficult form of security to overcome because it cannot be bypassed electronically and cannot be done remotely. An intruder must be in possession of a physical key and must be physically present at the site.

6. **a, c.** Fingerprint scan, retinal or iris scan, facial recognition, and voice recognition are all types of biometric security methods.

7. **b.** A cable lock is used to secure a laptop to an immovable object, such as a post. A token is any physical object used to gain access to a secure system. Key fobs, RFID cards, and smart cards are all types of tokens.

8. **c.** A firewall examines data packets being received by a network to determine whether they should be delivered to a network location or whether delivery should be blocked. Data packets can be allowed or blocked, depending on the threat level that is determined by the firewall programming.

9. **c, d.** A strong password should consist of eight or more characters, a combination of upper- and lowercase letters, symbols, and numbers. In addition, a strong password should not use real names or real words.

10. **c.** Phishing is a technique that involves tricking a user into revealing confidential information, such as a Social Security number or credit card information. The technique might involve a bogus security alert in the form of an email or a telephone warning that includes an offer of assistance. In social engineering, the hacker pretends to be a coworker or an IT professional in order to gain network access. Tailgating is getting through a secure door on the credentials of the person in front. Dumpster diving involves looking for physical clues to passwords or personal information around a workstation or in the trash. Shoulder surfing is an attempt to physically view confidential information (such as passwords or PINs) by looking over a user's shoulder.

11. **d.** BitLocker To Go can be used to encrypt a flash drive.

12. **b, c.** By changing the network name and disabling the SSID broadcast, Ellen can ensure that her neighbors can't see her network. MAC address filtering allows her to control who has access to the network.

13. **d.** Drive wiping is the most secure formatting technique. Using standard format and overwriting would work but can be reconstructed with recovery software. Low-level formatting is done by the manufacturer and not in the field.

14. **a.** Share permissions allow group access to folders. Password attempts do not impact user permissions. Options b and d cannot be true because Hiro could access his account.

15. **c.** The options for resetting the UEFI BIOS without a password include a jumper or a reset button. In the absence of those options, the CMOS coin-shaped battery can be removed for several minutes.

Chapter 8

1. **1a. b.** This is an error message from Windows 7. **1b. d.** To find the answer, search for the error message at the Microsoft website. **1c. b.** The most likely solution would be to uninstall the most recent app or hardware device and then install an updated app or a hardware device with an updated driver. Reinstalling the operating system is the last solution to try—but only after all other measures have been tried.

2. **b.** Free space on the system partition is used as a swap file when sufficient RAM is not available. If lack of space is the reason that your system has become unresponsive, you should clear space from the system partition by rebooting the computer to free up temporary files, emptying the Trash, or removing files and storing them on another drive or in the cloud. Upgrading to a newer macOS version can also help to improve responsiveness.

3. **a.** Use the System Recovery options and either select the **Startup Repair** option or open a command prompt and enter **bootrec /fixboot**. In Windows 10 use WinRE. Advanced Boot options are used to start Windows in Safe mode and other troubleshooting modes. Although a change in the BIOS startup settings to a different startup drive could cause this problem, it isn't likely. BOOTMGR cannot be downloaded from the Internet.

4. **b.** Press **Cmd+R** as soon as you hear the startup sound. After choosing your language, you have the option to restore, reinstall, get help, or open the Disk Utility. macOS uses the Cmd key in place of the Ctrl key used in Windows. Press **Ctrl+Alt+Del** on a Windows machine to display a menu that includes Task Manager and other options. Press **Alt+F1** to open the Applications menu in Ubuntu.

5. **a, b, c, d.** The drive containing the paging and temporary files must have at least 10% free space; 20% free space would be better. If dust and dirt build up around internal components, the CPU and system fans might not be able to adequately circulate the air and dissipate the heat that builds up, so the CPU might overheat. If your system is performing at a low level, you might try increasing the amount of RAM. Generally speaking, more RAM equals better performance. Too many programs and services at startup will slow the startup process and also slow down system performance.

6.

Step	Description
1.	g. Identify and research malware symptoms.
2.	d. Quarantine the infected systems.
3.	b. Disable System Restore (in Windows).
4. 4a. 4b.	c. Update the anti-malware software. h. Scan and use removal techniques (Safe mode, preinstallation environment).
5.	a. Schedule scans and run updates.
6.	f. Enable System Restore and create a restore point (in Windows).
7.	e. Educate the end user.

7. **b.** The Event Viewer contains the log files that Windows creates to record problems in the system. Device Manager stores information regarding hardware devices and their drivers. Recovery Environment is used in Windows 7/8/8.1/10 to diagnose and repair system failures. Finder is the file manager program in macOS.

8. **d.** Use the System Restore utility to create restore points before making major changes to your system. Then, if your system has a problem, you can revert to a restore point, and your computer will be configured as it was when the restore point was created.

9. **b.** msconfig is a troubleshooting tool that is used to configure system startup. You can use it to disable or enable any programs or services that run automatically when the system boots. You can also use it to configure a normal, diagnostic, or selective startup and to configure the order in which multiple operating systems boot. regedit can be used to change all Windows settings, but it is not the preferred tool. sfc, the system file checker, is used to replace damaged Windows system files. msinfo32 is used to display Windows and hardware configuration.

10. **c, d.** Safe mode is one of the selections in the Startup Settings menu. In Windows 8/8.1, you should reboot the system, hold down the **Shift** key, and then select **Restart**. You can also enter Safe mode from the Boot tab of the msconfig utility. In previous versions of Windows, you could press **F8** when rebooting, but that does not work in Windows 8/8.1.

11.

Option	When to Use This Option
a. Safe Mode	**3.** You have just upgraded a device driver, and Windows won't start.
b. Boot Logging	**1.** You want to determine which device or process is stopping startup.
c. Low Resolution	**5.** You have just installed a new video card, and Windows won't start.
d. Last Known Good Configuration	**2.** You have just installed new hardware or software, and Windows won't start.
e. Disable Automatic Restart	**4.** You frequently encounter STOP errors.

12. **b.** If your mobile devices use Bluetooth, you should configure those devices to request a code from any devices that attempt to pair with them. Using encryption, using a VPN, and disabling tethering are all good security measures, but they do not prevent pairing with unknown devices.

13. **a, b, c, d.** All of these problems could be caused by malicious software that was not downloaded from Google Play or the App Store.

14. **c.** The correct sequence is **Settings > Personal > Privacy and Safety > Location > Locating Method > GPS Only. Settings > Network > Wi-Fi > Disabled** turns off WiFi. **Settings > Privacy > Location Services > System Services >** is the correct answer for iOS. **Settings > Network > Airplane Mode** turns off all radio services.

Chapter 9

1. **a.** 6

   b. 3

   c. 5

   d. 2

   e. 4

   f. 1

   The object in this diagram is a 3-wire to 2-wire (grounded to ungrounded) adapter. You should only use it when the ground loop is to be connected to a metal grounding device such as a water pipe.

2. **c.** In this diagram, the outlet is wired incorrectly. The left light is on, and the center and right lights are off. According to the legend, this indicates that the outlet has an open neutral wire.

3. **b.** ESD (electrostatic discharge) is the sudden release of static electricity from one object to another. We are not usually aware of the fact that static electricity has built up in our bodies and on the objects around us. When we come in contact with electronic computer components and the static electricity in our bodies discharges into them, those components can be seriously damaged.

4. **a, c, d.** Electronic components come packaged in antistatic bags and should be stored in them when they are not installed in a computer. Technicians can use electrostatic mats and straps to safely handle computer components.

5. **a.** Carpet on the floor increases the likelihood of ESD, and a linoleum floor decreases it. Low humidity and low room temperature increase the likelihood of ESD, and increasing them will help to lower ESD. Rubber-soled shoes help to insulate the technician against ESD.

6. **d.** You should take all batteries to a recycling center. Many electronics stores also accept batteries for recycling. Never put batteries into the trash or even into a recycling bin.

7. **a.** A CRT monitor case should never be opened because it contains a capacitor that, if touched, can deliver a severe electric shock.

8. **c.** Use a Class C fire extinguisher for an electrical fire.

9. **c.** P = oil proof, R = oil resistant, N = not resistant to oil. A P100 mask is best, giving nearly 100% protection against oil and non-oil particulate aerosols. An R95 mask is next, with 95% protection against oil and non-oil particulate aerosols, and then an N95 mask, with 95% protection against non-oil particulate aerosols. There is no class A mask.

10. **b.** An MSDS contains information about dangerous chemicals. It describes how to store them, how to clean up spills, and which type of treatment should be used when you are exposed to them.

11. **d.** A short increase in AC voltage is known as a power surge. A brownout is a large drop in voltage. A blackout is a total loss of power. A whiteout occurs in a snowstorm and has nothing to do with computers.

12. **a.** UPS stands for *uninterruptable power supply*. A UPS is a battery backup that is used to power a system when the main AC power fails. A UPS is not designed to replace the AC power for a long period of time. It is only a backup battery. It is designed to keep a computer running long enough for you to shut down in an orderly manner so that your system does not crash.

13. **b.** The chain of custody documents who had possession of evidence relative to a legal investigation.

14. **a, b, c, d.** All of the options apply to open source software. Open source software may be freely used, and it may be modified. It may be sold, and it may be used for commercial purposes.

15. **a, b, d.** Storing sensitive information in cloud storage is more secure than storing it locally. BitLocker encryption encrypts the entire hard drive, not just selected files. You should install hardware and software firewalls to prevent intrusion. Files saved to a PC's hard drive, a laptop, or a backup file are all much more vulnerable to hackers than are the other methods listed.

16. **c.** Much of the success of your business (and your employer's business) depends on your customer skills. It is one of the most valuable assets that you bring to the job. You should always treat your customers with respect, listen carefully to what they have to say, and explain what you are doing in clear, easy-to-understand terms. Do not use a lot of technical jargon that the customer might not understand and do not act aloof.

17. **d.** The appropriate first response is to contact the violator's supervisor and get instructions on how to proceed. This is considered an incident and needs to be documented.

18. **c.** Active listening includes all three parts of Fatima's approach. Cultural sensitivity and dealing with difficult customers are important soft skills but are not demonstrated here. Presumptive listening is not a skill in good customer service.

19. **c.** RDP, or Remote Desktop Protocol, was likely used. Telnet is not secure. FTP is a protocol for transferring files. RDP is available in macOS.

20. **b.** .sh is the extension for Linux shell script. BASH is the most common shell in Linux. The other extensions listed are .js for JavaScript, .py for Python, and .bat for Windows batch file.

21. **b.** A whitepaper is a technical paper written to explain complex technical information to non-technical people. All three other answers demonstrate poor customer service skills on Josh's part.

22. **a.** The changes made by the healthcare provider unwittingly left Carla unable to do her job. When a major change is being implemented, an important step in change management is getting feedback from stakeholders who might potentially be affected. The other answers do not involve change management practices.

CompTIA A+ Core 1 (220-1001) and Core 2 (220-1002) Cert Guide Exam Updates

Over time, reader feedback allows Pearson to gauge which topics give our readers the most problems when taking the exams. To assist readers with those topics, the authors create new materials clarifying and expanding on those troublesome exam topics. As mentioned in the Introduction, the additional content about the exam is contained in a PDF on this book's companion website, at http://www.ciscopress.com/title/9780789760517.

This appendix is intended to provide you with updated information if CompTIA makes minor modifications to the exam upon which this book is based. When CompTIA releases an entirely new exam, the changes are usually too extensive to provide in a simple update appendix. In those cases, you might need to consult the new edition of the book for the updated content. This appendix attempts to fill the void that occurs with any print book. In particular, this appendix does the following:

- Mentions technical items that might not have been mentioned elsewhere in the book

- Covers new topics if CompTIA adds new content to the exam over time

- Provides a way to get up-to-the-minute current information about content for the exam

Always Get the Latest at the Book's Product Page

You are reading the version of this appendix that was available when your book was printed. However, given that the main purpose of this appendix is to be a living, changing document, it is important that you look for the latest version online at the book's companion website. To do so, follow these steps:

Step 1.   Browse to www.ciscopress.com/title/9780789760517.

Step 2.   Click the **Updates** tab.

Step 3.   If there is a new Appendix B document on this tab, download that document.

> **NOTE**   The downloaded document has a version number. Comparing the version of the print Appendix B (Version 1.0) with the latest online version of this appendix, you should do the following:
>
> - **Same version:** Ignore the PDF that you downloaded from the companion website.
> - **Website has a later version:** Ignore this Appendix B in your book and read only the latest version that you downloaded from the companion website.

Technical Content

The current Version 1.0 of this appendix does not contain additional technical coverage.

Index

Photo by marvent/Shutterstock

VIDEO TRAINING FOR THE **IT PROFESSIONAL**

LEARN QUICKLY
Learn a new technology in just hours. Video training can teach more in less time, and material is generally easier to absorb and remember.

WATCH AND LEARN
Instructors demonstrate concepts so you see technology in action.

TEST YOURSELF
Our Complete Video Courses offer self-assessment quizzes throughout.

CONVENIENT
Most videos are streaming with an option to download lessons for offline viewing.

Learn more, browse our store, and watch free, sample lessons at
informit.com/video

Save 50%* off the list price of video courses with discount code **VIDBOB**

the trusted technology learning source

To receive your 10% off
Exam Voucher, register
your product at:

www.pearsonitcertification.com/register

and follow the instructions.